Concise Dictionary of British Literary Biography
Volume One

Writers of the Middle Ages and Renaissance Before 1660

Concise Dictionary of British Literary Biography
Volume One

Writers of the Middle Ages and Renaissance Before 1660

A Bruccoli Clark Layman Book
Gale Research Inc.
Detroit, London

Advisory Board for
CONCISE DICTIONARY
OF BRITISH LITERARY BIOGRAPHY

Matthew J. Bruccoli and Richard Layman, *Editorial Directors*
Karen L. Rood, *Senior Editor*

Printed in the United States of America

Published simultaneously in the United Kingdom
by Gale Research International Limited
(An affiliated company of Gale Research Inc.)

The paper used in this publication meets the minimum requirements
of American National Standard for Information Sciences—Permanence
Paper for Printed Library Materials, ANSI Z39.48-1984. ∞™

ISBN 0-8103-7980-5
ISBN 0-8103-7981-3

10 9 8 7 6 5 4

Contents of Volume 1

Authors Included in This Series

Volume 2
Writers of the Restoration and Eighteenth Century, 1660-1789

Joseph Addison
James Boswell
John Bunyan
William Congreve
Daniel Defoe
John Dryden
Henry Fielding
Oliver Goldsmith
Thomas Gray
Samuel Johnson
Andrew Marvell
John Milton
Samuel Pepys
Alexander Pope
Samuel Richardson
Richard Brinsley Sheridan
Tobias Smollett
Richard Steele
Laurence Sterne
Jonathan Swift
William Wycherley

Volume 3
Writers of the Romantic Period, 1789-1832

Jane Austen
William Blake
Robert Burns
George Gordon, Lord Byron
Thomas Carlyle
Samuel Taylor Coleridge
Thomas De Quincey
William Godwin
John Keats
Charles Lamb
Sir Walter Scott
Mary Shelley
Percy Bysshe Shelley
Mary Wollstonecraft
William Wordsworth

Volume 4
Victorian Writers, 1832-1890

Volume 5
Late Victorian and Edwardian Writers, 1890-1914

Volume 6
Modern Writers, 1914-1945

Volume 7
Writers After World War II, 1945-1960

Volume 8
Contemporary Writers, 1960-Present

Plan of the Work

The eight-volume *Concise Dictionary of British Literary Biography* was developed in response to requests from school and college teachers and librarians, and from small- to medium-sized public libraries, for a compilation of entries from the standard *Dictionary of Literary Biography* chosen to meet their needs and their budgets. The *DLB*, which comprises more than one hundred volumes as of the end of 1991, is moving steadily toward its goal of providing a history of literature in all languages developed through the biographies of writers. Basic as the *DLB* is, many librarians have expressed the need for a less comprehensive reference work which in other respects retains the merits of the *DLB*. The *Concise DBLB* provides this resource.

The *Concise* series was planned by an eight-member advisory board, consisting primarily of secondary-school educators, who developed a method of organization and presentation for selected *DLB* entries suitable for high-school and beginning college students. Their preliminary plan was circulated to some five thousand school librarians and English teachers, who were asked to respond to the organization of the series. Those responses were incorporated into the plan described here.

Uses for the Concise DBLB

Students are the primary audience for the *Concise DBLB*. The stated purpose of the standard *DLB* is to make our literary heritage more accessible. *Concise DBLB* has the same goal and seeks a wider audience. What the author wrote; what the facts of his or her life are; a description of his or her literary works; a discussion of the critical response to his or her works; and a bibliography of critical works to be consulted for further information: these are the elements of a *Concise DBLB* entry.

The first step in the planning process for this series, after identifying the audience, was to contemplate its uses. The advisory board acknowledged that the integrity of *Concise DBLB* as a reference book is crucial to its utility. The *Concise DBLB* adheres to the scholarly standards established by the parent series; the *Concise DBLB* is a ready-reference source of established value, providing reliable biographical and bibliographical information.

It is anticipated that this series will not be confined to uses within the library. Just as the *DLB* has been a tool for stimulating students' literary interests in the college classroom—for comparative studies of authors, for example, and, through its ample illustrations, as a means of invigorating literary study—the *Concise DBLB* is a primary resource for high-school and junior-college educators.

Organization

The advisory board further determined that entries from the standard *DLB* should be presented complete—without abridgment. The board's feeling was that the utility of the *DLB* format has been proven, and that only minimal changes should be made.

The advisory board further decided that the organization of the *Concise DBLB* should be chronological to emphasize the historical development of British literature. Each volume is devoted to a single historical period and includes the most significant literary figures from all genres who were active during that time.

The eight period volumes of the *Concise DBLB* are: *Writers of the Middle Ages and Renaissance Before 1660; Writers of the Restoration and Eighteenth Century, 1660-1789; Writers of the Romantic Period, 1789-1832; Victorian Writers, 1832-1890; Late Victorian and Edwardian Writers, 1890-1914; Modern Writers, 1914-1945; Writers After World War II, 1945-1960; Contemporary Writers, 1960-Present.*

Form of Entry

The form of entry in the *Concise DBLB* is substantially the same as in the standard series. Entries have been updated and, where necessary, corrected.

It is anticipated that users of this series will find it useful to consult the standard *DLB* for information about those writers omitted from the *Concise DBLB* whose significance to contemporary readers may have faded but whose contribution to our cultural heritage remains meaningful.

Comments about the series and suggestions for its improvement are earnestly invited.

A Note to Students

The purpose of the *Concise DBLB* is to enrich the study of British literature. Besides being inherently interesting, biographies of writers provide a basic understanding of the various ways writers react in their works to the circumstances of their lives, the events of their times, and the cultures that envelop them.

Concise DBLB entries start with the most important facts about writers: what they wrote. We strongly recommend that you also start there. The chronological listing of an author's works is an outline for the examination of his or her career achievements. The biography that follows sets the stage for the presentation of the works. Each of the author's important works and the most respected critical evaluations of them are discussed in *Concise DBLB*. If you require more information about the author or fuller critical studies of the author's works, the references section at the end of the entry will guide you.

Illustrations are an integral element of *Concise DBLB* entries. Photographs of the author are reminders that literature is the product of a writer's imagination; facsimiles of the author's working drafts are the best evidence available for understanding the act of composition—the author in the process of refining his or her work and acting as self-editor; dust jackets and advertisements demonstrate how literature comes to us through the marketplace, which sometimes serves to alter our perceptions of the works.

Literary study is a complex and immensely rewarding endeavor. Our goal is to provide you with the information you need to make that experience as rich as possible.

Acknowledgments

This book was produced by Bruccoli Clark Layman, Inc. Karen L. Rood is senior editor for the *Dictionary of Literary Biography* series. David Marshall James was the in-house editor.

Production coordinator is James W. Hipp. Projects manager is Charles D. Brower. Photography editors are Edward Scott and Timothy C. Lundy. Layout and graphics supervisor is Penney L. Haughton. Copyediting supervisor is Bill Adams. Typesetting supervisor is Kathleen M. Flanagan. Systems manager is George F. Dodge. The production staff includes Rowena Betts, Teresa Chaney, Patricia Coate, Gail Crouch, Margaret McGinty Cureton, Bonita Dingle, Mary Scott Dye, Sarah A. Estes, Robert Fowler, Ellen McCracken, Kathy Lawler Merlette, John Myrick, Pamela D. Norton, Jean W. Ross, Laurrè Sinckler-Reeder, Thomasina Singleton, Maxine K. Smalls, Jennifer C. J. Turley, and Betsy L. Weinberg.

Walter W. Ross and Henry Cuningham did library research. They were assisted by the following librarians at the Thomas Cooper Library of the University of South Carolina: Jens Holley and the interlibrary-loan staff; reference librarians Gwen Baxter, Daniel Boice, Faye Chadwell, Jo Cottingham, Cathy Eckman, Rhonda Felder, Gary Geer, Jackie Kinder, Laurie Preston, Jean Rhyne, Carol Tobin, Virginia Weathers, and Connie Widney; circulation-department head Thomas Marcil; and acquisitions-searching supervisor David Haggard.

Concise Dictionary of British Literary Biography
Volume One

Writers of the Middle Ages and Renaissance Before 1660

Concise Dictionary of British Literary Biography

Francis Bacon

(22 January 1561 - 9 April 1626)

W. A. Sessions
Georgia State University

BOOKS: *Essayes: Religious Meditations. Places of perswasion and dissuasion. Scene and allowed* (London: Printed by J. Windet for Humfrey Hooper, 1597); revised and enlarged as *The Essaies of S[r] Francis Bacon Knight, the Kings Solliciter Generall* (London: Printed by John Beale, 1612); revised and enlarged as *The Essayes or Counsels, Civill and Morall, of Francis Lo. Verulam, Viscount St. Alban* (London: Printed by John Haviland for Hanna Barret & Richard Whitaker, 1625);

A Briefe Discourse, Touching the Happie Union of the Kingdomes of England, and Scotland, anonymous (London: Printed by R. Read for Felix Norton, to be sold by William Aspley, 1603);

Sir Francis Bacon His Apologie, in Certaine imputations concerning the late Earle of Essex: Written to the right Honorable his very good Lord, the Earle of Devonshire, Lord Lieutenant of Ireland (London: Printed by R. Field for Felix Norton, 1604);

Certaine Considerations touching the better pacification and Edification of the Church of England, anonymous (London: Printed by T. Purfoot for Henrie Tomes, 1604);

The Twoo Bookes of Francis Bacon: Of the proficience and advancement of Learning, divine and humane (London: Printed by T. Purfoot & T. Creede for Henrie Tomes, 1605); translated into Latin by Bacon as *Opera Francisci Baronis de Verulamo, Vice-Comitis Sancti Albani; Tomus Primus: Qui continet De Dignítate & Augmentis Scientiarum Libros IX* (London: Printed by John Haviland, 1623);

De Sapientia Veterum Liber (London: Printed by Robert Barker, 1609); translated by Sir Arthur Gorges as *The Wisdome of the Ancients* (London: Printed by John Bill, 1619);

The Charge of Sir Francis Bacon Knight, His Maiesties Attourney generall, touching Duells, upon an information in the Star-chamber against Priest and Wright: With The Decree of the Star-chamber in the same cause (London: Printed by G. Eld for Robert Wilson, 1614);

Summi Angliae Cancellarii Instauratio magna [Novum Organum] (London: Printed by B. Norton & John Bill, 1620);

Historia Naturalis et Experimentalis ad Condendam Philosophiam: Sive, Phaenomena Universi: Quae est Instaurationis Magnae Pars Tertia [Historia de Ventis] (London: Printed by John Haviland for Matthew Lownes & William Barret, 1622); translated by R. G. as *The Naturall and Experimentall History of Winds, &c.* (London: Printed for Humphrey Moseley, 1653);

The Historie of the Raigne of King Henry The Seventh (London: Printed by W. Stansby for Matthew Lownes & William Barret, 1622);

Historia Vitae & Mortis. Sive, Titulus Secundus in Historia Naturali & Experimentali ad condendam Philosophiam: Quae est Instaurationis Magnae Pars Tertia (London: Printed by John Haviland for Matthew Lownes, 1623); translated anonymously as *The*

Portrait of Bacon by William Marshall, from Gilbert Wats's 1640 edition of The Advancement of Learning

Historie of Life and Death. With Observations Naturall and Experimentall for the Prolonging of Life (London: Printed by I. Okes for Humphrey Mosley [*sic*], 1638);

Sylva Sylvarum or A Naturall Historie in ten Centuries, edited by William Rawley (London: Printed by John Haviland for William Lee, 1626)—includes "New Atlantis: A Worke unfinished";

Considerations Touching a Warre with Spaine (N.p., 1629);

The Elements of the Common Lawes of England, Branched into a double Tract: The One Containing a Collection of some principall Rules and Maximes of the Common Law, with their Latitude and Extent. Explicated for the more facile Introduction of such as are studiously addicted to that noble profession. The Other The Use of the Common Law, for preservation of our Persons, Goods, and good Names. According to the Lawes and Customes of this Land (London: Printed by the Assignes of John Moore Esq., 1630)—the attribution of "The Use of the Common Law" to Bacon seems to be spurious;

Cases of Treason (London: Printed by the Assignes of John More, sold by Matthew Walbancke & William Coke, 1641);

The Confession of Faith (London, 1641);

A Speech Delivered by Sir Francis Bacon, In the lower House of Parliament quinto Iacobi, concerning the Article of Naturalization of the Scottish Nation (London, 1641);

Three Speeches of The Right Honorable, Sir Francis Bacon Knight, then his Majesties Sollicitor Generall, after Lord Verulam, Viscount Saint Alban. Concerning the Post-Nati; Naturalization of the Scotch in England; Union of the Lawes of the Kingdomes of England and Scotland (London: Printed by Richard Badger for Samuel Broun, 1641);

A Wise and Moderate Discourse, Concerning Church-Affaires. As it was written, long since, by the famous Authour of those Considerations, which seem to have some reference to this. Now published for the Common good (London, 1641);

The Learned Reading of Sir Francis Bacon, One of her Majesties learned Counsell at Law, upon the Statute of Uses: Being his double Reading to the Honourable Society of Grayes Inne (London: Printed for Matthew Walbancke & Laurence Chapman, 1642).

Editions & Collections: *Certaine Miscellany Works of the Right Honourable, Francis Lo. Verulam, Viscount S. Alban*, edited by William Rawley (London: Printed by John Haviland for Humphrey Robinson, 1629);

Operum Moralium et Civilium, edited by Rawley (London: Printed by Edward Griffin for Richard Whitaker, 1638);

Scripta in Naturali et Universali Philosophia (Amsterdam: Printed by Ludwig Elzevier, 1653);

Resuscitatio, Or, Bringing into Publick Light Severall Pieces, of the Works, Civil, Historical, Philosophical, & Theological, Hitherto Sleeping; Of the Right Honourable Francis Bacon Baron of Verulam, Viscount Saint Alban. According to the best Corrected Coppies. Together, With his Lordships Life, edited, with biography of Bacon, by Rawley (London: Printed by Sarah Griffin for William Lee, 1657);

Opuscula Varia Posthuma, Philosophica, Civilia, et Theologica, edited by Rawley (London: Printed by R. Daniel, 1658);

The Philosophical Works of Francis Bacon, Baron of Verulam, Viscount St. Albans, and Lord High-Chancellor of England; Methodized, and made English, from the Originals, with Occasional Notes, to Explain what is Obscure; And shew how far the several Plans of the Author, for the Advancement of all the Parts of Knowledge, have been executed to the Present Time, 3 volumes, edited by Peter Shaw (London: Printed for J. J. and P. Knapton, D. Midwinter and A. Ward, A. Bettesworth and C. Hitch, J. Pemberton, J. Osborn and T. Longman, C. Rivington, F. Clay, J. Batley, R. Hett, and T. Hatchett, 1733);

The Works of Francis Bacon, Baron of Verulam, Viscount St. Alban. Lord High Chancellor of England. In Four Volumes. With several Additional Pieces, Never before printed in any Edition of his Works. To which is prefixed, A New Life of the Author, by Mr. Mallet, 4 volumes, edited by D. Mallet (London: Printed for A. Millar, 1740);

The Works of Francis Bacon, 14 volumes, edited by James Spedding, Robert Leslie Ellis, and Douglas Denon Heath (London: Longman, 1857-1874);

The Letters and the Life of Francis Bacon Including All His Occasional Works, Namely Letters, Speeches, Tracts, State Papers, Memorials, Devices and All Authentic Writings Not Already Printed among His Philosophical, Literary, or Professional Works, Newly Collected and Set Forth in Chronological Order with a Commentary Biographical and Historical, 7 volumes, edited by Spedding (London: Longman, Green, Longman & Roberts, 1861-1874);

Essays, Advancement of Learning, New Atlantis, and Other Pieces, edited by Richard Foster Jones (Garden City, N.Y.: Doubleday, Doran, 1937);

The New Organon, and Related Writings, edited by Fulton H. Anderson (New York: Lineral Arts Press, 1960);

The Essayes or Counsels, Civill and Moral, edited by Michael Kiernan (Cambridge, Mass.: Harvard University Press, 1985).

OTHER: *Apophthegmes New and Old*, collected by Bacon (London: Printed for Hanna Barret & Richard Whittaker, 1625);

The Translation of Certaine Psalmes into English Verse, translated by Bacon (London: Printed by Hanna Barret & Richard Whittaker, 1625).

"I have taken all knowledge to be my province," wrote Francis Bacon in 1592 to his uncle, Lord Burghley, the lord high treasurer. Bacon was just over thirty, but already he had begun the writing of his grand program for the renewal of human learning. It was to be nothing less than the reform of human epistemology itself—a reshaping of human perception through reforming its methods of perceiving, including the restoration of language and linguistic forms. The goal was vast. Its climactic text, Bacon's *Novum Organum* (New Instrument, 1620), revealed the dimensions of this task on its illustrated title page. Bacon's ship, with full-blown sails, is crossing the formerly forbidden strait between two huge pillars. The illustration represents what became one of Bacon's recurring commonplaces: his substitution of "plus ultra" (more beyond) for "ne plus ultra" (no more beyond), the motto that the Holy Roman Emperor Charles V had set to forbid exploration of the portion of his empire that stretched beyond the straits of Gibraltar. Bacon's audiences in England and on the Continent would have understood at once what this emblem meant. Bacon's grand Latin text was challenging all authority that denied exploration and the progression and movement of knowledge. The idea of progress would spread like fire, first in England in the later seventeenth and eighteenth centuries, in conjunction with that new center of science, the Royal Society, then in Europe, and then throughout the world in the nineteenth and twentieth centuries.

A quotation from the Latin Vulgate Bible appears at the base of the emblem: "Many will pass through and science will increase" (Dan. 12:4). *Scientia*, in the Renaissance, meant moral and philosophical knowledge, not just natural science. This sense of knowledge as the exploration of new worlds appears in the Columbus imagery throughout Bacon's texts; its apotheosis occurs in Bacon's prose fiction, "New Atlantis," published the year after his death in his *Sylva Sylvarum or A Naturall Historie in ten Centuries* (1626). The quotation from the prophet Daniel is appropriate: Bacon himself would become a prophet of a new world and would invent a new style of language and new images to reveal it to the existing world.

Bacon's prophetic texts—written, at their best, in one of the great prose styles of English literature (as well as in superb Renaissance Latin)—turn to experience, the actual world of human beings. They delineate that hope for human progress through knowledge that has fueled the modern world. If testimonies to these prophetic texts abound in England from John Milton and Thomas Hobbes, to John Locke and David Hume, to John Stuart Mill, Charles Darwin, and Thomas Carlyle, they also abound on the Continent in René Descartes, Gottfried Wilhelm Leibniz, the French philosophes, and reach on down to modern reconsiderations of epistemology. Perhaps the greatest tribute came at the onset of the revolution of modern critical thought when Immanuel Kant dedicated the second (1783) edition of the *Kritik der reinen Vernunft* (Critique of Pure Reason, 1781) to Bacon. For Kant, he was the "Verulamium" (Latin for one of Bacon's titles of nobility, Baron or Lord Verulam) whose elegant Latin and English texts of prophecy had entered powerfully, Kant thought, into the mainstream of modern world thought and modern consciousness. As these testimonies prove, the power of these prophetic texts sprang from Bacon's subtle control of language and imagery, which became a basis for modern prose style in English.

If it is certainly true that Bacon did not write the works of William Shakespeare, it is just as true that Shakespeare might have written the drama of Bacon's life. Living on the edge of court circles, with two monarchs demanding sycophancy of the most elaborate form, Bacon had to survive and prosper if he wanted to project his own images of power and knowledge. The 1592 assertion about knowledge to his uncle was typical: it was a gesture, of necessity, both political and intellectual. Bacon knew that only through politics could knowledge be augmented and history changed.

Bacon's letter of 1592 illustrates this strategy that would lead him by 1620 to the highest office in the land, outside that of the king himself: lord chancellor of the realm. Bacon, already a master of the Renaissance epistolary style, asks Burghley to help him find a job as a lawyer with the government, for "I do easily see, that place of any reasonable countenance doth bring commandment of more wits than a man's own." This sense of political control for a higher social purpose came naturally to Bacon. He was the son of Sir Nicholas Bacon, the lord chancellor at the time of Bacon's birth on 22 January 1561, the lord keeper of the Great Seal of the Realm, and, according to William Rawley, Bacon's chaplain, editor, and earliest biographer, "the second prop of the kingdom in his time"—the first being his wife's brother-in-law, William Cecil, Lord Burghley, the single individual who engineered the remarkable reign of Elizabeth I.

The Bacons had been simple gentry from Suffolk, and only since the time of Thomas Cromwell and the Reformation of the 1530s had Nicholas Bacon made his presence known on the political scene. Of course, he owed a great deal not only to his tenacity, natural prudence, and nouveau-riche drive but also to his teamwork with Burghley. Burghley himself had risen from comparatively humble sources in the Henrician and Edwardian upheavals, but at every stage he had identified himself with the new force of Renaissance humanism. Francis Bacon knew of this identification, as his classical allusions and Ciceronian prose style in his crucial letter of 1592 reveal. Bacon's mother, Anne, and her sister, Mildred, Burghley's wife, sprang from a family devoted both to humanism and its offspring, the Reformation.

Bacon's maternal grandfather, Sir Anthony Cooke, brought up his five daughters in the humanistic disciplines. Thus Anne Cooke Bacon was, says Rawley, "exquisitely skilled, for a woman, in the Greek and Latin tongues." To this discipline Cooke—who may or may not have taught the pious Edward VI but certainly did flee his sister, sitting out the Marian regime in Germany—added the Protestant religion. It was a particularly evangelical Christianity that the father intended for his daughters, and his possibly fatal political error occurred, once Elizabeth returned to power, when he refused to acknowledge the Act of Supremacy, which recognized Elizabeth as head of the English church. Bacon's mother emerged as "a choice lady, and eminent for piety, virtue, and learning," a woman almost ferocious in her religious fervor and a master of classical languages. On the one hand, her letters reveal, especially in the early 1590s, a mother who closely watched over her two children, the older Anthony and Francis, commenting on their questionable friends and their lack of proper religion. On the other hand, her translation of Bishop John Jewel's Latin defense (1562) of the English church as the true primitive church of Christ—a work often read with the English Bible and the Book of Common Prayer—marked her as the best of sixteenth-century translators, according to C. S. Lewis.

Bacon attended Trinity College, Cambridge, from April 1573 to March 1575. On 27 June 1576 he was admitted to Gray's Inn in London to study law, but soon left to serve on a diplomatic mission in Paris. His father died on 20 February 1579, leaving him virtually penniless. There being no hope for the scholarly life he envisioned in Cambridge and Paris, he returned to the study of common law at Gray's Inn, which would serve him as headquarters and occasional home for the rest of his life. He was first elected to Parliament in November 1584 and served until 1614. He became a reader (teacher) at Gray's Inn in 1588 and a "double" reader by 1600.

By the 1590s Bacon had begun to move into circles that would lead him into that center of all political and social reality in Elizabethan England, the court of the Virgin Queen herself. One of his means of selling himself, as his letter to Burghley indicates, was to play up his power of language, his ability to conceptualize new ideas—in short, the kind of intellectual prowess understood as necessary for power by Burghley and certainly by Elizabeth, with her own early grounding in humanism and languages from Roger Ascham and other masters of Tudor education. After a cool reception by his uncle, Bacon turned to the most dashing young courtier of his day, Robert Devereux, Earl of Essex, for whom he wrote a series of masques that were produced either at Gray's Inn or at court. These remarkable early works reflect the pervading influence of the recently published first three books of *The Faerie Queene* (1590), by Edmund Spenser, and conjoin both elaborate political praise of Elizabeth I with Bacon's own "praise of knowledge." Behind these early literary works appears already a political and philosophical agenda that would surface more overtly in the next two decades.

As Essex became more and more the central figure of Bacon's drive for power at court, so this chivalrous courtier, who flirted openly with the queen and she with him, turned to rely on his serious friend, the lawyer and clever courtier, for advice and direction. As the letters between the two men show, Bacon profited—quite literally—from this relationship, which had its roots in Bacon's physical attraction to Essex, or at least his enjoyment of the handsome young nobleman's presence and power. The letters also show that Bacon saw early the dangers of Essex's charms and warned him about his unstable ego, which would drive him on 8 February 1601 to his Sunday morning assault on the queen and cost him his head.

Bacon recovered from the loss of his court patron; his brother, Anthony, also attracted to Essex and more deeply entwined with him, did not, dying soon after Essex's execution and leaving his income to his younger brother. Part of that recovery stemmed from the trial, during which Elizabeth, in a characteristic gesture, asked Bacon to represent her in the case against Essex. At a dramatic moment in the trial Essex is supposed to have cried out: "I call Mr. Bacon against Mr. Bacon." How Bacon responded is not recorded; but, although he still received, as Rawley noted, no "place or means of honour and profit" from Elizabeth, he had survived the first great political debacle of his life.

In 1603 the advent of James I marked the resurgence of Bacon's political prospects. When James knighted him on 23 July, Bacon was over forty; except for his *Essayes* (1597) and many unpublished works, he had accomplished little in developing the advancement of knowledge he had outlined so boldly for his uncle in 1592. Then Bacon began to progress politically, and his momentum was remarkable for the next fifteen years. The years of silence and humiliation were paying off, and so was Bacon's patience with his own writing. In 1605 appeared *The Twoo Bookes of Francis Bacon: Of the proficience and advancement of Learning*—generally known as *The Advancement of Learning*—the text that he would later see as the first part of his grand program. Also, in 1605, Bacon married Alice Barnham, who was in her late teens. It was obviously a marriage of convenience to a wealthy and innocent daughter of a London alderman; there were no children.

Bacon is reputed to have said that King James was "that master to him, that had raised and advanced him nine times: thrice in dignity, and six times in office." He was made baron of Verulam in 1618 and, in the highest level of peerage, the Viscount Saint Albans in 1621. As he supported the doctrine of royal prerogative and the ascent of James's favorite, George Villiers, Duke of Buckingham, Bacon's rise to power was now meteoric. Moving from Counsel Learned Ordinary, Bacon became solicitor general in 1607, attorney general in 1613, counsellor of estate in 1616, lord keeper of the Great Seal in 1617, and finally lord chancellor in 1618.

In this last role Bacon was, with a household of almost three hundred retainers, the virtual head of the kingdom after the king, and he ruled like a Renaissance prince. On one occasion, when James I traveled to Scotland, Bacon opened Parliament, and the procession through London was immense: hundreds of soldiers and nobles walking before the coach in which he rode alone, solemnly waving his hand to the crowds, and hundreds of horsemen after him, all brightly liveried. At the same time, he pushed forward his grand agenda of knowledge, constantly preparing his *Novum Organum* for publication. The fact that its author possessed such political power made its intellectual content all the more significant for English and Continental audiences, and it was on the basis of its ideas that the work succeeded or not. For some it did not. James I is supposed to have said of Bacon's work: "it was like the peace of God: it passeth all understanding."

Within months after the publication of his great text, and within weeks of his elevation to viscount, Bacon fell from power. He had become an obvious liability in a fight between Parliament and Buckingham. The king and his beloved George traded Bacon off. He was accused of accepting bribes as lord chancellor; the trial was swift, and the conviction on 3 May 1621 was inevitable. Although the punishment was never really carried out—he only stayed in the Tower for four days—Bacon was banned from all centers of political power for the rest of his life. Within five years he was dead.

In that last fertile period Bacon composed, rewrote, and edited most of his works. He produced the last great edition of his essays in 1625. He translated *The Advancement of Learning* into Latin as *De Augmentis Scientiarum* (1623). He composed the innovative *The Historie of the Raigne of King Henry The Seventh* (1622), a model for new forms of historiography, as well as the *Historia Naturalis et Experimentalis* (1622) and *Historia Vitae & Mortis* (1623), in which he gathered experiments on the nature of winds, on the qualities of denseness and rareness and heaviness and lightness, on the magnet, and on the processes of life and death. He wrote political dialogues and legal digests, both setting models in their own fields; translated some of the Psalms into English; and composed some poetry. He also compiled, in aphoristic form, his lifetime catalogue of natural phenomena in *Sylva Sylvarum or A Naturall Historie in ten Centuries*. This work became the third part of his program for the restoration of knowledge. This work includes his popular utopian romance, "New Atlantis."

His death arose from just such experimentation and curiosity. Riding in his coach on the outskirts of London in late March 1626, he decided to stop and test the effects of refrigeration. A farmwoman killed and dressed a chicken, and Bacon stuffed it with snow. In the process he became chilled and stopped at the nearby Highgate villa of Thomas Howard, Earl of Arundel, where he was put in a room and bed that were as chilled as Bacon himself. He developed bronchitis and died on 9 April. A few months before his death he had revoked, in a codicil to his will, any provision for his wife. The incident is likely linked to the fact that, soon after Bacon's death, she married her gentleman-usher.

The sense of experience and experimentation that marked Bacon's life and death distinguish his essays, his most popular literary works. It would have been obvious to any reader of the essays in the last years of Elizabeth's reign—to a Shakespeare or a John Donne or a Ben Jonson, for example—that here was innovation on every level.

The response to Bacon's essays through the years has not been all positive, however. William Blake is said to have hurled Bacon's book away after scribbling in the margin: "Good advice for Satan's kingdom!" The myriad pieces of advice in the essays lend credence to the accusation that Bacon was a supermanipulator, a Machiavellian, or a clever lawyer, for whom the means always justified the end. To his Elizabethan and Stuart audiences, it must have been quite clear in 1597, even more so in the expanded edition of 1612, and most of all in the final edition of Bacon's lifetime in 1625 that Bacon was deliberately turning upside down the genre of the "courtesy-book," which provided advice to a courtier on how to succeed in the power centers of society. Here was no abstract exploration of the Aristotelian values of prudence or justice or fortitude, and certainly no exploration of social and personal virtue as transcendent and eternal, such as Christian teachers, including his contemporary Richard Hooker, had devised out of the teachings of Saint Thomas Aquinas.

Above all, the essays were light-years away from that traditional model of personal and internal virtue, Saint Augustine's *Confessions* (circa 400). What counted for Bacon was the immediate encounter with time. Thus, in his essay on death,

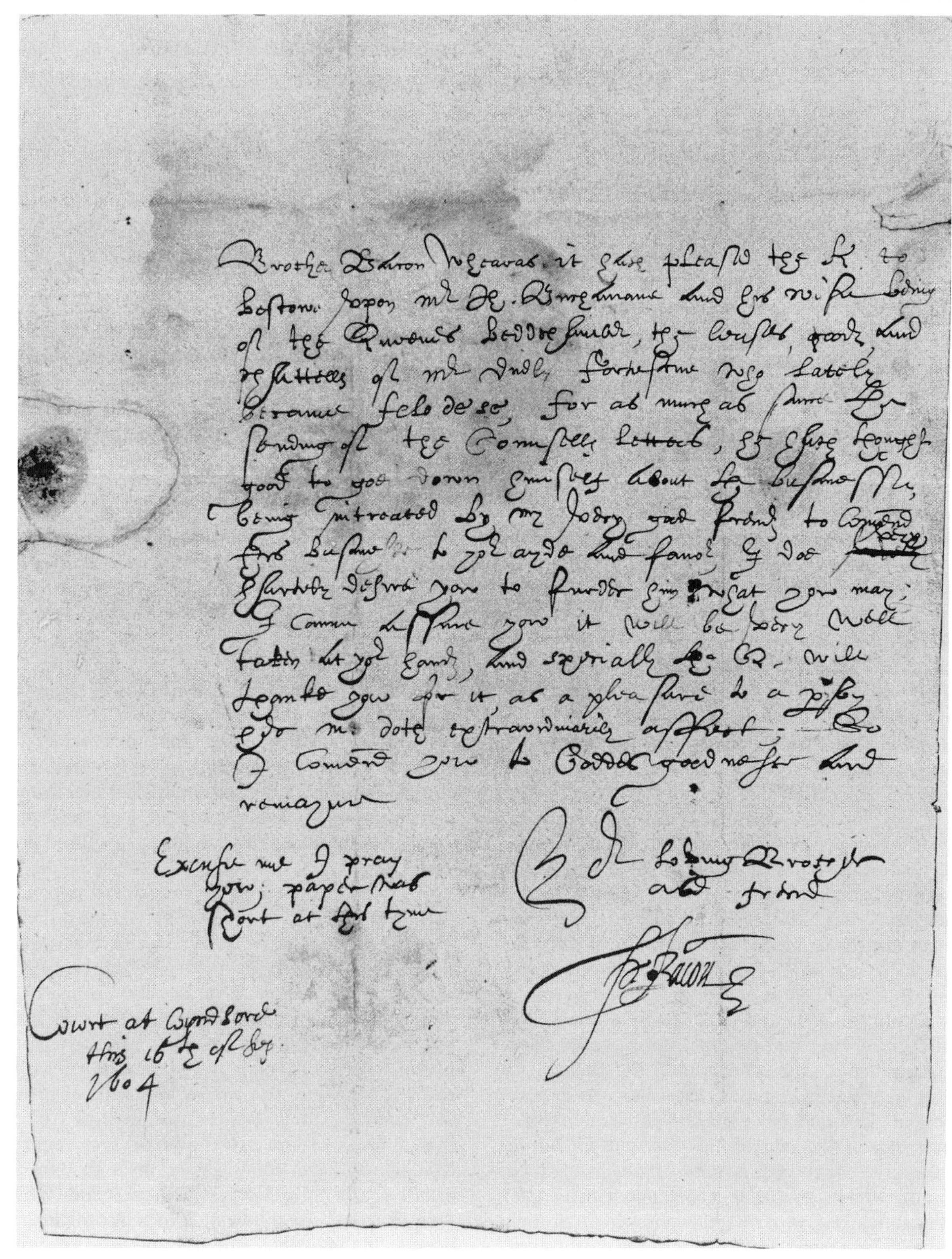

Brother Bacon whereas it hath pleased the K. to bestowe uppon Mr Th. Buchanane and his wife beinge of the Queenes beddechamber, the leases, goods and chattells of Mr Dudly Fortescue who lately became felo de se, for as much as since the sendinge of the Counsells letters, he hath thought good to goe down himselfe about the businesse, being intreated by my very good frend to commend his businesse to your ayde and favour I doe hartely desire you to further him in what you may; I can assure you it will be very well taken at your handes, and specially the K. will thanke you for it as a pleasure to a person who M. doth extraordinarily affect. So I commend you to Goddes good notice and remayne

Excuse me I pray you; paper was short at this tyme

Your lovinge brother and frend
Fr. Bacon

Court at Wyndsore this 16th of Sep. 1604

Letter from Bacon to his half-brother, Sir Nicholas Bacon, dated 16 September 1604 (MA 1215, Gift of Mr. Roland L. Redmond; Pierpont Morgan Library). Bacon requests Nicholas's assistance in the transferral of "the leases, goods, and chattells of Mr Dudly Fortescue," who had recently committed suicide, to Thomas Buchanane and his wife, who was a member of the "Queenes beddechamber."

Bacon stresses the art of dying; in his essay on studies, he marks not the ideal of knowledge but the practical process of how one learns; in his essay on friendship, he discusses its three uses. What is at issue for Bacon are not eternal values—or, if they are at issue, it is only as they are revealed in the utilitarian shifts and twists of time and in social reality, what Bacon calls in his last essay "the vicissitude of things."

Bacon devised a form to fit such a perspective on reality. The Baconian essay is a trial or attempt, not anything complete. Most follow the same pattern. There is generally a striking beginning: "*What is Truth?* said jesting Pilate; and would not stay for an answer"; "Men fear Death, as children fear to go in the dark; and as the natural fear in children is increased with tales, so is the other"; "I had rather believe all the fables in the Legend, and the Talmud, and the Alcoran, than that this universal frame is without a mind"; "Fortune is like the market; where many times, if you can stay a little, the price will fall"; "Travel, in the younger sort, is a part of education; in the elder, a part of experience"; "The joys of parents are secret; and so are their griefs and fears"; "He that hath wife and children hath given hostages to fortune; for they are impediments to great enterprises, either of virtue or mischief"; "Men in great place are thrice servants: servants of the sovereign or state; servants of fame; and servants of business."

The dramatic opening is followed by a series of practical proofs, usually laid out in sequential form, not unlike a Baconian series for an inductive argument. These proofs are more severe and rigorous in the earlier editions (single sentences appear as separate paragraphs in the austere 1597 essays) but increasingly more related and unified through transitional expressions in the editions of 1612 and 1625. These proofs, especially in the later editions, include quotations and allusions from classical texts and the Bible. It is as though Bacon is trying to include all experience, all knowledge, in these brief explorations. Such experience would be one more counter against the large abstractions of the Schoolmen against whom Bacon is rebelling. Finally, the essay fades out without real closure, as though Bacon is moving toward the next essay, the next challenge and trial. The method of incremental induction, the method of time itself is, he implies, not closure but openness.

The metaphysical concept behind Bacon's essays is that reality is unsettled, in motion, and always concrete. The theory for the literary form that best expresses this concept—Bacon's aphorism—can be found in *The Advancement of Learning*, which was probably written in the years just after the first edition of his essays. This theory was the basis for all of Bacon's prose style. Bacon's theory of the aphorism appears in the section of *The Advancement of Learning* where he is attempting to cleanse the mind of its diseases and distempers by recognizing them. He makes a catalogue—a favorite rhetorical device—of what he calls "peccant humours" rather "than formed diseases." Among these "humours" are "the over-early and peremptory reduction of knowledge into arts and methods; from which time commonly sciences receive small or no augmentation. But as young men, when they knit and shape perfectly, do seldom grow to further stature; so knowledge, while it is in aphorisms and observations, it is in growth. . . ." It is the progression of knowledge that the aphorism allows. And where there are no absolutes, or cultural authorities who can guarantee such absolutes, only the axiom of growth and the ability to evolve can guarantee any truth, however unfinished and incomplete. Lack of closure will lead to growth into another, possibly more inclusive, if also incomplete, truth. The form of the aphorism, for Bacon, guarantees this process; it is the only one by which language can arrive at truth. The very tentativeness of the aphorism thus acknowledges that human perception is a tentative and limited perception that grows incrementally, at best, and should be allowed to grow.

Bacon's essays may be considered expanded aphorisms. They are never to be viewed individually but only collectively, as a series that teaches young men-about-town how to be the best courtiers or lawyers, how to balance their lives and their careers within ethical and, at the same time, pragmatic perspectives. As in the body simile Bacon uses to develop his theory of the aphorism, young men with minds and wills in growth will survive better. The fifty-eight topics of the final edition of the essays portray the range of that growth from coming to terms with ultimates in "Of Truth," "Of Death," "Of Love," and "Of Nature in Men," to following the practical instructions in "Of Garden" (the only piece of literature that could be a seed catalogue), "Of Travel," "Of Masks and Triumphs," "Of Building," and "Of Regiment of Health." Between these two poles, Bacon examines the kind of experience a young man entering the job market and society in general will need to know. If Benjamin Franklin's *Poor Richard's Almanack* (1732-1757) and countless other books of advice and experience appear to follow Bacon, in actuality they do not. Bacon's close-knit synthesis of form and idea evolves with a structure all its own; the ideas cannot be separated from the carefully shaped prose. The essay builds, step-by-step, until it becomes a kind of linguistic cultural artifact that is a model of idea and image. At the same time, the language and radically new prose form imply a whole view of human perception and its limits and possibilities that Bacon's offspring could not.

"Of Studies" illustrates this evolution of design and unity within the single brief form. The essay begins with one of Bacon's favorite rhetorical devices, a tripartite division that adds to the dramatic assertion of this opening: "Studies serve for delight, for ornament, and for ability." Then, with his Ramist delight in outlining, Bacon continues: "Their chief use for delight, is in privateness and retiring; for ornament, is in discourse; and for ability, is in the judgment and disposition of business." He adds accumulation of details and observation that serve him as proof: "To spend too much time in studies is sloth; to use them too much for ornament, is affectation; to make judgment wholly by their rules, is the humour of a scholar." His brilliance in using similes—a Baconian trait that appears increasingly in the later editions—shows once more: studies "perfect nature, and are perfected by experience: for natural abilities are like natural plants, that need proyning by study; and studies themselves do give forth directions too much at large, except they be bounded in by experience." Bacon has turned his reader slowly and subtly with this simile, for now studies are seen as processes of nature, in growth, not fixed in any transcendental or eternal verity.

The metaphor that follows soon after takes up this process of studying and the practical matter of how to read: "Some books are to be tasted, others to be swallowed, and some few to be chewed and digested; that is, some books are to be read only in parts; others to be read, but not curiously; and some few to be read wholly, and with diligence and attention." This use of balanced sentences, with careful antitheses, is repeated in his statement "Reading maketh a full man; conference a ready man; and writing an exact man," followed by some practical—almost mundane—advice about what to do if the reader lacks any of the three.

His final advice is typical: linking problems of the body to problems of the mind in studying, he directly compares physical exercises that strengthen the body to mental exercises for curing weakness of the mind. The strategy completes his reduction of the transcendental notion of knowledge in both classical and Christian traditions. Learning is like physical exercise; mind (or soul) is really a form of body. The last line—"So every defect of the mind may have a special receipt"—provides the flat ending that Bacon wants. This subject is over, says Bacon to his reader; you have spent enough time; get on with it; go to the next subject, see the collective picture. Such is the method of time, Bacon had observed in his theory of the aphorism—the method of growth and progress. It is the method of the mechanical arts, he says elsewhere, that has produced the great inventions of his time.

The title of his next major publication, *Of the proficience and advancement of Learning, divine and humane*, develops this same sense of progression. As the title suggests, what is needed is not stasis but advancement, not knowledge but the active gerund, learning. For this text Bacon has a specific audience in mind, and it is not younger men such as Essex and his followers who need to know more about court. The text has two parts or books, and each begins with an elaborate, flattering dedication to the king: "for why should a few received authors stand up like Hercules' Columns, beyond which there should be no sailing or discovering, since we have so bright and benign a star as your Majesty to conduct and prosper us?" Bacon wants a society of intellectuals and scholars to be formed that will take on the task of reorganizing learning and knowledge. In the breakup, especially in England, of feudalism, humanism had provided schools; but there did not exist organizations devoted to learning as the old monasteries had been. So now, under the new supreme head of the church of England, whom Bacon calls the new Hermes Trismegistus (James as king, as priest, and as philosopher), the time is ripe to bring about "a conjunction of labors."

First, however, there must be cleansing and an authorizing once more of "the dignity of learning." The first book of *The Advancement of Learning* begins with this task. Learning must be delivered from ignorance, manifest in three forms: "the zeal and jealousy of divines"; "the severity and arrogancy of politiques"; and finally "the errors and imperfections of learned men themselves." It was a daring agenda at a time when all three forms wielded enormous political power over intellectual life.

In his attack on the religious hindrances to learning Bacon develops one of his best-known arguments: the equivalence of the book of God's word and the book of God's works. The argument's power originates no less in its brilliant manipulation of syntax and unique modern use of the ancient rhetorical figure of *homoeteleuton* (similar endings) than in its imagery, the latter focused on the humanist endeavor that dominated all Renaissance life—the book. With this image Bacon concludes the first attack with a metaphor that would reshape the Western world's attitude toward religion and science: "To conclude, therefore, let no man . . . think or maintain that a man can search too far or be too well studied in the book of God's word or in the book of God's works; divinity or philosophy; but rather let men endeavor an endless progress or proficience in both; only let men beware that they apply both to charity, and not to swelling; to use, and not to ostentation; and again, that they do not unwisely mingle or confound these learnings together."

In his second attack, on politicians, Bacon defends the man of learning against the charge that he cannot function in government. He demonstrates, primarily by examples from the ancient world, that this claim is not true.

In his third attack, on the ignorance of learned men, Bacon uses another tripartite division. He notes how such ignorance arises from the poverty of learned men; from their manners, which are eccentric in four ways that can be remedied; and finally, from the nature of their studies. Bacon takes more time with the last and, continuing his general anatomical metaphor, subdivides it into three "distempers" (fevers): fantastical learning, contentious learning, and delicate learning, or "vain imaginations, vain altercations, and vain affectations."

He begins his analysis of this illness of the body of learning with a passage that marks a watershed in Renaissance intellectual life. He attacks the development in his time of the Ciceronian prose style, an ornateness of language that inhibits clear meaning (he would add an attack on the more curt Senecan style in his 1623 translation of *The Advancement of Learning* into Latin, where he notes that Senecan language recoiled from the Ciceronian and itself became destructive). Bacon demonstrates how Martin Luther and the Reformation evolved through necessity a prose style in which "men began to hunt more after words than matter." The same kind of historical analysis dominates his attack on vain and contentious learning, seen particularly in the Schoolmen and the monks, for which Bacon invents the first of his insect images: "their wits being shut up in the cells of a few authors (chiefly Aristotle their dictator) as their persons were shut up in the cells of monasteries and colleges; and knowing little history, either of nature or time; did out of no great quantity of matter, and infinite agitation of wit, spin out unto us those laborious webs of learning which are extant in their books." Although the third attack is on the worst of the vanities, vain imagining of knowledge itself, Bacon concentrates largely on credit being given to false authorities. He then turns quickly to the next section, a kind of appendage to the three attacks on ignorance.

This section is the catalogue of "peccant" or unformed "humours" or illnesses. The brief paragraphs describing the "humours" read like expanded aphorisms, and they include some of Bacon's most spectacular images, such as the analogy of time and the river, Columbus as model experimenter, and the bodies of young men as knowledge, and arguments such as modern time being the real antiquity of the world. This catalogue ends in what would become Bacon's most elaborate use of the simile. Using anaphora, with the word *sometimes* marking the first term and *or* to signal the second term of the comparison, Bacon constructs six serial similes. They dramatize the human mistaking of the ends of knowledge, as, for example, when people seek knowledge "sometimes to entertain their minds with variety and delight . . . or [they seek in knowledge] a terrace, for a wandering and variable mind to walk up and down with a fair prospect." The goal of knowledge is none of the first five but—anticipating his utopia, "New Atlantis"—the sixth: for "the glory of the Creator and the relief of man's estate." Bacon ends this section with another of his recurring images, the female personification of knowledge: neither as courtesan nor bondwoman "but as a spouse, for generation, fruit, and comfort."

For the rest of the first book Bacon catalogues types that represent models of learning, first from the biblical world and then from the classical world. Bacon's parody of the old Christian device of typology culminates in his master figures of Alexander the Great and Julius Caesar, who represent both power and knowledge. The second book probably offered the next centuries in England their most accessible design of an encyclopedia of knowledge, for here Bacon seeks to organize all knowledge and to show areas that needed exploration and development. The impact of *The Advancement of Learning* and its Latin translation was immense throughout England, Europe, and America for centuries to come. Not only the eighteenth-century French philosophes but most of the modern institutes and centers of learning and intellectual life developed from this model.

Before and after publication of *The Advancement of Learning*, Bacon wrote tentative sketches that found their way into that work or derived from it. They also evolved into the grander and wider strategies of his masterwork, the *Novum Organum*. Posthumous works such as "Descriptio Globi Intellectualis" (Description of the Intellectual Globe, 1653) and "Valerius Terminus of the Interpretation of Nature, with Annotations of Hermes Stella" (1732) show how Bacon developed his ideas with startling images from around 1603 until 1620. The most complete of these works was his book of Hellenic mythology, *De Sapientia Veterum Liber* (1609). Here Bacon uses one of his most fascinating strategies, interpreting myth after myth in terms of his own new philosophy, politics, and ethics. Thus, for example, the myth of Cupid unveils, if properly understood, the mysteries of the atom; Pan, nature; Proteus, matter; Endymion, the court favorite; Perseus, war; Atalanta, profit; the Styx, treaties. Once more Bacon has used striking images to represent his own renewal of human learning.

This same sense of innovation marks the *Novum Organum*. Both in Latin and in the English translations that soon followed, Bacon's crucial text of 1620 embodies new form and new concepts, or at least ideas developed out of the matrix of *The Advancement of Learning*. The book begins with a series of introductory texts in which Bacon's universal scheme for the transformation of learning is given. The plan, which he calls *Instauratio Magna* (the Great Instauration [Restoration]), is to have six parts, corresponding to the six days of God's creation of the world: first, The Divisions of the Sciences; second, The New Organon, or Directions concerning the Interpretation of Nature; third, The Phenomena of the Universe, or a Natural and Experimental History for the foundation of Philosophy; fourth, The Ladder of the Intellect; fifth, The Forerunners, or Anticipations of the New Philosophy; and sixth, The New Philosophy, or Active Science. Bacon never completed this plan, leaving nothing but fragments of most of the parts; but he clearly indicated certain connections with his major texts. Thus, the first part of Bacon's plan for renewal can be found in the Latin version of *The Advancement of Learning*, the second in the *Novum Organum*, and the third in his various studies of natural and human phenomena; parts four and five are only hinted at in certain texts; and the utopia "New Atlantis" answers to the sixth part the most fully of any text of Bacon's.

The body of Bacon's 1620 text represents his attempt to establish a new logic of induction by following the strategies developed in his first major text of 1605: the first book of the *Novum Organum* cleanses and prepares the mind for the actual method of induction in the second part. Both books are written in aphorisms, either curt and direct, as in the first aphorism ("Man, being the servant and interpreter of Nature, can do and understand so much and so much only as he has observed in fact or in thought of the course of nature: beyond this he neither knows anything nor can do anything"), or quite long, even beyond the normal length of a Baconian essay.

There are several images, or image patterns, that date from earlier works but find their climactic structure here. The best known is Bacon's invention of the four Idols to show the false notions that have possessed the minds of human beings and must be removed before the true method of logic can take hold. Bacon calls the first of these the Idols of the Tribe, the measuring of all perception and reality by the human senses: "the human understanding . . . like a false mirror, which, receiving rays irregularly, distorts and discolours the nature of things by mingling its own nature with it." The Idols of the Den (Bacon draws here from Plato's *Republic*, in which people imprisoned in a cave mistake shadows for reality) make individual perception the measure of all reality. The Idols of the Market Place are formed by language: words are often either ambiguous or allow fictitious entities to be mistaken for real ones. The Idols of the Theatre are the bad philosophies the Renaissance had inherited, "so many stage-plays, representing worlds of their own creation after an unreal and scenic fashion."

Central recurring images in the *Novum Organum* include the insect imagery in which the bee represents the ideal scientist, not the ant of empiricism or the spider of abstract philosophy. Here too are the Greek myths, refurbished and descrip-

Engraved title page by Simon van de Passe for the first edition of Bacon's Summi Angliae Cancellarii Instauratio magna, *one of the most influential books in the history of scientific thought for its development of the inductive method of reasoning*

tive of Bacon's method of purifying the mind and rebuilding it through a new logic. In Aphorism 92 of book one Bacon takes his rhetorical skills to new heights to bring about a turning point in his argument: "I am now therefore to speak touching Hope; especially as I am not a dealer in promises, and wish neither to force nor to ensnare men's judgments, but to lead them by the hand with their good will." At the end of this aphorism Bacon gives fullest expression to his Columbus image. It explains the purpose of his book and, indeed, of his whole lifework: "And therefore it is fit that I publish and set forth those conjectures of mine which make hope in this matter reasonable; just as Columbus did, before that wonderful voyage of his across the Atlantic, when he gave the reasons for his conviction that new lands and continents might be discovered besides those which were known before; which reasons, though rejected at first, were afterwards made good by experience, and were the causes and beginnings of great events."

Bacon's sense of topos and imagery also dominates the very terms and procedure of his scientific method. Thus, the inductive method of scientific investigation that Bacon develops in the second book of the *Novum Organum* involves the regulating of observation by the setting up of three kinds of "Tables and Arrangements of Instances" or "Tables of Presentation." First, a "Table of Essence and Presence" will be used to note all observed instances of a given quality—what Bacon calls a "simple nature," such as heat, yellowness, malleability, heaviness, and so on—in diverse substances. Second, in a "Table of Deviation, or of Absence in Proximity" will be listed cases where the quality is absent. Finally, variations in the amount of a given quality in the same substance under different conditions, or in different substances, will be noted in a "Table of

Effigy of Bacon in St. Michael's Church, St. Albans

Degrees or Table of Comparisons." By means of such tables, the scientist's observations—whether of naturally occurring events or of the results of artificially contrived experiments—will not be random but will be guided systematically toward the discovery of causes and general laws. Other "helps of the understanding in the interpretation of nature" besides the tables include twenty-seven kinds of "prerogative instances," such as: "solitary instances," in which two kinds of a thing differ in only one quality; "glaring instances," where one quality is especially conspicuous in a thing, and "crucial instances," where the presence or absence of a given quality can help the scientist to decide between two equally convincing theories. Distrustful of wild leaps of the imagination, Bacon neglects the deductive method of hypothesis, by which most scientific discoveries are actually made.

Bacon's "New Atlantis" evolves from his Columbus imagery of the New World and exploration. Just as his other masterwork from his last five years, *The Historie of the Raigne of King Henry The Seventh,* revolutionized the method of historiography with its realistic and ambiguous portrayals of character and event, its superb use of old texts, its refusal to give transcendental meaning to events, and its clarity and continuity of prose style, so the "New Atlantis" set the pattern for most scientific utopias after the Renaissance.

Bacon's utopia is set in the frame of a first-person discourse exhibiting a pattern of conversion: a European sailor thrown upon the shores of a previously undiscovered island in the South Seas is drawn into the scientific world of Bensalem. The conversion takes place in a series of stages. There is first the storm that drives the ship off its course from Peru to China and Japan, and then the sight of the uncharted country. There follows the slow immersion in the exotic life of the island, with its mixture of the familiar and the utterly new. The languages of Hebrew, ancient Greek, scholastic medieval Latin, and the modern Spanish that the crew recognize, and the Christianity of the inhabitants, all provide a foundation that permits the Europeans to absorb the culture shock of the new technologies, medicines, materials, and dress. A third stage follows when the narrator learns the history of the island, especially how it miraculously received Christianity and the books of the Bible and how the good king Solamona transformed the society, bequeathing especially the scientific center called Solomon's House—"the noblest foundation," says the Governor of the Strangers' House to the narrator, "that ever was upon the earth, and the lanthorn [lantern] of this kingdom. . . . dedicated to the study of the Works and Creatures of God."

The final stage of the conversion occurs when a Father of Solomon's House travels to the city. The nameless European narrator is chosen to have a special audience with this sophisticated Father (a figure whose position in an order of scientists parodies that of a Jesuit priest). In this audience, the conversion is complete—that is, as complete as this unfinished narrative allows. The Father begins: "God bless thee, my son; I will give thee the greatest jewel I have. For I will impart unto three, for the love of God and men, a relation of the true state of Solomon's House."

Most of the rest of the science-fiction narrative is a catalogue of the wonders of this new society, whose end is "the knowledge of Causes, and secret motions of things; and the enlarging of the bounds of Human Empire, to the effecting of all things possible." The catalogue of wonders reads like one of Bacon's natural histories, listing, in aphoristic form, observations or inventions (among the latter are the telephone, airplane, and submarine). Most remarkable is the organization of science: the society of priest-scientists with its groups of three, extending from gatherers of experiments called "Depredators" to "Interpreters of Nature" who "raise the former discoveries by experiments into greater observations, axioms, and aphorisms."

After describing two significant aspects of the order—its gallery of statues of inventors and explorers, and its religious ceremonies in which God is praised for "his marvelous works" and implored "for aid and blessing for the illumination of our labours, and the turning of them into good and holy uses"—the Father rises, and the act of conversion is complete: ". . . and I, as I had been taught, knelt down; and he laid his right hand upon my head, and said, 'God bless thee, my son, and God bless this relation which I have made. I give thee leave to publish it, for the good of other nations; for we here are in God's bosom, a land unknown.' "

The effect of Bacon's message—especially as narrated in the persuasive science fiction of the "New Atlantis" and in the lively prose of his essays and *Advancement of Learning* and the elegant Latin of his *Novum Organum*—was immediate. From the Civil War to the French Revolution to Darwin and the intellectual debates of the nineteenth and twentieth centuries, Bacon has remained quite alive.

Bibliographies:

R. W. Gibson, *Francis Bacon: A Bibliography of His Works and of Baconiana to the Year 1750* (Oxford: Scrivener Press, 1950);

W. A. Sessions, "Recent Studies in Francis Bacon (1945-1984)," *English Literary Renaissance*, 17 (Spring 1987): 351-371;

Sessions, *The Essential Bacon: An Annotated Bibliography of Major Modern Studies* (New York: Macmillan, forthcoming).

Biographies:

Catherine Drinker Bowen, *Francis Bacon: The Temper of a Man* (Boston: Little, Brown, 1963);

Daphne du Maurier, *Golden Lads: Sir Francis Bacon, Anthony Bacon, and Their Friends* (Garden City, N.Y.: Doubleday, 1975);

Du Maurier, *The Winding Stair: Francis Bacon, His Rise and Fall* (London: Gollancz, 1976; Garden City, N.Y.: Doubleday, 1977).

References:

Fulton H. Anderson, *The Philosophy of Francis Bacon* (New York: Octagon Books, 1971);

Benjamin Farrington, *Francis Bacon: Philosopher of Industrial Science* (New York: Schuman, 1949);

Farrington, *Francis Bacon: Pioneer of Planned Science* (London: Weidenfeld & Nicolson, 1963);

Stanley Fish, "Georgics of the Mind: The Experience of Bacon's *Essays*," in his *Self-Consuming Artifacts* (Berkeley: University of California Press, 1972), pp. 78-155;

Lisa Jardine, *Francis Bacon: Discovery and the Art of Discourse* (Cambridge: Cambridge University Press, 1974);

C. S. Lewis, *English Literature in the Sixteenth Century, Excluding Drama* (Oxford: Oxford University Press, 1954);

Paolo Rossi, *Francis Bacon: From Magic to Science*, translated by Sacha Rabinovitch (London: Routledge & Kegan Paul, 1968);

W. A. Sessions, *Francis Bacon's Legacy of Texts: "The Art of Discovery Grows with Discovery"* (New York: AMS Press, 1990);

Brian Vickers, *Francis Bacon and Renaissance Prose* (New York & Cambridge: Cambridge University Press, 1968);

Vickers, ed., *Essential Articles for the Study of Francis Bacon* (Hamden, Conn.: Archon Books, 1968);

Charles Whitney, *Francis Bacon and Modernity* (New Haven: Yale University Press, 1986).

Francis Beaumont
(circa 1584 - 6 March 1616)
John Fletcher
(December 1579 - August 1625)

This entry was updated by Cyrus Hoy (University of Rochester) from his entry in DLB 58: Jacobean and Caroline Dramatists.

BOOKS: *Salmacis and Hermaphroditus*, by Beaumont (London: Printed by S. Stafford for J. Hodgets, 1602);

The Woman Hater, by Beaumont and Fletcher (London: Printed by R. Raworth & sold by J. Hodgets, 1607);

The Faithfull Shepheardesse, by Fletcher (London: Printed by E. Allde for R. Bonian & H. Walley, 1609?);

The Knight of the Burning Pestle, by Beaumont (London: Printed by N. Okes for W. Burre, 1613);

The Masque of the Inner Temple and Grayes Inne, by Beaumont (London: Printed by F. Kingston for G. Norton, 1613);

Cupid's Revenge, by Beaumont and Fletcher (London: Printed by T. Creede for Josias Harison, 1615);

The Scornful Ladie, by Beaumont and Fletcher (London: Printed by J. Beale for M. Partrich, 1616);

A King and No King, by Beaumont and Fletcher (London: Printed by J. Beale for T. Walkley, 1619);

The Maides Tragedy, by Beaumont and Fletcher (London: Printed by N. Okes for F. Constable, 1619);

Phylaster, or Love Lyes a Bleeding, by Beaumont and Fletcher (London: Printed by N. Okes for T. Walkley, 1621);

The Tragedy of Thierry King of France and His Brother Theodoret, by Beaumont, Fletcher, and Philip Massinger (London: Printed by N. Okes for T. Walkley, 1621);

Henry VIII, by Fletcher and William Shakespeare, in *Mr. William Shakespeares Comedies, Histories, & Tragedies* (London: Printed by Isaac Jaggard & Ed. Blount, 1623);

The Two Noble Kinsmen, by Fletcher and Shakespeare (London: Printed by T. Cotes for J. Waterson, 1634);

The Elder Brother, by Fletcher and Massinger (London: Printed by F. Kingston for J. Waterson & J. Benson, 1637);

The Bloody Brother, by Fletcher, Massinger, and others (perhaps Ben Jonson and George Chapman) (London: Printed by R. Bishop for T. Allott & J. Crook, 1639); republished as *The Tragœdy of Rollo Duke of Normandy* (Oxford: Printed by L. Lichfield, 1640);

Monsieur Thomas, by Fletcher (London: Printed by T. Harper for J. Waterson, 1639);

Wit Without Money, by Fletcher (London: Printed by T. Cotes for A. Crooke & W. Cooke, 1639);

Poems, by Beaumont (London: Printed by R. Hodgkinson for W. Wethered & L. Blaikelocke, 1640; enlarged edition, London: Printed for Laurence Blaikelocke, 1653); republished as *Poems: The Golden Remains of Francis Beaumont and John Fletcher* (London: Printed for W. Hope, 1660);

The Night-Walker, or The Little Theife, by Fletcher, revised by James Shirley (London: Printed by T. Cotes for A. Crooke & W. Cooke, 1640);

Rule a Wife and Have a Wife, by Fletcher (Oxford: Printed by L. Lichfield, 1640);

Comedies and Tragedies Written by Francis Beaumont and John Fletcher, Gentlemen. Never printed before, and now published by the Authours Originall Copies (London: Printed for Humphrey Robinson & Humphrey Moseley, 1647) —comprises *The Mad Lover, The Spanish Curate, The Little French Lawyer, The Custom of the Country, The Noble Gentleman, The Captain, Beggars' Bush, The Coxcomb, The False One, The Chances, The Loyal Subject, The Laws of Candy, The Lovers' Progress, The Island Princess, The Humourous Lieutenant, The Nice Valour or the Passionate Madman, The Maid in the Mill, The Prophetess, The Tragedy of Bonduca, The Sea Voyage, The Double Marriage, The Pil-*

John Fletcher (National Portrait Gallery, London) and Francis Beaumont (Knowle Estates)

grim, The Knight of Malta, The Woman's Prize or The Tamer Tamed, Love's Cure or The Martial Maid, The Honest Man's Fortune, The Queen of Corinth, Women Pleased, A Wife for a Month, Wit at Several Weapons, The Tragedy of Valentinian, The Fair Maid of the Inn, Love's Pilgrimage, The Masque of the Inner Temple and Gray's Inn, Four Plays or Moral Representations in One;

The Wild Goose Chase, by Fletcher (London, 1652);

A Very Woman, Massinger's revision of an unidentified play by Fletcher and Massinger of circa 1619-1622, in *Three New Playes . . . Written By Philip Massenger* (London: Printed for Humphrey Moseley, 1655);

Fifty Comedies and Tragedies. Written by Francis Beaumont and John Fletcher, Gent. All in one Volume. Published by the Authours Originall Copies, the Songs to each Play being added (London: Printed by J. Macock for John Martyn, Henry Herringman & Richard Marriot, 1679)—comprises the contents of the 1647 folio and *The Maid's Tragedy, Philaster, A King and No King, The Scornful Lady, The Elder Brother, Wit Without Money, The Faithful Shepherdess, Rule a Wife and Have a Wife, Monsieur Thomas, The Bloody Brother or Rollo Duke of Normandy, The Wild Goose Chase, The Knight of the Burning Pestle, The Night Walker, Cupid's Revenge, The Two Noble Kinsmen, Thierry and Theodoret, The Woman Hater* (the volume contains fifty-two plays, including erroneously James Shirley's *The Coronation*).

Editions and Collections: *The Works of Beaumont and Fletcher*, 11 volumes, edited by Alexander Dyce (London: Moxon, 1843-1846);

The Dramatic Works in the Beaumont and Fletcher Canon, 7 volumes to date, Fredson Bowers, general editor (Cambridge: Cambridge University Press, 1966-).

PLAY PRODUCTIONS: *The Woman Hater*, by Beaumont and Fletcher, London, Paul's theater, circa 1606;

The Knight of the Burning Pestle, by Beaumont, London, Blackfriars theater, circa 1607;

The Noble Gentleman, probably by Beaumont, later revised by Fletcher (and perhaps others), London, Paul's theater (?), circa 1607;

Love's Cure, or The Martial Maid, by Beaumont and Fletcher, later revised by Philip Massinger, London, Paul's theater (?), circa 1607;

The Faithful Shepherdess, by Fletcher, London, Blackfriars theater, circa 1608;

Philaster, or Love Lies a-Bleeding, by Beaumont and Fletcher, London, Blackfriars theater, circa 1609;

The Coxcomb, by Beaumont and Fletcher, London, Whitefriars theater, circa 1609;

Cupid's Revenge, by Beaumont and Fletcher, London, Whitefriars theater, circa 1611;

The Woman's Prize or The Tamer Tamed, by Fletcher, London, Whitefriars theater, circa 1611;

The Night Walker or The Little Thief, by Fletcher, London, Whitefriars theater, circa 1611;

The Maid's Tragedy, by Beaumont and Fletcher, London, Blackfriars theater, circa 1611;

A King and No King, by Beaumont and Fletcher, London, Blackfriars theater, circa 1611;

The Captain, by Beaumont and Fletcher, London, Blackfriars theater, circa 1611;

Bonduca, by Fletcher, London, Blackfriars theater, circa 1611;

Valentinian, by Fletcher, London, Blackfriars theater, circa 1612;

Monsieur Thomas, or Father's Own Son, by Fletcher, London, Whitefriars theater, circa 1612;

Four Plays, or Moral Representations in One, by Fletcher and Nathan Field, unknown theater, circa 1612;

Cardenio, by Fletcher and William Shakespeare, London, at Court, winter 1612-1613;

The Masque of the Inner Temple and Gray's Inn, verses by Beaumont, London, Whitehall Palace, Banqueting House, 20 February 1613;

The Two Noble Kinsmen, by Fletcher and Shakespeare, London, Blackfriars theater, circa 1613;

Henry VIII, by Fletcher and Shakespeare, London, Globe theater, 1613;

The Honest Man's Fortune, by Fletcher, Field, and Massinger, London, Whitefriars theater, circa 1613;

Wit Without Money, by Fletcher, London, Whitefriars theater, circa 1614;

The Scornful Lady, by Beaumont and Fletcher, London, Porter's Hall theater, circa 1615;

Thierry and Theodoret, by Beaumont, Fletcher, and Massinger, London, Blackfriars theater, circa 1615;

Beggars' Bush, by Beaumont, Fletcher, and Massinger, London, Blackfriars theater, circa 1615;

Love's Pilgrimage, by Beaumont and Fletcher, London, Blackfriars theater, circa 1616;

The Nice Valour, or the Passionate Madman, possibly by Fletcher, but mainly the work of Thomas Middleton, unknown theater, circa 1616;

Wit at Several Weapons, possibly by Fletcher, later revised by Middleton and William Rowley, unknown theater, circa 1616;

The Mad Lover, by Fletcher, London, Blackfriars theater, circa 1616;

The Queen of Corinth, by Fletcher, Massinger, and Field, London, Blackfriars theater, circa 1617;

The Chances, by Fletcher, London, Blackfriars theater, circa 1617;

The Jeweller of Amsterdam, by Fletcher, Massinger, and Field, London, Blackfriars theater, circa 1617-1619(?);

The Knight of Malta, by Fletcher, Massinger, and Field, London, Blackfriars theater, circa 1618;

The Loyal Subject, by Fletcher, London, Blackfriars theater, 1618;

The Humourous Lieutenant, or Demetrius and Enanthe, by Fletcher, London, Blackfriars theater, circa 1619;

The Bloody Brother, or Rollo Duke of Normandy, by Fletcher, Massinger, and others (perhaps Ben Jonson and George Chapman), London, Blackfriars theater, circa 1619;

Sir John van Olden Barnavelt, by Fletcher and Massinger, London, Blackfriars theater, August 1619;

The Custom of the Country, by Fletcher and Massinger, London, Blackfriars theater, circa 1619;

The False One, by Fletcher and Massinger, London, Blackfriars theater, circa 1620;

The Laws of Candy (perhaps the work of John Ford), London, Blackfriars theater, circa 1620;

Women Pleased, by Fletcher, London, Blackfriars theater, circa 1620;

The Island Princess, by Fletcher, London, Blackfriars theater, circa 1621;

The Double Marriage, by Fletcher and Massinger, London, Blackfriars theater, circa 1621;

The Pilgrim, by Fletcher, London, Blackfriars theater, circa 1621;

The Wild Goose Chase, by Fletcher, London, Blackfriars theater, circa 1621;

The Prophetess, by Fletcher and Massinger, London, Blackfriars theater, licensed 14 May 1622;

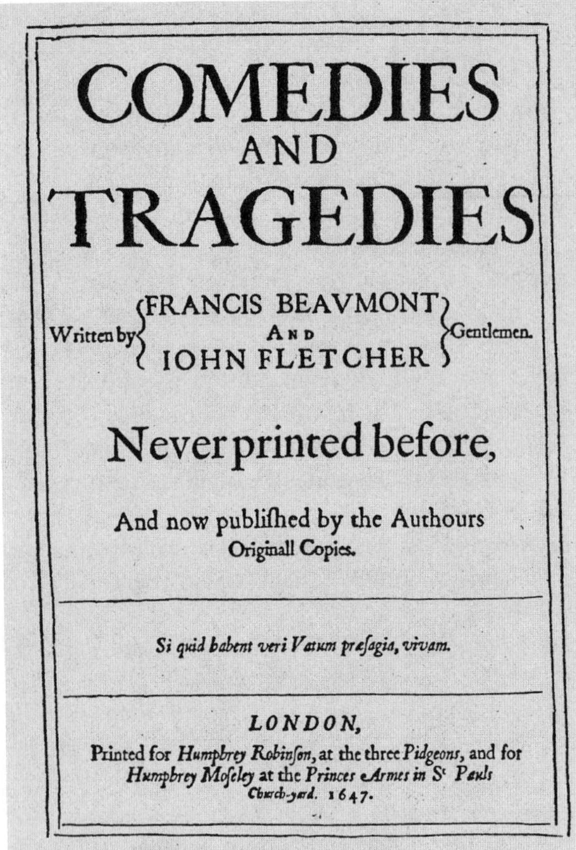

COMEDIES
AND
TRAGEDIES

Written by FRANCIS BEAVMONT And IOHN FLETCHER Gentlemen.

Never printed before,

And now publiſhed by the Authours Originall Copies.

Si quid habent veri Vatum præſagia, vivam.

LONDON,

Printed for *Humphrey Robinſon*, at the three *Pidgeons*, and for *Humphrey Moſeley* at the *Princes Armes in St Pauls Church-yard.* 1647.

Title page for the first of the folio collections that contributed to the impression that Beaumont and Fletcher always wrote as a team. In fact, Beaumont had a hand in only six of the thirty-five plays in this volume (American Art Association/Anderson Galleries auction catalogue, sale number 4240, 11-12 March 1936).

The Sea Voyage, by Fletcher and Massinger, London, Blackfriars theater, licensed 22 June 1622;

The Spanish Curate, by Fletcher and Massinger, London, Blackfriars theater, licensed 24 October 1622;

The Little French Lawyer, by Fletcher and Massinger, London, Blackfriars theater, circa 1623;

The Maid in the Mill, by Fletcher and Rowley, London, Blackfriars theater, licensed 29 August 1623;

The Devil of Dowgate, or Usury Put to Use, by Fletcher, London, Blackfriars theater, licensed 17 October 1623;

The Lovers' Progress, by Fletcher (apparently licensed 6 December 1623 as *The Wandering Lovers*; revised by Massinger as *Cleander*, licensed 7 May 1634), London, Blackfriars theater;

A Wife for a Month, by Fletcher, London, Blackfriars theater, licensed 27 May 1624;

Rule a Wife and Have a Wife, by Fletcher, London, Blackfriars theater, licensed 19 October 1624;

The Elder Brother, by Fletcher and Massinger, London, Blackfriars theater, circa 1625;

The Fair Maid of the Inn, by Fletcher, Massinger (and perhaps John Webster and John Ford), London, Blackfriars theater, licensed 22 January 1626;

A Very Woman (Massinger's revision of an unidentified play by Fletcher and Massinger of circa 1619-1622), London, Blackfriars theater, licensed 6 June 1634.

OTHER: *Certain Elegies Done by Sundrie Excellent Wits*, includes nondramatic poems by Beaumont (London: Printed by B. Alsop for M. Patriche, 1618).

Francis Beaumont and John Fletcher began to work together as dramatists around 1606-1607, and in the course of the next half-dozen years wrote some of the most successful plays of the Jacobean theater, plays that continued to hold the stage a century later. They wrote both comedies and tragedies, but they seem to have had their first success in the newly fashionable genre of tragicomedy, a form that provided a potentially tragic plot with a happy ending. Their emergence as playwrights coincided with the closing years of William Shakespeare's career in the theater, and critics have long noted the tragicomic shape of Shakespeare's last plays. Shakespeare's *Cymbeline* and Beaumont and Fletcher's *Philaster* display some notable similarities of plot and tone, but the date of each play is so uncertain (both seem to have been written circa 1609) that it is impossible to say which influenced the other. The vogue of tragicomedy was in the air. Shakespeare himself had experimented with it several years before, in *Measure for Measure* (circa 1603-1604), but the success of the younger dramatists with the form may have encouraged him to explore its possibilities even further in plays such as *Cymbeline* (1609), *The Winter's Tale* (1611), and *The Tempest* (1611). Tragicomedy dominated the London stage throughout the rest of the period, until the closing of the theaters in 1642, and the model for later Jacobean and Caroline tragicomedy was provided by plays such as Beaumont and Fletcher's *Philaster* and *A King and No King* (circa 1611), and the many plays Fletcher wrote either alone or in collaboration with other dramatists after his association with Beaumont ended.

The period of their collaboration did not, in fact, last long. Beaumont married an heiress sometime around 1613 or 1614, and his career as a playwright seems to have ended then. He died in 1616. By that time, Fletcher had succeeded Shakespeare as principal dramatist for London's leading acting company, the King's Men, and he wrote steadily for the stage until his death in August 1625. However, the initial impression of Beaumont and Fletcher as a team persisted. Beaumont, at most, could have had a share in no more than twelve of the fifty-four plays in the Beaumont and Fletcher canon, but when a collection of these plays was published in 1647, it bore the title *Comedies and Tragedies Written by Francis Beaumont and John Fletcher, Gentlemen.* There were those at the time who protested that many of the plays in this 1647 folio collection were the unaided work of Fletcher, or of Fletcher in collaboration with dramatists (especially Philip Massinger) other than Beaumont. The protests went unheeded, however, and when in 1679 the plays in the 1647 folio were republished together with the plays that had previously been printed in individual quarto editions (which the 1647 folio had excluded), this second, 1679 folio was titled *Fifty Comedies and Tragedies. Written by Francis Beaumont and John Fletcher, Gent.* The 1679 folio defined the corpus of plays adopted (with occasional additions and subtractions) in all later editions, and the canon continues to be designated as Beaumont and Fletcher's. The two playwrights seem fated to be irrevocably linked in English literary history, and the linkage is one that their contemporary audiences fostered. Thomas Fuller, writing in 1662 (in *The Histories of the Worthies of England*), compared them to "Castor and Pollux (most happy when in conjunction)."

Both dramatists were members of distinguished families, that of Beaumont being especially venerable: it was connected with some of the oldest and noblest families in England (Nevil, Hastings, Talbot, Cavendish), including a royal one (Plantagenet). The Beaumonts were landed gentry, some of the land in their country seat in Leicestershire having been recently acquired from the dissolution of the Nunnery of Grace-Dieu in Charnwood Forest. Beaumont's father (also named Francis) was a lawyer and judge; he was a member of Parliament in 1572, made sergeant at law in 1589, and in 1593 appointed one of the Queen's Justices of the Court of Common

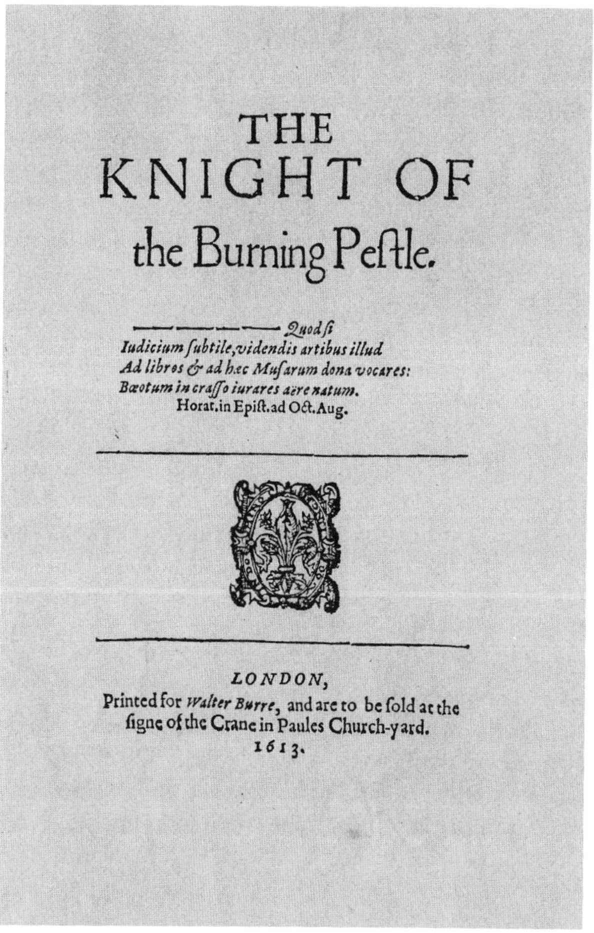
THE
KNIGHT OF
the Burning Peſtle.

Quod ſi
Iudicium ſubtile,videndis artibus illud
Ad libros & ad hæc Muſarum dona vocares:
Bœotum in craſſo iurares aere natum.
Horat.in Epiſt.ad Oct.Aug.

LONDON,
Printed for *Walter Burre*, and are to be ſold at the ſigne of the Crane in Paules Church-yard.
1613.

Title page for the 1613 edition of the only known play written by Beaumont alone (Bodleian Library)

Pleas. Beaumont the dramatist was born about 1584. On 4 February 1597 he (along with his two older brothers, Henry and John) entered Broadgates Hall (now Pembroke College), Oxford; the matriculation entry describes him as twelve years of age at the time of his admission. His father died a year later (22 April 1598); the funeral certificate gives the approximate ages of the dead man's four children: Henry, John, and Elizabeth are said to be, respectively, seventeen, fourteen, and nine years of age, "or thereabouts," and Francis is said to be "of thirteen years or more." On 3 November 1600 he entered the Inner Temple, where his two older brothers had preceded him and where their father and grandfather had prepared for legal careers. Though it is impossible to say how seriously Beaumont ever intended to study law, and while it is apparent that after about 1605 his interests had turned decisively to the theater, he maintained his identification with the Inner Temple throughout his career as a playwright. In 1613, not long before his marriage and retirement from the London theatrical scene, when the Inner Temple joined forces with Gray's Inn to present a masque in honor of the Princess Elizabeth's marriage, it was Beaumont who wrote it. London's inns of court provided an atmosphere that he would have found congenial. His fellow students were aristocrats like himself; there was much interest in poetry and the drama (students at the inns of court were notorious playgoers), and annually there was presented a series of high-spirited revels to celebrate the Christmas season. On one such occasion (sometime between around 1601 and 1605) Beaumont presented a burlesque, "Grammar Lecture," cast in the form of a mock-pedantic explication of the parts of speech amusingly wrenched to convey cynical admonitions to his audience of sophisticated fellow students. Its flashes of witty satire and its vein of extravagant mockery anticipate the ironic inventions that he would soon be putting on the stage.

This was not Beaumont's only literary performance in these early years. In 1602 his Ovidian narrative poem, *Salmacis and Hermaphroditus*, was published anonymously, the same year in which his brother John's mock-heroic poem, *The Metamorphosis of Tobacco*, was published, also anonymously, with some commendatory verses signed "F. B." *Salmacis and Hermaphroditus* contains an introductory sonnet signed "I. B." (that is, "J. B."). The brothers were evidently exchanging poetical compliments, and both were soon moving in literary circles. In the eighth eclogue of his *Poems Lyric and Pastoral* (entered in the Stationers' Register on 19 April 1606), Michael Drayton pays tribute to Mirtilla who is "in the Muses joyes" and who dwells in Charnwood by the river Soar, sister "to those hopefull Boyes," Thirsis and Palmeo: a tribute that is generally assumed to be a reference to Elizabeth Beaumont and her two brothers Francis and John. This suggests that Drayton's lines were written sometime after 10 July 1605, when Henry Beaumont, the eldest brother and head of the family, died. By his will, witnessed by Francis Beaumont and probated February 1606, Sir Henry left half of his private estate to his sister, Elizabeth, and the other half to be divided equally between John and Francis. John succeeded him as head of the family.

The Beaumont family had strong Roman Catholic loyalties. Francis Beaumont's grandmother, mother, uncle, and even his father, before he became a judge, had been active recusants. Before the end of the year 1605, the dramatist's cousin, Anne Vaux, would be implicated in the Gunpowder Plot. Soon after he succeeded to the family estate at Grace-Dieu in the summer of 1605, John Beaumont was penalized for his own recusancy. As a result, sometime before October 1605 the profits from this penalty had been allotted to Sir James Sempill, a boyhood companion of King James. Two-thirds of John Beaumont's lands and all his goods were forfeited to the king, and in 1607 they were formally granted to Sempill, who was still profiting from them as late as 1615. John Beaumont, as a recusant, was now required to live at Grace-Dieu and was confined to his house there. With the income from the family estate thus severely curtailed, Francis Beaumont's decision to write for the theater may have been prompted in part, at least, by financial need.

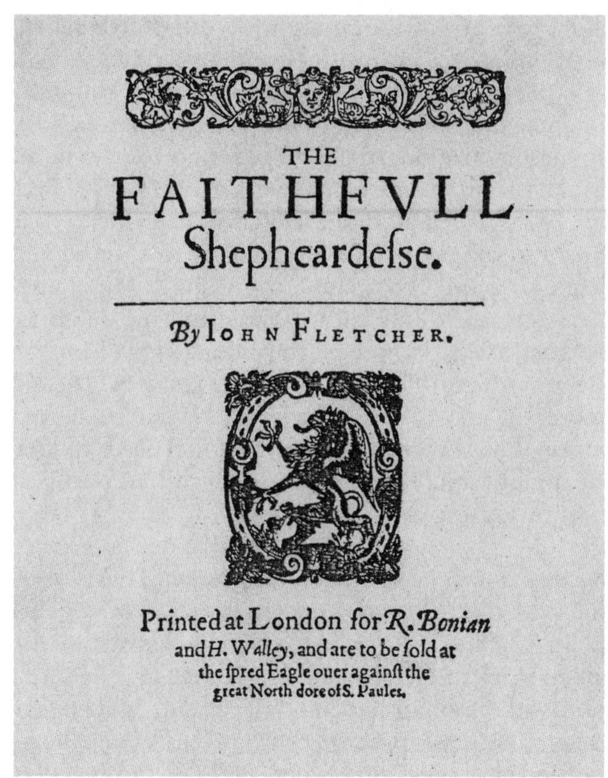
THE
FAITHFVLL
Shepheardesse.
By IOHN FLETCHER.
Printed at London for R. Bonian
and H. Walley, and are to be sold at
the spred Eagle ouer against the
great North doore of S. Paules.

Title page for the 1609(?) quarto edition of Fletcher's pastoral tragicomedy, prefixed by commendatory verses by Beaumont, Ben Jonson, George Chapman, and Nathan Field, all of whom assured potential readers that the play had failed in the theater because it made too great a demand on the intelligence of the average playgoer (Anderson Galleries auction catalogue, sale number 2077, 20-21 May 1926)

In the case of John Fletcher financial necessity seems almost certainly to have dictated the choice of his profession as a writer for the stage.

For the decade or so preceding the beginning of his career as a dramatist, Fletcher had been an orphan. His father had died in 1596, leaving a large burden of debts and nine children, of whom the future playwright, then aged seventeen, was one (his mother had died about 1594). The family fortunes had changed drastically since his birth in December 1579 at Rye, in Sussex, where his father, Richard Fletcher, was a minister of the local church. In the following years the father had had a career of some prominence in the Anglican church: he had been appointed successively chaplain to the queen, dean of Peterborough, bishop of Bristol, bishop of Worcester, and, in 1594, bishop of London. Richard Fletcher enjoyed the favor of the queen, who entrusted him with important missions (as dean of Peterborough he was chaplain to Mary, Queen of Scots, and had witnessed her execution); he had a house in Chelsea and counted among his friends such counselors to the queen as William Cecil, first Baron Burghley, Anthony Bacon, Sir Francis Drake, and Robert Devereux, second Earl of Essex. But in 1595 Richard Fletcher made a most improper second marriage with one Lady Baker, a widow with a notorious past. The queen suspended him from his office for a year, before the end of which he had died. Whether his son the future dramatist was the John Fletcher who entered Bene't College (now Corpus Christi), Cambridge, in 1591 is uncertain (the name was common), but plausible; Richard Fletcher had once been associated with that college. If the identification is allowed, then John Fletcher the dramatist became B.A. in 1595 and M.A. in 1598. He may have spent some of the years until he was able to fend for himself with his uncle Giles, the diplomat and author of a notable book on Russia (published in 1591), and with his young cousins Giles, Jr., and Phineas, who would earn minor places in English literary history as imitators of the poetical manner of Edmund Spenser.

The earliest extant play to exhibit Beaumont and Fletcher working together is a comedy titled *The Woman Hater*, entered in the Stationers' Register on 20 May 1607 and published that year in a quarto edition, the title page of which names no author (the 1648 edition attributed the play to Fletcher while the 1649 edition listed Beaumont and Fletcher as authors; uncertainty of this sort is characteristic of seventeenth-century title-page attributions). Though the play is substantially the work of Beaumont, Fletcher's hand can be traced in at least five scenes, chiefly through his use of certain linguistic forms (notably his preference for the pronoun *ye* for *you*) that Beaumont rarely if ever employed. The play's Italian setting provides the usual veil (familiar in so much of Renaissance English comedy) for satirizing the affectations and the humors of contemporary London life. Its models are the recent satiric comedies of John Marston (such as *The Dutch Courtesan*, 1605, and *The Fawn*, 1606), and the series of comedies of humors and "comical satires" that Ben Jonson had been presenting on the London stage between 1598 and 1605 (*Every Man in his Humour, Every Man Out of his Humour, Cynthia's Revel's, Poetaster*, and most recently, *Volpone*).

The Woman Hater seems to have made no particular impression on its initial audiences. John Dryden, writing many years later (in *An Essay of Dramatick Poesy*, 1668) reported that *Philaster* was the first play that brought Beaumont and Fletcher "in esteem . . . : for before that, they had written two or three very unsuccessfully." *The Woman Hater* was probably one of these. The two others were plays that each dramatist had written independently early in his career: Beaumont's *The Knight of the Burning Pestle*, and Fletcher's *The Faithful Shepherdess*. The composition date of each is uncertain. Nothing is known of either until it appeared in print, and neither play was published until some indeterminate time after it was first performed. *The Knight of the Burning Pestle* was probably written and unsuccessfully acted in 1607 (it was first printed in 1613). *The Faithful Shepherdess* seems to have been presented only to be rejected by audiences in 1608 (it was published in an undated quarto that was probably printed in 1609). Each play is highly characteristic of its author.

The Knight of the Burning Pestle is the only play of Beaumont's sole authorship that survives, and it provides a rare opportunity to witness the full ensemble of his comic artistry operating without interference from another quarter: his talents for satire, parody, and burlesque provide the play with a remarkably rich palette of comic shadings that complement and set each other off as effortlessly as the play's three principals (Grocer, Wife, and Apprentice) move back and forth between audience and stage, incorporating their own play into the one that the designated actors are trying to present. *The Knight* mocks the plot materials and the rhetoric of some of the most popular plays of the period: chauvinistic tales of young Englishmen engaged in chivalric exploits

PHYLASTER.

OR,

Loue lyes a Bleeding.

Acted at the Globe by his Maiesties Seruants.

Written by Francis Baymont and Iohn Fletcher. Gent.

Printed at London for Thomas Walkley, and are to be sold at his shop at the Eagle and Child in Brittaines Bursse. 1620.

Title page for the 1620 quarto edition of one of Beaumont and Fletcher's most successful tragicomedies (Bodleian Library)

in exotic landscapes, such as Thomas Heywood's *Four Prentices of London* (circa 1600), or John Day, William Rowley, and George Wilkins's *Travel of Three English Brothers* (1607); celebrations of the charitable and philanthropic acts of London citizens, such as Thomas Dekker's *The Shoemakers' Holiday* (1599); bourgeois comedies of love involving London citizens, their daughters, and their apprentices, and recounting the triumph of true affection over the objections of mercantile-minded parents (as again, in *The Shoemakers' Holiday*); plays of romantic adventure such as the anonymous *Mucedorus* (1598). In a prefatory note the printer of the 1613 edition of *The Knight* suggests that a reason why the play was "utterly rejected" when it was first acted was the failure of audiences to understand "the privy marke of *Ironie* about it." Irony in *The Knight* is not a matter of separate speeches or scenes directed to familiar satiric targets; rather, it is inherent in the very phenomenon Beaumont is out to represent, namely, the distance that separates the lives of ordinary London citizens from the various romantic fantasies—of knight-errantry, of love and marriage, of the means to fame and fortune—that dazzle their imaginations. However, plays of the sort that Beaumont is parodying in *The Knight* recognized no ironic distance between the facts of middle-class London life and the glamorous dreams that fed the imaginative life of its citizenry, and it is quite likely that the play's first audiences mistook it for another instance of the sort of play it satirizes. Its chief structural novelty—whereby its action has the appearance of being periodically derailed as the Grocer and his wife invade the stage from the audience—may have contributed to the incomprehension with which it was first greeted. Eventually audiences came to terms with the play, and it appears in theatrical repertoires throughout the rest of the period, until the closing of the theaters. It is Beaumont's finest achievement, and one of the most brilliant examples of the mock-heroic and of literary burlesque in English comic literature.

Fletcher's *The Faithful Shepherdess* is a very different kind of play: a pastoral tragicomedy inspired by Giovanni Battista Guarini's *Il Pastor Fido* (1590), though Fletcher's play has very little direct connection with that celebrated work. Where Beaumont's *Knight* is the product of the dramatist's amused observation of the humorous absurdities flourishing around him in contemporary London, *The Faithful Shepherdess* is very much a product of Fletcher's literary imagination. The play's setting is the conventional landscape of pastoral poetry—forests, arbors, bosky dells, with caves and charmed fountains and altars to the god Pan—populated with a typically pastoral dramatis personae: shepherds, shepherdesses, satyrs, river gods, and priests of Pan. The play celebrates the power of chastity (which accounts for its appeal to the young John Milton, a few years later, when he came to write *Comus*, 1634). The power is personified in the figure of Clorin, the faithful shepherdess of the title, who, her beloved having died, has vowed to lead a retired life of virginal purity; this preserves her knowledge, possessed since her youth, of "the dark hidden vertuous use of hearbs"; as a result, she is greatly gifted in the arts of healing. The other principal characters are arranged in a spectrum of passional self-control that extends from Clorin's awesome continence through various degrees of sexual indiscretion to uninhibited lust. Each prowls the forest darkness from dusk to dawn during the single night of the play's action, seeking a partner and encountering various forms of frustration and mayhem in the process (twice in the play a young man stabs the young woman whom he loves but believes to be unfaithful, thereby anticipating what would become a notorious scene in *Philaster*). The elaborate, often shrill, testimonials to the power of chastity contained in the play's poetry exist in strained opposition to the sexual frenzy that informs its action. When the play was published, no attempt was made to conceal its failure in the theater. Fletcher's fellow playwrights (Beaumont, Jonson, George Chapman, Nathan Field) rallied to the occasion by assuring him, in commendatory verses prefixed to the undated quarto edition, that what he had written had been too good for the stage; that its poetical excellencies had been, in effect, its undoing, since they made demands on the intelligence of the average audience that most members thereof were incapable of meeting. *The Faithful Shepherdess* never established itself on the seventeenth-century English stage, but if audiences found it unsatisfactory as a play, readers long admired it as a poem. It has a certain importance in the history of seventeenth-century English drama because it provided the occasion for Fletcher's famous definition of tragicomedy. In his address "To the Reader" printed in the undated quarto text of the play, he describes it as "a pastoral tragicomedy" and suggests that it failed in the theater because audiences came to it with false expectations concerning each term. As for "pastoral," audiences assumed "a play of country hired shepherds in gray cloaks, with curtailed dogs in strings, sometimes laughing together, and sometimes killing one another; and, missing Whitsun-ales, cream, wassail, and morris-dances, began to be angry." As for "tragi-comedy," such a play "is not so called in respect of mirth and killing, but in respect it wants deaths, which is enough to make it no tragedy, yet brings some near it, which is enough to make it no comedy, which must be a representation of familiar people, with such kind of trouble as no life be questioned; so that a god is as lawful in this as in a tragedy, and mean [that is, common] people as in a comedy."

Fletcher's comments are based on Guarini's *Il Compendio della poesia tragicomica*, published in 1601 in defense of his own pastoral tragicomedy, *Il Pastor Fido*. Tragicomedy had been attacked by Italian critics as illegitimate because Aristotle had made no provision for such a genre in his *Poetics*, where he had acknowledged only tragedy and comedy, and because tragicomedy has no distinct properties of its own but consists merely of a combination of tragic and comic elements. In defend-

A King and no King.
Acted at the Globe, by his Maiesties Seruants.
Written by Francis Beamount, and Iohn Flecher.
AT LONDON
Printed for Thomas Walkley, and are to bee sold at his shoppe at the Eagle and Childe in Brittans-Bursse. 1619.

Title page for the 1619 quarto edition of one of the Beaumont and Fletcher tragicomedies that served as models for later Jacobean and Caroline plays written in that popular genre (Bodleian Library)

ing the integrity of the genre Guarini explains how the author of a tragicomedy, far from mechanically combining the elements of tragedy and comedy, judiciously selects what is requisite from each: he takes from tragedy its great persons but not its great action, a plot which is verisimilar but not true, passions that have been moved but are tempered, tragedy's pleasure but not its sadness, "its danger but not its death; from comedy it takes laughter that is not excessive, modest amusement, feigned difficulty, happy reversal, and above all the comic order."

This selective combination of the requisite elements of tragedy and comedy, Guarini is prepared to claim, can result in a new dramatic genre that is superior to the two conventional ones: "It is much more noble than simple tragedy or simple comedy, as that which does not inflict on us atrocious events and horrible and inhumane sights, such as blood and deaths, and which, on the other hand, does not cause us to be so relaxed in laughter that we sin against the modesty and decorum of a well-bred man. And truly if today men understood well how to compose tragicomedy (for it is not an easy thing to do), no other drama should be put on the stage, for tragicomedy is able to include all the good qualities of dramatic poetry and to reject all the bad ones; it can delight all dispositions, all ages, and all tastes—something that is not true of the other two, tragedy and comedy, which are at fault because they go to excess." Tragicomedy was to be the genre in which Beaumont and Fletcher would have two of their most notable stage successes (*Philaster* and *A King and No King*), and it would be the genre which—after Beaumont's retirement—Fletcher, writing alone and in collaboration with other dramatists, would popularize to an extent that would profoundly influence the nature of English drama throughout the rest of the seventeenth century.

The composition date of *Philaster* is uncertain. It was not published until 1620, but a decade earlier John Davies of Hereford had referred to it under its subtitle, *Love Lies a-Bleeding* (along with *The Faithful Shepherdess*), in epigram 206 of his *Scourge of Folly*, entered in the Stationers' Register on 8 October 1610. Resemblances have often been noted between the titular figure and two of Shakespeare's most famous tragic heroes, Hamlet and Othello. Philaster, like Hamlet, is the son of a king whose kingdom has been usurped by a tyrant; the tyrant tolerates his continued residence at what had been his father's court because the kingdom's subjects love him, but he plans to divert the line of succession from Philaster to his daughter, the Princess Arathusa, whom he intends to marry to a Spanish prince. But Philaster also loves Arathusa and believes that she returns his love. When courtly slander causes him to doubt her faith, an Othello-like fury descends upon him, and he tries to kill the princess. The Shakespearean resemblances are certainly superficial, but ought not to be dismissed. Regularly in the Beaumont and Fletcher plays, there are signs that the authors are reworking situations from Shakespeare's recent plays, or placing one or another of his characters in altered dramatic circumstances. Philaster has a young page, Bellario, who unknown to him is in fact a young girl in disguise; she loves him, and finds herself—in the manner of Viola in Shakespeare's *Twelfth Night* (1601)—pleading the cause of the man she loves to the woman (Arathusa) whom he loves. Bellario is the person with whom, as courtly gossip would have it, Arathusa has been unfaithful to Philaster. There is a moment in the final act of *Twelfth Night* when the Duke, believing his page (the still-disguised Viola) to be his rival for the love of Olivia, threatens to kill the supposed boy. This is the sort of Shakespearean hint Beaumont and Fletcher were fond of developing. Philaster, having wounded Arathusa, wounds Bellario as well. The character of Philaster seems designed to represent a normally gentle prince driven to the brink of madness by melancholy occasioned by his displacement as heir to his father's kingdom and by sexual jealousy occasioned by his supposed displacement in the affections of Arathusa. His behavior is certainly erratic (as Hamlet's is, when the antic disposition is upon him), and his wild swings of mood—from trust to doubt, from proud confidence to pathetic helplessness—give to his movement through the play a quality of comic iteration. On this score, it is worth remembering that Guarini (in a passage already quoted) had stressed that, among the elements of comedy that the tragicomic dramatist will select for his work, he will include "above all the comic order." He will also include, according to Guarini, "feigned difficulty" and "happy reversal." In *Philaster* the feigned difficulty concerns the disguised Bellario and the accusations made against this character and Arathusa. When, at the end of the play, Bellario at last reveals her true identity, the charges against Arathusa fall to the ground, and Philaster's dark fortunes reverse themselves as happily as thought could wish. Arathusa is his, her father accepts him as son-in-law (the Spanish prince is dismissed) and restores to him his rightful place in the kingdom.

A King and No King, which was acted at court on 26 December 1611 and had been licensed for performance earlier in the same year, centers on another unstable protagonist, King Arbaces, whose pride in his self-sufficiency is severely shaken when he returns from his wars to find that his sister, Panthaea, has grown into a beautiful woman in his absence, and that he is falling in love with her, and she with him. Arbaces's desperate impulse to surrender to his incestuous desires at the same time that he is appalled by them is conveyed in some of Beaumont and Fletcher's most bravura scenes (they seem mainly to be the work of Beaumont). Arbaces is the sort of dramatic figure who—like a Medea or a Macbeth—knows what is the right way but yet is willfully

The Maides Tragedy.

AS IT HATH BEENE
diuers times Acted at the *Blacke-friers* by
the Kings Maieſties Seruants.

ASPATIA. AMINTOR.

LONDON
Printed for *Francis Conſtable* and are to be ſold
at the white Lyon ouer againſt the great North
doore of *Pauls Church.* 1619.

Title page for the 1619 quarto edition of the play that, with Philaster *and* A King and No King, *made Beaumont and Fletcher famous with London theatergoers (Bodleian Library)*

prepared to pursue the wrong one; his self-awareness on this score seals his march toward disaster with what would seem to be an inexorable finality, but in the manner of Guarinian tragicomedy, we discover as *A King and No King* nears its end that we have been in the presence of a feigned difficulty, and that a happy reversal is in prospect. Arbaces and Panthaea are not brother and sister after all. She is, in fact, the queen of what he has thought of as his realm, and, by being unkinged, he is free to marry her. For all the tense agonizing that has occurred at the center of the play, *A King and No King* preserves the comic order, as Guarini has said that a tragicomedy should, by surrounding Arbaces with a shrewdly observed group of friends, counselors, and court hangers-on whose response to his plight provides a critique by turns sympathetic and ironical of his extravagant behavior.

The Maid's Tragedy seems to have been written and acted in the period between Beaumont and Fletcher's most famous tragicomedies (it is assumed to have been in existence by 31 October 1611 when the Master of the Revels, licensing an anonymous play without a title, named it a "Second Maiden's Tragedy"). At the center of the play is another overwrought male protagonist, Amintor, who, though he has been betrothed to marry Aspatia, has at the king's command married instead Evadne, sister to his friend, the great general Melantius. What he does not know is that Evadne is the king's mistress, and that the marriage has been arranged to protect her reputation. She announces this fact to Amintor on their wedding night and goes on to declare her intention never to consummate their marriage. The play explores the consequences for all the parties to this sensational situation: Amintor's humiliation and rage, the grief of the abandoned Aspatia, the violent confrontation of brother and sister when Melantius learns why Evadne has married his friend. Amintor's impulse to avenge the dishonor by assaulting the man who has, in effect, made him a cuckold, is paralyzed by his reverence for the divinity that surrounds the person of a king. Melantius is not so awed; he works his sister to a proper sense of her shame with the result that she murders the king in his bed. Aspatia brings about her own death at the hands of Amintor, who thereupon commits suicide.

These three plays made Beaumont and Fletcher famous. That all three were produced by the King's Men (London's most prestigious acting company, of which Shakespeare was a principal shareholder and principal dramatist) is a measure of the success the two playwrights had achieved within a period of rather less than four years. Their first plays had been produced by companies of boy actors: *The Woman Hater* by Paul's boys, at their theater in the precincts of St. Paul's Cathedral; *The Knight of the Burning Pestle* and *The Faithful Shepherdess* by the Children of the Queen's Revels at their theater in Blackfriars. When, in the summer of 1608, the King's Men took over the lease of the enclosed Blackfriars theater for use as a winter headquarters and proceeded henceforth to produce plays in it as well as in their open-air Globe theater, it may have seemed to them wise to employ the services of a pair of dramatists whose skill at entertaining Blackfriars audiences was beginning to be noticed. Prior to *Philaster*, they had written other plays besides *The Woman Hater, The Knight of the Burning Pestle,* and *The Faithful Shepherdess,* though a good deal of uncertainty surrounds the composition of some of them.

There are plays in the Beaumont and Fletcher canon that seem to date from this early period, but there is no external evidence that might help to establish just when they were written; many of these did not appear in print until the folio collection of 1647, and some appear there in versions that have been revised by other hands (a prologue or epilogue frequently announces the fact of revision). A comedy such as *Love's Cure, or The Martial Maid*, for example, is very probably one of Beaumont and Fletcher's earliest collaborations (it has close ties of characterization and language to *The Woman Hater* and may have been written for the company at Paul's), but the 1647 folio text of the play has been extensively revised by Philip Massinger. *The Noble Gentleman* (circa 1607) seems originally to have been a play of Beaumont's sole authorship, but in its extant text it has been revised by Fletcher and perhaps by others. Even after they had been taken up by the King's Men, Beaumont and Fletcher continued to write for the Queen's Revels, now performing at a new theater in Whitefriars. It was for this children's company that they wrote (circa 1609) their very witty comedy of *The Coxcomb* (its plot suggested by the story of "The Curious Impertinent" in part 1 of Miguel de Cervantes' *Don Quixote*; it was performed at court on 2 or 3 November 1612). It was also for this boys' company that they wrote (circa 1611) their lurid tragedy, *Cupid's Revenge* (based on material from Sir Philip Sydney's *Arcadia*, 1593; performances at court recorded on 5 January 1612, 1 January 1613, and either 9 January or 27 February 1613). For the King's Men they wrote (circa 1611) another play about a woman hater, this one titled *The Captain* (circa 1611, it was performed at court during the season 1612-1613).

The court season of 1612-1613 was particularly rich in productions of plays, due to the festivities surrounding the marriage of the Princess Elizabeth to Frederick V, the Elector Palatine, and the head of the league of Protestant princes in Germany. Shortly after his arrival in England in October 1612, the festivities had been interrupted by the death of Prince Henry on 7 November 1612. After a suitable period of mourning the wedding took place on 14 February 1613. *The Masque of the Inner Temple and Gray's Inn* (1613, with verses by Beaumont), prepared by the members of those inns of court in honor of the occasion, was scheduled for performance on 16 February.

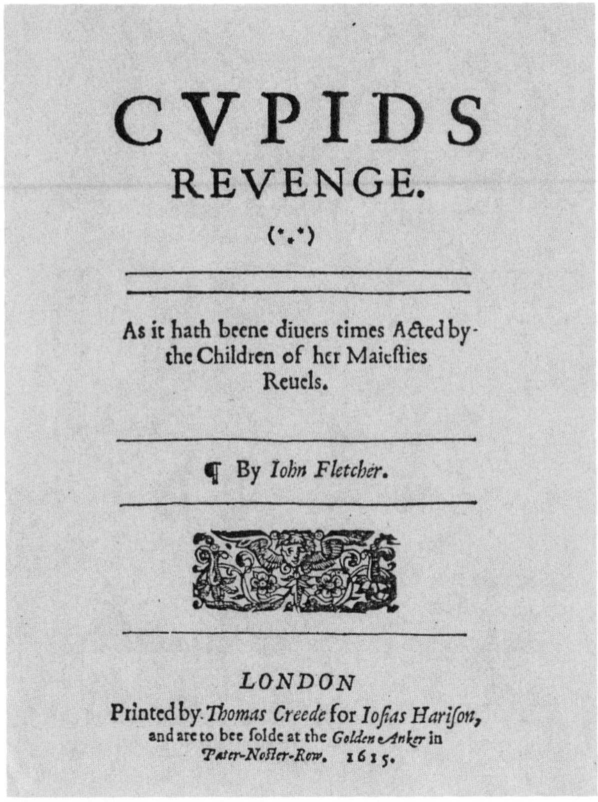
CVPIDS
REVENGE.
(*.*)

As it hath beene diuers times Acted by the Children of her Maiesties Reuels.

¶ By *Iohn Fletcher.*

LONDON
Printed by *Thomas Creede* for *Iosias Harison*, and are to bee solde at the *Golden Anker* in *Pater-Noster-Row*. 1615.

Title page for the 1615 quarto edition of the tragedy Beaumont and Fletcher based on material from Sir Philip Sidney's Arcadia. *Despite the title-page attribution to Fletcher alone, the play is the work of both playwrights (Anderson Galleries auction catalogue, sale number 2077, 20-21 May 1926).*

Since the "device" or theme of the masque was the marriage of the Thames to the Rhine, the masquers deemed it appropriate to go from their rendezvous at Winchester Place in Southwark to Whitehall Palace by water and did so in an elaborate (and very costly) procession of barges and galleys. Upon their arrival, however, they found the palace so crowded with people that it was impossible for them to make their way to the hall where they were to perform. Thus the explanation in the printed text of the masque, which may be true so far as it goes. But it was also rumored that King James, exhausted from having watched masques on the two previous nights (Thomas Campion's *The Lords Masque* on the 14th, and George Chapman's *Masque of the Middle Temple and Lincoln's Inn* on the 15th), pronounced himself incapable of watching another on this occasion. The masquers were invited back four nights later, and Beaumont's creation was staged in the Banqueting House at Whitehall on 20 February.

Beaumont's career as a dramatist was drawing to an end, and with it his life in London, including his life with Fletcher, which years later John Aubrey described (perhaps a bit fancifully) in a much-quoted passage: "They lived together on the Bankside, not far from the Play-house, both batchelors; lay together; had one Wench in the house between them, which they did so admire; the same cloathes and cloake, etc.; between them." But Beaumont—sometime during 1613 or 1614—put his bachelor life behind him and married an heiress, Ursula Isley, of Sundridge Hall, Kent. A daughter, Elizabeth, was born in either 1614 or 1615, and another daughter, named Frances, was born a few months after his death on 6 March 1616. He was buried in the Poet's Corner of Westminster Abbey, only the third English writer (after Geoffrey Chaucer and Spenser) to be so honored.

But either before retiring to his wife's country estate, or in the intervals of his life as a country gentleman during his last months, he contributed to four more plays. Beaumont and Fletcher's *The Scornful Lady* is a brilliant comedy of manners; according to the title page of the play's 1616 quarto edition, it was acted by the Children of the Queen's Revels in the Blackfriars, a statement which, if true, means that it was staged in 1615 during the brief period when the Queen's Revels company, having left Whitefriars, performed in a new theater in the precinct of Blackfriars known as Porter's Hall. Beaumont also has a share with Fletcher in three plays for the King's company that seem to have been staged after his death: *Love's Pilgrimage*, a romantic comedy; *Thierry and Theodoret* (circa 1615), a tragedy; and another comedy, *Beggars' Bush* (circa 1615). *Love's Pilgrimage* must have been one of the last plays on which the two dramatists collaborated. The source of the play, Cervantes' story, *Las dos doncellas*, in his *Novelas Exemplares*, was not allowed for publication in Spain until August 1613. A French translation was published in 1615. There is some evidence that the play was acted in 1616. It was not printed until the publication of the 1647 folio, where the text of the play's opening scene unaccountably contains two sizable passages (of 21 and 111 lines respectively) that duplicate passages in II.ii. and III.i. of Jonson's *The New Inn*, acted by the King's Men in January 1629 and printed in 1631, after the deaths of both Beaumont and Fletcher. Though Beaumont contributed, with Fletcher, to *Thierry and Theodoret*, and to *Beggars' Bush*, a third dramatist, Philip Massinger, has a share in each of these as well. In the years immediately following, Massinger would be Fletcher's principal collaborator, and it would appear that Fletcher joined forces with him now, either in anticipation of Beaumont's retirement, or to take over Beaumont's unfinished shares in these two plays.

In the last years of Beaumont and Fletcher's collaboration, from about 1611 on, Fletcher's career seems to have been moving in its own independent direction. Two signs are notable: Fletcher began to do what Beaumont never did in those years, write plays alone; Fletcher collaborated with Shakespeare on three plays, a suggestive sign that he was being groomed to succeed Shakespeare (who was about to retire) as principal dramatist for the King's Men. Shakespeare's *The Tempest* (produced in 1611) is often taken to be his valediction to the theater, but in fact he wrote three more plays, and Fletcher aided him in each of them. The first seems to have been *Cardenio*, acted at court during the busy Christmas-revels season of 1612-1613, and again before the Savoyard ambassador on 8 June 1613. The play is lost. From its title, one assumes it to have been based on the story of Cardenio in chapters 23-37 of part 1 of Cervantes' *Don Quixote*. The next Shakespeare-Fletcher collaboration was probably *The Two Noble Kinsmen*, a dramatization of Chaucer's "Knight's Tale." Since the play uses material from Beaumont's *The Masque of the Inner Temple and Gray's Inn*, it is usually assumed to have been written not long after the performance of that masque on 20 February 1613. The play was printed in 1634 with a title-page attribution to Shakespeare and Fletcher. The third Shakespeare-Fletcher collaboration was *Henry VIII*. Its date is well established since it is described as a new play in accounts of the performance of it that took place at the Globe on 29 June 1613, in the course of which fire broke out and destroyed the theater. The play was first printed (without reference to Fletcher) in the 1623 folio collection of Shakespeare's plays.

After the failure on stage of his *The Faithful Shepherdess*, Fletcher seems to have resumed his career as an independent dramatist with a series of comedies written for companies other than the King's. The first of these seems to be *The Woman's Prize or The Tamer Tamed*, a farcical exploitation of Shakespeare's *The Taming of the Shrew*, written sometime near the end of 1610 or early in 1611 for an unknown company (by 1633 it had passed into the possession of the King's).

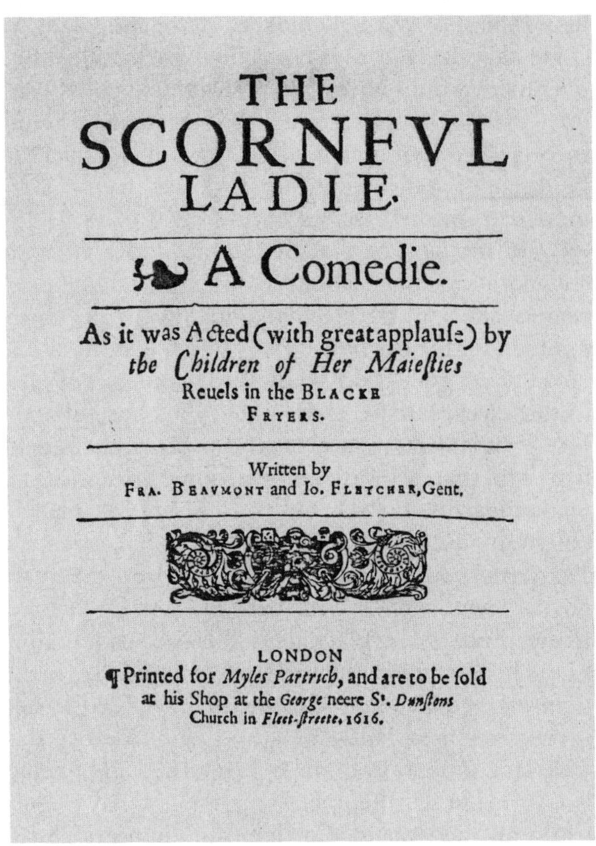

THE
SCORNFVL
LADIE.

A Comedie.

As it was Acted (with great applause) by
the Children of Her Maiesties
Reuels in the BLACKE
FRYERS.

Written by
FRA. BEAVMONT and IO. FLETCHER, Gent.

LONDON
Printed for *Myles Partrich*, and are to be sold
at his Shop at the *George* neere S^t. *Dunstons*
Church in *Fleet-streete*. 1616.

Title page for the 1616 quarto edition of one of the last plays that Beaumont wrote with Fletcher (Bodleian Library)

There follows a trio of lively comedies set in London and environs and centering on the amorous and/or monetary intrigues of feckless young gentlemen: *The Night Walker or The Little Thief* (circa 1611, for either the Queen's Revels or the newly formed company patronized by Lady Elizabeth; the text of the only extant substantive edition of the play, that of the 1640 quarto, had been revised by James Shirley in 1633); *Monsieur Thomas, or Father's Own Son* (circa 1612, for either the Queen's Revels or Lady Elizabeth's; one of the play's sources is the "Histoire de Cellidee, Thamyre et Calidon" in *L'Astrée de Messire Honoré d'Urfé*, part 2, published in Paris in February 1610); and *Wit Without Money* (circa 1614; probably for Lady Elizabeth's; the play seems to have been revised in 1620). Other work that Fletcher undertook with companies other than the King's during this period involved his collaboration with the actor turned dramatist Nathan Field, which seems to have begun in a series of one-act plays, framed with an induction and an epilogue, titled *Four Plays, or Moral Representations in One* (circa 1612; the auspices under which this was produced are unknown; the piece may have been designed for a private entertainment). The year 1613 found both Fletcher and Massinger aiding Field in a tragicomedy titled *The Honest Man's Fortune* for Lady Elizabeth's (the shares of Fletcher and Massinger are comparatively small).

Fletcher seems to have launched his work as an independent dramatist for the King's Men with *Bonduca* (circa 1611), a historical tragedy of Roman Britain. Another tragedy, *Valentinian*, shortly followed (circa 1612), for which he again turned for a source to part 2 of *L'Astrée de Messire Honoré d'Urfé* (the "Histoire d'Eudoxe, Valentinian, et Ursace"). With this play Fletcher's work in tragedy virtually ended. It had never loomed large in his output. He had helped Beaumont with *Cupid's Revenge* and *The Maid's Tragedy*; he would shortly be contributing (with Beaumont and Massinger) to *Thierry and Theodoret*; three of his future collaborations (*The Bloody Brother*, circa 1619; *Sir John van Olden Barnavelt*, August 1619; *The Double Marriage*, circa 1621) would be tragedies; but the remaining plays that he would write without a collaborator would be either comedies or tragicomedies.

One of his most successful tragicomedies, *The Mad Lover*, appeared in 1616 (it was acted at court on 5 January 1617). The play's bizarre plot it typical of the tendency in Fletcherian tragicomedy to deal in dramatic improbabilities with unabashed rhetorical assurance and to concoct histrionic effects that are a heady compound of sentiment and wit. The heroic and idealistic and more than a little naive protagonist of *The Mad Lover*, smitten with the beauty of a sophisticated court lady, offers her his heart, and she, in ironic mood, takes him at his word, whereupon, undaunted, he sets about making plans for having that organ removed from his body and sent to her. The play dramatizes—in terms at once tender and mocking—the means by which he is persuaded that he can go on living honorably without giving the lady what she had consented to receive.

The *Novelas Exemplares* of Cervantes had provided the plot for *Love's Pilgrimage*, and around this time (probably in 1617) Fletcher used another of these, *La Señora Cornelia*, for the plot of one of his best comedies, *The Chances* (the text of the play that appears in the 1647 folio was revised circa 1627, shortly after Fletcher's death).

The collaboration of Fletcher, Massinger, and Field that had produced *The Honest Man's Fortune* in 1613 continued in these years, now for the King's Men. In the period circa 1617-1619, the three dramatists wrote three plays together, though one (*The Jeweller of Amsterdam*, circa 1617-1619?) is lost. Of the two extant tragicomedies, *The Queen of Corinth* (circa 1617) is notable for the use in its plot of one of the *controversiae* of Seneca the Elder. *Controversiae* were declamations of a judicial kind, used in the oratorical schools of ancient Rome as rhetorical exercises in the training of young orators. The declamations consisted of arguments in support of or in opposition to hypothetical cases that posed legal or ethical dilemmas. The cases were contrived to be as intricate and as paradoxical as possible, the better to test the argumentative and rhetorical skills of the student. The *controversia* that provides the climax of *The Queen of Corinth* concerns the sentence that is to be meted out to a man who has raped two women; one woman demands his death, and the other demands that he marry her without a dowry, the law of the land permitting either penalty. This is the sort of difficulty that tragicomedy, as Guarini defined it, was created to solve. In the play the man (contrary to his belief) has not raped two women, but has raped one woman twice, she being in disguise on the second occasion. The problem concerning the conflicting penalties vanishes when this is revealed. The difficulty has been feigned, just as Guarini said it should be, and by the end of the play, matters have turned to "unexpected comedy," as one character puts it. In addition to *The Queen of Corinth*, at least two other plays in the Beaumont and Fletcher canon (*The Laws of Candy*, circa 1620, and *The Double Marriage*) are based on one or more of the *controversiae* of Seneca, and the example of these Latin oratorical exercises has had an effect on the design of Fletcherian tragicomedy, specifically with regard to the extravagantly contrived dramatic situations that often comprise its plots, and the elaborate rhetoric that ornaments its speeches in moments of dramatic crisis. Not long after *The Queen of Corinth*, Fletcher, Massinger, and Field wrote another tragicomedy, *The Knight of Malta*.

Field died in 1619 or 1620, and it may have been in an effort to replace him that about this time Fletcher and Massinger teamed up with two other dramatists (who have been conjectured to have been Jonson and Chapman) to produce a violent tragedy that is variantly titled *The Bloody Brother* (in a quarto edition published in 1639), and *Rollo Duke of Normandy* (in another quarto edition with a somewhat different text published in

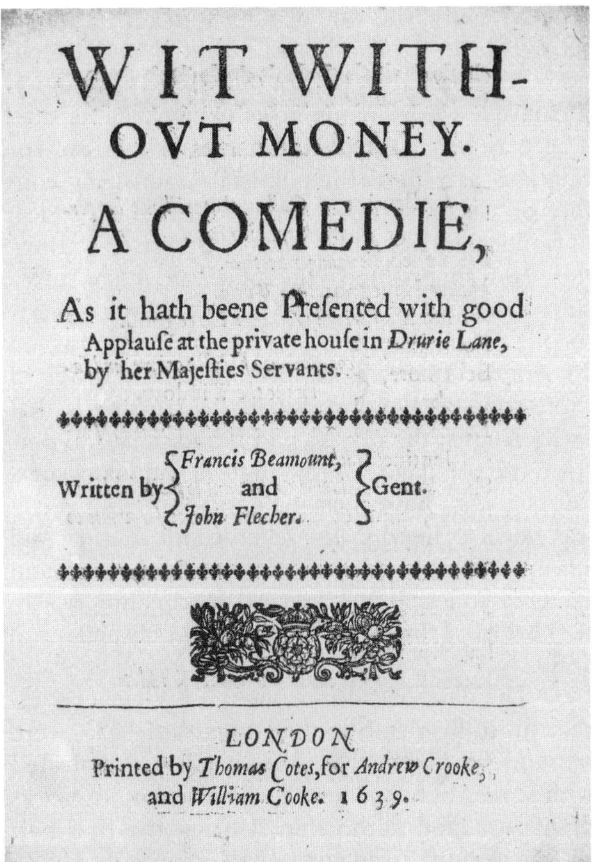
WIT WITH-
OVT MONEY.
A COMEDIE,
As it hath beene Preſented with good
Applauſe at the private houſe in *Drurie Lane*,
by her Majeſties Servants.

Written by *Francis Beamount*, and *John Flecher*. Gent.

LONDON
Printed by *Thomas Cotes*, for *Andrew Crooke*, and *William Cooke*. 1639.

Title page for the 1639 quarto edition of a play Fletcher wrote circa 1614 and probably revised in 1620 (Henry E. Huntington Library and Art Gallery)

1640). The play poses some of the most complicated problems, textual and authorial, in the Beaumont and Fletcher canon. In addition to having been one of its original authors, Massinger seems to have revised at least parts of it at some later date. And somebody has transported into the play (in a somewhat variant version) the song beginning "Take ô take those lips away" from Shakespeare's *Measure for Measure*.

After this experiment in a four-way collaboration, Fletcher seems to have preferred working with a single partner when he was not working alone. From around 1619 until his death six years later, his dramatic output alternates between plays of his own unaided authorship and collaborations with Massinger. After *The Mad Lover*, his next unaided play seems to have been *The Loyal Subject*, known to have been licensed for performance on 16 November 1618. For details concerning its Moscow setting, Fletcher drew on his uncle Giles's book (published in 1591) on the Russian "commonwealth." During the summer of 1619 Fletcher and Massinger quickly wrote another tragedy, this one dealing with recent political events in Holland: the downfall and execution of the Dutch patriot Sir John van Olden Barnavelt, whose name gives to the play its title. The play was of great contemporary interest, for religious as well as for political reasons: the conflict of Calvinism and Arminianism is an aspect of political intrigue that leads to Barnavelt's downfall. Not surprisingly, the play ran into censorship problems when the King's Men were ready to put it on the stage; its scheduled opening on 14 August 1619 was suppressed by the order of the bishop of London. What is surprising is that by 27 August the players had found means to perform the play, and it is said to have had many spectators and to have received applause. However, it was never printed in the seventeenth century and so appears in neither of the Beaumont and Fletcher folios. It is preserved in a manuscript in the British Library and was not published until 1883.

The last half-dozen years of Fletcher's career, until his death in the summer of 1625, were immensely productive. His name is associated with some twenty plays, of which seven are works of his unaided authorship. During the first half of this period (from circa 1619 until early 1622), evidence for determining the dates of these plays continues to be scant, as it is for many of the plays that conjecturally belong to the half-dozen years prior to 1619. After May 1622 evidence survives from the records of the Master of the Revels, Sir Henry Herbert, concerning the dates when plays were licensed for production, and this provides at least a basic chronology for the last two decades of the Jacobean and Caroline stage, before the closing of the theaters in September 1642. Thus the dates for Fletcher's plays in the last three years of his life can be established with far greater certainty than at any other period of his career.

The plays of Fletcher's unaided authorship that seem to belong to the period 1619-1622 are: *The Humourous Lieutenant* (the play's title in the 1647 folio; a somewhat longer manuscript text of the play exists with the title *Demetrius and Enanthe*), one of Fletcher's most enduringly popular tragicomedies; *Women Pleased* (Fletcher's dramatization of Chaucer's "Wife of Bath's Tale"; it has been suggested that the play is a revision of an earlier one, but the evidence is inconclusive); *The Island Princess* (performed at court on 26 December 1621); *The Pilgrim*, one of Fletcher's best comedies (written between 18 September 1621—when the English version of the play's principal source, Lope de Vega's *El Peregrino en su Patria*, was entered in the Stationers' Register—and New Year's Day, 1622, when the play was performed at court); *The Wild Goose Chase* (acted at court during the same 1621-1622 Christmas season as *The Island Princess* and *The Pilgrim*), Fletcher's most brilliant comedy, and one that seems to have been a particular favorite with contemporary audiences.

Interspersed with Fletcher's five unaided plays during the period 1619-1622 are four collaborations with Massinger (including *Barnavelt*, already mentioned). *The Custom of the Country* was probably written in either 1619 or 1620. The source of the play's main plot, Cervantes' *Persiles y Sigismunda*, was printed in Spanish in 1617, in French in 1618, and in English in 1619; the English translation was entered in the Stationers' Register on 22 February 1619, and the authors of the play made use of it. The play was popular and profitable, facts not inconsistent with the notorious reputation it gained for its scenes set in a male brothel. Dryden, at the end of the century, when the Restoration stage was under attack for immorality, replied indignantly (in his preface to *Fables Ancient and Modern*, 1700) that "There is more bawdry in one play of Fletcher's called *The Custom of the Country*, than in all ours together." *The False One*, Fletcher and Massinger's dramatization of the affairs of Caesar and Cleopatra, appears to date from the same period (circa 1620). *The Double Marriage* is probably a product of 1621. One of the most interesting tragedies in the Beaumont and Fletcher canon, it draws its plot material from a variety of sources: Thomas Danett's translation of *The Historie of Philip de Commines* (1596); Cervantes' *Don Quixote*, part 2, first published in English in 1620; and no less than two *controversiae* of Seneca ("The Daughter of the Pirate Chief" and "The Woman Tortured by the Tyrant because of Her Husband").

About this time another play printed in the 1647 Beaumont and Fletcher folio, *The Laws of Candy*, drew on a Seneca *controversia* for its source. Its authorship is a matter of considerable uncertainty. Massinger certainly had nothing to do with it, and Fletcher seems to have had very little. The play has been attributed to John Ford, whose career as a dramatist was getting under way in these years, and there is some internal (but no external) evidence for the attribution. It may be noted here that the status of two other plays printed in the 1647 folio is equally anomalous: *The Nice Valour or the Passionate Madman* (for which dates ranging from circa 1615 to 1625 have been posited) seems to be mainly the work of Thomas Middleton; Fletcher's share in it, if any, is minimal. The play may have been a Fletcherian original that Middleton had revised. *Wit at Several Weapons* (for which dates ranging from circa 1609 to 1620 have been suggested) seems—at least in the text that has come down to us—to be the work of Middleton and his frequent collaborator William Rowley.

The grounds for assigning dates to plays become very much more secure with the commencement in May 1622 of the surviving records of Sir Henry Herbert's licenses for the performance of new (or newly revised) plays. From now until the end of his career, Fletcher's unaided work and his collaboration with Massinger and others can be seen in a remarkably secure chronological sequence. Fletcher and Massinger's work together in the summer of 1622 is clear from Herbert's records. Their tragicomedy, *The Prophetess,* was licensed on 14 May; their romantic comedy, *The Sea Voyage,* on 22 June; and another romantic comedy, *The Spanish Curate,* on 24 October. In the months that followed, Fletcher and Massinger seem to have recast the dramatic design of *The Spanish Curate* in a new piece titled *The Little French Lawyer,* but the result is an uneasy and often incoherent blend of romantic comedy and farce. (*The Little French Lawyer* is not mentioned by Herbert, but the surviving transcript of his records is not complete.)

On 29 August 1623 Herbert licensed "a new Comedy," *The Maid in the Mill,* and reports it to have been "written by Fletcher, and Rowley," thereby announcing that Fletcher had taken on a new collaborator. William Rowley was a popular actor, who, in the course of the previous two decades, had written some unmemorable plays of his own, and—more memorably—had collaborated with Thomas Middleton on quite a good play, *A Fair Quarrel,* and on a great one, *The Changeling.* In 1621, two years before joining forces with Fletcher in *The Maid in the Mill,* Rowley had made a notable contribution (both as actor and part-author) to one of the finest plays of the 1620s, *The Witch of Edmonton,* in which he collaborated with Thomas Dekker and John Ford. Rowley specialized in playing fat, clownish young men, and he is presumed to have written for himself, and acted, the role of Bustofa, the miller's son, in the play that he and Fletcher wrote together.

That Fletcher should have turned to a new collaborator may suggest a change in his association with Massinger, who had virtually grown up professionally under Fletcher's wing. Since working with Fletcher and Field on *The Honest Man's Fortune* in 1613 (apparently his first assignment as a dramatist; he was thirty years old at that time), Massinger had been almost exclusively employed in assisting Fletcher in his various collaborative teams. Occasionally Massinger made moves in new directions. He and Field wrote a tragedy (*The Fatal Dowry*) together (circa 1619). He wrote another tragedy (*The Virgin Martyr*) with Dekker (1620). These were tentative moves in the direction of a career as an independent dramatist. It is difficult to judge the pace of his movement toward this goal because so many of his plays are lost, but by 1623, when Fletcher turned to Rowley to assist him in writing *The Maid in the Mill,* Massinger seems to have written three unaided plays (*The Maid of Honour, The Duke of Milan,* and *The Bondman*). The remaining plays with which his and Fletcher's names have been associated seem, as often as not, to be old plays Massinger revised after Fletcher's death rather than plays on which the two dramatists actively collaborated in the last years of Fletcher's life. This is certainly the case with the play known in the 1647 folio as *The Lovers' Progress;* it contains a prologue declaring it to be an old play of Fletcher's that has been extensively revised. It has been plausibly identified with the play titled *The Wandering Lovers,* licensed by Herbert and attributed by him to Fletcher on 6 December 1623. It has also been identified with "The tragedy of *Cleander*" which Herbert licensed and attributed to Massinger on 7 May 1634. "The Wandering Lovers" would be an apt title for *The Lovers' Progress;* and though the play is a strange mixture of tragedy and tragicomedy, it is a tragedy for the character named Cleander, who is killed in the course of it. Fletcher's *The Wandering Lovers* seems then to have been transformed by Massinger into *Cleander,* and that eventually came to be called *The Lovers' Progress,* a play that clearly contains the work of both dramatists.

A somewhat similar fate seems to have overtaken the play now known as *A Very Woman.* Herbert licensed a play of this title as the work of Massinger on 6 June 1634. Unlike *The Lovers' Progress,* it was not included in the 1647 Beaumont and Fletcher folio and did not appear in print until 1655 when it was included among Massinger's *Three New Playes,* where it is prefaced

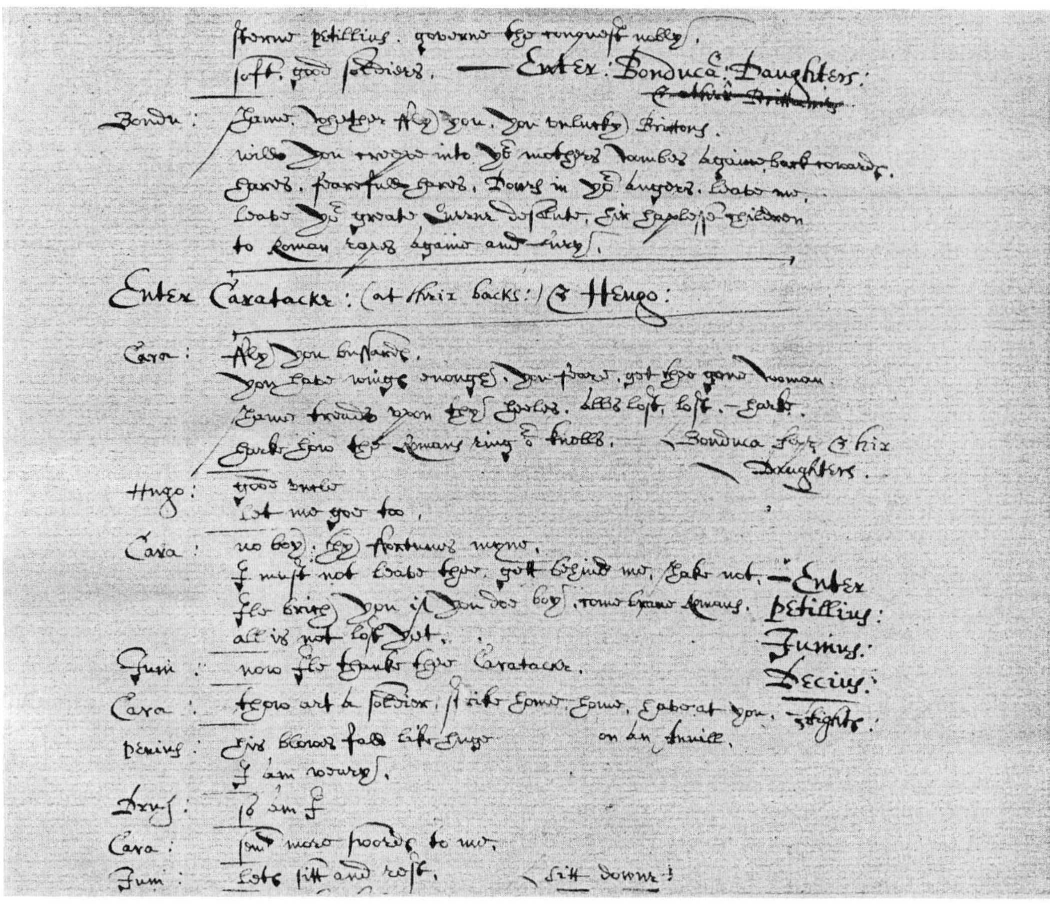

A portion of a page from the manuscript for Bonduca, *Fletcher's first unaided effort for the King's Men, that is preserved in the British Library. This manuscript is thought to be a fair copy made for a private collector some ten to twenty years before the play was published in the 1647 collection of Beaumont and Fletcher's plays (Add. MS 36758; British Library).*

with a prologue acknowledging it to be an old play that has been revised. The original play has not been identified, but there is evidence from the 1655 text to support the view that it was a Fletcher-Massinger collaboration, and that Massinger's revision of the play in 1634 (when it was licensed anew) was directed chiefly at his own share, and that he left Fletcher's original portion essentially intact.

The comedy titled *The Elder Brother* is sometimes said to be a play left unfinished at the time of Fletcher's death and completed by Massinger, but it seems more likely to be an actual collaboration between the two, with Massinger furnishing the first and last acts, as he often did in his collaborative work (such as in *The False One* and *The Queen of Corinth*) and as he would do again in *The Fair Maid of the Inn*. This seems to have been the last play on which Fletcher worked. In licensing it on 22 January 1626, Herbert attributed it to Fletcher alone, but by then the dramatist had been dead for five months, and his share in the play is suspiciously small. Massinger is certainly present in the play, and so, it would seem, are two other dramatists who have been conjecturally identified as John Webster and Ford. One or both may have been called in after Fletcher's death to complete his share. Before he died, however, Fletcher had written three more unaided plays. A comedy, *The Devil of Dowgate, or Usury Put to Use*, licensed by Herbert on 17 October 1623, is lost. There remains another tragicomedy, *A Wife for a Month*, licensed by Herbert on 27 May 1624, and one of Fletcher's liveliest comedies, *Rule a Wife and Have a Wife*, licensed on 19 October 1624.

Fletcher died in August 1625 at the height of the plague that had been gradually worsening in London since March. For the week ending 18 August the death toll was 4,463. It diminished a bit for the week ending 25 August, but still stood at a devastating 4,218. The theaters had been closed for months. According to Aubrey, "a knight of Norfolk (or Suffolke)" invited Fletcher

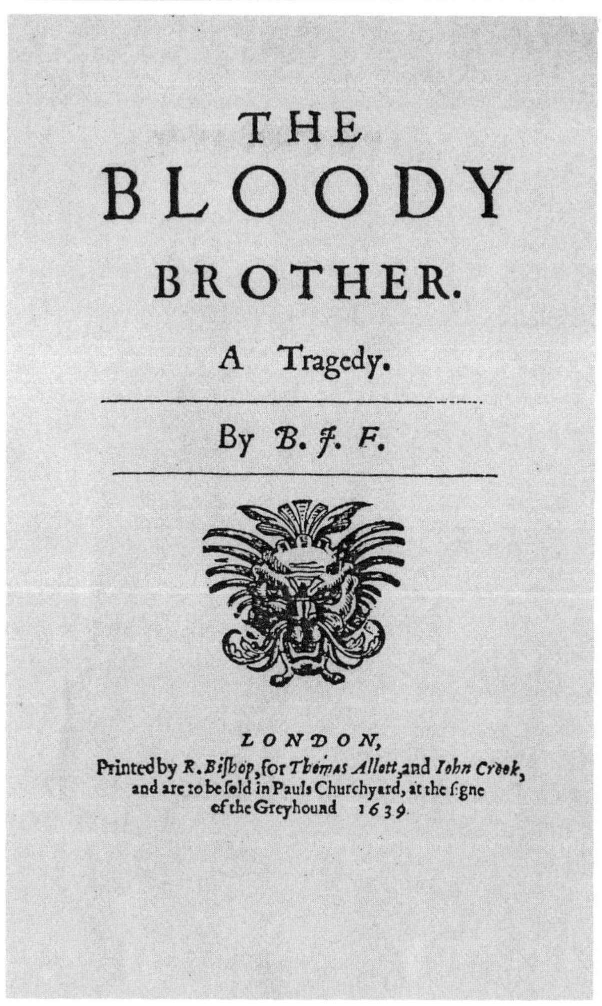
THE

BLOODY

BROTHER.

A Tragedy.

By B. J. F.

LONDON,

Printed by R. Bishop, for Thomas Allott, and Iohn Crook, and are to be sold in Pauls Churchyard, at the signe of the Greyhound 1639.

After Beaumont's retirement to the life of a country gentleman, Fletcher collaborated with Philip Massinger (and perhaps Ben Jonson and George Chapman) on this tragedy (from E. H. C. Oliphant, The Plays of Beaumont and Fletcher, *1927)*

into the country, but he stayed in London in order to have a suit of clothes made, "and while it was making, fell sick of the plague and died." He was buried in the Church of St. Saviour's, Southwark, on 29 August 1625.

At the time of his death, the Beaumont and Fletcher plays dominated the London stage. Virtually all of them were the property of the King's company, and the King's was the premier acting company in London. Also it was the company that performed most frequently at court. Between 1615 and 1624, the King's Men performed 114 times at court. Of these performances, 41 were plays from the Beaumont and Fletcher corpus, 15 were plays by Shakespeare, and 7 were plays by Ben Jonson. The preference for tragicomedy on the part of Jacobean and Caroline audiences has a great deal to do with the popularity of the Beaumont and Fletcher plays over those of Shakespeare and Jonson in these years. Tragicomedy presented audiences with interesting moral and ethical dilemmas that could arouse their fervent attention but spare them any really profound emotional involvement of the sort that tragedy at its most powerful would bring about. Tragedy was not the preferred dramatic form in the later Jacobean and Caroline theater. It did not disappear from the stage, but it cannot be said to have flourished in the final decades of English Renaissance drama (that is, from the death of Shakespeare to the closing of the theaters). What flourished in these years was tragicomedy. This is evident not only from the success of the Beaumont and Fletcher plays in themselves but from the extent to which other dramatists of the period imitated them. Once plays such as *Philaster, A King and No King, The Mad Lover*, and *The Loyal Subject* had made their impact, every dramatist of the period tried his hand at tragicomedy at one time or another, including Webster (*The Devil's Law Case*); Middleton (*More Dissemblers Besides Women, No Wit, No Helps Like a Woman's, The Witch, A Fair Quarrel*); Dekker (*Match Me in London*); Heywood (*The Captives, A Challenge to Beauty*); Ford (*The Lover's Melancholy*). Tragicomedy is central to the work of the principal dramatists writing for the stage in the late 1620s and the 1630s (Massinger, James Shirley, Richard Brome, Sir William Davenant), and it looms large in the offerings of the period's minor dramatists (Lodowick Carlell, Henry Glapthorne, Thomas Killigrew, William Cartwright).

As for Beaumont and Fletcher's comedy, it is a happy transference of Shakespeare's comedy of romantic love from Illyria and the Forest of Arden to the sort of fashionable urban society that Jonson had brought on the stage in *Epicoene*. Beaumont and Fletcher's admiration for Jonson is a matter of record. Both wrote commendatory verses for the published editions of Jonson's *Volpone* (1607) and *Catiline* (1611), and Beaumont contributed a prefatory poem to the 1609 edition of *Epicoene*. The 1647 folio contains Beaumont's famous verse letter to Jonson, written during a visit to the country where he finds himself thinking longingly of his meeting with Jonson and others at the Mermaid Tavern, and of the brilliant conversation that went forth there. By contrast, he ruefully considers how rusticated his own wit is growing in the absence of such stimulating com-

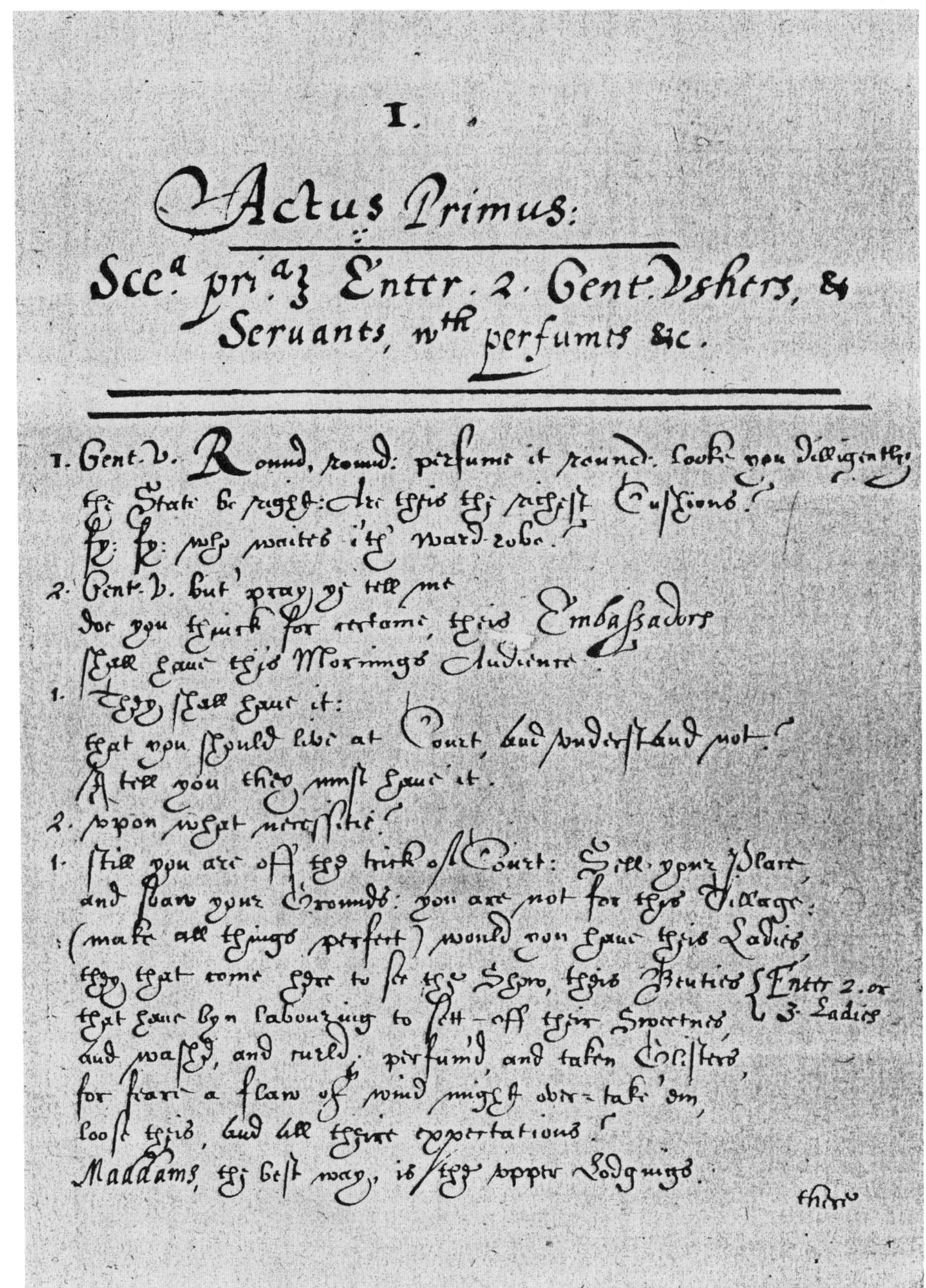

I.

Actus Primus:

Scea. pria. Enter. 2. Gent. Vshers, & Seruants, wth perfumes &c.

1. Gent. V. Round, round: perfume it round. Look you dilligently
the State be right: Are these the richest Cushions?
fie: fie: who waites i'th' ward-robe.
2. Gent. V. but pray ye tell me
doe you think for certaine, theis Embassadors
shall haue this Mornings Audience.
1. they shall haue it:
that you should liue at Court, and vnderstand not!
I tell you they must haue it.
2. vpon what necessitie?
1. still you are off the trick of Court: Sell your Place,
and sow your Grounds: you are not for this Tillage.
(make all things perfect) would you haue theis Ladies,
they that come here to see the Show, theis Beauties { Enter 2. or 3. Ladies
that haue been labouring to sett-off their Sweetnes,
and wash'd, and curl'd: perfum'd, and taken Glisters,
for feare a flaw of wind might ouer-take 'em,
loose theis, and all their expectations?
Maddams, the best way, is the vpper Lodgings.
there

Page from Demetrius and Enanthe, *the longer manuscript version of the play by Fletcher published in the 1647 folio collection of Beaumont and Fletcher's plays as* The Humourous Lieutenant. *This manuscript is a fair copy made by the scribe Ralph Crane in 1625 and is now in the library of Lord Harlech (Brogyntyn MS 42; Collection of Lord Harlech).*

panions. He is dazzled to remember the wit that blazed at the Mermaid:

> wit that might warrant be
> For the whole City to talke foolishly
> Till that were cancel'd, and when that was gone,
> We left an aire behind us, which alone,
> Was able to make the two next companies
> Right witty; though but downright fools, more wise.

There is much mention of the wit of both Beaumont and Fletcher in the forty-odd folio pages of commendatory verses that preface the 1647 edition of their *Comedies and Tragedies*. Aubrey, on the authority of John Earle, reports that Fletcher had an overabundance of the quality, and that "Beaumont's maine Businesse was to lop the overflowings of Mr. Fletcher's luxuriant Fancy and flowing Witt." Throughout the seventeenth century, wit (in the sense of imaginative ingenuity, and an ability to make connections among incongruous elements) is a convenient means of signifying what is special about the Beaumont and Fletcher plays. One of the speakers in Dryden's *An Essay of Dramatick Poesy* observes that Beaumont and Fletcher "had with the advantage of *Shakespeare*'s wit, which was their precedent, great natural gifts, improv'd by study," and he goes on to praise their special excellencies:

> Their plots were generally more regular than *Shakespeare*'s, especially those which weremade before *Beaumont*'s death; and theyunderstood and imitated the conversation of Gentlemen much better; whose wilde debaucheries, and quickness of wit in reparties, no Poet before them could paint as they have done. Humour, which *Ben. Johnson* deriv'd from particular persons, they made it not their business to describe: they represented all the passions very lively, but above all, Love.... Their Playes are now the most pleasant and frequent entertainments of the Stage; two of theirs being acted through the year for one of *Shakespeare*'s or *Johnsons*: the reason is, because there is a certain gayety in their Comedies, and Pathos in their more serious Playes, which suits generally with all mens humours. *Shakespeares* language is likewise a little obsolete, and *Ben. Johnson*'s wit comes short of theirs.

If anything had been needed to make Beaumont and Fletcher jointly one with Shakespeare and Jonson in the triumvirate of great English dramatists, it was the publication of the 1647 folio edition of their plays: an edition that matched the 1616 collection of Jonson's and the 1623 collection of Shakespeare's. It is ironic, therefore, that by the time the second folio volume of their plays was published in 1679, their great reputation had begun to dim. Dryden's own later criticism is far more severe concerning the Beaumont and Fletcher plays than the remarks in *An Essay of Dramatick Poesy* had been. In the preface to *An Evening's Love* (1671), after acknowledging that "no man ever will decry wit, but he who despairs of it himself," he goes on to declare (on the authority of Abraham Cowley) that one may have too much of a good thing ("rather than all wit let there be none"), and he deplores "the superfluity and wast of wit" in Fletcher and Shakespeare. Later still, in 1679, in the preface to *Troilus and Cressida* ("The Grounds of Criticism in Tragedy"), Dryden, commenting on "manners" (that is, the inclinations that move a character to action), finds both Shakespeare and Fletcher inferior to Jonson on this score, but Fletcher is decidedly inferior to Shakespeare:

John Fletcher (Collection of the Earl of Clarendon)

> 'Tis one of the excellencies of *Shakespear*, that the manners of his persons are generally apparent; and you see their bent and inclinations. *Fletcher* comes far short of him in this, as indeed he does almost in every thing: there are but glimmerings

> of manners in most of his Comedies, which run upon adventures: and in his Tragedies, *Rollo, Otto* [in *Rollo Duke of Normandy*], the *King and No King, Melantius* [in *The Maid's Tragedy*], and many others of his best, are but Pictures shown you in the twi-light; you know not whether they resemble vice, or virtue, and they are either good, bad, or indifferent, as the present Scene requires it.

In this last point Dryden sounds a note that persists in criticism of the Beaumont and Fletcher plays to the present day: the Protean nature of their characters, with their striking capacity to change from one scene to the next, may make for continually surprising stage situations, but these are often achieved at the expense of a character's dramatic consistency and motivation.

As for Dryden's reference to Fletcher (rather than to Beaumont and Fletcher) in discussing the weaknesses of these plays: he anticipates the tendency of later critics to spare Beaumont and to hold Fletcher accountable for all the defects on exhibit in the plays of the Beaumont and Fletcher corpus, despite the fact that his sense of authorial divisions within the corpus is very uncertain (none of the three plays to which he alludes is the unaided work of Fletcher).

Twentieth-century studies of the problems of authorship which these plays pose have made possible a more just appraisal of the poetic and dramatic talents of the two playwrights. Since Fletcher wrote a large number of unaided plays, the characteristics of his poetic and dramatic style can be studied with considerable thoroughness. The case of Beaumont is more difficult. We have only one play that is solely his (*The Knight of the Burning Pestle*). The language of his masque does not shed much light on the language of the plays to which he contributed; nor do his nondramatic poems (*Salmacis and Hermaphroditus*, "The Remedy of Love," the verse letter to Jonson, his various commendatory poems, his "Elegy on the Lady Markham," his "Epistle to the Countess of Rutland" and his "Elegy" on her death, his "Funeral Elegy on the Death of Lady Penelope Clifton"). Beaumont's nondramatic poems are not themselves without authorial problems. Those poems that have just been named are the ones that seem most likely to be his, but they appear in posthumous collections (1618, 1640, 1653, 1660) amid other poems whose attribution to Beaumont seems very questionable. Massinger's share in the Beaumont and Fletcher plays is now fully recognized, and the extent of it is clearly defined, since Massinger, like Fletcher, has left a large number of unaided plays that provide criteria for identifying his work in plays of divided or uncertain authorship. What now emerges clearly from an examination of the Beaumont and Fletcher corpus is that Fletcher's collaboration with Beaumont was different from his collaboration with Massinger or any other dramatist with whom he worked.

The Beaumont-Fletcher collaboration was obviously very close. Beaumont seems usually to have given the final form to their plays (perhaps in the process of bringing Fletcher's reputedly luxuriant fancy and overflowing wit under control), but the plays themselves seem to have been jointly designed, and the language of the two dramatists has been carefully blended to make for a virtually seamless verbal text. Perhaps if one had a clearer idea of Beaumont's unaided style, his share in the collaborative works could be more readily determined, but this is by no means certain, for Fletcher's own very distinctive style, which emerges with great clarity from his unaided work, is much less readily apparent in the collaborated with Beaumont. When Fletcher collaborated with Massinger, however, their respective shares of a given play could not be more apparent, not only because of their stylistic differences one from another, but because they divided the various acts and scenes of the play on distinctly authorial lines. Beaumont and Fletcher often seem to have sat together in the same room and worked together on the same scene. Fletcher and Massinger seem to have drawn up a scenario for a play and then, on the basis of it, having decided which dramatist would write which scenes, gone their separate ways. When Massinger's work appears in the same scene with Fletcher's it is a sign, not that the two are writing the scene together, but that Massinger is revising (probably after Fletcher's death) what Fletcher originally wrote.

Fletcher is the constant in the fifty-odd plays of the Beaumont and Fletcher corpus, but Fletcher writing with Beaumont is one thing, Fletcher writing alone is another, and Fletcher writing with his various post-Beaumont collaborators is something else again. The Beaumont-Fletcher collaborations such as *Philaster, The Maid's Tragedy*, and *A King and No King* have a rare blend of pathos and irony along with a poetic subtlety that vanishes from the corpus when Beaumont withdraws. Fletcher's own plays have a histrionic and rhetorical extravagance that makes one understand how indeed Beaumont may have exercised a controlling force on Fletcher's wit. They are products of a very shrewd instinct for theatrical artifice, with their improbable plots, volatile characters, and bravura emotional range that extends from sentimental passion to heroic self-control, and that provides occasion for the display of the most effulgent virtue and sinister vice. The best of them—*Valentinian, The Mad Lover, The Loyal Subject, The Humourous Lieutenant, A Wife for a Month*—prepare the way for the baroque tragedy and tragicomedy of the Restoration theater. Fletcher's collaborations with Massinger are most successful when his comic energies can be played off against Massinger's moral earnestness, as in *The Custom of the Country, The Spanish Curate, The Prophetess, The Sea Voyage.*

The Beaumont and Fletcher plays have never regained the esteem in which they were held during the half century after Fletcher's death, and it is unlikely that they will ever hold the stage again. They are, nonetheless, theatrical artifacts of considerable aesthetic interest, for they are products of an important cultural moment in the history of the English stage. After Christopher Marlowe's and Shakespeare's work in tragedy, after Shakespeare's and Jonson's work in comedy, what direction was English drama to take? The Beaumont and Fletcher plays are the threefold answer. They seek to refine the heritage of Marlowe and Shakespeare in tragedy (as in *The Maid's Tragedy*); they seek to accommodate the romantic and satiric traditions of Shakespearean and Jonsonian comedy in a new comic blend (as in *The Scornful Lady, Monsieur Thomas, The Wild Goose Chase, The Pilgrim, The Chances, Rule a Wife and Have a Wife*); and they seek to explore and to define the space between the classically sanctioned tragic and comic genres by addressing themselves to the creation of a new, third genre (in the celebrated series of tragicomedies produced over a fifteen-year period, from *Philaster* to *A Wife for a Month*). Whatever audiences of future centuries might think of these plays, there is ample evidence that audiences of the middle decades of the seventeenth century found them highly satisfactory. When, during the Interregnum, it was not possible to see them on the stage, sometime-audiences could find pleasure in reading them in the 1647 folio. When, at the Restoration, the theaters were reopened, it was the Beaumont and Fletcher plays which, for the next twenty years, dominated the repertoire, and the heroic tragedies and the double-plot tragicomedies of Dryden and his contemporaries were created in their image. No one who seeks to understand the course of English dramatic history in the seventeenth century can afford to ignore them.

Bibliographies:

Samuel A. Tannenbaum, *Beaumont and Fletcher: A Concise Bibliography* (New York: Privately printed, 1938); supplement, by Samuel A. and Dorothy R. Tannenbaum (New York: Privately printed, 1946);

C. A. Pennel and William P. Williams, *Elizabethan Bibliographies, Supplement VIII: Francis Beaumont and John Fletcher, 1937-1965* (London: Nether Press, 1968);

Terence P. Logan and Denzell S. Smith, eds., *A Survey and Bibliography of Recent Studies in English Renaissance Drama: The Later Jacobean Dramatists* (Lincoln: Nebraska University Press, 1978).

References:

Joseph Quincy Adams, ed., *The Dramatic Records of Sir Henry Herbert, Master of the Revels, 1623-1673* (New Haven: Yale University Press, 1917);

John Aubrey, *Brief Lives: Edited from the Original Manuscripts and With a Life of John Aubrey by Oliver Lawson Dick* (Ann Arbor: University of Michigan Press, 1957);

Gerald Eades Bentley, *The Jacobean and Caroline Stage*, 7 volumes (Oxford: Oxford University Press, 1941-1986);

E. K. Chambers, *The Elizabethan Stage*, 4 volumes (Oxford: Clarendon Press, 1923);

John Dryden, *An Essay of Dramatick Poesy*, in *The Works of John Dryden*, volume 17: *Prose 1668-1691*, edited by Samuel Holt Monk, A. E. Wallace Maurer, Vinton A. Dearing, R. V. LeClercq, and Maximillian E. Novak (Berkeley, Los Angeles & London: University of California Press, 1971), pp. 3-81;

Dryden, Preface to *An Evening's Love*, in *The Works of John Dryden*, volume 10: *Plays: The Tempest, Tyrannick Love, An Evening's Love*, edited by Novak and George Robert Guffey (Berkeley, Los Angeles & London: University of California Press, 1970), pp. 202-213;

Dryden, Preface to *Troilus and Cressida*, in *The Works of John Dryden*, volume 13: *Plays: All for Love, Oedipus, Troilus and Cressida*, edited by Novak, Guffey, and Alan Roper (Berkeley, Los Angeles & London: University of California Press, 1984), pp. 225-248;

Mark Eccles, "A Biographical Dictionary of Elizabethan Authors," *Huntington Library Quarterly*, 5 (April 1942): 281-302;

Philip J. Finkelpearl, *Court and Country Politics in the Plays of Beaumont and Fletcher* (Princeton: Princeton University Press, 1990);

Charles Mills Gayley, *Beaumont, the Dramatist* (New York: Century, 1914);

Allan H. Gilbert, ed., *Literary Criticism: Plato to Dryden* (New York: American Book Co., 1940);

Cyrus Hoy, "The Shares of Fletcher and his Collaborators in the Beaumont and Fletcher Canon," 7 parts, *Studies in Bibliography*, 8 (1956): 124-146; 9 (1957): 143-162; 11 (1958): 85-99; 12 (1959): 91-116; 13 (1960): 77-108; 14 (1961): 45-67; 15 (1962): 71-90;

Arthur Colby Sprague, *Beaumont and Fletcher on the Restoration Stage* (Cambridge, Mass.: Harvard University Press, 1926);

Eugene M. Waith, *The Pattern of Tragicomedy in Beaumont and Fletcher* (New Haven: Yale University Press, 1952).

Papers:

Beaumont's "Grammar Lecture" is preserved in Sloane MS. 1709 in the British Library and has been published by Mark Eccles in *Review of English Studies*, 16 (October 1940): 402-414. The manuscripts for seven of the plays in the Beaumont and Fletcher corpus have been preserved: *Sir John van Olden Barnavelt* (BL MS Add. 18653 in the British Library), *Beggars' Bush* (MS in the Lambarde volume, Folger Shakespeare Library), *Bonduca* (Add. MS 36758 in the British Library), *The Honest Man's Fortune* (MS Dyce 9 in the Victoria and Albert Museum), *The Elder Brother* (MS Egerton 1994 in the British Library), *The Humourous Lieutenant* (titled *Demetrius and Enanthe*; Brogyntyn MS 42 in the library of Lord Harlech at Brogyntyn, Oswestry), *The Woman's Prize* (MS in the Lambarde volume, Folger Shakespeare Library).

Beowulf

(circa 900-1000 or 790-825)

Jeffrey Helterman
University of South Carolina

Manuscript: The only extant transcription, in the hands of four scribes and dating from circa 975-1025, is in the British Library (Cotton Vitellius, A. xv). Facsimile: *Beowulf: Reproduced in Facsimile from the Unique Manuscript, British Museum MS. Cotton Vitellius A. xv, with a Transliteration and Notes by Julius Zupitza, Second Edition, Containing a New Reproduction of the Manuscript*, intro—by Norman Davis (London, New York & Toronto: Published for the Early English Text Society by the Oxford University Press, 1967).
First publication: *De Danorum rebus getis secul. III & IV. Poema danicum dialecto anglo-saxonica. Ex bibliotheca cottoniana Musaei britannici*, edited by Grimur Johnson Thorkelin (Havnia: Typis T. E. Rangel, 1815).
Edition: *Beowulf and The Fight at Finnsburg*, edited by Friedrich Klaeber (Boston & New York: D. C. Heath, 1922; third edition, with supplements, 1950).

The knotty problem of the date of *Beowulf* tells us a great deal about how we think of the past and the kinds of assumptions that are made in confronting history. In the first edition of the poem (1815), Grimur Thorkelin identified the historical events as occurring in the third and fourth centuries and the poem, because of the detail in such allusions, as having been written not more than a century later. This date is the earliest that has been assigned to the poem. The last composition date for the poem, the terminus ad quem, is the date of the unique manuscript for the poem. Based on the two copyists' hands, this manuscript date has been established, with some certainty, as around 975-1025. The last date would put the poem within half a century of the Norman invasions and the consequent end of the Old English language. The date of the manuscript is accepted by most scholars, but until recently most of them have argued that the poem predates the manuscript by at least two hundred years. This assumption has led to some interesting attitudes toward the manuscript.

Thorkelin's early date for the poem derives from a bias that controlled the response to it in the nineteenth century. Following investigations showing how the Homeric poems were based on earlier shorter poems that reflected the spirit of the ancient Greek people, there was a movement in early studies of *Beowulf* to see it as derivative of the Germanic *Volk*. Any Christian attitudes in the poem were presumed to be monkish interpolations. Such a reading of the poem allowed Thorkelin to ignore the date of 597, the year when Saint Augustine of Canterbury carried out his missionary work and undertook the conversion of England to Christianity. Since the poem seems quite comfortable in its Christianity (there are no direct New Testament references and no naming of Christ, though the frequent Old Testament references make it seem clear that the poet was a Christian) and free of missionary zeal, it would seem likely that the poem was written at least several generations after the conversion, which would put the earliest date for the composition of the poem at about 700. At this point, the subject matter of the poem comes into play.

This English epic has no action which takes place in England, and the bulk of the action takes place in Denmark, the home of the Vikings, who were raiding the English coast from 834 to the end of the disastrous reign of Aethelred the Unready (978-1014). Until recently, all those who dated the poem started with the basic assumption that *Beowulf* could not have been composed in this period, so if its language is early and the manuscript is eleventh century, there must be two hundred years between the manuscript and the composition of the poem. This "Viking age Englishmen must hate poems about Scandinavia" attitude is based on assumptions about grudge holding that are not testified to explicitly in the period. There were already Danes who owned English farms in the ninth and tenth centuries, and the Viking raids, though an ever-present threat, were not constant. It does not seem impossible that a pro-Danish poem could have been written in this period, though a pro-Viking one is a different matter.

The poem has been dated by internal evidence, using linguistic forms, primarily case endings which are then matched against externally datable texts. Such analysis reveals oddly contradictory evidence, as if a modern formal, printed text included the fifteenth-century form *axeth* (asks), the seventeenth century *thou saist*, and the only recently acceptable *ain't*. One way to account for these discrepancies was to posit that the poem went through the hands of several copyists who lived at different times and in different regions in England. This assumption is made by Frederick Klaeber, whose 1922 edition of the poem is still the standard school text. Because Klaeber assumes that the poem has gone through at least four copyists, the manuscript is fair game for any linguistically justifiable emendation, the assumption always being that the copyist mistook a form he did not recognize. This explanation is given even when the reading of the manuscript is clear. It should be noted that the arguments against the composition of the poem in the Viking period militate even more heavily against the copying of the poem in this period (the time when Klaeber says it was done). The copying of a long poem was not a matter of interest or preference but an institutional event that took place in copying rooms called scriptoria. The copying of a text such as *Beowulf* would be an official act assigned by one monk, probably with the approval of at least one superior, to another. Since the extant *Beowulf* manuscript is in two hands, it is likely the decision to copy it this one time needed the approval of at least four men, which would have been the case each time the poem was copied before. If one would not be likely to compose a pro-Dane poem in the Viking period, it would be more unlikely that one could copy it.

Recent criticism has argued for a late date of composition for the poem, probably closely coinciding with the date of the manuscript. These scholars view the existence of antique linguistic forms in *Beowulf* as part of a poetic word stock rather than as a reflection of the composition date of the poem.

The oral-formulaic theory of the composition of Anglo-Saxon poetry supports the possibility of a late date for *Beowulf*: this theory states that most Anglo-Saxon poetry, even epics as long as *Beowulf*, were composed orally. The basic poetic unit is a four-stressed line in which three of the four stressed words alliterate. The poetry is filled with appositions and frequent modification by adverb and adjective so that a poet could instantly turn a sentence into verse. For example, the Old English bard, or scop, could look at the headline "Bush defeats Hussein in Kuwaiti desert" and turn it into:

> **B**old-hearted **B**ush. **B**ravest of **M**en
> **K**icked the **I**raqi, most **C**raven of **C**owards,
> **S**addam **s**lipped away, **s**cudding into **i**nfamy.

The only full surviving discussion of Anglo-Saxon poetic creation is Bede's story of the inspiration of Caedmon, an illiterate cowherd who was told by an angel to sing (to make up a song). Caedmon responded with a nine-line alliterative hymn of creation. The monks at the local monastery were so impressed with this gift that they kept feeding Caedmon doctrine which he transformed into poetry. The monks stood at his mouth and wrote down his every word. The story, no matter how apocryphal, tells of a culture where the composition of poetry was thought to be oral and writing it down was already seen to be copyists' work. Caedmon's poems, however, are lyrics, and it is not certain that an epic could be composed this way. Early oral-composition theories of *Beowulf* saw it as an aggregate of episodic lays, poems of the same size and kind as *The Fight at Finnsburg*, in which the Danish scop makes up a song of "Beowulf" (which we do not hear), praising the hero's victories over Grendel and his mother. A very different notion of the possibilities of oral composition followed the researches of Albert Bates Lord and Milman Parry in the mountains of Yugoslavia. In *The Singer of Tales* (1960) Lord reports on Yugoslav folk poets who could compose extemporaneously epics longer than *Beowulf*. None of these poems, however, is nearly as good as *Beowulf*. A problem that has not been addressed in the oral theory of composition is how the poems were then written down. Caedmon had a small army of monks writing down his every word, but these were lyrics. How could a long oral secular poem be written down as it was being recited in a day of quill pens and vellum? The poem would either have to be written by someone who had the whole poem in his head, either the scop himself, which would mean he could not be unlettered like Caedmon, or else by some literate man, most likely a cleric, who had learned or was an apprentice at the art of oral composition. In either case the poem as literary artifact would be differ-

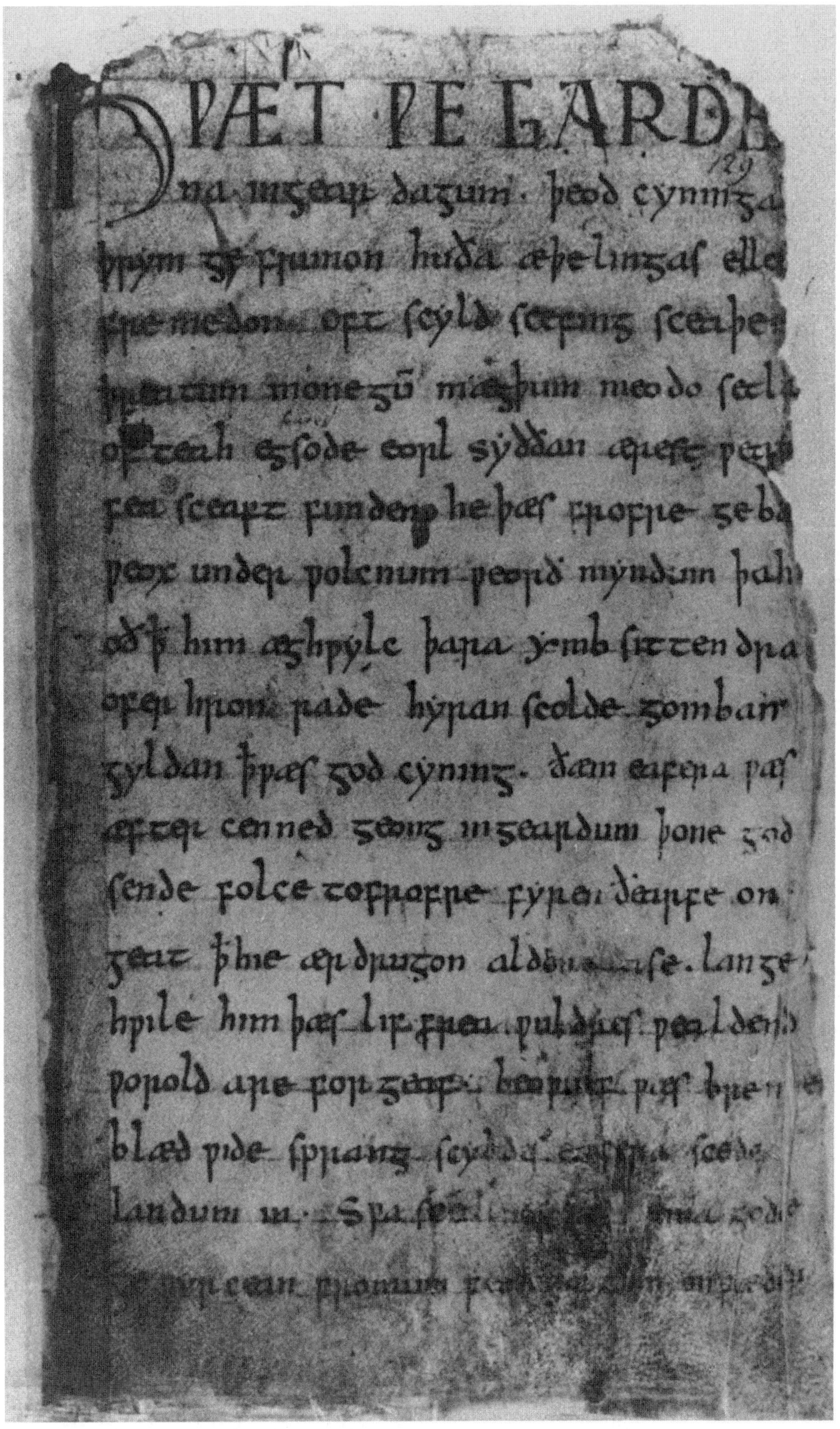

First page of the only surviving manuscript for Beowulf, *a copy made by two scribes circa 975-1025 (Cotton Vitellius, A. xv; British Library)*

ent from the oral poem, if it ever existed. The likelihood of an oral stage of the poem would help explain the existence of antique words and case endings in the poem. Contrary to expectation, illiteracy is far more conservative than literacy. A phrase such as "wait *on* opposing traffic" or a pronunciation of *hep* for *help* will survive from grandfather to grandson as long as it is not exposed to the printed word. Oral generation of the text tends to preserve antique locutions even in fairly late tellings of a story.

In any case the Viking-gap theory of dating the composition of *Beowulf* assumes that the poem is strongly pro-Danish in its leanings. This assumption is based on many "brave Spear-Dane" phrases and the reports of the splendors of the Danish court, but those who accept this theory ignore the plot and setting of the Grendel episodes. Rather than existing triumphantly, the Danes are moping around impotently while they await a stranger who will defeat the monster that has rendered their glorious mead hall useless. One of the difficult determinations in this text is the establishing of tone of the war poetry of this period. *Beowulf* has often been linked with elegiac poetry such as *The Wanderer* and *The Seafarer* which laments the loss of the glories of the hall and the hearth companions. In fact, *Beowulf* may be closer to a *yielp* such as "The Battle of Brunnanburh," which mocks the defeat of one's enemies. *The Battle of Brunnanburh* says that the losers have no need to laugh or boast of their victory, a statement which implies that the winners do laugh and boast. That, in fact, is the point of the *yielp*. The spirit of *Schadenfreude*, joyful malice, is everywhere. It is quite possible to imagine that an audience which has just heard about a Viking attack on the English coast in *The Battle of Maldon* would greet the story of Grendel's meal of one fully armed Dane with uproarious laughter. In fact, the epic depths of *Beowulf* seem to intertwine the elegiac with the military *yielp*, but it is quite difficult to tell where one ends and the other begins.

The threefold structure of Beowulf's confrontations with the monsters must give us pause since the three battles—with Grendel, with Grendel's mother, and with the dragon—seem anticlimactic. Though the dragon in "real life" may be more powerful than either of the Grendels, he is clearly less original or fearsome. Beowulf's battles with the monsters must be read in an oddly foregrounded context. The background to these battles is in the stories and songs often told in celebration of victory or told as exempla: "You should not be as hardhearted as X who. . . ." The so-called digressions produce an anecdotal portrait of the Germanic society out of which the Anglo-Saxon society arose. Beowulf's battles tell of the collapse of that society—a society based on the principle of feud. Such a society is out of harmony with the principles of Christianity—a point that is too often ignored. Other poems, such as *The Wanderer* and *The Seafarer*, come to the same conclusion, but then include a specific moral: "thus should a man. . . ." Beowulf has no such moral, though its characters do moralize, and it is perhaps for this reason, as much as any other, that the poem is set in the pre-Christian past. The values of the society in *Beowulf* will have to stand or fall on their own merits.

These values are based on the interrelations of the *comitatus*, the king and his warrior household. In the ideal society, the king (gold friend, ring giver) gives treasure to his thanes and they, in turn, give service to their king. There is no sense of payment here but of generosity on both sides. In order to distribute treasure, the king must have a center of power, a mead hall with a giving chair (throne) at its very center. He must also have treasure in the form of rings (gold arm bands) or ancient and often famous arms and armor. This treasure is obtainable from three primary sources: directly from military victories, indirectly from the subjugation of neighboring tribes in the form of tribute, or from inheritance, though it should be noted that this last requires ancestors who have done the first two, and *no one ever forgets*. In the beginning of *Beowulf* the eponymous founder of the Danish (Scylding) line, Scyld Scefyng, starts his nation by subjugating his neighbors and leaving a large treasure for his son. For this he earns simple but unqualified praise from the poet: That was a good king.

The mead hall is the social and spiritual center of the Anglo-Saxon culture, and the loss of the joys of the hall is seen as a fate worse than death. In the hall the king distributes treasures to his hearth companions, and they in turn pledge their loyalty to him. The fact that these pledges are made with the mead cup in hand is not lost on the Anglo-Saxon poet: the value of the *beot* (pledge) is based on its successful completion. If a man fulfills his *beot*, it is an "oath," and he is a man of his word; if he fails, his *beot* is merely a "boast," and his courage in the mead hall was no more than the liquor talking. The most basic pledge was not to outlive the ring giver on the battlefield, and the greatest cowards, like the sons of Offa in *The Battle of Maldon*, are those who flee before the battle is done. The duty imposed on the survivors (those who were not there, in fact, even those who were not born yet) is to pay back those who killed their kinsmen. It is then the duty of *their* relatives to get even for the deaths of their kin. Everywhere the principle of feud is kept alive; a sword taken two generations earlier from an ancestor is enough to ignite it again.

In theory there are two ways of escaping from this endless cycle of feud. The first is the payment of *wergeld* (a man's price). Each man in the society was given a price based on his rank in society. Upon the receipt of this amount the aggrieved family was supposed to give up the need to continue the feud. The second solution was a marriage between important representatives of the feuding parties, the equivalent of the prince and princess of feuding tribes marrying. The woman was seen as the bringer of peace in these circumstances, and two words for *woman* in Anglo-Saxon, which translate as "peaceweaver" and "peacecontract," attest to this function.

In *Beowulf* both these methods to disengage the feud mentality are measured and found wanting. Their inherent failure is seen first in Beowulf 's trip to Denmark and then, even more poignantly, in his return home. The end of his reign almost certainly marks the end of the Geatish nation, which has become inextricably bound in international feud.

As a hero, Beowulf goes to the court of Hrothgar, the man who has apparently mastered the system only to discover that his mastery is for nought. Hrothgar, King of the Danes, has built the ultimate mead hall, a place from which he can distribute treasure and fulfill his function as ring giver. Hrothgar's hall, Heorot (the Hart, Stag), is the biggest that has ever been, but it has been rendered useless by the incursions of Grendel, who occupies it at night and has killed and eaten thirty Danish thanes. In his role as wanderer of the trackless fens and as a creature of night, "forscrifen . . . / in Cāines cynne" (proscribed as a member of the race of Cain), Grendel appears to represent all of the aspects of chaos in Anglo-Saxon society. For that reason, it is not surprising that he is enraged by the song of the scop. The scop sings the song of creation, which is probably similar to the song known as "Caedmon's Hymn." To Grendel the ordering of chaos is anathema, and he attacks its center and the hall joys from which he has been excluded. Perhaps the greatest irony is that, despite Grendel's epic depradations, it is not he who destroys Heorot. Beowulf will save the mead hall this time, but the end of Heorot is predicted. It will be destroyed by the uncle of Hrothgar's son. The man who will burn it is, in fact, at dinner when Beowulf comes. Beowulf can protect Heorot from monstrous, man-eating enemies; he cannot defend it against friends and relatives.

One of the odd situations of Beowulf's rescue mission is how difficult the Danes make it for Beowulf to kill their monster. Beowulf is stopped by a Coast Guardian, then by a Hall Guard, and then finally he is challenged by Unferth, the spokesman (*thyle*) of the Danish court. Unferth's basic question is who are you to presume to challenge our monster? At this point the Danes expect Beowulf to lose, and in a world where reputation is everything, they do not want him getting cheap—even at the price of his life—glory. Even a loss to Grendel would go down in song and story, and such a glorious end is not to be earned lightly. Unferth, as *thyle*, seems to be the court insulter, whose job is to test Beowulf in the two things that count in Anglo-Saxon culture: words and works. Unferth says that Beowulf has no reason to challenge Grendel since he was not even able to defeat the warrior Breca in a swimming race. Beowulf replies that it was not a swimming race, but two men testing themselves against the sea and its monsters. In the process Beowulf defeated many monsters, reopening the seas to commerce, an act which establishes him as a civilizer versus chaos, a principal symbolic role he will take on in his struggle against Grendel. Beowulf 's answer also puts Unferth and the Danes in their place. If you are so brave, he asks Unferth, why are you still safely alive while the monster is ravaging your kingdom? Then, in a final turn of the screw, Beowulf notes that Unferth's only act of courage was the murder of his own brother. This fratricide makes Unferth, like Grendel, of the race of Cain and casts Grendel's shadow on the whole Danish court.

In his fight with Grendel, Beowulf disdains armor, stating rather gentlemanly reasons for his decision. The monster does not know the use of armor so the hero too will refrain from wearing it. The odd turn is that Beowulf later uses armor against Grendel's mother, who supposedly is weaker than her son. Beyond his stated reason of courtesy, Beowulf 's decision not to wear armor allows the audience to confuse man and monster in the description of the fight with Grendel, which does not happen in the fight against Grendel's mother. The hand-to-hand combat of Grendel and Beowulf appears to be a fair one. Grendel has eaten thirty men, and Beowulf has the strength of thirty in his arm. The immediate effect of Beowulf 's not wearing armor or carrying a sword is that he does not kill Grendel outright; he merely tears off his arm. Both of these situations—the confusion of Beowulf and Grendel in the tangle of flailing opponents and the hanging up of Grendel's arm as a token of victory in Heorot—point to the same thing, that Grendel is less alien to the Danish society than anyone would like to admit. His being of the race of Cain (there is a tradition that the mark God put upon Cain after he killed Abel was some kind of monstrous malformation) puts Grendel only one generation from the ancestry of all of mankind. Nothing is said about the naming of Heorot (the stag), but it would not be unlikely that a stag's horns might be used to mark the spot. It is clear that, when Beowulf puts up Grendel's Grip as a token (though he never says what it betokens), Grendel has in a real sense co-opted Heorot by becoming the fratricidal spirit of the place—even though he has lost the fight and run back to his lair to die.

Though Grendel's mother quickly redeems her son's arm, one can imagine the unlettered Danish tourist looking for the memorial of the Great Battle. Where can I find Grendel's Grip?, he might ask, and in a few years the great mead hall would be known as Grendel's. Though Grendel's mother retrieves the hand, it will soon be replaced by Grendel's head so the tourist's question will hardly change. He had better hurry though, for the hall will be destroyed within this generation by internecine familial hate. The spirit of Cain is the equal possession of the Grendels and the Danish royal family.

The place of Grendel's mother arises out of the function of women and mothers in this society and is related to three stories about women that are told in the time surrounding her descent upon the mead hall. The first of these women is Wealhtheow, the wife of Hrothgar, who seems to be the ideal queen and woman, but her danger to Beowulf stems from this idealness. It is Wealhtheow who cements the bond between the Danes and their not-quite-welcome guests by passing the mead cup among them. Later, when Beowulf defeats her enemies, she gets him to pledge his support for her sons, in case any new enmity should come to them. We do not know if she already suspects the uncle's treachery, and we never hear of Beowulf coming to their aid, but it is important that Beowulf has bound himself for the first time in the web of feud. At this point Wealhtheow is designated as *frithowebbe* or weaver of peace.

At the same time two stories are told about the failure of marriage as a way to end feud. In both cases the woman's presence becomes the spark for new violence rather than the ender of the old. In the first, a sketched version of events which are also told in *The Fight at Finnsburg*, Hildeburh, the daughter of the Danish king, Hoc, is married to Finn, the king of the enemy Frisians, to cement peace between two warring tribes. A generation later, Hnaef, now king of the Danes, goes to visit his sister at Finn's fortress. As a king, Hnaef does not travel alone, but with a band of armed retainers. Their presence rekindles the old flames, and war breaks out, killing Hildeburh's brother, Hnaef, and her warrior son. These deaths, in turn, are avenged when Hengest, Hnaef 's chief thane, spends the winter in Finn's land (a thing never done among Scandinavian tribes) and, with the coming of spring, slays his host and enemy.

The other marriage story is told by Beowulf on his return home to his own country. He tells his king, Hygelac, that the Danish princess, Freawaru, is about to marry Ingeld, the king of the Heathobards, in another of these peace-insuring unions. Then, in a tricky piece of narration, Beowulf tells what will happen to this marriage. The events he foretells are in fact history to the audience, and what is shocking about Beowulf 's narration is the detail in which he recounts the future. The story he tells is as follows: Freawaru will come to the Heathobard court, and one of her retainers will be wearing a sword that was taken from the grandfather of one of the young men in the court; an old man will recognize the sword and will incite the young man to murder with an incendiary speech. Then Beowulf provides verbatim the words of a speech that has not yet been made. The poet seems to be saying that the pattern of woman as institutional peacemaker is so flawed that one can predict exactly how it will go wrong in the future. Within this pattern of woman as the net that binds together the corrosive energy of society, Grendel's mother appears. If Grendel is the deadly force that implements the murderous acts of feud, then she is the institution itself, and so it is that her killing of one man is not the unmotivated wrath and hunger of her son, but rather an act sanctioned by the society she attacks. She had been content to dwell in her lair, but the code of retribution demands that she take one life for her son's.

After Beowulf 's return home, the historical digressions shift from a generalized vision of the Anglo-Saxon way to the specific history of the Geatish line which leads to Beowulf's becoming king. The history of the Geatish royal line provides a paradigm for the self-destruction inherent in the feud system. Beowulf 's grandfather, Hrethel, is a successful warrior king. He rules over the *comitatus* with the aid of his three sons, all proven warriors. Then his eldest son, Herebeald, is killed in an archery accident. In the normal state of affairs Hrethel could then claim *wergeld* in lieu of punishment from the family of his son's slayer. This solution will not work, nor will the option of feud, since his son's slayer is also his son and now the heir to the throne. Hrethel suffers the ultimate frustration of a tribal leader, an unavenged son. The poet tells us that Hrethel's grief drove him from the world, that is, he either died from morbid sorrow, or he took his grief into the monastery, where he then died. In any case the options and obligations of revenge incumbent on a tribal leader are closed to him.

Beowulf 's actual reign of fifty years is never discussed, only the conditions—a series of disastrous wars against the Swedes—which remove the three-man line for the throne ahead of him and allow him to become king. When we meet Beowulf as king, his reign of half a hundred years (fifty years seems to indicate that he has ruled his whole life rather than to designate the specific length of his reign) is almost at an end. The strength of Beowulf 's right arm has apparently guaranteed the Geats a reign of tranquility despite their being surrounded by powerful neighbors waiting to swallow them up. This peace is shattered by the awakening of a dragon that has held its own peace for three hundred years. Once again it is the mechanism of the feud system which causes the uproar in the land of the Geats. The dragon is disturbed by someone designated as "niththa nathwylc" (no one in particular), a man who steals a plated cup from the dragon's treasure hoard, presumably for the purpose of paying off *wergeld*.

The dragon, therefore, puts Beowulf in the position of Hrothgar, a king whose kingdom is besieged by a monster, but Beowulf does not wait for a hero. Instead he seeks out the dragon himself. As has been his custom, Beowulf goes with an armed troop of men, and this time he carries an iron shield. Beowulf, still operating in the heroic rather than royal mode, tells his men that the dragon is his fight, not theirs. They conveniently accept this determination and skulk off to the wood to hide. That their action is wrong is confirmed by Wiglaf, the one warrior who comes to Beowulf 's aid. Wiglaf condemns Beowulf 's hearth companions, both before the dragon fight and after. He accuses them of failure to do service for ring giving. His condemnation of these men is a condemnation of the system itself and renders Beowulf 's tragic end pathetic. Beowulf 's death in the face of the dragon's fiery wrath is inevitable. He is already an old man, but he does accomplish, with Wiglaf 's help, the killing of the dragon. This feat is all Beowulf could hope for but he hopes for more. He wants the treasure to leave to his people so that a ring giver—someone like Wiglaf—could rule over his people the way the original Scyld ruled over the Danes. Beowulf, literally on his deathbed, holds on long enough to luxuriate in the treasure he has won for his people. But all is in vain; the treasure is cursed and will prove useless. With all his virtues Beowulf has left the Geats neither an heir with a strong right arm (which Hrethel did in begetting Haethcyn and Hygelac) nor a treasure for ring giving (as Scyld did for his son, the first Beowulf). As the treasure is returned to the earth, Wiglaf 's condemnation reminds us of the pathetic decline of the whole enterprise. Even if the treasure remained to be distributed, it would have been left to men like these, who were too craven to honor the treasure they had been already given.

The Beowulf manuscript, which provides the basis of all editions, has led a kind of charmed life. It survived from its tenth-century birth until the sixteenth century almost certainly in some monastic library. During the terrible depredations upon monastic holdings during the reign of Henry VIII (1509-1547), it came into the hands of the antiquarian scholar Lawrence Novell, whose name, and the date 1563, are written on the manuscript. Soon after, it became the property of Sir Robert Cotton (1571-1631), in whose library it was listed as Cotton Vitellius A. xv (in the Cottonian library, in the book press under the bust of the Roman Emperor Aulus Vitellius, first shelf down, fifteenth volume in). The library remained in the Cotton family for several generations, until it was donated to the British nation in 1700. The Cottonian Library was eventually designated as the manuscript collection of the British Museum when that library was founded in 1753.

By 1722, the Cotton house was considered so dilapidated that the library was moved to Essex House, and then—because this building was considered unsafe—the collection was taken to Ashburnham House, which burned in 1731. The codex survived, and the manuscript, which was bound between several other works, remained remarkably intact. The manuscript, whose importance no one recognized, should have been rebound after the fire, but no one knew its significance and the fire-damaged vellum began to decay. Fortunately, the Danish scholar Thorkelin had some sense of what the manuscript was, and had it hand-copied in 1790. Thorkelin eventually produced an edition and a Latin translation. Though the many inaccuracies of Thorkelin's edition were recognized by the first great *Beowulf* scholar, N. F. S. Grundtvig, the Thorkelin transcription of the manuscript has proved invaluable in preserving readings lost by the gradual deterioration of Cotton Vitellius A. xv. It was not until the mid nineteenth century that the manuscript was rebound, so that it could be once again available to scholars.

References:

Stephen C. Bandy, "*Beowulf*: the Defense of Heorot," *Neophilologus*, 56 (January 1972): 86-92;

Adrien Bonjour, *The Digressions in Beowulf* (Oxford: Blackwell, 1950);

Arthur G. Brodeur, *The Art of Beowulf* (Berkeley: University of California Press, 1959);

Alan K. Brown, "The Firedrake in *Beowulf*," *Neophilologus*, 64 (July 1980): 439-460;

Allen Cabaniss, "*Beowulf* and the Liturgy," *Journal of English and Germanic Philology*, 54 (April 1955): 195-201;

R. W. Chambers, *Beowulf: An Introduction to the Study of the Poem*, third edition, with a supplement by C. L. Wrenn (Cambridge: Cambridge University Press, 1959);

Robert P. Creed, "A New Approach to the Rhythm of *Beowulf*," *PMLA*, 81 (March 1966): 23-33;

Norman E. Eliason, "Beowulf's Inglorious Youth," *Studies in Philology*, 76 (April 1979): 101-108;

Margaret E. Goldsmith, "Christian Perspective in *Beowulf*," *Comparative Literature*, 14 (Winter 1962): 71-90;

Stanley B. Greenfield, "A Touch of the Monstrous in the Hero, or Beowulf Re-Marvellized," *English Studies*, 63 (1982): 294-300;

Marie Padgett Hamilton, "The Religious Principle in *Beowulf*," *PMLA*, 61 (June 1946): 309-330;

Jeffrey Helterman, "*Beowulf*: The Archetype Enters History," *ELH*, 35 (March 1968): 1-20;

Bernard F. Huppé, *The Hero in the Earthly City: A Reading of Beowulf* (Binghamton: Medieval & Renaissance Texts & Studies, State University of New York at Binghamton, 1984);

Edward B. Irving, Jr., *A Reading of Beowulf* (New Haven: Yale University Press, 1968);

Stanley J. Kahrl, "Feuds in *Beowulf*: A Tragic Necessity?," *Modern Philology*, 69 (February 1972): 189-198;

R. E. Kaske, "*Sapientia et Fortitudo* as the Controlling Theme of *Beowulf*," *Studies in Philology*, 55 (July 1958): 423-456;

Kevin S. Kiernan, *Beowulf and the Beowulf Manuscript* (New Brunswick, N.J.: Rutgers University Press, 1981);

Albert Bates Lord, *The Singer of Tales* (Cambridge, Mass.: Harvard University Press, 1960);

Kemp Malone, "Young Beowulf," *Journal of English and Germanic Philology*, 36 (January 1937): 21-23;

M. B. McNamee, "*Beowulf*—An Allegory of Salvation?," *Journal of English and Germanic Philology*, 59 (April 1960): 190-207;

Charles Moorman, "The Essential Paganism of *Beowulf*," *Modern Language Quarterly*, 28 (March 1967): 3-18;

John D. Niles, *Beowulf: The Poem and its Tradition* (Cambridge, Mass.: Harvard University Press, 1983);

Donald H. Reiman, "Folklore and Beowulf's Defense of Heorot," *English Studies*, 42 (August 1961): 231-232;

James L. Rosier, "The Uses of Association: Hands and Feasts in *Beowulf*," *PMLA*, 78 (March 1963): 8-14;

Kenneth Sisam, *The Structure of Beowulf* (Oxford: Clarendon Press, 1965);

J. R. R. Tolkien, "*Beowulf*: The Monsters and the Critics," in *Proceedings of the British Academy*, volume 22 (London: Oxford University Press, 1936); pp. 245-295;

Jacqueline Vaught, "*Beowulf*: The Fight at the Center," *Allegorica*, 5 (Winter 1980): 125-137;

Dorothy Whitelock, *The Audience of Beowulf*, corrected edition, (Oxford: Clarendon Press, 1958).

Thomas Campion

(12 February 1567 - 1 March 1620)

This entry was updated by David Lindley (University of Leeds) from his entry in DLB 58: Jacobean and Caroline Dramatists.

BOOKS: *Thomæ Campiani Poemata* (London: Printed by R. Field, 1595);

A Booke of Ayres, by Campion and Philip Rosseter (London: Printed by P. Short, by the assent of T. Morley, 1601);

Observations in the Art of English Poesie (London: Printed by R. Field for A. Wise, 1602);

The Discription of a Maske, Presented before the Kinges Maiestie at White-Hall on Twelfth Night last, in honour of the Lord Hayes, and his Bride, Daughter and Heire to the Honourable the Lord Dennye (London: Printed by J. Windet for J. Brown, 1607);

A Relation Of The Late Royall Entertainment given By The Right Honourable The Lord Knowles, at Cawsome House neere Redding: to our most Gracious Queene, Queene Anne in her Progresse toward the Bathe, upon the seven and eight and twentie dayes of Aprill 1613. Whereunto is annexed the Description, Speeches and Songs of the Lords Maske, presented in the Banqueting House on the Mariage night of the High and Mightie, Count Palatine, and the Royally descended the Ladie Elizabeth (London: Printed by W. Stansby for J. Budge, 1613);

Songs of Mourning (London: Printed by T. Snodham for J. Browne, 1613);

Two Bookes of Ayres (London: Printed by T. Snodham for M. Lownes & J. Browne, 1613?);

The Description of a Maske. Presented in the Banqueting roome at Whitehall on Saint Stephens Night last, at the Mariage of the Right Honourable the Earle of Somerset: And the right noble the Lady Francis Howard (London: Printed by E. Allde & T. Snodham for L. Lisle, 1614);

OBSERVATIONS
in the Art of Engliſh
Poeſie.

By *Thomas Campion.*

Wherein it is demonſtra-
tiuely prooued, and by example
confirmed, that the Engliſh toong
will receiue eight ſeuerall kinds of num-
bers, proper to it ſelfe, which are all
in this booke ſet forth, and were
neuer before this time by any
man attempted.

Printed at London by RICHARD FIELD
for *Andrew Wiſe.* 1602.

Title page for the 1602 octavo edition of Campion's treatise on poetic meter (Bodleian Library, Oxford)

The Third and Fourth Bookes of Ayres (London: Printed by T. Snodham, 1617?);

A New Way of Making Fowre parts in Counter-point (London, 1617?);

The Ayres that were sung and played, at Brougham Castle in Westmerland in the Kings Entertainment (London: Printed by Thomas Snodham, 1618);

Thomæ Campiani Epigrammatum Libri II (London: Printed by E. Griffin, 1619).

Editions: *Campion's Works*, edited by Percival Vivian (Oxford: Clarendon Press, 1909);

The Lords' Masque, edited by I. A. Shapiro, in *A Book of Masques*, edited by T. J. B. Spencer and Stanley Wells (Cambridge: Cambridge University Press, 1967), pp. 95-124;

The Works of Thomas Campion, edited by Walter R. Davis (Garden City, N.Y.: Doubleday, 1967; London: Faber & Faber, 1969);

Four Hundred Songs and Dances from the Stuart Masque, edited by Andrew J. Sabol (Providence: Brown University Press, 1968);

The Lord Hay's Masque and *The Lords' Masque*, in *Inigo Jones: The Theatre of the Stuart Court*, volume 1, by Stephen Orgel and Roy Strong (London: Sotheby Parke Bernet / Berkeley: University of California Press, 1973), pp. 115-121, 241-252;

De Puluerea Coniuratione (On The Gunpowder Plot), edited by David Lindley, with translations and additional notes by Robin Sowerby, *Leeds Texts and Monographs*, new series 9 (1987).

PLAY PRODUCTIONS: *The Lord Hay's Masque*, London, at Court, 6 January 1607;

The Lords' Masque, London, at Court, 14 February 1613;

The Caversham Entertainment, near Reading, Caversham House, 27-28 April 1613;

The Somerset Masque, London, at Court, 26 December 1613.

Thomas Campion made a varied contribution to the arts of his period. Perhaps best known today as the composer of music and lyrics for more than one hundred songs for voice and lute, he was equally celebrated in his own time for his Latin poetry. He wrote a theoretical treatise on versification urging the adoption of classical quantitative meters in English, and a music textbook which was sufficiently forward-looking to be republished throughout the seventeenth century. His contribution to the dramatic literature of the age consists of four masques, works which have been unjustly condemned by most modern critics. While there can be no doubt that Ben Jonson is the dominant figure in the history of the Jacobean masque, Campion's works are fine examples of the genre.

Campion was born on 12 February 1567 in the parish of St. Andrew's, Holborn. By 1580 his father, John Campion, a cursitor (official clerk) of the Court of Chancery, and his mother, Lucy, were both dead, leaving him in the care of his mother's third husband, Augustine Steward, and his new wife, Anne Sisley. In 1581 he was sent to Peterhouse, Cambridge, where he remained until 1584, leaving without taking a degree. Two years later he was admitted to Gray's Inn. He acquired no legal qualification, but during the time of his connection with the inn he must have begun his writing career. His connection with drama and the masque also began at this time. In 1588 he acted a part in a comedy presented before Lord Burleigh and other noblemen, and in 1594 he contributed at least one lyric to *The Masque of Proteus*, a highly significant work in the establishing of the masque form. It is probable that in 1591-1592 Campion joined Robert Devereux, second Earl of Essex, on his unsuccessful expedition to aid Henry IV of France against the Catholic League in Normandy.

In 1595 Campion's publishing career began with the appearance of *Thomæ Campiani Poemata* (though five songs probably by Campion had been included with other poems appended to Thomas Newman's unauthorized edition of Sir Philip Sidney's *Astrophel and Stella* in 1591). In 1601 Campion and his friend Philip Rosseter jointly published *A Booke of Ayres*, the first half of which was by Campion. Rosseter's dedication of this work to Sir Thomas Monson indicates that Campion had for some time been under the protection of this important musical patron, who was himself a client of the powerful Howard family. This relationship was to be of considerable significance for Campion's future. After the publication in 1602 of his treatise on meter, *Observations in the Art of English Poesie*, it is assumed that Campion traveled on the Continent. In any event he received the degree of M.D. from the University of Caen in February 1605 and practiced medicine for the rest of his life.

Campion's masque-writing career began in 1607, when on 6 January *The Lord Hay's Masque*

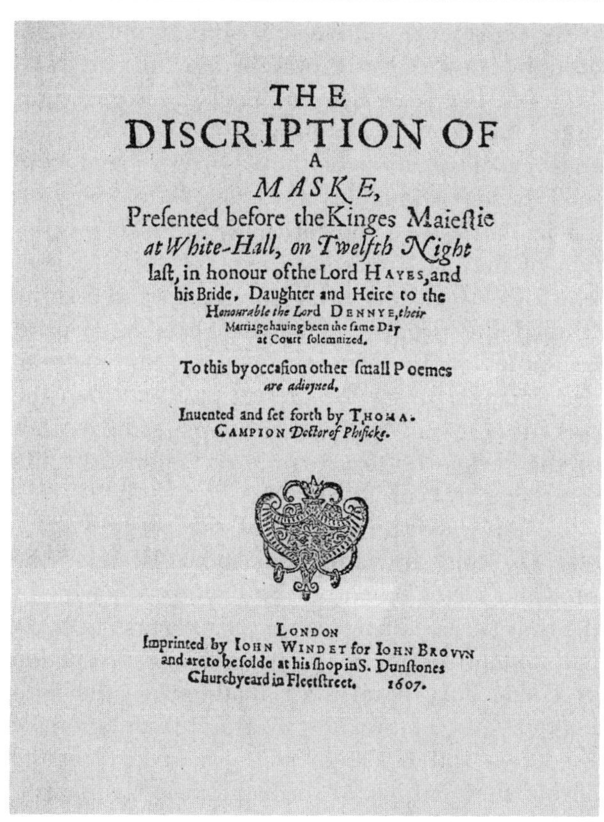

THE
DISCRIPTION OF
A
MASKE,
Presented before the Kinges Maiestie
at White-Hall, on Twelfth Night
last, in honour of the Lord HAYES, and
his Bride, Daughter and Heire to the
Honourable the Lord DENNYE, *their*
Marriage hauing been the same Day
at Court solemnized.

To this by occasion other small Poemes
are adioyned.

Inuented and set forth by THOMA.
CAMPION *Doctor of Phisicke.*

LONDON
Imprinted by IOHN WINDET for IOHN BROWN
and are to be solde at his shop in S. Dunstones
Churchyeard in Fleetstreet. 1607.

Title page for the 1607 quarto edition of Campion's first masque (British Library)

was performed at court to celebrate the marriage of King James's Scottish favorite James Hay to Honora Denny. Summarizing a masque text, its meaning and significance, is no easy task. Music and spectacle, which play a vital role in the genre, are not easy to reconstruct in the imagination. Furthermore, the poet's ambition to lay hold on some more-removed mystery (in Jonson's phrase) means that the critic is involved in the explication of myth and symbol. Finally, since a masque grows out of a specific occasion, it is only when the context of an individual work is fully understood that layers of political implication can be uncovered.

The Lord Hay's Masque is notable for the detail with which its musical arrangements are described. Three separate groups of musicians were disposed in different places, their antiphonal sound contributing to the work's dramatic effect, and their climactic conjunction in full chorus to praise James I emphatically underlining the masque's panegyric. The published text also contains an amusing record of a failure in the scene designer's art, when trees that parted to reveal the masquers within failed to disappear "either by the simplicity, negligence, or conspiracy of the painter," as Campion testily remarked.

The narrative of the masque concerns nine Knights of Apollo who have been imprisoned in trees by Diana, goddess of chastity, for their temerity in seeking to seduce her nymphs. By the mediation of Hesperus, Diana is reconciled, the knights are released, and, after paying homage to Diana's tree, they are free to join in the revels to celebrate the marriage.

The device is appropriate to its occasion in that the concord of the three deities, Apollo, Venus (Hesperus), and Diana, figures the elemental concord between male heat and female cold that marriage brings about. The masque urges on the couple a temperate and lasting love.

This marriage between a Scotsman and an Englishwoman also served as an emblem of the union between Scotland and England that James had urgently prosecuted since 1603, when, already James VI of Scotland, he had become James I of Great Britain. Campion shows himself fully aware of this political dimension. For while the overall direction of the masque serves to commend the union, much of its detail shows an awareness of the problems that hindered the success of the scheme. Most notably, in choosing Diana as the defender of the female (English) side of the match he alludes to the memory of Queen Elizabeth, and by making the knights' homage to her tree the climax of their restoration he articulates the English concern at the intemperance of James's court and his excessive reward of Scottish followers. At the same time, however, English spectators are reminded that Elizabeth had consented to James's succession and therefore to the union of countries it brought about. The masque as a whole indicates the need for love to replace ancient hostility between the nations. The balanced attitude Campion strikes suited Robert Cecil and Thomas Howard, who probably commissioned and paid for the masque, but it seems typical also of the author's personality as it reveals itself in his poetry and in his later masques.

After this work Campion published virtually nothing for six years, but late in 1612 he was commissioned to provide a masque for the extensive celebrations of the wedding of Princess Elizabeth to Frederick, Elector Palatine. Perhaps it was Jonson's absence from the country that made room for him, and his connection, through Monson, with Thomas Howard, the lord chamberlain, that secured this prestigious responsibility. The preparations were, however, interrupted by

Engraving of a Knight of Apollo published in the 1607 quarto edition of The Lord Hay's Masque *(from Stephen Orgel and Roy Strong,* Inigo Jones, *1973)*

the death of Prince Henry on 6 November 1612. To this sad event Campion responded by publishing his *Songs of Mourning* with music by Giovanni Coprario. In his dedication of this work to Frederick he promised that he would soon be singing "delayed wedding songs," and the promise was fulfilled on 14 February 1613, with the performance of *The Lords' Masque*.

For this work Campion collaborated with Inigo Jones. Where in his previous masque he had cause for complaint against the scene designer, here he was full of praise for Jones's "extraordinarie industrie and skill," especially in his contrivance of a ballet of moving stars. This particularly ingenious device elicited admiring comment from the Venetian ambassador. It is not only the setting of this masque which marks an advance on earlier work, for the work begins with an antimasque of madmen as foil to the main masque, following the formal innovation introduced by Jonson some four years previously.

The masque itself is complex. Two sets of masquers are involved. The first set, eight lords, represents the dancing stars, and they are brought down by Prometheus, the mythical stealer of fire from heaven. The second set, eight ladies, has been turned into statues by Jove in his anger at Prometheus's theft. Jove relents, and four by four the ladies are brought to life, joining in dance with the lords. In a striking variation of the usual masque form the social dances which follow do not bring the masque to a close. Instead the prophetess Sibylla appears, flanked by statues of the bride and groom. She prophesies a happy future for the couple, and then the spectators are invited to contemplate the statues of the couple before turning to honor "the life those figures bear."

The elaborate surface of the masque shadows a serious and ambitious moral design. The program seems based on the Platonic doctrine of the four furies which lead men from earth to celestial contemplation. It begins with the distinction of Poetic Fury from mere madmen in the antimasque and culminates in the presentation of Frederick and Elizabeth as types of Love at the end of the masque. At the same time Campion is able to explore the problem of how such mysteries may be revealed in art, as Orpheus and Entheus, representing poetry and music, are joined by Prometheus the maker of images. Campion's part in the contriving of the masque is figured in the first two, Inigo Jones's in the third.

Throughout this masque Campion addresses the question of the relationship of masque image to the reality it idealized, and he insists upon the necessity of the masquers' remembering the significance of the roles they play, making clear his didactic purpose.

This marriage was, of course, a highly significant political event. The wedding of Elizabeth to a Protestant was seen as committing James to the anti-Spanish cause in Europe and raised hopes among some fervent souls of a new crusade against Catholicism. Campion presents a much more restrained attitude. The work as a whole seems to support a pacific line that accorded much more closely with James's own inclinations, and perhaps alludes to his policy of balancing this Protestant match with a Catholic marriage for his son. But whether or not that is the case, there can be no doubt that Campion responded to this most demanding commission with an extraordinarily ambitious work, whose meaning is only available after detailed consideration of its iconology and political address.

Inigo Jones's costume design for the lords who played dancing stars in Campion's The Lords' Masque *(from Stephen Orgel and Roy Strong,* Inigo Jones, *1973)*

The political attitude of this masque must have commended itself to the Howard family, since Campion was entrusted by them with two more commissions within the next twelve months. Queen Anne, on her progress to Bath after her daughter's wedding, stayed at Caversham near Reading, the home of Sir William Knollys, who was related to the Howards by marriage.

The Caversham Entertainment is a slighter piece than the other masques. When the Queen approached the house on 27 April she was greeted by a Cynick who attempted to bar the way. A Traveller countered his arguments, and the Queen proceeded toward the house to be greeted at various points by a Keeper and a Gardiner with appropriate verses, songs, and dances. Campion here manipulates fairly standard pastoral figures with grace, for the sequence of meetings is so contrived that the nearer the Queen approached to the house the more sophisticated her welcome became.

The following night the Queen was entertained after supper by a masque indoors. Cynick, Traveller, and Gardiner reappear in a brief, almost Jonsonian antimasque which is interrupted by Silvanus. He then introduces the eight masquers in their elegantly pastoral attire.

The lack of any scenic device and the somewhat old-fashioned role of Sylvanus as presenter of the disguising are typical of the necessarily more limited scope of masques away from the court. Within these limits Campion contrived a graceful if not profound work exploiting rather different conventions from those of his larger-scale masques.

It was probably in this same year (1613) that Campion brought out his *Two Bookes of Ayres*, dedicated to the earl of Cumberland and his son. But at the end of the year it was again to a Howard commission that Campion responded, with his masque for the marriage of Suffolk's daughter Frances to Robert Carr, Earl of Somerset.

The Somerset Masque, presented on 26 December 1613, is interesting in several ways. Because Inigo Jones was away, Campion had to avail himself of the services of Constantine de' Servi, and once again he had cause for complaint. He wrote: "he, being too much of him selfe, and no way to be drawne to impart his intentions, fayled so farre in the assurance he gave, that the mayne invention, even at the last cast, was of force drawne into a farre narrower compasse then was from the beginning intended." One can only conjecture how seriously this affected the masque, but the comment does serve to underline the extent to which any court masque was a collaborative enterprise, and it alerts a text-orientated critic to the significance of the scene designer's part in the work's devising.

Also noteworthy is the fact that Nicholas Lanier began his career as a composer of masque music with a setting of the lyric "Bring away this Sacred Tree" in a highly declamatory style. The masque is significant in the history of the evolution of musical style, and this song marks a major step in the advance toward a quasi-operatic manner.

Campion himself signaled a departure from his earlier style when in the prologue to the published text he dismissed old-fashioned myth, instead grounding his "whole Invention upon Inchauntments and several transformations." He is here following closely the tendencies of French court entertainment and reflecting his career-long interest in French music and poetry.

Catullus's narrative of the marriage of Peleus and Thetis underlies *The Somerset Masque*. Twelve masquers have been prevented by enchantment from attending the marriage. The consequences of the enchanters' power are demonstrated in a series of discordant dances, but their disharmony is dispelled by the entrance of Eternitie and the Destinies. Queen Anne is invited to pluck a bough from their sacred tree, and the knights are thus freed to dance in honor of the couple. After the revels a brief coda sees skippers emerge from Thames barges and perform a dance before the masque draws to its close.

This masque has an altogether more rhetorical and assertive character than the earlier works, with much less emphasis upon the education of the masquers themselves. The reason is not far to seek, for the circumstances of its composition were peculiarly difficult.

The marriage of Frances Howard to Robert Carr, the king's chief favorite, was a signal triumph in political terms for the Howard clan. It was made possible by Frances's divorce from the earl of Essex, to whom she had been married as a child in 1606. The divorce hearing, blatantly rigged by the king, granted Frances her freedom on the grounds of Essex's impotence toward her. It occasioned a great deal of salacious gossip and many outbursts of moral indignation.

It was this scandal that *The Somerset Masque* confronted directly. Error, Rumour, Curiosity, and Credulity are the enchanters whose inhibition of the celebrations the masque overcomes. The work is therefore directed out at the audience in a defiant attempt to persuade them of the propriety of the marriage. Queen Anne's blessing on the marriage was more than conventional flattery, since it was the relaxation of her opposition to the match that allowed it to be celebrated in London rather than at the bride's home. Furthermore, the gift of children that the Destinies promised the couple is itself an explicit defense of the divorce, since Essex's impotence would have denied Frances the legitimate possibility of procreation.

It is tempting to see this masque as a glaring example of the obsequious and unthinking flattery proffered to his patron by a court poet. But a case can be made that Campion, like George Chapman in his poem *Andromeda Liberata* (which has significant similarities with the masque), saw the marriage as a real attempt to bring court faction together, and as a morally defensible liberation of a woman from the prison of a nonmarriage.

But though such an attitude was possible in 1613, it could scarcely be sustained when, in 1615, it was revealed that Frances Howard, possibly with Carr's collusion, had caused the murder of Sir Thomas Overbury in the Tower of London just before the divorce was granted. These disclosures had important consequences for Campion. His patron Thomas Monson had been instrumental in replacing William Wade as lieutenant of the Tower with Sir Gervase Elwes, a man more amenable to Frances's designs. Campion himself had collected a large sum of money from Elwes to be given to Monson as payment for procuring the position. He was questioned, but cleared of any guilty knowledge. Monson was not so fortunate. Though never charged, and protesting his innocence, he was imprisoned until 1617. While it is impossible to be absolutely certain, it would seem unlikely that Campion or Monson had any inkling of the dark consequences of their actions.

When Monson was released Campion published his *The Third and Fourth Bookes of Ayres* with a dedication congratulating Monson on his fortitude, which the poet had been able to observe when attending him as his physician. Many of the lyrics in *The Third Booke* speak of disillusionment with the faithlessness of the world, perhaps reflecting something of Campion's own feelings at the betrayal of the idealized picture of Frances Howard and of court society he had created in *The Somerset Masque*.

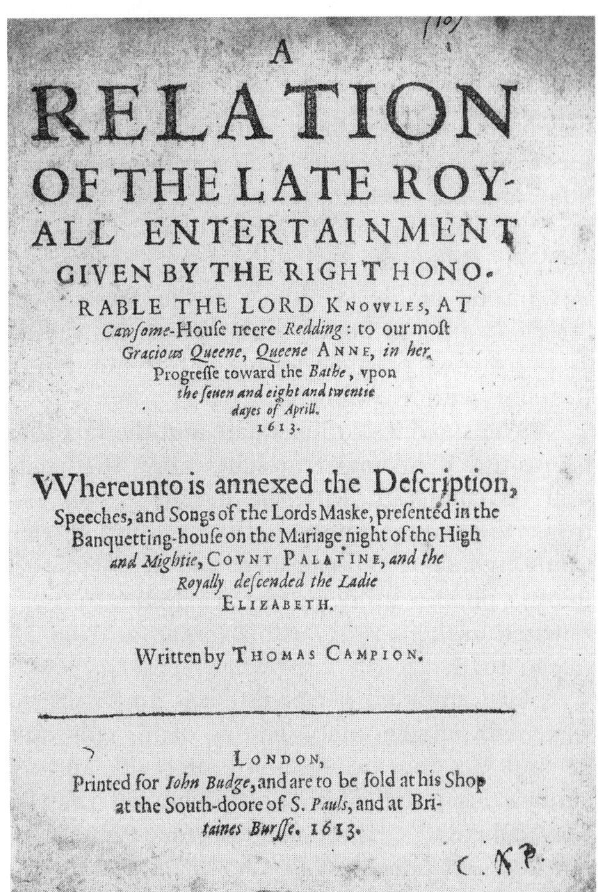
A RELATION OF THE LATE ROYALL ENTERTAINMENT GIVEN BY THE RIGHT HONORABLE THE LORD KNOWLES, AT *Cawsome*-House neere *Redding*: to our most *Gracious Queene*, *Queene* ANNE, *in her* Progresse toward the *Bathe*, vpon *the seuen and eight and twentie dayes of Aprill.* 1613.

Whereunto is annexed the Description, Speeches, and Songs of the Lords Maske, presented in the Banquetting-house on the Mariage night of the High *and Mightie*, COVNT PALATINE, *and the Royally descended the Ladie* ELIZABETH.

Written by THOMAS CAMPION.

LONDON, Printed for *Iohn Budge*, and are to be sold at his Shop at the South-doore of S. *Pauls*, and at Britaines *Bursse*. 1613.

Title page for the 1613 quarto edition of the first masque on which Campion collaborated with Inigo Jones (Henry E. Huntington Library and Art Gallery)

It is possible that Campion contributed to the entertainment of King James when he visited the earl of Cumberland in August 1617 on his return from Scotland. *The Ayres that were sung and played, at Brougham Castle* were published the following year with music by George Mason and John Earsden but no acknowledgment of the writer of the words. Campion had been connected with the Clifford family; a letter cited by Percival Vivian, the editor of the 1909 edition of Campion's works, seems to indicate some degree of involvement with the entertainment of the king, and one or two of the lyrics echo Campion's Latin poems faintly. Unfortunately, whether or not Campion did write these poems, it is impossible to reconstruct from them any real idea of the character of the entertainment in which they figured.

Campion's last work, *Epigrammatum Libri II*, revising and considerably extending his first Latin publication, appeared in 1619. This publication did not, however, include the recently discovered *De Puluerea Coniuratione*, which survives in a single manuscript (Sidney Sussex MS 59). Probably written between 1615 and 1618, it is Campion's most ambitious Latin work. The epical treatment of the Gunpowder Plot is dedicated to the king, and may well represent an effort to regain the favor lost in the aftermath of the Overbury murder. Campion died on 1 March 1620 and was buried at St. Dunstan's in the West, Fleet Street. In his will he left his entire estate, valued at twenty-two pounds, to his old friend Philip Rosseter, wishing that it "had bin farr more."

The smallness of his estate and the fact that he produced no major masques after 1613 may well be connected with the decline of his patrons' fortunes that followed the Overbury trial. Monson suffered financially, and the Howard family's political influence began a decline that culminated in the earl of Suffolk's removal from office in 1618.

Of Campion's personality it is impossible to write with any certainty. In one of his epigrams he indicates that he was spare of build, and an anonymous poem of circa 1611 implies that he was talkative: "How now Doctor Champion, musicks and poesies stout Champion, / Will you nere leave prating?" The masques suggest that he was balanced in his political attitudes, conservative in temperament, yet able to criticize the excesses of the Jacobean court.

Campion's masques are significant examples of their kind. In them may be traced the evolution of the early Jacobean masque, its music and scene design. Each of them offers an interesting gloss on the significant political events they celebrated. If their symbolism is fully and sympathetically understood, then often-repeated criticism of Campion's lack of structural ability is shown to be false and Stephen Orgel's censure of Campion's political flaccidity revealed as unjust. For though *The Somerset Masque* exposes the strains that any poet must have felt in idealizing the increasingly unideal court of King James, Campion managed in all his works to serve his patrons, satisfy the panegyric necessity of the form, and yet not lose sight of the didactic and moral seriousness that alone could give weight to these transitory shows and preserve his own integrity.

References:

A. Leigh DeNeef, "Structure and Theme in Campion's *The Lords Maske*," *Studies in English Literature*, 17 (Winter 1977): 95-103;

Jerzy Limon, *The Masque of Stuart Culture* (Newark: University of Delaware Press / London & Toronto: Associated University Presses, 1990);

David Lindley, "Campion's *Lord Hay's Masque* and Anglo-Scottish Union," *Huntington Library Quarterly*, 43 (Winter 1979): 1-11;

Lindley, *Thomas Campion* (Leiden, Netherlands: E. J. Brill, 1986);

Lindley, "Who Paid for Campion's *Lord Hay's Masque*?," *Notes and Queries*, new series 27 (April 1979): 144;

Edward Lowbury, Timothy Salter, and Alison Young, *Thomas Campion* (London: Chatto & Windus, 1970);

Wilfred Mellers, *Harmonious Meeting* (London: Dobson, 1965);

Stephen Orgel, *The Jonsonian Masque* (Cambridge, Mass.: Harvard University Press, 1967);

John Orrell, "The agent of Savoy at *The Somerset Masque*," *Review of English Studies*, 28 (1977): 301-304;

Paul Reyher, *Les Masques Anglais* (Paris & London: Hachette et Cie, 1909);

Ian Spink, "Campion's Entertainment at Brougham Castle, 1617," in *Music in English Renaissance Drama*, edited by John H. Long (Lexington: University of Kentucky Press, 1968), pp. 57-74;

Enid Welsford, *The Court Masque* (Cambridge: Cambridge University Press, 1927);

Christopher R. Wilson, "Some Musico-Poetic Aspects of Campion's Masques," in *The Well Enchanting Skill: Music, Poetry and Drama in the Culture of the Renaissance, Essays in Honour of F. W. Sternfield* (Oxford: Clarendon Press, 1990), pp. 91-106.

Geoffrey Chaucer

(1340? - 1400)

Jeffrey Helterman
University of South Carolina

MAJOR WORKS: Guillaume de Lorris, *The Romance of the Rose*, translated by Chaucer (early 1360s)

Manuscript: The only Middle English manuscript is *Romaunt of the Rose*, MS. V.3.7, in the Hunterian Museum, Glasgow.

First publication: In *The Workes of Geffray Chaucer Newly Printed, with dyuers Workes neuer in print before*, edited by W. Thynne (London: Printed by T. Godfray, 1532).

The Book of the Duchess (circa 1368-1369)

Manuscripts: There are three extant transcriptions, included in three manuscripts in the Bodleian Library, Oxford: Fairfax 16 (circa 1450), Tanner 346 (circa 1450), and Bodley 638 (circa 1430-1440).

First publication: In *The Workes of Geffray Chaucer Newly Printed, with dyuers Workes neuer in print before*, edited by W. Thynne (London: Printed by T. Godfray, 1532).

The House of Fame (circa 1378-1381)

Manuscripts: There are two texts. Two manuscripts at the Bodleian Library, Bodley 638 (circa 1430-1440) and Fairfax 16 (circa 1450), both include transcriptions in the hand of the "A" copyist, while Pepys 2006 (circa 1450-1500) at Magdalene College, Cambridge, includes a copy in the hand of scribe "B." Most modern editions are based on the "A" text.

First publication: *The Book of Fame Made by G. Chaucer*, edited by William Caxton (Westminster: Printed by William Caxton, 1483).

The Parliament of Birds (circa 1378-1381)

Manuscripts: All of the fourteen extant manuscripts seem deficient. Modern editions are largely based on the texts in Cambridge University Library Gg 4.27 (circa 1420-1440) and in Fairfax 16 (circa 1450), in the Bodleian Library.

First publication: In *The lyf so short the craft so lōge to lerne* (Westminster: Printed by William Caxton, 1477?).

Miniature of Geoffrey Chaucer in the Ellesmere Manuscript of The Canterbury Tales, *a transcription dating from 1400-1410 (EL 26 C9, f.153v; Henry E. Huntington Library and Art Gallery)*

Boethius, *Consolation of Philosophy* (*Boece*), translated by Chaucer (circa 1380s)

Manuscripts: There are ten extant manuscripts, including two at Cambridge University Library—Ii.i.38 and Ii.iii.21—on which modern editions are largely based.

First publication: *Boecius de consolacione* (Westminster: Printed by William Caxton, 1478?).

Troilus and Criseyde (circa 1382-1386)

Manuscripts: There are twenty extant manuscripts of which four represent fragments. Most modern editions are based on Corpus Christi College, Cambridge, MS. 61 (circa

1400) or Pierpont Morgan Library MS. 817 (formerly the Campsall Manuscript), a transcription made for Henry V when he was Prince of Wales (1399-1413).

First publication: *tThe* [sic] *double sorrow of Troylus to telle* (Winchester: Printed by William Caxton, 1483).

The Legend of Good Women (circa 1386)

Manuscript: Modern editions are usually based on the transcriptions in Fairfax 16 (circa 1450) at the Bodleian Library and Gg 4.27 (circa 1420-1440) at Cambridge.

First publication: In *The Workes of Geffray Chaucer Newly Printed, with dyuers Workes neuer in print before,* edited by W. Thynne (London: Printed by T. Godfray, 1532).

The Canterbury Tales (1386-1394)

Manuscripts: Of the more than eighty whole or partial transcriptions of *The Canterbury Tales,* the bases for most editions are two of the earliest: the Hengwrt Manuscript at the National Library of Wales and the Ellesmere Manuscript at the Henry E. Huntington Library, both dating from 1400 to 1410 and thought to be the work of the same copyist, working under different editors. While some recent scholars consider the Hengwrt Manuscript to be the more accurate of the two, the Ellesmere Manuscript is the more complete, and its ordering of the tales is widely accepted. John M. Manly and Edith Rickert, editors of the comparative edition based on all known manuscripts of *The Canterbury Tales,* see the Hengwrt Manuscript as the earliest attempt—after the death of Chaucer—to arrange the unordered tales, and so closest to Chaucer's intentions. N. F. Blake, in *The Textual Tradition of The Canterbury Tales* (1985), has presented the strongest case for the primacy of the Hengwrt Manuscript. The Ellesmere Manuscript, more regular in spelling and dialect—as well as more complete—remains the choice of most modern editors.

First publication: *wHan that Apprill with his shouris sote* (Westminster: Printed by William Caxton, 1477).

EDITIONS: *The Complete Works of Geoffrey Chaucer,* edited by F. N. Robinson (Boston: Houghton Mifflin, 1933); revised as *The Works of Geoffrey Chaucer, Second Edition* (Boston: Houghton Mifflin, 1957); revised as *The Riverside Chaucer, Third Edition,* edited by Larry D. Benson (Boston: Houghton Mifflin, 1987);

The Text of The Canterbury Tales, Studied on the Basis of All Known Manuscripts, 8 volumes, edited by John M. Manly and Edith Rickert (Chicago: University of Chicago Press, 1940);

The Complete Poetry and Prose of Geoffrey Chaucer, edited by John H. Fisher (New York: Holt, Rinehart & Winston, 1977; second edition, 1989);

A Variorum Edition of the Works of Geoffrey Chaucer, 3 volumes to date, Paul G. Ruggiers, general editor (Norman: University of Oklahoma Press, 1979-).

Perhaps we must first realize what a curious phenomenon it is that Geoffrey Chaucer became the first English author. It would have been surprising in the fourteenth century for anyone to think of writing in his native tongue, and this was particularly true for Chaucer's role models. The first impulse for a medieval writer who was writing something he wanted remembered was to write it in Latin. Latin was considered to be the *grammatica,* the language which would not change, the indestructible language. Cicero wrote in it a millennium and a half ago, and we still read Cicero, so it is not surprising that around 1307-1314, when Dante started out to write the *Commedia,* he started in Latin. Fortunately for us, he started in Hell not in Heaven, because when he discovered he did not know enough Latin words for mud, dirt, and most political intrigues, he found that he could do it better in Italian.

Though Petrarch wrote his sonnets about his beloved Laura in Italian, he expected to be remembered for his Latin epic poems. In England during Chaucer's time, Latin was not so much the language of choice as was French. Since the Normans had ruled England for three hundred years, everyone who was anyone spoke and wrote in French. Chaucer's friend and rival, "moral Gower," wrote a treatise in Latin, the *Vox Clamantis* (circa 1379-1381), and one in French, the *Mirour de l'Omme* (circa 1376-1378), to match his great English work the *Confessio Amantis* (circa 1386). And so it was not at all assumed that an English writer would write in English, especially not someone in the odd personal circumstances of Chaucer.

We can assume Chaucer was quite comfortable with Latin since he translated Boethius's *Consolation of Philosophy* into English, and yet we have a suspicion that he did not have John Gower's fluency. For example, we often find him using French translations of Latin texts, the French *Livre Griseldis* instead of Petrarch's Latin version of the story of Griselda or the *Ovide Moralise* instead of the Latin *Metamorphoses*. Though his Latin was certainly better than that of William Shakespeare, whom Ben Jonson twitted about his small Latin and less Greek, it seems unlikely that he had the fluency even if he had the desire to write in Latin. That Chaucer did not write in French is more surprising; his French must have been quite good. In addition to the evidence of his translation of *The Romance of the Rose*, it is clear that the upper class of England still spoke French in their daily lives. They were still Normans, and their French separated them from the lower-class Saxons. Though Chaucer was not of the upper class, he married into it and shockingly high up. His wife, Philippa, was the sister of Katherine Swynford, the third wife of John of Gaunt, and so Chaucer was the brother-in-law of the most powerful man in England, even, as Shakespeare reminds us in *Richard II* (1595), more powerful than the king himself.

Because of Chaucer's unlikely alliance with the center of Norman power, one might suppose that Chaucer would write in French to impress his in-laws and their circle. After all, he could never be as rich or powerful as John of Gaunt, but he could write better—even in French—than his Norman relatives. Chaucer, as far as we can tell, was of an age with Gaunt, who was born in 1340, and both were married to daughters of the French knight Sir Paon de Roet. For Chaucer, the marriage appears to have been a small step up; for Gaunt, this marriage, his third, was such a long step down that many of the wives of his peers refused to appear in court any longer. Gaunt had married his mistress of many years, probably to legitimize the offspring of their union (all the English kings after Henry VI came from this line). No one was shocked at his having a mistress, but they were horrified that Gaunt married the daughter of a poor French knight. Some historians suggest that he had gotten both sisters pregnant, and that Chaucer's marriage to Philippa, on or before 12 September 1366, helped Gaunt out of some difficulty. Though some critics have attributed Chaucer's perceived bitterness toward the institution of marriage to this "loveless" union, one might better understand his motives by realizing that marriages, even at Chaucer's relatively low social level, had nothing to do with love and everything to do with property and rank. Despite the views of Anya Seton's romantic novel, John did not marry his mistress out of love, but to legitimize her sons.

Chaucer must have seen his own marriage as a way into the world of the aristocracy. Of all the Canterbury pilgrims (and there is a "Chaucer"), the one who most closely approximates his situation is the social-climbing Franklin, a man heartily concerned with the gentility of his son. Chaucer's own son, Thomas, became one of the richest men in London, and *his* great-grandson (who died on the battlefield) was named heir apparent to the throne of England.

Chaucer had all these incentives to write in French, but he chose instead to write in English, the language of Saxon England. As Sir Walter Scott pointed out, the Saxon language can name only barnyard animals on the hoof. If one fed a domestic animal, one called it by its Saxon name, *sheep*, but if one ate it, one called it by its French name, *mouton*, which soon became *mutton*. This distinction, in a nutshell, is linguistic class distinction in Chaucer's England: if one raised a farm animal, one was a Saxon and called it by its English name; if one were rich enough to eat it, one named it in French: *calf / veau (veal); chicken / poulet (pullet); pig / porc (pork)*. Chaucer did not try, however, to impress his relatives with his French, and when he wrote about farm animals he stood Scott on his head. True to Scott's model, the widow who raises Chauntecleer and Pertelote lives in a world of one-syllable Saxon words, "Milk and broun breed, . . . / Seynd bacoun, and somtyme an ey [egg] or tweye," while her Norman chickens exist in a Frenchified world where the "faire damoysele Pertelote" is "Curteys . . . , discreet, and debonaire, / And compaignable." But Chaucer gives the Saxons their first revenge for 1066. Chauntecleer, for all his French words and fancy manners, escapes only the French fox, Reynard; one day he will be stuffed and roasted for the widow's table.

One of the best ways of imagining the world in which Chaucer grew up is to picture him as a character in Shakespeare's *Richard II*. Although Chaucer belonged to the previous generation, the world of Richard's uncles, Duke Lionel and John of Gaunt, it is important that we understand that he was always on the fringes of this world of political intrigue. There is still a nineteenth-century image of Chaucer in his father's London tavern preparing to write *The Canterbury Tales* by analyzing the customers. The fact that he was the descendant of a man named Le Taverner certainly plays a part in this misconception, and the poet himself has fostered this image by his self-portraits in *The Book of the Duchess* and *The House of Fame* as an innocent, overweight bookworm. Nothing could be further from the truth.

The son of John and Agnes (de Copton) Chaucer, Geoffrey Chaucer was descended immediately from two generations of wealthy vintners who had everything but a title, a thing that no amount of money they could imagine could buy. What could be bought was position, and in 1357 Chaucer began pursuing this assiduously as a squire in the court of Elizabeth, Countess of Ulster, the wife of Lionel, Earl of Ulster (later Duke of Clarence). Also in service at this court was Philippa Pan, probably his own age; that is, both were teenagers. She is probably the same Philippa, daughter of Paon (hence Pan) de Roet, whom Chaucer eventually married in 1366. As an esquire, Chaucer would have served as a gentleman's gentleman in a time before this phrase designated a butler. A young man in this position would be in service to the aristocrats of the court. Their duties would include such butlerly tasks as making beds and fastening shirts. Since there were always twenty young men on duty in this household, such duties could not have been very onerous, and we must conclude that one of the burdens that fell on these young men was the entertainment of nobles. For a young man who could both tell stories and compose songs the way must have opened quickly. The countess was French, so French poets such as Guillaume de Machaut and Eustache Deschamps provided an early inspiration, and we find his earliest poems, *The Book of the Duchess* and *The Parliament of Birds*, resting on a heavy French base. At the duchess's castle at Hatfield, Chaucer made the acquaintance of the man who would most deeply influence his political career, John of Gaunt, Duke of Lancaster.

Chaucer's first major work, *The Book of the Duchess*, is an elegy on the death of Blanche, John of Gaunt's first wife. For this reason we can date the poem with some certainty. Blanche died of the plague in 1368, and Gaunt married Constance of Castile in 1372. The poem must have appeared between these two dates for Gaunt to be portrayed as an inconsolable widower.

The poem, though filled with traditional French flourishes, develops its originality around the relationship between the narrator, a fictionalized version of the poet, and the mourner, the Man in Black, who represents Gaunt. Though there has been some interest in the source of the allegory—the death of Blanche is seen as the loss of a game of chess—Chaucer's originality is seen in his handling of the naive narrator. In all his incarnations, this narrator is always meant to be a cartoon version of Chaucer (in *The House of Fame* he is called Geoffrey), and his naiveté is a tool that Chaucer exploits everywhere.

In *The Book of the Duchess*, the narrator seems to miss the point of everything. He reads the story of Ceys and Alcione, a story whose point is consolation, and appears to think that it is a story about cures for sleeplessness. The narrator's chief naiveté is in relation to the Man in Black. Although he hears the Man complain that Death has taken his Lady, he acts as if he has never heard this lament. He becomes particularly obtuse when the Man in Black says that he has lost a game at chess with Fortune. The obtuseness, however, forces the Man in Black to face his loss without the comfortable protection of allegory. The narrator's naiveté becomes a sounding board against which the Man in Black must assert both the value of his love and the reality of losing her.

In *The Book of the Duchess*, especially through the instrument of the naive narrator, Chaucer begins to develop a concealment model of the language of fiction rather than a communication model. What becomes most interesting and, oddly enough, most useful to characters is what they misunderstand. At the beginning of this poem, the narrator is suffering from an unknown malady (which we may guess is unrequited love). Since he cannot deal with the malady, the narrator sets out to deal with the symptom—sleeplessness. From here on, he always misinterprets. He reads a story of consolation, but finds in it only a sleeping potion; he dreams of a hunt where the "hert" (stag) disappears and thinks he has missed the "hert-huntyng." For this reason, he is content to follow a puppy instead of the hounds, but the puppy leads him to the Man in Black whose "herte" (heart) is in hiding. The narrator acts as if he thinks the Man in Black is mourning the lost hart, while he finds (invents) a tale to recover the man's lost heart.

It is at this point that we begin to realize that the narrator's mistakes are necessary. For example, if he sees the issue of consolation in Ceys and Alcione, the problem will be settled before

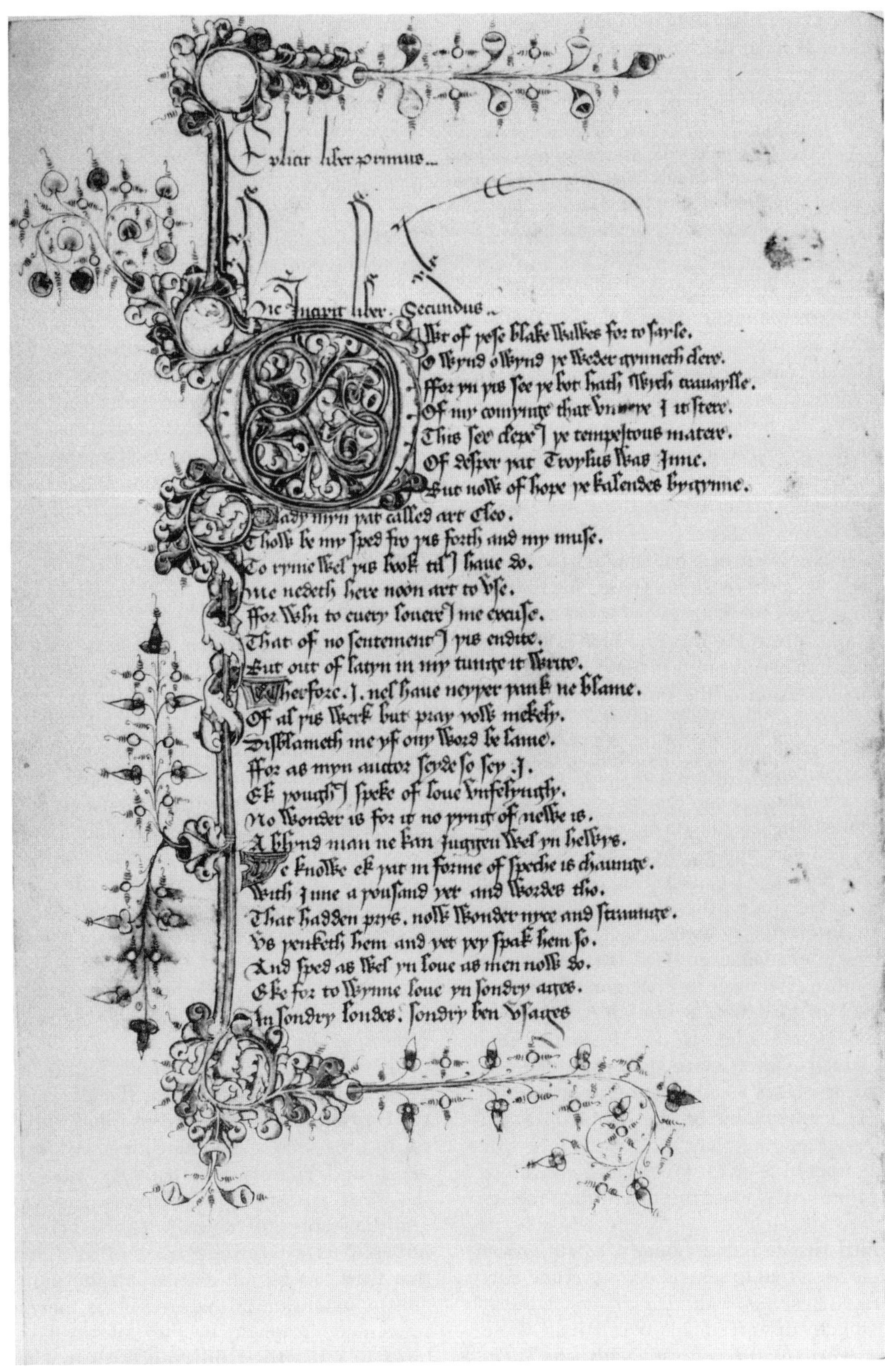

Explicit liber primus.

Incipit liber Secundus.

Owt of þese blake wawes for to sayle.
O wynd o wynd þe weder gynneth clere.
ffor yn þis see þe boot hath swych trauaylle.
Of my connyng that vnneþe I it stere.
This see clepe I þe tempestous matere.
Of desper þat Troylus was inne.
But now of hope þe kalendes bygynne.
O lady myn þat called art Cleo.
Thow be my sped fro þis forth and my muse.
To ryme wel þis book til I haue do.
Me nedeth here noon art to vse.
ffor why to euery louere I me excuse.
That of no sentement I þis endite.
But out of latyn in my tunge it write.
Wherfore .I. nel haue neyþer þank ne blame.
Of al þis werk but pray yow mekely.
Disblameth me yf ony word be lame.
ffor as myn auctor seyde so sey .I.
Ek þough I speke of loue vnfelyngly.
No wonder is for it no þyng of newe is.
A blynd man ne kan juggen wel yn hewys.
Ye knowe ek þat in forme of speche is chaunge.
With inne a þousand yer and wordes tho.
That hadden prys. now wonder nyce and straunge.
Vs þenketh hem and yet þey spak hem so.
And sped as wel yn loue as men now do.
Eke for to wynne loue yn sondry ages.
In sondry londes. sondry ben vsages

First page of a transcription of Troilus and Criseyde *made for Henry V at some time between 1399 and 1413, when he was Prince of Wales (MS. 817, Lewis Cass Ledyard Fund; Pierpont Morgan Library)*

he gets to the Man in Black. If he openly acknowledges that the Man in Black's loss is his heart, he will only be able to offer empty words of consolation. Instead, his irritating misunderstanding forces the Man in Black to re-create his love, to deallegorize his loss (Blanche as the "goode faire White" was too easy to allegorize as the losing side in a chess game), and finally to recognize that it would have been a greater sorrow never to have loved her than to have loved her and lost her. In searching (cleansing) the Black Knight's wound, the narrator finally faces his own; that is, the love that he seeks is worth the pain that it costs in the seeking. Thus, when the narrator says near the end of this poem, "al was doon, / For that tyme, the hert-huntyng," he is no longer talking about deer hunting, but about the cure for a broken heart.

Chaucer also makes use of the naive narrator in *The House of Fame* (circa 1378-1381), a poem which has been tied by scholars to events in the courts of Richard II, of Gaunt, or of Lionel, but none of these theories has been convincing enough to refute the others. What is clear is that Chaucer had been reading Dante, and he provided a comic version of the guide-narrator relationship of Dante and Virgil in the *Commedia*. The talkative Eagle guides the naive "Chaucer" just as the naive Dante is guided by the gossipy Virgil. There are many comic touches as the Eagle gives new meaning to the term *captive audience*. Though it seems as though the Eagle's lecture is going to be boring, "Chaucer," in the grasp of the Eagle's talons, is hardly in a position to say "no I'm not interested in your story."

In this poem Chaucer tries on the role he would use more effectively in *Troilus and Criseyde*—the historian of love who is himself a failure in love. The Eagle takes him to the House of Fame (Rumor), which is even more the house of tales. Here Chaucer makes a case for the preeminence of story. The inhabitants of the House of Fame are asked whether they want to be great lovers or to be remembered as great lovers, and all choose the latter: the story is more important than the reality.

A third dream-vision poem, *The Parliament of Birds*, has been tied to several occasions and corresponding dates. As with *The House of Fame*, there is much disagreement over what these events are. Perhaps the accuracy with which *The Book of the Duchess* can be dated has led literary historians to expect too much of the allegory. *The Book of the Duchess* is datable because of the elaborate puns on "Blanche" and "Lancaster" in the poem. There is no comparable evidence in either *The House of Fame* or *The Parliament of Birds*, so scholars have had to look for parallel situations where the primary question is "In what ways is Anne of Bohemia like this bird?" The problematics of such an approach has led some critics to see the poem as a beast fable with no particular occasional reference and only a debate about the running of parliamentary government.

The Parliament of Birds (circa 1378-1381) has as its subject a flock of birds of the noble class (eagles and hawks) arguing over who has priority in a love match with a female eagle. After a long wrangle in which the lower orders of birds get involved, the hoped-for wedding is put off. This conclusion has led historians to try to figure out to which delayed betrothal contract the poem refers. The occasion for the poem has been seen as the negotiations for the betrothal of Richard II to Marie, Princess of France, in 1377 or his successful betrothal to Anne of Bohemia in 1379, or the end of further negotiations which culminated in the marriage in 1381. Taking a different approach to dating (whose end is establishing the order of composition of the texts), it has been noted that in *The Parliament of Birds* Chaucer changed from the eight-syllable couplets he was using in *The Book of the Duchess* and *The House of Fame* and started using the seven-line pentameter stanza that he would use in *Troilus*. If we can assume that the change is an abandonment of an old form and style, then the order of these poems is *The Book of the Duchess*, *The House of Fame*, *The Parliament of Birds*, and *Troilus and Criseyde*.

Despite frequent echoes from Guillaume de Lorris's section of *The Romance of the Rose*, *The Parliament of Birds* seems to be an indictment of courtly love as Chaucer had found it in the French poem, so that when the dreamer enters the Garden of Love he finds it filled with allegorical figures such as Foolhardiness, Bribery of Servants, and Flattery and Jealousy, who represent the worst aspects of love. Opposed to Venus, the guardian spirit of courtly love, is Nature, who hopes to effect the marriage of all the birds so that they can go out and propagate their species and by extension all nature. Their marriages are prevented, however, by the failure of the noble birds to settle their differences over a matter of courtly love: who has priority in love? Each of the male eagles has a different answer: the one who loves first; the one who loves most; or the one who suffers most. The other birds, exasperated by the courtly love quandary of the noble birds, get into the act with views of love that represent their social classes. Chaucer appears to have divided the birds into four classes that match the standard medieval conception of the social hierarchy. The hunting birds (eagles, hawks) represent the nobles, the worm eaters (cuckoos) represent the bourgeois, the water fowl are the merchants, and the seed eaters (turtle doves) are the landed farming interests. Each class is given a distinctive voice, so that when the sparrow hawk complains sarcastically about the "parfit resoun of a goos," we know what he means: the goose, in his examples of, and metaphors for, love has made love mercantile and goose foolish.

The disorder caused by courtly love ruins the scheme of "commune profyt" that would keep this commonwealth of birds functioning, and as such it touches one of Chaucer's favorite social issues: in "The Clerk's Tale" Walter forgoes the "commune profyt" of his realm so that he can pursue his obsessive testing of Griselda's love. In *The Parliament of Birds* Chaucer examines themes that will pervade his later work. The conflict between Nature and courtly love will be a major issue in *Troilus and Criseyde* and especially in "The Knight's Tale," where Palemon and Arcite's argument about who has priority in loving Emily comes right out of the arguments for the "hand" of the female eagle. Perhaps more significant is the experiment with different voices for all the characters and social classes of birds. Such differentiation would become the benchmark of *The Canterbury Tales.*

As a courtier of some rank, Chaucer found his service to the nobility quickly escalating beyond making beds. In the late 1350s he was in military service in France with John of Gaunt. Chaucer was soon to serve England in peace as well as war, as part of several embassies to France and Italy. These often involved delicate personal matters of the royal family, such as the betrothal of Richard II, who succeeded his grandfather, Edward III, to the throne in 1377, at the age of nine.

By 1374 Chaucer was firmly involved in domestic politics and was granted the important post of controller of customs taxes on hides, skins, and wool. In addition to the direct income of ten pounds a year, the position had the added remuneration of fees and fines for those who tried to evade customs. The position was no sinecure, and Chaucer had to keep the records himself as well as oversee the collectors. It is notable that the collectors themselves became important men in the business life of London, with at least one of them becoming lord mayor. These were prosperous times for Chaucer; his wife had gotten a large annuity, and they were living rent free in a house above the city gate at Aldgate. This Chaucer would have felt comfortable with the men of substance on the Canterbury pilgrimage, where he would have ridden in company with the Merchant, Franklin, and Man of Law.

Chaucer's love affair with the Italian language, nurtured by his visits in 1372-1373 to Genoa and Florence and in 1378 to Lombardy, flowered in the following decade with his composition of *Troilus and Criseyde* (circa 1382-1386). This poem, considered by some to be the first English novel, takes its story line from Giovanni Boccaccio's *Il Filostrato* (1335-1340), but its inspiration from Dante's love for Beatrice as told in the *Convito* (1307) and from Petrarch's love for Laura as manifested in the sonnets. Though many critics have insisted that the poem presents an ironic view of romantic love in which Troilus confuses passion (*cupiditas*) with celestial love (*caritas*), Chaucer is presenting a case for ennobling passion which fits with the French romances he had read in his youth; only in *Troilus and Criseyde* this romance takes a particularly Italian turn. The most telling demonstration of this development is an odd piece of borrowing done by Chaucer, in which a passage from Boccaccio is deliberately put in the wrong poem.

When Chaucer borrowed his plot for "The Knight's Tale" from Boccaccio's *Teseida* (1341), he left out the apotheosis of Arcite. In Boccaccio, Arcite's spirit ascends to a sphere of a classical heaven. Not only does Chaucer leave out Arcite's flight to heaven, but the knight claims that his source says nothing about the fate of Arcite's soul. It has been suggested that Chaucer left out Arcite's ascent to heaven because heaven has no place at the beginning of *The Canterbury Tales* and only becomes significant as the pilgrims approach Canterbury.

Chaucer, however, did not forget the passage, and he inserted it, not in "The Knight's Tale," but into *Troilus and Criseyde*, immediately after Troilus's death. At this point in his poem he is translating almost word for word from Boccaccio. The result of this insertion is that a situation which is desperate in *Il Filostrato* becomes sublime in *Troilus and Criseyde*. In Boccaccio, Troilo is killed, and the narrator says over and over that this is the end of Troilo's "ill-conceived" love for Criseyda. In the English poem Troilus is killed; then Chaucer inserts the passage from the *Teseida*, so that Troilus ascends to heaven (with words meant originally for Arcite); then the narrator says such an end Troilus had for love, but this end is now triumph not tragedy. If books were not so expensive, one could imagine Chaucer cutting out the passage from the *Teseida* and pasting it in the appropriate spot in *Il Filostrato*.

This alteration allowed Chaucer to use brilliantly the naive narrator in this poem. The narrator considers himself above love and sets as his task to tell the double sorrow of Troilus in love: the pain of falling in love with Criseyde and the pain of losing her. The narrator's standpoint is that of a moral, Christian man who has forsaken earthly love for the hope of divine love. His assumption is that Troilus has sacrificed heaven for his ill-conceived love for Criseyde. After all, he has read Boccaccio's version where Troilo simply dies—better to eschew love and go to heaven. Nevertheless, the narrator is sorely tried when he watches Troilus and Criseyde consummate their love, and he, who was once proud of his lack of experience in love, says, "O blisful nyght of hem so longe isought, / . . . . / Why nad I swich oon with my soule ybought / . . . ?" Yet this gasp of desire is stifled by his knowledge that ultimately he is right and Troilus is wrong. Imagine his surprise when he finds Troilus in heaven. This was not supposed to happen; the story—Boccaccio's story—says that Troilus just dies, but Chaucer has changed the ending, and the moral superiority of the narrator is in for a shock when he discovers that Troilus has all this and heaven too.

The claim that *Troilus and Criseyde* is the "first English novel" is based on the way Chaucer handled the psychology of the main characters. They are always operating at two levels of response, verbal and intellectual. For Criseyde, this usually comes out as a she thought/she said duality, which happens so often that the reader comes to wonder what she is thinking anytime she says anything. This duality is less common in the men, but only because they have each other to confide in. Their duality is between what they say to Criseyde and what they say to each other.

The poem analyzes the artifices of love as well as the complex motivations of lovers. This analysis often has been seen as an ironic view of romantic love, but this interpretation assumes that falling in love is as simple as it is for Tristan and Isolde. The first half of the poem, the seduction of Criseyde, is necessitated by the literary models followed by Pandarus, her uncle. There is, for example, no good reason why the love of Troilus and Criseyde has to be secret. Unlike Tristan and Isolde or Launcelot and Guinevere, there is no adultery involved. Pandarus, however, has been getting his notion of love from literary models such as Andreas Capellanus's *Art of Courtly Love* (circa 1174). Andreas insists there can be no love between partners in an arranged marriage and so sets up an elaborate system for adulterous love. Pandarus, a self-confessed failure in love, promotes the affair by the book until his involvement pushes the limits of vicarious pleasure, "And so we may ben gladed [gladdened], alle thre."

The seduction of Criseyde is programmed to exploit her tenuous position as the daughter of a traitor and to force her to turn to Troilus for protection. Two plots are set in motion: the Poliphete plot, in which rumors are spread that Poliphete wants her, as the traitor Calchas's daughter, out of Troy; and the Horaste plot, in which she is accused of being the lover of Horaste (Orestes). Both plots put Troilus, Criseyde, and a bed in the same place. In each case Troilus is set up as a rock in a stormy sea of politics. Criseyde is never allowed to forget that he is the king's son and, after Hector, the strongest man in Troy. While Pandarus and Troilus are manipulating her, Criseyde is in many ways their match. She is, for example, always aware that they are less than frank with her. Criseyde is actually more experienced than either of the men. She is, after all, a widow not a virgin, and her responses to Pandarus's devices are always complex. In this situation, Troilus is the emotional virgin. He is the one who swoons first, and who falls in love at first sight. In a typical reaction, when Pandarus tells Criseyde that Troilus must see her at night, she agrees because his condition seems wretched, because Pandarus's story sounds like the truth, because she loves Troilus more than anything, because the dark night will hide his coming, and because he is coming through a secret entrance. She is always both passionate and practical.

Perhaps Pandarus's most despicable device is his reifying of the metaphor of heartbreak. It is given of the Petrarchan view of love as well as of *The Romance of the Rose* that the lady's coldness will break the lover's heart. Pandarus accuses Criseyde of desiring Troilus's death. One might say that Pandarus is overplaying the metaphor, but

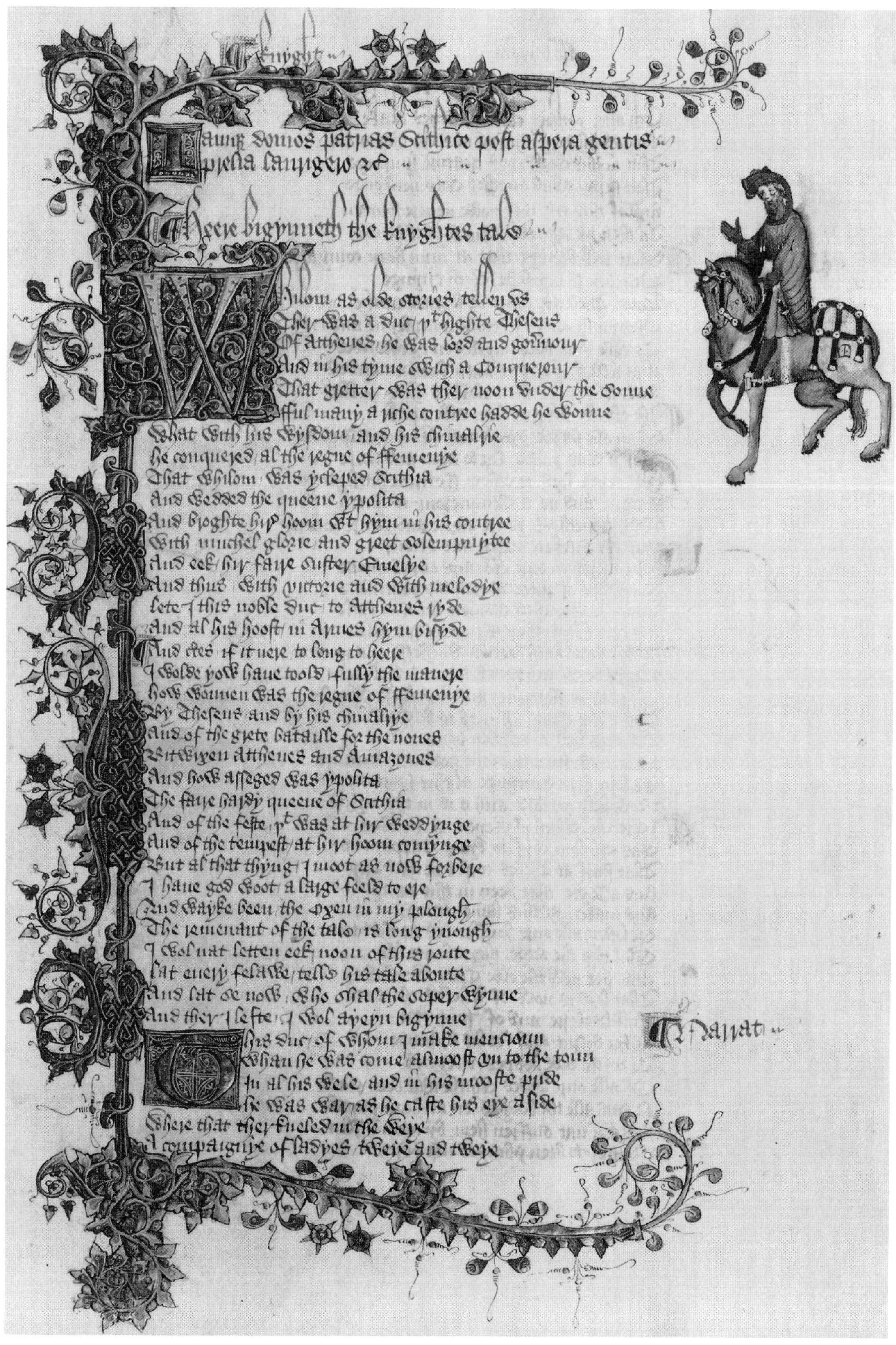

The beginning of "The Knight's Tale" in the Ellesmere Manuscript of The Canterbury Tales *(EL 26 C9, f. 10r; Henry E. Huntington Library and Art Gallery)*

then he makes the metaphor real by drawing his dagger and threatening to stab himself if Troilus dies of a broken heart due to Criseyde's coldness. Whatever she thinks of the metaphoric "death" of Troilus, her uncle's threat is with a real knife. In this way guilt is added to Criseyde's fear in an effort to destabilize her and throw her into the arms of Troilus.

The elaborate fictions that have been used to establish this romance become the reason for its destruction. When Calchas demands his daughter in exchange for a Trojan prisoner of war, only Hector stands up to the Trojan council. He equates the giving up of Criseyde with the sanctioning of prostitution, "We usen here no wommen for to selle," and it is clear that if Troilus added his voice to his brother's then Criseyde would not be sent to the Greek camp. The secrecy—unnecessary in its origins—of the affair makes it impossible for Troilus to stand up for Criseyde, and she is sent to her father.

It has been said that she falls too quickly for the Greek warrior Diomedes, but her actions are entirely explainable by the way Troilus and Pandarus have programmed her behavior. They have deliberately undermined her sense of security and stability so that she would fall for Troilus as a tower of strength, a strong man in any enemy camp. Diomedes simply pushes the same buttons, and she is his. In a comic scene, we see the huge Greek champion as he echoes Troilus, the swooning swain. Diomedes quavers and blushes as he proffers his tender love to Criseyde with teeny nods and gestures.

Though the subtlety of the love games and the deviousness of the players is greater than in Boccaccio, Chaucer's understanding of love takes on a new quality when he leaves that model altogether. Both Dante and Petrarch begin by seeing love as artifice and then show how love breaks free of that artifice. In the *Convito,* Dante tells of using a screen lady when he becomes enamored of Beatrice. This is a woman who sits between him and Beatrice at church. Because of her position, Dante can pretend to be looking at her while in fact he is looking at Beatrice. Then Dante writes sonnets "to" this lady. He has to learn to be a love poet before he can be Beatrice's poet. Dante then reports that he becomes Love's poet, that is, the celebrant of Cupid and love in the abstract. Finally, a voice tells him it is time to put away simulacra (false idols), and he becomes the poet in love with Beatrice. Troilus follows three similar steps. Under Pandarus's guidance, he becomes a courtly lover by the book, who uses all the conventional attitudes expected of lovers. Then Troilus emulates Criseyde's metaphysical expectations of love: love becomes a wall of steel, the stone of certainty, and he becomes the lover of Love. Finally, Troilus goes beyond both of his mentors to something at once higher and lower. He loves Criseyde for herself, for no reason at all. This love is not shaken by Pandarus's doubts or by Criseyde's betrayal; he says "I ne kan nor may . . . unloven yow a quarter of a day" at a point where Boccaccio's Troilo condemns and curses her.

Troilus goes essentially from being Romeo in love with Rosaline to Romeo in love with Juliet, a distinction already made by Petrarch. Petrarch's poems *(rime)* to Laura are in two groups divided by a simple fact, her death. The sonnets in "Vita di ma donna Laura" are artificial conventional poems filled with such tropes as oxymoron, antithesis, hyperbole, and conceit. The style was so conventional that the French poets had a verb, *Petrarquizer,* to write like Petrarch. The sonnets change radically after Laura's death, *"in morte,"* as the artifices fall away in his attempt to re-create the true Laura. The same change occurs in Troilus after the absence of Criseyde. He has been a Petrarchist, who in fact spouts Petrarch. His first song, *Cantus Troili,* is a sonnet of Petrarch's, but after Criseyde's absence these artifices will not serve to re-create the missing Criseyde, and, in fact, the first physical description of Criseyde occurs only in book 5. Until this point, she had merely been the ideal beloved. Only in the last book does she become a real woman. She even has a flaw in her beauty: her eyebrows are too close together. Through his trials Troilus learns, as have Dante and Petrarch before him, that loving a real woman is the only real love.

In the prologue to *The Legend of Good Women* (circa 1386), Chaucer castigates himself for doing a disservice to love by publishing the unfaithfulness of women. In this poem, the poet figure responds to this charge from the god of love by telling stories of faithful women, love's martyrs. It was at about this time (1386) that Chaucer's friend John Gower was writing his work on a similar theme, *Confessio Amantis* (The Lover's Confession), and there is some sense of rivalry between the two poets. Gower, however, turned his poem into his masterpiece, while Chaucer seemed to tire quickly of *The Legend of Good*

Women and left it unfinished. The most original and interesting part of this poem is the prologue, which, among other things, names and sometimes critiques the poems that Chaucer had written up to this time. The list is particularly interesting because it includes some works, such as *Troilus and Criseyde*, that critics see as stylistically more advanced than *The Legend of Good Women*. If critics see this poem as more primitive than poems that certainly antedate it by virtue of being on this list, then the list calls into question the whole enterprise of the dating of Chaucer's works by cues such as style or literary influence (a French or Italian period). The legends themselves, of such martyrs to love as Dido, Cleopatra, and Ariadne, are treated with such an unsympathetic voice that some critics have seen the poem as a parody of such collections of stories of martyred women that Chaucer left off when the joke got old.

Although there has been movement in this century to see the finished (Chaucer would say "parfit") *Troilus and Criseyde* as his masterpiece, it is *The Canterbury Tales* that is the measure of his greatness. Though this fact is not surprising, the reasons for it may be. Although unfinished, the work is a brilliant advance on the frame tale as practiced by Boccaccio in *The Decameron* (1349-1351). We should note that Petrarch, who knew Boccaccio fairly well, did not know of *The Decameron*, so there is no certainty that Chaucer knew of its existence either. Since, in the days before printing, fragments of a manuscript were gathered with no concern for a whole work or even an individual author, it would be possible to prove that Chaucer knew a tale from *The Decameron* without assuming he was aware of the whole book. This seems to be the case with Petrarch, who knew Boccaccio from his Latin works. Both Italians were prouder of their Latin achievements than their work in the vernacular. Chaucer's favorite works of Boccaccio, *The Teseida* (source of "The Knight's Tale") and *Il Filostrato* (source of *Troilus and Criseyde*), are in Italian, and it makes sense that Chaucer, avid book collector that he was, would have sought a copy of *The Decameron* if he knew of its existence. In any case, it is helpful to set out *The Decameron* as a model of the frame-tale narrative so we can see what Chaucer is doing in *The Canterbury Tales*.

The pretext for storytelling in Boccaccio is a plague in Florence which sends a group of ten nobles to the country to escape the Black Death. For each of ten days, they each tell a tale. Each day's tales are grouped around a common topic or narrative subject. Boccaccio, perhaps straitened by the need to tell ten tales on the same topic, has one escape valve each day: one teller who can improvise a subject. The tales, all one hundred of them, are completed; the plague ends in Florence; and the nobles return to the city.

Set against this model, we can see Chaucer's innovation. Far from being noble, his tale-tellers run the spectrum of the middle class, from the Knight to the Pardoner and the Summoner. In the "General Prologue," the Pilgrims are introduced in order of their rank, not their physical place in line. The Knight and the wealthy ecclesiastics (Prioress, Monk, Friar) are introduced first. The Summoner, who tells an obscene tale, and the Pardoner, from whom one is expected, are described last. If this list were mere reportage of the events, the Miller, who leads them out of town, should be the first person described, and the Reeve, who brings up the rear (partly to stay away from the Miller), should be the last. When the tales begin, it looks as if this social order will be followed. Though straws are drawn to determine the first teller, Chaucer gives the first straw to the Knight, and when he is finished, place is given to the Monk, one of the high-ranking ecclesiastics. But the Monk is doomed never to tell his story.

Though George Lyman Kittredge, the dean of American Chaucerians, sees most of the tales as centering on discussions of marriage, what we may be seeing in the frame tale of Canterbury storytelling is the social-climbers' revenge. "The Knight's Tale," for all its Italian origins, is a tale that Jean Froissart, the chronicler of Edward III and the Hundred Years' War, would approve—it is an upper-class entertainment. Though it is nominally set in ancient Greece, the details, especially of the tournament, are fourteenth-century English. It is unlikely that Chaucer would have been aware of this anachronism, but he would have been aware that "The Knight's Tale" is just the kind of tale that Froissart might have told to the approval of Chaucer's father-in-law, Sir Paon de Roet, and that this sort of tale was the typical entertainment in the courts of Duke Lionel of Gaunt, and of the king. When "The Knight's Tale" is finished, it is established as a noble tale, one, in fact, that the better class of pilgrims should memorize. In a sense it would seem that the storytelling contest is over before it begins. Yet before the Knight is allowed to rest on his laurels, the Miller

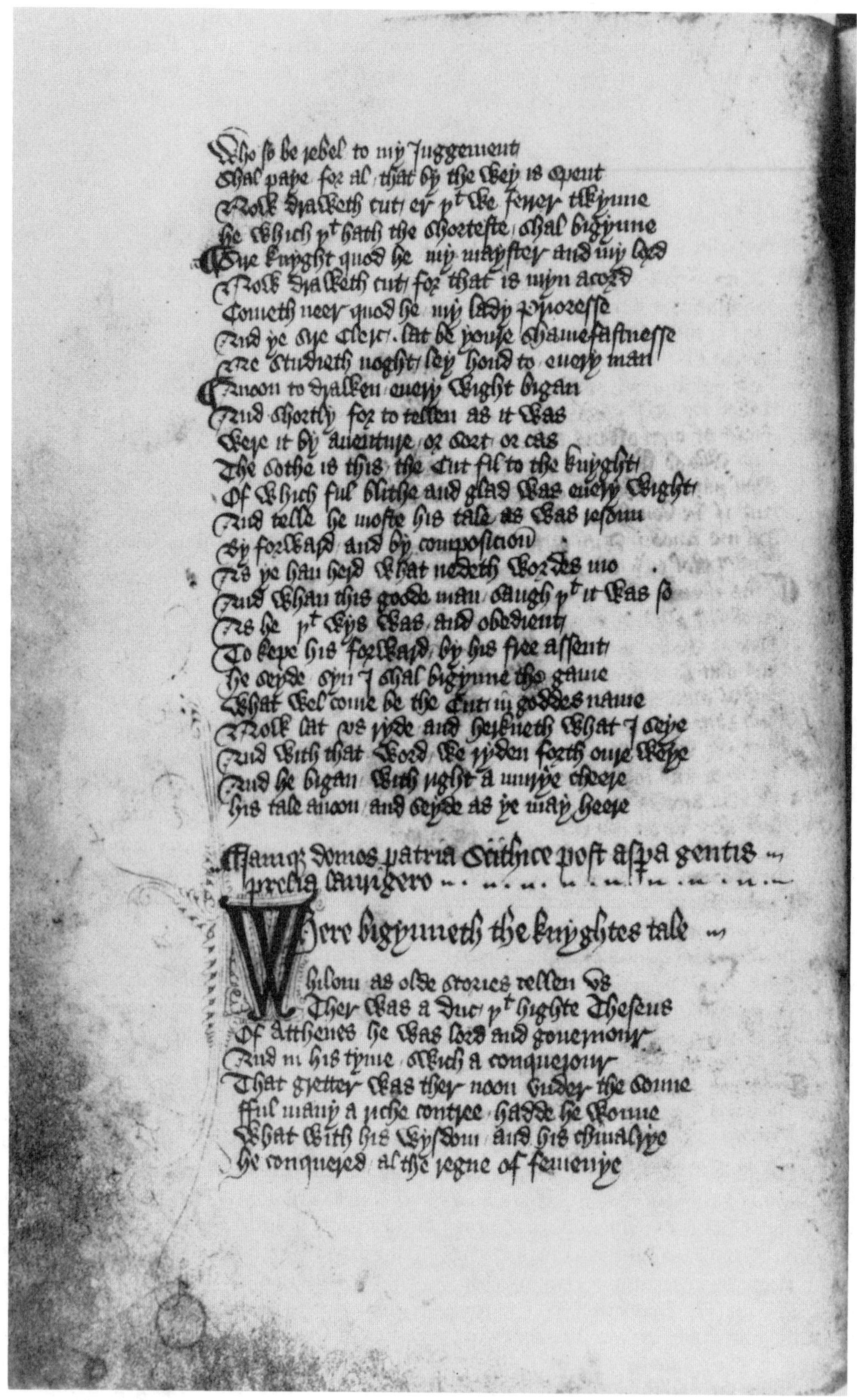

Who so be rebel to my Iuggement
Shal paye for al that by the wey is spent
Now draweth cut er þt we ferrer twynne
He which þt hath the shorteste shal bigynne
Sire knyght quod he my mayster and my lord
Now draweth cut for that is myn acord
Cometh neer quod he my lady Prioresse
And ye sire clerk lat be youre shamefastnesse
Ne studieth noght / ley hond to euery man
Anoon to drawen euery wight bigan
And shortly for to tellen as it was
Were it by auenture or sort or cas
The sothe is this the cut fil to the knyght
Of which ful blithe and glad was euery wight
And telle he moste his tale as was resoun
By forward and by composicioun
As ye han herd what nedeth wordes mo
And whan this goode man saugh þt it was so
As he þt wys was and obedient
To kepe his forward by his free assent
He seyde syn I shal bigynne the game
What wel come be the cut in goddes name
Now lat vs ryde and herkneth what I seye
And with that word we ryden forth oure weye
And he bigan with right a murye cheere
His tale anoon and seyde as ye may heere

Iamque domos patrias Cithice post aspera gentis
Prelia laurigero

Here bigynneth the knyghtes tale

Whilom as olde stories tellen vs
Ther was a duc þt highte Theseus
Of Athenes he was lord and gouernour
And in his tyme swich a conquerour
That gretter was ther noon vnder the sonne
Ful many a riche contree hadde he wonne
What with his wysdom and his chiualrye
He conquered al the regne of femenye

The beginning of "The Knight's Tale" in the Hengwrt Manuscript of The Canterbury Tales, *a copy made at about the same time as the Ellesmere Manuscript (Peniarth 392, ff.12v and 13r; Aberystwyth, National Library of Wales)*

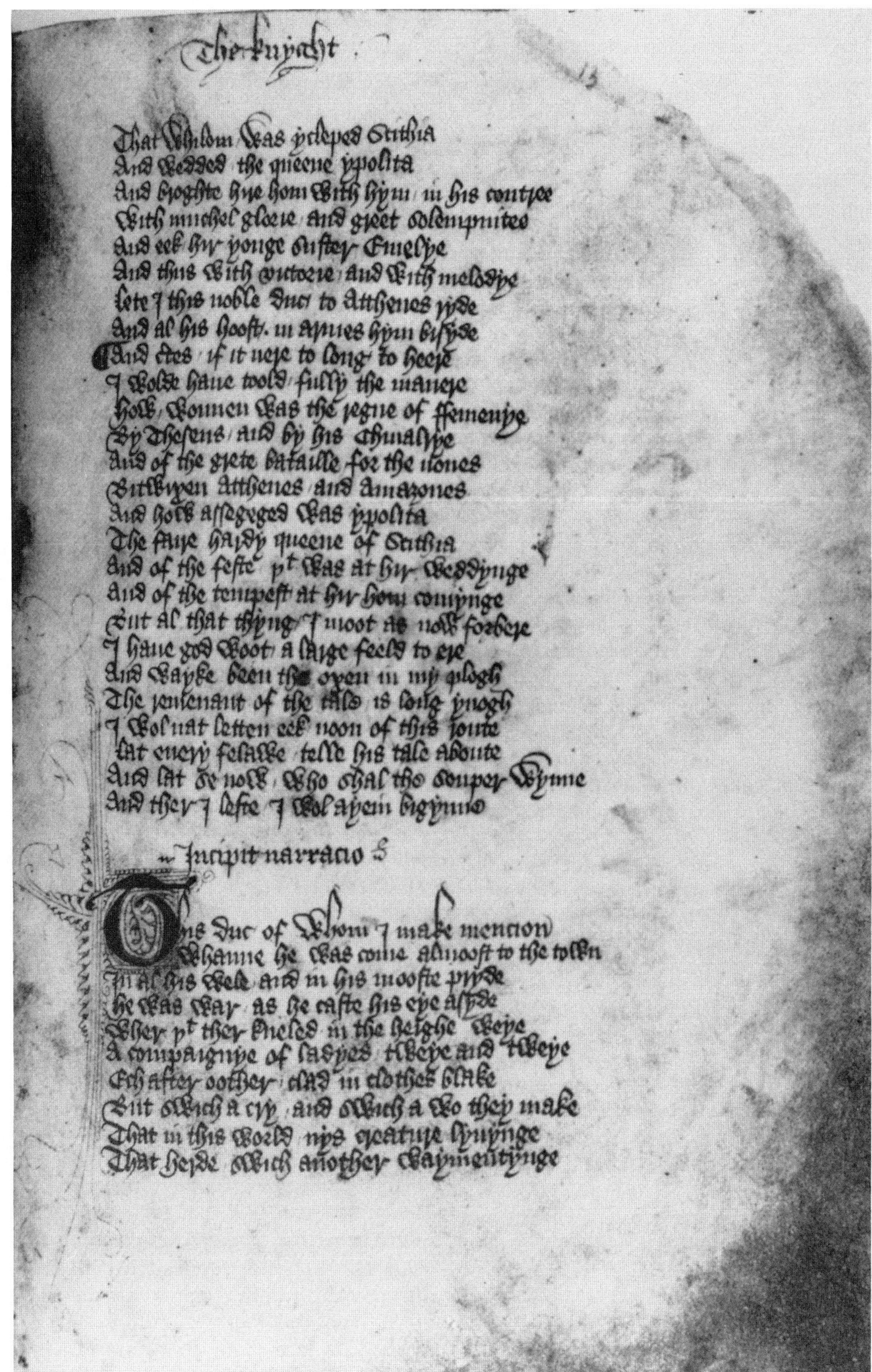

The knyght

That whilom was ycleped Scithia
And wedded the queene ypolita
And broghte hire hom with hym in his contree
With muchel glorie and greet solempnitee
And eek hir yonge suster Emelye
And thus with victorie and with melodye
Lete I this noble duc to Atthenes ryde
And al his hoost in armes hym bisyde
And certes if it nere to long to heere
I wolde haue told fully the manere
How wonnen was the regne of ffemenye
By Theseus and by his chiualrye
And of the grete bataille for the nones
Bitwixen Atthenes and Amazones
And how asseged was ypolita
The faire hardy queene of Scithia
And of the feste pt was at hir weddynge
And of the tempest at hir hom comynge
But al that thyng I moot as now forbere
I haue god woot a large feeld to ere
And wayke been the oxen in my plogh
The remenant of the tale is long ynogh
I wol nat letten eek noon of this route
Lat euery felawe telle his tale aboute
And lat se now who shal the souper wynne
And ther I lefte I wol ayein bigynne

Incipit narracio

This duc of whom I make mencion
Whanne he was come almoost to the town
In al his wele and in his mooste pryde
He was war as he caste his eye asyde
Wher pt ther kneled in the heighe weye
A compaignye of ladyes tweye and tweye
Ech after oother clad in clothes blake
But swich a cry and swich a wo they make
That in this world nys creature lyuynge
That herde swich another waymentynge

interrupts with a "noble" tale of his own. His tale—among other things, a lower-class parody of the plot outlined in "The Knight's Tale" (two apparently similar men fight over the same woman)—becomes the first tale motivated by answering the previous tale. The Miller's word *quite* (requite) becomes the energizing force behind the tale-telling. Each character uses his tale as a weapon or tool to get back at or even with the previous tale-teller. Compare this linkage with *The Decameron*, where the tales of the day hang statically on the pegs of topic; not even the plague impacts much on Boccaccio's tale-telling. His tales, clever as they are, just sit there.

Not so in Chaucer. Once the Miller has established the principle of "quiting," each tale generates the next. The Reeve, who takes offense because "The Miller's Tale" is about a cuckolded carpenter (the Reeve had been a carpenter in his youth), tells a tale about a cuckolded miller, who also gets beaten up after his daughter is deflowered. As in many of the tales, subtle distinctions of class become the focal point of the story. The social-climbing miller, Simkyn, is upset mostly that his daughter has slept with the wrong class of man. It is not so much that she has been deflowered, but disparaged (had sex with a man of a lower social class). From this point in the tale-telling, each tale becomes the motive for the tale or several tales which follow it.

The neatest example of this quiting principle is seen in the group of tales beginning with the Wife of Bath's and ending with the Clerk's. In her long prologue, the Wife stirs up first the Pardoner and then the Friar, but she also issues a challenge to the Clerk which says that clerks, because they are men, are incapable of praising women. Therefore, she challenges the Clerk to tell a tale which praises women. After the Wife's tale, the Friar and Summoner have at each other, the Friar telling of a rascally summoner and the Summoner of an evil friar. In their tales the two tellers reflect the personalities ascribed to them in the "General Prologue." "The Friar's Tale" is as elegant as he is, and the gross, garlic-eating Summoner tells an obscene tale filled with ill winds of all kinds. The last turn in this grouping is the Clerk's tale of patient Griselda. Though the Clerk does nothing but praise Griselda, thus responding to the Wife's challenge, he does it in such a way that Griselda's wifely virtue, her perfect obedience to her husband, seems a monstrous kind of womanly and motherly behavior. Though Chaucer provides a framework in which Griselda's behavior—allowing her children to be taken to what she believes to be their deaths according to her husband's whim—is acceptable, he will then undercut this frame with another ending. Chaucer first offers what is essentially Petrarch's idea of the tale, which reads Griselda's behavior allegorically: Griselda's incomprehending obedience to Walter is a model for man's unquestioning acceptance of God's judgments. Just when Griselda's behavior is normalized as allegory, Chaucer adds a second ending, which warns men that they had better not test their wives the way Walter tested Griselda because they may find that they have married not Patient Griselda but the irritable Alice of Bath.

Chaucer's refusal to let his tale end conventionally is typical of the way he handles familiar stories. He wants to have it both ways, and he reminds the reader of this constantly. In "The Nun's Priest's Tale," for example, he argues both against an allegorical reading of the tale, "My tale is of a cok," and for it, "Taketh the fruyt, and lat the chaf be stille."

At work in the presentation of Griselda as a good woman is an important Chaucerian device, a false syllogism based on the movement from the specific to the general back to the specific again, although the specific now occupies a new moral ground. The Clerk praises Griselda, who as a good wife (specific) is also a good woman (general). The Clerk never spells out the inference that results from the movement back to the specific. Griselda, the good wife and woman, leaves her children to be murdered. If she is a bad mother, then she should also be a bad woman, but the Clerk, in his "contract" with the Wife, will never dispraise women, so he never completes the syllogism.

Almost every time Chaucer offers a list of examples, he is playing with this disparity between the general and the specific. In "The Merchant's Tale," when January, in his haste to get married, offers examples of good women from the Bible, he misses the fact that all of his good women were deceivers or destroyers of their husbands or "lovers." Rebecca deceived her husband, as did Esther, and Judith chopped off the head of Holofernes; good women . . . certainly, but not, as January thinks, a very convincing argument to get married. Chaucer often combines this trick with a basic notion about the way stories are used to avoid confrontations with the truth. In "The Franklin's Tale," Dorigen promises the squire Aurelius that she will sleep with him if he accomplishes the impossible task of removing the rocks from along the coast of Brittany. By a trick, Aurelius removes the rocks, and Dorigen, a married woman, sees only one out: death before dishonor—but then, instead of plunging the blade into her breast, she begins regaling herself with tales of good wives who chose death before dishonor. Gradually, her list drifts to good wives who chose death after dishonor, and finally, moving from the specific to the general, stories of good wives. She then concludes that, since good wives are obedient to their husbands, she will run and ask her husband what to do, hoping he will not recommend death before dishonor. Dorigen spends three days "purposing ever" to die, and then, as a good wife, she runs and asks her husband for guidance, even though, in a unique arrangement, he had made her sovereign in their marriage.

As Chaucer worked against the impossibility of finishing *The Canterbury Tales* according to the original plan—120 tales, 4 told by each of thirty pilgrims (in the Middle Ages, which had many systems based on 12, 120 was as round a number as the 100 of *The Decameron*)—he began to consider the nature of finishing an act of storytelling. In *The Canterbury Tales*, in addition to several unfinished tales (the Cook's, the Squire's), there are two tales that are interrupted by other pilgrims: Chaucer's own "Tale of Sir Thopas" and "The Monk's Tale." In handling these tales, Chaucer moves into issues, particularly that of closure, that are only now appearing in the theory of fiction. In "The Franklin's Tale" Chaucer had shown how Dorigen avoids the moral imperative of suicide by telling tales about the moral imperative of suicide. In "The Monk's Tale" we get a complicated meditation on what a tale is: when does an episode or an embedded tale become a tale itself ? The Monk had been chosen as the second teller, but had been interrupted and silenced. When he is invited, later on in the pilgrimage, to take his turn and tell his story, he promises to tell a collection of stories, which have in common the fact that they are all tragedies. He says he has a hundred of these stories, and he will tell them all as his tale. Perhaps this is his payback for being interrupted by the Miller. Though such a project would be as long as *The Decameron*, no one interrupts the Monk at first because his tales, the Fall of Lucifer and the Fall of Adam—that is, the plot of John Milton's *Paradise Lost* (1667)—are only a stanza long. Gradually, however, his tales begin to get tales embedded within them (the tale of Hercules has twelve labors, each a potential tale) so that they become multistanzaic. Finally, the Knight has to interrupt the Monk. Though the Knight says that the dreariness of the tragedies is the reason for the interruption, we remember that the Knight, in his own tale, insisted on not adding digressive embedded tales because he wants everyone to get a chance to tell his tale. The Monk is interrupted because his tale is potentially endless, and his hundred tragedies could scuttle the whole Canterbury tale-telling enterprise.

Conversely, the pilgrim Chaucer's "Tale of Sir Thopas" is filled with problems of not knowing how to start a tale and, for that reason, presents as much of a hazard to the tale-telling as the Monk's. "Chaucer's" tale-telling constantly suffers narrative letdown as sentences and stanzas build up to jarring anticlimaxes. As the knight errant, Sir Thopas, rides out in search of adventure, the phrase "Ther spryngen" promises a tiger or at least a panther, but typical of the pattern of the story, the only things that leap out at the doughty knight are grass and weeds: "Ther spryngen herbes grete and smale." If "The Monk's Tale" is interrupted because he does not know how to end it, then Chaucer's tale is interrupted by Harry Bailey because "Chaucer" does not know how to begin it. The poet Chaucer, with stories told in different styles by distinct storytellers, plays games with the idea of narration. He tells tales such as the Clerk's and then offers conflicting interpretive conclusions to the tale. The second interpretation is based on a completely different way of reading the tale; it is to be read as an allegory / it is not to be read as an allegory.

Chaucer worries both about what a story can mean and what a story can be. The Wife of Bath—whose tale follows the Man of Law's claim that Chaucer has used up all the stories and that he, the Man of Law, is going to tell the last available story—seems to want to tell her own life as an original story. The men on the pilgrimage refuse to allow her life to be a story for several reasons. The most important is that stories *exist*; people did not make up stories in the Middle Ages; they retold them—they offered new versions of old stories. The Monk says he has a hundred stories in his cell; he is planning on drawing on his stock of old stories, not on making up new ones. The second reason for the protest against the Wife's use of her life as a story—"This is a long

Miniature of the Miller in the Ellesmere Manuscript of The Canterbury Tales *(EL 26 C9, f.34v; Henry E. Huntington Library and Art Gallery)*

preamble of a tale!"—is that in the Middle Ages, one's life was not a story. Painters did not paint self-portraits, and writers did not write autobiographies. Perhaps Augustine's autobiography was accepted by the Middle Ages because it was called a confession. Clearly no one on the Canterbury pilgrimage would have accepted it as an entry in Harry's storytelling contest.

When he invents a way for the Miller to use his tale as a weapon against the Knight, Chaucer moves toward a very modern conception of the function of speech. In a book with an oddly primitive title, *How to do Things with Words* (1962), J. L. Austin points out that there are certain acts that one can perform with words: one can promise, swear, threaten, curse, and so forth. These speech acts are so solid that they often acquire legal standing, so that one can be sued for breach of promise, and all testimony must be preceded by an oath because perjury is not lying in court but rather breaking one's oath to tell the truth. In considering the ramifications of an invented teller telling about other invented tellers telling stories whose main purpose is to get back ("quite") at other tellers, Chaucer finds himself with a new conception of fiction. This idea of the use of story puts him at odds with the patristic tale readers of his day as well as those modern critics who use the methods of the Church Fathers to read medieval fiction. The Fathers (Augustine, Ambrose, Jerome, and the millennium of scholars who followed them) asked exclusively what does a story mean ultimately?—to the extinction of the story itself. "Taketh the fruyt, and lat the chaf be stille," in "The Nun's Priest's Tale," refers to this doctrine. The meaning of the story was the fruit, or kernel of the wheat, and the story was the chaff, to be blown away by the wind once one had gotten the meaning out. Chaucer, seeing the Miller take up his story in arms against the Knight, is impressed by the power of the story-act. The Miller's weapon, the cudgel, would be useless against the Knight's lance, but his "noble tale" puts him on equal footing against the noble tale of the Knight.

Once this principle is established, it is often more fruitful to ask about each pilgrim's tale, what is he doing with it rather than what does it mean. This can be seen in one of the most vexing of the tales, the Pardoner's, which raises many questions about the meaning and characterization of the teller. "The Pardoner's Tale" is one of several (the others are the Wife of Bath's and the Canon's Yeoman's) which include an extensive confessional self-portrait as a prologue to the tale proper. In his prologue, the Pardoner confesses to being a vicious, evil man who cheats his customers, the purchasers of his pardons. There has been much speculation about the reason for this confession, usually centering around the likelihood that he is drunk, or that he is mimicking the Wife's confession of her lustfulness, or that the confession of evil is a way to assert his suspect masculinity. Though there is some validity to each of these claims, one must consider what the Pardoner was trying to do with his tale. One of the notable aspects of the pilgrims is their perfection—the Knight is "parfit," the physician is a "parfit praktisour," and the Friar is the best beggar in his house. We should note that his concept does not at all designate moral perfection, but only completion; the perfect one is whatever he is to the nth degree. This is most easily seen in the designation of the Friar as the best beggar. He is a member of a mendicant order whose essence, therefore, is begging. To be the best beggar is to be able to beg the most money and, even better, in the smallest begging district. This notion of expertise, of being the best *at* whatever one does, is everywhere in *The Canterbury Tales*. The Wife is the best wife, if being good at being a wife means marrying and subjugating the greatest number of husbands.

In the tales, the best example of such a character is the summoner in "The Friar's Tale." For him, summoning means using his ecclesiastical office to gouge parishioners through the threat of a summons to the archdeacon's court. When the summoner finds himself in the company of a devil, he does not try to run as do all the characters in his position in analogous tales. Rather he stays to show up the devil, to outsummon him. When he sees the devil fail to get a horse that a carter has consigned to the devil, the summoner is filled with condescension. He tells the devil that he may be good at what he does in his neck of the woods, but if he wants to see how it is done, he should watch the summoner at work. This spirit of expertise energizes many of the pilgrims and their characters: they are so good at what they do that they can outdo the devil, even if it is doing evil.

The Pardoner then raises this notion of doing evil to new heights. His plan is to use the Great Magician's trick of showing his audience how he does the trick, then pulling it off anyway. In this case, the ultimate act of a pardoner would be to tell the pilgrims how he sells his pardons dishonestly, then sell them pardons anyway. In this tale, the Pardoner plans the ultimate act of requital; he wants to get back at the whole pilgrimage. That he has been designated as the lowest of the low is seen in his position in the "General Prologue." He is the last pilgrim to be introduced in a sweep that goes down the social order to him. This scorn is resurrected at the beginning of his tale when the "gentils" put strictures on him, insisting that he "Telle us som moral thyng," with the implication that an obscene story is to be expected from such a low, obscene fellow. What better revenge than to sell these people his pardons. For them to buy the pardons would be for them to acknowledge that they are evil, and for them to buy them after he has told them the tricks of his trade would certify them as fools. And the genius of the Pardoner is that he almost pulls it off.

Walter Clyde Curry has argued that the Pardoner's confession works partly as a smoke screen for his real secret, that he is a eunuch. Most critics have accepted this analysis and have noted that many of his actions come out of an attempt to hide his true nature. It is for this reason that the Pardoner interrupts the Wife's prologue to announce that he is about to get married. Also for this reason he confesses to a desire to have a wench in every town; that is, he is proclaiming he can do that which nature has left him unable to do. Though there is a moral dilemma for the Pardoner in his eunuchry because he believes eunuchs are cursed in the Bible and therefore unpardonable, Chaucer will use his condition for the last twist in his use of language as a weapon.

The Pardoner's trick in selling pardons to his usual flock is to tell them that his pardons will work only for people who have *not* committed vicious sins, like adultery. Since his usual trade is families out for market day, both husband and wife rush up to buy his pardons. Once one couple comes up to purchase pardon, the rest will fall in line. Silence or inactivity appears to admit guilt. The Pardoner plans the same method of attack in his plot to sell his pardons to the pilgrims: he needs just one pilgrim to bite, and they will all fall into his net. He determines that Harry Bailey is his target, and this version of his tale has only one purpose: to force Harry into purchasing pardon. The interest in the tale is in what it does rather than what it means.

The interruption of the pilgrimage by the Canon and his Yeoman signifies a radical change in the narrative plan for *The Canterbury Tales*. The introduction of a teller who does not belong to the original company assembled at the Tabard Inn breaks down all notions of what the finished *Tales* should be. In contrast to *The Decameron*, a collection of tales named for the number of sets of tales (ten) which it comprises, *The Canterbury Tales* will not now be so easily rounded off. The medieval reader liked the roundedness of *The Decameron*: ten tellers x ten days = one hundred tales. But Chaucer's symmetry breaks down with the arrival of the Canon's Yeoman. Suddenly, simply multiplying the number of pilgrims by the number of tales will not yield the number of tales that there are supposed to be. It is not clear if the new teller is to be included in the number of pilgrims or if he will be expected to tell four tales and be a legitimate entrant in the storytelling contest. Furthermore, the number of tellers is no longer stable. There is nothing to prevent another stranger from joining the pilgrimage, or, in fact, to keep an original pilgrim from leaving.

As if to underscore how radical the change is, Chaucer does not have the interrupter tell the tale, but rather his assistant. Everyone expects the Canon to tell the tale; as if to qualify him as a storyteller, the Canon is introduced with an elaborate description of the kind given to the pilgrims in the "General Prologue." When the Canon is frightened away, the Yeoman tells his master's tale, the story of alchemy. The Yeoman is the only pilgrim who does not present himself as an expert. In fact, one of the points he makes in delivering his lecture on alchemy is how little he knows about the subject. Though the Yeoman is not an expert, he is in a position to claim expertise. He has served his master for seven years, which is the time it takes for a journeyman to become the master of a trade, and with his master fled he could claim the position of master himself. Instead he rejects the art he has almost mastered, swears off alchemy, and advises everyone else to do the same.

"The Canon's Yeoman's Tale" then marks a major turning point in *The Canterbury Tales,* so by the end of the next tale (the Manciple's), the narrator announces, "Now lakketh us no tales mo than oon" to "knytte up wel a greet mateere." Chaucer is bringing things to an end, though the tales have not gone the original distance planned. In fact, not all of the pilgrims have told even one tale.

There is much speculation as to why Chaucer left *The Canterbury Tales* unfinished. He seems to have left off writing them in the mid 1390s, some five or six years before his death. At that time he was about fifty-five years old and, from the record of his business activities, apparently in good health. Since he was writing tales, rather than a long unified work like *Troilus and Criseyde,* there would not seem to be a problem of getting stuck in a narrative. It is possible that the enormousness of the task overwhelmed him. He had been working on *The Canterbury Tales* for some ten years, and he was not one quarter through his original plan. He may have felt he could not divide his time successfully between his writing and his business interests.

Chaucer himself offers an explanation in the "Retraction" which follows "The Parson's Tale," the last of *The Canterbury Tales.* In it Chaucer disclaims apologetically all of his impious works, especially "the tales of Caunterbury, thilke that sowen into synne." There has been some speculation of "deathbed confession" about the "Retraction": Chaucer in ill health confesses his impieties; and some belief that the "Retraction" is merely conventional: the apologetic voice allows Chaucer to list all his works while taking on the persona of the humble author, a stance favored in the Middle Ages.

Miniature of the Wife of Bath in the Ellesmere Manuscript of The Canterbury Tales *(EL 26 C 9, f.72r; Henry E. Huntington Library and Art Gallery)*

If we are to take Chaucer at his word, he seems to suggest that his works were being misread, that people were mistaking the sinful behavior in *The Canterbury Tales* for its message (for example, seeing the Wife's lechery—instead of the empty life to which it leads—as the point of her tale). If this is the case, then he must, like his favorite Latin poet, Ovid (in the *Tristia,* A.D. 8-18), disclaim all the works that he believed could be read immorally. It may be that a more anguished version of the calm, valedictory tone of the "Retraction" is found in "The Manciple's Tale," where Apollo takes away the voice and tears out the feathers (quills) of the crow because he has told the *truth.* The crow seems to be exactly like Chaucer, the poet of *The Canterbury Tales,* when it is said that he could "countrefete the speche of every man / . . . when he sholde telle a tale." The crow's problem is that his truths are mistaken, and in the conclusion of "The Manciple's Tale," we are told, "be noon auctour newe / Of tidynges, whither they been false or trewe." Here, as in the "Retraction," Chaucer excludes explicitly didactic works, but here the flaw is seen in the misreading of the tales; in the "Retraction," Chaucer, in the guise of the humble author, puts the blame on himself.

The last thirteen years of Chaucer's life correspond almost exactly to the span of years covered by Shakespeare's *Richard II*, that is, the period marked by Richard's claiming his majority (he had become king at nine) and his assumption of the power of the throne in 1389 until his deposition and death in 1399. Though the realm was marred by the power struggles of the Lancastrian (Gaunt and his son, the eventual Henry IV) and Court (Richard) parties, it must be remembered that in presenting this strife Shakespeare squeezes thirteen years of intrigue into one five-act play. Chaucer had connections in both camps, and over a dozen years it was possible to be of the court without being Gaunt's enemy. That Chaucer was able to do this is indicated by the fact that Henry renewed annuities granted to Chaucer during Richard's reign.

Nonetheless, these appear to have been financially trying times for Chaucer. His wife received the last payment of her annuity in 1387, which suggests she died in the following year. Although Chaucer lost his post as controller of customs in 1386, he had been appointed justice of peace for the County of Kent in 1385, and in 1389, following the coming to power of Richard, Chaucer was named clerk of public works. This post, which amounted to being a kind of general contractor for the repair of public buildings, was more lucrative than the controller's job that he had lost, but it caused him no end of headaches. One of the duties of this position required him to carry large sums of money, and in 1390 he was robbed of both his and the king's money three times in the space of four days. Though there was no direct punishment of Chaucer, he was appointed subforester of North Pemberton in Somerset. It appears that in 1390 or 1391 he was eased out of his clerk's job and rusticated. Chaucer seems to have missed the bustle of court and public life for his writing dried up when he moved away from London. In a short poem from this period, "The Letter to Scogan," Chaucer says, "thynke I never of slep to wake my muse, / That rusteth in my shethe stille in pees." Chaucer eventually got into financial trouble. In 1398 Chaucer borrowed against his annuity and was sued for debt. His last poem is "The Complaint to his Purse," a letter asking King Henry for money. It is not surprising that at least one manuscript of this poem calls it the "Supplication" to King Richard. It is quite likely that in the last years of his life, he was constantly asking the king, whoever he was, for money. The poem, or his connections to the Lancastrians, must have worked because Chaucer was granted a sizable annuity by Henry. Nonetheless, Chaucer moved to a house in the Westminster Abbey Close because a house on church grounds granted him sanctuary from creditors. And so, from the fact of Chaucer's debts comes the tradition of burying poets, or erecting memorials to them, in Westminster Abbey. Chaucer died in 1400, the year after the accession of Henry to the throne and also the year after the death of John of Gaunt, the king's father, Chaucer's almost exact contemporary and once the most powerful man in England. That Chaucer was buried in Westminster Abbey was due primarily to the fact that his last residence was on the abbey grounds. So important was he deemed as a poet, that the space around his tomb was later dubbed the Poets' Corner, and luminaries of English letters were laid to rest around him.

Bibliographies:

Eleanor Hammond, *Chaucer: A Bibliographical Manual* (New York: Macmillan, 1908);

Dudley Griffith, *Bibliography of Chaucer, 1908-1953* (Seattle: University of Washington Press, 1955);

William Crawford, *Bibliography of Chaucer, 1954-63* (Seattle: University of Washington Press, 1967);

Lorrayne Y. Baird, *A Bibliography of Chaucer, 1964-1973* (Boston: G. K. Hall, 1977);

Lorrayne Baird-Lange, *A Bibliography of Chaucer, 1974-1985* (Hamden, Conn.: Archon, 1988).

Biographies:

Martin M. Crow and Clair C. Olson, eds., *Chaucer Life-Records* (Oxford: Clarendon Press, 1966; Austin: University of Texas Press, 1966);

John C. Gardner, *The Life and Times of Chaucer* (New York: Knopf, 1976);

Derek Brewer, *Chaucer and His World* (New York: Dodd, Mead, 1977);

Donald R. Howard, *Chaucer: His Life, His Work, His World* (New York: Dutton, 1987).

References:

Ruth Ames, *God's Plenty: Chaucer's Christian Humanism* (Chicago: Loyola University Press, 1984);

C. David Benson, *Chaucer's Drama of Style: Poetic Variety and Contrast in The Canterbury Tales* (Chapel Hill: University of North Carolina Press, 1986);

N. F. Blake, *The Textual Tradition of the Canterbury Tales* (London: Arnold, 1985);

Muriel Bowden, *A Commentary On the General Prologue to the Canterbury Tales* (New York: Macmillan, 1948);

Derek Brewer, *Chaucer in his Time* (London: Nelson, 1964);

W. F. Bryan and Germaine Dempster, eds., *Sources and Analogues of Chaucer's Canterbury Tales* (Chicago: University of Chicago Press, 1941);

Nevill Coghill, *The Poet Chaucer* (London & New York: Oxford University Press, 1949);

Walter Clyde Curry, *Chaucer and the Mediæval Sciences* (New York & London: Oxford University Press, 1926);

Alfred David, *The Strumpet Muse: Art and Morals in Chaucer's Poetry* (Bloomington: Indiana University Press, 1976);

Rodney Delasanta, "The Theme of Judgment in *The Canterbury Tales*," *Modern Language Quarterly*, 31 (September 1970): 298-307;

Bert Dillon, *A Chaucer Dictionary* (Boston: G. K. Hall, 1974);

Carolyn Dinshaw, *Chaucer's Sexual Poetics* (Madison: University of Wisconsin Press, 1989);

John Ganim, *Chaucerian Theatricality* (Princeton: Princeton University Press, 1990);

John Gardner, *The Poetry of Chaucer* (Carbondale: Southern Illinois University Press, 1977);

Jeffrey Helterman, "The Dehumanizing Metamorphoses of the Knight's Tale," *ELH*, 38 (December 1971): 493-511;

Richard Hoffman, *Ovid and the Canterbury Tales* (Philadelphia: University of Pennsylvania Press, 1966);

Donald Howard, *The Idea of the Canterbury Tales* (Berkeley: University of California Press, 1976);

Bernard Huppé and D. W. Robertson, Jr., *Fruyt and Chaf: Studies in Chaucer's Allegories* (Princeton: Princeton University Press, 1963);

Robert M. Jordan, *Chaucer and the Shape of Creation: The Aesthetic Possibilities of Inorganic Structure* (Cambridge, Mass.: Harvard University Press, 1967);

Stanley J. Kahrl, "Chaucer's *Squire's Tale* and the Decline of Chivalry," *Chaucer Review*, 7 (Winter 1973): 194-209;

R. E. Kaske, "The Knight's Interruption of the *Monk's Tale*," *ELH*, 24 (December 1957): 249-268;

Robert Kellogg, "Oral Narrative, Written Books," *Genre*, 10 (Winter 1977): 655-665;

George Lyman Kittredge, *Chaucer and His Poetry* (Cambridge, Mass.: Harvard University Press, 1915);

V. A. Kolve, *Chaucer and the Imagery of Narrative: The First Five Canterbury Tales* (Stanford: Stanford University Press, 1984);

W. W. Lawrence, *Chaucer and the Canterbury Tales* (New York: Columbia University Press, 1950);

C. S. Lewis, *The Allegory of Love: A Study in Medieval Tradition* (Oxford: Clarendon Press, 1936);

R. M. Lumiansky, *Of Sondry Folk: the Dramatic Principle of The Canterbury Tales* (Austin: University of Texas Press, 1955);

Francis Magoun, *A Chaucer Gazetteer* (Chicago: University of Chicago Press, 1961);

John Manly, *Some New Light on Chaucer* (New York: Holt, 1926);

J. Mitchell Morse, "The Philosophy of the Clerk of Oxenford," *Modern Language Quarterly*, 19 (March 1958): 3-20;

Charles Muscatine, *Chaucer and the French Tradition: A Study in Style and Meaning* (Berkeley: University of California Press, 1957);

Charles A. Owen, Jr., "The Problem of Free Will in Chaucer's Narratives," *Philological Quarterly*, 46 (October 1967): 433-456;

Russell A. Peck, "Chaucer and the Nominalist Questions," *Speculum*, 53 (October 1978): 745-760;

Robert A. Pratt, "Chaucer and the Hand that Fed Him," *Speculum*, 41 (October 1966): 619-642;

Edmund Reiss, "Medieval Irony," *Journal of the History of Ideas*, 42 (1981): 209-226;

D. W. Robertson, Jr., *A Preface to Chaucer: Studies in Medieval Perspectives* (Princeton: Princeton University Press, 1962);

Beryl Rowland, *Blind Beasts: Chaucer's Animal World* (Kent, Ohio: Kent State University Press, 1971);

Paul Ruggiers, *The Art of the Canterbury Tales* (Madison: University of Wisconsin Press, 1965);

James Sledd, "The Clerk's Tale; The Monsters and the Critics," *Modern Philology*, 51 (1954): 73-82;

Paul Strohm, *Social Chaucer* (Cambridge, Mass.: Harvard University Press, 1989);

Joseph Westlund, "The *Knight's Tale* as Impetus for Pilgrimage," *Philological Quarterly*, 43 (October 1964): 526-537;

Trevor Whittock, *A Reading of the Canterbury Tales* (London & New York: Cambridge University Press, 1968);

Arnold Williams, "Chaucer and the Friars," *Speculum*, 28 (July 1953): 499-513;

Chauncey Wood, *Chaucer and the Country of the Stars: Poetic Uses of Astrological Imagery* (Princeton: Princeton University Press, 1970).

Thomas Dekker

(circa 1572 - August 1632)

This entry was updated by Cyrus Hoy (University of Rochester) from his entry in DLB 62: Elizabethan Dramatists.

BOOKS: *The Pleasant Comedie of Old Fortunatus* (London: Printed by S. Stafford for W. Apley, 1600);

The Shoemakers Holiday. Or The Gentle Craft. With the Life of Simon Eyre, Shoomaker, and Lord Maior of London (London: Printed by V. Sims, 1600);

Blurt Master-Constable. Or The Spaniard's Night-Walke, by Dekker and perhaps Thomas Middleton (London: Printed by E. Allde for H. Rockytt, 1602);

Satiro-Mastix. Or The Untrussing of the Humorous Poet (London: Printed by E. Allde for E. White, 1602);

The Pleasant Comodie of Patient Grissell, by Dekker, Henry Chettle, and William Haughton (London: Printed by E. Allde for H. Rocket, 1603);

1603. The Wonderfull Yeare. Wherein Is Shewed the Picture of London, Lying Sicke of the Plague (London: Printed by T. Creede, sold by N. Ling, J. Smethwick & J. Browne, 1603);

Newes from Graves-End: Sent to Nobody (London: Printed by T. Creede for T. Archer, 1604);

The Meeting of Gallants at an Ordinarie: or The Walkes in Powles, by Dekker and perhaps Middleton (London: Printed by T. Creede, sold by M. Lawe, 1604);

The Honest Whore, with, the Humours of the Patient Man, and the Longing Wife [part 1], by Dekker and Middleton (London: Printed by V. Simmes & others for J. Hodgets, 1604); republished as *The Converted Curtezan* (London: Printed by V. Simmes, sold by J. Hodgets, 1604);

The Magnificent Entertainment: Given to King James upon His Passage through London (London: Printed by T. Creede, H. Lownes, E. Allde & others for T. Man the younger, 1604);

The Double PP. A Papist in Armes. Encountred by the Protestant. A Jesuite Marching before Them (London: Printed by T. Creede, sold by J. Hodgets, 1606);

Newes from Hell; Brought by the Divells Carrier (London: Printed by R. Blower, S. Stafford & V. Simmes for W. Ferebrand, 1606); enlarged as *A Knights Conjuring. Done in Earnest: Discovered in Jest* (London: Printed by T. Creede for W. Barley, 1607);

The Seven Deadly Sinnes of London: Drawne in Seven Severall Coaches, Through the Citie Bringing the Plague with Them (London: Printed by E. Allde & S. Stafford for N. Butter, 1606);

Jests to Make You Merie: With the Conjuring Up of Cock Watt, by Dekker and George Wilkins (London: Printed by N. Okes for N. Butter, 1607);

North-ward Hoe, by Dekker and John Webster (London: Printed by G. Eld, 1607);

The Famous History of Sir T. Wyat. With the Coronation of Queen Mary (presumably the same play as *Lady Jane*), by Dekker, Webster, Thomas Heywood, Chettle, and Wentworth

Smith (London: Printed by E. Allde for T. Archer, 1607);

West-ward Hoe, by Dekker and Webster (London: Printed by W. Jaggard, sold by J. Hodgets, 1607);

The Whore of Babylon (London: Printed at Eliot's Court Press [?] for N. Butter, 1607);

The Dead Tearme. Or Westminsters Complaint for Long Vacations and Short Termes (London: Printed by W. Jaggard, sold by J. Hodgets, 1608);

The Belman of London: Bringing to Light the Most Notorious Villanies Now Practised in the Kingdome (London: Printed by N. Okes for N. Butter, 1608);

Lanthorne and Candle-light. Or the Bell-mans Second Nights Walke (London: Printed by G. Eld for J. Busbie, 1608; corrected and amended edition, London: Printed by E. Allde for J. Busby, 1609); enlarged as *O per se o, or a new crier of Lanthorne and Candle-Light* (London: Printed by T. Snodham for J. Busbie, 1612); enlarged again as *Villanies Discovered by Lanthorne and Candle-Light* (London: Printed by W. Stansby for J. Busby, 1616; enlarged again, London: Printed by A. Mathewes, 1620); enlarged again as *English Villanies* (London: Printed by A. Mathewes, sold by J. Grismond, 1632);

Foure Birds of Noahs Arke (London: Printed by H. Ballard for N. Butter, 1609);

The Guls Horne-Booke (London: Printed by N. Okes for R. S., 1609);

The Ravens Almanacke Foretelling of a Plague, Famine, and Civill Warre (London: Printed by E. Allde for T. Archer, 1609);

Worke for Armorours: or, The Peace Is Broken (London: Printed by N. Okes for N. Butter, 1609);

The Roaring Girle. Or Moll Cut-purse, by Dekker and Middleton (London: Printed by N. Okes for T. Archer, 1611);

If It Be Not Good, The Divel Is in It. A New Play (London: Printed by T. Creede for J. Trundle, sold by E. Marchant, 1612);

Troia-Nova Triumphans. London Triumphing, or, The Solemne, Receiving of Sir J. Swinerton After Taking the Oath of Maioralty (London: Printed by N. Okes, sold by J. Wright, 1612);

A Strange Horse-Race, at the End of Which, Comes in the Catch-Pols Masque (London: Printed by N. Okes for J. Hunt, 1613);

The Artillery Garden (London: Printed by G. Eld, 1616);

Dekker His Dreame. In Which, the Great Volumes of Heaven and Hell to Him Were Opened (London: Printed by N. Okes, 1620);

The Virgin Martir, A Tragedie, by Dekker and Philip Massinger (London: Printed by B. Alsop for T. Jones, 1622);

A Rod for Run-Awayes. Gods Tokens, of His Feareful Judgements, upon This City (London: Printed by G. Purslowe for J. Trundle, 1625);

Brittannia's Honor: Brightly Shining in Severall Magnificent Shewes or Pageants, to Celebrate R. Deane, at His Inauguration into the Majoralty of London, October the 29th. 1628 (London: Printed by N. Okes & J. Norton, 1628);

Warres, Warres, Warres (London: Printed by N. Okes for J. G., 1628);

Londons Tempe, or The Feild of Happines. To Celebrate J. Campebell, at His Inauguration into the Maioralty of London, the 29 of October, 1629 (London: Printed by N. Okes, 1629);

London Looke Backe, at That Yeare of Yeares 1625 (London: Printed by A. Mathewes, sold by E. Blackmoore, 1630);

The Blacke Rod: and the White Rod (London: Printed by B. Alsop & T. Fawcet for J. Cowper, 1630);

The Second Part of the Honest Whore (London: Printed by Eliz. Allde for N. Butter, 1630);

A Tragi-Comedy: Called, Match Mee in London (London: Printed by B. Alsop & T. Fawcet for H. Seile, 1631);

Penny-Wise Pound Foolish or, a Bristow Diamond, Set in Two Rings, and Both Crack'd (London: Printed by A. Mathewes for E. Blackmoore, 1631);

The Noble Souldier. Or, A Contract Broken, Justly Reveng'd. A Tragedy (London: Printed by J. Beale for N. Vavasour, 1634);

The Wonder of a Kingdome (London: Printed by R. Raworth for N. Vavasour, 1636);

The Sun's-Darling: A Moral Masque, by Dekker and John Ford (London: Printed by J. Bell for Andrew Penneycuicke, 1656);

Lust's Dominion, or The Lascivious Queen (presumably the same play as *The Spanish Moor's Tragedy*), by Dekker, Haughton, John Day, and John Marston (London: Printed by F. K., sold by Robert Pollard, 1657);

The Witch of Edmonton, by Dekker, Ford, and William Rowley (London: Printed by J. Cottrel for Edward Blackmoore, 1658).

Editions: *The Non-Dramatic Works of Thomas Dekker*, 5 volumes, edited by A. B. Grosart (London, 1884-1886);

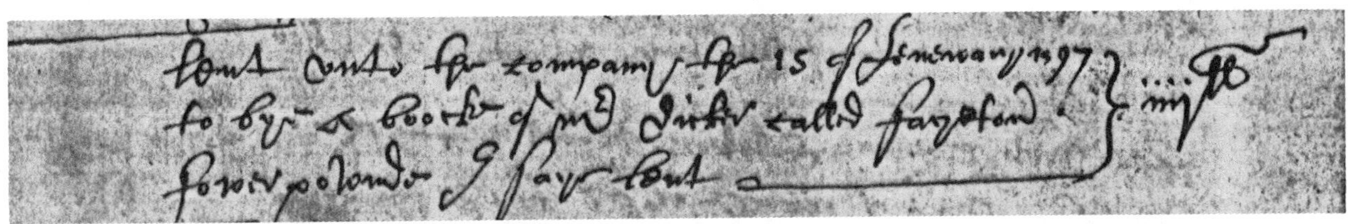

Entry in the diary of Philip Henslowe recording a payment on 15 January 1598 (1597 according to the calendar then in use) for Dekker's play Phaeton, *now lost (MS VII, l. 44ʳ; Dulwich College, London)*

The Plague Pamphlets of Thomas Dekker, edited by F. P. Wilson (Oxford: Clarendon Press, 1925);

The Dramatic Works of Thomas Dekker, 4 volumes, edited by Fredson Bowers (Cambridge: Cambridge University Press, 1953-1961);

Thomas Dekker: Selected Prose Works, edited by E. D. Pendry (London, 1968);

Cyrus Hoy, *Introductions, Notes, and Commentaries to texts in 'The Dramatic Works of Thomas Dekker,'* 4 volumes (Cambridge: Cambridge University Press, 1980-1981).

PLAY PRODUCTIONS: *Sir Thomas More*, probably by Anthony Munday, with revisions by Dekker, Henry Chettle, probably William Shakespeare, and perhaps Thomas Heywood, probably not produced, circa 1598;

Phaeton, London, Rose theater, January 1598;

The Triangle (or Triplicity) of Cuckholds, London, Rose theater, March 1598;

The Famous Wars of Henry I and the Prince of Wales (also known as *The Welshman's Prize*), by Dekker, Chettle, and Michael Drayton, London, Rose theater, March 1598;

Earl Godwin and his Three Sons, parts 1 and 2, by Dekker, Drayton, Chettle, and Robert Wilson, London, Rose theater, spring 1598;

Black Bateman of the North, part 1, by Dekker, Drayton, Chettle, and Wilson, London, Rose theater, May 1598;

The Mad Man's Morris, by Dekker, Drayton, and Wilson, London, Rose theater, July 1598;

Hannibal and Hermes, part 1 (also known as *Worse Afeard than Hurt*), by Dekker, Drayton, and Wilson, London, Rose theater, July 1598;

Pierce of Winchester, by Dekker, Drayton, and Wilson, London, Rose theater, July-August 1598;

Worse Afeard than Hurt (presumably part 2 of *Hannibal and Hermes*), by Dekker and Drayton, London, Rose theater, September 1598;

Conan, Prince of Cornwall, by Dekker and Drayton, London, Rose theater, October 1598;

The Civil Wars of France, parts 1, 2, and 3, by Dekker and Drayton, London, Rose theater, September to December 1598;

The First Introduction of the Civil Wars of France, London, Rose theater, January 1599;

Troilus and Cressida, by Dekker and Chettle, London, Rose theater, April 1599;

Agamemnon (apparently the same play as *Orestes' Furies*), by Dekker and Chettle, London, Rose theater, May 1599;

The Shoemakers' Holiday, London, Rose theater, summer 1599;

Page of Plymouth, by Dekker and Ben Jonson, London, Rose theater, September 1599;

The Tragedy of Robert II, King of Scots, by Dekker, Chettle, Jonson, and perhaps John Marston, London, Rose theater, September 1599;

The Stepmother's Tragedy, by Dekker and Chettle, London, Rose theater, October 1599;

Old Fortunatus, London, Rose theater, November 1599;

Patient Grissell, by Dekker, Chettle, and William Haughton, London, Rose theater, January 1600;

Lust's Dominion (possibly a revision of an earlier play and presumably the same play as *The Spanish Moor's Tragedy*), by Dekker, John Day, Haughton, and Marston, London, Rose theater, spring 1600;

The Seven Wise Masters, by Dekker, Chettle, Haughton, and Day, London, Rose theater, March 1600;

The Golden Ass, or Cupid and Psyche, by Dekker, Chettle, and Day, London, Rose theater, May 1600;

Fair Constance of Rome, part 1, by Dekker, Drayton, Munday, Wilson, and Richard Hathway, London, Rose theater, June 1600;

Fortune's Tennis, London, Rose or Fortune theater, September 1600;

Sebastian, King of Portugal, by Dekker and Chettle, London, Fortune theater, May 1601;

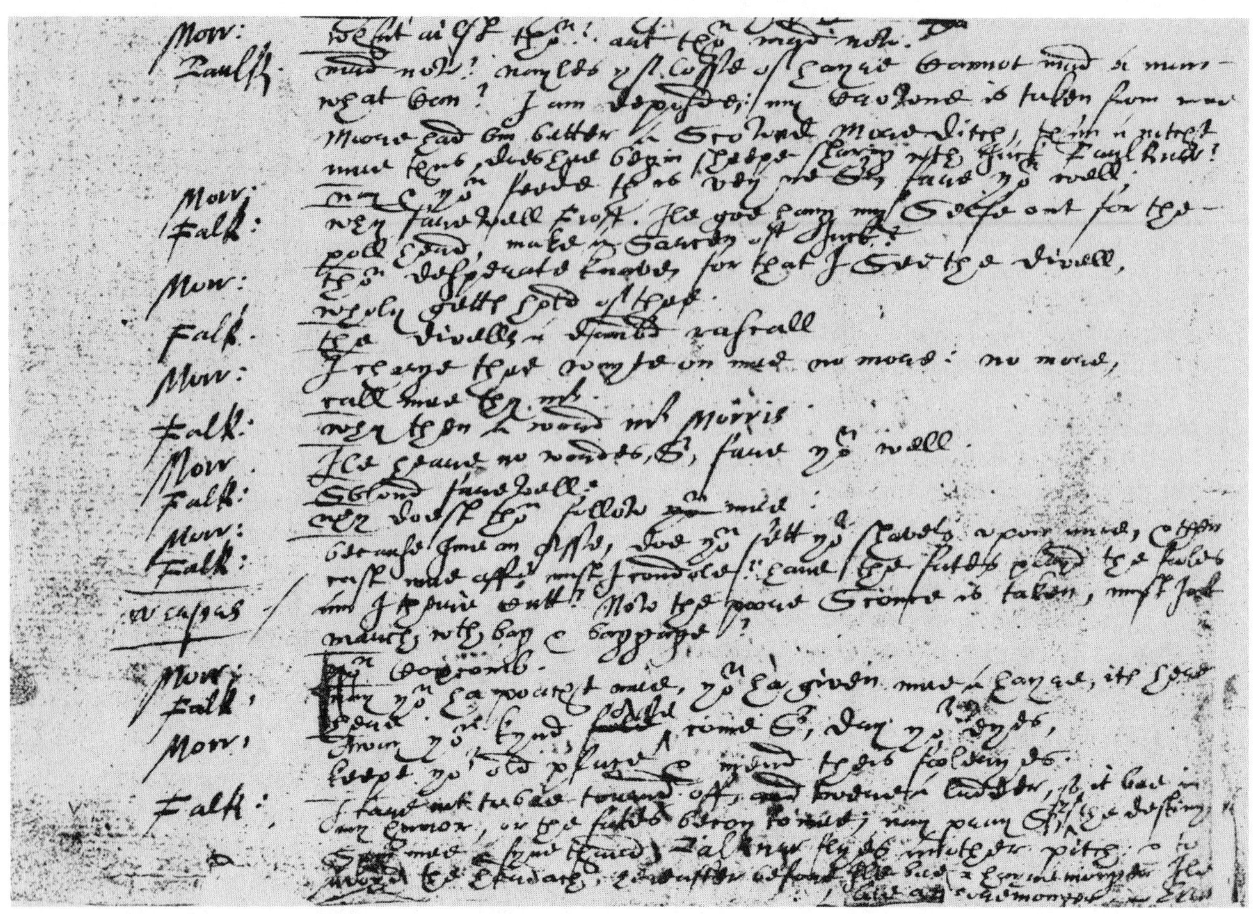

Dekker's addition to Sir Thomas More, *in the manuscript preserved at the British Library (Harleian MS 7368, l. 13ᵛ; British Library). These lines are the only preserved example of a dramatic composition in Dekker's hand.*

Satiromastix, London, Globe theater and Paul's theater, autumn 1601;

Blurt, Master Constable, by Dekker and perhaps Thomas Middleton, London, Paul's theater, circa 1601-1602;

Pontius Pilate (anonymous play of circa 1597), prologue and epilogue added by Dekker, London, Fortune theater, January 1602;

Tasso's Melancholy (anonymous play of circa 1594), revised by Dekker, London, Fortune theater, January 1602;

Jephthah, by Dekker and Munday, London, Fortune theater, May 1602;

Caesar's Fall (also known as *Two Shapes*), by Dekker, Drayton, Munday, Middleton, and John Webster, London, Fortune theater, May 1602;

Sir John Oldcastle, part 2, by Drayton, Hathway, Munday, and Wilson (1600), revised by Dekker, London, Boar's Head or Rose theater, September 1602;

A Medicine for a Curst Wife, London, Boar's Head or Rose theater, September 1602;

Sir Thomas Wyatt (presumably the same play as *Lady Jane*), by Dekker, Webster, Chettle, Heywood, and Wentworth Smith, London, Boar's Head or Rose theater, autumn 1602;

Christmas Comes but Once a Year, by Dekker, Chettle, Heywood, and Webster, London, Boar's Head or Rose theater, November 1602;

The Magnificent Entertainment, by Dekker (with Zeal's speech by Middleton), streets of London, 15 March 1604;

The Honest Whore, part 1, by Dekker and Middleton, London, Fortune theater, spring 1604;

Westward Ho, by Dekker and Webster, London, Paul's theater, late 1604;

The Honest Whore, part 2, London, Fortune theater, circa 1604-1605;

Northward Ho, by Dekker and Webster, London, Paul's theater, 1605;

The Whore of Babylon, London, Fortune theater, winter 1605-1606;

The Roaring Girl, by Dekker and Middleton, London, Fortune theater, April-May 1611;

If This Be Not a Good Play, the Devil Is in It, London, Red Bull theater, May-June 1611;

Troia-Nova Triumphans, streets of London, 29 October 1612;

Guy of Warwick, by Dekker and Day (Stationers' Register, 15 January 1620), unknown theater;

The Virgin Martyr, by Dekker and Philip Massinger, London, Red Bull theater, October 1620;

Match Me in London, London, Red Bull theater, circa 1621;

The Witch of Edmonton, by Dekker, John Ford, and William Rowley, London, Cockpit theater, 1621;

The Noble Spanish Soldier (perhaps a revision of an earlier, circa 1600, collaboration with Day), unknown theater, circa 1622;

The Wonder of a Kingdom (apparently a revision and abridgment of a collaboration with Day), unknown theater, circa 1623;

The Bellman of Paris, by Dekker and Day, London, Curtain or Red Bull theater, licensed 30 July 1623;

The Welsh Ambassador (in part a revision of *The Noble Spanish Soldier* and perhaps a collaboration with Ford), unknown theater, circa 1623;

The Sun's Darling, by Dekker and Ford, London, Cockpit theater, licensed 3 March 1624;

The Fairy Knight, by Dekker and Ford, London, Red Bull theater, licensed 11 June 1624;

The Late Murder of the Son upon the Mother, by Dekker, Ford, Rowley, and Webster, London, Red Bull theater, September 1624;

The Bristow Merchant, by Dekker and Ford, London, Fortune theater, licensed 22 October 1624;

Lord Mayor's pageant, streets of London, 29 October 1627;

Britannia's Honor, streets of London, 29 October 1628;

London's Tempe, streets of London, 29 October 1629.

Thomas Dekker was one of the most versatile of Renaissance English writers, and the plays and the nondramatic pamphlets (usually cast in

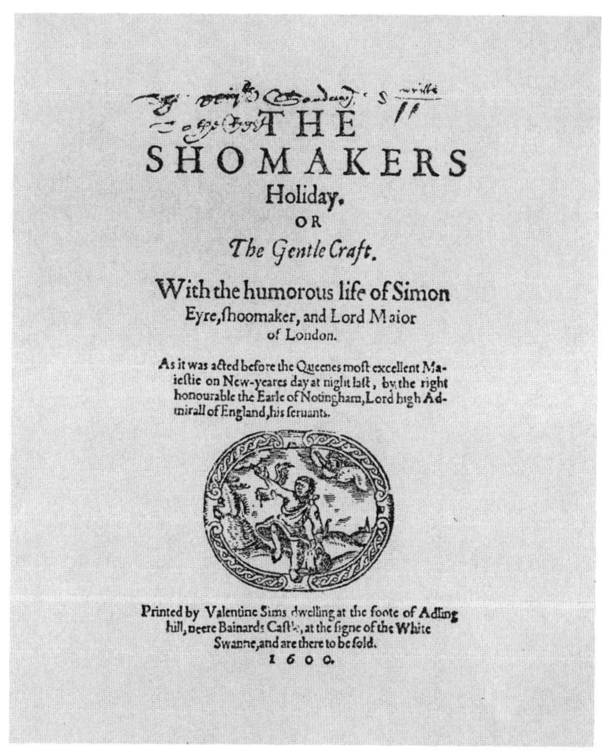
THE
SHOMAKERS
Holiday.
OR
The Gentle Craft.
With the humorous life of Simon
Eyre, ſhoomaker, and Lord Maior
of London.
As it was acted before the Queenes moſt excellent Ma-
ieſtie on New-yeares day at night laſt, by the right
honourable the Earle of Notingham, Lord high Ad-
mirall of England, his ſeruants.
Printed by Valentine Sims dwelling at the foote of Adling
hill, neere Bainards Caſtle, at the ſigne of the White
Swanne, and are there to be ſold.
1600.

Title page for the 1600 quarto edition of the earliest surviving play solely written by Dekker (Anderson Galleries auction catalogue, sale number 2077, 20-21 May 1926)

the form of journalistic essays and narratives) that he produced during a career extending from the late 1590s to the early 1630s provide a record of popular taste during the last years of the reign of Queen Elizabeth I, through the reign of James I, and into the early years of Charles I. Dekker earned his living by his pen, and nearly everything he wrote shows signs of haste. Only rarely, as in such plays as *The Shoemakers' Holiday* or *The Honest Whore*, or such nondramatic pieces as *The Gull's Horn Book* or *Four Birds of Noah's Ark* does a single work of his seem entirely satisfactory, but nearly everything that he wrote bears witness to a sensitive and shrewd imagination and to a remarkable verbal range. His descriptive manner is by turns lyrical and boisterous. Where depiction of human feeling is concerned, he writes with a simplicity and a directness that carry great eloquence. At the other extreme of style, his accounts of human folly and error and vice and the lurid imbroglio these often make of worldly affairs exhibit a raucous delight in grotesquely personified detail. His work presents a striking blend of romantic sentiment and worldly awareness, a representation of the way things are combined with a vision of the way they ought to be. He is a compassionate but by

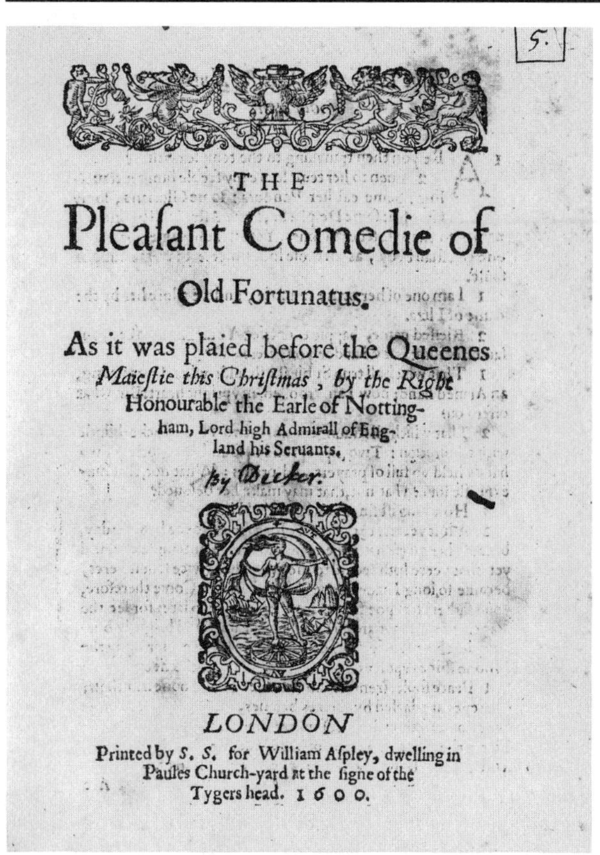
THE
Pleaſant Comedie of
Old Fortunatus.
As it was plaied before the Queenes
Maieſtie this Chriſtmas, by the Right
Honourable the Earle of Notting-
ham, Lord high Admirall of Eng-
land his Seruants.
LONDON
Printed by S. S. for William Aſpley, dwelling in
Paules Church-yard at the ſigne of the
Tygers head. 1600.

Title page for the 1600 quarto edition of Dekker's version of an old play, which he wrote in autumn 1599 and revised for a court performance during the Christmas season of 1599-1600 (Henry E. Huntington Library and Art Gallery)

no means uncritical commentator on the life of his times, and he mirrors it in language that, both in its quiet lyricism and its verbal exuberance, is typically Elizabethan.

The exact date of Dekker's birth is unknown. In the epistle to *English Villanies*, the 1632 edition of his *Lanthorn and Candlelight*, he speaks of his "three-score years," and this is the basis for the assumption that he was born in or around the year 1572. In his writings he several times makes reference to London as the place of his birth and his upbringing, and his devotion to the city is manifest both in his plays and in his nondramatic works. Nothing is known of his life prior to January 1598, when his name begins to appear among the entries for payments to dramatists in the diary (that is the manuscript account book) of Philip Henslowe, theater owner and financier of two of the companies of players (the Lord Admiral's Men and the Earl of Worcester's Men) with whom Dekker was associated in the early years of his career.

The early 1590s witnessed the formation of a regular, theatergoing audience in London. The possibility of attending plays on anything like a regular, day-to-day basis had been available to the public only since 1576, when James Burbage built the first commercial theater in the vicinity of London. More theaters were built in the years that followed: the Curtain in 1577, the Rose in 1587, the Swan in 1595 or 1596, the Fortune in 1600. As their number increased, so the need increased for plays to be acted on their stages. Henslowe, who owned shares in the Rose and the Fortune, kept in his employment a virtual crew of playwrights, who turned out comedies, histories, and tragedies, sometimes of an individual's own devising but more often by collaborative teams that might number anywhere from two to five or six members. We first hear of Dekker when his name appears in Henslowe's list of dramatists in January 1598, but, since it was only in that year that Henslowe began to include the names of dramatists in his diary entries (prior to then he had listed only the names of plays), one may assume that Dekker's career as a playwright had begun several years before. By January 1598 he was well launched as a professional dramatist. Frances Meres, surveying the English literary scene at just that time, cited Dekker (along with such contemporary dramatists as William Shakespeare, Michael Drayton, George Chapman, and Ben Jonson) as one of "our best for Tragedy" in his *Palladis Tamia* (1598; the book was entered for publication in the Stationers' Register on 7 September 1598).

During the four-and-a-half-year period from January 1598 to June 1602, Henslowe's records show Dekker to have been associated in one way or another with some forty plays for the Admiral's Men. Between July and December 1602 he was engaged on five more for Worcester's Men. His services were variously employed, as the dated entries in Henslowe's diary indicate. Occasionally, he is found writing a play unaided, as in the case of *Phaeton* (January 1598), or *The Triangle (or Triplicity) of Cuckholds* (March 1598), or *The Shoemakers' Holiday* (July 1599), or *A Medicine for a Curst Wife* (September 1602). Sometimes he was employed to alter an old play by another dramatist or dramatists, as he did to *Tasso's Melancholy* in January and again in November and December 1602, or to *Sir John Oldcastle* (a 1600 play by Michael Drayton, Richard Hathway, Anthony Munday, and Robert Wilson) in August and September 1602. Or he might be hired to supply a

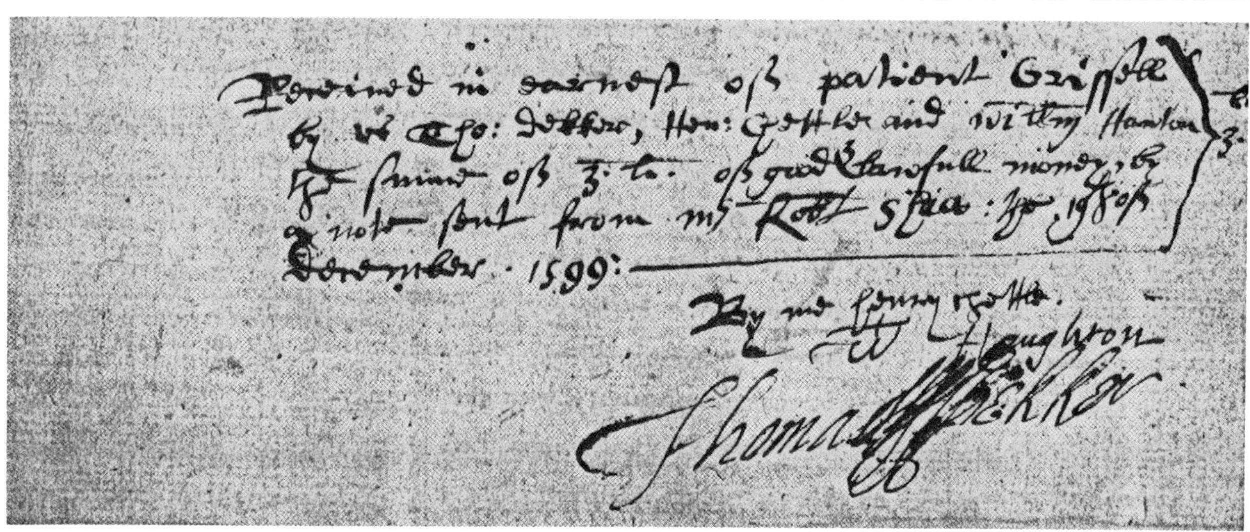

Receaved in earnest of patient Grissell by us Tho: Dekker, Hen: Chettle and Willm Haughton the summe of 3 li. of good & lawfull money, by a note sent from Mr Robt Shaa: the 19th of December 1599.

By me Henry Chettle.
W Haughton
Thomas Dekker

Receipt in the hand of Henry Chettle for an advance on the play Patient Grissell, *signed by Chettle, William Haughton, and Thomas Dekker (from the diary of Philip Henslowe; MS VII, l. 31ʳ; Dulwich College, London)*

prologue and an epilogue for someone else's play, as he did for *Pontius Pilate* (January 1602). Sometimes he is found revising an old play, but revising it so thoroughly as to make it virtually his own, as with *Old Fortunatus* (November 1599). More often he is found working in collaboration with one or more other dramatists.

One of his more notable collaborators during this period was the poet Michael Drayton. The two of them were coauthors of a three-part play titled *The Civil Wars of France* (September to December 1598), and of *Conan, Prince of Cornwall* (October 1598). Dekker and Henry Chettle were a frequent team (for example, *Troilus and Cressida*, April 1599; *Agamemnon*, also apparently known as *Orestes' Furies*, May 1599; *The Stepmother's Tragedy*, October 1599; *Sebastian, King of Portugal*, May 1601). Dekker collaborated with Ben Jonson on *Page of Plymouth* in August-September 1599; with Anthony Munday on *Jephthah* (May 1602). But in Henslowe's factory for the assembling and production of plays, collaborative pairs could readily become trios. Thus Dekker, Chettle, and Drayton wrote *The Famous Wars of Henry I and the Prince of Wales*, also known as *The Welshman's Prize* (March 1598). Dekker, Drayton, and Robert Wilson put together *The Mad Man's Morris* (July 1598), *Hannibal and Hermes*, part 1 (July 1598; part 2, also known as *Worse Afeard than Hurt*, was the work of Dekker and Drayton only, September 1598), and *Pierce of Winchester* (July-August 1598). Dekker, Chettle, and William Haughton wrote *Patient Grissell* (January 1600). Dekker, Chettle, and John Day wrote *The Golden Ass, or Cupid and Psyche* (May 1600). Dekker, Day, and Haughton collaborated on *The Spanish Moor's Tragedy* (Spring 1600). Trios grew into quartets: Dekker, Chettle, Jonson, and another (perhaps John Marston) wrote *The Tragedy of Robert II, King of Scots* (September 1599); Dekker, Drayton, Chettle, and Wilson put together a two-part play titled *Earl Godwin and his Three Sons* between March and June 1598. In April of the same year, the same foursome was at work on *Pierce of Exton*, though this play may not have been finished. In May of that year they produced part 1 of *Black Bateman of the North* (Chettle and Wilson wrote part 2 a month later). Dekker, Chettle, Haughton, and Day wrote *The Seven Wise Masters* (March 1600); Dekker, Chettle, Thomas Heywood, and John Webster assembled *Christmas Comes but Once a Year* (November 1602). Quartets could bloom into quintets: Dekker, Chettle, Heywood, Webster, plus Wentworth Smith wrote part 1 of what may have been a projected two-part play dealing with Lady Jane Grey (titled *Lady Jane*, but also known, it seems, as *The Overthrow of Rebels*, autumn 1602). Dekker, Drayton, Munday, Wilson, and Richard Hathway wrote *Fair Constance of Rome*, part 1 (June 1600; whether or not part 2 was ever completed is uncertain). Dekker, Drayton, Munday, Webster, and Thomas Middleton together wrote *Caesar's Fall*, also known as *Two Shapes* (May 1602).

All but five of these plays are lost. *The Shoemakers' Holiday or the Gentle Craft, Old Fortunatus*, and *Patient Grissell* survive under their own titles. *Lady Jane* is preserved in part at least in the play ti-

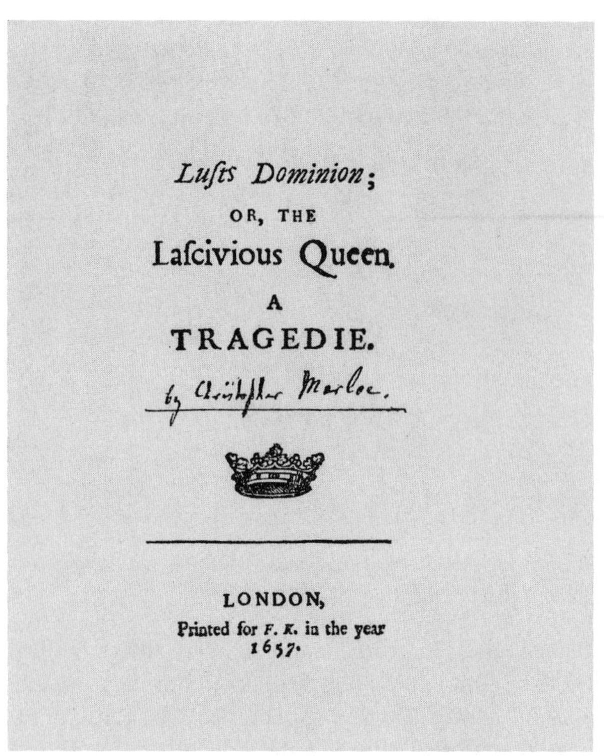
Lufts Dominion;

OR, THE

Lafcivious Queen.

A

TRAGEDIE.

LONDON,

Printed for *F. K.* in the year 1657.

Title page for the unique copy of the first issue of the 1657 quarto edition of the play that is probably The Spanish Moor's Tragedy, *produced at the Rose theater in 1600 (Library of Congress). The play was first attributed to Christopher Marlowe, but that attribution is now generally rejected.*

tled *Sir Thomas Wyatt. The Spanish Moor's Tragedy* is almost certainly the play now known as *Lust's Dominion.* It is possible that portions of one or another of Dekker's other plays for Henslowe are preserved in altered form in later work, either his own or another's. For example, two passages attributed to Dekker in Robert Allot's anthology of "the choicest flowers of our modern poets," *England's Parnassus* (1600), are reprinted in part in the 1636 text of Heywood's *Love's Mistress.* Two of Dekker's later plays, *The Noble Spanish Soldier* (circa 1622) and *The Wonder of a Kingdom* (circa 1623), seem to derive in some way from earlier collaborations with Day. Certain anonymous plays that survive either in printed editions or in manuscript (such as *The Telltale, Look About You, The Weakest Goeth to the Wall, The London Prodigal, Captain Thomas Stukeley, The Merry Devil of Edmonton*) have been claimed to be either wholly or partially Dekker's, but such claims, based as they are on stylistic evidence, are difficult to establish with any certainty.

Insofar as the titles of Dekker's lost plays yield any clues to their subjects, one gets the impression that he (like most of Henslowe's playwrights) could work in any dramatic genre. He wrote plays—or helped to write plays—on subjects drawn from English history (*The Famous Wars of Henry I, Earl Godwin, Lady Jane*), from recent European political events (*The Civil Wars of France* and *Sebastian, King of Portugal*), from classical legend (*Phaeton, Troilus and Cressida, Agamemnon,* and *The Golden Ass, or Cupid and Psyche*), from biblical history (*Jephthah*), and he could produce tragedy of various kinds (*The Stepmother's Tragedy, The Tragedy of Robert II, King of Scots,* to say nothing of *Agamemnon*) as well as comedy (*The Shoemakers' Holiday* and *Old Fortunatus* among his extant plays bear witness to this fact, and so presumably would such lost plays as *The Triangle (or Triplicity) of Cuckholds* and *A Medicine for a Curst Wife*). This sort of eclecticism is characteristic of the whole of his career as a dramatist.

What may be the earliest surviving example of Dekker's work is perhaps his contribution to a play not mentioned by Henslowe titled *Sir Thomas More,* a work commissioned, it would seem, by the joint companies of Lord Strange and the Lord Admiral during the period when they were acting together (circa 1590-1594). The play seems to have run into difficulties both with the company, which found it dramatically unsatisfactory, and with the Master of the Revels, who found it politically objectionable and declined to license it for production. The company attempted to salvage the play (the original version of which seems to have been the work of Munday) by hiring at least four different dramatists to revise or rewrite portions of it. The additions made to the play by way of revision have sometimes been dated as late as 1601, but a date circa 1593-1594 best fits the evidence. The manuscript of the play, together with the additions designed for it, is preserved in the British Library, London, and is one of the most important theatrical documents to survive from the Elizabethan period, not only for the notes by the censor that it contains concerning objectionable matter but for the handwriting of the various authors contained in the additions. One of the hands is almost certainly Shakespeare's, another may be Heywood's, a third is certainly Chettle's, and a fourth is certainly Dekker's (he seems to have revised one scene and added some thirty lines in his own hand).

The earliest surviving play of Dekker's sole authorship is *The Shoemakers' Holiday.* It is his most famous play, and it is one of his best. The setting is London, a place that Dekker found every

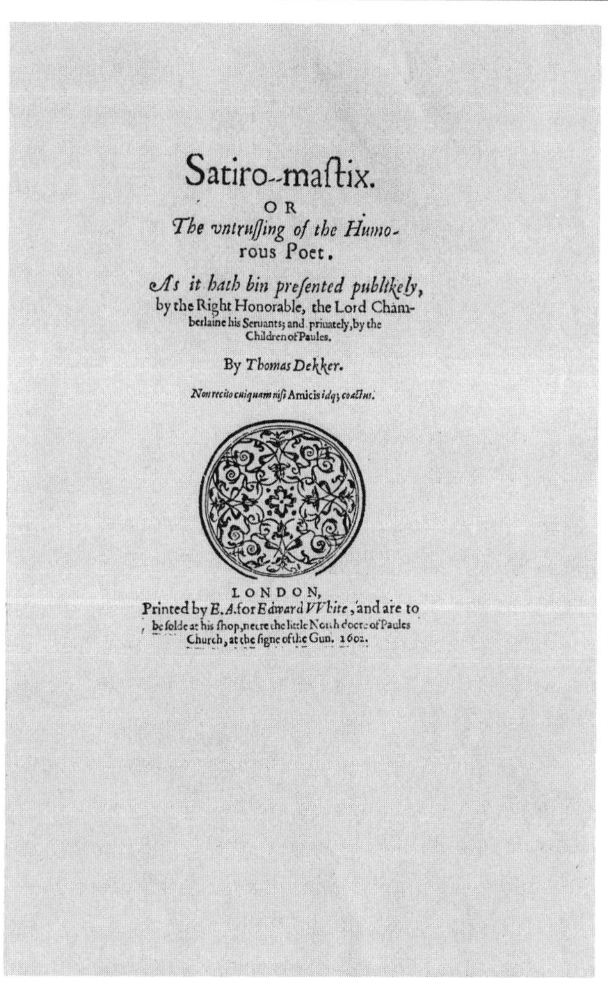

Satiro-mastix.

OR

The vntrussing of the Humorous Poet.

As it hath bin presented publikely, by the Right Honorable, the Lord Chamberlaine his Seruants; and priuately, by the Children of Paules.

By *Thomas Dekker.*

Non recito cuiquam nisi Amicis *idq; coactus.*

LONDON,
Printed by *E. A.* for *Edward VVhite*, and are to be solde at his shop, neere the little North doore of Paules Church, at the signe of the Gun. 1602.

Title page for the 1602 quarto edition of Dekker's contribution to the "war of the theaters," written in response to Ben Jonson's Every Man out of His Humour, Cynthia's Revels, *and* Poetaster *(Fredson Bowers, ed.,* The Dramatic Works of Thomas Dekker, *volume 1, 1953)*

bit as appropriate for the scene of a comedy as Shakespeare found the Forest of Arden in the exactly contemporary *As You Like It.* Here is a principal clue to the romantic quality of Dekker's literary imagination. Born and bred in London, he is as well acquainted with the city's capacity to breed vice and disease as he is with the daily toil required to make a living there; yet the city remained for him a place of wonders where honest industry combined with a shrewd business sense can raise a man from humble tradesman to offices of civic dignity, where the turbulence and chicanery of city life can issue in the festivity of a communal feast, and where a sense of social harmony and order are seen to be the direct result of those forces of good government with which England's capital city and England itself are blessed. At the end of *The Shoemakers' Holiday*, the King of England himself comes to the feast that Simon Eyre makes for his apprentices after he has risen from shoemaker to Lord Mayor of London. Like any Shakespearean comedy, *The Shoemakers' Holiday* has two pairs of lovers, and part of the play's comic design is to eliminate the obstacles to their love. One pair, Rafe and Jane, are distinctly proletarian. He is one of Simon Eyre's journeymen, and she is his humble wife. He is drafted for service in the wars in France, and word comes back that he is dead; but he returns, a cripple, just in time to save Jane from being forced into marriage with another. Differences of social class separate the other pair, Lacy and Rose, for a time. He is of the nobility, nephew to the Earl of Lincoln; she is but a citizen's daughter though her father is a wealthy citizen, being in fact the Lord Mayor of London who precedes Simon Eyre in that office. Their families oppose their match, and Lacy plays truant from his colonelcy in the English armies in France and remains in London, disguised as a Dutch shoemaker in the employment of Simon Eyre, in order to pursue his love. The King pardons him in the final scene, affirms the union of the pair, and reconciles their elders to their match. But it is the madcap, merry-hearted but worldly-wise Simon Eyre, with his lusty crew of singing and dancing apprentices swirling around him like so many attendant spirits of mischief, who is the center of the play, generating the air of festival and mirth and tolerant good cheer that is the life of the play. *The Shoemakers' Holiday* had the distinction of being acted at court before Queen Elizabeth I on New Year's night 1600. Something of its contemporary popularity is suggested by the six printed editions of the play's text that were published between 1600 and 1657. The play continues to be staged from time to time, the most notable twentieth-century productions being the one performed at the Old Vic theater in London in 1926 and the one presented by Orson Welles and John Houseman at the Mercury theater in New York in 1938.

Old Fortunatus presents a similar blend of moral earnestness and quirky humor, but it is a sterner play than *The Shoemakers' Holiday.* The spirit of revelry may rule in it for a season, but by the end a series of punishments has been meted out against those who have abused life's gifts and have willfully strayed from the path of virtue. The play has its source in the German folktale of Fortunatus, to whom the goddess of Fortune gives a purse that will never be empty of

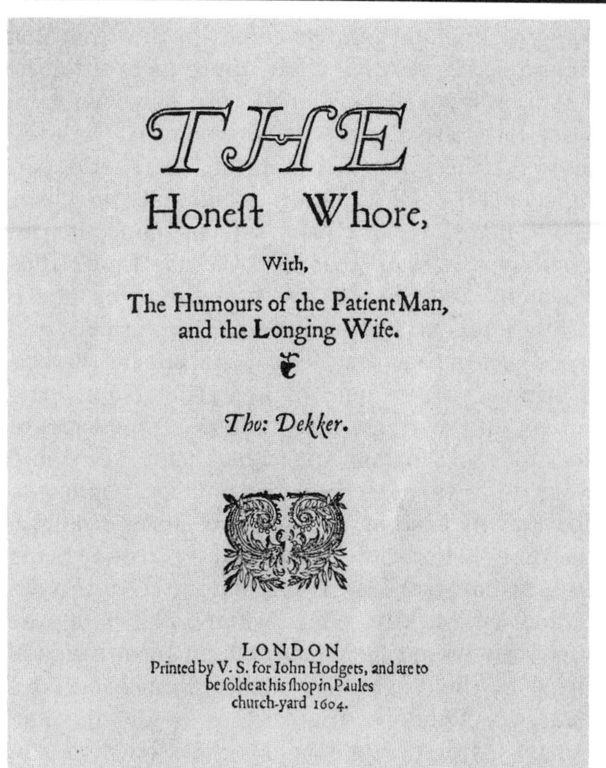

THE

Honeſt Whore,

With,

The Humours of the Patient Man,
and the Longing Wife.

Tho: Dekker.

LONDON
Printed by V. S. for Iohn Hodgets, and are to
be ſolde at his ſhop in Paules
church-yard 1604.

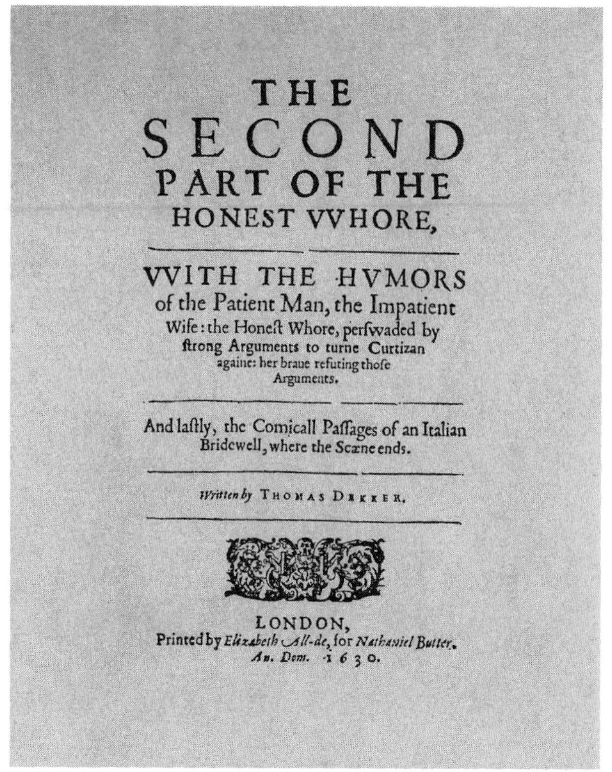

THE
SECOND
PART OF THE
HONEST VVHORE,

VVITH THE HVMORS
of the Patient Man, the Impatient
Wife: the Honeſt Whore, perſwaded by
ſtrong Arguments to turne Curtizan
againe: her braue refuting thoſe
Arguments.

And laſtly, the Comicall Paſſages of an Italian
Bridewell, where the Scæne ends.

Written by THOMAS DEKKER.

LONDON,
Printed by *Elizabeth All-de*, for *Nathaniel Butter*.
An. Dom. 1630.

Title pages for the first 1604 quarto edition of part 1 and the only quarto edition of part 2 (1630) of Dekker's play about the reformation of a prostitute and her efforts to maintain her virtue (Fredson Bowers, ed., The Dramatic Works of Thomas Dekker, *volume 2, 1955). Both parts were written in 1604-1605, the first with the assistance of Thomas Middleton.*

money. To this treasure Fortunatus adds another, a wonderful hat which will convey the wearer to any point in the world where he wishes to be (Fortunatus has stolen it from the Soldan of Babylon). When midway through the play Fortunatus dies, he leaves the purse and the hat to his two sons, and the last half of the play traces the manner in which the gifts reduce them to wretchedness and death. Like *The Shoemakers' Holiday, Old Fortunatus* was acted at court in the presence of the Queen during the Christmas season 1599-1600. Henslowe's records indicate that Dekker was paid to make alterations in the play for the court performance, and these are preserved in the printed edition that appeared in 1600. They include a prologue and an epilogue, each consisting of a dialogue in praise of the Queen and her court; and a specially designed ending to the play, wherein the Queen is complimented when the debate among Fortune, Vice, and Virtue as to which is most powerful is referred directly to her for a decision. In her presence Vice flees, and Fortune admits herself overcome by the Queen's superior power, leaving Virtue, who represents what the Queen herself embodies, the victor.

Henslowe's records indicate that most of the work on *Patient Grissell* was done by all three collaborators (Dekker, Chettle, and Haughton) during the last weeks of December 1599. On 26 January 1600 Henslowe recorded payment of twenty shillings "to buy a grey gown for Grissell," so presumably the play was on the stage shortly thereafter. The story of patient Griselda was already famous in European literature. Giovanni Boccaccio had told it in the closing tale of the *Decameron*, and Geoffrey Chaucer's Clerk had related it in English in *The Canterbury Tales*. The figure of Griselda—raised from the condition of her humble birth to high estate through marriage to a marquess who, though he loves her, persists in subjecting her to repeated trials in order to test her constancy—had become for Renaissance writers something of an exemplum for Christian humility and patience and for the rewards that attend on the successful pursuit of these virtues. Griselda never demurs at the trials to which she is put, and her devotion to her husband remains steadfast despite her distress at his repeated testings. By the time Dekker and his collaborators wrote their play, her story was well known in ballad and song and drama of a moralizing bent.

Dekker's share in the play seems to have been chiefly confined to the treatment of Grissell's family: her simple, loving father, who stands staunchly by her through all her adversities; her brother, who strongly resents the marquess's treatment of her; and their devoted clown of a serving man.

The two other plays that survive from this period of Dekker's work for Henslowe are *Lady Jane* (in the play now known as *Sir Thomas Wyatt*) and *The Spanish Moor's Tragedy* (in the play now known as *Lust's Dominion*). *Sir Thomas Wyatt* treats of events from English history of half a century before: the plot to put Lady Jane Grey on the English throne upon the death of King Edward VI in 1553, together with the failure of this plan and the accession of Mary Tudor to the crown, and the subsequent rebellion of Sir Thomas Wyatt in protest against the Queen's alliance (specifically through her marriage to Philip of Spain) with foreign Roman Catholic powers. The text in which the play is preserved has been severely cut and may represent an abridgement of an original two-part play; further, the surviving text seems to have been put together from memory by a group of actors, and much of it is badly garbled. It is impossible to determine with any real precision Dekker's share in the play as it stands.

Lust's Dominion seems to be a revision of an older play. It is a revenge tragedy of the sort that came into vogue in the late 1580s with such plays as Thomas Kyd's *Spanish Tragedy*, Christopher Marlowe's *Jew of Malta*, and Shakespeare's *Titus Andronicus*. Eleazer the Moor of *Lust's Dominion* (presumably the titular figure of the play's original title, *The Spanish Moor's Tragedy*) is closely modeled on Aaron the Moor in Shakespeare's *Titus Andronicus*, and the Queen Mother of Spain, whose lust for him wrecks the kingdom, is a copy of Tamora, Queen of the Goths, whose erotic involvement with Aaron is the source of much of the violence that descends on Rome in Shakespeare's early tragedy. Henslowe's records suggest that the play was being worked on in the course of the fall and winter of 1599-1600, and that in addition to Dekker, Day, and Haughton, a fourth dramatist, Marston, may have had a hand in it. There is some internal evidence from vocabulary and idiom for Marston's presence in the play. The point is of some importance for it provides our only basis for associating Dekker and Marston, and it is just at this time that the two playwrights come under attack from Ben Jonson, who parades them through three of his plays as a singularly ill-matched pair of would-be poet-dramatists.

Jonson's attack began with his *Every Man out of His Humour* (in existence by April 1600), continued in *Cynthia's Revels* (in existence by May 1601), and reached a virulent peak in *Poetaster* (in existence by December 1601). Marston seems to have been Jonson's original target: the language of his recent satiric poems (*Certain Satires* and *The Scourge of Villainy*, both published in 1598) had brought him a certain notoriety; Jonson parodies it in Clove's speeches in act 3 of *Every Man out of His Humour.* Marston had recently begun to write for the theater, urged in that direction perhaps by the ban on satire in June 1599, when his own books had been prominent among others of a scandalous or politically subversive nature that had been called in by the censor and burned. Two more disparate figures than Dekker and Marston are hard to imagine: Dekker with his humble London background, toiling away for a living in Henslowe's factory; Marston, son of an old Shropshire family, educated at Oxford and now living in London, leading the privileged life of a member of the Middle Temple, where he was supposedly preparing himself for a legal career. The depiction of the pair in *Every Man out of His Humour* as the extravagantly verbal Clove (Dekker) and Orange (Marston), his all-but-silent companion who only speaks clichés, was but a preliminary sketch for what would follow. In *Cynthia's Revels*, Hedon (Marston) is presented as a frivolous fop, given over entirely to the pursuit of voluptuous pleasures. Anaides (Dekker), his constant companion, is a coarser type whose impudence and ignorance are stressed; he is much given to ridiculing what he does not understand. Both are notably envious of the honorable Crites, whom contemporary audiences regarded as Jonson's flattering portrait of himself. Hedon and Anaides try to detract from Crites' reputation for virtue, but to no avail, and they are increasingly frustrated by the high-minded manner in which he rises above their mean-spirited efforts to slander him. *Poetaster* contains the most open attack on the pair. Again Marston is represented as a reveler who plays at being a poet when he is not gossiping or flirting; he is now called Crispinus. In need of money, he takes to writing for the players, and it is through them that he meets Demetrius (Dekker), a down-at-the-heels hack, described at one point as "a dresser of plays about the town," where "dresser" is an apt description of the alterations often performed by Dekker and his cowork-

THE
WHORE OF
BABYLON.

As it was acted by the Princes
Seruants.

Vexat Censura Columbas.

Written by THOMAS DEKKER.

LONDON
Printed for Nathaniel Butter.
1607.

Title page for the 1607 quarto edition of Dekker's dramatic response to the discovery of the Gunpowder Plot, an allegory in which Titania (Elizabeth I) triumphs over the Empress of Babylon (the Roman Catholic church) (Fredson Bowers, ed., The Dramatic Works of Thomas Dekker, *volume 2, 1955)*

ers on old plays being refurbished as new ones to be acted in Henslowe's theaters. The envy and hatred directed by Hedon and Anaides against Crites in *Cynthia's Revels* is now directed by Crispinus and Demetrius against Horace (another piece of Jonsonian self-portraiture) in *Poetaster.* In the end both are accused of slander and found guilty: in a famous scene, pills are administered to Crispinus, who shortly vomits up the more outrageous gobbets of his vocabulary; Demetrius is forgiven but made to wear a fool's coat and cap; both are made to take an oath never again to slander Horace.

Much is made in *Poetaster* of a play attacking Horace that a company of players has hired Demetrius to write; Crispinus is hired to help him with it. Such a play—Dekker's *Satiromastix* (1601)—in fact was written. Marston may (and probably did) help with the strategy of counterattack, but there is no evidence in the extant text of the play that he participated in the actual writing. He was busy throughout this period with his own responses to Jonson, in *Jack Drum's Entertainment* and *What You Will.* Dekker, in *Satiromastix,* replied to Jonson's satiric attacks by simply appropriating the two characters—Crispinus and Demetrius—who had been the vehicles of Jonson's satire, together with Jonson's admiring representation of himself in the figure of the high-minded Horace. Crispinus, Demetrius, and Horace all appear in *Satiromastix,* but their characters are completely changed. Here Crispinus and Demetrius are sober, responsible young men who look on in dismay as Horace (who is represented as a toady to the rich and powerful) demeans the genuine poetic talent which they acknowledge him to possess as he scrambles after wealthy patrons and vilifies anyone whom he suspects of standing in his way. *Satiromastix* makes the pretense that the bill of complaints drawn up against Jonson/Horace is lodged more in sorrow than in anger; but the complaints are pressed firmly, and in detail. His associates make it clear to the Horace of *Satiromastix* that they are tired of indulging him in his hypocrisy, tired of the high moral line he takes with all the world but never lives up to himself, tired of his efforts to pass himself off as a fearless champion of virtue when in fact he is as vicious as the next man and a sniveling coward into the bargain. As a piece of satiric retaliation, *Satiromastix* is an extremely clever play, and its effect seems to have been devastating: at any rate, Jonson made no attempt to answer it, and Dekker may be said to have had the last word in the famous war of the theaters.

This "stage quarrel" has been much discussed in histories of the Elizabethan theater. There was of course more to it than the quarrel between Jonson on the one hand and Marston and Dekker on the other. On the basic level of box-office economics, it was a competition for London theater audiences. Essentially, the competition was between companies of adult actors, performing in large, open-air public theaters such as the Globe (where Shakespeare's plays were being acted at this time) or those owned by Henslowe, and companies of child actors performing in smaller, enclosed, private theaters where the price of admission was higher and the general tone of the audience more fashionable than at the public theaters. Companies of child actors (the children were choirboys) had performed in

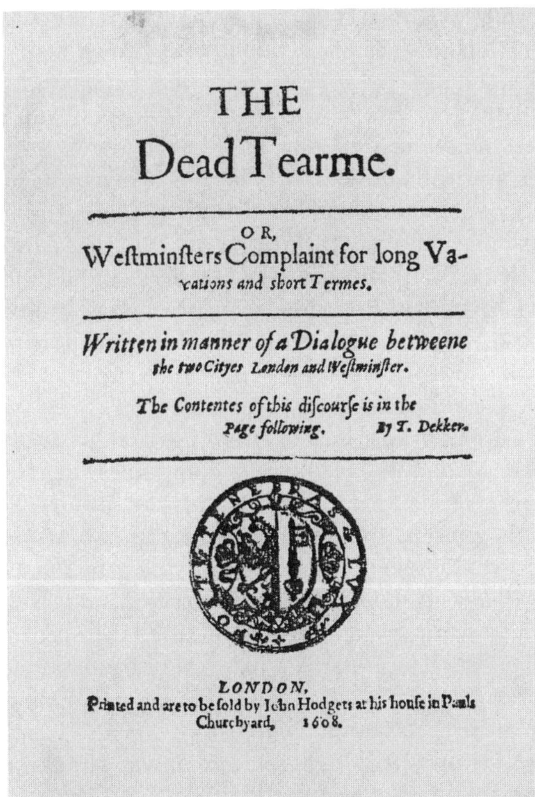
THE
Dead Tearme.
OR,
Weſtminſters Complaint for long Vacations and ſhort Termes.
Written in manner of a Dialogue betweene the two Cityes London and Weſtminſter.
The Contentes of this diſcourſe is in the Page following. By T. Dekker.
LONDON.
Printed and are to be ſold by Iohn Hodgets at his houſe in Pauls Churchyard, 1608.

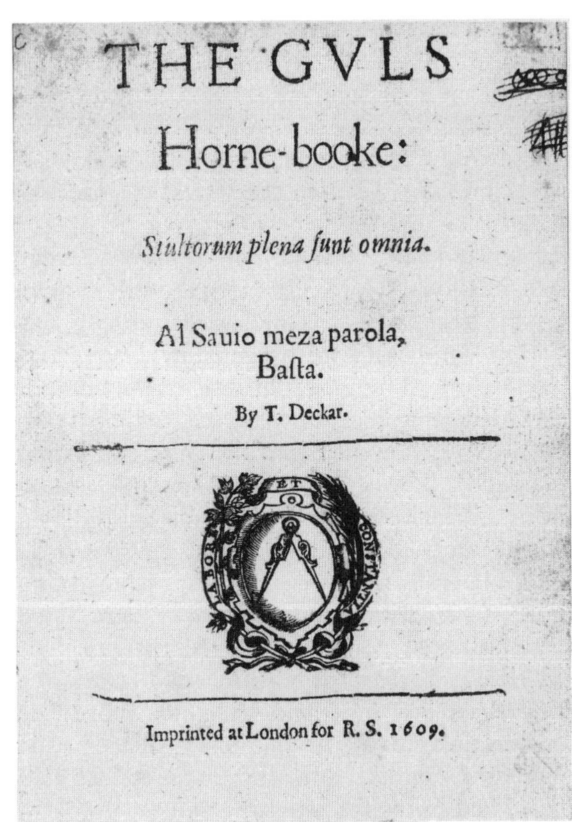
THE GVLS
Horne-booke:
Stultorum plena ſunt omnia.
Al Sauio meza parola, Baſta.
By T. Deckar.
Imprinted at London for R. S. 1609.

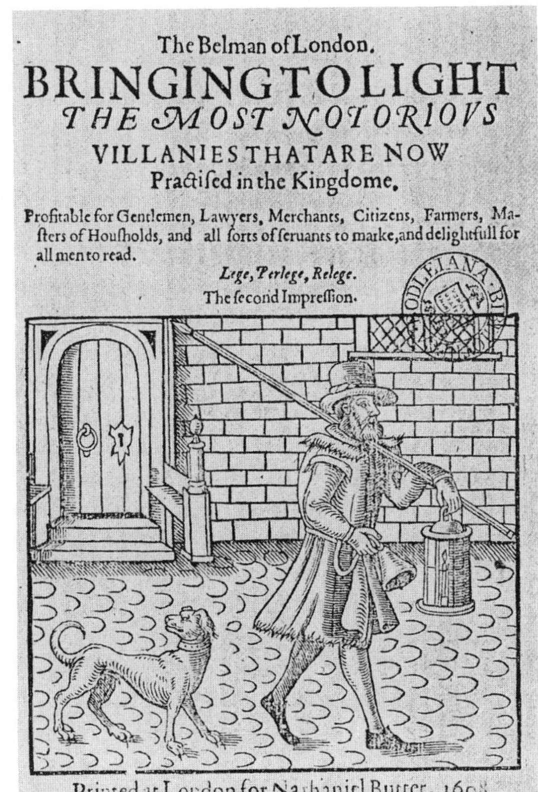
The Belman of London.
BRINGING TO LIGHT
THE MOST NOTORIOVS
VILLANIES THAT ARE NOW
Practiſed in the Kingdome.
Profitable for Gentlemen, Lawyers, Merchants, Citizens, Farmers, Maſters of Houſholds, and all ſorts of ſeruants to marke, and delightfull for all men to read.
Lege, Perlege, Relege.
The ſecond Impreſſion.
Printed at London for Nathaniel Butter. 1608.

LANTHORNE
and Candle-light.
Or
The Bell-mans ſecond Nights walke.
In which
Hee brings to light, a Broode of more ſtrange Villanies, then euer were till this yeare diſcouered.
--Decet nouiſſe malum; feciſſe, nefandum.
By Thomas Dekker.
LONDON
Printed for Iohn Busbie, and are to be ſold at his ſhop in Fleet-ſtreet, in Saint Dunſtans Church-yard.
1608.

Title pages for four of the prose pamphlets Dekker wrote between 1605 and 1611 (top left: Anderson Galleries auction catalogue, sale number 2077, 20-21 May 1926; top right: Henry E. Huntington Library and Art Gallery; bottom left and right: Bodleian Library)

London before, but not for nearly a decade, when in 1599 the Children of Paul's began to perform plays in their song school near St. Paul's Cathedral; the following year the Children of the Chapel Royal began to perform in Blackfriars. A novelty on the London theatrical scene, the children's companies enjoyed a vogue in the years around the turn of the century. Shakespeare, in *Hamlet* (II.ii.), alludes to the stiff competition the companies of boy actors were giving the adult companies in, presumably, the season of 1600-1601. The stage history of *Satiromastix* (performed it would seem in the fall of 1601) makes it clear, however, that the competition was not simply between child and adult acting troupes performing respectively in private and public theaters. There also seems to have been rivalry between the two children's companies. Jonson's *Cynthia's Revels* and *Poetaster* were acted by the Chapel Children at Blackfriars. *Satiromastix* was performed both by child actors in a private theater (Paul's) and by adult actors (the Chamberlain's Men) in a public theater (the Globe). *Satiromastix*, with the prospect it held forth to audiences for satirizing Jonson the well-known satirist, must have seemed a sufficiently promising box-office success for Paul's Boys and the Chamberlain's Men, erstwhile rivals, to join forces in a common enterprise.

From the summer of 1600 to the end of 1601, Dekker's name appears less and less frequently in Henslowe's records, and the title page of *Satiromastix*, with its advertisement that the play had been acted by both Paul's and the Chamberlain's companies, suggests why: Dekker had begun to write for other companies besides Henslowe's. His only recorded play for Henslowe during the whole of 1601 is a collaboration with Chettle (*Sebastian, King of Portugal*) in May. But sometime during the late fall or winter of 1601-1602, presumably in the aftermath of his *Satiromastix* assignment, he wrote another play for Paul's, a comedy titled *Blurt, Master Constable* (it was in existence by 7 June 1602 when it was licensed for printing). No author is named on the title page of the only edition of the play, and it was long attributed to Thomas Middleton. Only in recent years have scholars put forth an argument in support of Dekker's authorship of *Blurt, Master Constable*, and it is now generally acknowledged to be his (it may be a collaboration with Middleton, but if so, Middleton's share is a relatively small one). The play is unlike any of Dekker's extant work to this time, but that is not surprising in view of the fact that it was written for a private theater and not a public one. It is a fashionable comedy, populated with witty ladies and the elegant gentlemen who are their lovers and the pert maids and cheeky pages who serve the ladies and the gentlemen. There is also a collection of low-comedy figures including the bumbling constable who gives the play its title and who is modeled on Shakespeare's Dogberry, and a fantastical Spaniard (referred to in the play's subtitle) whose efforts to make his way through the thickets of amorous intrigue which make up the play's plot are ridiculed.

Dekker resumed something like his former work load for Henslowe's companies in 1602. Henslowe records payments to him for one sort of assignment or another throughout that year: for providing a prologue and epilogue for *Pontius Pilate* in January; for altering *Tasso's Melancholy* in January (and for "mending" it in November and December); for collaborating with Munday on *Jephthah* in early May; for collaborating with Drayton, Middleton, Webster, and Munday on *Caesar's Fall* or *Two Shapes* later in the same month; for writing his own *A Medicine for a Curst Wife* from mid July to the beginning of September; for providing new additions to *Sir John Oldcastle* in August and September; for work on *Lady Jane* in October; for collaborating on *Christmas Comes but Once a Year* with Heywood, Webster, and Chettle in November.

Performances in all London theaters abruptly ceased on 19 March 1603, when Queen Elizabeth I became gravely ill; she died on 24 March. The theaters had hardly reopened following the period of official mourning before they were closed again on account of the plague, which had been raging since early April. They remained closed throughout the rest of the year and until the spring of 1604. Dekker, with his means of livelihood from the stage temporarily shut off, turned to writing nondramatic pamphlets. The first of these, *The Wonderful Year*, appeared near the end of 1603. It presents a vivid account of the changing climates of feeling during the events of the past momentous year: the anxiety of the opening months as the Queen's death approached; the relief felt throughout the land when James VI of Scotland succeeded peacefully to the English throne as James I; the sense of relief interrupted when the plague descended on the capital city like some heaven-sent reminder of the loss the land had suffered in the death of the great Queen. The latter half of *The Wonderful*

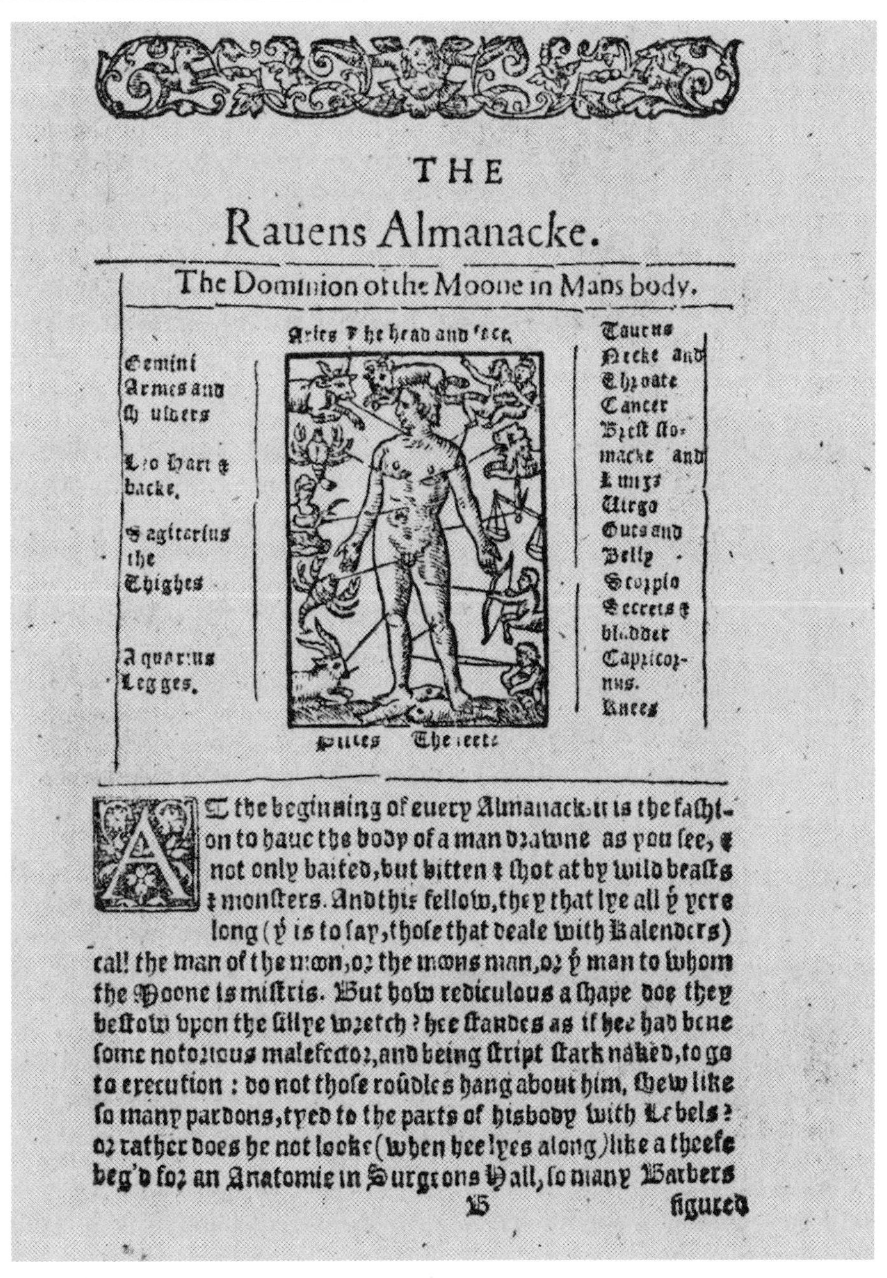

THE

Rauens Almanacke.

The Dominion of the Moone in Mans body.

Aries The head and face.

Gemini Armes and Shoulders

Leo Hart & backe.

Sagitarius the Thighes

Aquarius Legges.

Taurus Necke and Throate

Cancer Brest stomacke and Lungs

Virgo Guts and Belly

Scorpio Secrets & bladder

Capricornus. Knees

Pisces The feete.

AT the beginning of euery Almanacke, it is the fashion to haue the body of a man drawne as you see, & not only baited, but bitten & shot at by wild beasts & monsters. And this fellow, they that lye all ẏ yere long (ẏ is to say, those that deale with Kalenders) call the man of the moon, or the moons man, or ẏ man to whom the Moone is mistris. But how rediculous a shape doe they bestow vpon the sillye wretch? hee standes as if hee had bene some notorious malefactor, and being stript stark naked, to go to execution: do not those roũdles hang about him, shew like so many pardons, tyed to the parts of his body with Lebels? or rather does he not looke (when hee lyes along) like a theefe beg'd for an Anatomie in Surgeons Hall, so many Barbers

B figured

First page of text from Dekker's almanac "foretelling of a plague, famine, and civill warre" for 1609 (Bodleian Library)

Year presents (as the title page advertises) "the picture of London lying sick of the plague"; it is a grimly moving account of the appalling death tolls, and of the gallantry that the citizens of London displayed in enduring their ordeal. Early in 1604 Dekker published two further pamphlets dealing with London life during the plague: *News from Gravesend* and *The Meeting of Gallants at an Ordinary* (perhaps with Middleton).

The plague had caused the postponement of the coronation of King James, originally scheduled for the summer of 1603. It eventually took place on 15 March 1604, and the dramatists commissioned by the City of London to devise the pageants and compose the poetic speeches that would comprise the occasion were, ironically enough, Dekker and Ben Jonson. They had evidently not made their peace in the years since the stage quarrel, for Jonson published his share of the so-called *Magnificent Entertainment* separately, and when Dekker published the text of his own share together with a description of the

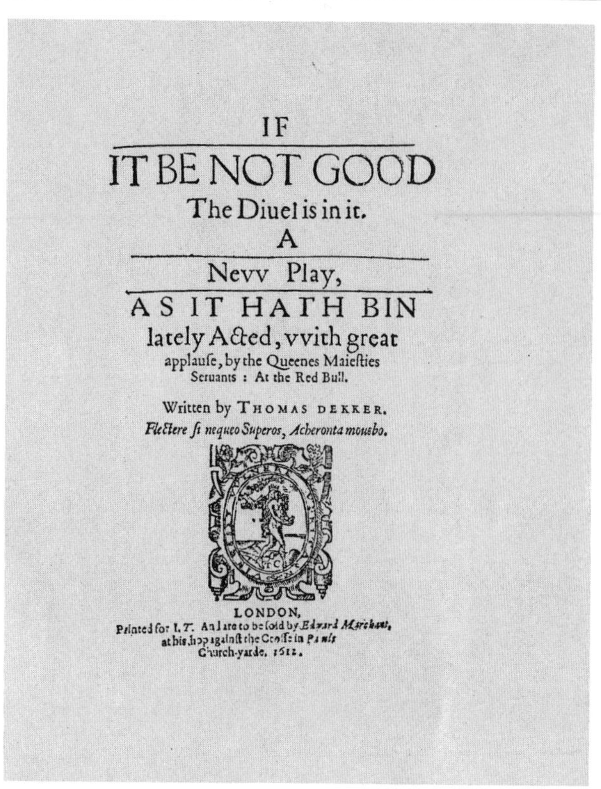

IF
IT BE NOT GOOD
The Diuel is in it.
A
Nevv Play,
AS IT HATH BIN
lately Acted, vvith great
applauſe, by the Queenes Maieſties
Seruants : At the Red Bull.

Written by THOMAS DEKKER.
Flectere ſi nequeo Superos, Acheronta mouebo.

LONDON,
Printed for I. T. And are to be ſold by *Edward Marchant*,
at his ſhop againſt the Croſſe in *Pauls*
Church-yarde. 1612.

Title page for the 1612 quarto edition of the play that marked the end of Dekker's association with the Prince's Men (Fredson Bowers, ed., The Dramatic Works of Thomas Dekker, *volume 3, 1958)*

whole affair, he merely summarized Jonson's contribution without naming him. He was careful, however, to acknowledge the share of Middleton, who contributed one speech to Dekker's part. Dekker's association with Middleton, which may have begun with *Blurt, Master Constable* in 1601, is a matter of record by the spring of 1604. At the same time Middleton was assisting Dekker with *The Magnificent Entertainment* he was also collaborating with him on a play that is now known as part 1 of the two-part play titled *The Honest Whore.* Henslowe's records for what had been the Admiral's Men but now, since the accession of James I, was known as Prince Henry's Men, end with his entry for 14 March 1604; just before this final entry, he records payments to Dekker and Middleton for a play called "The Patient Man and the Honest Whore." It is one of Dekker's best (Middleton's share in it is comparatively small): a romantic, somewhat sentimental, but fiercely earnest account of the prostitute Bellafront's conversion to the ways of virtue, and her determined effort to persist in her reform despite all sensual and economic pressures to revert to her former life. The play's sequel, *The Honest Whore*, part 2, is entirely the work of Dekker. It continues Bellafront's uphill battle to preserve her integrity, and it is chiefly notable for two of Dekker's finest pieces of characterization: that of Orlando Friscobaldo, Bellafront's father, who renounced her when she became a fallen woman and is skeptical when he hears of her conversion but is gradually brought to believe in the sincerity of her repentance and is reconciled with her; and that of Matheo, the lively but entirely unprincipled rogue who first led Bellafront astray and who, in her converted state, she feels constrained to marry.

During 1604-1605 Dekker was writing both for the Prince's Men (which produced the two parts of *The Honest Whore*) and for the Children of Paul's. For the latter company, near the end of 1604, he and John Webster (with whom he had worked on *Lady Jane/Sir Thomas Wyatt*) wrote *Westward Ho*, a satiric comedy set in contemporary London and dealing with the manner in which a group of citizens' wives outwit the amorous designs that a group of gallants have on them. It seems to have been popular enough to cause the rival comedy of boy actors, the Children of Her Majesty's Revels, performing at the Blackfriars, to produce a similar kind of comedy with a similar title, *Eastward Ho* (a three-part collaboration by Jonson, Chapman, and Marston, who was now reconciled with Jonson). The notoriety of this play (its unflattering remarks about the Scots brought down on the company the wrath of King James) must have encouraged Dekker and Webster to write another comedy of London life, this time titled *Northward Ho*, a lively account of how age outwits youth when a young gallant tries to seduce the virtuous wife of a London citizen. Dekker's remaining play for this period is *The Whore of Babylon*, acted by the Prince's Men and written either in late 1605 or early 1606. The play is a product of the anti-Roman Catholic passions that gripped England in the weeks following the discovery of the Gunpowder Plot in November 1605. It bears similarities with Dekker's anti-Roman tract, *The Double PP*, published in December 1606, in which the double *P* of the title alludes to the Pope. *The Whore of Babylon* is a religious and historical allegory. Its heroine is Titania (Queen Elizabeth I), and it dramatizes the many plots engineered by her enemy, the Empress of Babylon (the Roman church) to assassinate her and subvert her country and its religion.

The Whore of Babylon seems to have been Dekker's last play for some five years. Perfor-

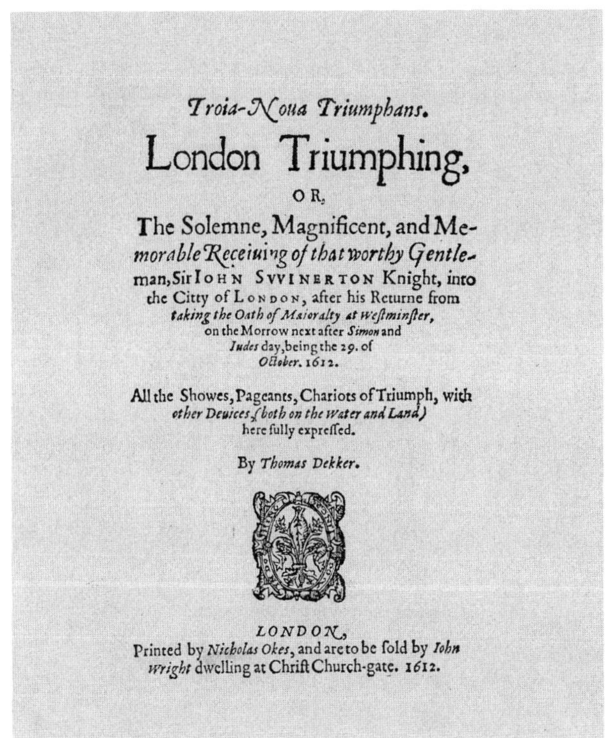

Troia-Noua Triumphans.

London Triumphing,

OR,

The Solemne, Magnificent, and Memorable *Receiuing of that worthy Gentleman*, Sir IOHN SVVINERTON Knight, into the Citty of LONDON, after his Returne from *taking the Oath of Maioralty at Westminster*, on the Morrow next after *Simon* and *Iudes* day, being the 29. of *October*. 1612.

All the Showes, Pageants, Chariots of Triumph, with *other Deuices, (both on the Water and Land)* here fully expressed.

By *Thomas Dekker*.

LONDON,

Printed by *Nicholas Okes*, and are to be sold by *Iohn Wright* dwelling at Christ Church-gate. 1612.

Title page for the 1612 quarto edition of Dekker's first Lord Mayor's pageant (Fredson Bowers, ed., The Dramatic Works of Thomas Dekker, *volume 3, 1958)*

mances by the Paul's Boys gradually ceased after the summer of 1606 (the company came to an end in 1608), and this may have had something to do with Dekker's decision to give over (temporarily at least) writing for the stage. But it is also possible that he was discovering that writing his nondramatic pamphlets was more profitable than writing plays. In any case, it would seem (unless he wrote some plays that have vanished without a trace) that his pamphlets occupied him exclusively during the next five years. He turned out at least ten of them during this period: *News from Hell* (1606; revised in the following year as *A Knight's Conjuring*), *The Seven Deadly Sins of London* (1606), *Jests to Make You Merry* (1607, with George Wilkins), *The Dead Term* (1608), *The Bellman of London* (1608), *Lanthorn and Candlelight* (1608), *Four Birds of Noah's Ark* (1609), *The Gull's Hornbook* (1609), *The Raven's Almanac* (1609), and *Work for Armorers* (1609). *Four Birds of Noah's Ark* is a collection of prayers and meditations. The rest are, in effect, journalistic essays and narratives on various aspects of the contemporary London scene, written in a vein that is by turns pleasantly humorous, satiric, didactic, and grotesquely jocular. The pamphlets are invaluable for the detailed evidence they provide concerning Jacobean London and its people. There are depictions of the city and its neighbor, Westminster, bustling with activity when the law courts are in session and all but deserted during the long summer vacation (*The Dead Term*); there are lively accounts of the latest fashions and fads and villanies (*News from Hell, The Raven's Almanac*); exposés of the confidence games—the so-called cony-catching schemes—practiced by rogues (*The Bellman of London, Lanthorn and Candlelight*); a shrewd appraisal of the social gulf that separates poverty and wealth (*Work for Armorers*); an account of an average day in the life of a would-be gentleman of fashion (*The Gull's Hornbook*). *The Bellman of London* and its sequel, *Lanthorn and Candlelight*, were immensely successful. *The Bellman of London* went through four separate editions in the year of its publication and appeared in subsequent editions in 1616 and 1640. *Lanthorn and Candlelight*, after its original edition in 1608, immediately went into a revised second edition in 1609; thereafter, Dekker periodically revised and expanded it in new editions with differing titles throughout the rest of his life: in 1612 (when it appeared as *O per se o, or a new crier of Lanthorn and Candlelight*); in 1616 (as *Villanies Discovered by Lanthorn and Candlelight*; reprinted with slight additions in 1620); in 1632 (as *English Villanies;* reprinted in 1638 and 1648). Dekker's indebtedness in *The Bellman of London* and *Lanthorn and Candlelight* to Robert Greene's cony-catching pamphlets of the early 1590s is considerable, but he manages to update Greene's material to a degree that stamps both works with his own distinctive style. The Elizabethan predecessor to whom that style owes most is Thomas Nash. Dekker is not so aggressively witty as Nash, and his satire is not so devastating; there is a gentleness, sometimes a sentimentality, in Dekker's nondramatic pamphlets that is quite foreign to the work of Nash; but Nash's verbal fecundity, the torrents of epithets and extravagantly developed metaphors that proceed from his pen by a sort of free association, clearly provided the rhetorical model that Dekker sought to emulate.

Dekker returned to writing for the stage in the spring of 1611 with *The Roaring Girl*, a collaboration with Middleton based on a contemporary figure, Mary Frith, known as Moll Cutpurse, who had achieved a certain notoriety for her exploits on the fringes of the London underworld. *The Roaring Girl* was acted by the Prince's Men, but a prefatory note to the published text of Dekker's next play, *If This Be Not a Good Play, the Devil Is in*

It, written in the summer of 1611, indicates that a breach had occurred between the author and the company with which he had been associated for well over a decade. The Prince's Men seem to have rejected *If This Be Not a Good Play,* and it is in fact one of Dekker's weakest plays: an uneasy combination of raucous humor and moral didacticism concerning three devils sent to earth by Satan to corrupt mankind, and finding themselves outdone by mankind's superior deviltry. The play was performed by the Queen's Men at the Red Bull theater.

In October 1612 Dekker was commissioned to prepare the pageant celebrating the inauguration of London's new Lord Mayor (an annual event, occurring each October twenty-ninth). His pageant, *Troia-Nova Triumphans,* has for its motif the myth of London's founding by descendants of the ancient Trojans, who called their capital city Troynovant or New Troy: a myth that Dekker frequently alludes to in his nondramatic works. Not long after this, however, in Michaelmas Term 1612, Dekker's fortunes took a ruinous turn when he was arrested for debt and committed to the King's Bench prison. There he remained for nearly seven years. Though his career as a playwright was brought to a halt, he did manage to do a certain amount of literary work during these years. In 1616 he wrote a poetical pamphlet, *The Artillery Garden,* praising the London militia, in the dedication to which he alludes to his present imprisonment. In the same year he brought out a new edition of *Lanthorn and Candlelight* to which he added six new chapters dealing, appropriately enough, with prison life. In one of these he states that he has been in prison for more than three years. There is reason to believe that he contributed six new character descriptions (of "A Prison, A Prisoner, A Creditor, A Sargeant, His Yeoman, and A Jailor") to the ninth impression of Sir Thomas Overbury's collection *Sir Thomas Overbury His Wife, with New Elegies,* published in 1616. He may have contributed as well to *Certain Characters and Essays of Prisons and Prisoners,* compiled by Geoffray Mynshul, his fellow prisoner in the King's Bench, and published in 1618. Dekker was apparently released from prison sometime before 11 October 1619, when another of his poetical pamphlets, *Dekker his Dream,* was entered in the Stationers' Register (it was published in 1620). In the preface to it he refers to "the bed on which seven years [he] lay dreaming," and to the "long sleep, which for almost seven years together, seized all [his] senses."

THE VIRGIN MARTIR, A TRAGEDIE.

AS IT HATH BIN DIVERS times publickely Acted with great Applaufe,

By the feruants of his Maieflies Reuels.

Written by Phillip Meffenger and Thomas Decker.

LONDON, Printed by Bernard Alfop for Thomas Iones. 1622.

Title page for the 1622 quarto edition of the play that Dekker and Philip Massinger based on the life of Saint Dorothea (Fredson Bowers, ed., The Dramatic Works of Thomas Dekker, *volume 3, 1958)*

Dekker seems to have resumed his playwriting activities by collaborating with Philip Massinger on a dramatization of the life of Saint Dorothea in a play titled *The Virgin Martyr,* licensed for acting on 6 October 1620. The play is a strange and often disconcerting mixture of tender sentiment and raucous vulgarity. The mixture is in some degree inherent in the saint's life on which the play is based; most of those among whom Dorothea dwells in the still-pagan Roman world that she inhabits would violate her if they could. Most of the low-comedy scenes involving Dorothea's two vicious servants (one described as a drunkard and the other as a whoremaster) and the evil spirit who savagely urges on her chief persecutor are Dekker's, but so too is the gently lyrical scene between Dorothea and the angelic spirit who serves her: a passage that prompted Charles Lamb's famous assertion that Dekker "had poetry enough for anything." The play was acted by the company at the Red Bull (where Dekker's last play before his imprisonment, *If This Be Not a Good Play,* had been performed) and was evidently successful. There were editions printed in 1622, 1631, 1651, and 1661. Though the Red

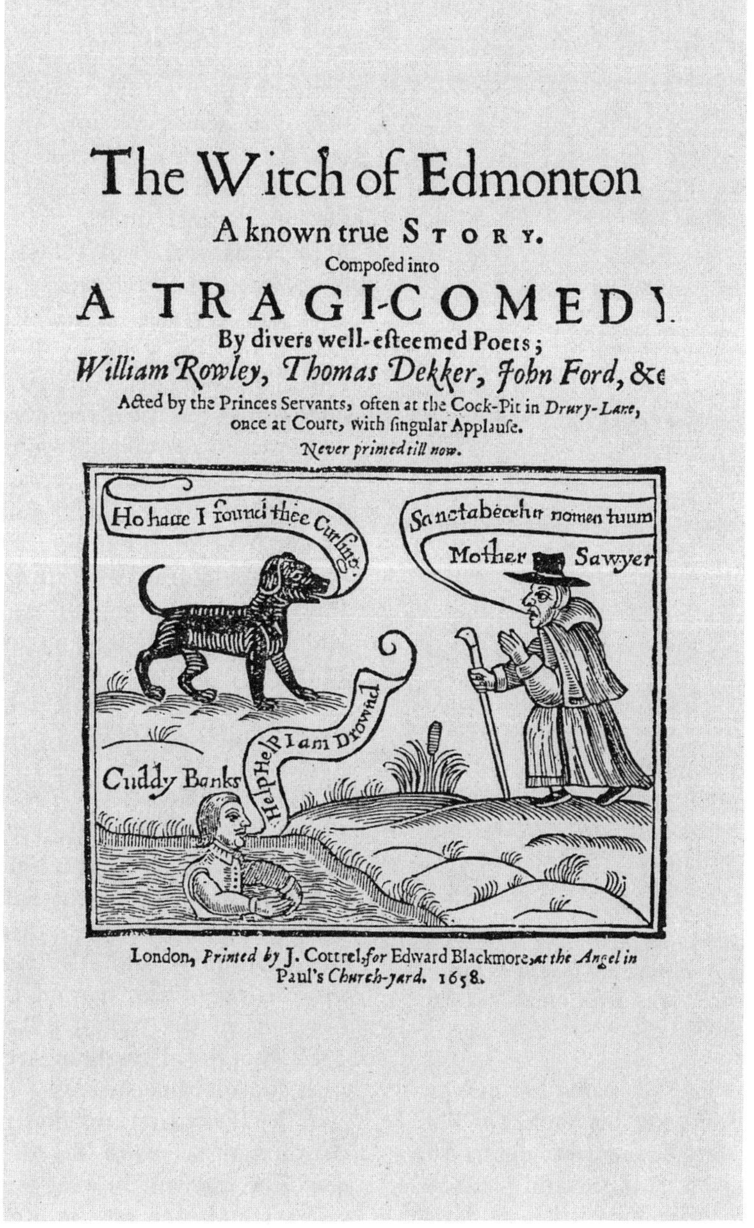

The Witch of Edmonton

A known true STORY.

Compoſed into

A TRAGI-COMEDY.

By divers well-eſteemed Poets;

William Rowley, Thomas Dekker, John Ford, &c.

Acted by the Princes Servants, often at the Cock-Pit in *Drury-Lane*, once at Court, with ſingular Applauſe.

Never printed till now.

London, *Printed by* J. Cottrel, *for* Edward Blackmore, *at the Angel in* Paul's *Church-yard.* 1658.

Title page for the 1658 quarto edition of the play that Dekker, William Rowley, and John Ford based on Henry Goodcole's 1621 account of Elizabeth Sawyer's trial and execution for witchcraft (Fredson Bowers, ed., The Dramatic Works of Thomas Dekker, *volume 3, 1958)*

Bull company had broken up by the summer of 1623, *The Virgin Martyr* had evidently passed into the repertory of another company; a new scene was licensed for it in the summer of 1624, but this was never printed. *The Virgin Martyr* is the only play in the Dekker canon to have been revived on the Restoration stage.

What seems to have been Dekker's next play, *The Witch of Edmonton,* is also a collaboration, this time with two others: the actor-dramatist William Rowley and John Ford, whose career as a dramatist may have begun with this play and who would emerge in the course of the next decade as the most significant figure in the later Jacobean and Caroline theater. The central plot of *The Witch of Edmonton* was based on a recent event: the trial and condemnation for witchcraft of one Elizabeth Sawyer in the spring of 1621, and her execution on 19 April of that year. An account of her case was written by the Rever-

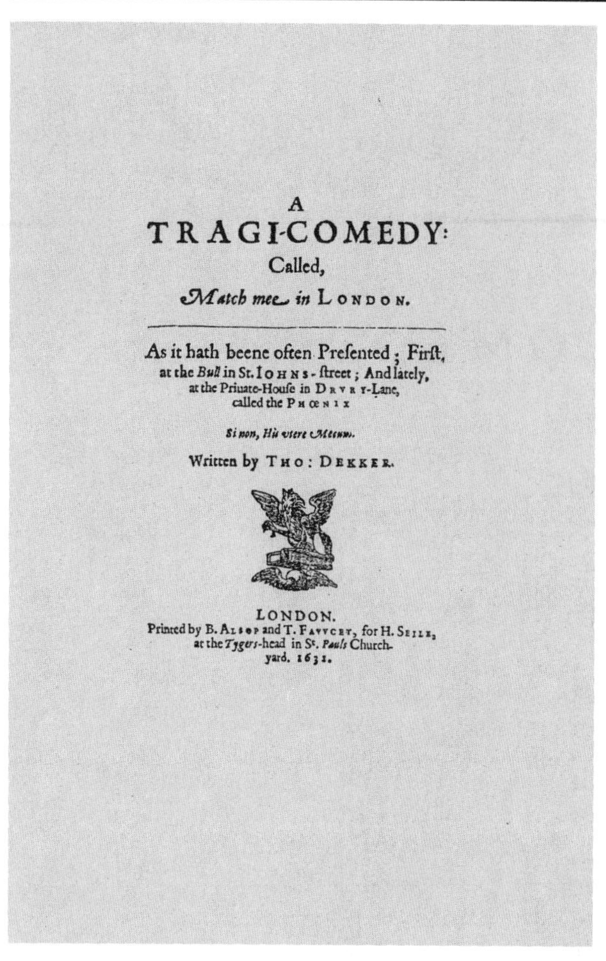

A
TRAGI-COMEDY:
Called,
Match mee in LONDON.

As it hath beene often Presented; First,
at the *Bull* in St. IOHNS-street; And lately,
at the Priuate-House in DRVRY-Lane,
called the PHŒNIX

Si non, His vtere Mecum.

Written by THO: DEKKER.

LONDON.
Printed by B. ALSOP and T. FAVVCET, for H. SEILE,
at the *Tygers*-head in St. *Pauls* Church-
yard. 1631.

Title page for the 1631 quarto edition of Dekker's first play in the genre popularized by Beaumont and Fletcher (Fredson Bowers, ed., The Dramatic Works of Thomas Dekker, *volume 3, 1958)*

end Henry Goodcole, who had visited her in Newgate during her imprisonment; his book, *The Wonderful Discovery of Elizabeth Sawyer*, was entered in the Stationers' Register on 27 April and provided the principal source for this one of the play's two plots. The play was in existence by 29 December 1621, when it was acted at Court by the Prince's Men. The figure of Mother Sawyer in the play is the work of Dekker, and it is his greatest piece of dramatic portraiture. She is presented as a lonely and tormented old woman whose neighbors have so long accused her of being a witch that she begins to believe that in fact she is one. The devil sends a familiar spirit to her in the form of a black dog. It represents a great rarity in her life, a creature that loves her and will do her bidding; it indulges her crazed fantasies of vengeance on her enemies, and then, having lured her to damnation, deserts her. The play's other plot (chiefly the work of Ford) concerns Frank Thorney, a well-meaning but weak-willed young man who commits bigamy and, in an effort to extricate himself from this offense, murders his second wife. The demonic dog is put to extraordinarily effective use as it wanders from Mother Sawyer's scenes into the presence of Frank Thorney as his murderous intentions take shape. It makes another notable appearance in the scene where Thorney's guilt is discovered by the sister and father of his dead wife. The dog also strays across the path of a clownish yokel named Cuddy Banks, a part played on the stage by Rowley and written by him. The whiff of the diabolic that the dog's presence brings has the effect of turning scenes of conventional low-comic buffoonery into disquietingly bizarre and sinister episodes. *The Witch of Edmonton* is a remarkably unified play for a work of tripartite authorship, and much of the credit for its structural coherence must go to Dekker, for it is the scenes concerning Mother Sawyer and her dog, which he created, that provide the connective tissue linking all the play's principal strands of action, over which they cast that peculiarly combined glow of tenderness and grotesquerie which is a Dekker specialty. The play continues to be staged from time to time, at least in England. Sybil Thorndike acted the role of Mother Sawyer in a London production in 1921, and Edith Evans took the part in the Old Vic production of 1936 in a cast that also included Michael Redgrave and Alec Guinness. There was a production of the play at the Mermaid theater, London, in the fall of 1962, and in the fall of 1982 the Royal Shakespeare Company staged it with considerable success.

Dekker's first unaided play following his imprisonment seems to have been *Match Me in London.* The date of the play is uncertain. Sir Henry Herbert, Master of the Revels, whose office it was to license plays for performance, refers to it in August 1623 as an old play, but that could mean no more than that it had been previously licensed by one of his predecessors; Herbert had assumed his office only the month before. The text was not published until 1631, and the title page of that edition may tell us something when it prominently advertises the play as "A Tragicomedy." "Tragicomedy" is the most conspicuous word on the page; it appears at the top, and in far larger and bolder type than any other word. The vogue of romantic tragicomedy on the Jacobean stage may be said to have been launched in the years between 1608 or 1609 and 1611 (just prior to Dekker's imprisonment) with the great success

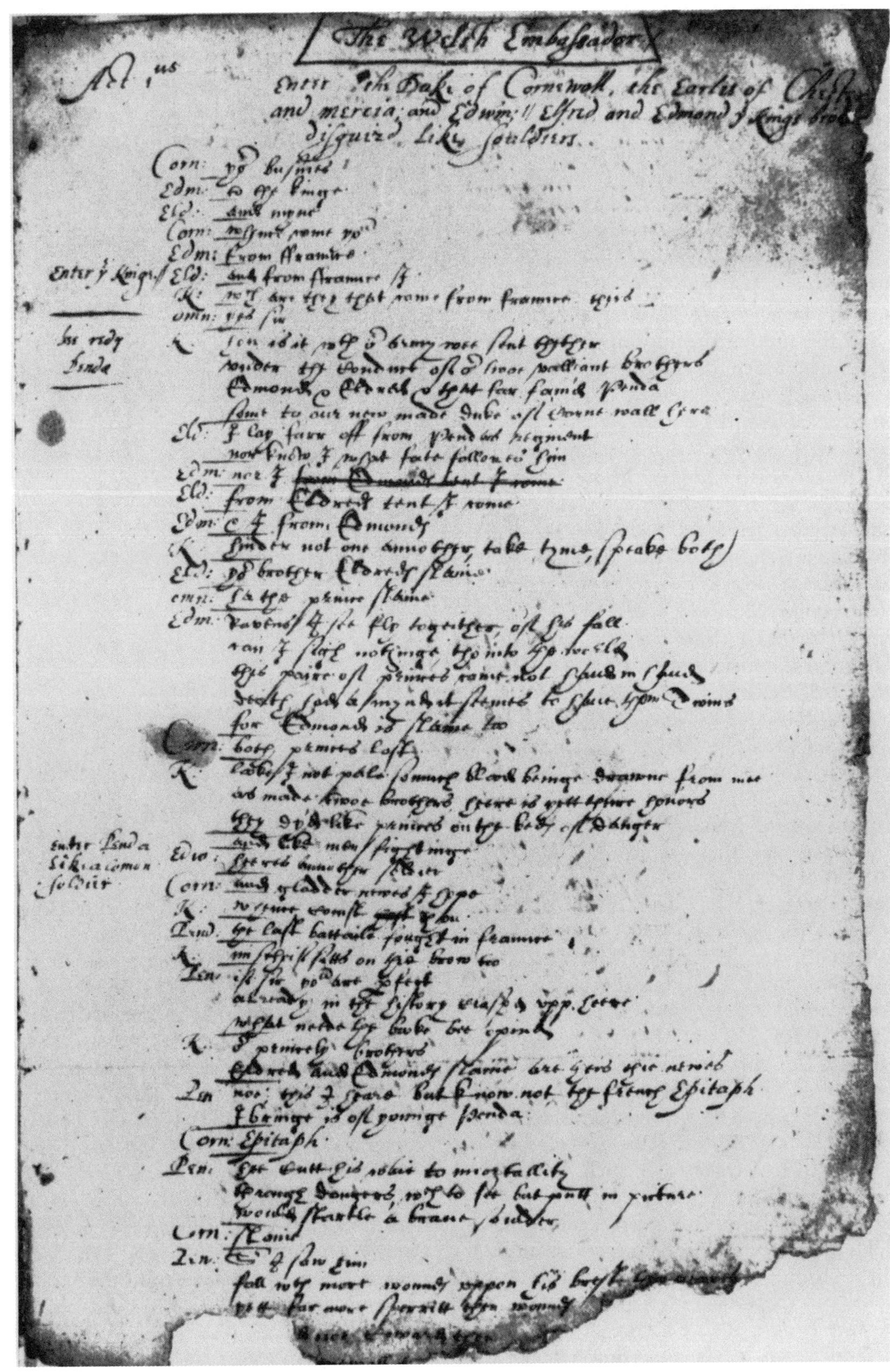

The Welsh Embassador

Actus 1us

Enter the Duke of Cornwall, the Earles of Chester and Mercia, and Edwin, Elfred and Edmond the kings brothers disguised like souldiers.

First page of the manuscript, written in the hand of a scribe, for The Welsh Ambassador *preserved in the Public Library of Cardiff, Wales*

achieved by such Francis Beaumont and John Fletcher tragicomedies as *Philaster* and *A King and No King.* During the years of Dekker's imprisonment the popularity of tragicomedy continued apace, and, when around 1619 or 1620 he resumed his career as a playwright, tragicomedy was the favorite dramatic form with London's theatergoers. *Match Me in London* is Dekker's attempt to produce a play in the new style. Its subject is the familiar tragicomic one: a lustful tyrant attempts to seduce a virtuous wife. Dekker seeks to develop his plot by means of the surprising disclosures and the sudden shiftings of a character's mood or motive which Beaumont and Fletcher handled with such easy virtuosity, but *Match Me in London* is an awkwardly contrived and derivative piece of work. It amply demonstrates how ill equipped Dekker was to master the new fashion in play making.

What survives from the work Dekker produced in his last decade is not distinguished. Some of his plays are lost, known to us only from licensing entries in Sir Henry Herbert's office book. These include *The Bellman of Paris,* a collaboration with John Day (licensed 30 July 1623), and two further collaborations with John Ford: *The Fairy Knight* (licensed 11 June 1624) and *The Bristow Merchant* (licensed 22 October 1624). In the summer of 1624 Dekker, Ford, and Rowley (the trio that had produced *The Witch of Edmonton*) joined forces again, together with Webster, to write a play that would combine two highly publicized recent events (a murder and a scandalous marriage). The play's title—*The Late Murder of the Son upon the Mother*—glanced at both news items, and it was performed at the Red Bull in September 1624, but the play is lost, and we know about it only from the lawsuits that followed in its wake. *The Sun's Darling* (licensed 3 March 1624) is the only certain Dekker-Ford collaboration that survives in addition to *The Witch of Edmonton.* It is a masque written for the public theater in emulation of the elaborate masques that by the 1620s had come to be such a notable feature of Stuart court entertainment. *The Sun's Darling* is a moral allegory of a prodigal's progress through the seasons of the year (and, by implication, through life), from spring to winter. It is full of songs and spectacle and might, in its original form, have been quite a pleasing show, but in the version in which it has come down to us (it was not printed until 1656) the ending has been altered so that the masque's original conclusion and thus its total design can no longer be discerned. Two plays connected with Dekker's last years—*The Wonder of a Kingdom* and *The Noble Spanish Soldier* (both entered together in the Stationers' Register on 16 May 1631)—seem to be based in some degree on earlier collaborations with John Day. Passages from both plays appear in Day's *Parliament of Bees.* The central plot situation of *The Noble Spanish Soldier* (which seems in its extant version to date from circa 1622) was reworked by Dekker circa 1623 in *The Welsh Ambassador.* None of these three plays seems to have met with success. Two of them were published after Dekker's death (*The Noble Spanish Soldier* in 1634, *The Wonder of a Kingdom* in 1636). *The Welsh Ambassador* was never published until the twentieth century and is preserved in manuscript in the Public Library of Cardiff, Wales.

Brittannia's Honor:
Brightly Shining in seuerall Magnificent Shewes or Pageants, to Celebrate the Solemnity of the Right Honorable RICHARD DEANE, At his Inauguration into the Majoralty of the Honourable Citty of *London*, on Wednesday, October the 29th. 1628.
At the particular Cost, and Charges of the Right Worshipfull, Worthy and Ancient Society of *Skinners.*
Mart. lib. 7. Ep. 5. *Rursus Io, Magnos clamat noua-Troia Triumphos.*
Inuented by THO. DEKKER.

Title page for the unique copy of the 1628 quarto edition of Dekker's fourth Lord Mayor's pageant (British Library)

In 1627 Dekker was commissioned to provide the pageant for the Lord Mayor's inauguration. The show he provided is lost; we know that he wrote it from his statement in the dedication to his poetical pamphlet *Wars, Wars, Wars* (published in 1628). He went on to provide Lord Mayor's shows for the next two years: *Britannia's Honor* in 1628, *London's Tempe* in 1629. Both are feeble performances, though it may be said in Dekker's defense that there is a general falling off in the quality of mayoral pageants in the 1620s. The form was becoming hackneyed. Dekker offered to prepare an inaugural pageant for Lord Mayor's Day in 1630, but no pageant—only a triumphal procession—was presented that year. The committee in charge of the occasion, however, paid him twenty shillings for his offer.

Just as in 1603 the death of Elizabeth I and the accession of James I had been accompanied by an outbreak of plague, so in 1625 the death of James and the accession of Charles I had been similarly attended. Dekker produced another plague pamphlet, *A Rod for Runaways*, for the occasion. When another epidemic of plague threatened in 1630, he put together two more: *The Black Rod and the White Rod*, and *London Look Back*. In 1631 he published *Penny Wise, Pound Foolish*, a piece of prose fiction retailing the amorous adventures of a Bristow (that is, Bristol) merchant. Scholars have wondered what, if any, relation the story may have had to Dekker and Ford's lost play of a Bristow merchant. In the same year Dekker dedicated the published text of *Match Me in London* to Lodowick Carlell, the young courtier-dramatist and favorite of King Charles. He speaks poignantly of his advancing age: "I have been a priest in Apollo's temple many years, my voice is decaying with my age." In the following year, in the dedication to *English Villanies* (the 1632 edition of *Lanthorn and Candlelight*), he speaks of his "three-score years."

It is in this year that Dekker is last heard of, and thus he was almost certainly the "Thomas Decker, householder" buried at St. James's, Clerkenwell, on 25 August 1632. The administration of his estate was renounced by his widow, Elisabeth, on 4 September 1632; this implies that Dekker died in debt. A few years before, in 1626 and 1628, he had been indicted for recusancy; fear of process for debt may explain why he had not been attending church. His widow, Elisabeth, was not his first wife. Years before, on 24 July 1616, while Dekker was in prison, "Mary wife of Thomas Deckers" had been buried in the same London parish (Clerkenwell) where sixteen years later Dekker died.

Dekker's work has elicited a varied range of critical response over the four hundred years since he wrote. Lamb said he had poetry enough for anything. Swinburne admired his capacity to fuse humor with pathos, but he deplored the carelessness that mars so much of his work. The phrase "hack writer" has been hurled at him in one form or another since the days of Ben Jonson. There is some truth in all these responses. Much of Dekker's work is hack writing. He is a prime example of a writer who made his living by his pen. This means that he was often working in haste and often writing about subjects that could not have interested him very much. This is especially true of some of the nondramatic pamphlets, especially those of the poetical kind, such as *Wars, Wars, Wars* or *The Artillery Garden* or *The Double PP*. Dekker's poetry on such occasions is mainly doggerel, and pieces such as these seem clearly to have been produced to capitalize on public excitement over some such special occasion as the Gunpowder Plot, or to secure some gift of patronage from the persons or groups to whom they are dedicated. The best of the nondramatic pieces, *The Gull's Hornbook* and *Four Birds of Noah's Ark*, demonstrate the dual strands of Dekker's literary personality with great clarity: *The Gull's Hornbook* is a lively, shrewd, and ironically amusing description of the swinging life-style to which sophisticated young men aspired in Jacobean London. The prayers and meditations of *Four Birds of Noah's Ark*, on the other hand, exhibit just how eloquent and affecting the simplicity of Dekker's style can be.

Financial need evidently caused him to cease writing plays and to devote himself to writing nondramatic pamphlets for the five years or so from 1606 to 1611, but the interruption clearly did his career as a playwright no good. Just when he might have been expected to have consolidated all that he had gained from his early experience in the theater and to have built on such success as he had heretofore achieved to create more mature plays, his work for the stage ceased, and his career as a dramatist never regained the momentum that was driving it in the years from 1599 to 1605. When, in 1611, he resumed his activity as a playwright only to have it interrupted a year or so later by the half-dozen years of his imprisonment, his prospects for adding in any considerable way to the body of work he had already managed to produce for the stage were finished. Only *The Witch of Edmonton*, among the surviving plays with which he was associated after 1620, has any claim to real distinction. It is to this play, and to those earlier ones writ-

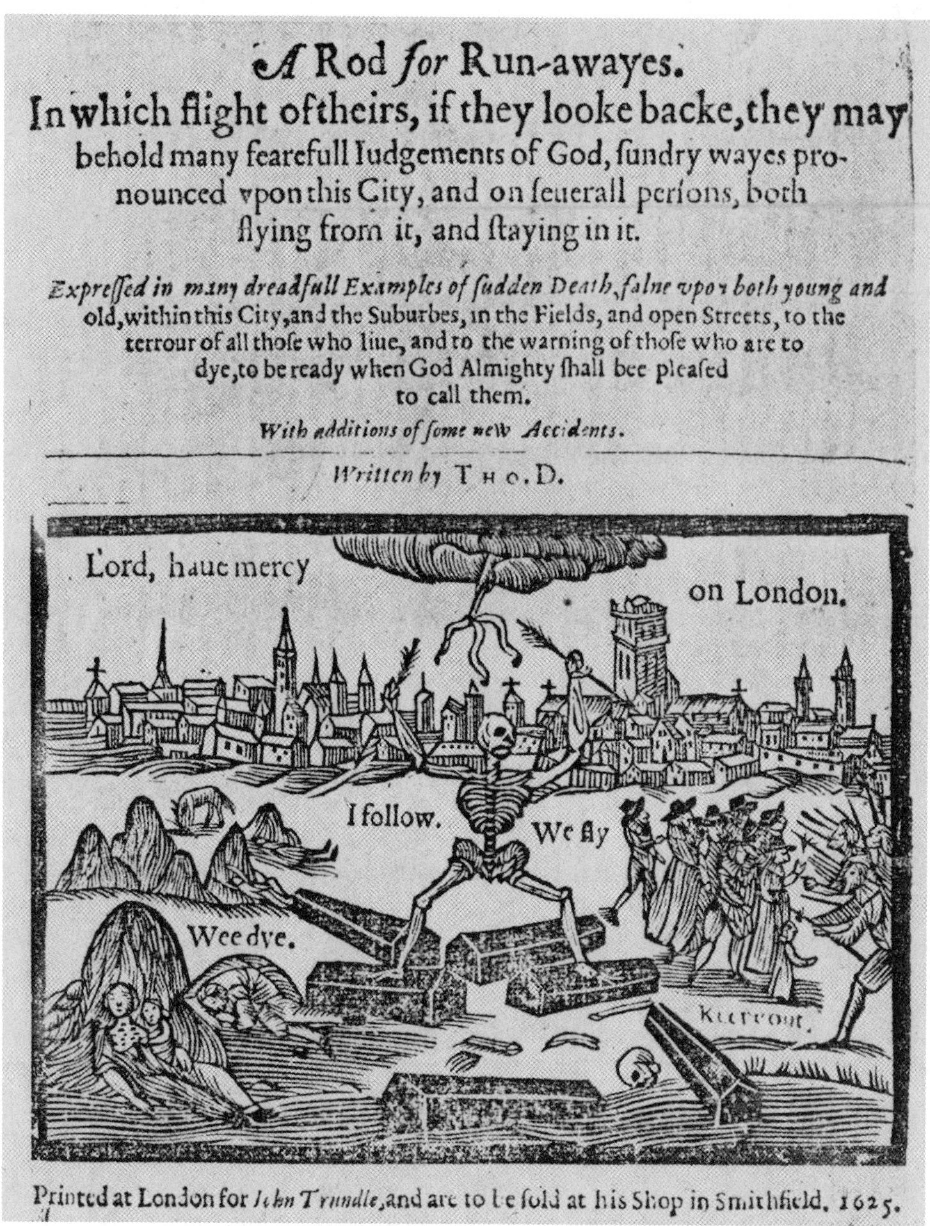
A Rod for Run-awayes.
In which flight oftheirs, if they looke backe, they may behold many fearefull Iudgements of God, ſundry wayes pronounced vpon this City, and on ſeuerall perſons, both flying from it, and ſtaying in it.

Expreſſed in many dreadfull Examples of ſudden Death, falne vpon both young and old, within this City, and the Suburbes, in the Fields, and open Streets, to the terrour of all thoſe who liue, and to the warning of thoſe who are to dye, to be ready when God Almighty ſhall bee pleaſed to call them.

With additions of ſome new Accidents.

Written by Tho. D.

Printed at London for *Iohn Trundle*, and are to be ſold at his Shop in Smithfield. 1625.

Title page for the 1625 revised quarto edition of the pamphlet Dekker wrote during the London plague at the time of the death of James I and the accession of Charles I to the British throne (Bodleian Library)

ten in the period 1599-1605, that one must look to find the qualities that critics such as Charles Lamb and William Hazlitt and Algernon Charles Swinburne so much admired. They can be summarized under two heads: Dekker's compassion, and his humor. The compassion is most evident in the sympathy Dekker manages to generate for simple people who find themselves in the grip of very powerful feelings: feelings such as the guilt and shame aroused in Bellafront in *The Honest Whore*, part 1; the fury and grief which her fall from virtue causes her father, Orlando Friscobaldo, and the renewed love and respect which he feels for his daughter when he is assured of her repentance in *The Honest Whore*, part 2; the indignation that Grissell's brother, Laureo, feels in behalf of his sister's treatment by her royal husband, and by contrast the deep but uncomplaining sorrow felt by the father, Janicola, for his daughter, in *Patient Grissell;* the humiliation and outrage that drive Mother Sawyer to crazed visions of revenge on the neighbors who have persecuted her in *The Witch of Edmonton.*

As for Dekker's humor, it is of the genial kind that delights in eccentricities of personality and manner, and in his best work he has a fine gift for capturing his subject's typical quirks, fancies, and preoccupations in speech that is a compound of catch phrases and extravagant imaginative flights combined with the sort of nuances that particularize and characterize. The gift is most fully displayed in the character of Simon Eyre and his shop full of apprentices in *The Shoemakers' Holiday*, and in the titular character in *Old Fortunatus*. But nothing that Dekker wrote is ever entirely devoid of his energizing powers of language. They vitalize his nondramatic pamphlets, with their elaborate and often fantastic personifications (for example, *The Seven Deadly Sins*, the account of the armies of the poor in *Work for Armorers*, the grotesque description of the rout of thieves and rogues and the officers of the law who have them in chase in *A Strange Horse Race*). Side by side with the strain of eccentric fantasy in Dekker's art there is his clear-sighted vision of human strengths and weaknesses, and he gives voice to these in accents of the utmost simplicity. His powers of compassion and pathos exist in natural harmony with the genial humor of his comic manner, and together they give him a place in the tradition of English comic artists that includes such greater but nonetheless kindred spirits as Chaucer and Shakespeare, Henry Fielding and Laurence Sterne and Charles Dickens. Though his artistry is seldom equal to theirs, his poignant sense that human life contains much to be amused with and much to pity matches theirs.

Bibliographies:

Samuel A. Tannenbaum, *Dekker: A Concise Bibliography* (New York: Privately printed, 1939);

Samuel A. and Dorothy R. Tannenbaum, *Supplement to a Bibliography of Thomas Dekker* (New York: Privately printed, 1945);

Dennis Donovan, *Thomas Dekker, 1945-1965: Elizabethan Bibliographies Supplements, No. 2* (London: Nether Press, 1967);

A. F. Allison, *Thomas Dekker, c. 1572-1632. A Bibliographical Catalogue of the Early Editions to the end of the 17th Century* (Folkestone & London: Dawsons of Pall Mall, 1972);

Terence P. Logan and Denzell S. Smith, eds., *A Survey and Bibliography of Recent Studies in English Renaissance Drama: The Popular School* (Lincoln: University of Nebraska Press, 1975).

References:

Gerald Eades Bentley, *The Jacobean and Caroline Stage*, volume 3 (Oxford: Clarendon Press, 1956), pp. 241-275;

R. A. Foakes and R. T. Rickert, eds., *Henslowe's Diary* (Cambridge: Cambridge University Press, 1961);

M. T. Jones-Davies, *Un peintre de la vie londonienne: Thomas Dekker*, Collection des Etudes Anglaises, no. 6, 2 volumes (Paris, 1958).

Papers:

The manuscript for the play *Sir Thomas More*, containing Dekker's addition in his own hand, is preserved as Harleian MS 7368 in the British Library, London. The manuscript for *The Welsh Ambassador* is in the Public Library of Cardiff, Wales. The manuscript of Philip Henslowe's diary, with its many references to Dekker, is preserved among the papers of Edward Alleyn in the library of Dulwich College, London. Also preserved among the Alleyn papers are two letters in Dekker's hand, both written while he was a prisoner in the King's Bench prison. One is dated 12 September 1616; the other is undated. A commonplace book in the Folger Shakespeare Library, Washington, D.C. (MS V.a.160), contains two poems attributed to Dekker: "A New Ballad of the Dancing on the Ropes" and "Paul his Temple Triumphant." Both poems are reprinted by F. D. Hoeniger in "Thomas Dekker, the Restoration of St. Paul's, and J. P. Collier, the Forger," *Renaissance News*, 16 (1963): 181-200. Dekker's deposition (dated 3 February 1625) in the legal suit arising from the lost play titled *The Late Murder of the Son upon the Mother* is preserved in the Public Records Office, London. See C. J. Sisson, *Lost Plays of Shakespeare's Age* (Cambridge: Cambridge University Press, 1936), pp. 81ff.

John Donne

(1572 - 31 March 1631)

A. J. Smith
University of Southampton

BOOKS: *Pfevdo-Martyr* (London: Printed by W. Stansby for Walter Burre, 1610);

An anatomy of the World (London: Printed for Samuel Macham, 1611);

Ignatius his Conclaue (London: Printed by N. O. for Richard More, 1611);

A Sermon Vpon The XV. Verfe Of The XX. Chapter Of The Booke Of Iudges (London: Printed by William Stansby for Thomas Jones, 1622);

A Sermon Vpon The VIII. Verfe Of The I. Chapter of The Acts Of The Apoftles (London: Printed by A. Mat for Thomas Jones, 1622);

Three Sermons Vpon Speciall Occasions (London: Printed for Thomas Jones, 1623);

Deuotions Vpon Emergent Occasions (London: Printed by A. M. for Thomas Jones, 1624);

The Firft Sermon Preached To King Charles (London: Printed by A. M. for Thomas Jones, 1625);

Foure Sermons Vpon Speciall Occafions (London: Printed for Thomas Jones, 1625);

Fiue Sermons Vpon Speciall Occafions (London: Printed for Thomas Jones, 1626);

A Sermon, Preached To The Kings Mtie. At Whitehall, 24. Febr. 1625 (London: Printed for Thomas Jones, 1626);

A Sermon Of Commemoration Of The Lady Dãuers (London: Printed by I. H. for Philemon Stephens and Christopher Meredith, 1627);

Deaths Duell (London: Printed by Thomas Harper for Richard Redmer and Benjamin Fisher, 1632);

Iuuenilia (London: Printed by E. P. for Henry Seyle, 1633);

Poems (London: Printed by M. F. for John Marriot, 1633);

Six Sermons Vpon Severall Occafions (London: Printed by the Printers to the Universitie of Cambridge, 1634);

Sapientia Clamitans (London: Printed by I. Haviland for R. Milbourne, 1638);

Wifdome crying out to Sinners (London: Printed by M. P. for John Stafford, 1639);

Donne in 1616; miniature by Isaac Oliver at Windsor Castle (Collection of Her Majesty the Queen)

LXXX Sermons (London: Printed for Richard Royston and Richard Marriot, 1640);

Biathanatos (London: Printed by John Dawson, 1647);

Essayes in Divinity (London: Printed by T. N. for Richard Marriot, 1651).

Editions and Collections: *Fifty Sermons* (London: printed by Ja. Flesher for M. F. J. Marriot and R. Royston, 1649);

XXVI. Sermons (London: Printed by T. N. for James Magnes, 1660);

The Works of John Donne, D.D., Dean of Saint Pauls 1621-1631, With a memoir of his life, 6 volumes, edited by Henry Alford (London: John W. Parker, 1839);

The Poetical Works of Dr. John Donne, with a memoir, edited by James Russell Lowell (Boston: Little, Brown & Co., 1855);

The Poems of John Donne, edited by E. K. Chambers (London: Lawrence & Bullen, 1896);

The Life and Letters of John Donne, 2 volumes, edited by Edmund Gosse (London: Heinemann, 1899);

The Love Poems of John Donne, edited by Charles Eliot Norton (Boston: Houghton, Mifflin, 1905);

The Poems of John Donne, edited by Herbert J. C. Grierson (Oxford: Clarendon Press, 1912);

Donne's Sermons: Selected Passages, edited, with an introduction, by Logan Pearsall Smith (Oxford: Clarendon Press, 1919);

The Poems of John Donne, edited by Hugh I'Anson Fausset (London & Toronto: Dent, 1931);

The Complete Poems of John Donne, edited by Roger E. Bennett (Chicago: Packard & Co., 1942);

The Complete Poetry and Selected Prose of John Donne, edited by Charles M. Coffin (New York: Modern Library, 1952);

Essays in Divinity, edited by Evelyn M. Simpson (Oxford: Clarendon Press, 1952);

The Sermons of John Donne, 10 volumes, edited by George R. Potter and Evelyn M. Simpson (Berkeley & Los Angeles: University of California Press, 1953-1962);

John Donne: The Anniversaries, edited by F. Manley (Baltimore: Johns Hopkins Press, 1963);

John Donne's Sermons on the Psalms and Gospels. With a Selection of Prayers and Meditations, edited by E. M. Simpson (Berkeley & Los Angeles: University of California Press, 1963);

The Complete Poetry of John Donne, edited by John T. Shawcross (New York: Doubleday, 1967);

Donne's Prebend Sermons, edited by Janel M. Mueller (Cambridge, Mass.: Harvard University Press, 1971);

John Donne: The Complete English Poems, edited by A. J. Smith (Harmondsworth, U.K.: Penguin, 1971);

Devotions Upon Emergent Occasions, edited by Anthony Raspa (Montreal: McGill-Queen's University Press, 1975);

Biathanatos, edited by Ernest W. Sullivan II (Newark: University of Delaware Press / London: Associated University Presses, 1984);

John Donne, edited by John Carey (Oxford & New York: Oxford University Press, 1990).

John Donne's standing as a great English poet, and one of the greatest of all writers of English prose, is now assured. However, it has been confirmed only in the present century. The history of Donne's reputation is the most remarkable of any major writer in English; no other body of great poetry has fallen so far from favor for so long and been generally condemned as inept and crude. In Donne's own day his poetry was highly prized among the small circle of his admirers who read it as it was circulated in manuscript, and in his later years he gained wide fame as a preacher. For some thirty years after his death successive editions of his verse stamped his powerful influence upon English poets. During the Restoration his writing went out of fashion and remained so for several centuries. Throughout the eighteenth century, and for much of the nineteenth century, he was little read and scarcely appreciated. Commentators followed Samuel Johnson in dismissing his work as no more than frigidly ingenious and metrically uncouth. Some scribbled notes by Samuel Taylor Coleridge in Charles Lamb's copy of Donne's poems make a testimony of admiration rare in the early nineteenth century. Robert Browning became a known (and wondered-at) enthusiast of Donne, but it was not until the end of the nineteenth century that Donne's poetry was eagerly taken up by a growing band of avant-garde readers and writers. His prose remained largely unnoticed until 1919.

In the first two decades of the twentieth century Donne's poetry was decisively rehabilitated. Its extraordinary appeal to modern readers throws light on the Modernist movement itself, as on our intuitive response to our own times. Donne may no longer be the cult figure he became in the 1920s and 1930s, when T. S. Eliot and William Butler Yeats among others discovered in his poetry the peculiar fusion of intellect and passion, and the alert contemporariness, which they aspired to in their own art. He is not a poet for all tastes and times, yet for many readers Donne remains what Ben Jonson judged him: "the first poet in the world in some things." His poems continue to engage the attention and challenge the experience of readers who come to him afresh. His high place in the pantheon of the English poets now seems secure.

Donne's love poetry was written nearly four hundred years ago, yet one reason for its appeal is that it speaks to us as directly and urgently as if we overhear a present confidence. For instance, a lover who is about to board ship for a long voyage turns back to share a last intimacy with his mistress: "Here take my picture" (*Elegy 5*). Two lovers who have turned their backs upon a threatening world in "The Good Morrow" celebrate their discovery of a new world in each other:

Let sea-discoverers to new worlds have gone,
Let maps to others, worlds on worlds have shown,
Let us possess one world, each hath one, and is one.

In "The Flea" an importunate lover points out a flea that has been sucking his mistress's blood and now jumps to suck his; he tries to prevent his mistress from crushing it:

Oh stay, three lives in one flea spare,
Where we almost, nay more than married are.
This flea is you and I, and this
Our marriage bed, and marriage temple is;
Though parents grudge, and you, we' are met,
And cloistered in these living walls of jet.

This poem moves forward as a kind of dramatic argument in which the chance discovery of the flea itself becomes the means by which they work out the true end of their love. The incessant play of a skeptical intelligence gives even these love poems the style of impassioned reasoning.

The poetry inhabits an exhilaratingly unpredictable world in which wariness and quick wits are at a premium. The more perilous the encounters of clandestine lovers, the greater zest they have for their pleasures, whether they seek to outwit the disapproving world, or a jealous husband, or a forbidding and deeply suspicious father, as in *Elegy 4*, "The Perfume":

Though he had wont to search with glazed eyes,
As though he came to kill a cockatrice,
Though he have oft sworn, that he would remove
Thy beauty's beauty, and food of our love,
Hope of his goods, if I with thee were seen,
Yet close and secret, as our souls, we have been.

Exploiting and being exploited are taken as conditions of nature, which we share on equal terms with the beasts of the jungle and the ocean. In "Metempsychosis" a whale and a holder of great office behave in precisely the same way:

He hunts not fish, but as an officer,
Stays in his court, as his own net, and there
All suitors of all sorts themselves enthral;
So on his back lies this whale wantoning,

Portrait of Donne, circa 1595, by an unknown artist (Collection of the Marquis of Lothian)

And in his gulf-like throat, sucks everything
That passeth near.

Donne characterizes our natural life in the world as a condition of flux and momentariness, which we may nonetheless turn to our advantage, as in "Woman's Constancy":

Now thou hast loved me one whole day,
Tomorrow when thou leav'st, what wilt thou say?
. . . .
Vain lunatic, against these 'scapes I could
Dispute, and conquer, if I would,
Which I abstain to do,
For by tomorrow, I may think so too.

In such a predicament our judgment of the world around us can have no absolute force but may at best measure people's endeavors relative to each other, as Donne points out in "Metempsychosis":

There's nothing simply good, nor ill alone,
Of every quality comparison,
The only measure is, and judge, opinion.

The tension of the poetry comes from the pull of divergent impulses in the argument itself. In "A Valediction: Of my Name in the Window," the lover's name scratched in his mistress's window ought to serve as a talisman to keep her chaste; but then, as he explains to her, it may instead be an unwilling witness to her infidelity:

> When thy inconsiderate hand
> Flings ope this casement, with my trembling name,
> To look on one, whose wit or land,
> New battery to thy heart may frame,
> Then think this name alive, and that thou thus
> In it offend'st my Genius.

So complex or downright contradictory is our state that quite opposite possibilities must be allowed for within the scope of a single assertion, as in *Satire 3*: "Kind pity chokes my spleen; brave scorn forbids / Those tears to issue which swell my eye-lids."

The opening lines of *Satire 3* confront us with a bizarre medley of moral questions. Should the corrupted state of religion prompt our anger or our grief ? What devotion do we owe to religion, and which religion may claim our devotion? May the pagan philosophers be saved before Christian believers? What obligation of piety do children owe to their fathers in return for their religious upbringing? Then we get a quick review of issues such as the participation of Englishmen in foreign wars, colonizing expeditions, the Spanish auto-da-fé, and brawls over women or honor in the London streets. The drift of Donne's argument holds all these concerns together and brings them to bear upon the divisions of Christendom that lead men to conclude that any worldly cause must be more worthy of their devotion than the pursuit of a true Christian life. The mode of reasoning is characteristic: Donne calls in a variety of circumstances, weighing one area of concern against another so that we may appraise the present claim in relation to a whole range of unlike possibilities: "Is not this excuse for mere contraries, / Equally strong; cannot both sides say so?" The movement of the poem amounts to a sifting of the relative claims on our devotion that commonly distract us from our absolute obligation to seek the truth.

Some of Donne's sharpest insights into erotic experience, as his insights into social motives, follow out his sense of the bodily prompting of our most compelling urges, which are thus wholly subject to the momentary state of the physical organism itself. In "Farewell to Love" the end that lovers so passionately pursue loses its attraction at once when they have gained it:

> Being had, enjoying it decays:
> And thence,
> What before pleased them all, takes but one sense,
> And that so lamely, as it leaves behind
> A kind of sorrowing dullness to the mind.

Yet the poet never gives the impression of forcing a doctrine upon experience. On the contrary, his skepticism sums up his sense of the way the world works.

Donne's love poetry expresses a variety of amorous experiences that are often startlingly unlike each other, or even contradictory in their implications. In "The Anniversary" he is not just being inconsistent when he moves from a justification of frequent changes of partners to celebrate a mutual attachment that is simply not subject to time, alteration, appetite, or the sheer pull of other worldly enticements:

> All kings, and all their favourites,
> All glory of honours, beauties, wits,
> The sun itself, which makes times, as they pass,
> Is elder by a year, now, than it was
> When thou and I first one another saw:
> All other things, to their destruction draw,
> Only our love hath no decay;
> This, no tomorrow hath, nor yesterday,
> Running it never runs from us away,
> But truly keeps his first, last, everlasting day.

The triumph the lovers proclaim here defies the state of flux it affirms.

Some of Donne's finest love poems, such as "A Valediction: forbidding Mourning," prescribe the condition of a mutual attachment that time and distance cannot diminish:

> Dull sublunary lovers' love
> (Whose soul is sense) cannot admit
> Absence, because it doth remove
> Those things which elemented it.
>
> But we by a love, so much refined,
> That our selves know not what it is,
> Inter-assured of the mind,
> Care less, eyes, lips, and hands to miss.

Donne finds some striking images to define this state in which two people remain wholly one while they are separated. Their souls are not divided but expanded by the distance between them, "Like gold to airy thinness beat"; or they move in response to each other as the legs of twin compasses, whose fixed foot keeps the moving foot steadfast in its path:

> Such wilt thou be to me, who must
> Like th' other foot obliquely run;
> Thy firmness makes my circle just,
> And makes me end, where I begun.

A supple argument unfolds with lyric grace.

It must be borne in mind that the poems editors group together were not necessarily produced thus. Donne did not write for publication, and no more than seven poems and a bit of another poem were published during his lifetime, and only two of these publications were authorized by him. The poems he released were passed around in manuscript versions and transcribed by his admirers singly or in gatherings, some copies of which have survived. When the first printed edition of his poems was published in 1633, two years after his death, the haphazard arrangement of the poems gave no clue to the order of their composition. Many modern editions of the poetry impose categorical divisions that are unlikely to correspond to the order of writing, separating the love poetry from the satires and the religious poetry, the verse letters from the epithalamiums and funeral poems. No more than a handful of Donne's poems can be dated with certainty. The *Elegies* and *Satires* are likely to have been written in the early 1590s. The "Metempsychosis" is dated 16 August 1601. The two memorial *Anniversaries* for the death of Elizabeth Drury were certainly written in 1611 and 1612; and the funeral elegy on Prince Henry's death must have been written in 1612. But the *Songs and Sonnets* were evidently not conceived as a single body of love verses and do not appear so in early manuscript collections. Donne may well have composed them at intervals and in unlike situations over some twenty years of his poetic career. Some of them may even have overlapped with his best-known religious poems, which are likely to have been written about 1609, before he took holy orders.

Poems so vividly individuated invite attention to the circumstances that shaped them. Yet we have no warrant to read Donne's poetry as a record of his life or the expression of his inner disquiets. Donne's career and personality are nonetheless arresting in themselves, and they cannot be kept wholly separate from the general thrust of his writing, for which they at least provide a living context. Donne was born in London between 24 January and 19 June 1572 into the precarious world of English recusant Catholicism, whose perils his family well knew. His mother, a lifelong Catholic, was the great-niece of the martyred Sir Thomas More; his uncle Jasper Heywood headed an underground Jesuit mission in England from 1581 to 1583 and when he was caught was imprisoned and then exiled; his younger brother Henry died from the plague in 1593 while being held in Newgate Prison for harboring a seminary priest. Yet at some time in his young manhood Donne himself converted to Anglicanism and never went back on that reasoned decision, although controversy remained his element. He trained as a lawyer at Lincoln's Inn following early studies at Oxford and possibly Cambridge. After sailing as a gentleman adventurer with the English expeditions to Cadiz and the Azores, he entered the service of Sir Thomas Egerton, the lord keeper of England. As Egerton's highly valued secretary he developed the keen interest in statecraft and foreign affairs that he retained throughout his life.

His place in the Egerton household also brought him into acquaintance with Egerton's domestic circle. Egerton's brother-in-law was Sir George More, parliamentary representative for Surrey, whose family seat was Loseley House near Guildford in Surrey. More came up to London for an autumn sitting of Parliament in 1601, bringing with him his daughter Ann, then seventeen. Ann More and Donne may well have met and fallen in love during some earlier visit to the Egerton household; they were clandestinely married in December 1601 in a ceremony conducted hugger-mugger between a small group of Donne's friends. Some months elapsed before Donne dared to break the news to the girl's father, which he did at last by letter, provoking a violent response. Donne and his helpful friends were briefly imprisoned, and More set out to get the marriage annulled, demanding that Egerton dismiss his amorous secretary.

The marriage was eventually upheld; indeed, More became reconciled to it and to his son-in-law, but Donne lost his job in 1602 and did not find regular employment again until he took holy orders more than twelve years later. Throughout his middle years he and his wife brought up an ever-increasing family with the aid of relatives, friends, and patrons, and on the uncertain income he could bring in by polemical hackwork and the like. His anxious attempts to

Old St. Paul's Church and Bow Church, as seen from the Thames (detail of an engraving from C. J. Visscher's View of London, *circa 1616). Donne served as dean of St. Paul's from November 1621 until his death in March 1631. Old St. Paul's was destroyed in the Great Fire of 1666.*

gain secular employment in the queen's household in Ireland, or with the Virginia Company, all came to nothing, and he seized the opportunity to accompany Sir Robert Drury on a diplomatic mission in France in 1612. Nevertheless, from these frustrated years came most of the verse letters, funeral poems, epithalamiums, and holy sonnets, as well as the prose treatises *Biathanatos* (1647), *Pseudo-Martyr* (1610), and *Ignatius his Conclave* (1611).

In the writing of Donne's middle years, skepticism darkened into a foreboding of imminent ruin. Such poems as the two memorial *Anniversaries* and "To the Countess of Salisbury" register an accelerating decline of our nature and condition in a cosmos that is itself disintegrating. In "The First Anniversary" the poet declares

> mankind decays so soon,
> We' are scarce our fathers' shadows cast at noon.
> . . . .
> And freely men confess that this world's spent,
> When in the planets, and the firmament
> They seek so many new; they see that this
> Is crumbled out again to his atomies.
> 'Tis all in pieces, all coherence gone.

Donne contends that at this late stage of creation we exhibit a pitiful falling off from the early state of humankind:

> There is not now that mankind, which was then,
> When as the sun, and man, did seem to strive,
> (Joint tenants of the world) who should survive.
> . . . .
> Where is this mankind now? who lives to age,
> Fit to be made Methusalem his page?
> Alas, we scarce live long enough to try
> Whether a true made clock run right, or lie.

Our attempts to know the world by means of our natural powers are inevitably misconceived. For we seek to order a degenerating cosmos with our decaying faculties and to impose a stable pattern upon a condition of continual flux that we cannot even adequately measure, as Donne claims in "The Second Anniversary":

> And what essential joy canst thou expect
> Here upon earth? what permanent effect
> Of transitory causes? Dost thou love
> Beauty? (and beauty worthiest is to move)
> Poor cozened cozener, that she, and that thou,
> Which did begin to love, are neither now;
> You are both fluid, changed since yesterday;
> Next day repairs, (but ill) last day's decay.
> Nor are, (although the river keep the name)
> Yesterday's waters, and today's the same.
> So flows her face, and thine eyes, neither now
> That saint, nor pilgrim, which your loving vow
> Concerned, remains; but whilst you think you be
> Constant, you'are hourly in inconstancy.

In this condition of gathering uncertainty the very latest of our so-called discoveries are likely to be the most unsettling, as shown in these lines from "The First Anniversary":

And new philosophy calls all in doubt,
The element of fire is quite put out;
The sun is lost, and th'earth, and no man's wit
Can well direct him where to look for it.

Yet Donne is not counseling despair here. On the contrary, the *Anniversaries* offer us a sure way out of our spiritual dilemma: "thou hast but one way, not to admit / The world's infection, to be none of it" ("The First Anniversary"). Moreover, the poems propose that a countering force is at work that resists the world's frantic rush toward its own ruin. Such amendment of corruption is the true purpose of our worldly being: "our business is, to rectify / Nature, to what she was" ("To Sir Edward Herbert, at Juliers"). But in the present state of the world, and ourselves, the task becomes heroic and calls for a singular resolution.

The verse letters and funeral poems celebrate those qualities of their subjects that stand against the general lapse toward chaos: "Be more than man, or thou'art less than an ant" ("The First Anniversary"). The foremost of these qualities must be innocence itself, for that is just the condition which Adam and Eve forfeited at the Fall. As an innocent person presents a pattern of our uncorrupted state, so an innocent death is an ambiguous event; for in itself it is no death at all, and yet in its effects it reenacts the primal calamity. Elizabeth Drury's departure from the world left us dying but also better aware of our true state, as depicted in "The First Anniversary":

This world, in that great earthquake languished,
For in a common bath of tears it bled,
Which drew the strongest vital spirits out
But succoured them with a perplexed doubt,
Whether the world did lose, or gain in this.

With the loss of her preserving balm the world falls sick and dies, even putrefies, leaving the poet only the task of anatomizing it so as to demonstrate its corruption. Donne uncompromisingly carries this complex conceit of an innocent death right through the two anniversary poems for Elizabeth Drury, disregarding the practical disadvantage that he is thus led to attribute a great deal to a young girl he had not even met. Ben Jonson assured William Drummond "That Donne's *Anniversary* was profane and full of blasphemies," and said "That he told Mr. Donne, if it had been written of the Virgin Mary it had been something; to which he answered that he described *The Idea* of a woman and not as she was."

Donne does not seek to celebrate a uniquely miraculous nature or a transcendental virtue. He shows us how an innocent young girl effectively embodied in her own human nature the qualities that alone preserve the natural creation, and why her death reenacts the withdrawal of those qualities from the world. He pointedly declines to take the girl for an emanation of the divine spirit, another Beatrice who rose above the flesh in her life and transcends the world finally in her death. On the contrary, Elizabeth Drury is celebrated for human excellences that are spiritually refined in themselves. She was a being in whom body and spirit were at one.

Most of the people Donne praised, alive or dead, were past the age of innocence. Yet the burden of the *Anniversary* poems is that Elizabeth Drury's death has shown us all how to resist the corrupting force of the world. A tried election of virtue is possible, though rarely achieved, which resists the common depravity of the Fall. Donne consoles a mourning woman with the conceit that she now incorporates her dead companion's virtues with her own, and has thus acquired the power to preserve both their beings from corruption: "You that are she and you, that's double she" ("To the Countess of Bedford"). He claims that a woman embodies all virtue in herself and sustains the world, so that "others' good reflects but back your light" ("To the Countess of Huntingdon"). He excoriates a blind world that unknowingly owes what little vitality it still retains to the virtue of a few moral prodigies who mediate Christ's own virtue, having the quasi-alchemic power to turn "Leaden and iron wills to good" and make "even sinful flesh like his" ("Resurrection, Imperfect"). Such virtuous beings rectify nature to what it was in their own bodies, so interfusing sense and spirit as to make an intelligent organism of the body itself, as depicted in "The Second Anniversary":

we understood
Her by her sight, her pure and eloquent blood
Spoke in her cheeks, and so distinctly wrought,
That one might almost say, her body thought.

These poems of Donne's middle years are less frequently read than the rest of his work, and they have struck readers as perversely obscure and odd. There is clearly some justification for that response, as seen in these lines from "The Second Anniversary":

Immortal Maid, who though thy would'st refuse
The name of mother, be unto my Muse
A father, since her chaste ambition is,
Yearly to bring forth such a child as this.

The poems flaunt their creator's unconcern with decorum to the point of shocking their readers. In his funeral poems Donne harps on decay and maggots, even venturing satiric asides as he contemplates bodily corruption: "Think thee a prince, who of themselves create / Worms which insensibly devour their state" ("The Second Anniversary"). He shows by the analogy of a beheaded man how it is that our dead world still appears to have life and movement ("The Second Anniversary"); he compares the soul in the newborn infant body with a "stubborn sullen anchorite" who sits "fixed to a pillar, or a grave / . . . / Bedded, and bathed in all his ordures" ("The Second Anniversary"); he develops in curious detail the conceit that virtuous men are clocks and that the late John Harrington, second Lord of Exton, was a public clock ("Obsequies to the Lord Harrington"). Such unsettling idiosyncrasy is too persistent to be merely wanton or sensational. It subverts our conventional proprieties in the interest of a radical order of truth.

Donne's reluctance to become a priest, as he was several times urged to do, does not argue a lack of faith. The religious poems he wrote years before he took orders dramatically suggest that his doubts concerned his own unworthiness, his sense that he could not possibly merit God's grace, as seen in these lines from *Divine Meditations 4*:

Yet grace, if thou repent, thou canst not lack;
But who shall give thee that grace to begin?
Oh make thyself with holy mourning black,
And red with blushing, as thou art with sin.

These *Divine Meditations*, or *Holy Sonnets*, make a universal drama of religious life, in which every moment may confront us with the final annulment of time: "What if this present were the world's last night?" (*Divine Meditations 13*). In *Divine Meditations 10* the prospect of a present entry upon eternity also calls for a showdown with ourselves and with the exemplary events

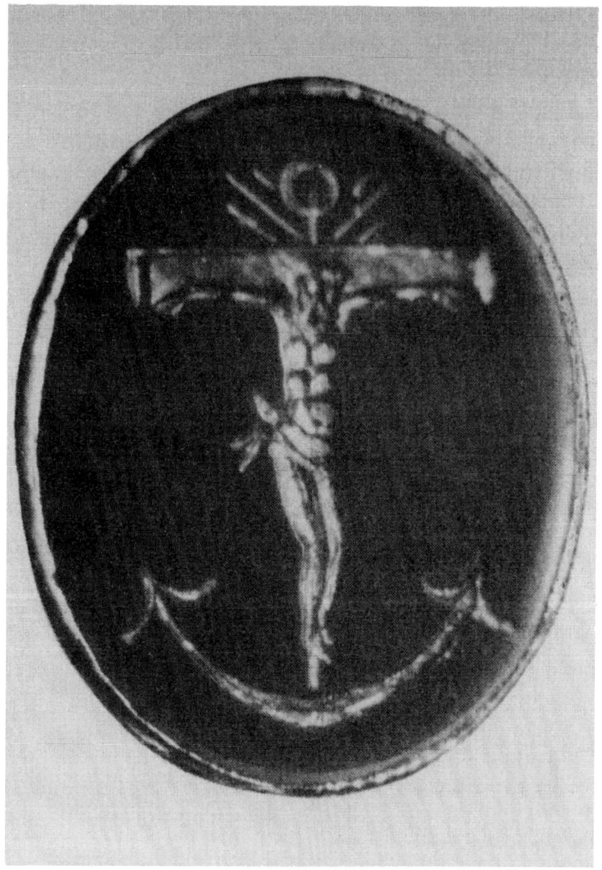

Donne's seal, which he had made in 1615, when he began his career as a cleric (Salisbury Cathedral Library)

that bring time and the timeless together in one order:

Mark in my heart, O soul, where thou dost dwell,
The picture of Christ crucified, and tell
Whether that countenance can thee affright.

Christ's double nature, as God and man at once, assures his power to transform events in time; and it also confirms our power to outbrave our last enemy: "Death be not proud, though some have called thee / Mighty and dreadful, for, thou art not so." The ringing rhetoric sustains a mighty shout of defiance in *Divine Meditations 7*, proclaiming the possibility of a heroic triumph snatched from likely defeat:

At the round earth's imagined corners, blow
Your trumpets, angels, and arise, arise
From death, you numberless infinities
Of souls, and to your scattered bodies go.

Such a magnificent declamation gives our moral life the grandeur of a universal drama that is perpetually reenacted; it sets the trumpets blowing here and now to proclaim the sudden irruption of the Day of Judgment.

The poet is always fearfully aware that we cannot command such triumphs for ourselves, and that we may have part in them at all only by submitting ourselves to a course of repentance that will open us to God's grace at last. In *Divine Meditations 1* he states

> But let them sleep, Lord, and me mourn a space,
> For, if above all these, my sins abound,
> 'Tis late to ask abundance of thy grace,
> When we are there; here on this lowly ground,
> Teach me how to repent.

The present moment may define us forever. We make our predicament immediate by imagining ourselves in mortal sickness, or at the point of final judgment, bringing ourselves sharply up against a reality that our daily lives obscure from us:

> I run to death, and death meets me as fast,
> And all my pleasures are like yesterday,
> I dare not move my dim eyes any way,
> Despair behind, and death before doth cast
> Such terror.

These *Divine Meditations* make self-recognition a necessary means to grace. They dramatize the spiritual dilemma of errant creatures who need God's grace in order that they may deserve it; for we must fall into sin and merit death even though our redemption is at hand, yet we cannot even begin to repent without grace. The poems open the sinner to God, imploring God's forceful intervention by their willing acknowledgment of the need for a drastic onslaught upon his present hardened state, as in *Divine Meditations 14*:

> Batter my heart, three-personed God; for, you
> As yet but knock, breathe, shine, and seek to mend;
> That I may rise, and stand, o'erthrow me, and bend
> Your force, to break, blow, burn, and make me new.

The force of the petition measures the dire extremity of his struggle with himself and with God's adversary. Donne pleads with God that He too has an interest in this contention for the sinner's soul: "Lest the world, flesh, yea Devil put thee out" (*Divine Meditations 17*). The drama brings home to the poet the enormity of his ingratitude to his Redeemer, confronting him bodily with the irony of Christ's self-humiliation for us. In *Divine Meditations 11* Donne wonders why the sinner should not suffer Christ's injuries in his own person:

> Spit in my face ye Jews, and pierce my side,
> Buffet, and scoff, scourge, and crucify me,
> For I have sinned, and sinned, and only he,
> Who could do no iniquity, hath died.

On the death of his wife in 1617 Donne's poetic response in *Divine Meditations 17* was movingly restrained and dignified:

> Since she whom I loved hath paid her last debt
> To nature, and to hers, and my good is dead,
> And her soul early into heaven ravished,
> Wholly in heavenly things my mind is set.

He turns his worldly loss to an occasion of final good in that he now finds only one sure way to be reunited with her. She becomes the means by which Christ woos his soul toward a remarriage in heaven: "But why should I beg more love, when as thou / Dost woo my soul for hers; offering all thine."

Donne's religious poems turn upon a paradox that is central to our hope for eternal life: Christ's sacrificing himself to save mankind. God's regimen is paradoxical, and in *Divine Meditations 13* Donne sees no impropriety in entreating Christ with the casuistry he had used on his "profane mistreses" when he assured them that only the ugly lack compassion:

> so I say to thee,
> To wicked spirits are horrid shapes assigned,
> This beauteous form assures a piteous mind.

In *Divine Meditations 18* he resolves his search for the true Church in a still bolder sexual paradox, petitioning Christ as a "kind husband" to betray his spouse to our view so that the poet's amorous soul may "court thy mild dove": "Who is most true, and pleasing to thee, then / When she'is embraced and open to most men." The apparent indecorum of making the true Church a whore and Christ her complaisant husband at least startles us into recognizing Christ's own catholicity. The paradox brings out a truth about Christ's Church that may well be shocking to those who uphold a sectarian exclusiveness.

Wit becomes the means by which the poet discovers the working of Providence in the casual traffic of the world. A journey westward from

Portrait of Donne by an artist in the school of Cornelius Janssen, presumably a copy of a portrait in the Deanery of St. Paul's (Dyce Collection, Victoria and Albert Museum)

one friend's house to another over Easter 1613 brings home to him the general aberration of nature that prompts us to put pleasure before our due devotion to Christ. We ought to be heading east at Easter so as to contemplate and share Christ's suffering; and in summoning up that event to his mind's eye, he recognizes the shocking paradox of the ignominious death of God upon a Cross: "Could I behold those hands, which span the poles, / And turn all spheres at once, pierced with those holes?" ("Good Friday, 1613. Riding Westward"). An image of Christ's degradation is directly imposed upon an image of God's omnipotence. We see that the event itself has a double force, being at once the catastrophic consequence of our sin and the ultimate assurance of God's saving love. The poet's very journey west may be providential if it brings him to a penitent recognition of his present unworthiness to gaze directly upon Christ:

O Saviour, as thou hang'st upon the tree;
I turn my back to thee, but to receive
Corrections, till thy mercies bid thee leave.
O think me worth thine anger, punish me,
Burn off my rusts, and my deformity,
Restore thine image, so much, by thy grace,
That thou mayest know me, and I'll turn my face.

A serious illness that Donne suffered in 1623 produced a still more startling poetic effect. In "Hymn to God, my God, in my Sickness" the poet presents his recumbent body as a flat map over which the doctors pore like navigators to discover some passage through present dangers to tranquil waters; and he ponders his own destination as if he himself is a vessel that may reach the desirable places of the world only by negotiating some painful straits:

Is the Pacific Sea my home? Or are
The eastern riches? Is Jerusalem?
Anyan, and Magellan, and Gibraltar,
All straits, and none but straits, are ways to them.

By this self-questioning he brings himself to understand that his suffering may itself be a blessing, since he shares the condition of a world in which our ultimate bliss must be won through well-endured hardship. The physical symptoms of his illness become the signs of his salvation: "So, in his purple wrapped receive me Lord, / By these his thorns give me his other crown." The images that make him one with Christ in his suffering transform those pangs into reassurance. The flushed face of the fevered man replicates Christ's bloodied flesh, which is also the purple robe of Christ's saving dominion; the sufferer's spasms of pain become the thorns of Christ's crown, which is also a true crown of glory. By intertwining Christ's agony and loving power with the circumstances of his own desperate illness, Donne identifies the travails of a holy death with Christ's anguish on the Cross, making such a death a means to bliss. His witty conceit seeks to catch the working of Providence itself, which shapes our human accidents in the pattern of timeless truth.

In Donne's poetry, language may catch the presence of God in our human dealings. The pun on the poet's name in "A Hymn to God the Father" registers the distance that the poet's sins have put between himself and God, with new kinds of sin pressing forward as fast as God forgives those already confessed: "When thou hast done, thou hast not done, / For, I have more." Then the puns on "sun" and "Donne" resolve these sinful anxieties themselves:

I have a sin of fear, that when I have spun
My last thread, I shall perish on the shore;
But swear by thy self, that at my death thy son
Shall shine as he shines now, and heretofore;

> And, having done that, thou hast done,
> I fear no more.

For this poet such coincidences of words and ideas are not mere accidents to be juggled with in jest. They mark precisely the working of Providence within the order of nature.

The transformation of Jack Donne the rake into the Reverend Dr. Donne, dean of St. Paul's Cathedral, no longer seems bizarre. To impose such clear-cut categories upon a man's career may be to take too rigid a view of human nature. That the poet of the *Elegies* and *Songs and Sonnets* is also the author of the *Devotions* and the sermons need not indicate some profound spiritual upheaval. One reason for the appeal of Donne in modern times is that he confronts us with the complexity of our own natures.

Donne took holy orders in January 1615, having been persuaded by King James himself of his fitness for a ministry "to which he was, and appeared, very unwilling, apprehending it (such was his mistaking modesty) to be too weighty for his abilities." So writes his first biographer, Izaak Walton, who had known him well and often heard him preach. Once committed to the church, Donne devoted himself to it totally, and his life thereafter becomes a record of incumbencies held and sermons preached.

His wife died in childbirth in 1617. He was elected dean of St. Paul's in November 1621, and he became the most celebrated cleric of his age, preaching frequently before the king at court as well as at St Paul's and other churches. A hundred and sixty of his sermons have survived. The few religious poems he wrote after he became a priest show no falling off in imaginative power, yet the calling of his later years committed him to prose, and the artistry of his *Devotions* and sermons at least matches the artistry of his poems.

The magnificent prose of Donne's *Devotions* embodies a way of thinking that gives it both its character and its power. The impassioned development of a thought through metaphor sets up links and correspondences that are caught in the structure of the sentences themselves, as witnessed in this prayer, number 20 in *Devotions Upon Emergent Occasions*:

> I am come by thy goodness, to the use of thine ordinary means for my *body*, to wash away those *peccant humours*, that endangered it. I have, *O Lord*, a *River* in my *body*, but a *Sea* in my *soul*, and a *Sea* swollen into the depth of a *Deluge*, above the *sea*. Thou hast raised up certain *hills* in me heretofore, by which I might have stood safe, from these *inundations* of *sin* . . . and to the *top* of all these *hills*, thou has brought me heretofore; but this *Deluge*, this *inundation*, is got above all my *Hills*; and I have sinned and sinned, and multiplied *sin* to *sin*, after all these thy assistances against *sin*, and where is there *water* enough to wash away this *Deluge*?

The highly dramatic counterpointing of the syntax follows out an elaborate pattern of understanding. This set of twenty-three *Devotions* presents a prime example of the attempt to find an eternal significance in the natural occurrences of the world, even such a down-to-earth proceeding as a forced evacuation of the bowels to relieve a physical malady.

Donne wrote his *Devotions* in his convalescence from a protracted bout of relapsing fever that brought him very near to death in November and December 1623. He plots in formal stages the day-to-day physical progress of the illness, discovering in it nothing less than a universal pattern of ruin and (as it turns out) recovery. By taking his own constitution for a little world that reproduces the economy of the larger world, he works out in elaborate detail the correspondence between his present predicament and the disordered state of nature. As his illness is no mere physical accident but the embodiment of a spiritual condition, so the whole of nature itself now decays in consequence of reiterated sin. At the very nadir of his being Donne contemplates the prospect of his imminent death, as well as the final ruination of the world, by occasion of the death of another human being whose funeral bell he hears tolling close at hand. The celebrated passage from number 17 in *Devotions Upon Emergent Occasions* gains power in its context:

> Perchance he for whom this *Bell* tolls, may be so ill, as that he knows not it *tolls* for him; And perchance I may think my self so much better than I am, as that they who are about me, and see my state, may have caused it to toll for me, and I know not that. The *Church* is *Catholic*, *universal*, so are all her *Actions*; *All* that she does, belongs to *all*. When she *baptizes a child*, that action concerns me . . . who bends not his *ear* to any *bell*, which upon any occasion rings? But who can remove it from that *bell*, which is passing a *piece of himself* out of this *world*? No Man is an *Island*, entire of it self; every man is a piece of the *Continent*, a part of the *main*; if a *Clod* be washed away by the *Sea*, *Europe* is the less, as well as if a *Promontory* were, as well as if a *Manor* of thy *friends*, or

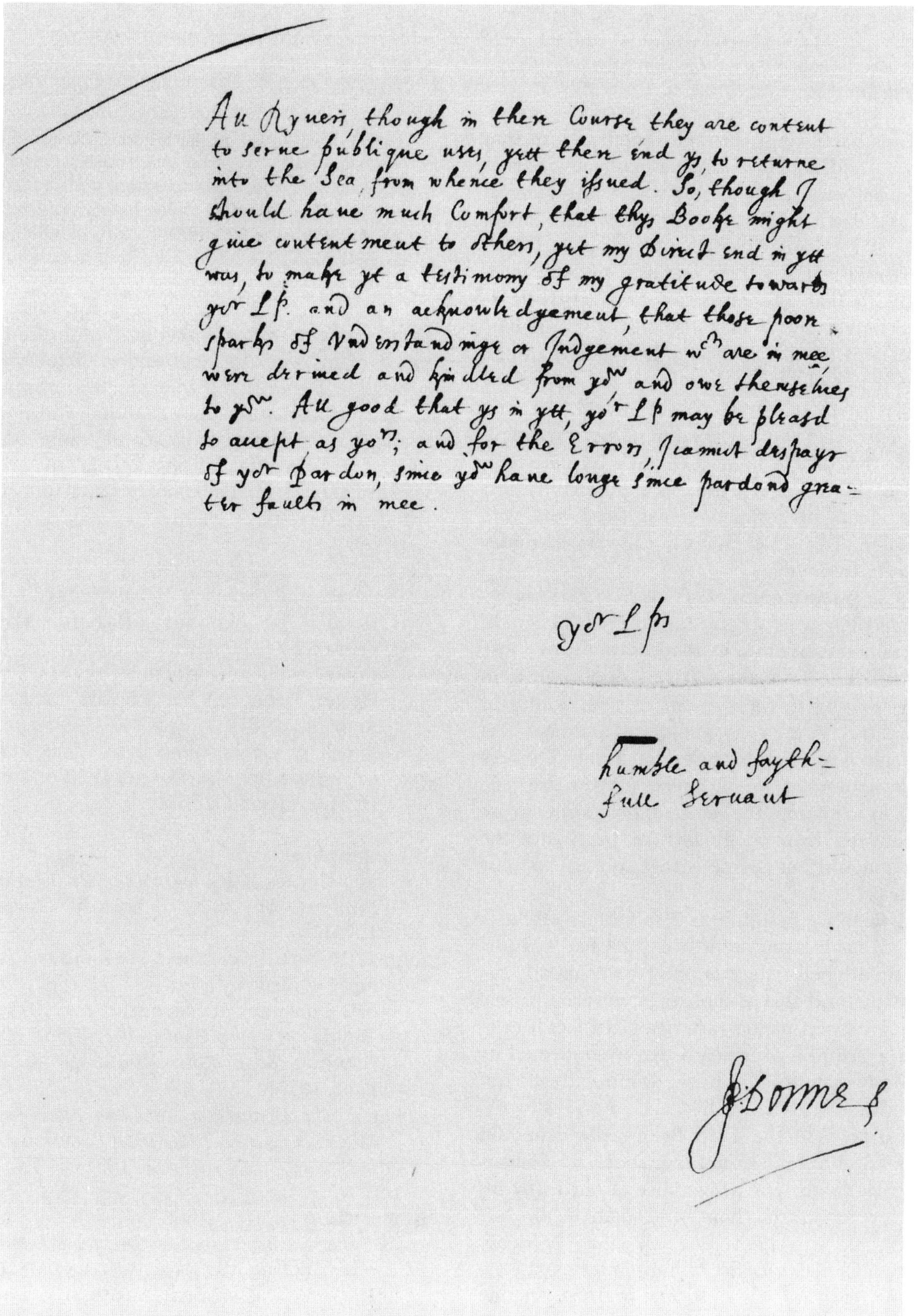

All Ryvers though in their Course they are content to serve publique uses, yett their end ys, to returne into the Sea, from whence they issued. So, though I should have much Comfort, that thys Booke might give contentment to others, yet my Direct end in ytt was, to make yt a testimony of my gratitude towards yor Lp. and an acknowledgement, that those poore sparks of Vnderstandinge or Judgement wch are in mee, were derived and kindled from you and owe themselves to you. All good that ys in ytt, yor Lp may be pleased to accept as yors; and for the Errors, I cannot despayre of yor Pardon, since you have longe since pardoned greater faults in mee.

Yor Lps

humble and faythfull Servant

J. Donne

Letter from Donne to Sir Thomas Egerton, his former employer, in 1610 (private collection lent to the Pierpont Morgan Library). The letter was attached to the back of a copy of Donne's Pseudo-Martyr *(1610), which the author presented to Egerton.*

> of *thine own* were; Any Man's *death* diminishes *me*, because I am involved in *Mankind*; And therefore never send to know for whom the *bell* tolls; It tolls for *thee*.

It is thus harrowingly brought home to him that his own predicament is not particular to himself but shared with the whole of nature. All funeral bells toll for us all, as well as for our dying world.

However, the sudden and unexpected remission of his fear also realizes a spiritual truth. A countermovement against the rush to ruin may save us and the world if we will sustain it in our lives. Christ's blood can counteract the seas of sin that threaten to inundate the world. In one man's extremity the universal design of Providential love discloses itself, and Donne's formal meditation of his sickness stands as a powerfully sustained feat of thinking that discovers the coherence of God's creation in the very fortuities that seem to deny it.

The publication in 1919 of *Donne's Sermons: Selected Passages*, edited by Logan Pearsall Smith, came as a revelation to its readers, not least those who had little taste for sermons. Reviewer John Bailey, writing in the *Quarterly Review*, found in these extracts "the very genius of oratory . . . a masterpiece of English prose." Sir Arthur Quiller-Couch, in *Studies in Literature*, judged the sermons to contain "the most magnificent prose ever uttered from an English pulpit, if not the most magnificent prose ever spoken in our tongue."

Donne's best-known sermon, "Death's Duel," is his last one, which he preached at court just a month before he expired. He was already visibly dying, and this sermon is often taken to seal his long preoccupation with death. In fact it celebrates a triumph over death that is confirmed by the Resurrection of Christ. Donne draws out three distinct senses of his text from Psalm 68, "And unto God the Lord belong the issues Of death." God has power to bring about our deliverance *from* death; our deliverance *in* death (by his care for us in the hour and manner of our death); and our deliverance *by means of* death (through Christ's sacrifice of himself for us). By examining each of these senses in turn, Donne shows that they finally cohere in Christ's life. The sermon culminates in a meditation upon Christ's last hours and sufferings, inviting the reader to acquiesce in oneness with Christ's own condition, just because he is the second Adam who redeems the sin of the first Adam:

> There we leave you, in that blessed dependency, to hang upon him, that hangs upon the cross. There bathe in his tears, there suck at his wounds, and lie down in peace in his grave, till he vouchsafe you a Resurrection, and an ascension into that Kingdom which he hath purchased for you, with the inestimable price of his incorruptible blood.

Over a literary career of some forty years Donne moved from the skeptical naturalism of so much of his work to a conviction of the shaping presence of the divine spirit in the natural creation. Yet his mature understanding did not contradict his earlier vision. He simply came to anticipate a Providential disposition in the restless whirl of the world. The amorous adventurer nurtured the dean of St. Paul's.

Letters:

Letters to Severall Persons of Honour, edited by John Donne, Jr. (London: Richard Marriott, printed by J. Flesher, 1651; reprinted in facsimile, with introduction by M. Thomas Hester, Delmar, N.Y.: Scholars' Facsimiles & Reprints, 1977);

A Collection of Letters, Made by Sr Tobie Mathews, Kt., edited by John Donne, Jr. (London: For H. Herringman, 1660).

Bibliographies:

Geoffrey Keynes, *A Bibliography of Dr. John Donne: Dean of St. Paul's* (Oxford: Clarendon, 1973);

John R. Roberts, *John Donne: An Annotated Bibliography of Modern Criticism, 1912-1967* (Columbia: University of Missouri Press, 1973);

A. J. Smith, ed., *John Donne: The Critical Heritage* (London & Boston: Routledge & Kegan Paul, 1975);

Roberts, *John Donne: An Annotated Bibliography of Modern Criticism, 1968-1978* (Columbia: University of Missouri Press, 1982).

Biographies:

Izaak Walton, *The Lives of Dr. John Donne, Sir Henry Wotton, Mr. Richard Hooker, Mr. George Herbert, and Robert Sanderson* (London: Printed by Tho. Newcomb for Richard Marriott, 1670; the *Life of Dr. John Donne* first appeared in the 1640 edition of Donne's *LXXX Sermons*);

Effigy of Donne made by Nicholas Stone in 1631, located in St. Paul's Cathedral.

Augustus Jessopp, *John Donne, Sometime Dean of St. Paul's A. D. 1621-1631* (London: Methuen, 1897);

Sir Edmund Gosse, *The Life and Letters of John Donne*, 2 volumes (London: Heinemann, 1899);

Hugh I'Anson Fausset, *John Donne: A Study in Discord* (London: Cape, 1924; New York: Harcourt, Brace & Co., 1925);

R. C. Bald, *Donne and the Drurys* (Cambridge: Cambridge University Press, 1959);

Edward LeComte, *Grace to a Witty Sinner: A Life of John Donne* (New York: Walker & Co., 1965);

Bald, *John Donne: A Life* (New York & Oxford: Oxford University Press, 1970).

References:

N. J. C. Andreasen, *John Donne: Conservative Revolutionary* (Princeton: Princeton University Press, 1967);

John Bailey, "The Sermons of a Poet," *Quarterly Review*, 463 (April 1920): 317-328;

R. C. Bald, *Donne's Influence in English Literature* (Morpeth, U.K.: St. John's College Press, 1932);

Joan Bennett, *Four Metaphysical Poets: Donne, Herbert, Vaughan, Crashaw* (Cambridge: Cambridge University Press, 1934);

Louis I. Bredvold, "The Naturalism of Donne in Relation to Some Renaissance Traditions," *JEGP*, 22 (1923): 471-502;

Douglas Bush, *English Literature in the Earlier Seventeenth Century, 1600-1660* (Oxford: Clarendon, 1945);

John Carey, *John Donne: Life, Mind and Art* (New York: Oxford University Press, 1981);

Dwight Cathcart, *Doubting Conscience: Donne and the Poetry of Moral Argument* (Ann Arbor: University of Michigan Press, 1975);

Charles Monroe Coffin, *John Donne and the New Philosophy* (Morningside Heights, N.Y.: Columbia University Press, 1937);

Rosalie L. Colie, *Paradoxia Epidemica: The Renaissance Tradition of Paradox* (Princeton: Princeton University Press, 1966);

Patrick Cruttwell, *The Shakespearean Moment and Its Place in the Poetry of the 17th Century* (London: Chatto & Windus, 1954);

Joseph E. Duncan, *The Revival of Metaphysical Poetry: The History of a Style, 1800 to the Present* (Minneapolis: University of Minnesota Press, 1959);

T. S. Eliot, "The Metaphysical Poets," *TLS*, 20 October 1921, pp. 669-670;

William Empson, "Donne the Space Man," *Kenyon Review*, 19 (Summer 1957): 337-399;

Barbara Everett, *Donne: A London Poet* (London: Oxford University Press, 1972);

Anne Ferry, *All in War with Time: Love Poetry of Shakespeare, Donne, Jonson, Marvell* (Cambridge, Mass.: Harvard University Press, 1975);

Ferry, *The "Inward" Language: Sonnets of Wyatt, Sidney, Shakespeare, Donne* (Chicago: University of Chicago Press, 1983);

Peter Amadeus Fiore, ed., *Just So Much Honor: Essays Commemorating the Four-Hundredth Anniversary of the Birth of John Donne* (University Park: Pennsylvania State University Press, 1972);

Dennis Flynn, "Donne and the Ancient Catholic Nobility," *English Literary Renaissance*, 19 (Autumn 1989): 305-323;

Flynn, "Donne's Catholicism: I," *Recusant History*, 13 (April 1975): 1-17; "Donne's Catholicism: II" (April 1976): 178-195;

Helen Gardner, ed., *John Donne: A Collection of Critical Essays* (Englewood Cliffs, N.J.: Prentice-Hall, 1962);

K. W. Gransden, *John Donne* (London & New York: Longmans, Green, 1954);

Donald L. Guss, *John Donne, Petrarchist* (Detroit: Wayne State University Press, 1966);

M. Thomas Hester, *Kinde Pitty and Brave Scorn: John Donne's Satyres* (Durham, N.C.: Duke University Press, 1982);

Hester and R. V. Young, Jr., eds., *John Donne Journal*, 1982- ;

Merritt Y. Hughes, "Kidnapping Donne," *University of California Publications in English*, 4 (1934): 61-89;

Richard E. Hughes, *The Progress of the Soul: The Interior Career of John Donne* (New York: William Morrow, 1968);

Clay Hunt, *Donne's Poetry: Essays in Literary Analysis* (New Haven: Yale University Press, 1954);

Robert S. Jackson, *John Donne's Christian Vocation* (Evanston, Ill.: Northwestern University Press, 1970);

Frank Kermode, "Dissociation of Sensibility," *Kenyon Review*, 19 (Spring 1957): 169-194;

F. R. Leavis, "The Influence of Donne on Modern Poetry," *Bookman*, 79 (March 1931): 346-347;

Pierre Legouis, *Donne the Craftsman* (Paris: Didier, 1928);

J. B. Leishman, *The Monarch of Wit: An Analytical and Comparative Study of the Poetry of John Donne* (London: Hutchinson University Library, 1951);

C. S. Lewis, *English Literature in the Sixteenth Century Excluding Drama* (Oxford: Clarendon, 1954);

Anthony Low, *Love's Architecture: Devotional Modes in Seventeenth-Century English Poetry* (New York: New York University Press, 1978);

M. M. Mahood, *Poetry and Humanism* (New Haven: Yale University Press, 1950);

Arthur F. Marotti, *John Donne, Coterie Poet* (Madison: University of Wisconsin Press, 1986);

Louis L. Martz, *The Poetry of Meditation: A Study in English Religious Literature of the Seventeenth Century* (New Haven: Yale University Press, 1954);

Marjorie Hope Nicolson, *The Breaking of the Circle: Studies in the Effect of the "New Science" upon Seventeenth Century Poetry* (Evanston, Ill.: Northwestern University Press, 1950);

David Novarr, *The Disinterred Muse: Donne's Texts and Contexts* (Ithaca, N.Y.: Cornell University Press, 1980);

Douglas L. Peterson, *The English Lyric from Wyatt to Donne* (Princeton: Princeton University Press, 1967);

Sir Arthur Quiller-Couch, *Studies in Literature* (Cambridge: Cambridge University Press, 1920); pp. 96-117;

John R. Roberts, ed., *Essential Articles for the Study of John Donne's Poetry* (Hamden, Conn.: Archon, 1975);

Murray Roston, *The Soul of Wit: A Study of John Donne* (Oxford: Clarendon Press, 1974);

Terry G. Sherwood, *Fulfilling the Circle: A Study of John Donne's Thought* (Toronto & Buffalo: University of Toronto Press, 1984);

Evelyn M. Simpson, *A Study of the Prose Works of John Donne* (Oxford: Clarendon, 1924);

Thomas O. Sloane, *Donne, Milton, and the End of Humanist Rhetoric* (Berkeley: University of California Press, 1985);

A. J. Smith, ed., *John Donne: Essays in Celebration* (London: Methuen, 1972);

Smith, *The Metaphysics of Love: Studies in Renaissance Love Poetry from Dante to Milton* (Cambridge & New York: Cambridge University Press, 1985);

James Smith, "On Metaphysical Poetry," *Scrutiny*, 2 (December 1933): 222-239;

Theodore Spencer, ed., *A Garland for John Donne, 1631-1931* (Cambridge, Mass.: Harvard University Press, 1931);

Arnold Stein, *John Donne's Lyrics: The Eloquence of Action* (Minneapolis: University of Minnesota Press, 1962);

Claude J. Summers and Ted-Larry Pebworth, eds., *The Eagle and the Dove: Reassessing John Donne* (Columbia: University of Missouri Press, 1986);

Edward W. Tayler, *Donne's Idea of a Woman: Structure and Meaning in "The Anniversaries"* (New York: Columbia University Press, 1991);

Rosemond Tuve, *Elizabethan and Metaphysical Imagery: Renaissance Poetic and Twentieth-Century Critics* (Chicago: University of Chicago Press, 1947);

Leonard Unger, *Donne's Poetry and Modern Criticism* (Chicago: Henry Regnery, 1950);

Helen C. White, *The Metaphysical Poets: A Study in Religious Experience* (New York: Macmillan, 1936);

Baird W. Whitlock, "Donne's University Years," *English Studies*, 43 (February 1962): 1-20;

George Williamson, *The Donne Tradition: A Study in English Poetry from Donne to the Death of Cowley* (Cambridge, Mass.: Harvard University Press, 1930);

Yvor Winters, "The 16th Century Lyric in England: A Critical and Historical Reinterpretation," *Poetry*, 53 (February 1939): 258-272.

Papers:
With the exception of the *Anniversaries*, almost none of Donne's poems were published during his lifetime; only one poem survives in his holograph. The texts for all others derive from more than two hundred pieces of manuscript evidence, the majority of which are recorded by Peter Beal in *Index to English Literary Manuscripts*, volume one (London: R. R. Bowker, 1980). A forthcoming project under the general editorship of Gary Stringer, *The Variorum Edition of the Poetry of John Donne* (Columbia: University of Missouri Press, 1991-), aims to account for the complete textual and critical history of Donne's poems.

John Ford

(circa April 1586 - ?)

This entry was updated by Paul A. Cantor (University of Virginia) from his entry in DLB 58: Jacobean and Caroline Dramatists.

BOOKS: *Fames Memoriall, or The Earle of Devonshire Deceased* (London: Printed by R. Bradock for C. Purset, 1606);

Honor Triumphant. Or the Peeres Challenge, By Armes Defensible, At Tilt. Also the Monarches Meeting (London: Printed by G. Eld for F. Burton, 1606);

Christes Bloodie Sweat. Or the Sonne of God in His Agonie, attributed to Ford (London: Printed by R. Blower, 1613);

The Golden Meane, attributed to Ford (London: Printed by H. Lownes for J. Chorlton, 1613);

A Line of Life. Pointing at the Immortalitie of a Vertuous Name (London: Printed by W. Stansby for N. Butter, 1620);

The Lovers Melancholy (London: Printed by F. Kingston for H. Seile, 1629);

The Broken Heart. A Tragedie (London: Printed by J. Beale for H. Beeston, 1633);

'Tis Pitty Shee's a Whore (London: Printed by N. Okes for R. Collins, 1633);

Loves Sacrifice. A Tragedie (London: Printed by J. Beale for H. Beeston, 1633);

The Chronicle Historie of Perkin Warbeck (London: Printed by T. Purfoot for H. Beeston, 1634);

The Fancies, Chast and Noble (London: Printed by E. Purslowe for H. Seile, 1638);

The Ladies Triall (London: Printed by E. Griffin for H. Shephard, 1639);

The Queen, or The Excellency of Her Sex, attributed to Ford (London: Printed by T. N. for Thomas Heath, 1653);

The Sun's-Darling: A Moral Masque, by Ford and Thomas Dekker (London: Printed by J. Bell for Andrew Penneycuicke, 1656);

The Witch of Edmonton, by Ford, Dekker, and William Rowley (London: Printed by J. Cottrel for Edward Blackmore, 1658).

Editions: *The Works of John Ford*, 3 volumes, edited by Alexander Dyce and William Gifford (London: J. Toovey, 1869)—comprises *The Lover's Melancholy, 'Tis Pity She's a Whore, The Broken Heart, Love's Sacrifice, Perkin Warbeck, The Fancies Chaste and Noble, The Lady's Trial, The Sun's Darling, The Witch of Edmonton, Fame's Memorial, Poems, Honor Triumphant, A Line of Life*;

John Ford, edited by Havelock Ellis (London: T. Fisher Unwin, 1888)—comprises *The Lover's Melancholy, 'Tis Pity She's a Whore, The Broken Heart, Love's Sacrifice, Perkin Warbeck*;

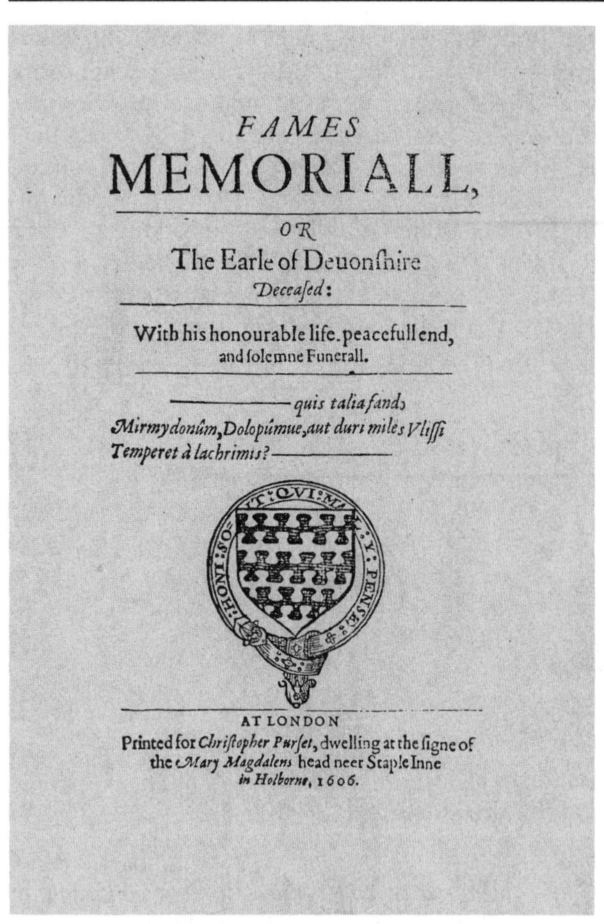

FAMES

MEMORIALL,

OR

The Earle of Deuonshire

Deceased:

With his honourable life, peacefull end, and solemne Funerall.

———*quis talia fando*
Mirmydonum, Dolopumue, aut duri miles Vlissi
Temperet à lachrimis?———

AT LONDON

Printed for *Christopher Purset*, dwelling at the signe of the *Mary Magdalens* head neer Staple Inne *in Holborne*, 1606.

Title page for the 1606 quarto edition of Ford's first book, an elegy for Charles Blount, Earl of Devonshire (Bodleian Library)

John Ford: Three Plays, edited by Keith Sturgess (Harmondsworth, U.K.: Penguin, 1970)—comprises *'Tis Pity She's a Whore, The Broken Heart, Perkin Warbeck.*

PLAY PRODUCTIONS: *An Ill Beginning Has a Good End*, attributed to Ford, London, at Court, winter 1612-1613;

The Witch of Edmonton, by Ford, Thomas Dekker, and William Rowley, London, Cockpit theater(?), 1621;

The Welsh Ambassador (perhaps a revision of *The Noble Spanish Soldier* by Dekker and John Day), by Dekker and perhaps Ford, unknown theater, circa 1623;

The Sun's Darling, by Ford and Dekker, London, Cockpit theater, March 1624;

The Fairy Knight, by Ford and Dekker, London, Red Bull theater, licensed 11 June 1624;

The Late Murder of the Son upon the Mother, by Ford, Dekker, Rowley, and John Webster, London, Red Bull theater, September 1624;

The Bristow Merchant, by Ford and Dekker, London, Fortune theater, licensed 22 October 1624;

The Lover's Melancholy, London, Blackfriars theater, licensed 24 November 1628;

Beauty in a Trance, London, Cockpit (Whitehall Palace), 28 November 1630;

The Broken Heart, London, Blackfriars theater, circa 1630-1633;

'Tis Pity She's a Whore, London, Phoenix theater, circa 1630-1633;

Love's Sacrifice, London, Phoenix theater, circa 1632-1633;

Perkin Warbeck, London, Phoenix theater, circa 1633-1634;

The Fancies Chaste and Noble, London, Phoenix theater, circa 1635-1636;

The Lady's Trial, London, Phoenix theater, licensed 3 May 1638.

John Ford is arguably the last major dramatist of the English Renaissance. Though he is usually discussed along with the Jacobean playwrights, most of his dramatic work falls into the Caroline period. Judging by his plays, Ford himself seems to have had a sense of being a latecomer to the Renaissance dramatic scene. Coming as he did at the end of one of the most productive eras in the history of drama, Ford had a rich heritage to draw upon in shaping his own art. He clearly derived inspiration from his great predecessors, above all, William Shakespeare, and his plays often have a reflective character, as if he were consciously harking back to earlier achievements in the genres in which he was working.

And yet the artistic heritage which sustained Ford also presented a challenge to him, the challenge of finding novel themes and stage effects long after writers from Christopher Marlowe to Thomas Middleton seemed to have exhausted the possibilities of Renaissance theater. Ford's attraction to normally taboo themes, such as incest, may be accounted for by his need to get the attention of audiences who thought they had already seen everything there was to see on the stage. It was once common to attribute Ford's choice of subject matter to a kind of moral decadence, as if in portraying incest on the stage he were advocating it in real life. But Ford's exploration of exotic subjects is best explained in aesthetic rather than in moral terms. He had to find a way of revitalizing themes and motifs that had grown stale through repetition in the hands of his predecessors. In his most famous and most shocking play, *'Tis Pity She's a Whore* (circa 1630-1633), Ford takes the potentially hackneyed theme of star-crossed young lovers and gives it a new twist by making the Romeo and Juliet of his play brother and sister. In many respects, Ford pushed Renaissance drama to its limits, and the course his work took suggests that, even if the Puritans had not closed the London theaters in 1642, the Elizabethan dramatic impulse had finally played itself out in the Caroline era.

As is the case with many Renaissance dramatists, little is known about Ford's life. He was born in Ilsington, Devonshire, and baptized on 17 April 1586, the second son of Thomas and Elizabeth Ford. The Fords were evidently a family of country gentlemen; one of Ford's ancestors was granted a coat of arms, and his father was a landowner. Ford seems to have been relatively well educated. A John Ford from Devon is listed on the rolls of Exeter College, Oxford, in 1601. In 1602 Ford enrolled at one of the Inns of Court, the Middle Temple, with which he was associated for many years. The Inns of Court provided a general education and specific legal training. We have no way of knowing whether Ford ever actually practiced law, but at the time it was one of the few professions open to young gentlemen who hoped to rise in the world. What evidence we have suggests that Ford ran into a few difficulties. He was expelled from the Middle Temple in the 1605-1606 term for not paying his buttery bill and was not reinstated until 10 June 1608. In 1617 he was suspended along with forty other members of the Middle Temple for wearing mere hats in place of the traditional lawyer's caps. One hesitates to read too much into such a minor incident, but it does suggest that Ford had trouble fitting himself into the conventional role of a lawyer.

The one other piece of evidence perhaps suggesting a rebellious nature in the young John Ford is his father's will. When Thomas Ford died in 1610, he left ten pounds to John but larger sums to John's two younger brothers, an action which hints at some form of parental displeasure with the future dramatist. Ford's older brother, Henry, died in 1616 and left John a legacy amounting to twenty pounds a year for the rest of his life. As sketchy as the details of Ford's life are, the profile he presents is a familiar one: a young man setting out for London to make his fortune but not succeeding in conventional paths, gradually drifting into literary endeavors, and finally hitting upon the theater as his means of livelihood. Ford's career as a dramatist is fairly well documented. At the height of his dramatic powers, he worked for the King's Majesties Servants (Shakespeare's old company) and then joined Hugh Beeston's companies at the Phoenix theater in Drury Lane. Among the few contemporary references to Ford, the closest we come to a glimpse into his personality is in an epigram in William Heminges's *Elegy on Randolph's Finger*: "Deep in a dumpe Jack Ford alone was got / With folded arms and melancholy hat." The last work of Ford's to be published under his name appeared in 1639. After that date no records of Ford can be found; we do not even know when or where he died.

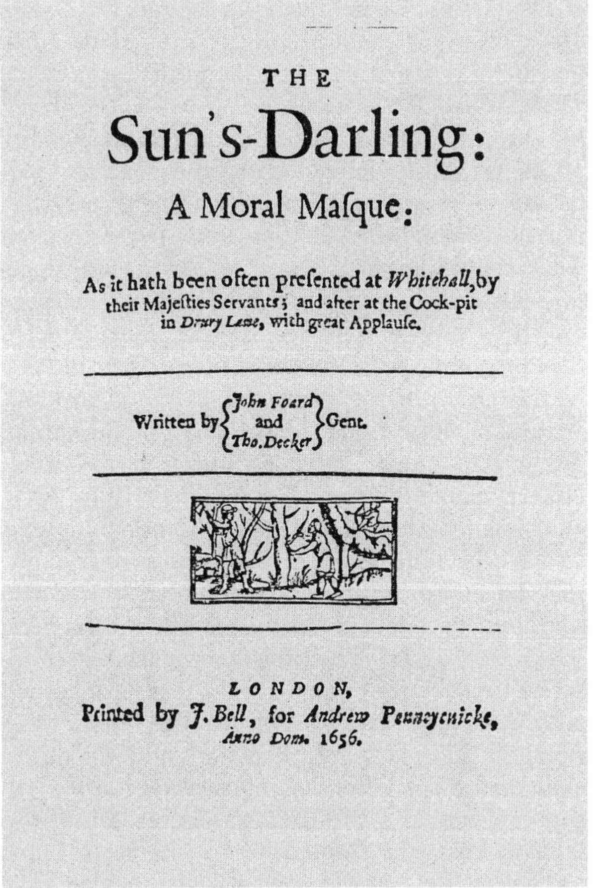

THE

Sun's-Darling:

A Moral Masque:

As it hath been often presented at *Whitehall*, by their Majesties Servants; and after at the Cock-pit in *Drury Lane*, with great Applause.

Written by {*John Foard* and *Tho. Decker*} Gent.

LONDON,
Printed by *J. Bell*, for *Andrew Pennycuicke*, *Anno Dom.* 1656.

Title page for the 1656 quarto edition of Ford and Dekker's masque (from Fredson Bowers, ed., The Dramatic Works of Thomas Dekker, *volume 4, 1961)*

Before turning to drama, Ford tried his hand at a few other literary forms. He is generally credited with five nondramatic works: two poems, *Fame's Memorial* (1606) and *Christ's Bloody Sweat* (1613); and three pamphlets, *Honor Triumphant* (1606), *The Golden Mean* (1613), and *A Line of Life* (1620). *Christ's Bloody Sweat* and *The Golden Mean* are only conjecturally attributed to Ford, and he may also have been the author of a prose work called *Sir Thomas Overbury's Ghost* (entered in the Stationers' Register on 25 November 1615), now lost. None of these works has any particular literary merit, and they would probably not be remembered if they were not associated with an author who went on to become an important dramatist. *Fame's Memorial* (1606), an elegy on the death of Charles Blount, Earl of Devonshire, and Lord Mountjoy, is of some interest because the poem is dedicated to Blount's widow, Lady Penelope Rich, the Stella of Sir Philip Sidney's sonnet sequence, *Astrophil and Stella* (1591). Some scholars believe that Lady Rich, who was married against her will and who seems to have become involved in a romantic triangle, may have provided a model for several of Ford's heroines, particularly Penthea in *The Broken Heart* (circa 1630-1633). The prose pamphlets are of interest because they show Ford already concerned with models of virtuous conduct and questions of nobility. The kind of rhetorical and dialectical skill Ford displays in arguing such typical Renaissance topics as "Fair lady was never false" was later to be at the disposal of his characters, such as Giovanni in *'Tis Pity She's a Whore*.

In his nondramatic works, Ford was writing as a literary amateur. Unfortunately the beginnings of his career as a professional dramatist are obscure. In the first of his surviving works he was collaborating with older and more established playwrights. But he may have written plays on his own earlier. For many of Ford's "works" all that survive are the titles and in some cases records of their having been staged; in most cases the attribution to Ford is speculative, and even if he did have a hand in these works, he may not have been the sole author. All one can do is to record the titles of lost works which have been associated with Ford's name: *An Ill Beginning Has a Good End* (winter 1612-1613), *Beauty in a Trance* (28 November 1630), *The London Merchant, The Royal Combat, The Fairy Knight* (written with Thomas Dekker, licensed 11 June 1624), *The Late Murder of the Son upon the Mother* (with Dekker, William Rowley, and John Webster, September 1624), and *The Bristow Merchant* (with Dekker, licensed 22 October 1624). To complicate the picture further, some scholars have tried to ascribe to Ford works credited to other playwrights, such as *The Spanish Gypsy*, published originally as a work by Middleton and Rowley. Even in the case

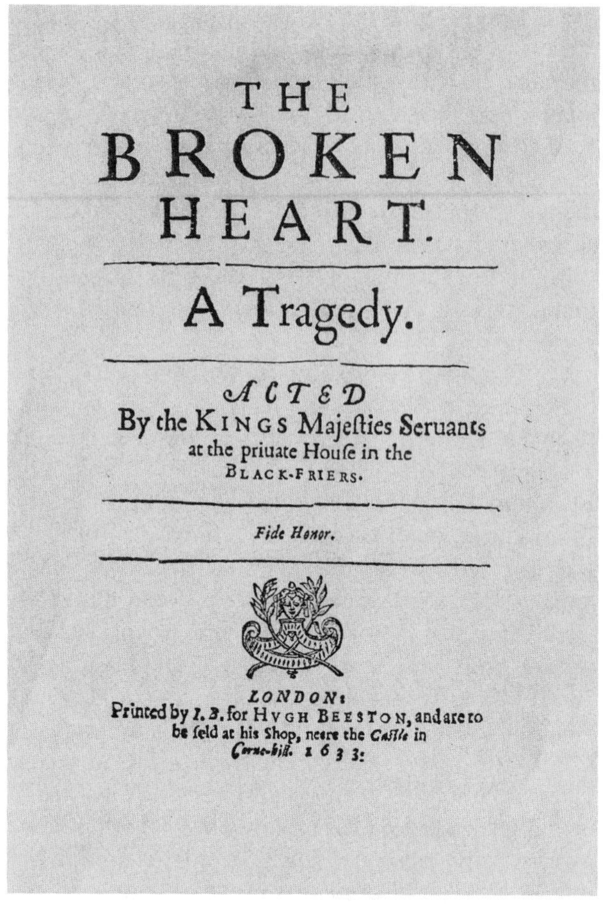
THE BROKEN HEART.

A Tragedy.

ACTED By the KINGS Majesties Seruants at the priuate House in the BLACK-FRIERS.

Fide Honor.

LONDON: Printed by I. B. for HVGH BEESTON, and are to be sold at his Shop, neere the Castle in Corne-hill. 1633.

Title page for the 1633 quarto edition of what is probably the last play Ford wrote for the King's Majesties Servants (Bodleian Library)

of the established Ford canon, it has proven impossible to determine conclusively the dates of composition for the plays, or even the precise order in which they were written. Thus any attempt to analyze Ford's dramatic career must rest on shaky foundations. It is very difficult to substantiate any hypothesis about his development as a playwright since most of his early works have been lost and we cannot be sure which are his final compositions. The titles of his lost works suggest that the range of his subject matter was greater than appears in his surviving work. In particular, he seems to have devoted more attention to middle-class subjects than one would conclude from the works we have by him. Given the significant gaps in our knowledge about Ford's output as a playwright, the only safe course is to take up his surviving works in their order of publication, which is firmly established.

Though his output is uneven in quality, Ford was in general a consummate man of the theater. The governing principle of his dramas seems to be theatrical effect. For the sake of a striking scene or turn of events, he will sacrifice dramatic probability or consistency of character. Rather than exploring a single plot in depth, he tends to load his plays with multiple plots, so that he can always keep one story line or another moving. In a quintessentially Fordian moment in *Love's Sacrifice* (circa 1632-1633), a "wanton Courtier" named Ferentes is confronted by not just one but three women he has seduced with promises of marriage and abandoned with child. In *The Broken Heart,* the heroine Calantha learns in the space of less than ten lines of the deaths of her father, her best friend, and her betrothed lover.

In terms of subject matter, Ford staked out for himself the theme of thwarted love. He frequently portrays the conflict between romantic passion and other obligations, usually of a social nature. His plays often deal with romantic triangles, and he seems particularly drawn to the theme of sexual jealousy, especially when a man's close friend is the one to arouse his suspicions. Of all the earlier plays which seem to hover in the background of Ford's works, *Othello* (1604) casts the broadest shadow.

What is perhaps most distinctive about Ford as a playwright is the clarity, directness, fluidity, and (at its best) the limpid beauty of his dramatic verse, together with his talent for mood painting, especially moods of exquisite sorrow and suffering. His characters are perpetually frustrated in their desires either because they are simply confused about what they want or because their passions pull them in two directions at once. He loves to create characters with an almost self-conscious aristocratic bearing, who pride themselves on maintaining their self-possession in the face of the most calamitous turns of fortune. Noble death scenes, filled with stoic rhetoric, are one of Ford's specialties. At times his characters can become theatrical in their nobility, as if they somehow knew they were on stage playing a part and had decided to play it to the hilt, observing all the proper forms and gestures. In a way Ford's characters seem to share their creator's sense of being a latecomer. They appear to have learned how to behave from watching plays; they are governed in their lives by theatrical models of what it is to be a tragic lover, a noble prince, a jealous husband, or a loyal friend. It is no accident that *Perkin Warbeck* (circa 1633-1634) is the most nearly perfect of Ford's creations, for in choosing the theme of a pretender to the throne for this play he finally hit upon the ideal dramatic vehicle for his distinctive vision. Striving to act out the noble role of a storybook king in a world of realpolitik, Perkin becomes an emblem for all of Ford's characters, whose often overheated poetic imaginations are constantly running afoul of the coolly prosaic reality in which they find themselves.

The first play of Ford's which survives is *The Witch of Edmonton,* written in 1621 with the seasoned Elizabethan playwright Dekker and the perennial collaborator Rowley. It may have been first performed by the Prince's Servants at the Cockpit theater before the court production at Whitehall Palace on 29 December 1621. The play is in part based on an actual contemporary incident, recounted in Henry Goodcole's *The Wonderfull Discoverie of Elizabeth Sawyer A Witch Late of Edmonton* (1621). The play weaves together two plots. One is the story of Mother Sawyer, an old woman who is accused by the local townspeople of witchcraft so often that she turns to the devil to gain revenge and actually becomes a witch, a crime for which she is eventually sentenced to death. The other plot is the story of a young man named Frank Thorney, who has secretly married a serving maid named Winnifride. When Frank's father insists for financial reasons that he marry a rich yeoman's daughter, Susan Carter, he knowingly commits bigamy and, sinking further into crime, eventually kills Susan in order to be able to escape with Winnifride and his newly acquired wealth. Though Frank temporarily manages to place the blame for the murder on two innocent men, his guilt is discovered in the end, and he too is led off to be executed.

In trying to parcel out the different sections of *The Witch of Edmonton* among its three authors, scholars have quarreled, but the consensus is that Dekker basically handled the Mother Sawyer plot and Ford the Frank Thorney plot (though Dekker may have been largely responsible for creating the character of Susan Carter). As was often the case in his collaborations, Rowley probably did not contribute much to the play: he seems to have written the few comic scenes between a rustic clown named Cuddy Banks and the devil in the form of Mother Sawyer's dog. Though at times crude and simplistic, *The Witch of Edmonton* is in many respects one of the most successful of the few Renaissance attempts at domestic tragedy. With its rural setting and the inevitability with which its protagonists are drawn to their destruction, the play has something of the feel of a Thomas Hardy novel. In its sympathy

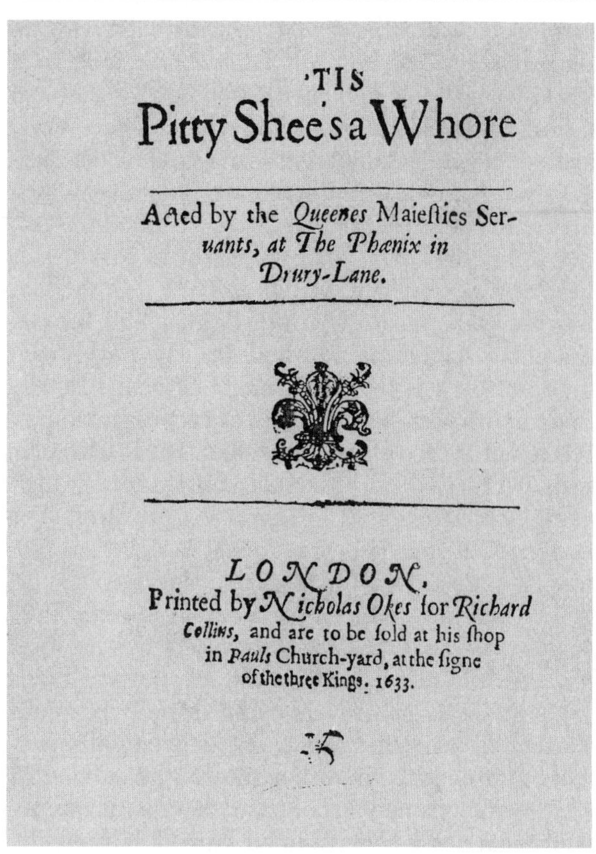
'TIS

Pitty Shee's a Whore

Acted by the Queenes Maieſties Seruants, at The Phœnix in Drury-Lane.

LONDON.

Printed by Nicholas Okes for Richard Collins, and are to be ſold at his ſhop in Pauls Church-yard, at the ſigne of the three Kings. 1633.

Title page for the 1633 quarto edition of Ford's best-known play (Folger Shakespeare Library)

for the outcast and the financially troubled, *The Witch of Edmonton* comes as close as any English Renaissance drama to social protest. Frank is basically a decent young man who is led into bigamy and other crimes in order to save his father's land (and hence his own inheritance). Initially, Mother Sawyer's only crime is being old, and when she is accused of being a witch, she pointedly turns the tables on her accusers by claiming that the real witches are the beautiful women at court, who bewitch men with their sensual arts, and the wives of London merchants, who magically transform hard-earned wealth into worthless luxuries.

But *The Witch of Edmonton* stops short of being a modern problem play or sociological drama. Though at times it strongly suggests that the upper classes get away with precisely the crimes for which the middle and lower classes are punished, in the end the play reimposes conventional moral categories on its action. The authors were not quite ready for a purely sociological explanation of events. They have to account for the tragedy they are telling by the only explanatory system they have available: evil spirits, not socioeconomic conditions, are ultimately responsible for what Mother Sawyer and Frank Thorney do. For example, Frank kills Susan as a result of the promptings of the witch's familiar. Despite the effort to associate Frank with evil spirits, he is allowed a sincere repentance at the end and receives forgiveness from all the characters he has injured. Though Ford did not write the whole of *The Witch of Edmonton*, many critics believe that he was responsible for the play's overall construction. In any case the play is unique in the Ford canon as we have it and adds to our sense of his range as a dramatist. Set in the country rather than in the court, with a cast of common people rather than of aristocrats, and dealing with simple and basic human problems and emotions rather than the convoluted psyches and hypersophisticated sentiments of Ford's usual characters, *The Witch of Edmonton* is proof that when he wanted to, Ford could work within the ordinary range of human experience.

Ford continued his collaboration with Dekker in a masque called *The Sun's Darling*, licensed on 3 March 1624 and presumably performed at the Cockpit theater and at court. The work was not printed until 1656, and we do not know if what we have is the original version. There are signs that the masque was revised in 1638 or 1639, perhaps for a new court performance. *The Sun's Darling* is a typical court masque, with elements of a morality play mixed in. It tells the story of the Sun's favorite, Raybright, who tries to cure his melancholy by turning to the world of nature. Moving through the four seasons from spring to winter, Raybright foolishly abandons the natural gifts symbolized by his companions Youth, Health, and Delight for the sake of a variety of false pleasures to which he is led by his squire Folly and which are chiefly represented by a figure named Humour. When read, the work comes across as an obvious and on the whole rather tedious allegory; when performed, it was no doubt enlivened by the use of stage spectacle, music, singing, and dancing.

The first of Ford's solo efforts as a dramatist which has come down to us is *The Lover's Melancholy*, a tragicomedy licensed in 1628, performed according to the title page by the King's Majesties Servants privately at the Blackfriars and publicly at the Globe, and published in 1629. The play tells the story of two mental illnesses which must be cured, in true comic fashion, by means of a series of disguises and mistaken identities. Prince

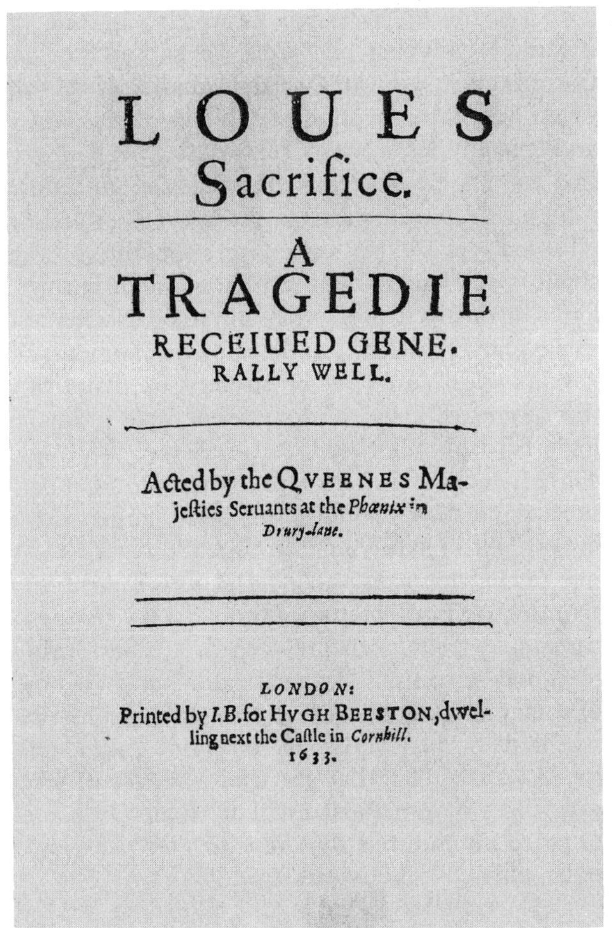
LOUES
Sacrifice.
A
TRAGEDIE
RECEIUED GENE-
RALLY WELL.

Acted by the QVEENES Ma-
jesties Seruants at the Phœnix in
Drury-lane.

LONDON:
Printed by I.B. for HVGH BEESTON, dwelling next the Castle in Cornhill.
1633.

Title page for the 1633 quarto edition of the play that has been called Ford's attempt to rewrite William Shakespeare's Othello *(Bodleian Library)*

Palador of Cyprus is suffering from the lover's melancholy of the title as a result of losing his betrothed Eroclea in a series of intrigues involving his now dead father, King Agenor. Eroclea's father, Lord Meleander, has lost his reason as a result of her disappearance. Into this sorrowful and nearly paralyzed world Ford introduces a young lord named Menaphon, who has returned from Greece to see the woman he loves, Thamasta, cousin to Palador. Menaphon is accompanied by a youth from Greece named Parthenophil, whose good looks enchant Thamasta. Though Parthenophil rejects Thamasta's advances, Menaphon grows increasingly jealous of his young friend. When events threaten to take a tragic turn, Parthenophil is revealed to be Eroclea in disguise, thus resolving all difficulties. Eroclea in reunited with Palador, helps to restore her father's mental balance, and permits Menaphon to be reconciled with Thamasta.

Much of the criticism of *The Lover's Melancholy* has focused on Ford's debt to Robert Burton's *The Anatomy of Melancholy* (1621), the great Renaissance compendium of medical, scientific, and psychological knowledge, which Ford does draw upon in portraying the symptoms and cure of his melancholy characters. But Ford's greatest debt is to Shakespeare. *The Lover's Melancholy* is basically a reworking of *Twelfth Night* (1601), with Palador corresponding to Orsino and Eroclea to Viola. Though Ford does not fully grasp Shakespeare's profound understanding of the pitfalls of romantic love, he does follow his master in portraying the way people get locked into sterile poses as a result of living by artificial ideals of conduct generated by literature, especially Petrarchan love poetry. The Prince's physician, Corax, complains that he is failing to follow the regimen of physical exercise his doctor prescribed and is instead wrapped up in books, with the result that his princely activities are "all changed into a sonnet." His courtiers even accuse the Prince of narcissism, claiming that his melancholy, like Orsino's in *Twelfth Night*, is a form of self-indulgence (you are "wrapt up in self-love" he is told in II.i). By using the comic device of mistaken identity to jumble up his characters, Ford is able to break them out of the ruts into which they have fallen and thus to restore psychic health to their community. As in Shakespeare's romantic comedies, the multiple marriages at the end of Ford's play signify the triumph of a realistic and fruitful conception of male-female relationships over the self-imposed melancholy and abstract idealism of the Petrarchan love tradition: "Sorrows are changed to bride-songs."

Ford's other principal debt is to *King Lear* (circa 1605-1606). The mad old Meleander is clearly modeled on Lear, as is evident from striking verbal parallels, such as Meleander's reaction in II.ii when several characters come to see him: "I am a weak old man. All these are come / To jeer my ripe calamities / . . . But I'll outstare ye all." Meleander's contempt in his madness for the luxuries of the court, the way he is finally cured of his madness, and, above all, his reunion scene with his daughter all hark back to *King Lear*. Naturally the comparison cannot work to Ford's advantage. He misses all the tragic complexity and grandeur of Lear and exploits the situation of a mad old man largely for its potential for sentiment. *The Lover's Melancholy* shows how readily Ford was able to adapt Shakespearean material to his own purposes. But the fact that he chose to mix material from one of Shakespeare's greatest tragedies indiscriminately with material from the romantic comedies suggests that Ford's appropriation of Shakespeare resulted not from any deep aesthetic affinity or sympathetic understanding, but from a practical playwright's sense of what in the work of his predecessor had been effective with audiences.

The play Ford probably wrote after *The Lover's Melancholy* is *The Broken Heart*, published in 1633 and evidently the last of his works to be performed by the King's Majesties Servants. *The Broken Heart* is set supposedly in ancient Sparta, but one would search in vain in Thucydides for any Spartans acting as do Ford's. Like so many of Ford's plays, *The Broken Heart* tells a story of love thwarted and vengeance delayed but eventually executed. In a peculiar twist, seemingly more appropriate to comedy than tragedy, the characters have "names fitted to their Qualities." Perhaps Ford was experimenting with the idea of a tragedy of humors. The proud young hero Ithocles ("Honour of loveliness") has incurred the hatred of Orgilus ("Angry") by forcing his sister Penthea ("Complaint") to break her betrothal to Orgilus and marry instead an older and thoroughly distasteful man named Bassanes ("Vexation"). Insanely jealous, Bassanes has made Penthea's life miserable with his suspicions, and in order to ease her burden Orgilus pretends to leave for Athens. In reality he remains in Sparta disguised as a philosophy student, but Penthea rejects his secret advances, even though she still loves him. Meanwhile, Ithocles has grown to regret what he did to his sister and has himself fallen hopelessly in love with Princess Calantha ("Flower of beauty"). When Bassanes discovers Penthea and Ithocles in private conference he accuses Ithocles of having committed incest with his sister. Though grotesquely unjust this charge drives Penthea to despair and destroys her will to live. Before she starves herself to death, however, she manages to win Calantha's love for her brother. But before Ithocles can be wed to Calantha, Penthea's death provokes Orgilus to murder him. Having just become queen of Sparta, Calantha sentences Orgilus to die, and he chooses to do so by bleeding himself to death onstage. Calantha then expires by the side of her dead lover Ithocles. The deaths of Orgilus and Calantha fulfill two mysterious oracles uttered earlier in the play: "Revenge proves its own executioner" and "The lifeless trunk shall wed the broken heart."

The Broken Heart has proven to be one of the most enduring of Ford's works and has attracted more critical attention than any of his plays, with the exception of *'Tis Pity She's a Whore* and *Perkin Warbeck*. No source has ever been identified for *The Broken Heart*, and it seems to be the most original and perhaps the most personal of all Ford's plays. For once, he steps out of the shadow of Shakespeare and finds his own voice, and a distinctive voice it turns out to be. No Renaissance play focuses so unrelievedly on moments of psychological suffering or sustains so plaintively the accents of grief. With an inexorable dramatic logic Ford pursues his favorite theme: the tragic consequences of any attempt to divert human passions from their chosen paths and channel them instead into lawful but unwanted directions. As one of the characters says: "affections injur'd / By tyranny, or rigor of compulsion, / Like tempest-threaten'd trees unfirmly rooted, / Ne'er spring to timely growth." The frustration and twisting of romantic passion in *The Broken Heart* is so pervasive that the play verges at times on sentimentality. And the fact that the characters' suffering can find no vent in action but is merely something to be endured threatens to give the play a static, almost monotonous quality.

Nevertheless, Ford manages to give a kind of stateliness to the sorrow he portrays. Though a mood of grief suffuses the whole play, the grief is restrained, especially in the way it is expressed. In general the characters tend to understate their sorrows; Calantha sums up the mode of the play when she speaks of "the silent griefs which cut the heartstrings." The laments of Ford's characters, and above all their death scenes, have a ritual air about them, in part because he creates self-conscious characters, who seem to sense that they are on display. Penthea says at one point: "On the stage / Of my mortality, my youth hath acted / Some scenes of vanity," and as Bassanes graciously opens one of Orgilus' veins, he comments on the impression the scene is making: "This pastime / Appears majestical; some high-tun'd poem / Hereafter shall deliver to posterity / The writer's glory and his subjects's triumph." For what may be the first time in Ford theatricality becomes both means and end. Wanting to achieve a certain kind of stage effect, Ford creates characters whose theatrical attitude toward their own emotions and circumstances ensures that he will get just the ritualized pattern of grief he wants.

To my truest friend, my worthiest Kinsman, IOHN FORD of *Grayes-Inne, Esquire.*

THE Title of *this little worke* (may good Cozen) is in sence but the argument of a Dedication; which being in most writers a *Custome,* in many a *complement,* I question not but your cleere knowledg of my intents, will in me read as the *earnest of affection.* My ambition herein aimes at a faire flight, borne vp on the double wings of gratitude, for a receiued, and acknowledgement for a continued loue. It is not so frequent to number many kinsmen, & amongst them some friends; as to presume on some friends, and amongst them little friendship. But in euery fulnesse of these particulars, I doe not more partake *through you* (my Cozen) the delight, then enioy the benefit of them. This *Inscription to your name,* is onely a faithfull deliuerance to *Memory* of the truth of my respects to *vertue,* and to the equall

A in

The Epistle Dedicatory:

in honour with vertue, *Desert.* The contempt throwne on *studies of this kinde,* by such as dote on their owne singularity, hath almost so out-fac'd *Inuention,* and prescrib'd *Iudgement*; that it is more safe, more wise, to be *suspectedly silent,* then *modestly confident* of opinion, herein. Let me be bold to tell the seuerity of *censurers,* how willingly I neglect their practise, so long as I digresse from no becomming thankfulnesse. Accept then (my Cozen) this *witnesse to Posteritie* of my constancy to your Merits; for no *Ties* of blood, no ingagements of *Friendship* shall more justly liue a *President,* then the sincerity of *Both* in the Heart of

IOHN FORD.

To my friend Mr. IOHN FORD.

VNto this Altar, rich with thy owne spice,
I bring one graine, to thy Loves Sacrifice:
And boast to see thy flames ascending, while
Perfumes enrich our Ayre from thy sweet Pile.

Looke here THOV *that hast* malice *to the Stage,*
And Impudence *enough for the whole Age;*
Voluminously-Ignorant! *be vext*
To read this Tragedy, and thy owne be next.

James Shirley.

The Sceane *PAVYE.*

The Speakers in this TRAGEDY.

Phillippo Caraffa.	Duke of Pavy.
Paulo Baglione,	Vnckle to the Dutchesse.
Fernando	Favorite to the Duke.
Ferentes	A wanton Courtier.
Roseilli	A young Nobleman.
Petruchio / *Nibrassa*	Two Counsellors of State.
D'auolos	Secretary to the Duke.
Mauruccio	An old Antike.
Giacopo	Servant to *Mauruccio.*
Attendants.	

Women.

Biancha	The Dutchesse.
Fiormonda	The Dukes Sister.
Colona	Daughter to *Petruchio.*
Julia	Daughter to *Nibrassa.*
Morona	an old Lady.

Dedicatory letter, commendatory verse by James Shirley, and dramatis personae from the 1633 quarto edition of Love's Sacrifice *(Bodleian Library)*

The Broken Heart may have provided the germinal idea for Ford's best-known play, *'Tis Pity She's a Whore*. In the earlier work Ford merely toys with the idea of brother-sister incest; audience reaction may have suggested to him the shock value of building a whole play around the theme. *'Tis Pity She's a Whore* was first published in 1633; because Ford refers to it as "these first fruits of my leisure" in the dedication, some scholars have argued that it was the first of his major plays and have claimed that it must have been written and performed well before its publication date. But the fact that the title page asserts that the play was performed by the Queen's Majesties Servants suggests that it came later than *The Broken Heart* and may in fact have been the first result of Ford's switch to a new theater company.

The hero of *'Tis Pity She's a Whore* is an impetuous young man named Giovanni, who develops an incestuous longing for his beautiful sister, Annabella. Despite the warnings of a friar named Bonaventura, Giovanni pursues his love for his sister and quickly wins her assent to a passionate affair. In order to conceal the unlawful romance Annabella eventually consents to marry a nobleman named Soranzo. Soranzo has a guilty secret himself, having seduced and abandoned a married woman named Hippolita. Much of the play is devoted to unsuccessful attempts by Hippolita and her husband, Richardetto, to gain revenge on Soranzo. Ford also includes a comic subplot involving a fool named Bergetto who vainly woos Annabella. The secret love of Giovanni and Annabella is finally revealed when Soranzo discovers that he has married a pregnant woman. By the end of the play almost all the characters have been killed off in a sequence of revenges and counterrevenges. Giovanni has the most spectacular death of all. After killing Annabella to preserve the purity of their love, he enters the last scene with her heart on his dagger, murders Soranzo, and is finally killed himself by a gang of banditti specifically hired by Soranzo for the purpose.

Most of the critical debate concerning *'Tis Pity She's a Whore* has understandably centered on Ford's treatment of incest. The play contains many explicit attacks on such an unconventional love, and of course the catastrophic outcome of the romance of Giovanni and Annabella suggests that Ford was warning against the breaking of so basic a social taboo. And yet Ford allows Giovanni to make an unusually spirited and eloquent defense of forbidden love. Moreover,

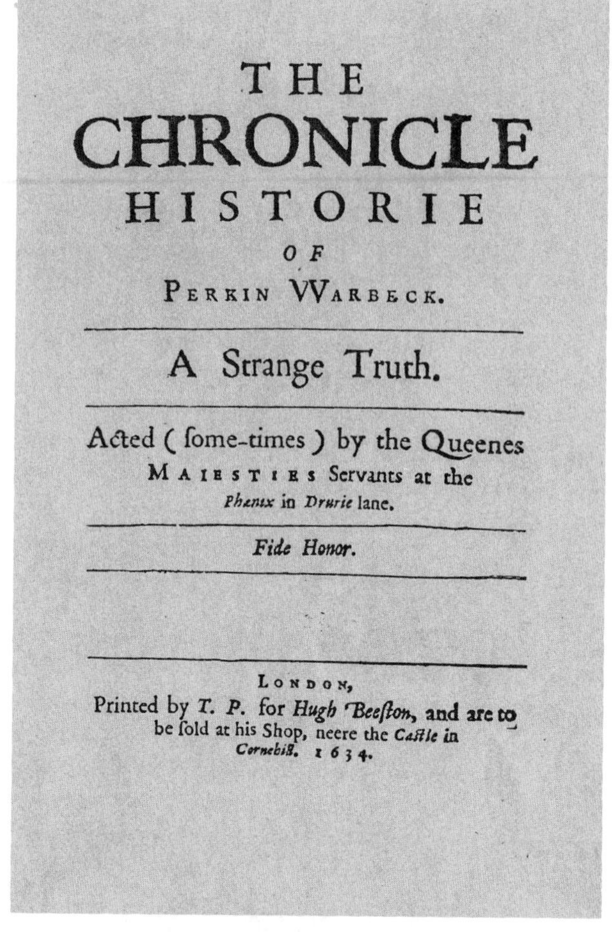
THE
CHRONICLE
HISTORIE
OF
PERKIN WARBECK.

A Strange Truth.

Acted (ſome-times) by the Queenes
MAIESTIES Servants at the
Phœnix in *Drurie* lane.

Fide Honor.

LONDON,
Printed by *T. P.* for *Hugh Beeſton*, and are to
be ſold at his Shop, neere the *Caſtle* in
Cornehill. 1634.

Title page for the 1634 quarto edition of Ford's history play about the last major challenger to the legitimacy of the Tudor line of the British monarchy (King's College, Cambridge)

Giovanni and Annabella are by far the most vibrant characters in the play, and, even though their love destroys them, there are strong suggestions that they have in the process attained an intensity of experience from which the crassly conventional characters in the play are barred. *'Tis Pity She's a Whore* has a Marlovian quality: the protagonists are overreachers and perish in their attempts to go beyond the limits of normal humanity, but the forces which oppose them in the scheme of the play hardly have a solid moral basis for their opposition, being involved as they are in a shabby web of sexual intrigue and assassination plots. In the end, *'Tis Pity She's a Whore* seems to turn on the opposition between one grand crime of romantic passion and a series of petty crimes fueled by lust and vengefulness.

Perhaps Ford simply was not interested in analyzing and resolving the moral problem of incest. Had he wished to explore the topic in depth, he would have shown Giovanni's incestuous passion gradually developing and concentrated on Annabella's moral dilemma of whether or not to yield to her brother's advances. But in fact by the second scene Ford already has Giovanni and Annabella pledging their love to each other, and he chooses to fill up the rest of the play with revenge plots instead of giving us further insights into the characters of the young lovers. In short, brother-sister incest is the dramatic premise of *'Tis Pity She's a Whore*, not its sole focus. One might then argue that Ford was driven to the theme by the logic of his historical position as a latecomer in Renaissance drama. Romantic passion thrives on opposition: lovers derive the strength of their emotion from the strength of the obstacles they have to overcome in order to be united. When Shakespeare wrote *Romeo and Juliet* (circa 1595-1596), it was enough that the lovers' parents opposed the match. But Ford was writing in and for a world that had already, as it were, digested the message of *Romeo and Juliet*—that romantic love must be allowed some legitimacy. In *The Broken Heart*, for example, when the young prince Nearchus learns that Calantha is in love with Ithocles, he abandons his suit to her and is willing to let a social inferior take precedence over him because Ithocles has passion on his side. In *'Tis Pity She's a Whore* itself, Annabella's father, unlike Juliet's, makes it clear that he will not force her into a marriage against her wishes: "I would not have her marry wealth but love." In this newly permissive and parentally indulgent environment Ford must search for a form of love that will *not* have the endorsement of society.

Love between brother and sister is the answer to Ford's need for a passion that can still totally isolate his protagonists and drive them to a tragic death. With this one change Ford is able to rewrite *Romeo and Juliet* even to the point of companioning his young hero with a meddling friar and his heroine with a coarse nurse. Supplied with the fresh context of an incestuous situation, all the old clichés of Petrarchan love poetry suddenly regain their vitality, as the lovers really must keep their relationship a secret and face danger and the prospect of death wherever they turn. The situation thus permits Ford's characters the kind of theatricality he savors. Giovanni, for example, seems obsessed with playing the role of a Romeo. As he marches off to the final scene, he prompts himself: "Shrink not, courageous hand, stand up, my heart, / And boldly act my last and greater part." An incestuous love proves to be the only way Giovanni can act the part of a tragic lover in a world that has come to grant more conventional forms of romantic passion their legitimate place in society.

The last of Ford's plays to be published in 1633 is *Love's Sacrifice*. If *'Tis Pity She's a Whore* rewrites *Romeo and Juliet, Love's Sacrifice* is Ford's most sustained effort at rewriting the play that seems to have obsessed him more than any other: *Othello*. *Love's Sacrifice* tells the story of a peculiar love triangle involving Philippo Caraffa (Duke of Pavia), his beautiful wife, Bianca, and his best friend, Fernando. An Iago-like character named D'Avolos convinces Philippo that Fernando is having an affair with Bianca behind his back. To arouse the Duke's suspicions D'Avolos uses many of Iago's strategies, such as taunting Philippo with the prospect of actually seeing himself cuckolded: "Would you desire, my lord, to see them exchange kisses, sucking one another's lips, nay, begetting an heir to the dukedom?" The difference from *Othello* is that in Ford's play there is a genuine basis for the husband's suspicions. Fernando and Bianca have fallen in love but have taken a vow to keep their relationship platonic. But when Philippo discovers them in each other's arms, he accuses his wife of adultery and kills her. Protesting their innocence of literal adultery, Fernando poisons himself at Bianca's funeral. Realizing that he has unjustly destroyed his wife and his friend, Philippo also commits suicide, leaving D'Avolos to be punished for his role in precipitating the tragedy.

On the face of it *Love's Sacrifice* ought to be a more plausible drama than *Othello*. After all, D'Avolos can point to real evidence in substantiating his accusations, whereas Iago must manufacture his proofs out of thin air and Othello's jealous imagination. Perhaps Ford was trying to correct Shakespeare and show how a true tragedy of jealousy should be written. And yet of the two, it is *Othello* which makes by far the more convincing impression as a drama. Shakespeare makes his tragedy grow out of the natures of his characters so that the story unfolds with a sense of dramatic inevitability. Ford, by contrast, attempts to generate interest, not by following a single intense plot line, but by continually playing with his audience: misleading them, arousing false expectations, springing shocking reversals on them, and in general working to keep them off-balance at all times. In the process, he bends his characters to fit a contrived dramatic pattern to the point where they begin to dissolve as people

The Scene,

The Continent of Great Britayne.

The Perſons preſented.

Henry the ſeaventh.	*Iames* the 4th King of *Scotl.*
Dawbney.	Earle of *Huntley.*
Sir *William Stanly.*	Earle of *Crawford.*
Oxford.	Lord *Daliell.*
Surrey.	*Marchmount* a Herauld.
Biſhop of *Durham.*	
Vrſwicke Chaplaine to King *Henry.*	*Perkin Warbeck.*
Sir *Robert Clifford.*	*Frion* his Secretarie.
Lambert Simnell.	Mayor of Cork.
Hialas a *Spaniſh* Agent.	*Heron* a Mercer.
Conſtable, Officers, Servingmen, and Souldiers.	*Sketon* a Taylor.
	Aſtly--a Scrivener.

Women.

Ladie *Katherine Gourdon*, —wife to *Perkin*,
Counteſſe of *Crawford.*
Iane Douglas —Lady *Kath.* mayd.

TO

PROLOGVE.

Studyes haue, of this Nature, been of late
So out of faſhion, ſo vnfollow'd; that
It is become more Iuſtice, to reviue
The antick follyes of the Times, then ſtriue
To countenance wiſe Induſtrie: no want
Of Art, doth render witt, or lame, or ſcant,
Or ſlothfull, in the purchaſe of freſh bayes;
But want of Truth in Them, who giue the prayſe
To their ſelfe-loue, preſuming to out-doe
The Writer, *or (for need) the* Actor's *too.*
But ſuch THIS AVTHOVR'S *ſilence beſt beſitt's,*
Who bidd's Them, be in loue, with their owne witt's:
From Him, *to cleerer Iudgement's, wee can ſay,*
Hee ſhew's a Hiſtorie, couch't in a Play:
A Hiſtorie of noble mention, knowne,
Famous, and true: moſt noble, 'cauſe our owne:
Not forg'd from Italie, *from* Fraunce, *from* Spaine,
But Chronicled at Home; *as rich in ſtrayne*
Of braue Attempts, as ever, fertile Rage
In Action, could beget to grace the Stage.
Wee cannot limitt Scenes, *for the whole Land*
It ſelfe, appeard too narrow to with-ſtand
Competitors for Kingdomes: *nor is heere*
Vnneceſſary mirth forc't, to indeere
A multitude; on theſe two, *reſt's the Fate*
Of worthy expectation; TRVTH *and* STATE.

THE

THE
CHRONICLE
HISTORIE OF
PERKIN WARBECK.

Actus primus, Scæna prima.

Enter King Henry, Durham, Oxford, Surrey, *Sir* William Stanly, *Lord Chamberlaine, Lord* Dawbny. *The King ſupported to his Throne by* Stanly *and* Durham. *A Guard.*

King. STill to be haunted; ſtill to be purſued,
Still to be frighted with falſe apparitions
Of pageant Majeſtie, and new-coynd greatneſſe,
As if wee were a mockery King in ſtate;
Onely ordaind to lauiſh ſweat and blond
In ſcorne and laughter to the ghoſts of *Yorke*,
Is all below our merits; yet (my Lords,
My friends and Counſailers) yet we ſit faſt
In our owne royall birth-right; the rent face
And bleeding wounds of *England's* ſlaughterd people,
Haue beene by vs (as by the beſt Phyſitian)
At laſt both throughly Cur'd, and ſet in ſafetie;
And yet for all this glorious worke of peace
Our ſelfe is ſcarce ſecure.

B *Dur.* The

Epilogue.

HEre ha's appear'd, though in a ſeverall faſhion,
The Threats of Majeſtie; the ſtrength of paſſion;
Hopes of an Empire; change of fortunes; All
What can to Theater's of Greatneſſe fall;
Proving their weake foundations: who will pleaſe
Amongst ſuch ſeverall Sight's, to cenſure Theſe
No birth's abortiue, nor a baſtard-brood
(Shame to a parentage, or foſterhood)
May warrant by their loues, all juſt excuſes,
And often finde a welcome to the Muſes.

FINIS.

Dramatis personae, prologue, first page of act 1, and epilogue from the 1634 quarto edition of Perkin Warbeck *(King's College, Cambridge)*

with firm characters and turn into a series of flexible stage reactions. For example, one comes away from the play with no consistent impression of Bianca. At first she seems to resist Fernando's advances completely, then she seems to want to yield to him completely, and finally she seems determined to resist him completely again. One gets the impression that Ford was thinking in terms of individual brilliant scenes without considering how they might add up to a coherent dramatic whole. Critics have argued that *Love's Sacrifice* achieves a certain consistency through an underlying philosophy of platonic love derived from a cult which flourished in the court of Charles I under the patronage of his French queen, Henrietta Maria. But once again this seems to be a case of critics looking for a moral message in Ford, when he was largely concerned with keeping his audience on the edges of their seats.

The one play Ford wrote with any genuine depth is *Perkin Warbeck,* published in 1634. *The Broken Heart* may be the most distinctively "Fordian" of his works and *'Tis Pity She's a Whore* the most theatrically exciting, but *Perkin Warbeck* is his most satisfying work of art, coherent in conception, consistent in execution, and thought-provoking in its implications. It tells the story of the last of the major challenges to the legitimacy of the Tudor line, the appearance of the Yorkist pretender Perkin Warbeck, who claimed to be the younger of Edward IV's two sons (the princes Richard III was supposed to have murdered in the Tower of London). Striving for historical accuracy, Ford based his account on two sources, Thomas Gainsford's *True and Wonderful History of Perkin Warbeck* (1618) and Francis Bacon's *History of the Reign of King Henry VII* (1622). Following Bacon's lead, Ford portrays Henry VII as the model of a modern king, efficient in his administration, concerned about the financial basis of his rule, and never letting any idealistic principles or romantic illusions stand in the way of the realistic securing and exercising of his power. What is lacking in Henry VII is the poetry of kingship, and that is just what the pretender Perkin is able to supply in abundance. Perkin has all the trappings of a king without the substance: he knows how to speak nobly, always has the right gesture at his command, and maintains a regal bearing even in defeat. Though Ford leaves little doubt that Perkins is in fact an impostor, he departs from his sources and never shows the pretender admitting that he is not what he claims to be. We are never sure whether Perkin is consciously trying to deceive the world or is somehow himself deluded by the role he had adopted.

As a result, *Perkin Warbeck* takes on a very modern quality, as if it were a play by Luigi Pirandello or perhaps the William Butler Yeats who wrote *The Player Queen* (1922). Ford's theme seems to be that the player king is in some respects more kinglike than the real king. It is Perkin who inspires the kind of personal loyalty in his followers that one associates with feudal monarchy in all its glory. To add to the romantic aura that surrounds Perkin, Ford gives him the one love interest in the play. He is married to a kinswoman of the Scottish king, Lady Katherine Gordon, who remains faithful to him even when he is captured and sentenced to death by Henry. But Perkins's nobility has a fairy-tale quality to it. He can sound regal in his speeches, but he cannot perform the deeds needed to back up those speeches. In the end he seems to have stepped out of the pages of some book of Arthurian romance and unfortunately to have wandered into a very real world of Machiavellian statecraft and diplomacy, which swiftly destroys him. His chivalry and courtliness, however admirable as personal qualities, are no match for the hardheaded, down-to-earth politics of Henry VII. As a measure of Perkin's failure in worldly terms, Ford shows King James IV of Scotland, who initially supports the pretender's claim to the throne, gradually coming over to the Tudor party and abandoning the would-be Yorkists. But even in defeat—one might say above all in defeat—Perkin wins our sympathy. His is the pathos of a perpetually lost cause, and one inevitably thinks of *Waverley* (1814) when reading Ford's play and of the parallels in Walter Scott's romantic treatment of the doomed supporters of the Stuart pretender. (Both the Ford play and the Scott novel contrast a modern, bourgeois England with a Scotland more in touch with a heroic, aristocratic past.) Living in a world of dreams and poetic aspirations, Perkin has the luxury of never having to dirty his hands with the kind of difficult deeds real kings are called upon to perform. It is easy to be perfectly noble if one never has to get down to the business of actually ruling.

In writing a history play in the 1630s Ford realized that he was attempting to revive a genre that had long been "out of fashion" (to quote his prologue). He clearly had Shakespeare's history plays in mind; one might in fact argue that Ford's choice of subject matter was an attempt to fill in the one gap Shakespeare had left in his sequence, the period between *Richard III* (circa 1591-1592) and *Henry VIII* (1613). The history play which seems to have influenced *Perkin Warbeck* most is *Richard II* (circa 1595). Many critics have seen the contrast between Perkin and Henry VII as a re-creation of the contrast between Richard II and Henry Bolingbroke. Though coming late in the development of the genre, indeed at the very end, *Perkin Warbeck* can justifiably lay claim to being the finest history play in English after Shakespeare. If Ford does not equal Shakespeare's achievement it is because, unlike Shakespeare's protagonists, his main character is not as actively engaged in the process of history. Though Perkin is a historical figure, in a sense history has passed him by; he is a walking anachronism trying to live by a code of kingship now outmoded by the English Civil War. Thus Perkin imperceptibly passes out of the realm of historical action into the realm of pure poetry. His antagonist, Henry, finally expresses his contempt for the pretender in theatrical terms: "The player's on the stage still, 'tis his part; / 'A does but act. . . . The lesson, prompted and well conn'd, was moulded / Into familiar dialogue, oft rehearsed / Till, learnt by heart, 'tis now receiv'd for truth." As a man for whom life has become an act, Perkin Warbeck is arguably the quintessential Fordian dramatic figure.

If one had to select a single play that brings the great era of Renaissance drama to a close, *Perkin Warbeck* would be an excellent choice. The era in effect began with the titanic figure of Marlowe's Tamburlaine, who is able to conquer cities merely with the power of his words. Perkin speaks the language of a king, but when he and his party try to talk one of Henry's strongholds into yielding, its defenders stand firm. In Ford's play reality no longer yields to the power of poetry: in fact, reality and poetry seem to be separating out into two distinct realms, with Henry ruling one and Perkin the other. Thus in *Perkin Warbeck* the interaction of poetry and reality, which had given life to so many Renaissance dramas, ceases to be a viable possibility. With reality becoming prosaic and poetry losing touch with reality, it becomes difficult to write the kind of poetic drama that had made Renaissance theater so powerful. Ford himself never seems to have been able to equal his level of achievement in *Perkin Warbeck*. His two plays published after *Perkin Warbeck* show a sad decline in quality, but whether this is to be attributed to the exhaustion of his creative powers we cannot be sure, especially since they may have been written earlier and merely published later.

The Fancies Chaste and Noble, a tragicomedy published in 1638, is Ford's one genuinely repellent work. He titillates his audience with all sorts of sexual innuendo and then in the end tries to show that everything in the play was actually innocent. Set in Siena, the play seems to portray a thoroughly corrupt world in which a young man named Livio is willing to advance his own career by making a whore out of his sister Castamela. He sends her off to the court of the Marquis Octavio, where she joins three young ladies collectively known as "the Fancies." All sorts of rumors circulate concerning the Marquis's collection of females, from the suggestion that he is running a harem to supply his lust to the equally damning assertion that he is impotent and merely keeps the women around for show. Ford fills the play with characters with equally sordid reputations. In the end we learn that the "Fancies" are actually Octavio's nieces, three orphans he has brought up carefully and chastely. All the other characters with reputations for lewdness turn out to be equally misrepresented in Siena.

Based on the epilogue, one could try to read a moral lesson out of *The Fancies Chaste and Noble* about not trusting first impressions or common opinion. But judging by the way Ford handles the material, he seems to have been interested solely in exploiting it for its prurient interest. The audience cannot help feeling cheated by the end of the play. What drama Ford generates depends wholly on his withholding of information from his characters and the audience. In its dramaturgy, *The Fancies Chaste and Noble* resembles the work of Francis Beaumont and John Fletcher rather than that of Shakespeare. Ford is skillful in the way he manipulates and misleads his viewers or readers, but the skill serves no real artistic purpose. Despite its title, *The Fancies Chaste and Noble* comes as close to pornography as any English Renaissance drama. That all turns out to have been chaste does not make the play noble; indeed it only underlines its hollowness.

The Lady's Trial, published in 1639, is probably Ford's last attempt to come to terms with *Othello*. He tells the story of a Genoese nobleman and soldier named Auria, who has to leave behind his beautiful wife, Spinella, while, like Othello, he goes off to war against the Turks (as a reward for his services Auria becomes governor of Corsica, rather than Cyprus). Auria's best

THE

LADIES TRIALL.

ACTED By both their Majesties Servants at the private house in *DRVRY LANE.*

FIDE HONOR

LONDON,
Printed by E. G. for *Henry Shephard*, and are to be sold at his shop in *Chancery-Lane* at the signe of the Bible, between Sarjants Inne and Fleet-street, neare the Kings-head Taverne. 1639.

Title page for the 1639 quarto edition of what is believed to be the last play by Ford staged during his lifetime (Cambridge University Library)

friend, Aurelio, warns him against leaving Spinella alone and unprotected, and in Auria's absence Aurelio becomes convinced that she is having an affair with a young lord named Adurni, especially when he breaks in upon them having supper together. As usual Ford fills the play with subplots which add to the atmosphere of sordidness and sexual infidelity. But Spinella is innocent and was in fact rejecting Adurni's advances when Aurelio discovered them together. Nevertheless, goaded into suspicion by Aurelio, Auria, once he returns to Genoa, feels that he has to subject Spinella to a mock trial. She acquits herself well and in the end is reconciled with her husband.

Ford seems to be going out of his way to write a play in which sexual jealousy does *not* lead to violence and tragedy. Once again, one might read *The Lady's Trial* as an attempt to "correct" *Othello*. As in *Love's Sacrifice*, Ford provides a more substantial basis for his hero's jealousy, and this time the lady's accuser is no villain but a friend genuinely interested in Auria's welfare. Ford might be trying to show a couple coping rationally with a situation that destroyed Othello and Desdemona. Auria has cause to distrust Spinella: he, like Othello, has married a woman much younger than he and, as he says: "disaproportion / In years, amongst the married, is a reason / For change of pleasures." Nevertheless, Auria struggles hard to maintain his faith in Spinella and argues to Aurelio: "he deserves no wife / Of worthy quality who does not trust / Her virtue in the proofs of any danger," which might serve as Ford's comment on Othello. In contrast to Desdemona, Spinella will not let anyone get away with falsely accusing her and gives a spirited defense of herself at her "trial." In a way, *The Lady's Trial* is *Othello* with a happy ending presented as the more likely outcome of such a domestic broil. All that is missing from the play is, of course, Othello and Desdemona, he with the profound anguish of his great soul and she with her unquestioning faith in her chosen lord. But perhaps Ford is not consciously commenting on *Othello* in *The Lady's Trial*, but simply searching, as in *The Fancies Chaste and Noble*, for any new dramatic formula to keep his audiences interested. When the theatrical convention was that the slightest hint of sexual infidelity might lead to marital tragedy, to show a couple working out their problems with a degree of candor and emotional restraint became a real novelty on the stage.

One remaining play has come to be included in the Ford canon, a tragicomedy called *The Queen*, published anonymously in 1653. There is no external evidence for attributing the play to Ford, but on the basis of a few verbal parallels and a general resemblance to the situation in some of Ford's plays, several twentieth-century scholars have claimed that Ford is the author of *The Queen*. The play weaves together two basic plots. One is the story of the Queen of Arragon, who saves a rebel named Alphonso from a sentence of death and marries him, only to have him banish her from his presence, until his adviser Muretto awakens his love for her by first awakening his jealousy, falsely accusing the Queen of having an affair with a young lord at court. The other is the story of the Queen's great general, Velasco, who, out of devotion to his beloved Salassa, consents to refuse all fighting and act like a coward, much to his public disgrace. The two plots come together when Velasco is called upon to serve as the Queen's champion once Alphonso formally accuses her of infidelity. The Queen's name is cleared, and all problems are resolved as Velasco weds Salassa and the Queen and Alphonso are reunited. The fact that *The Queen* has certain elements of *Othello* in it, in particular Muretto's Iago-like role in arousing Alphonso's suspicions, suggests that Ford may have had a hand in the play, but it is hardly conclusive. The way the play deals with the perversities of romantic love, and especially Muretto's scheme for curing Alphonso of his misogyny, suggests that *The Queen* may be a companion piece to *The Lover's Melancholy*. But the aesthetic quality of the play is so low that it could just as easily be the work of an imitator of Ford. One wonders why anyone would go out of his way to include the play in the Ford canon: it adds nothing to our understanding of his art or to our appreciation of his skill or range as a playwright.

The large number of titles associated with Ford's name, as well as the substantial number of plays which have actually come down to us, suggests that he was one of the most successful dramatists of his era. Though his plays have not become standard theatrical repertory, neither have they suffered the total eclipse many Renaissance dramas have undergone. Ford was occasionally revived in the Restoration era: Samuel Pepys attended both *'Tis Pity She's a Whore* and *The Lady's Trial*, neither of which he liked. There are records of performances of *The Lover's Melancholy* and *Perkin Warbeck* in the eighteenth century. The Jacobite threat seems to have kept interest in *Perkin Warbeck* alive. It was reprinted in 1714 and was performed at the Goodman's Fields theater on 19 December 1745, presumably as a warning against the latest Stuart uprising. Given its purpose, the play was revised to make Perkin a less attractive character in this production.

In the nineteenth century, Charles Lamb rediscovered Ford and championed him in his *Specimens of English Dramatic Poets* (1808), calling him "of the first order of poets." Ford was soon attacked by some powerful critics, including Francis Jeffrey and William Hazlitt, who said that Ford's plays "seem painted on gauze, or spun out of cobwebs." Critical opinion has swung back and forth between these two extremes ever since, with some critics hailing Ford as a major dramatic and poetic talent and others assailing his works as superficial and empty. The truth lies somewhere in between these two positions. At his worst, Ford could be very bad indeed, but at his best, he was a master dramatic craftsman, and even in the face of the massive accumulated achievement of English Renaissance drama, he managed to carve out a distinctive place for himself. He clearly deserves his current ranking as the best of the Caroline dramatists and one of the most important in the whole Renaissance era. He continues to attract a great deal of attention from critics, and interpretations of his work as a whole and of individual plays have been proliferating. Measured by the demanding standard which in a way he himself invites—the plays of Shakespeare—Ford inevitably appears inferior and lacking in depth. But to be forced to create in the wake of Shakespeare was no easy task, and Ford did not shun the challenge. In two of his best plays, *'Tis Pity She's a Whore* and *Perkin Warbeck*, he showed that something could still be done in genres Shakespeare seemed to have staked out for himself, and in *The Broken Heart* Ford created a work uniquely his own in style and subject matter. Though not uniform in quality, Ford's plays are at least varied in theme and tone and together constitute one of the most impressive bodies of achievement in Renaissance drama.

References:

Donald K. Anderson, Jr., "John Ford," in *The Later Jacobean and Caroline Dramatists*, edited by Terrence P. Logan and Denzell S. Smith (Lincoln: University of Nebraska Press, 1978), pp. 120-151;

Anderson, *John Ford* (New York: Twayne, 1972);

Anne Barton, "He That Plays the King: Ford's *Perkin Warbeck* and the Stuart History Play," in *English Drama: Forms and Development*, edited by Marie Axton and Raymond Williams (Cambridge: Cambridge University Press, 1977), pp. 69-93;

T. S. Eliot, "John Ford," in his *Selected Essays* (New York: Harcourt, Brace, 1950), pp. 170-180;

Una Ellis-Fermor, *The Jacobean Drama* (London: Methuen, 1936);

Arthur Kirsch, Jacobean Dramatic Perspectives (Charlottesville: University Press of Virginia, 1972);

Clifford Leech, *John Ford and the Drama of His Time* (London: Chatto & Windus, 1957);

Michael Neill, ed., *John Ford: Critical Re-Visions* (Cambridge: Cambridge University Press, 1988);

Robert Ornstein, *The Moral Vision of Jacobean Tragedy* (Madison: University of Wisconsin Press, 1960);

Irving Ribner, *Jacobean Tragedy* (London: Methuen, 1962);

L. G. Salingar, "The Decline of Tragedy," in *The Age of Shakespeare*, edited by Boris Ford (Harmondsworth, U.K.: Penguin, 1955);

George F. Sensabaugh, *The Tragic Muse of John Ford* (Stanford: Stanford University Press, 1944).

George Herbert

(3 April 1593 - 1 March 1633)

Sidney Gottlieb
Sacred Heart University

BOOKS: "In Obitum Henrici Principis" and "Ulteriora timens cum morte paciscitur Orbis," in *Epicedium Cantabrigiense, In obitum immaturum Henrici, Principis Walliae* (Cambridge, 1612);

Oratio Qua auspicatissimum Serenissimi Principis Caroli (Cambridge, 1623);

Memoriae Matris Sacrum, printed with *A Sermon of commemoracion of the ladye Danvers by John Donne . . . with other Commemoracions of her by George Herbert* (London: Philemon Stephens and Christopher Meredith, 1627);

The Temple. Sacred Poems and Private Ejaculations (Cambridge: Printed by Thomas Buck and Roger Daniel, 1633);

Herbert's Remains, Or, Sundry Pieces Of that sweet Singer of the Temple (London: Printed for Timothy Garthwait, 1652) [contains *A Priest to the Temple: Or, The Country Parson His Character, and Rule of Holy Life* and *Jacula Prudentum Or Outlandish Proverbs, Sentences, &c.* as well as a letter, several prayers, and three Latin poems].

Editions and Collections: *The Poetical Works of George Herbert*, edited by George Gilfillan (Edinburgh: J. Nichol, 1853);

The Works of George Herbert in Prose and Verse, 2 volumes, edited by William Pickering (London: W. Pickering, 1853);

The Complete Works in Verse and Prose of George Herbert, 3 volumes, edited by Alexander B. Grosart (London: Robson & Sons, 1874);

The English Works of George Herbert, 3 volumes, edited by George Herbert Palmer (Boston & New York: Houghton Mifflin, 1905; revised, 1907);

The Works of George Herbert, edited by F. E. Hutchinson (Oxford: Clarendon Press, 1941; revised, 1945);

The Latin Poetry of George Herbert, translated by Mark McCloskey and Paul R. Murphy (Athens: Ohio University Press, 1965);

The Selected Poetry of George Herbert, edited by Joseph H. Summers (New York: New American Library, 1967);

Major Poets of the Earlier Seventeenth Century, edited by Barbara K. Lewalski and Andrew J. Sabol (New York: Odyssey Press, 1973);

The English Poems of George Herbert, edited by C. A. Patrides (London: Dent, 1975);

George Herbert and Henry Vaughan, edited by Louis L. Martz, The Oxford Authors series (Oxford: Oxford University Press, 1986).

OTHER: Luigi Cornaro, *A Treatise of Temperance and Sobrietie*, translated into English by Herbert, in *Hygiasticon* (Cambridge: Printed by R. Daniel, 1634);

Briefe Notes on Valdesso's Considerations, in *The Hundred and Ten Considerations of Signior Iohn Valdesso* (Oxford: Printed by Leonard Lichfield, 1638);

Outlandish Proverbs Selected by Mr. G. H. (London: Printed by T. P. for Humphrey Blunden, 1640);

Musae Responsoriae, in *Ecclesiastes Solomonis* by James Duport (Cambridge: Printed for John Field, 1662);

George Herbert; drawing by Robert White (Houghton Library, Harvard University)

The Williams Manuscript of George Herbert's Poems, edited by Amy M. Charles (Delmar, N.Y.: Scholars' Facsimiles & Reprints, 1977) [contains early versions of some of the poems in *The Temple* as well as two collections of Latin poems, *Lucus* and *Passio Discerpta*].

Nestled somewhere within the Age of Shakespeare and the Age of Milton is George Herbert. There is no Age of Herbert: he did not consciously fashion an expansive literary career for himself, and his characteristic gestures, insofar as these can be gleaned from his poems and other writings, tend to be careful self-scrutiny rather than rhetorical pronouncement; local involvement rather than broad social engagement; and complex, ever-qualified lyric contemplation rather than epic or dramatic mythmaking. This is the stuff of humility and integrity, not celebrity. But even if Herbert does not appear to be one of the larger-than-life cultural monuments of seventeenth-century England—a position that virtually requires the qualities of irrepressible ambition and boldness, if not self-regarding arrogance, that he attempted to flee—he is in some ways a pivotal figure: enormously popular, deeply and broadly influential, and arguably the most skillful and important British devotional lyricist of this or any other time.

There is, as Stanley Stewart has convincingly demonstrated, a substantial School of Herbert cutting across all ages. Stewart focuses on the seventeenth-century poets who professed allegiance to Herbert and whose works are markedly indebted to his techniques, subjects, and devotional temperament. He comes up with an impressive list, including some admittedly minor poets, such as Henry Colman, Ralph Knevet, Mildmay Fane, Christopher Harvey, and Thomas Washbourne, and some considerably more talented poets, such as Henry Vaughan, Richard Crashaw, and Thomas Traherne. Extended through modern times, the School of Herbert includes Samuel Taylor Coleridge, Ralph Waldo Emerson, Emily Dickinson, Gerard Manley Hopkins, T. S. Eliot, W. H. Auden, Elizabeth Bishop, Anthony Hecht, and perhaps Robert Frost—although these later poets are far less simply derivative and single-minded in their devotion to Herbert than were his seventeenth-century followers.

Herbert is also important, especially in the seventeenth century, not only as a poet but as a cultural icon, an image of religious and political stability held up for emulation during tumultuous times. Much of his early popularity—there were at least eleven editions of *The Temple* in the seventeenth century—no doubt owes something to the carefully crafted persona of "holy Mr. Herbert" put forth by the custodians of his literary works and reputation. In the preface to the first edition of *The Temple*, published in 1633, shortly after Herbert died, his close friend Nicholas Ferrar established the contours of Herbert's exemplary life story, a story that not only validated but was also presumably told in the poems of the volume. In a few short pages Ferrar indelibly sketches Herbert as one who exchanged the advantages of noble birth and worldly preferment for the strains of serving at "Gods Altar," one whose "obedience and conformitie to the Church and the discipline thereof was singularly remarkable," and whose "faithfull discharge" of the holy duties to which he was called "make him justly a companion to the primitive Saints, and a pattern or more for the age he lived in." This is not only high praise, but praise with political as well as religious implications: in 1633 the church was a place of contention as well as worship, and Ferrar helped establish Herbert as a model of harmonious, orderly, noncontroversial devotion for whom faith brought answers and commitment to the social establishment, not divisive questions and social fragmentation.

By 1652, the time of the next major biographical statement about Herbert, the tensions of the 1630s had erupted into a devastating civil war: the army of King Charles I had been decisively defeated, and the king himself executed; the bishops had been disenfranchised from their high place in both church and state government; and the maintenance of peace depended on a coalition of parties—old and new landowners, merchants, religious enthusiasts, army commanders, and soldiers—with conflicting interests. Little wonder, then, that Barnabas Oley, a Royalist divine, envisioned Herbert as a "primitive . . . holy and heavenly soul" who could instruct a later generation living in much-deserved chastisement and exile. Herbert seemed to be a fit subject for nostalgia, one who lived and died in peace. In Oley's introduction to *Herbert's Remains* (1652), containing among other works *A Priest to the Temple: Or, The Country Parson*, Herbert's prose description of the ideal way a priest would serve his country parish (written during the last years of his life when he was a country parson at Bemerton), Oley pictures Herbert as one who embodies traits that the current age has left behind: a person of charity, a lover of traditional, time-honored worship, church music and ceremonies, and a master of "*modest, grave and Christian reproof*." Oley's preface is apocalyptic throughout, and he frames Herbert's image in such a way that it may lead mid-century England to holiness and repentance, "Recovery, and Profit."

Izaak Walton, who wrote the first extensive biography of Herbert, follows the lead of Ferrar and Oley in shaping Herbert's life. Walton's *Life of Mr. George Herbert*, first published in 1670 and then revised in 1674 and 1675, does not have Ferrar's austerity nor Oley's urgency: by 1670 the king had been restored, the Anglican church was reestablished as the official religious institution of the country, and—despite inevitable exceptions—there seemed to be a growing respect for the advantages of toleration and accommodation rather than confrontation. Herbert was still needed, but not so much for reproof in perilous times as for gentle guidance in times of relative calm. For Walton, Herbert was not only a "primitive Saint"—that is, a throwback to the church of a simpler era—but a prefiguration of the ideal Restoration clergyman: well-born but socially responsible, educated but devout, experienced in the ways of the world but fully committed to the ways of the church, and knowledgeable about both the pains and joys of spiritual life.

In Walton's hands Herbert comes alive, and it would be nice to believe everything he tells us. But it would be safer to approach Walton's biography as one of the great works of seventeenth-century prose fiction. All subsequent examinations of Herbert inevitably rely on Walton: he is the source of much valuable information available nowhere else. But his story is picturesque, compelling, and more than occasionally unreliable. Some of the most memorable anecdotes he relates may not be untrue, but they are unverified and upon close examination seem to be stitched together from Herbert's own writings.

Walton has a habit of treating Herbert's writings as literal and factually accurate autobiographical statements, and much of the *Life* seems to be a fanciful embellishment of such poems as "Affliction" (I), "The Collar," and "The Crosse," and the prose character-sketch *The Country Parson.* Like so many other biographers, Walton's logic seems to be that if certain events did not happen in his subject's life, they should have, and he therefore feels free to frame the life as he sees fit as long as he is faithful to his subject—especially if he is prompted by one of the subject's own works. (At one point Walton parenthetically describes an anecdote about Herbert rebuilding a church at his own cost—an event that is in fact documented by other sources besides Walton—as "a real Truth," as if to acknowledge that there are different levels of truth in his *Life.*) In addition, everything in Walton's story seems to be shaped according to a unifying theme: Herbert's disappointed "Court hopes" and his ensuing turn to the church. While this is unquestionably a key topic, as a frame for an entire life it is too restrictive. Herbert's life and work are much more varied, complex, and in some respects inscrutable than Walton or the other early biographers imagined.

George Herbert was born on 3 April 1593 at Black Hall in Montgomery, Wales. His family on his father's side was one of the oldest and most powerful in Montgomeryshire, having settled there in the early thirteenth century and improving and consolidating its status by shrewd marriage settlements and continuous governmental service. The surviving stories about the patriarchs focus, not surprisingly, on their bravery and valor as they fought to civilize the countryside, administer justice, and keep peace in an area that had a well-deserved reputation for wildness. Herbert no doubt grew up with these tales but could not have had much contact with the men themselves: his grandfather, evidently a remarkable courtier, warrior, and politician, died the month after Herbert was born; and his father, also an active local sheriff and member of Parliament, died when Herbert was three and a half years old.

Herbert may have spent his early years in a home without a strong father figure, but this is not to say that the household lacked a commanding presence. His mother, Magdalen, from the Newport family of Shropshire, was by all accounts an extraordinary woman, fully capable of managing the complex financial affairs of the family, moving the household when necessary, and supervising the academic and spiritual education of her ten children. There is evidence of Herbert's deep attachment to, and even identification with, his mother throughout his works: his earliest surviving poems, which attempt to outline his direction as a poet, were written and sent to her as a gift; he mourned her death (and celebrated her life) with a collection of Latin and Greek poems, *Memoriae Matris Sacrum* (1627); and *The Temple* (1633) is filled with images of childlike submissiveness and maternal love, devotion, and authority. John Donne's funeral sermon on Magdalen focuses quite a bit on her melancholy, and one wonders whether this too—not necessarily religious despair, but a kind of spiritual vulnerability and sadness—is a crucial part of her legacy to her son.

Magdalen did not keep the family long in Wales. Shortly after the birth of her last child, Thomas, in 1597, she moved the family first to Shropshire, then to Oxford—primarily to oversee the education of the oldest son, Edward—and then finally to a house at Charing Cross, London. This last move also facilitated the education of the other children. George was tutored at home and then entered Westminster School, probably in 1604, a distinguished grammar school that not only grounded him in the study of Latin, Greek, Hebrew, and music, but also introduced him to Lancelot Andrewes, one of the great churchmen and preachers of the time. From Westminster, Herbert went up to Trinity College, Cambridge, in 1609 and began one of the most important institutional affiliations of his life, one that lasted nearly twenty years.

At Cambridge, Herbert moved smoothly through the typical stages of academic success: he gained a B.A. then an M.A.; a Minor fellowship then a Major fellowship, which involved increasing responsibilities as a tutor and lecturer; and was made university orator in 1620, a position of great prestige within the university that was often a stepping-stone to a successful career at court. The orator was the spokesperson for the university on a variety of occasions, making speeches and writing letters, and the little evidence that survives of Herbert's activities as orator indicates that he served in this capacity with both ceremonious wit and independent boldness. He was well able to offer the required fatuous compliments to the king: in a letter thanking King James I for the gift of his Latin works to Cambridge, he compared these volumes themselves to a library far grander than that of the Vatican or

Magdalen Newport Herbert, the poet's mother, who inspired his Memoriae Matris Sacrum *(portrait possibly by Sir William Segar; Collection of the Earl of Bradford)*

the Bodleian Library at Oxford. But he was also willing to dare to offer some unwanted advice when it was needed: in an oration on 8 October 1623 capping the university's celebration of the safe return of Prince Charles (later Charles I) and George Villiers, first Duke of Buckingham, from Spain, Herbert made a forceful plea for the value of keeping the peace, even though it was clear that the failure to marry off the prince to the Spanish Infanta made war with Spain more desirable and likely. It is unclear whether Herbert helped or hurt his chances for secular advancement by being both witty and principled.

During the Cambridge years Herbert wrote much of his poetry. He began, auspiciously enough, with a vow, made in a letter accompanying two sonnets sent to his mother as a New Year's gift in 1610, "that my poor Abilities in *Poetry*, shall be all, and ever consecrated to Gods glory." The sonnets are written at a high pitch of enthusiasm—there are nine astonished rhetorical questions in the first poem alone—as Herbert yearns to be a fiery martyr, burning with love of God, not women. Herbert was not alone in wanting to redirect poetry from Venus to God: Sir Philip Sidney, Robert Southwell, and Donne, among others, urged the same thing, and even King James helped encourage this kind of revolution by writing and publishing his own religious poems. But these two sonnets have the force of personal discovery behind them, and they are a preview of a cluster of later poems in *The Temple* that examine his willingness and ability to write religious verse, a continuing problem in Herbert's life. As in so many of his best poems, exuberance betrays a deep sense of disorder and nervousness.

These sonnets are disturbing declarations, filled with aching desire—"My God, where is that ancient heat"—but based on contemptuous dismissals of erotic love, love poetry, and women. As a present to his mother these verses are particularly curious. Magdalen Herbert was strikingly beautiful, if we can gauge this by her portrait and by contemporary accounts, and inescapably vital, with ten children and a dashing new husband half her age (she had married John Danvers in 1609). One wonders how Herbert expected her to respond to the anatomy of a woman that concludes his second sonnet:

> Open the bones, and you shall nothing find
> In the best *face* but *filth*, when, Lord, in thee
> The *beauty* lies in the *discovery*.

Perhaps Magdalen would not have read the poem from the position of one of the women being so anatomized, and would have simply appreciated the closing celebration of the Lord's beauty. Donne evidently trusted her as a reader not easily offended and capable of discerning the sincere motive of a poem. In sending her "The Autumnall," a poem presumably about her that contains some remarkably audacious and severe praise, Donne seems to have relied on certain qualities of her as a reader on which Herbert also counted. (Magdalen herself may have been a model for this kind of forthright and uncompromising directness: even as he writes her epitaph in *Memoriae Matris Sacrum* number 13, Herbert describes her as "seuera parens" [strict parent].) In any event, Herbert's earliest poems announce his dedication to sacred poetry in a startling fashion.

It is difficult to date most of Herbert's poems with certainty, but it is clear that not all his early poetic efforts were the kind of impassioned sacred lyrics promised by the sonnets he sent to his mother. His various occasional pieces—poems on the death of Prince Henry (oldest son of James I) in 1612 and Queen Anne (wife of James I) in 1619, to the queen of Bohemia in exile, to his friends Francis Bacon and Donne—show that Herbert, like his contemporaries, viewed and used poetry as a medium of social discourse, not just self-analysis and devotion. And even the bulk of Herbert's early religious poetry is public and didactic rather than introspective and meditative. His modern reputation rests almost exclusively on the devotional lyrics collected in "The Church," the middle section of *The Temple*, and while some of these lyrics may have been written as early as 1617, there is good reason to believe that most of them date from much later, from the mid 1620s to the last years of his life at Bemerton. But "The Church" is carefully positioned between two long poems, "The Church-porch" and "The Church Militant," both of which are early pieces much different from the later lyrics.

Amy M. Charles, Herbert's most thorough and meticulous biographer, suggests that "The Church-porch" was perhaps written as early as 1614 and that at least on one level it is a poem of advice addressed to his brother Henry, one year younger than George but already a man of the world and living in France. The two brothers shared a love of proverbs, and indeed what saves the poem from turning into a plodding collection of "thou shalt nots" is Herbert's ability to release the dramatic as well as the moral potential of some of these proverbs. In the context of *The Temple*, "The Church-porch" is intended as a kind of secular catechism, instructing a young man in basic moral principles and manners to prepare him for life in society and, more important, entrance into the church, a place where he will encounter moral and spiritual problems of a different sort.

Herbert's premise, as he announces in two of his most frequently quoted lines, is that "A verse may finde him, who a sermon flies, / And turn delight into a sacrifice." But the poem would not be delightful at all if it only contained seventy-seven stanzas of prudential bullying: *Beware of lust, Lie not, Flie idlenesse, Be thriftie, Laugh not too much* and so on. What enlivens the poem is Herbert's ability to complement the moral tags with striking images and brief dramatizations (techniques that characterized the best, or at least the most appealing and effective, sermons of the time as well). "Drinke not the third glasse" is an abstract, easily disregarded bit of advice until it is capped by a vivid personal illustration: "It is most just to throw that on the ground, / Which would throw me there, if I keep the round." And Herbert's passionate apostrophe "O England! full of sinne, but most of sloth" is transformed from a forgettable traditional complaint to a memorable chastisement by a homely but stunning figure of speech:

> Thy Gentrie bleats, as if thy native cloth
> Transfus'd a sheepishnesse into thy storie:
> Not that they are all so; but that the most
> Are gone to grasse, and in the pasture lost.

"The Church-porch" has something in common with manuals of conduct that aim to prepare a young man not so much for moral behavior as for social advancement. Many of the traits that Herbert warns against are defects in the eyes of God but also disadvantages in the company of other men, particularly one's competitors and superiors. At this time in his life Herbert undoubtedly had high ambitions for himself, and it does not paint him as a mere place-seeker to suggest that he was shrewdly aware that a morally self-controlled and cautious person might gain both earthly and heavenly rewards. Still, we should not overemphasize the secular context of "The Church-porch." For all its descriptions of life in the social arena and comments on how to act in company, it concludes with advice about charity, prayer, and proper worship. The structure of the poem thus entices the imagined reader from where he lives to where he should live, from superficial concern for the pleasure of this world, a joy that "fades," to a much deeper awareness of holy joy that "remains." At this time Herbert may not have been ready to write the poems that describe the rhythm of pain and joy that define a spiritual life, but he was well able to lead himself and his reader close to "The Church."

He was also ready to envision the corporate life of the church. In the broad plan of *The Temple*, the reader "sprinkled" by the "precepts" of "The Church-porch" and then transported by the twists and turns of faith in "The Church" still needs to see the fate of the institutional church, dramatized in "The Church Militant." This concluding section of *The Temple* is considered to be an early poem for several reasons: it is written in a combative, assertive tone like that which dominates much of Herbert's early Latin verse, and many of its satiric targets and topical allusions link it to other of his writings of the early 1620s that are vehemently controversial and impatient with a church establishment that is faulty and decaying but unable to heal itself. "The Church Militant," like his oldest brother Edward Herbert's satire *The State Progress of Ill* (1608) and Donne's *Second Anniversary: Of the Progres of the Soule* (1612), turns time into space and charts the historical development of the Christian church as a trip around the world, with Sin following close behind every move made by Religion. Like each individual believer, the church as a whole is bound to a rhythm of rising and falling, simple purity followed inevitably by excessive embellishment, wholeness turned into fragmentation.

After an invocation to God's beneficent creation of the church as an instrument of divine love, not earthly power—an outspoken political comment, especially during an age when the church was being counted on more and more as a subordinate but nevertheless vital ally of the king and administrator of his power—the poem is broken up into five main sections, each concluding with the lines "How deare to me, O God, thy counsels are! / Who may with thee compare?" For all that this psalm-based refrain captures the speaker's heartfelt submissive praise of God, these lines are ironic because they set up a model that the world at large is unable to follow. Despite the success that Christianity has in transforming pagan religion and culture into something beautiful and worthy of worship, sin is always capable of sneaking in to turn faith to "infidelitie," peace to controversy, and light to darkness.

Sin is imagined in broad terms as superstition, pride, and disorderly pleasure, but its most current and insidious form is Roman Catholicism. Herbert seems to align himself with the apocalyptic Protestant militants of late-sixteenth- and early-seventeenth-century England as he energetically and somewhat venomously satirizes the pope as Antichrist, Rome as "Western *Babylon*," the Jesuits as the Devil's army, priests as crafty wizards, and Roman Catholicism in general as a religion of shameless glory rather than grace. And England is by no means a secure fortress: reformed though it is, the British church is all but ready to succumb to the darkness that has afflicted all previous churches.

Herbert's prophetic vision of the beleaguered true church poised and ready to depart England for America was quoted repeatedly by his seventeenth-century readers:

> Religion stands on tip-toe in our land,
> Readie to passe to the *American* strand.
> When height of malice, and prodigious lusts,
> Impudent sinning, witchcrafts, and distrusts
> (The marks of future bane) shall fill our cup
> Unto the brimme, and make our measure up;
> When *Sein* shall swallow *Tiber*, and the *Thames*
> By letting in them both pollutes her streams:
> When *Italie* of us shall have her will,
> And all her calender of sinnes fulfill;
> Whereby one may foretell, what sinnes next yeare
> Shall both in *France* and *England* domineer:
> Then shall Religion to *America* flee:
> They have their times of Gospel, ev'n as we.

For many, these lines accurately predicted a new age of Protestant martyrdom and exile, and the demise of the Protestant church in England at the hands of King Charles I; his French wife, Henrietta Maria, a Roman Catholic with a large entourage; and Archbishop William Laud, a High Churchman and anti-Calvinist (though not a Roman Catholic) with little taste or tolerance for Reformation theology or notions of church government. But for all Herbert's historical accuracy and prescience, his eyes were on the end of history, which promised a happy consummation of his "progress." Redemption, a final escape from the repetitive cycle of "vertuous actions" and "crimes," comes not in time but beyond time, on a day of judgment when the church and the sun overcome sin and darkness.

The two long early poems that frame "The Church" are thus substantially different from the lyrics that are Herbert's greatest achievement. But they serve an important function in the overall structure of *The Temple*, helping Herbert to present a multidimensional, comprehensive examination of moral, spiritual, and institutional history, and situating the persona (and reader) alternately in the world, in the church, and then finally in the midst of a macrocosmic struggle between religion and sin that begins in time but ends out of it. And in a curious way these two long poems do share something with the poems of "The Church." Like Herbert's most characteristic lyrics, they are "self-consuming," to use Stanley E. Fish's phrase: that is to say, the premises from which they begin are suspended by their conclusions. In "The Church-porch" adjustment to life in the social world of "plots" and "pleasures" is rendered if not inconsequential then at least of secondary importance by the concluding turn to life within the church, where "vain or busie thoughts have . . . no part." In "The Church Militant" outraged satire of the foolish spectacle of sin dogging the church is superseded by an abrupt but all-important vision of a day of judgment that takes us well beyond sin and satire.

During this time at Cambridge, Herbert also composed a substantial amount of Latin poetry. This, of course, should be no surprise: grammar school and university education was largely a matter of immersion in classical texts and repeated exercise in copying, translating, and imitating Latin authors. The Renaissance turn to distinctively national literature and the Reformation turn to vernacular Bible translations and church services by no means displaced Latin as the international language for diplomats and scholars, and the common vehicle for many types of serious disputation, religious devotion, and intellectual and poetic wit and playfulness. Writing Latin poetry was a natural development of Herbert's day-to-day activities at Cambridge and—because of the particular traditions of Latin and Neo-Latin literature that he knew intimately and the learned audience that Latin works would be directed to—allowed him to use different poetic voices than the ones he cultivated in his English lyrics.

Musae Responsoriae (1662) is a series of energetically witty and satiric "Epigrams in Defense of the Discipline of Our Church" meant to counter the attacks of Scottish Presbyterian Andrew Melville, whose poem *Anti-Tami-Cami-Categoria* pictured the British church as insufficiently reformed and still too beholden to Roman Catholic ceremonies, rituals, and accompaniments to worship. The publication of Melville's poem in 1620 perhaps provided Herbert with an opportunity to assert himself as the newly appointed orator of Cambridge—the universities were, after all, under siege by Melville, who criticized both Oxford and Cambridge for not supporting Puritan reform—and an occasion to clarify his own notion of the ideal British church. As in "The Church Militant," Herbert was deeply critical of what he felt were the many excesses of Roman Catholicism, but he was not sympathetic to Melville's "vain fears of the Vatican She-wolf" and the puritanical drive to purge the church of music, traditional prayers, vestments, and bishops.

For Herbert, Roman Catholics and Puritans are brothers, twin dangers like Scylla and Charybdis between which the British church must navigate: the *via media* is best, a theme that he returns to in one of the poems in *The Temple*, "The British Church." *Musae Responsoriae* is filled with comic caricatures of abrasive Puritan preachers and disorderly worshipers; respectful addresses to King James, Prince Charles, and Lancelot Andrewes as custodians of the peace threatened by the Puritans; and satiric analysis of Melville's ridiculous desire to create a church of nakedness and noise to replace one of visual beauty and music. It is a witty volume aimed to tease and please, but it is also an integral part of Herbert's lifelong attempt to define his church—no mean feat, since neither Scylla nor Charybdis can nor should be banished—and his place within it, as defender and worshiper.

Herbert's other two collections of Latin poems written during the early 1620s are comprised primarily of sacred rather than satiric and controversial epigrams. *Lucus* (a "Sacred Grove") is a somewhat loosely arranged miscellany that includes poems on Christ, the pope, the Bible, and several biblical episodes and figures, including Martha and Mary, and examines an assortment of topics such as love, pride, affliction, and death. Several of the poems, like those in *Musae Responsoriae*, use irony for satiric purposes.

The decrepit fate of Rome is ingeniously discovered in its very name, "Roma," which can be construed as an anagram depicting its decline from the glorious days of Virgil ("Maro") to the present day, when hate has banished love ("Amor"). But in most of the poems irony and paradox are used to convey the miraculous and mysterious power of Christ. Herbert's emphasis is not on careful, rational argumentation but bold, dramatic astonishment, as in the brief but dazzling lines "On the stoning of Stephen": "How marvelous! Who pounds rock gets fire. But Stephen from stones got heaven." The longest poem in the collection, "The Triumph of Death," indicts man's ironic misuse of intelligence to create weapons and other instruments of death, but the greater irony, revealed in the following poem, "The Christian's Triumph: Against Death," is that benign images of Christ—the lamb, the Cross—overwhelm even the most threatening spears, bows, and battering rams.

The twenty-one poems of *Passio Discerpta* are much more unified than those in *Lucus*, each focusing on some aspect of Christ's Crucifixion. Like Richard Crashaw's sacred epigrams, written some ten years later, these poems are intensely, even grotesquely, visual, but unlike Crashaw, Herbert's prevailing emotion is calm wonderment rather than ecstatic excitement. The description of the Passion of Christ is remarkably dispassion-

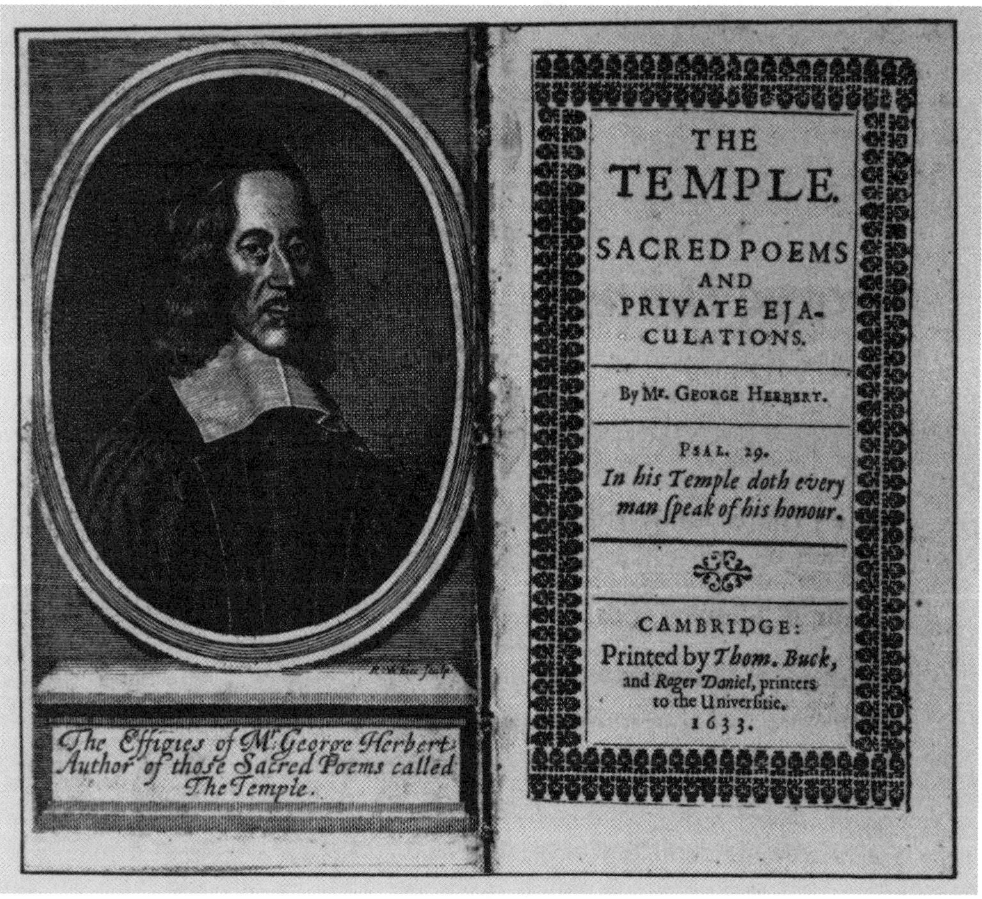

The Effigies of Mr George Herbert
Author of thoſe Sacred Poems called
The Temple.

THE
TEMPLE.
SACRED POEMS
AND
PRIVATE EJA-
CULATIONS.

By M^r. George Herbert.

Psal. 29.
In his Temple doth every man ſpeak of his honour.

CAMBRIDGE:
Printed by *Thom. Buck*,
and *Roger Daniel*, printers
to the Univerſitie.
1633.

Frontispiece and title page for Herbert's best-known work. John Wesley adapted many of these sacred poems during the eighteenth century for use in hymnals.

ate: the poetic witness is not cold or distant but is moved primarily by the redemptive purpose rather than the melodramatic circumstances of the Crucifixion. He is transfixed and indelibly marked by what he sees—"I, joyous, and my mouth wide open, / Am driven to the drenched cross"—and he is well aware that the death of Christ crushes the world and, as he imagines it, grinds the human heart to powder. But these poems, as baroque and intense as they may seem to be on the surface, are written from the secure perspective of one who feels at every moment that the inimitable sacrifice of Christ "lightens all losses."

Though the Latin poems of *Musae Responsoriae, Lucus*, and *Passio Discerpta* are relatively early works in Herbert's canon and represent a distinctive stage in the development of his style and ideas, they are by no means mere apprentice work, disconnected from his later efforts. Thematically, these collections have much in common with the poems of "The Church" and illustrate that these later lyrics are the result of lifelong meditation on certain themes, not spontaneous or occasional poeticizing. And stylistically, the Latin poems, relying heavily on compression, paradox, wordplay, and climactic moments of understated surprise, are at least in some ways the foundation of what has been called Herbert's "metaphysical wit." Such poems as "The Agonie" and "Redemption" may be more finely crafted and powerful than any of the verses in *Passio Discerpta*, but they are deeply akin to them.

Poetry was not all that was on Herbert's mind at Cambridge. He was worried about money: not for any extravagant purposes, but simply to live on. His university position paid him modestly, and the yearly portion assigned him in his father's will was administered by his brother Edward and usually sent late and begrudgingly. He sought and probably got help from his stepfather, but especially for someone who, as Ferrar describes him, valued his "independencie," financial insecurity was a great source of frustration.

And he worried about his health. In several of his letters he tells of being sick, restricted to a very careful (and expensive) diet, and too weak to fulfill his daily duties. "I alwaies fear'd sickness more then death," he wrote to his mother, "because sickness has made me unable to perform those Offices for which I came into the world."

Ill health troubled him for his entire adult life, and although many of the "afflictions" he describes in *The Temple* are spiritual, his intimate knowledge of the precarious state of the human body makes such poems as "Church-monuments" and "The Flower" particularly moving. Though he sometimes felt the ravages of "Consuming agues" that left him "thinne and leane" ("Affliction" [I]), he turned himself into an emblem confirming that physical sickness need not be an impediment to spiritual health, as seen in "The Size":

A Christians state and case
Is not a corpulent, but a thinne and spare,
Yet active strength: whose long and bonie face
Content and care
Do seem to equally divide.

The face that appears in Robert White's portrait of Herbert, copied from a lost original and printed in the first edition of Walton's *Life*, has these qualities: it is thin and spare, long and bony, and radiates both content and care.

However, Herbert's primary concern during the 1620s, more than health or money, was choosing his vocation, a recurrent theme in "The Church." Walton describes Herbert's path as a kind of involuntary conversion. His noble birth, upbringing, and education nurtured "ambitious Desires" for "the painted pleasures of a Court-life" and "the outward Glory of this World," but serious illness coupled with the death of his most influential friends at court led him to brood over his "many Conflicts with himself." "At last," Walton relates, "God inclin'd him to put on a resolution to serve at his Altar," and Herbert entered the church. Despite Walton's effort to praise Herbert's holiness and enviable commitment to church service, he stops just short of demonstrating that Herbert became a priest largely out of frustration and impatience.

Walton's analysis discounts the fact that well before the mid 1620s Herbert was preparing himself for a career in the church and believed that secular advancement was not necessarily antithetical to holy living. In a letter to John Danvers, dated 18 March 1618, he mentions his plans for a spiritual vocation as a long-acknowledged fact, not an agonizing crisis: "You know, Sir, how I am now setting foot into Divinity, to lay the platform of my future life." But this did not keep him from other pursuits: his public position as orator, which he defended as having "no such earthiness in it, but it may very well be joined with Heaven"; and friendships with ambitious and powerful men at court, such as Francis Bacon and John Williams. These two men bolstered Herbert's hope that secular and sacred interests could be fruitfully reconciled: Bacon was lord chancellor and translator of *Certain Psalmes* (1625), dedicated to Herbert; and Williams was a holy bishop and a formidable power broker and patron at court, for a time Herbert's greatest benefactor.

Walton is right to note that after many early successes Herbert's chances for advancement began to falter. His highly placed friends died (Ludovick Stuart, second Duke of Lennox, in 1624 and James Hamilton, second Marquis of Hamilton, in 1625) or tumbled as a result of political infighting (Bacon's fall into disgrace after going to trial for accepting bribes may have taught Herbert a great deal about the vagaries of power and the difficulty of reconciling morality and public greatness; and Williams went into retreat after losing battles with first Buckingham and then Laud.) His stepfather and his good friend Ferrar struggled in vain to save one of their pet projects and investments, the Virginia Company, formed to both colonize the New World and help spread the Gospel. After the king dissolved the corporation, Ferrar removed himself to a life of devotion at Little Gidding, while John Danvers, much more volatile and angry, intensified both his gardening at his house in Chelsea and his political agitating. Two decades later he was actively fighting against Charles I and ultimately became one of the regicides, directly responsible for the king's execution.

The power and reputation of some of Herbert's influential friends and family members were thus certainly being challenged and weakened at this time, but Walton drastically oversimplifies Herbert's character by identifying thwarted ambition as his primary motivation in moving closer to the priesthood. Although we cannot know for sure, it is just as likely that Herbert was deeply influenced by firsthand experience of the world of business, political intrigue, and court maneuvering and discovered not so much that it did not offer him a place as that it did not suit him. His youthful confidence that the sacred and the secular could be harmonized was not confirmed by the lives of those around him, and his attendance at the particularly tumultuous Parliament of 1624 more likely stifled than fanned any desire for a public political career. Years later, in *The Country Parson*, he recommended political service as a necessary part of the education of a gentleman: "for there is no School to a Parliament." But the lesson he learned there may be one stated simply in his poem "Submission," where he finds that worldly success and divine service are not easily blended: "Perhaps great places and thy praise / Do not so well agree."

Late in 1624 Herbert was preparing to take holy orders. Doing so would preclude any further service in Parliament and cut him off from many types of secular employment, but would be necessary for him to remain at Cambridge. (Fellows and other officials at the universities were required to take holy orders, normally within seven years of obtaining a master's degree, a vestige of the medieval origin of the university as primarily a training ground for church service). But at this time Herbert was leaving both Parliament and Cambridge behind. He was largely absent from Cambridge and delegated most of his duties to others. He did not return even to deliver the funeral oration commemorating the death of King James on 27 March 1625, and though he was not officially replaced as the university orator until January 1628, he had basically begun his removal from the Cambridge community by late 1623.

Ordination as a deacon, which Amy M. Charles suggests occurred in late 1624, by no means resolved the major problems of Herbert's life and in fact may have coincided with a heightening of them. He was presented by Bishop John Williams with several church livings, one at Llandinam in his home county of Montgomeryshire in 1624, and another at Lincoln Cathedral in Huntingtonshire near Little Gidding in 1626, and these brought him at least modest income and required only minimal effort of supervising some church functions and preaching once a year at Lincoln Cathedral. But this was not enough to support him, and between 1624 and 1629, with no house of his own, he stayed with a succession of friends and relatives: with "a friend in Kent," his stepfather and mother at Chelsea, his brother Henry at Woodford, and Henry Danvers, Earl of Danby (John Danvers's brother), at Dauntesey House in Wiltshire.

His financial condition improved substantially when in July 1627 a Crown grant made him part owner (with his brother Edward and Thomas Lawley, a cousin) of some land in Worcestershire, which was then sold to his brother Henry. The grant, about which little is known, may have assured Herbert that his family was not completely neglected (perhaps his estimate of his own current fate) nor out of royal favor (the frequent state of Edward, whose life as a courtier and diplomat oscillated between royal grace and disgrace), and the money he gained from the sale of the land was certainly welcome. Amy M. Charles suggests that it allowed him to resign his position at Cambridge and gave him the wherewithal to turn toward one of the favorite projects of his later life, rebuilding churches, an activity he undertook not only at Leighton Bromswald but also at Bemerton. But the fact remains that at this time Herbert was still without a settled vocation.

Many of the poems of "The Church" focus on the problems of finding a proper vocation. Some, such as "Affliction" (I) and "Employment" (I) and (II), seem to be early meditations on Herbert's uneven progress toward finding a position that might satisfy both his and God's desires. Others, such as "The Priesthood" and "Aaron," are undoubtedly later poems reflecting on the specific implications of his decisions to become a priest. "The Crosse," though, describes an intermediate stage, one at which Herbert was distressingly stuck in 1626, the probable date of this poem. The speaker seeks "some place, where I might sing, / And serve thee," but he comes to realize that the consequences of this desire are far more overwhelming than he had anticipated. "Wealth and familie," and indeed any sense that even the most dedicated believer brings something useful to Christ, prove to be irrelevancies and must be set aside. This "strange and uncouth thing," the Cross, completely disrupts one's normal life, and any potentially heartening illusions about "My power to serve thee" are replaced by an awareness that "I am in all a weak disabled thing."

One of the deepest ironies of the poem is that even when one's hesitancies about serving God are resolved, the basic impossibility of doing so still remains. As in so many of his other poems, Herbert finds himself on receding ground: God takes him up only to throw him down; devotion is not a release from physical and spiritual pain but an introduction to an even more devastating experience of "woe"; and the fulfillment of one's desire is never finally satisfying or peaceful—the speaker can "have my aim, and yet . . . be / Further from it then when I bent my bow." But after trying so hard to plan his own life, the speaker finally discovers his role in a life planned for him. There are various images and patterns of crosses in this poem, not the least of which is the intersection between man choosing God and God choosing him. The pains of life—"these crosse actions" that "cut my heart"—link one inextricably to Christ, particularly as a model of patient suffering and devoted service to man and God. Despite the plea "Ah my deare Father, ease my smart!" in the conclusion of the poem, Herbert is ultimately less concerned with escaping suffering than he is with finding meaning for it, and he does so by speaking Christ's words on the Cross, simultaneously letting Christ speak these words through him: "*Thy will be done.*"

As a logical conclusion, this will not do: Herbert fails to spell out exactly how one goes about following "thy will," details that would be especially important during a time of decision for him, such as the mid 1620s. But the last four words are a sign of devotional assent: a leap from, rather than a culmination of, rational analysis. This sudden imagination of the impossible—a characteristic movement in Herbert's most dynamic poems, such as "Prayer" (I) and "The Collar"—allows "The Crosse" to end with at least a momentary stay against confusion, as Frost might describe it. Weaving Scripture into his verses was an integral part of Herbert's attempt to forge a vocation as a servant of the Word of God, as both poet and priest. Here it allows him a sudden intuition into the blending of "mine" and "thine" as not one of the great problems, but one of the great joys, of religious experience. My will and thy will, my words and thy words, my voice and thy voice prove to be, as it were, intersecting beams in this poem about not the adoration, but the cooperative construction, of a cross.

Joseph H. Summers describes the years between 1626 and 1629 as "the blackest of all for Herbert," filled with anxious concern—conveyed in such poems as "The Crosse"—not only about his spiritual duties but also his physical health. In Walton's words, Herbert was "seized with a sharp *Quotidian* Ague" in 1626 that required a full year of careful diet and convalescence. And not long after, in June of 1627, his mother died, an event that affected him in complex, even contradictory ways. The death of a parent—and in Herbert's case, of his one parent—can be an emotional shock that is both devastating and liberating, confusing and clarifying. Herbert indeed moves through this wide range of response in the nineteen Latin and Greek poems that make up *Memoriae Matris Sacrum*, registered for publication along with Donne's funeral sermon on Magdalen Herbert on 7 July 1627, a month after her death. Mourning in general is highly ritualized, and such poems are usually formal and traditional rather than spontaneous and directly personal. We should therefore not expect these poems to record Herbert's unmediated feelings about the death of his mother, and we cannot know for sure when the poems are conventional exercises and when they are somewhat more telling autobiographical outbursts.

Even with these cautions in mind, *Memoriae Matris Sacrum* is an extremely revealing collection, giving important insight into his relationship with his mother and his corresponding sense of himself. Interestingly, it is the only collection of poems he published during his lifetime. (Although *Lucus, Passio Discerpta,* and the poems of *The Temple* were carefully copied out in manuscript, no doubt in preparation for eventual publication, they did not appear until after his death.) This may be explained by the prevailing norms of poetic practice for nonprofessionals at the time, which allowed for the publication of heroic, historical, and occasional poems, particularly of public celebration and mourning, but discouraged anything more than the circulation of other poems in manuscript, followed perhaps by posthumous publication. But Herbert's sense of himself as a poet was deeply intertwined with his relationship to his mother—as indicated by the early sonnets announcing to her his fiery poetic devotion—and not only writing but publishing *Memoriae Matris Sacrum* may have been part of a complex process of poetic self-assertion and self-definition as well as mourning.

It is common in elegiac and memorial poems to dwell on the impossibility of satisfactorily praising and mourning the person departed, but far more than this Herbert's poems examine the ways his mother both authorizes and threatens his poetry. "You taught me to write," he says in the second poem, and when he comes to write about important topics, such as her praise, "that skill, unloosed, / Floods the paper." And in the ninth poem he imagines himself in perennial com-

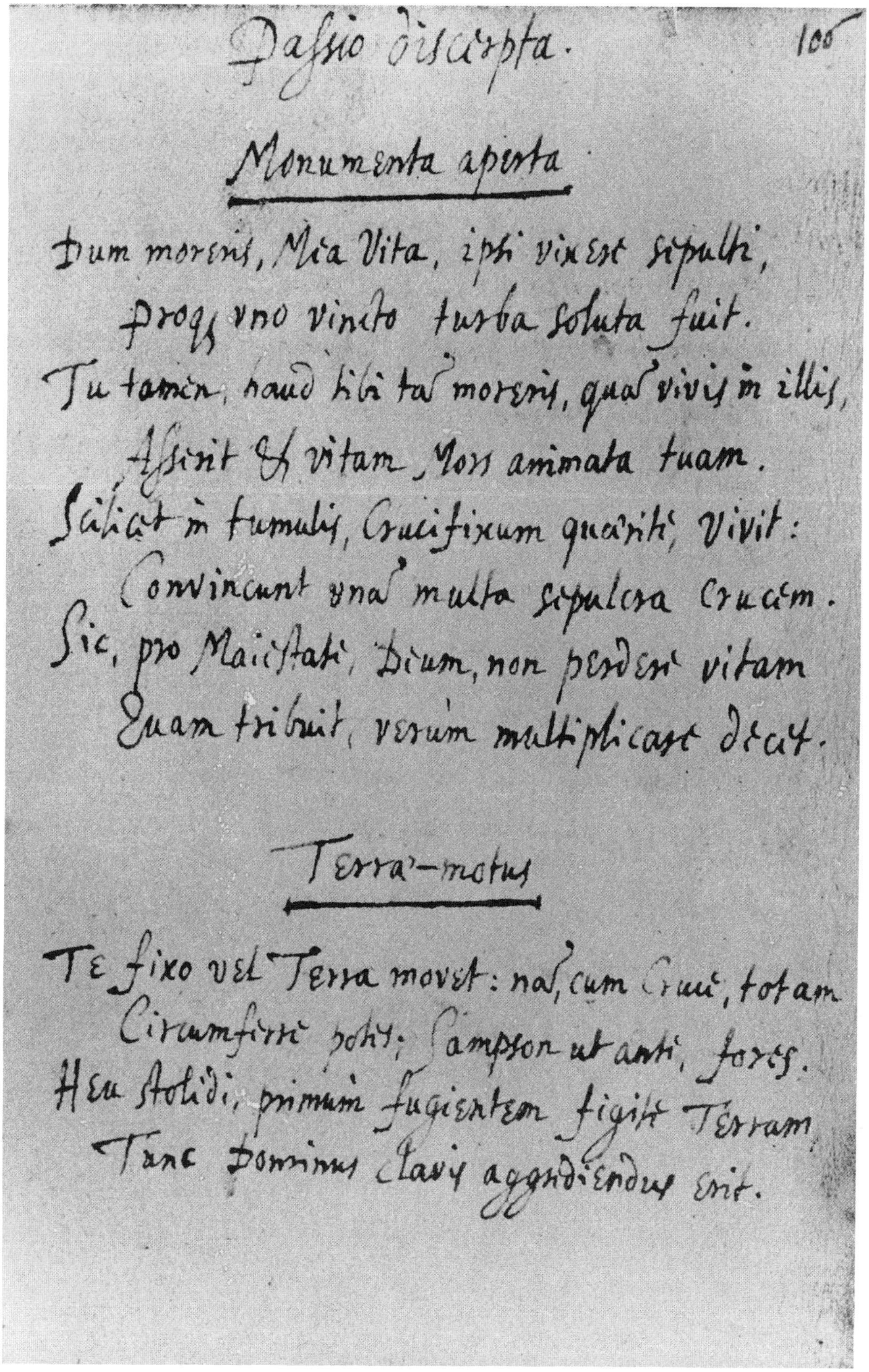

Passio discerpta. 100

Monumenta aperta

Dum moreris, Mea Vita, ipsi vixere sepulti,
Proq; uno vincto turba soluta fuit.
Tu tamen, haud tibi tota moreris, quae vivis in illis,
Asserit et vitam, Mors animata tuam.
Scilicet in tumulis, Crucifixum quaerite; vivit:
Convincunt unam multa sepulcra Crucem.
Sic, pro Maiestate, Deum, non perdere vitam
Quam tribuit, verum multiplicare decet.

Terra-motus

Te fixo vel Terra movet: nam, cum Cruce, totam
Circumferre potes; Sampson ut ante, fores.
Heu stolidi, primum fugientem figite Terram,
Tunc Dominus clavis aggrediendus erit.

Page from the manuscript for Passio Discerpta *(MS. Jones B 62; Dr. Williams's Library, London)*

munication with her, a "zealous child" sending her poems that she takes time off from her heavenly singing to read. She is integral to his fame: "For how can there be laurels for me, / How Nectar, unless with you / I pass the day in song?" But he also associates her with deep suspiciousness of language—"language being chaos since the time of Babel"—and complains that she failed to educate her children in a particular kind of verbal skill that might have made life easier: "manners' smooth / Mellifluous gift, the charm of words / To beat the lion back from us."

In the sixth poem Herbert confirms that poetry is his only remaining vehicle of contact with his mother and his only way of attempting to heal his deep distress, but the almost hallucinatory imagery conveys not only grief but also the intensity of Herbert's intertwined feelings about his mother and himself as a poet. After dismissing traditional medicine and suicide as possible sources of relief, he focuses on the act of writing in terms that are of great psychological interest. He pictures his arm swollen with the heat of "writing's fever," and anyone attempting to check his pulse would feel "the beating vein / My mother's residence." His swelling, setting aside its sexual suggestiveness, is both sickness and pregnancy, as his body now contains his mother, and his condition is, to say the least, precarious and unique: "Not sure my state: / My quality of flesh is not another's." But this same fever of creation is his best medicine, not an "Ill heat, but the only thing that heals the heart."

Memoriae Matris Sacrum is of course not exclusively about poetry. It contains many poignant expressions of sorrow and both directly and indirectly presents an interesting character sketch of Magdalen Herbert. Alongside conventional praise of her beauty, modesty, wide knowledge (especially in practical matters), charity, love of music, and fine penmanship, we catch glimpses of her somewhat more intimidating qualities: she "besieges" the Lord with "Sharp and fiery prayer," has a "Stern winsomeness," is a "strict mother," "Proud / and meek at once," and a "source of fiery contention / Of lord and commoner alike." Herbert's poems not only mourn and memorialize her but attempt to analyze and express the burden of a mother's love, a love that can both encourage and overwhelm, inspire and inflame. Not surprisingly, these dynamics recur in Herbert's later poems—despite his vow in the concluding poem that "This one time I write / To be forever still"—and the God that he loves and contends with in "The Church" is frequently not God the Father but God the Mother, at least as described in *Memoriae Matris Sacrum*.

It is sometimes difficult to determine what is a coincidence and what is a consequence, but in any event the death of his mother was followed by some decisive changes in Herbert's life. He separated himself finally from Cambridge (another of his mothers, alma mater) and went to stay at Dauntesey House in the countryside, where he recovered his health, probably wrote and revised some of the poems that would be gathered in "The Church," and got married. Walton tells a fanciful tale of how Jane Danvers, his stepfather's cousin, wooed by her father's deep respect for Herbert, fell in love with him sight unseen. They first met only three days before their wedding, he says, "at which time a mutual affection entered into both their hearts, as a Conqueror enters into a surprized City, and made there such Laws and Resolutions, as neither party was able to resist."

The romantic overlay seems to be Walton's invention, uncorroborated by any other evidence and surprisingly dissonant with what we know of Herbert's emotional life from his own writings, but there is little reason to doubt Walton's fundamental assertion that the marriage was one thoughtfully negotiated and arranged, not uncommon during this time. Several sections in *The Country Parson* suggest that Herbert put a high value on companionate marriage, based on mutual love and shared work, and such a marriage with Jane Danvers at this time in his life may have served a variety of purposes: besides affording him emotional support, it perhaps also consolidated his relationship with the Danvers family, with whom he seemed to be very attached; eased his transition to life in Wiltshire, where he seemed to be gravitating; and allowed him to make practical plans for setting up his own household and accepting the vocation at which he had long aimed. Herbert and Jane were married on 5 March 1629, and although they lived for a year with her family at Baynton House, by the end of 1630 he was an ordained priest settled in the small parish of Bemerton, where he spent the few remaining years of his life.

Even after he had been presented with the living at Bemerton—probably through the influence of his relative William Herbert, the third Earl of Pembroke, whose estate in Wilton was close to the tiny country parish of Bemerton—Herbert delayed entering the priesthood. He may have been, as Amy M. Charles suggests, occupied with wrapping up bits of business of the life he was ready to leave behind: perhaps traveling to Lincoln Cathedral to deliver the last of his yearly sermons, and to Little Gidding for a visit with Ferrar, something he might not have the luxury of doing once his full duties commenced at Bemerton. Or this may have been a final period of spiritual wrestling, with Herbert still needing to argue himself into a final conviction that he was worthy, willing, and able to be God's servant. Walton is frequently melodramatic, but some of the melodrama may be authentic: he describes Herbert on the day of his induction at Bemerton lying "prostrate on the ground before the Altar," devising rules for his own future conduct and making "a vow, to labour to keep them." His long-awaited ordination as a priest on 19 September 1630 surely did not mark the end of all his spiritual worries or sense of personal frailty, but it may well have signified a new accommodation of them, a deepened understanding of how weakness and worry (which in any event can never be erased from human experience) can be integrated into one's spiritual life.

While at Bemerton, Herbert was extremely busy with a wide range of activities. *The Country Parson* documents that for Herbert the priesthood was not only a spiritual vocation but a social commitment, and although this work was intended as an idealized portrait—"a Mark to aim at," he tells us in the preface—rather than an autobiographical statement, Herbert undoubtedly was much like the parson he describes: charitable, conversant with his parishioners outside as well as inside the church, an arbiter of local squabbles, and a familiar example rather than a formal sermonizer. Walton tends to describe Herbert's life at Bemerton as a kind of intentional humbling of himself. He describes Herbert's first sermon as a learned and witty exercise that confounded his parishioners, but he concluded with a promise never to preach that way again: he would from that point on "be more plain and practical in his future Sermons."

This illustrates Herbert's dramatic conversion from university orator to parish priest. But while *The Country Parson* implicitly acknowledges that he had to make strenuous adjustments to enter into the life—and barns and houses—of common country people, there is little indication that he did this grudgingly. The model for condescension (literally "stepping down") is Christ, a model Herbert readily accepts. Throughout *The Country Parson* and in other poems (such as "Whitsunday," "Sunday," "Lent," and "The Elixir") he shows himself to be a sincere "Lover of old Customes," common charity, and daily labor quite unlike any he would have done at Cambridge or court.

This is not to say that life at Bemerton was a continual round of conversations with farmers and catechizing the uneducated. Wilton House was nearby, and Herbert was a confidant of Lady Anne Clifford, wife of his kinsman Philip Herbert, fourth Earl of Pembroke. Salisbury was also within walking distance, and some of Walton's most charming tales describe Herbert's love of music and his visits twice a week to evensong at the magnificent cathedral in Salisbury. Herbert was also busy directing the rebuilding of the church and rectory at Bemerton and entertaining guests, such as Arthur Woodnoth, Ferrar's cousin and an important intermediary between him and Herbert.

As deeply involved as he was in the social life of the parish, Herbert still had time for private meditation and writing. *The Country Parson* is dated 1632 in his preface. At or near this time he was also annotating John Valdesso's *The Hundred and Ten Considerations*, a book of Catholic devotion sent him by Ferrar. In his "Briefe Notes," eventually included in an edition of Valdesso published in 1638, Herbert describes Valdesso as a "true servant of God," but one whose "defects" need correction. Herbert's careful attention to such a book indicates not his attraction to Roman Catholicism but his willingness to appreciate and learn from spiritual advice from a wide range of authors, a devotional openness that thwarts critics who try to define Herbert's theology too precisely. He was also engaged in translating *A Treatise of Temperance and Sobrietie*, by Luigi Cornaro, which shortly before his death he sent to Ferrar, who published it in 1634 as part of a larger work, *Hygiasticon*. Herbert's editor F. E. Hutchinson speculates that Bacon may have proposed the idea of translating this work, but no matter who set the task for him, the subjects of temperance, sobriety, and careful diet were of lifelong interest to Herbert. During this time Herbert probably also continued to work on another lifelong interest, his collection of proverbs, published as *Outlandish Proverbs Selected by Mr. G. H.* in 1640 and in an expanded version in 1652 as *Jacula Prudentum*.

More important, though, is his final work at Bemerton composing, revising, and structuring

The Temple. According to Walton, Herbert described it as containing *"a picture of the many spiritual conflicts that have past betwixt God and my Soul, before I could subject mine to the will of* Jesus, my Master: *in whose service I have now found perfect freedom*." But this is an incomplete and misleading picture in several respects. First, it gives the impression that *The Temple* is primarily a miscellany of assorted poems on wavering faith, unstable devotion, and human resistance, problems at last securely overcome by strenuous efforts not described by the poems. On the contrary, *The Temple* dramatizes both "spiritual Conflicts" and the achievement of "perfect freedom." Second, Herbert's brief description sets up a simple division between the troubles of the past and the peaceful obedience of the present, a division that *The Temple* repeatedly undermines. Many of the troubled narratives and complaints in "The Church" ("The Collar," for example) are retrospective, presumably spoken from a position of strength or recovery, but the pains are conveyed with such vivid force and immediacy that they infiltrate the present. The past rarely stays past for Herbert: "perfect freedom," obedience, peace, and joy are powerful realities in the poems, but they never become completely disengaged from the threats they overcome.

Herbert's understanding of this dialectical relationship between worry and assurance and his corresponding insight into the rhythms of the spiritual life remain somewhat veiled if we examine the poems randomly and individually instead of as parts of an intricately interconnected whole. It is clear that Herbert carefully planned the arrangement of the poems in *The Temple* and intended it to be read in its entirety. An early version of nearly half of the poems eventually printed in the first edition of 1633 appears in a manuscript copied probably in the mid 1620s, and this so-called Williams Manuscript indicates that Herbert had not only outlined the basic structure of the volume by this time but also that he was constantly tinkering with it. Some of the poems in the manuscript are set in different places in the printed arrangement, and Herbert made changes in the texts and titles to fit these poems into their new positions.

Even a casual reader could hardly miss the many clues that *The Temple* is a carefully constructed artifact or sequence, but Herbert virtually announces his plans in one of the poems placed early in "The Church," titled "The H. Scriptures II." Here he not only praises the Bible for its penetrating insight into human life but notes that its wisdom may be somewhat mysterious unless one knows how it is structured:

> This verse marks that, and both do make a motion
> Unto a Third, that ten leaves off doth lie:
> Then as dispersed herbs do watch a potion,
> These three make up some Christians destinie.

Scriptural interpreters of the time stressed that the Bible is best understood as a unified work: difficult passages could be explicated by comparison with other places in the text, and in general the many repetitions and parallels written into the Bible linked not only the Old and New Testaments but the lives of all Christians. In this as in so many other ways, *The Temple* is modeled after the Bible.

There are many levels of structure in *The Temple*, some broad or obvious, others subtle or minute. The three main sections, "The Church-porch," "The Church," and "The Church Militant" of course indicate that the entire volume will move through stages of secular preparation, sacred initiation, and prophetic vision. Within "The Church" itself there is also a variety of clearly defined sequences of poems. The sense of temporal sequence is particularly strong in the first part of "The Church," perhaps because Herbert wants immediately to call attention to the fact that his poems trace out stages in a devotional life, but also perhaps because he wants to accustom his readers to a simple notion of poetic order before he goes on to more complicated patterns. "The Church" begins with a series of poems that concentrates on Easter week and dramatizes not only Christ's Crucifixion but the difficulties one faces in responding properly to this all-important event. Herbert starts his Christian calendar not with the birth of Christ, explored later in "The Church" in a two-part poem titled "Christmas," but with poems that describe Christ's death and how it allows his followers to live, including "The Sacrifice," "The Agonie," "Good Friday," "Redemption," "Easter," and "Easter-wings." And immediately after this sequence Herbert places another cluster of poems with a readily apparent linear plot. Even the titles of this group tell a familiar story: "H. Baptisme" (I) and (II), "Nature," "Sinne" (I), "Affliction" (I), "Repentance," "Faith," "Prayer" (I), and "The H. Communion."

Some of the sequences are not temporal narratives. For example, "Church-monuments," "Church-musick," "Church-lock and key," "The Church-floore," and "The Windows" are grouped together not so much because they describe a literal walk through the physical church but because each of these subjects prompts a meditation on interior qualities, a temple within. And other sequences allow Herbert to give sustained attention not to a plot but to a particular theme: the poems "Content," "The Quidditie," "Humilitie," "Frailtie," "Constancie," and "Affliction" (III) comprise a kind of anticourt sequence in which Herbert contrasts the sacred and secular worlds. No one poem could convey so well Herbert's complex understanding of the continuing allure of a life-style he sought to reject and the continuing difficulties and pains of a devotional style he sought to accept.

Just as it begins with a highly articulated temporal sequence, "The Church" ends with a series of poems that seems to confirm that all along Herbert has been tracing the life of an exemplary, though more than occasionally troubled, believer, and that at last these troubles are falling away. The final poems are filled with images of comfort and joy, and even potential worries are almost miraculously transformed into occasions for celebration. "Discipline" is an argumentative plea for God to "Throw away thy rod," and its boldness betrays not lingering pride but confident intimacy with the God of Love. "The Invitation" issues a call to "Come ye hither All" to join with God in a splendid feast, a call answered in the following poem, "The Banquet." "The Posie," "A Parodie," "The Elixir," and "A Wreath" dramatize God's presence in dedicated human labor, and in particular stress that poetry can be a fit vehicle for praise of God, a recurrent concern for Herbert.

The next four poems focus on the Last Things, but the traditional gloomy meditation on Death, Judgment, Heaven, and Hell becomes, in the best sense of the term, a comedy: Hell is not even mentioned; "Death" pictures not physical decay but the everlasting life made possible by Christ toward which one should rush at "Doomsday"; the day of "Judgement" is a time when human sins are accepted as "thine"; and "Heaven," written as an echo poem, describes a place of light, joy, pleasure, and leisure that calls out to us. Finally, the real Last Thing, first and last for Herbert, is "Love," and in the third of the poems with this title in "The Church," Herbert dramatizes the persona's last resistance to God, acceptance of communion, and reception into the heaven promised by the God of Love.

In broad terms, then, the entire sequence of poems in "The Church" follows the spiritual progress of one who "groneth" to be "holy, pure, and cleare" ("Superliminare"), and although the path is difficult and uneven, the end is sure. But sometimes the groaning and the unevenness seem more prominent than the promised end. Unlike some of his followers—including Henry Colman and Christopher Harvey in the seventeenth century and John Keble in the nineteenth, who doggedly elaborate a Christian Year or a physical Church in their volumes and in the process flatten out the devotional life—Herbert's sequence is by no means simple and linear, and the path traversed by "The Church" is filled with interruptions, backslidings, and sudden rises and falls. Lessons need to be repeated and relearned, and in some respects linear progress throughout "The Church" is an illusion: the persona at the end of the sequence is still working on many of the same problems as at the beginning. The all-too-human but wrongheaded enthusiasm and evasiveness of the speaker of "The Thanksgiving," who does everything but look directly at his real task at hand—confronting the inimitable example of Christ—is akin to the shortsightedness of the speaker in "Miserie"; the forgivable boldness of the speaker in "Discipline," who tries to tell God what to do; and the stubbornness of the speaker in "Love" (III), who to the very end tries to resist the irresistible.

Nothing happens once and for all in "The Church," and every mood is transitory, liable to pass into its opposite. Sometimes this can be heartening. There are many moments of physical and spiritual recovery in the sequence, as one poem of worry is answered by another of wonderful consolation. "Church-monuments" relentlessly pictures the wearing away of the body to death and dust, but the next poem, "Church-musick," lifts the released, bodiless soul toward heaven. "Longing" is a prolonged poem of complaint by a tormented person who can hardly even imagine relief, but the opening line of "The Bag" announces a dramatic—though not final—end to all this: "Away despair! my gracious Lord doth heare." And in one of the most remarkable instances of sudden healing and consolation in the entire collection, the accumulating worries, pains, and sorrows of "The Search," "Grief," and "The Crosse" give way to "The Flower"—"How fresh, O Lord, how sweet and clean / Are thy returns!"—

which turns even the cycle of joy and pain into a joy.

But joy, comfort, and recovery often seem to be as fleeting as pain and despair. "The Glimpse" opens with an emotional but not particularly surprised statement about the evanescence of comfort and assurance:

> Whither away delight?
> Thou cam'st but now; wilt thou so soon depart,
> And give me up to night?

The "but now" could be a specific reference within the imaginary narrative constructed by the poems of "The Church": the preceding poem, "The Collar," ends with the sudden interruption of the consoling voice of the Lord calling to a rebellious child he claims rather than disowns, a "delight" that "The Glimpse" perhaps suggests is gone almost as soon as it is received. Even if "The Glimpse" is not responding directly to the experience of "The Collar," it describes a feeling of loss common in "The Church," one dramatized and interpreted in the paired poems titled "The Temper." The first of these poems ends with a vision of a universe of perfect unity and comfort, where God's "power and love, my love and trust, / Make one place ev'ry where." But the inevitable falling off happens in the short space between the end of the first and the beginning of the second poem, which opens in a voice that Herbert is a master of, blending astonishment and matter-of-factness: "It cannot be. Where is that mightie joy, / Which just now took up all my heart?"

These rises and falls, falls and rises, are apparently an inescapable and even a necessary part of the devotional life for Herbert. They torment—"O rack me not to such a vast extent" in "The Temper" (I) is a plea for release from an implement of torture—but also comprise part of a "tempering" process that ultimately tests and strengthens one: like metals heated to high temperatures and then suddenly cooled, the experience of emotional and spiritual extremes, no matter how painful, improves us. There is something to William Empson's provocative claim that Herbert's God, like Milton's, is a savage God indeed if torment characterizes divine example and human fate. But the backslidings and nearly interminable emotional ups and downs in "The Church" are not indictments of a cruel God nor dramatizations of impossible devotional responsibilities. They are, though, reminders that spiritual progress is extremely complex, demanding,

18 *The Church.*

The Altar.

A broken ALTAR, Lord, thy ſervant reares,
Made of a heart, and cemented with teares:
Whoſe parts are as thy hand did frame;
No workmans tool hath touch'd the ſame.
A HEART alone
Is ſuch a ſtone,
As nothing but
Thy pow'r doth cut.
Wherefore each part
Of my hard heart
Meets in this frame,
To praiſe thy name.
That if I chance to hold my peace,
Theſe ſtones to praiſe thee may not ceaſe.
O let thy bleſſed SACRIFICE be mine,
And ſanctifie this ALTAR to be thine.

The

Page from the first edition of The Temple, *with one of the poems that was typographically structured to resemble its subject*

and in some ways unpredictable—terms that also provide an apt description of Herbert's artistry in arranging his poems to describe that progress.

This structural artistry is abundantly evident in the individual poems as well as in the plan of the entire collection. Herbert experimented constantly with poetic forms and meters: he shaped his poems carefully, rarely repeated stanzaic patterns or rhyme schemes, and frequently established patterns in order to break or vary them. This versatility may have been influenced by collections of poems such as the *Greek Anthology*, constantly consulted by Renaissance poets as a handbook of poetic practice, but the Bible also offered a model of stylistic diversity. The Book of Psalms in particular was frequently described as an encyclopedia of poetic genres and voices, and Herbert undoubtedly felt that the psalms licensed and instructed him in his formal experimentation. Contemporary metrical translations of the psalms, especially by Sir Philip Sidney and his sister, Mary Herbert, Countess of Pembroke, perhaps also played a great role in reinforcing Herbert's sense that the variety of religious experience requires a variety of poetic forms.

"The Church" is characterized not only by formal variety and experimentation but also by what may be called structural play: Herbert frequently relies on the form of a poem to embody and convey much of the meaning and effect. Some of the patterns are easily visible: "The Altar" is typographically shaped like an altar, and the two stanzas of "Easter-wings" look like angels' wings seen from behind. Later critics such as John Dryden ridiculed such poems, not only because they were unsympathetic to the visual dimensions of a verbal genre but also because they missed some of the complexities of what at first glance seem to be simple picture-poems. "The Altar" pictures not only an altar of poetic devotion but also a large "I," one of the great impediments to devotion. And the stanzas of "Easter-wings" look like wings only when they are turned on end: as the poem is read, the stanzas look like hourglasses. These poems are thus emblems or pictorial representations not so much of simple objects as of a complex process that recurs throughout "The Church": a shifting figure-ground relationship that confirms the instability of perception and interpretation. Because of this instability, Herbert's poems are frequently about reconsiderations—looking at, hearing, or otherwise evaluating or responding to something again. The first glance, figuratively speaking, is typically naive, insufficient, incomplete; the second is deeper, corrected, more properly informed.

Several of Herbert's pattern poems focus directly on this particular drama. "Jesu" pictures a broken "frame"—the human heart carved with the name of "Jesu" imagined as a printer's device holding individual letters—and describes the shifting stages of perception whereby a first glance of random letters turns to an awareness that they spell "*I ease you*" and then finally "JESU." (The fact that the letter *I* was used interchangeably with *J* at this time makes possible the pun at the heart of this poem.) And "Coloss. 3.3" literally embodies the "double motion" and double look it describes: the normal sequential reading of the lines must be supplemented by a separate reading of the statement embedded diagonally in the poem. The plodding and prosaic couplets are much in contrast with the italicized biblical quotation that is the dramatic revelation of the poem: "*My Life Is Hid In Him, That Is My Treasure.*"

Herbert's "hieroglyphic" patterns, to use Joseph H. Summers's term, do not always rely on direct pictorial or visual representation. Form creates or supports meaning throughout "The Church" in many ways. "Prayer" (I) is comprised of a tumbling together of apparently random epithets that have a disorienting effect and raise the suspicion that prayer may well be indefinable. But gradually the poem shapes itself as a sonnet, and the assertion of regular poetic form (there are two couplets, for example, in the last five lines) helps manage the extraordinary energy of the descriptions and allows for a peaceful conclusion: "something understood" is more the culmination of an emotional drama than a rational process of analysis, and perhaps suggests that our attempt to define prayer is subsumed by a sudden awareness of how prayer defines us.

"The Collar" similarly uses a kind of free verse that is ultimately reined in by orderly and regular poetic form. The rebelliousness of the speaker is of course mirrored by the apparent disorder of his speech, a disorder that he flaunts: "My lines and life are free; free as the rode / Loose as the winde, as large as store." But the "fierce and wilde" complaints not only express but also exhaust this rebelliousness, and never far from the centrifugal energy on the surface of the poem is a substratum of order ready to emerge. The real plot of the poem is not the momentary flight from, but the inevitable movement toward, obedience and order, and this movement is underscored by the gradual achievement of structural stability culminating in the last four lines, a controlled, alternately rhyming quatrain. For all its formal pyrotechnics and structural play, though, "The Collar," like "Prayer" (I), is no mere five-finger exercise. These poems are devotional, not mechanical, fugues, and much of their extraordinary power comes from Herbert's ability to embody rather than merely describe dramas of faith and doubt, resistance and assent.

Herbert's structural artistry is matched by his verbal skill. His long-standing interest in rhetoric perhaps betrays not only his deep fascination with words but also his awareness of the connection between language and power, both secular and sacred. Verbal language is the primary, though not the only, vehicle of communication, exchange, and contact among people and between one person and God. In addition it may not be too much of an overstatement to say that the language of the self *is* the self, providing a necessary mode of construction as well as access and expression. For all that this proposition reeks of contemporary linguistic theorizing, we should note how closely it accords with Herbert's incarnational view of the world: an understanding of Christ as the Word made flesh undoubtedly reinforced Herbert's serious concern for the relationship between verbal expression and devotion and heightened his awareness of how his own self and the world he inhabited were, if not verbal artifacts, then at least inevitably shaped by words.

Herbert's wordplay, then, is often as philosophical as it is playful, and his poetic voice and style—really voices and styles—are not matters of convenience but careful devotional choices. He is most often praised for his simplicity, contrasted with Shakespeare's tortuous ambiguity, Donne's rugged obscurity, and Jonson's learned allusiveness, but Herbert's simplicity is artful, studied, and less simple than it appears. He delights in the rich multiplicity of reference in words. "I like our language," he says in "The Sonne," not because words set up stable one-to-one relationships between signifier and signified but because they set up correspondences between the one and the many, which when properly traced out reveal a deeper one-to-One connection, between man and God. The word *son* refers not only to "parents issue and the sunnes bright starre" but ultimately to Christ, the Son of God and sun of our life—all of this neatly contained in a *sonnet*.

Key words in Herbert's poems often set off explosions of meaning, and this multiplicity frequently offers relief from, as well as a description of, the tensions and ironies of the human predicament. The "collar" in Herbert's poem of that name brings to mind a chafing yoke around the neck, rebellious anger ("choler"), and perhaps even the "color" of rhetorical embellishment used to plead a difficult case forcefully, the speaker's exact situation here. It also sounds like "the caller," and in this way subtly foreshadows the climactic "Me thoughts I heard one Calling, *Child!* / And I reply'd, *My Lord*." The first part of "Christmas" is a somewhat uneasy poem attempting to fathom the mystery of the Christ-child, but the description of the baby's "contracted light" simultaneously increases the witness's awe at the spectacle of immensity made small and eases his worry about future "relief" by recalling the ineradicable contract between man and God. And in "The Crosse" one of the figures of speech that conveys the speaker's deepest depression—"To have my aim, and yet to be / Further from it then when I bent my bow"—imagines not only a bow and arrow helpless to shoot him closer to his target but also the bow of devotional obedience that concludes the poem, itself an imitation of Christ's bow on the Cross.

Herbert's art of plainness thus does not preclude purposeful ambiguity, and his wit thrives on assertions of multiple references for words. But as some of his poems about poetry indicate, he was deeply critical of showy and excessively self-assertive wit and obsessively concerned with the relationship between problems of style and problems of devotion. Poetry is a mode of holy service for Herbert and an index of spiritual health or affliction. Full recovery at the end of "The Flower" is imagined as a blend of organic rebirth, renewed sensuality, and poetic activity, the latter perhaps the most prominent:

> And now in age I bud again,
> After so many deaths I live and write;
> I once more smell the dew and rain,
> And relish versing.

Behind these lines is the memory of another fact, visible in other poems, that despair is registered as a disruption of his ability to write: in "Deniall" distance from God breaks "my heart" and "my verse." Nearly all his devotional problems are analogous to stylistic problems: this reminds us that his poems on poetry are thus never about poetry alone. His worries cover a wide range. In "Grief" he wonders whether poetry is an adequate vehicle for his pain—"Verses, ye are too fine a thing, too wise / For my rough sorrows"—and in fact the poem ends with a dramatic assertion of the limits of poetry: his final sigh "Alas, my God!" literally falls outside the poem, a sigh evidently too powerful to be contained by "measure, tune, and time."

He also frequently questions whether poetry can be an adequate vehicle for praise of God. The act of poetry is double-moated with irony for Herbert: it perhaps represents the best, even all we have to offer God, and yet it is still not enough; and even though it is all that we have, it too is not ours but a gift from God. Secular poets frequently play on these tropes—that even the highest praise is insufficient, and that it is derivative, not original, a return of beneficence already given by a lord who thus not only occasions, but in effect authors, the praise. With an infinitely more powerful Lord as his subject, this situation is potentially infinitely more humiliating for Herbert. As a poet and a worshiper he must face up to the devastating implications of the fact, stated most succinctly in "The Holdfast," that "nothing is our own."

Throughout "The Church" this assertion and variants of it threaten virtually to annihilate the self and in the process silence all poetry. The response of the persona in "The Holdfast" is typical: "I stood amaz'd at this, / Much troubled." But here and elsewhere such turmoil is the prelude to an all-important interpretive discovery: to say that "nothing is our own" or even that "to have nought is ours" disclaims sole ownership but not shared possession. The soothing voice of a friend at the end of the poem advises that the process of letting go is the best way of holding and being held fast: "all things were more ours by being his," kept by Christ. If one loses absolute independence by depending on Christ, one gains, in Ferrar's fine phrase describing Herbert, "independencie upon all others." One loses selfishness, not the self.

Many of Herbert's poems on poetry follow the same pattern as "The Holdfast," because while he feels the necessity of writing—"The shepherds sing; and shall I silent be?" he notes in "Christmas"—all writing is almost inescapably an act of self-assertion. The traditions and conventions of poetry reinforce this: a "good" poem is normally one that calls attention to itself by fine phrases; inevitable lies; false flattery; and indulgent wit, learning, or obscurity. Herbert attempts to reject all these qualities in such poems as "Jordan" (I) and (II), "A true Hymne," "The Posie," "The Forerunners," "A Parodie," and "A Wreath," but renunciation is always imperfect—poetic pride, like sin in general, is ineradicable and surfaces even in poems that aim to be simple and submissive—and even when it is momentarily successful, it raises further difficulties. What will take the place of all these banished qualities of conventional poetry?

The safest recourse is to construct poetry from God's words. Both "Jordan" poems end with advice to abandon a poetics of invention for one of quotation, ventriloquism, or direct imitation: one should "plainly say, *My God, My King*" (I) and humbly accept that "*There is in love a sweetnesse readie penn'd: / Copie out onely that, and save expense*" (II). And "The Forerunners" compresses a manifesto into a statement of rather strict limits: "For, *Thou art still my God*, is all that ye / Perhaps with more embellishment can say." Herbert's actual poetic practice indicates that he followed such advice both faithfully and creatively. Instead of weaving his "self into the sense," one of the dangers noted in "Jordan" (II), he attempted to weave the Bible into his poems, a process of literary allusion and devotional absorption studied in fine detail by Chana Bloch. In a powerful way the Bible created rather than stifled Herbert's poetic voice, stimulating him to find many ways to say "My God, My King." And despite his distrust of easily abused poetic fancy, he allowed himself the "embellishment" mentioned in "The Forerunners," decking the sense not to "sell" but to serve. For Herbert, devotion chastens but finally engages all human powers, and we see the results of this in the art and the artlessness, the strain and the wondrously achieved calm, the prayer and the poetics of "The Church."

Herbert did not publish *The Temple* during his lifetime, although it is clear that he intended it to be published. Walton writes that when Herbert was on his deathbed, he gave his volume to a friend, Edmund Duncon, to deliver to Ferrar for publication, leaving these instructions: "*if he can think it may turn to the advantage of any dejected poor Soul, let it be made publick: if not, let him burn it.*" Literary fame was not on Herbert's mind. Still, *The Temple* was instantly well received: Walton noted in 1674 that "there have been more than Twenty Thousand of them sold since the first Impression." Herbert's immediate popularity cut across a wide range of readers, including Puritans, Anglicans, and Roman Catholics as well as Royalists, Parliamentarians, and republicans, but waned by the end of the seventeenth century. Early-eighteenth-century readers either avoided him or spoke respectfully of his piety but condescendingly of his false wit and grotesque imagery, and there was no new edition of his poems between 1709 and 1799.

Herbert's poems began to resurface in hymnals, primarily through the efforts of John Wesley, who adapted and rewrote many poems from *The Temple* and also published an edition of Herbert's selected sacred poems. Yet the real revival of interest came in the nineteenth century, buoyed by fine critical comments, allusions, and appreciations by such influential writers as Coleridge, Emerson, and John Ruskin. Several important editions of Herbert's complete works in the latter part of the century testified to and also helped spread the renewed interest, culminating in a dramatic twentieth-century revival of

Herbert—as well as the other Metaphysical poets—led in part by T. S. Eliot, whose poems and critical writings illustrate his lifelong attraction to Herbert. Book-length critical studies of Herbert began to appear in the early 1950s and have continued unabated to the present day.

Many early analyses of Herbert—and some more current ones—draw his range much too narrowly, defining him in effect as the quintessential minor poet: extremely talented, but noticeably restricted. However, he is not nearly as limited as some imagine. His poems are of course deeply Christian, but contrary to what Coleridge and others suggest, one need not be a dutiful worshiper of the Anglican religion to find them powerful and relevant, and one not need be a Christian at all to respond deeply to many of his dramatizations of emotional loss, pain, joy, and recovery.

Herbert's simplicity has also been overstated, and while it has led some to view him as a refreshing contrast to Donne, it has tamed him too much. His formal simplicity is deceptive and challenging. Anyone who would speak of his temperamental simplicity is missing the variety in the poems, which includes near-hysterical worry, hallucinatory clarity (especially in visionary allegorical poems such as "Love unknown"), and both sweet acquiescence ("H. Baptisme" [II]) and sweet resistance ("Love" [III]). And although the lyric, Herbert's main genre, is sometimes thought of as too slight a form to sustain poetic greatness, Herbert stretches the form considerably not only by constant inventiveness but also by linking the individual lyrics into much broader patterns.

Perhaps more damaging to any attempt to amplify Herbert's stature is the perception that his poems are private and that they reflect a narrow range of interests and experience. The "spiritual Conflicts" of *The Temple*, though, are not Herbert's alone: they are deeply personal, even autobiographical, but also typical, shared; and the poems are acts of communion with a human as well as heavenly audience. Furthermore, the conflicts in *The Temple* are social and institutional as well as personal. Even in the devotional lyrics of "The Church," Herbert casts his eyes on the social and political as well as the religious turmoil of the early seventeenth century: this is most obvious in such poems as "The British Church," "Divinitie," and "Church-rents and schismes," which focus specifically on controversies of the day. Even though he is not a political poet in the way that Milton and Andrew Marvell are, many of his poems reflect his constant meditation on public affairs.

Finally, critics who feel that Herbert's range excludes secular issues also suggest that he is somewhat limited by lack of attention to secular love. For Donne we have not only sacred poems but also the *Songs and Sonets*; for Herbert we have only sacred poems in "The Church," marked by the exclusion of and contempt for secular love and sexual attention to women. This unquestionably cuts him off from an important part of human experience. But he does give remarkably full expression to the erotic aspect of his relationship with God, a relationship marked by physical intimacy, patient wooing, and a sensation of "sweetness." Throughout "The Church" the persona is a lover, and the height of spiritual success is experienced as loving and being loved.

By most standards Herbert is both a major and a great poet. These standards involve the following qualities: a high level of analytical intelligence; a close but dynamic and innovative relationship to literary traditions and conventions; technical versatility; an ability to dramatize key crises of emotional and spiritual life; a distinctive style and voice; an extensive body of work; sustained popularity and influence; a strong sense of the physical nature of life; a sense of comedy (somewhat different from a sense of humor); and density of thought and expression.

To say that Herbert is one of the masters of the devotional lyric is high praise but may be misleading if that term qualifies as well as specifies his achievement. It is somewhat bolder but still justifiable to say simply that he is one of the great English poets. *The Temple* stands up to repeated readings and detailed analysis as a work that, as Ferrar felt it would, continues to "*enrich the World with pleasure and piety*."

Bibliography:

John R. Roberts, *George Herbert: An Annotated Bibliography of Modern Criticism: Revised Edition, 1905-1984* (Columbia: University of Missouri Press, 1988).

Biographies:

Izaak Walton, *The Lives of John Donne, Sir Henry Wotton, Richard Hooker, George Herbert, and Robert Sanderson* (London: Oxford University Press, 1927) [The life of Herbert was originally published in 1670];

Margaret Bottrall, *George Herbert* (London: John Murray, 1954);

Marchette Chute, *Two Gentle Men: The Lives of George Herbert and Robert Herrick* (New York: Dutton, 1959);

Amy M. Charles, *A Life of George Herbert* (Ithaca, N.Y.: Cornell University Press, 1977).

References:

Heather A. R. Asals, *Equivocal Predication: George Herbert's Way to God* (Toronto: University of Toronto Press, 1981);

Diana Benet, *Secretary of Praise: The Poetic Vocation of George Herbert* (Columbia: University of Missouri Press, 1984);

Chana Bloch, *Spelling the Word: George Herbert and the Bible* (Berkeley: University of California Press, 1985);

Ira Clark, *Christ Revealed: The History of the Neotypological Lyric in the English Renaissance* (Gainesville: University of Florida Press, 1982);

Donald R. Dickson, *The Fountain of Living Waters: The Typology of the Waters of Life in Herbert, Vaughan, and Traherne* (Columbia: University of Missouri Press, 1987);

T. S. Eliot, *George Herbert* (London: Longmans, Green, 1962);

Stanley E. Fish, *The Living Temple: George Herbert and Catechizing* (Berkeley: University of California Press, 1978);

Fish, *Self-Consuming Artifacts: The Experience of Seventeenth-Century Literature* (Berkeley: University of California Press, 1972);

Coburn Freer, *Music for a King: George Herbert's Style and the Metrical Psalms* (Baltimore: Johns Hopkins University Press, 1972);

Sidney Gottlieb, "The Social and Political Backgrounds of George Herbert's Poetry," in *The Muses Common-Weale": Poetry and Politics in the Seventeenth Century* (Columbia: University of Missouri Press, 1989), pp. 107-118;

Gottlieb, ed., *George Herbert Journal*, 1977- ;

Patrick Grant, *The Transformation of Sin: Studies in Donne, Herbert, Vaughan, and Traherne* (Amherst: University of Massachusetts Press, 1974);

William Halewood, *The Poetry of Grace: Reformation Themes and Structures in English Seventeenth-Century Poetry* (New Haven: Yale University Press, 1970);

Barbara Leah Harman, *Costly Monuments: Representations of the Self in George Herbert's Poetry* (Cambridge, Mass.: Harvard University Press, 1982);

Barbara K. Lewalski, *Protestant Poetics and the Seventeenth-Century Religious Lyric* (Princeton: Princeton University Press, 1979);

Anthony Low, *Love's Architecture: Devotional Modes in Seventeenth-Century English Poetry* (New York: New York University Press, 1978);

Janis Lull, *The Poem in Time: Reading George Herbert's Revisions of "The Church"* (Newark: University of Delaware Press, 1990);

Mary Maleski, ed., *A Fine Tuning: Studies of the Religious Poetry of Herbert and Milton* (Binghamton, N.Y.: Medieval and Renaissance Texts and Studies, 1989);

Leah Sinanoglou Marcus, *Childhood and Cultural Despair: A Theme and Variations in Seventeenth-Century Literature* (Pittsburgh: University of Pittsburgh Press, 1978);

Louis L. Martz, *The Poetry of Meditation: A Study in English Religious Literature of the Seventeenth Century*, revised edition (New Haven: Yale University Press, 1962);

Edmund Miller and Robert Diyanni, eds., *"Like Season'd Timber": New Essays on George Herbert* (New York: Peter Lang, 1987);

A. D. Nuttall, *Overheard by God: Fiction and Prayer in Herbert, Milton, Dante and St. John* (London: Methuen, 1980);

William H. Pahlka, *Saint Augustine's Meter and George Herbert's Will* (Kent, Ohio: Kent State University Press, 1987);

C. A. Patrides, ed., *George Herbert: The Critical Heritage* (London: Routledge, 1983);

Robert H. Ray, ed., "The Herbert Allusion Book: Allusions to George Herbert in the Seventeenth-Century," *Studies in Philology*, 83 (Fall 1986): 1-182;

Mary Ellen Rickey, *Utmost Art: Complexity in the Verse of George Herbert* (Lexington: University of Kentucky Press, 1966);

John R. Roberts, ed., *Essential Articles for the Study of George Herbert's Poetry* (Hamden, Conn.: Archon, 1979);

Malcolm M. Ross, *Poetry and Dogma: The Transfiguration of Eucharistic Symbols in Seventeenth-Century English Poetry* (New York: Octagon Books, 1969);

Michael C. Schoenfeldt, *Prayer and Power: George Herbert and Renaissance Courtship* (Chicago: University of Chicago Press, 1991);

Robert B. Shaw, *The Call of God: The Theme of Vocation in the Poetry of Donne and Herbert* (Cambridge, Mass.: Cowley Publications, 1981);

Terry G. Sherwood, *Herbert's Prayerful Art* (Toronto: University of Toronto Press, 1989);

Marion White Singleton, *God's Courtier: Configuring a Different Grace in George Herbert's "Temple"* (Cambridge: Cambridge University Press, 1987);

Camille Wells Slights, *The Casuistical Tradition in Shakespeare, Donne, Herbert, and Milton* (Princeton: Princeton University Press, 1981);

Arnold Stein, *George Herbert's Lyrics* (Baltimore: Johns Hopkins University Press, 1968);

Stanley Stewart, *George Herbert* (Boston: Twayne, 1986);

Richard Strier, *Love Known: Theology and Experience in George Herbert's Poetry* (Chicago: University of Chicago Press, 1983);

Claude J. Summers and Ted-Larry Pebworth, eds., *"Too Rich to Clothe the Sunne": Essays on George Herbert* (Pittsburgh: University of Pittsburgh Press, 1980);

Joseph H. Summers, *George Herbert: His Religion and Art* (Cambridge, Mass.: Harvard University Press, 1954);

Mark Taylor, *The Soul in Paraphrase: George Herbert's Poetics* (The Hague: Mouton, 1974);

Richard Todd, *The Opacity of Signs: Acts of Interpretation in George Herbert's "The Temple"* (Columbia: University of Missouri Press, 1987);

Rosemond Tuve, *A Reading of George Herbert* (Chicago: University of Chicago Press, 1952);

Gene Edward Veith, Jr., *Reformation Spirituality: The Religion of George Herbert* (Lewisburg, Pa.: Bucknell University Press, 1985);

Helen Vendler, *The Poetry of George Herbert* (Cambridge, Mass.: Harvard University Press, 1975);

John N. Wall, Jr., *Transformations of the Word: Spenser, Herbert, Vaughan* (Athens: University of Georgia Press, 1988);

Bart Westerweel, *Patterns and Patterning: A Study of Four Poems by George Herbert* (Amsterdam: Rodopi, 1984);

Helen C. White, *The Metaphysical Poets: A Study in Religious Experience* (New York: Macmillan, 1936).

Papers:

There are two important manuscripts of Herbert's writings still in existence. The Williams manuscript, held in Dr. Williams's Library, London, contains an early version and arrangement of nearly one-half of the poems of *The Temple*, with some corrections in Herbert's own hand, and two Latin collections, *Lucus* and *Passio Discerpta*, written in Herbert's hand. The Bodleian manuscript, held in the Bodleian Library, Oxford, is the manuscript distributed to the licensers prior to the publication of *The Temple*. Other letters, orations, and records containing Herbert's signature are located in the British Library, the Ferrar Papers at Magdalene College, Cambridge, Dr. Williams's Library, and the Salisbury Diocesan Registry. Izaak Walton reports that Herbert's widow preserved many of her husband's papers but that these were burnt during the English Civil War.

Ben Jonson

(11 June 1572? - 6 August 1637)

This entry was written by Kevin J. Donovan (University of New Hampshire) for DLB 62: Elizabethan Dramatists.

BOOKS: *The Comicall Satyre of Every Man out of His Humor* (London: Printed by Adam Islip for William Holme, 1600);

Every Man in His Humor (London: Printed by Simon Stafford for Walter Burre, 1601);

The Fountaine of Selfe-Love. Or Cynthias Revells (London: Printed by Richard Read for Walter Burre, 1601);

Poetaster or the Arraignment (London: Printed by Richard Braddock for Matthew Lownes, 1602);

B. Jon: His Part of King James His Royall and Magnificent Entertainement through His Honorable Cittie of London, Thurseday the 15. of March. 1603 . . . Also, A Briefe Panegyre of His Maiesties First and Well Auspicated Entrance to His High Court of Parliament, on Monday, the 19. of the Same Moneth. With Other Additions (London: Printed by Valentine Simmes and George Eld for Edward Blount, 1604);

Seianus His Fall (London: Printed by George Eld for Thomas Thorpe, 1605);

Eastward Hoe, by Jonson, George Chapman, and John Marston (London: Printed by George Eld for William Aspley, 1605);

Hymenaei: or The Solemnities of Masque, and Barriers (London: Printed by Valentine Simmes for Thomas Thorpe, 1606);

Ben: Jonson His Volpone or the Foxe (London: Printed by George Eld for Thomas Thorpe, 1607);

The Characters of Two Royall Masques. The One of Blacknesse, the Other of Beautie. . . . The Description of the Masque. With the Nuptial Songs. Celebrating the Happy Marriage of Iohn, Lord Ramsey, Vicount Hadington, with the Lady Elizabeth Ratcliffe (London: Printed by George Eld for Thomas Thorpe, 1608);

Ben: Jonson, His Case Is Altered (London: Printed by Nicholas Okes for Bartholomew Sutton, 1609);

The Masque of Queenes Celebrated from the House of Fame (London: Printed by Nicholas Okes for Richard Bonion & Henry Wally, 1609);

Catiline His Conspiracy (London: Printed by William Stansby? for Walter Burre, 1611);

The Alchemist (London: Printed by Thomas Snodham, for Walter Burre & sold by John Stepneth, 1612);

The Workes of Benjamin Jonson (London: Printed by William Stansby, 1616)—comprises *Every Man in His Humour, Every Man out of His Humour, Cynthia's Revels, Poetaster, Sejanus, Volpone, Epicoene, The Alchemist, Catiline, Epigrams, The Forrest, The King's Coronation Entertainment, A Panegyre, The Entertainment at Althorp, The Entertainment at Highgate, The Entertainment of the Two Kings at Theobalds, An Entertainment of the King and Queen at Theobalds, The Masque of Blackness, The Masque of Beauty, Hymenaei, The Haddington Masque, The Masque of Queens, Prince Henry's Barriers, Oberon the Fairy Prince, Love Freed From Ignorance and Folly, Love Restored, A Challenge at Tilt, The Irish Masque, Mercury Vindicated from the Alchemists, The Golden Age Restored;*

Lovers Made Men. A Masque (London, 1617);

Epicoene, or The Silent Woman. A Comoedie (London: Printed by William Stansby & sold by John Browne, 1620);

The Masque of Augures. With Several Antimasques (London, 1621);

Time Vindicated to Himselfe and to His Honors (London, 1623);

Neptunes Triumph for the Returne of Albion, A Masque 1623 (London, 1624);

The Fortunate Isles and Their Union. A Masque 1624 (London, 1625);

Love's Triumph through Callipolis. A Masque, by Jonson and Inigo Jones (London: Printed by John Norton, Jr., for Thomas Walkley, 1630);

Chloridia, Rites to Chloris and Her Nymphs (London: Printed for Thomas Walkley, 1631);

Bartholmew Fayre. The Divell Is an Asse. The Staple of Newes (volume 2 of Jonson's works) (London: Printed by John Beale for Robert Allot, 1631);

Portrait by an unknown artist (National Portrait Gallery, London)

The New Inne. Or, The Light Heart (London: Printed by Thomas Harper for Thomas Alchorne, 1631);

Ben: Jonson's Execration against Vulcan. With Divers Epigrams (London: Printed by John Okes for John Benson & Andrew Crooke, 1640);

Q. Horatius Flaccus: Horatius Flaccus: His Art of Poetry. Englished by Ben: Jonson. With Other Workes of the Author, Never Printed Before (London: Printed by John Okes for John Benson, 1640);

The Workes of Benjamin Jonson, volume 1 (London: Printed by Richard Bishop & sold by A. Crooke, 1640)—a reprint of *The Workes of Benjamin Jonson* (1616); volumes 2-3 (London: Printed for Richard Meighen & Thomas Walkley, 1640)—comprises the sheets of the 1631 works (volume 2) together with *The Magnetic Lady, A Tale of a Tub, The Sad Shepherd, The Fall of Mortimer, Christmas His Masque, Lovers Made Men, The Vision of Delight, Pleasure Reconciled to Virtue, For the Honor of Wales, News from the New World Discovered in the Moon, The Gypsies Metamorphosed, The Masque of Augurs, Time Vindicated, Neptune's Triumph, Pan's Anniversary, The Masque of Owls, The Fortunate Isles, Love's Triumph through Callipolis, Chloridia, The Entertainment at Welbeck, Love's Welcome at Bolsover, The Underwood, Horace, His Art of Poetry, The English Grammar, Discoveries* (volume 3) (London: Printed by John Dawson, Jr., for Thomas Walkley, 1640).

Editions: *Ben Jonson,* 11 volumes, edited by C. H. Herford and Percy and Evelyn Simpson (Oxford: Clarendon Press, 1925-1952)—comprises *A Tale of a Tub, The Case Is Altered, Every Man in His Humour* (original and revised texts), *Every Man out of His Humour, In Memoriam: Charles Harold Herford, Cyn-*

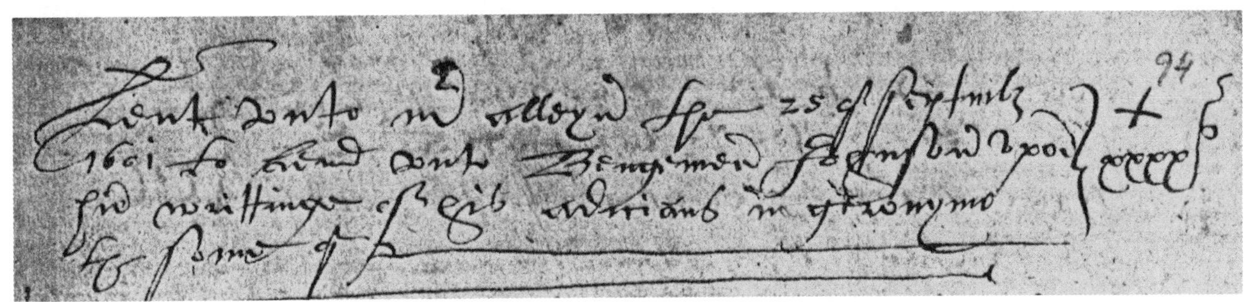

An entry in Philip Henslowe's diary recording a payment on 25 September 1601 for Jonson's additions to The Spanish Tragedy, *which Henslowe calls "geronymo" (MSS VII, l. 94ʳ; Dulwich College, London)*

thia's Revels, Poetaster, Sejanus, Eastward Ho, Volpone, Epicoene, The Alchemist, Catiline, Bartholomew Fair, The Devil Is an Ass, The Staple of News, The New Inn, The Magnetic Lady, The Sad Shepherd, The Fall of Mortimer, Masques and Entertainments, The Poems, The Prose Works.

PLAY PRODUCTIONS: *The Isle of Dogs,* by Jonson, Thomas Nashe, and others, London, Swan theater, August 1597;

The Case Is Altered, London, unknown theater, 1597-1598;

Every Man in His Humour, London, Curtain theater, September (?) 1598;

Every Man out of His Humour, London, Globe theater, November or December, 1599;

Cynthia's Revels, London, Blackfriars theater, late 1600;

Poetaster, London, Blackfriars theater, early 1601;

The Entertainment at Althorp, Althorp, 25 June 1603;

Sejanus, London, Globe theater, late 1603 or early 1604;

The King's Coronation Entertainment, London, 15 March 1604;

A Panegyre, London, 19 March 1604;

The Entertainment at Highgate, Highgate, 1 May 1604;

Eastward Ho, by Jonson, George Chapman, and John Marston, London, Blackfriars theater, 1604-1605;

The Masque of Blackness, Westminster, Whitehall, 6 January 1605;

Hymenaei, Westminster, Whitehall, 5 and 6 January 1606;

Volpone, London, Globe theater, February-March 1606;

The Entertainment of the Two Kings at Theobalds, Theobalds, 24 July 1606;

An Entertainment of the King and Queen at Theobalds, Theobalds, 22 May 1607;

Entertainment for the Merchant Taylors' Company, London, 16 July 1607;

The Masque of Beauty, Westminster, Whitehall, 10 January 1608;

The Haddington Masque, Westminster, Whitehall, 9 February 1608;

Entertainment at Salisbury House, Westminster, Salisbury House, May 1608;

The Masque of Queens, Westminster, Whitehall, 2 February 1609;

Entertainment at Britain's Burse, London, 11 April 1609;

Epicoene, London, Whitefriars theater, December 1609 or January 1610;

The Speeches at Prince Henry's Barriers, Westminster, Whitehall, 6 January 1610;

The Alchemist, London, Globe theater, 1610;

Oberon, the Fairy Prince, Westminster, Whitehall, 1 January 1611;

Love Freed from Ignorance and Folly, Westminster, Whitehall, 3 February 1611;

Catiline, London, Globe theater, 1611;

Love Restored, Westminster, Whitehall, 6 January 1612;

The Irish Masque at Court, Westminster, at Court, 29 December 1613;

A Challenge at Tilt, Westminster, at Court, 1 January 1614;

Bartholomew Fair, London, Hope theater, 31 October 1614;

The Golden Age Restored, Westminster, Whitehall, 6 January 1615;

Mercury Vindicated from the Alchemists, Westminster, Whitehall, 1 January 1616;

Entertainment for the New Company of Merchant Adventurers, London, 14 June 1616;

The Devil Is an Ass, London, Blackfriars theater, November or December 1616;

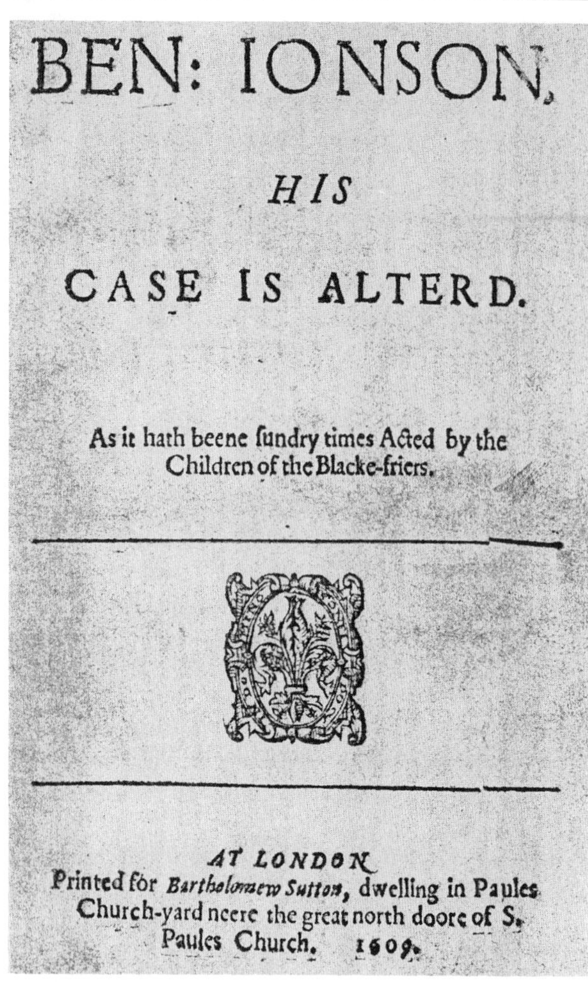
BEN: IONSON,

HIS

CASE IS ALTERD.

As it hath beene ſundry times Acted by the Children of the Blacke-friers.

AT LONDON

Printed for *Bartholomew Sutton*, dwelling in Paules Church-yard neere the great north doore of S. Paules Church. 1609.

Title page for an unauthorized 1609 quarto edition of Jonson's first surviving play (British Library)

Christmas, His Masque, Westminster, Whitehall, Christmas season 1616;

The Vision of Delight, Westminster, Whitehall, 6 January 1617;

Lovers Made Men, London, Essex House, 22 February 1617;

Pleasure Reconciled to Virtue, Westminster, Whitehall, 6 January 1618; revised as *For the Honor of Wales,* Westminster, Whitehall, 17 February 1618;

News from the New World Discovered in the Moon, Westminster, Whitehall, 7 January 1620;

Entertainment at the Blackfriars, London, May 1620(?);

Pan's Anniversary, Westminster, at Court, 19 June 1620(?);

The Gypsies Metamorphosed, Burley-on-the-Hill, 3 August 1621;

The Masque of Augurs, Westminster, Whitehall, 6 January 1622;

Time Vindicated to Himself and to His Honors, Westminster, Whitehall, 19 January 1623;

The Masque of Owls, Kenilworth, 19 August 1624;

The Fortunate Isles and Their Union, Westminster, Whitehall, 9 January 1625;

The Staple of News, London, Blackfriars theater, February 1626;

The New Inn, London, Blackfriars theater, early 1629;

Love's Triumph through Callipolis, Westminster, Whitehall, 9 January 1631;

Chloridia, Westminster, Whitehall, 22 February 1631;

The Magnetic Lady, London, Blackfriars theater, autumn 1632;

A Tale of a Tub, London, Cockpit theater, May 1633;

The King's Entertainment at Welbeck, Welbeck, 21 May 1633;

Love's Welcome at Bolsover, Bolsover, 30 July 1634.

By turns turbulent and weighty, scatological and refined, boisterous and delicate, Ben Jonson's works have always excited strong reactions among his readers and his playgoing audiences, just as his personality strongly impressed or offended his contemporaries. Jonson's life displays some of the same apparent contradictions as his work. He was a branded felon and for much of his life a recusant, whose career was punctuated by trouble with the officials of the church and state. Yet he rose to be a favored court poet, a companion of some of the most prominent men and women in the country, and a champion of royal authority. He was the greatest playwright of his age (with one notable exception) and one of the greatest English dramatists of all time; yet he seems to have distrusted the theater as a vehicle for the ethical program that informs his art.

Despite the contradictory impulses found in his life and work—or perhaps because of them—"honest Ben" is a more distinct personality than almost any of his contemporaries. Jonson was a man of strong convictions and equally strong prejudices. He was convinced of the necessity for rational control of the passions, especially for a poet; yet he often failed to manage his own notoriously unruly passions and appetites. In a censorious and aggressive age he was notably censorious and aggressive. However, he was also loyal and generous, and he had a special talent for making firm friendships.

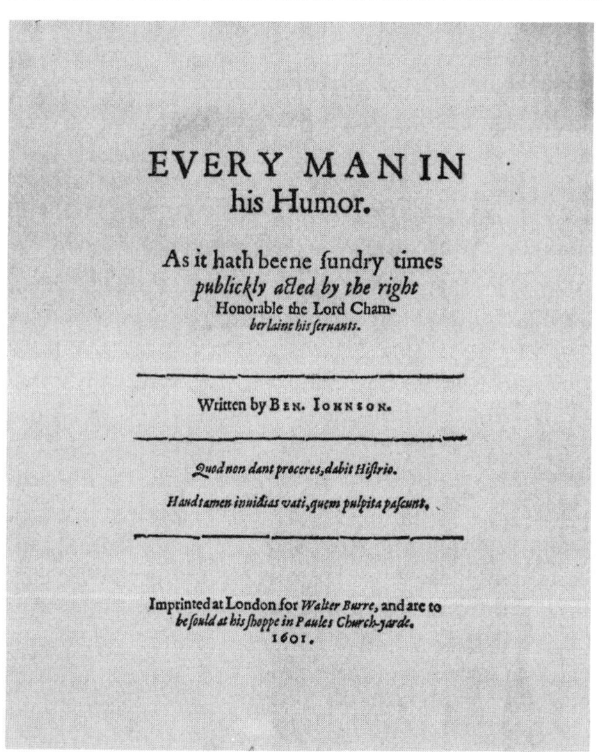
EVERY MAN IN
his Humor.

As it hath beene sundry times
publickly acted by the right
Honorable the Lord Cham-
berlaine his seruants.

Written by BEN. IOHNSON.

Quod non dant proceres, dabit Histrio.
Haud tamen inuidias vati, quem pulpita pascunt.

Imprinted at London for Walter Burre, and are to
be sould at his shoppe in Paules Church-yarde.
1601.

Title page for the 1601 quarto edition of the play that Jonson considered his first theatrical success (Anderson Galleries auction catalogue, sale number 2077, 20-21 May 1926)

Of Jonson's early life and family background relatively little is known. He told the Scottish poet William Drummond of Hawthornden, whose account of his conversations with Jonson is a valuable source of information about Jonson's life, that his grandfather was a gentleman who came from Carlisle and before that from Annandale. His father, a minister who lost his estate under Queen Mary, died in 1572, not long before the birth of his son Benjamin, near London, between 5 May 1572 and 19 January 1573 (probably on 11 June 1572). The character of his mother can be glimpsed in an anecdote about Jonson that is related in the *Conversations with Drummond* (1842). In 1604 Jonson was arrested along with the playwrights John Marston and George Chapman for some satirical passages in their collaborative play *Eastward Ho,* and, after their release, Jonson feasted his friends in celebration: "at the midst of the Feast his old Mother Dranke to him & shew him a paper which she had (if the Sentence had taken execution) to have mixed jn ye Prisson among his drinke, which was fūll of Lūstie strong poison & that she was no chūrle she told she minded first to have Drunk of it herself." Such a mother does much to explain the temperament of her famous son.

Within a few years of Jonson's birth, his mother remarried. Jonson's stepfather was a master bricklayer, a worker in one of the humbler crafts in the highly stratified society of Elizabethan England. According to tradition, the family lived in Westminster, in Hartshorn Lane, where Jonson attended St. Martin's Parish School. Thus Jonson's stepfather may have been the bricklayer Robert Brett, who is found to have lived in Hartshorn Lane and whose name appears with Jonson's in the parish accounts of St. Martin's-in-the-Fields in 1597. In the normal course of affairs, Jonson would have followed his stepfather's trade immediately after finishing his studies at St. Martin's. However, as Jonson told Drummond, he was "putt to school by a friend" and attended Westminster School, where he studied under the great antiquarian William Camden. His affection and regard for Camden were expressed later in life in his dedication of the 1616 folio text of *Every Man in His Humour* to his former teacher, and in his Epigram 14, "To William Camden."

Although Jonson's experience at Westminster was brief, it profoundly affected him. Westminster School gave Jonson access to those Roman writers whose ethical and artistic ideals exerted so powerful an influence on his art. In addition he acquired there a love of classical literature and scholarship that would remain with him all his life. (One of Jonson's last surviving letters asks Sir Robert Cotton for the loan of a book that would tell "the true site, & distance betwixt *Bauli* or *portus Baiarum,* and *Villa Augusta.*") And Jonson was proud of his scholarship, as the marginal notes in the quarto editions of *Sejanus* and *The Masque of Queens* testify. We should also note that Westminster introduced Jonson to the drama; the Westminster scholars regularly performed three plays a year.

Jonson's formal education ended with Westminster, and he may not have even completed the course of studies there. He was taken out of school and set to work at his stepfather's trade. Drummond recorded Jonson's telling him that he was "taken from [school], and put to ane other Craft (I thinke was to be a Wright or Bricklayer) which he could not endure, then went he to ye low Countries, but returning soone he betook himself to his wonted studies." Jonson's apparent vagueness on the subject of his "other Craft" suggests a certain sensitivity; his early career as a bricklayer later provided a convenient source of jibes for his enemies. Of his service in the Nether-

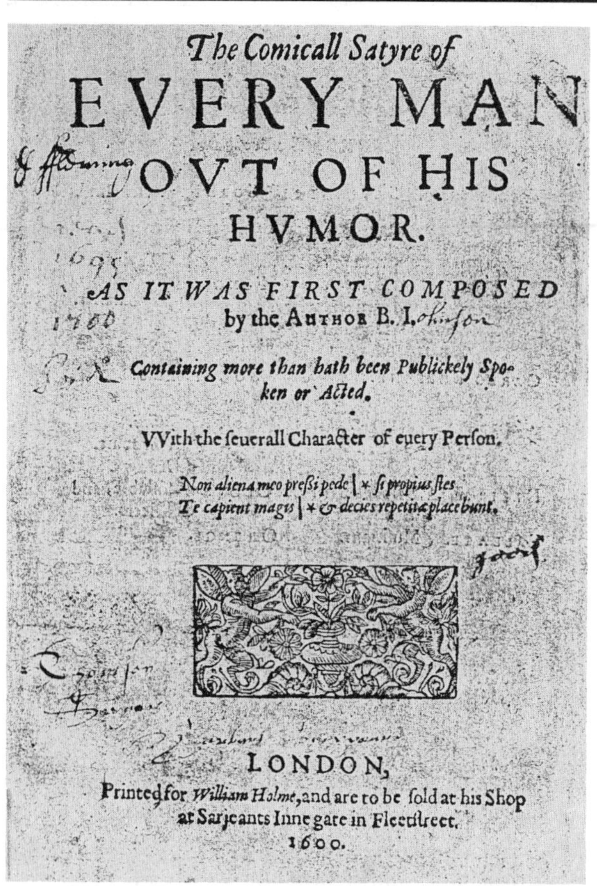

The Comicall Satyre of

EVERY MAN

OVT OF HIS

HVMOR.

AS IT WAS FIRST COMPOSED by the Avthor B. I.

Containing more than hath been Publickely Spoken or Acted.

VVith the seuerall Character of euery Person.

Non aliena meo pressi pede | * si propius stes
Te capient magis | * & decies repetita placebunt.

LONDON,

Printed for William Holme, and are to be sold at his Shop at Sarjeants Inne gate in Fleetstreet.

1600.

Title page for a 1600 quarto edition of the play that includes Jonson's opening salvo in the "war of the theaters," a satiric portrait of John Marston in the minor character Clove (British Library)

lands, Drummond recorded a famous anecdote: "he had jn the face of both the Campes Killed ane Enimie & taken opima spolia from him." Jonson probably refers to this exploit in Epigram 108, "To true Souldiers."

The lengths of Jonson's service in the Netherlands and of his career as a bricklayer as well as the nature of the "wonted studies" to which he returned are uncertain. Jonson left Westminster probably about 1589, was married in 1594, and appears as a playwright in Henslowe's diary in 1597. Besides these sketchy details, all that is known of him in these years is that he worked as an actor, at first probably in a touring provincial troupe and later at Paris Garden, a bear-baiting pit that doubled as a theater. The source of this information is not impartial; it appears in Thomas Dekker's *Satiromastix,* where Jonson is lampooned in the character of "Horace." Another character several times taunts "Horace" with references to his acting career: "I ha seene thy shoulders lapt in a Plaiers old cast Cloake, like a Slie knaue as thou art. . . . thou hast forgot how thou amblest (in a leather pilch) by a play-wagon, in the high way, and took'st mad Ieronimoes part, to get seruice among the Mimickes." Horace is also said to have played the part of "Zulziman" at Paris Garden.

Jonson was married to Anne Lewis on 14 November 1594 in the London parish of St. Magnus Martyr. Relatively few facts are known about this marriage. Jonson told Drummond in 1618 or 1619 that his wife was "a shrew yet honest" and that he had lived apart from her for five years. Her "shrewishness" may well have been exacerbated by her marriage to a difficult man: Jonson narrated with evident glee some of his episodes as a philanderer. As for her other epithet, Drummond also records that "of all stiles [Jonson] loved most to be named honest." At least two children were born of the marriage, Mary, "the daughter of [her parents'] youth," whose infant death is commemorated in Epigram 22, and Benjamin, the subject of Epigram 45, who died in 1603 at the age of seven. Other children were probably born of the marriage, including a Joseph Johnson, baptized on 9 December 1599, and another Benjamin, who was baptized on 20 February 1608 and died on 18 November 1611. "Elisib. daughter of Ben. Johnson," baptized on 25 March 1610, was probably an illegitimate daughter. Yet another Benjamin, described in the church records as "fil. Ben," was baptized on 6 April 1610; obviously this Benjamin and Elisabeth had different mothers if not different fathers. None of these children seems to have lived to adulthood.

By 1597 Jonson was earning a living as a playwright. In that same year he experienced the first of his many troubles with the authorities, this time over a lost play, *The Isle of Dogs.* The play was mainly written by Thomas Nashe, but Jonson seems to have supplied the play's conclusion. The Privy Council found that it contained "very seditious and sclandrous matter," and Jonson was arrested along with two fellow actors for his role as actor and part author. Nashe fled to Yarmouth and so escaped arrest. The incident caused a great stir; the Privy Council ordered the destruction of all the stages in London, an order which, fortunately, was rescinded; the theaters were closed for a time but soon reopened. The Privy Council also appointed a team of investigators, headed by the notorious recusant hunter Richard Topcliffe, to try to get the imprisoned actors to incriminate each other. Years later Jonson

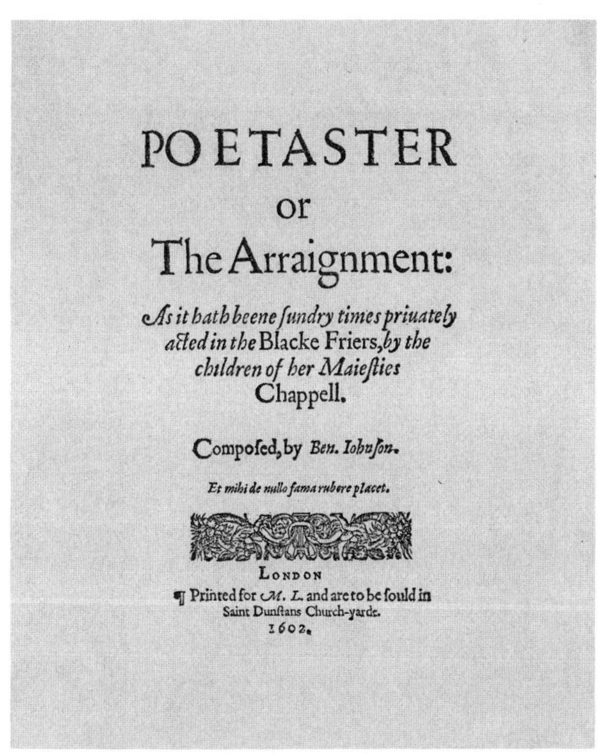
POETASTER
or
The Arraignment:
As it hath beene sundry times priuately acted in the Blacke Friers, by the children of her Maiesties Chappell.
Composed, by Ben. Iohnson.
Et mihi de nullo fama rubere placet.
LONDON
Printed for M. L. and are to be sould in Saint Dunstans Church-yarde.
1602.

Title page for the 1602 quarto edition of the play in which Jonson satirized Thomas Dekker as Demetrius, a writer of doggerel verse and "a dresser of plays about town," and John Marston as Crispinus, a vain fop who "pens high, loftie, in a new stalking strain" (Anderson Galleries auction catalogue, sale number 2077, 20-21 May 1926)

would still express contempt for the "two damn'd Villans" sent to trap him. Epigram 59, "On Spies," was written in response to this incident.

Jonson was imprisoned for more than two months. While still in prison he entered the employ of the theatrical entrepreneur Philip Henslowe. Henslowe, who owned the Rose and who eventually acquired other playhouses, financed the Lord Admiral's Men, a leading Elizabethan company whose foremost actor, Edward Alleyn, was Henslowe's son-in-law. From the evidence of Henslowe's diary, we know that Jonson wrote plays for Henslowe. In July of 1597 he sold Henslowe his share of an unknown play, and in December of the same year he was working on an unnamed "boocke" for the Admiral's Men. In 1598 he cowrote with Henry Chettle and Henry Porter a comedy called *Hot Anger Soon Cold* and supplied the "plotte" for an unknown tragedy written by Chapman. In the following year he was working on a tragedy called *Robert II* and cowrote with his future enemy Thomas Dekker the tragedy *Page of Plimoth.* The year 1601 found him writing additions to Thomas Kyd's *The Spanish Tragedy* for Henslowe, and in 1602 he was writing a play called *Richard Crookback* and "new adicyons for Jeronymo."

Except for the additions to *The Spanish Tragedy,* which may or may not be those appearing in the play's 1602 edition, none of Jonson's work for Henslowe has survived. Jonson later told Drummond "that the half of his comedies were not jn Print," though at that date (1618-1619) the "half " would include *Bartholomew Fair, The Devil Is an Ass,* and also perhaps *The Case Is Altered,* which was published in 1609 without Jonson's approval. Jonson's lost tragedies were admired by the uncritical Francis Meres, who in *Palladis Tamia* (1598) groups Jonson among "our best for Tragedie." However, Jonson chose not to include any of the works written for Henslowe, or *The Case Is Altered,* written in 1597-1598 for the Children of the Chapel, in his 1616 collected works. Apparently these plays were not consistent with the image of his artistic development that Jonson wished to present to the world.

The entries in Henslowe's diary provide a valuable supplement to the image of Jonson's career which he consciously cultivated. Jonson always emphasized his departure from the practice of his contemporaries and immediate predecessors. Thus he would later refer to "those Comick Lawes / Which I . . . first did teach the Age." However, the titles of the plays in Henslowe's diary suggest the standard fare of Elizabethan theater: popular comedy, chronicle history, domestic tragedy, and revenge tragedy. It is fascinating to observe that Jonson wrote *Richard Crookback* for Henslowe as late as 1602, by which time he had written both *Every Man* plays, *Cynthia's Revels,* and *Poetaster,* and was working on *Sejanus.*

The first play by Jonson to survive is *The Case Is Altered.* Jonson deliberately multiplied incidents and characters in the play, combining plots from two comedies by Plautus (*Captivi* and *Aulularia*) with a romantic love story and some clowning by Onion the servingman and Juniper the cobbler. Juniper seems to have been popular with Elizabethan audiences; Nashe refers in *Lenten Stuffe* to "the merry coblers cutte in that witty Play of *the Case is altered.*" The text of the play as it has survived also includes a scene burlesquing playwright Anthony Munday, which was probably written at a later date than the play's original composition.

In its mingling of clowns and counts, its emphasis on love, its comic horseplay, and its reliance on such "romantic" plot elements from New

SEIANVS

HIS FALL.

Written
by
BEN: IONSON.

MART. Non hîc *Centauros*, non *Gorgonas*, *Harpyasq;*
Inuenies: Hominem pagina noſtra ſapit.

AT LONDON
Printed by *G. Elld*e, for *Thomas Thorpe.* 1605.

SEIANVS.

ACTVS PRIMVS.

SABINVS. SILIVS. NATTA. LATIARIS. CORDVS. SATRIVS. ARRVNTIVS. EVDEMVS. HATERIVS. &c.

SAB. HAile [a] *Caius Silius.* SIL. [b] *Titius Sabinus*, Hayle.
Yo'are rarely met in Court! SAB. Therfore, well met.
SIL. 'Tis true: Indeed, this Place is not our Sphære.
SAB. No *Silius*, we are no good Inginers;
We want the fine Artes, and their thriuing vſe
Should make vs grac'd, or fauor'd of the Times:
We haue no ſhift of Faces, no cleft Tongues,
No ſoft, and glutinous bodies, that can ſtick,
Like Snailes, on painted walls; or, on our breſts,
Creepe vp, to fall, from that proud height, to which
We did by [c] ſlauerie, not by ſeruice, clime.
We are no guilty men, and then no Great;
We haue nor place in Court, Office in ſtate,
That we [d] can ſay, we owe vnto our Crimes;
We burne with no [e] black ſecrets, which can make
Vs deare to the pale Authors; or liue fear'd
Of their ſtill waking iealoſies, to raiſe
Our ſelues a Fortune, by ſubuerting theirs.
We ſtand not in the lines, that do aduance
To that ſo courted point. SIL. But yonder leane
A paire that doe. (SAB. Good Coſſen [f] *Latiaris.*)
SIL. [g] *Satrius Secundus*, and [h] *Pinnarius Natta*,
The great *Seianus* Clients; There be two,
Know more, then honeſt Councells: whoſe cloſe breſts
Were they rip'd vp to light, it would be found
A poore, and idle ſinne, to which their Trunkes
Had not beene made fit Organs: Theſe can lie,
Flatter, and ſweare, forſweare, depraue, [i] informe,
Smile, and betray; make guilty men; then beg

De Caio Silio, *vid.* Tacit, Lipſ. edit. 4°. *Anna, lib.* 1. *pag.* 11. *lib.* 2. *pag.* 28. & 33.
[b] *De* Titio Sabino. *vid* Tac. *lib.* 4. *pag.* 79.
[c] Tac. *Annal. lib* 1. *pag.* 2.
[d] Iuuenal. *Sat.* 1. *ver.* 75.
[e] *Et* Sat. 3. *ver.* 49. &c.
[f] *De* Latiari, *cõſ.* Tac. *Annal, lib.* 4 *pag.* 94. & Dion. Step. edit. *fol. lib.* 58. *pag.* 711.
[g] *De* Satrio Secundo, &
[h] Pinnario Natta, *Leg* Tacit. *Annal. lib.* 4. *pag.* 83. *Et de* Satrio. *conſ.* Senec. *cõſol. ad Marciam.*
[i] *Vid.* Sen. *de Benef. lib* 3 *cap.* 26.

B The

Variant title page for the 1605 quarto edition of the play Jonson wrote after deciding, "since the Comick *MVSE / Hath prou'd so ominous to me, I will trie / If* Tragoedie *haue a more kind aspect," and the first page of the text with scholarly notes that Jonson included to demonstrate the "truth of argument" he considered a criterion for tragedy (Bodleian Library)*

Comedy as the finding of long-lost children—all of which are characteristic of Elizabethan popular comedy—*The Case Is Altered* is very different from the kind of comedy for which Jonson is most remembered. As Jonson mastered a more classical dramatic idiom in his maturity, he came to prefer that this earlier work be forgotten. When in 1616 Jonson published his collected works, *The Case Is Altered* was omitted. However, in his later career Jonson would return to writing romantic comedy with *The New Inn,* a play which the Caroline public rejected.

In 1598 Jonson also wrote another play, *Every Man in His Humour,* this time for the Lord Chamberlain's Men at the Curtain. As the list of actors appended to the text of *Every Man in His Humour* in the 1616 folio edition of Jonson's collected works shows, Shakespeare acted in the original performance. Jonson regarded *Every Man in His Humour* as his first success. He chose it to head his collected works, although he first thoroughly revised it, changing the setting from Florence to London. At the end of his career, while writing *The Magnetic Lady* and contemplating "the close, or shutting up of his Circle," he described himself as "beginning his studies of this kind, with *every man in his Humour.*"

The play's title exploits the popularity of the term "humour," which had become a fashionable catchword. Originally a medical term, "humours" were the fluids believed to regulate the body and by extension the temperament or "complexion" of man. An imbalance of one of them was supposed to cause a disturbance in man's body and his mind. However, the emphasis of Elizabethan psychology is always moral, rather than physiological. A person who allowed his passions to overwhelm his rational powers was considered morally guilty.

In popular speech the term had become less specific and was used to refer to any dominant trait or quirk of character. Chapman had al-

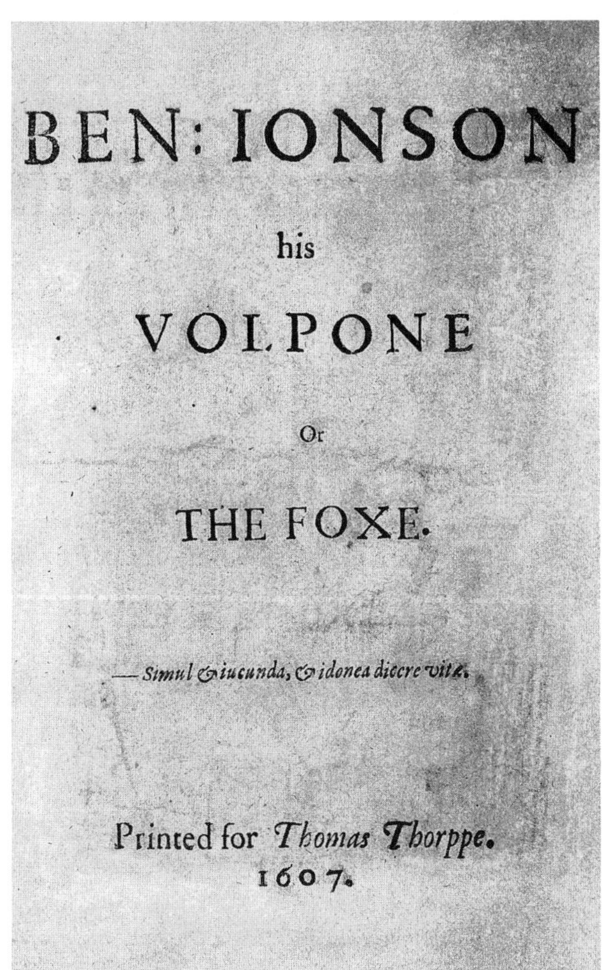
BEN: IONSON

his

VOLPONE

Or

THE FOXE.

—Simul & iucunda, & idonea dicere vitæ.

Printed for *Thomas Thorppe.*
1607.

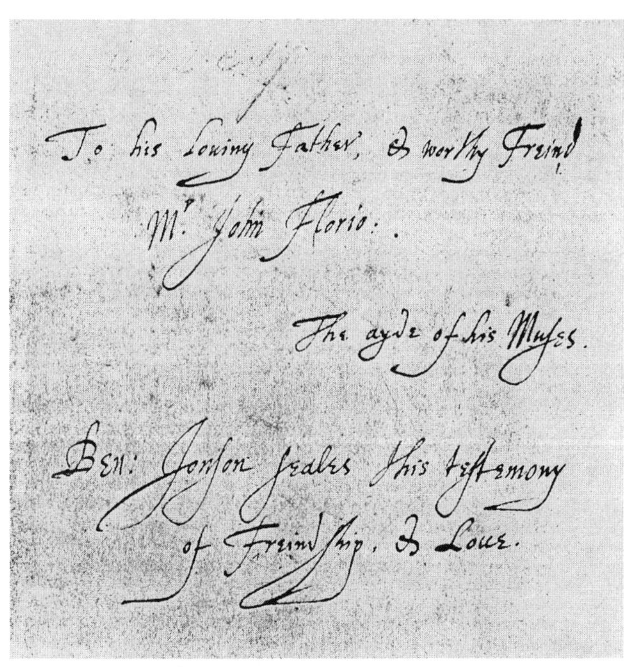
To his loving Father, & worthy Freind
Mr. John Florio:

The ayde of his Muses.

Ben: Jonson seales this testimony
of Freindship, & Love.

Title page for the 1607 quarto edition of the comedy that proved immensely popular with audiences at the Globe, where it was staged in early 1606, and at both Oxford and Cambridge, where it was performed later in the same year (Henry E. Huntington Library and Art Gallery); and Jonson's inscription to John Florio, groom of the privy chamber in the Court of James I and the first English translator of Montaigne's Essays, *in another copy of the same edition of the play (British Library)*

ready exploited the word's popularity with his comedy *A Humorous Day's Mirth.* However, in *Every Man in His Humour* and *Every Man out of His Humour,* which followed it, Jonson made the term forever his own.

The concept of "humour" was well suited to Jonson's comic vision. Typically Jonsonian comic characters are obsessed with a single idea or desire and pursue it to absurd lengths, spinning monstrous fantasies out of their imaginations. The emphasis on a single trait or folly tends to reduce characters in one direction, but the exaggeration often attains a unique monstrous grandeur. "Humour" provided an explanation of sorts for such character types that was consistent with the classical principles espoused by Jonson. The imagery in Jonson's plays, poems, and masques shows that he had fully absorbed traditional Roman ethics, in which folly and vice are described as variable and liquid, and virtue as stable and solid. In the induction to *Every Man out of His Humour,* Jonson advocates the use of the term "humour" to describe the effect "when some one peculiar quality / Doth so possesse a man, that it doth draw / All his affects, his spirits, and his powers, / In their confluctions, all to runne one way."

The plot of *Every Man in His Humour* is original, but in its main outlines it owes a great debt to New Comedy. A young gallant (in this case a would-be poet) and his boon companion scheme with the aid of a tricky servant to outwit the young man's father and gain a pair of pretty brides. The play adheres to those infamous bugbears of neoclassical criticism, "the unities," and Jonson made much of the play's "correctness" in the prologue he wrote for the revised version of

Costume designs by Inigo Jones for a Daughter of Niger (left) and a torchbearer, an Oceania (right), in The Masque of Blackness *(from Stephen Orgel and Roy Strong,* Inigo Jones, *1973)*

the play that appears in the 1616 folio. The fun of the play lies in its "humorous" characters, the braggart soldier Bobadill, the jealous husband Kitely, the country gull Stephen and the city gull Matthew, Downright the irascible country squire, and Justice Clement, "an old, merry Magistrate." In comparison to the comical satires that followed this play, *Every Man in His Humour* is genial and relaxed rather than satirical. The play "sport[s] with humane follies," as the prologue says. Fittingly it ends with the classic ritual affirmation of social harmony, the wedding feast.

Jonson had little time to celebrate the success of *Every Man in His Humour.* On 22 September 1598, probably within days of the first production of *Every Man in His Humour,* he killed a man in a duel and found himself on trial for murder. The victim, Gabriel Spencer, was an actor in Henslowe's company who had been arrested with Jonson over the *Isle of Dogs* affair the previous year. Jonson's Latinity saved his life; he escaped the gallows by pleading benefit of clergy (a privilege extended to all who could read enough Latin to construe a passage from the Bible). As it was, he suffered branding as a felon and the confiscation of all his property.

According to his statement to Drummond, Jonson was converted to Roman Catholicism while in prison for murder and continued in that faith for twelve years. The "priest who Visited him jn Prisson" and who converted him may have been Thomas Wright, the author of *The Passions of the Minde in Generall,* for which Jonson wrote a prefatory sonnet. Like Wright, Jonson maintained his loyalty to the Crown despite his religion. The authorities seem to have been aware of this fact, for in November 1605, within days of the discovery of the Gunpowder Plot, Robert Cecil, first Earl of Salisbury, then Secretary of State, employed Jonson to help find a priest willing to cooperate with the government's investigation.

Jonson spent only a few weeks in prison and was released in October 1598. In January 1599, however, Jonson was again committed to prison, this time to the Marshalsea in Southwark for a debt of ten pounds owed to a player named Robert Browne. Throughout his life Jonson had trouble making ends meet. At this time, having just suffered the loss of his goods to the Crown, he must have been in particularly dire straits. However, this debt must have been paid soon, because Jonson did not remain in prison for very long.

HYMENAEI:
OR
The Solemnities of
Masque, and *Barriers,*
Magnificently performed on the eleventh, and twelfth Nights, from Christmas;
At Court:
To the auspicious celebrating of the Marriage-*vnion,* betweene *Robert,* Earle of *Essex,* and the Lady *Frances,* second Daughter to the most noble Earle of *Suffolke.*

By BEN: IONSON.

Iam veniet Virgo, iam dicetur Hymenaeus.

AT LONDON
Printed by *Valentine Sims* for *Thomas Thorp.*
1606.

Title page for the 1606 quarto edition of the second masque Jonson wrote for performance at the Court of James I (Anderson Galleries auction catalogue, sale number 2077, 20-21 May 1926)

Part of 1599 was spent writing for Henslowe, but his most important work of that year was written for the Lord Chamberlain's Men. The title of *Every Man out of His Humour* capitalizes on the popularity of *Every Man in His Humour.* However, the play is in no sense a sequel; in fact, it is unlike anything previously presented on the Elizabethan stage. The character Cordatus, who is Jonson's mouthpiece in the play, describes it as "strange, and of a particular kind by it selfe, somewhat like *Vetus Comœdia.*"

The play is the first of three "comicall satires" written by Jonson. Satire was much in vogue in the 1590s. However, a decree by the archbishop of Canterbury and the bishop of London on 1 June 1599 had banned the printing of satires and epigrams because of the uproar raised by the works of Joseph Hall, John Marston, Thomas Nashe, and others. Jonson satisfied the public's hunger for satire by bringing it on the stage. However, he was not merely catering to the taste of his audience. The satirist's role of castigating vice strongly appealed to Jonson, who was convinced that responsible poetry, like philosophy, was supposed to educate its hearers, to teach them to love virtue and to shun vice. In addition he clearly enjoyed the linguistic license and exuberance characteristic of Elizabethan satire.

Elizabethan satire is a strange phenomenon. Because Renaissance critics had confused the classical terms *satura* and *satyra*, many spurious notions were attached to satire. The satirist was conceived of as a morally outraged satyr. Harshness was held to be "decorous" in terms of the genre, and satirists frequently took great liberties with language and with literary conventions. Some of this creative license is apparent in *Every Man out of His Humour*. The "scene" of the play is treated in a fluid way; at the outset of the play a satirist figure, Asper, appears, and we are told that the action which will follow is his own creation. A chorus frequently breaks in to comment on the main action of the play, shattering any dramatic illusion. Character, too, is fluid. Asper the censor plays a role, that of Macilente the envious man, in the drama that he supposedly creates.

Compared to *Every Man in His Humour* and *The Case Is Altered,* which are comedies of intrigue, *Every Man out of His Humour, Cynthia's Revels,* and *Poetaster* are relatively static. In the words of the prologue to *Cynthia's Revels,* these plays present "Words, aboue action: matter, aboue words." Another notable feature of the comical satires is their pronounced didacticism; the audience is invited to sit in judgment on the fools and knaves who are paraded out and systematically castigated. The didactic emphasis and static quality of these plays have not endeared them to later ages. The comical satires have virtually no stage history since the early seventeenth century. However, *Every Man out of His Humour* was a great success in its own day. Three editions of the play were published in 1600, and the many contemporary allusions to Jonson as the poet of "humours," where the context emphasizes satire, show how important the play was in establishing Jonson's literary reputation in London at the turn of the century.

In *Every Man out of His Humour,* Jonson's powers are most clearly shown in the frequent descriptions of the dramatis personae. Carlo Buffone, who is the embodiment of scurrility in the play, nearly steals the show with his "stabbing *simile's.*" Like the Theophrastan "characters" prefixed to the text of the play, Carlo's descriptions of his fellow "humorists" display the fertility of Jonson's imagination in their teeming mass of disparate images grotesquely yoked together. It is interesting to note that the same phrase used to characterize Carlo, "hee will sooner lose his soule then a iest," reappears only slightly modified in the *Conversations with Drummond* in reference to Jonson himself: "given rather to losse a friend, than a Jest." If the play's programmatic didacticism suggests the ordered, dispassionate ethos that Jonson adopts so often in his critical statements about poetry and true poets, Carlo's speeches show the more turbulent side of the mind of their maker, who told Drummond that "he heth consumed a whole night jn lying looking to his great toe, about which he hath seen tartars & turks Romans and Carthaginions feight in his jmagination."

The original ending of *Every Man out of His Humour* caused some unwelcome controversy for Jonson. The motive force in the play's slender plot is the envy of Macilente, who forces the other "humorists" into situations where their "humours" are purged. His own "humour," envy, was originally purged from him at the sight of the Queen, who was the embodiment of ideal virtue in Elizabethan literary convention. A boy actor dressed up as the Queen marched onto the stage of the Globe; at the sight of "the Queen" Macilente found himself completely dishumored. To many the impersonation of the queen by a mere stage player was utterly distasteful, and Jonson revised the ending, cutting the offensive appearance of the Queen and having Macilente proclaim that his "humour" was gone now that his envy had no more objects upon which to feed. However, in typical fashion Jonson included the original ending as an appendix when the quarto edition of the play was published in 1600, "that a right-ei'd and solide *Reader* may perceiue it was not so great a part of the Heauen awry, as [many] would make it."

Jonson's next play, *Cynthia's Revels,* which was performed in late 1600 by the Children of the Chapel at Blackfriars, is extraordinarily ambitious. While *Every Man out of His Humour* sought the acclaim of Elizabethan wits by castigating the

Lucy Harington, Countess of Bedford, wearing a costume designed by Inigo Jones for Hymenaei *(Bedford Estate)*

follies and vices of various social classes, *Cynthia's Revels* bade directly for the queen's recognition by the remarkable strategy of ridiculing the faults of the court. Not surprisingly the attempt to win royal approbation was unsuccessful. If the two motives of the play—an appeal for royal favor and satire of courtiers—seem at odds, so do some of the play's formal elements. Jonson borrows elements of the Lylyan model of the courtly play, which had been so well suited both to complimenting the queen and to performance by a company of boy actors. Thus *Cynthia's Revels* employs deliberately artificial groupings of allegorical and symbolic characters, passages of repartee between witty pages, and very pretty lyrics that have often been anthologized. However, it is difficult to integrate this delicate mode of comedy with the demands of satire. Jonson's experiment is consciously daring; the play's prologue announces that,

> In this alone, his MVSE her sweetness hath,
> Shee shunnes the print of any beaten path,
> And proues new wayes to come to learned
> eares.

However, Jonson's experiment is not entirely successful. At its best the play's blend of mythological allegory and dramatic satire provokes an intriguingly complicated aesthetic response. All too often, however, the mythology seems perfunctory and irrelevant, and the satire labored and tedious.

Also problematic is the role of Jonson's spokesman in the play, Crites (called Criticus in the quarto text). On the one hand he is a paragon, "A creature of a most perfect, and diuine temper." On the other, his resemblance to the author is discomfiting: he is a poor and obscure scholar who earns the gratitude of the Queen by purging her court of its vanity by the efficacy of the revels over which he presides.

Certainly Jonson's enemies read the character of Crites as an idealized self-portrait. Some of Jonson's fellow playwrights were sufficiently annoyed by what they perceived as Jonson's arrogance that they were willing to satirize him personally. The grounds of Jonson's quarrels with John Marston and Thomas Dekker may go back farther than *Cynthia's Revels;* Jonson told Drummond that his quarrels with Marston had begun when Marston represented him on the stage. Apparently the character Chrisogonus in Marston's *Histriomastix* was meant to be a complimentary portrait of Jonson. However, Jonson resented the intended compliment and introduced into *Every Man out of His Humour* a minor character, Clove, intended to ridicule Marston. The attacks then went back and forth, with Marston lampooning Jonson in his *Jack Drum's Entertainment,* Jonson responding in *Cynthia's Revels* with the character Hedon, and Marston again retorting with the character Lampatho Doria in *What You Will.* The whole affair is rather murky up to this point. At any rate the Chamberlain's Men, angered at Jonson's having gone over to their new rivals, the Children of the Chapel, hired Dekker to write a play attacking him. Jonson learned of the coming attack, and in fifteen weeks he wrote *Poetaster,* which lampoons Dekker and Marston, and got it on the boards at the Blackfriars before the

Chamberlain's Men could produce Dekker's *Satiromastix.* Thus was fought the famous "war of the theaters" obliquely alluded to in *Hamlet.*

In *Poetaster* Augustan Rome is the scene of Jonson's personal satire of Dekker and Marston. Jonson defends himself against his enemies by showing that the Roman poets whom he most admired, "VIRGIL, HORACE, and the rest / Of those great master-spirits," suffered from detraction just as he did. Jonson represents himself in the character of the Roman poet Horace, whom he greatly esteemed; Jonson later translated the *Ars Poetica,* and his nondramatic poetry is greatly indebted to Horatian precept and practice. Dekker and Marston are lampooned in the characters of Demetrius and Crispinus. Demetrius is a writer of witless doggerel verse and "a dresser of plays about the town" hired to abuse Horace. Crispinus is a vain fop who "pens high, loftie, in a new stalking strain"; a specimen of his verse is an obvious parody of Marston's style in his satires, characterized by such uncouth words as "lubricall," "glibberie," "snotteries," and "bespawles." The purgative function of comical satire is wittily translated into stage action in the play's final scene, when Crispinus is given an emetic and forced to vomit up his bizarre vocabulary onstage.

Poetaster is not merely an attack on Marston and Dekker. Most of the characters in the play do not refer to any of Jonson's contemporaries, and attempts by earlier scholars to identify Ovid and Virgil in the play with other Elizabethan poets have not met with acceptance. The larger concerns of *Poetaster* are with the proper role of the poet in society. The ridicule of Crispinus and Demetrius occurs in the context of a general evaluation of poetry in which Ovid, Virgil, Horace, and Tibullus are also judged. However, the play's stinging satire is the quality most remembered by posterity and by Jonson's contemporaries as well. *Poetaster* created yet more controversy for Jonson. Besides the attacks on Marston and Dekker, the play also satirizes lawyers, military braggarts, and professional actors. The satire of lawyers and the law seems to have riled certain government officials, and once again Jonson was threatened with prosecution. However, a friend, Richard Martin, intervened and defended Jonson. The author expressed his gratitude by dedicating the folio text of the play to Martin.

Jonson himself had sought to defend *Poetaster* in an "Apologeticall Dialogue" appended to the play. However, the dialogue was performed only once before being "suppressed by authority," and it was not included in the 1600 quarto edition of the play, although it was restored in the folio of 1616. In the "Apologeticall Dialogue" Jonson announces the end of his experimentation with comical satire:

> since the *Comick* MVSE
> Hath prou'd so ominous to me, I will trie
> If *Tragoedie* haue a more kind aspect.

THE
MASQVE OF QVEENES
Celebrated
From the Houſe of Fame:
By the moſt abſolute in all State,
And Titles.
ANNE
Queene of Great *Britaine*, &c.
With her Honourable Ladies.
At VVhite Hall,
Febr. 2. 1609.
Written by BEN: IONSON.
Et memorem famam, quæ bene geßit, habet.
LONDON,
Printed by N. OKES. for *R. Bonian* and *H. VValley*, and are to be sold at the Spred Eagle in Poules Church-yard. 1609.

Title page for the 1609 quarto edition of the masque whose production cost James I more than three thousand pounds (Anderson Galleries auction catalogue, sale number 2077, 20-21 May 1926)

The result would be *Sejanus.* Meanwhile Jonson needed some means of support. In 1602 his name appeared for the last time in Henslowe's accounts for work on the lost *Richard Crookback* and on additions to *The Spanish Tragedy.* In addition Jonson was seeking noble patronage. In February 1603 the law student John Manningham recorded in his diary that "Ben Johnson the poet nowe lives upon one Townesend and scornes the world."

The year 1603 ushered in a new reign. The ascension of James I to the throne of England would prove to be auspicious to Jonson, for under the new sovereign he would find royal favor and patronage. In addition, Jonson was now coming to know many noble men and women of the kingdom. Dekker had charged him in *Satiromastix* with trying to "skrue and wriggle himselfe into great Mens famyliarity," but the record of Jonson's friendship with highly prominent people suggests an easy familiarity rather than servility on his part. Jonson's self-assurance among the great is seen not only in several anecdotes in the *Conversations with Drummond* but also in the tone in which he addresses such patrons as Lucy, Countess of Bedford (Epigrams 76 and 84), Sir Robert Wroth (*The Forrest* 3), Sir Robert Sidney (*The Forrest* 2), and William Herbert, third Earl of Pembroke (dedications to *Catiline* and *Epigrams*). Other nobles with whom Jonson was familiar included Lady Elizabeth Rutland, the daughter of Sir Philip Sidney; and Esmé Stuart, Lord D'Aubigny, a cousin of King James, with whom Jonson lived for five years. His relations with Salisbury, the secretary of state, and Thomas Howard, first Earl of Suffolk, the lord chamberlain, were more ambiguous; epigrams of praise are addressed to both, but the *Conversations with Drummond* show that Jonson was not on the best of terms with either man.

Although the new reign was to bring Jonson fame and success, it began inauspiciously, with a personal loss, the death of his first son, commemorated in Epigram 45. Drummond recorded a fascinating anecdote concerning the death. While the new king was journeying to London, the plague was raging in the city, and Jonson was staying in the country, at the house of the great antiquarian Sir Robert Cotton, with his old schoolmaster Camden. There one night he had a vision of his son Benjamin with the mark of a bloody cross on his forehead. The next morning he related the incident to Camden, who tried to reassure him that "it was but ane appreehension of his fantasie at which he sould not be disjected." Then a letter arrived from his wife telling of the boy's death of the plague. Jonson said that his son, who was seven years old at his death, appeared to him in "a Manlie shape & of yt Grouth that he thinks he shall be at the resurrection."

Another disappointment came with the first performance of *Sejanus* in late 1603 or early 1604. If Jonson had hoped to find "a more kind aspect" in tragedy than he had found in comedy, then he was greatly disappointed; *Sejanus* was hissed off the stage by the audience at the Globe. And once again Jonson found himself in trouble with the government, accused this time of popery and treason. Jonson believed that his troubles were due to Henry Howard, first Earl of Northampton, with whose servant he had brawled. However, members of the Privy Council, who summoned Jonson to appear before them, tended to be wary on principle of plays dealing with conspiracy against monarchs. Fortunately no serious consequences ensued.

Sejanus is an unremittingly grim play. From beginning to end all power rests with the evil, crafty emperor Tiberius. Sejanus, his power-hungry underling, is as evil as his master and nearly his equal in intrigue, but his ambition proves fatal, and he is cruelly destroyed. The death of this villain at the close of the play, however, merely ushers in a worse, Macro. The play's good characters are wholly passive, "good, dull, noble lookers on," in the words of one of them.

The play as we have it differs from the version performed at the Globe, "wherein a second Pen had good share." Jonson replaced the work of the unnamed second poet (perhaps George Chapman) with passages of his own writing and published in 1605 a quarto edition of the play notable for its plethora of scholarly notes testifying to the "truth of argument" which he strongly emphasized as a criterion for tragedy. Having failed to please the populace in the theater, Jonson now appealed to the more literate sectors of society for their approbation. That this move was successful is shown by the many admiring references to the play by Jonson's contemporaries.

A new phase of Jonson's career, his employment as a writer of court masques and courtly entertainments, began in June 1603, when Jonson was commissioned to write an entertainment to greet the queen and prince at Althorp, the house of Sir Robert Spencer, on their way south from Scotland. In 1604, when the king arrived in London, the city hired Jonson to write speeches of greeting as part of its formal welcome of the new monarch; he also wrote a "Panegyre" for James's opening of Parliament a few days later. In the same year he wrote *The Entertainment at Highgate,* which welcomed the king and queen to the house of Sir William Cornwallis. The king and queen

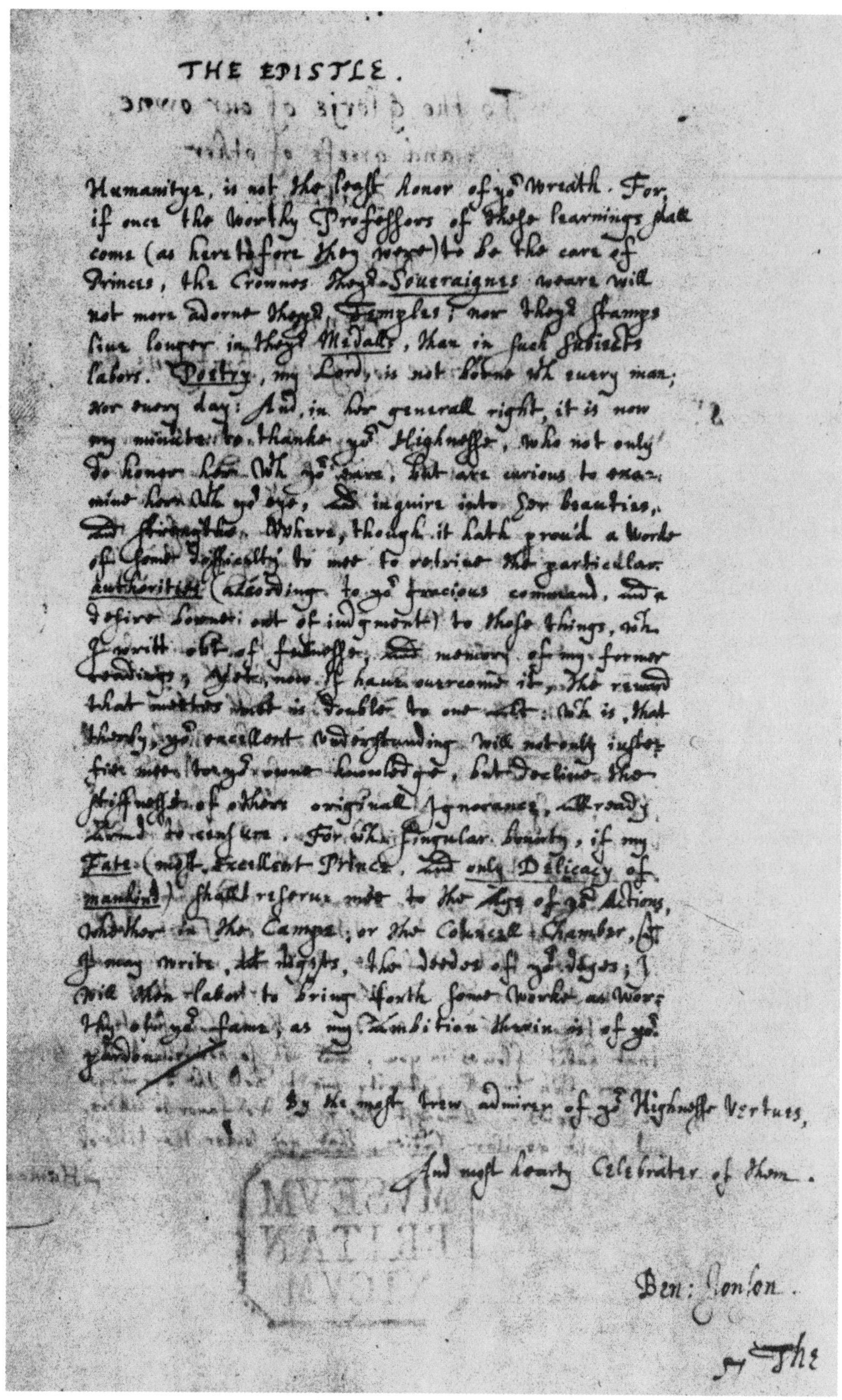

THE EPISTLE.

Humanitye, is not the least honor of yor wreath. For, if once the worthy Professors of these learnings shall come (as heretofore they were) to be the care of Princes, the Crownes theyr Soueraignes weare will not more adorne theyr Temples; nor theyr stamps liue longer in theyr Medalls, than in such subiects labors. Poetry, my Lord, is not borne wth euery man; nor euery day: And, in her generall right, it is now my minute to thanke yor Highnesse, who not only do honor her wth yor eare, but are curious to examine her wth yor eye, and inquire into her beauties, and strengths. Where, though it hath prou'd a worke of some difficulty to mee to retriue the particular authorities (according to yor gracious command, and a desire borne out of iudgment) to those things, wch I writt out of fullnesse, and memory of my former readings; Yet, now I haue ouercome it, the reward that meetes mee is double to one act: wch is, that therby, yor excellent vnderstanding will not only iustify mee to myne owne knowledge, but decline the stiffnesse of others originall Ignorance, already arm'd to censure. For wch singular bounty, if my Fate (most excellent Prince, and only Delicacy of mankind) shall reserue mee to the Age of yor Actions, whether in the Campe, or the Councell-Chamber, that I may write, at nights, the deedes of yor dayes; I will then labor to bring forth some worke as worthy of yor fame, as my ambition therein is of yor pardon.

By the most trew admirer of yor Highnesse Vertues,

And most hearty Celebrater of them.

Ben: Jonson.

The

Letter of dedication from a presentation copy of The Masque of Queens, *entirely in Jonson's hand (Royal MS 18 A xlv, f.2ᵛ; British Library)*

were sufficiently impressed by these performances that Jonson was commissioned to write the court masque for the next Christmas season's customary Twelfth Night revels.

Queen Anne requested a masque in which she and her chief ladies could appear disguised as "Black-mores." The result, *The Masque of Blackness,* performed on Twelfth Night 1605, launched Jonson's career as a deviser of court masques. Thereafter Jonson would produce a masque for the court's Christmas festivities every year of the reign except for Christmas 1606-1607, when Thomas Campion's *Masque of Lord Hayes* was written for that lord's wedding, which replaced the usual Christmas celebration; 1613, when he was in France; and Christmas 1620-1621.

Jonson is the most important writer of court masques, largely because he approached masque writing so seriously. Court masques were celebrations of royalty designed to impress foreign and domestic observers by their magnificence, and most people considered them to be primarily spectacles. Samuel Daniel, whose *Vision of the Twelve Goddesses* was performed at court in January 1604, had ridiculed those who attempted "to shew most wit about these Puntillos of Dreames and shewes." However, Jonson insisted that masques be true poems, that they not only entertain but also move the spectators to virtue. The introduction to *Hymenaei* (produced on 5 and 6 January 1606) provides the clearest account of Jonson's lofty conception of the function of masques. There the spectacular elements of masques are compared to the body, and the intellectual elements to the soul. Jonson claims that the grounding of masques upon solid intellectual and moral ideas "hath made the most royall *Princes,* and greatest *persons* (who are commonly the *personaters* of these *actions*) not onely studious of riches, and magnificence in the outward celebration, or shew; (which rightly becomes them) but curious after the most high, and heartie *inuentions,* to furnish the inward parts: (and those grounded vpon *antiquitie,* and solide *learnings*) which, though their *voyce* be taught to sound to present occasions, their *sense,* or doth, or should alwayes lay hold on more remou'd *mysteries.*"

Jonson recognized that poetry was only part of the masque; elaborate costumes and stage scenery, music, and dance were all integral parts of the form. However, he insisted that all spectacular elements should contribute to communicating a principal theme. And he believed that it was the poet's job to supply the theme around which the masque would be structured.

The opportunity to write court masques greatly attracted Jonson. For one thing, masque writing paid well. In 1620 Jonson was paid one hundred pounds for writing *News from the New World Discovered in the Moon;* in contrast he told Drummond in 1619 that "of all his Playes he never Gained 2 hundred pounds." However, Jonson was attracted by more than the financial rewards. The courtly masque satisfied both his desire for a more refined audience than was available in the public theater and his belief that poetry should serve the commonwealth. In the comical satires he had tried unsuccessfully to reform society from the stage. In the masques he could help to inform royalty with virtue, thus potentially reforming society from the top.

The royal entertainments and court masques of 1604-1605 were the beginning of a happy relationship between Jonson and King James. However, Jonson came very close to losing the foothold to royal favor that he had gained. In late 1604 or early 1605 he collaborated with Chapman and with his former adversary Marston on the play *Eastward Ho.* Imprudently the authors inserted some passages ridiculing the Scots, probably during an unlicensed production sometime between July and September 1605, while the king was on his Oxford progress. When James learned of the offense he was outraged. The three authors were imprisoned, and as Jonson told Drummond, "the report was that they shoūld then had their ears cutt & noses." The three playwrights appealed to various powerful noblemen, Chapman even writing to the king himself, Jonson to the earl of Salisbury. The intervention of Suffolk, the lord chamberlain, and of Lord D'Aubigny helped to bring about the release of the three authors.

A few months later Jonson found himself caught up in the government's response to a national crisis. The Gunpowder Plot to blow up Parliament on 5 November 1605 was thwarted just as the conspirators were about to put their plan into action. Jonson knew several of the conspirators; he had been at a supper party hosted by the conspirator Robert Catesby and attended by fellow Catholics sometime around 9 October. However, Jonson was loyal to the crown. On 7 November Lord Salisbury commissioned Jonson to convey a promise of safe conduct to a priest "that offered to do good service to the State." Jonson sought him out unsuccessfully and was forced to

Costume designs by Inigo Jones for The Masque of Queens: *left (top) Penthesileia, (bottom) Camilla; right (top) Zenobia, (bottom) Atalanta (from Stephen Orgel and Roy Strong,* Inigo Jones, *1973)*

write to Salisbury that "that Party will not be found, (for soe he returnes answere.)."

Jonson's cooperation did not keep him from trouble during the official reaction to the plot. In April of 1606 he and his wife were summoned before the Consistory Court for absenting themselves from Anglican communion; Jonson was also charged with being "a seducer of youthe to popishe religion." Jonson denied the latter charge on his own behalf and also denied all charges against his wife. With characteristic self-confidence, the poet told his examiners that his nonattendance at communion was due to "some scruple of conscience" and requested that learned men be appointed to resolve him in the matter.

In 1605 Jonson was living in a house in the district of the Blackfriars. There in five weeks he wrote *Volpone,* an undisputed masterpiece and his first unqualified success. The play was immensely popular at the Globe in early 1606; more gratifying still was the play's success at both universities later that year. The former bricklayer and itinerant actor who for years had demanded recognition of his scholarship and artistry had won the approval of the most prestigious centers of learning in the land. When Jonson published *Volpone* in 1607 he included a lengthy dedication to the universities expressing his gratitude.

Volpone marks a new phase in Jonson's struggle to develop a moral comedy. The comical satires had deliberately subordinated plot to characterization and to moral instruction. At the center of each stood an arbiter of morals—Asper, Crites, or Horace—surveying folly and vice from a position of lofty detachment while deftly managing the onstage action that exposes the fools and knaves. In the comedies from *Volpone* to *Bartholomew Fair,* there are no virtuous characters controlling the action. More often than not the rogues call all the shots; the virtuous Celia and Bonario seem relatively helpless in the world of *Volpone.* After this play the depiction of ideal virtue disappears entirely from the comedies and is reserved for the masques and nondramatic poems of praise.

In *Volpone* and the comedies which follow it, the role of intrigue returns to the foreground as the plane of the ideal disappears. Plot becomes much more important in the middle and late comedies than in the comical satires. And the willingness to experiment with comic form seen in *Every Man out of His Humour* is replaced by an emphasis on critical orthodoxy: the prologue to *Volpone* promises "quick *comœdie,* refined, / As best Criticks haue designed."

Volpone has much in common with *Sejanus.* In both plays the action is wholly dominated by a crafty villain whose tricky henchman tries unsuccessfully to snatch power from him. Both Sejanus and Volpone are masters of theatricality. And in both plays virtue is helpless to deal with the machinations of the wicked.

The plot of *Volpone* is inspired by the Roman practice of *captatio,* whereby would-be legatees gave lavish gifts to old or sickly rich men in hopes of being named their heirs. The scene is not ancient Rome, however, but Renaissance Venice, which Jonson invests with all of the splendor and corruption that the Elizabethans associated with Italy. Elements from the genre of beast fable are woven into the plot, emphasizing the brutality of the world of the play. Thus most of the human characters have animal names, such as Volpone or fox, Mosca or fly, and Voltore, Corbaccio, and Corvino—"vulture . . . Rauen, and gor-crow."

Brutality does not sufficiently qualify the description of the characters, however. Volpone and his assistant Mosca have intelligence and imagination as well. Volpone especially is not merely the crafty villain implied by the epithet "fox." He is a magnifico who combines the ruthless intelligence of Tiberius in *Sejanus* with the passionate will and daring imagination of a Marlovian overreacher, so that he attains a kind of perverse grandeur. Jonson gives him magnificent speeches packed with imagery that dazzles and glitters. Under the spell of his rhetoric we almost forget his villainy.

In the early part of the play Volpone also gains much of our sympathy because his victims are no better morally than he, while they lack his intelligence and imagination. They deceive themselves by their own greed and deserve to be cheated. However, Jonson forces his audience to condemn Volpone when "the fox" attempts to rape an innocent woman and then tries to calumniate her equally innocent defender, Bonario. Volpone almost succeeds; but when he is betrayed by Mosca, who almost grabs all of his master's loot, he chooses to reveal his guilt in court and thus destroy himself along with Mosca, rather than allow himself to be cheated.

The play's catastrophe has excited a good deal of critical debate, for *Volpone* has one of the harshest endings of any comedy. Volpone is condemned "to lie in prison, crampt with irons"

THE

ALCHEMIST.

VVritten
by
BEN. IONSON.

——*Neque, me vt miretur turba, laboro:*
Contentus paucis lectoribus.

LONDON,
Printed by *Thomas Snodham*, for *Walter Burre*,
and are to be sold by *John Stepneth*, at the
West-end of Paules.
1612.

TO THE READER.

IF thou beest more, thou art an Vnderstander, and then I trust thee. If thou art one that tak'st vp, and but a Pretender, beware at what hands thou receiu'st thy commoditie; for thou wert neuer more fair in the way to be cos'ned (then in this Age, in Poetry, *especially in Playes: wherein, now, the Concupiscence of Jigges, and Daunces so raigneth, as to runne away from Nature, and be afraid of her, is the onely point of art that tickles the* Spectators. *But how out of purpose, and place, doe I name Art? when the Professors are growne so obstinate contemners of it, and presumers on their owne Naturalls, as they are deriders of all diligence that way, and, by simple mocking at the termes, when they vnderstand not the things, thinke to get of wittily with their Ignorance. Nay, they are esteem'd the more learned, and sufficient for this, by the Multitude, through their excellent vice of iudgement. For they commend Writers, as they doe Fencers, or Wrastlers; who if they come in robustuously, and put for it with a great deale of violence, are receiu'd for the brauer fellowes: when many times their owne rudenesse is the cause of their disgrace, and a little touch of their Aduersary giues all that boisterous force the foyle. I deny not, but that these men, who alwaies seeke to doe more then inough, may some time happen on some thing that is good, and great; but very seldome: And when it comes it doth not recompence the rest of their ill. It sticks out perhaps, and is more eminent, because all is sordide, and vile about it: as lights are more discern'd in a thick darknesse, then a faint shadow. I speake not this, out of a hope to doe good on any man, against his will; for I know, if it were put to the question of theirs, and mine, the worse would finde more suffrages:*

A 3 *because*

because the most fauour common errors. But I giue thee this warning, that there is a great difference betweene those, that (to gain the opinion of Copie) vtter all they can, how euer vnfitly; and those that vse election, and a meane. For it is onely the disease of the vnskilfull, to thinke rude things greater then polish'd: or scatter'd more numerous then compos'd.

To my friend, M[r]. *Ben: Ionson.* vpon
his Alchemist.

A Master, read in flatteries great skill,
Could not passe truth, though he would force his (*will,*
By praising this too much, to get more praise
In his Art, then you out of yours doe raise.
Nor can full truth be vttered of your worth,
Vnlesse you your owne praises doe set forth:
None else can write so skilfully, to shew
Your praise: Ages shall pay, yet still must owe.
All I dare say, is, you haue written well,
In what exceeding height, I dare not tell.

George Lucy.

The Persons of the Comœdie.

SVBTLE. The Alchemist.
FACE. The House-keeper.
DOL: Common. Their Colleague.
DAPPER. A Clearke.
DRVGGER. A *Tabacco*-man.
LOVE-Wit. Master of the House.
EPICVRE MAMMON. A Knight.
SVRLY. A Gamster.
TRIBVLATION. A Pastor of *Amstredam*.
ANANIAS. A Deacon there.
KASTRIL. The Angry Boy.
DA: PLIANT. His sister: A Widdow.
Neighbours.
Officers.
Mutes.

THE ARGVMENT.

T he Sicknesse hot, A Master quit, for feare,
H is House in Towne: and left one Seruant there.
E ase him corrupted, and gaue meanes to know
A Cheater, and his Punque; who now brought low,
L eauing their narrow practise, were become
C os'ners at large: and, onely wanting some
H ouse to set vp, with him they here contract,
E ach for a share, and all begin to act.
M uch company they draw, and much abuse
I n casting Figures, telling Fortunes, Newes,
S elling of Flyes, flat Bawdry, with the *Stone*:
T ill It, and They, and All in *fume* are gone.

Title page, epistle to the reader, commendatory verse by George Lucy, dramatis personae, and the Argument from the 1612 quarto edition of one of Jonson's best-known plays (King's College Library, Cambridge)

Costume design by Inigo Jones for Oberon in the first of two Jonson masques performed at Court during the 1610-1611 Christmas season (from Stephen Orgel and Roy Strong, Inigo Jones, *1973)*

until he is truly lame and sick; Mosca is to be whipped and sentenced to life in the galleys; their dupes are also punished severely. Apparently Jonson still felt that, in order to point the moral of the play, retributive justice like that in the comical satires was necessary.

After *Volpone,* Jonson remained absent from the stage for a period of four years. Meanwhile several masques appeared. January 1606 had seen the performance of *Hymenaei,* written for the wedding of Frances Howard to Robert Devereux, third Earl of Essex, which supplanted the usual Twelfth Night revels. The masque was performed on two consecutive nights, the first night's performance presenting the subjugation of the Humors and Affections to Reason at the behest of the god Hymen, and the second the victory of Truth over Opinion in a mock combat. That summer, on 24 July, *The Entertainment of the Two Kings at Theobalds* was performed to welcome James and his brother-in-law, King Christian of Denmark, to the earl of Salisbury's house. On 22 May 1607 *An Entertainment of the King and Queen at Theobalds* was performed to mark the earl of

Salisbury's turning his house over to the king. That summer Jonson was also engaged by the Merchant Taylors' Company to provide an entertainment for the king, the queen, and Prince Henry when they came to attend the annual election of the company's Master and Warders.

On 10 January 1608 *The Masque of Beauty,* designed as a sequel to *The Masque of Blackness,* was performed in the newly completed Banqueting House at Whitehall, followed by *The Haddington Masque* on 9 February 1608, to celebrate the marriage of a favorite of the king's, Sir John Ramsay, Viscount Haddington. Both masques were very costly, but both were highly successful. A few months later Jonson was commissioned by the earl of Salisbury to write a lesser piece, an entertainment welcoming King James to Salisbury House in the Strand. The text of this entertainment has not survived.

Jonson wrote *The Masque of Queens* for the next year's Twelfth Night festivities at the court. However, because of diplomatic wrangling among the foreign ambassadors who were to attend the performance (a frequent problem during Jonson's tenure as a writer of court masques), the performance was postponed until 2 February 1609. When it was finally performed it made a great impression. However, it was also quite expensive, costing the king over three thousand pounds. Another entertainment, now lost, was performed before the royal family on 11 April 1609, to celebrate the opening of "Britain's Burse," later known as the New Exchange. Jonson received over thirteen pounds for his share in devising the entertainment.

A prominent feature of Jonson's life during these years was his social activity. During the first half of the reign of King James, Jonson was one of a circle of literary men and wits who gathered in the famous Mermaid Tavern, whose "rich Canary wine" is mentioned in Epigram 101, "Inviting a Friend to Supper." A verse epistle from Francis Beaumont to Jonson has immortalized the gatherings at the tavern, and the tradition was embellished by Jonson's early biographers. Thomas Fuller (1608-1661) recorded that the tavern was the setting for "wit-combats" between Jonson and Shakespeare, "which two I behold like a *Spanish great Gallion,* and an *English man of War*; Master *Johnson* (like the former) was built far higher in Learning; *Solid,* but *Slow* in his performances. *Shake-spear,* with the *English man of War,* lesser in *bulk,* but lighter in *sailing,* could turn with all tides, tack about and take advantage of all winds, by the quickness of his Wit and Invention."

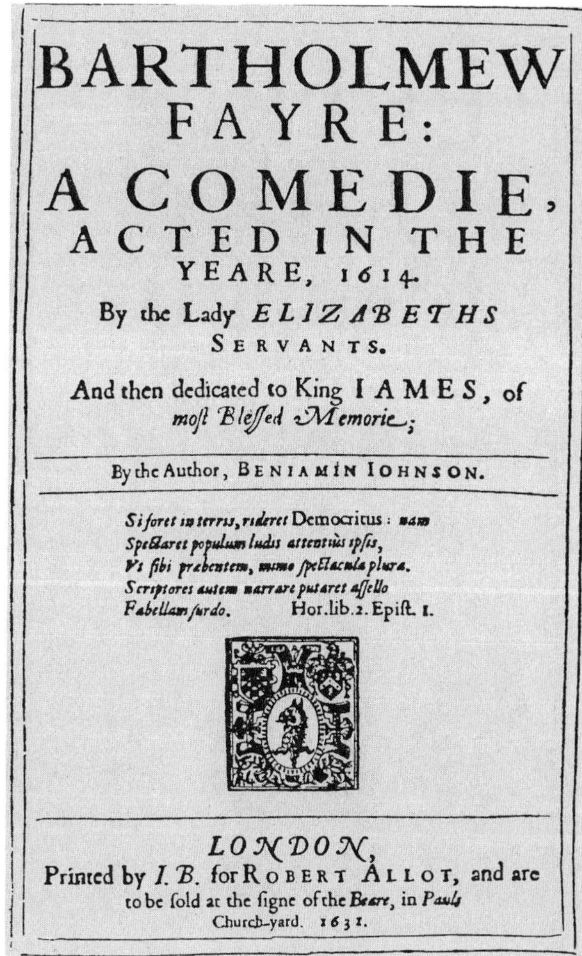

BARTHOLMEW
FAYRE:
A COMEDIE,
ACTED IN THE
YEARE, 1614.
By the Lady *ELIZABETHS*
SERVANTS.
And then dedicated to King IAMES, of
most Blessed Memorie;

By the Author, BENIAMIN IOHNSON.

Si foret in terris, rideret Democritus: *nam*
Spectaret populum ludis attentiùs ipsis,
Vt sibi præbentem, mimo spectacula plura.
Scriptores autem narrare putaret asello
Fabellam surdo. Hor.lib.2.Epist.1.

LONDON,
Printed by *I. B.* for ROBERT ALLOT, and are
to be sold at the signe of the *Beare,* in *Pauls*
Church-yard. 1631.

Title page for the first printing of Jonson's comedy, produced in 1614, from the 1631 folio edition of volume 2 of his works (from C. H. Herford, Percy and Evelyn Simpson, eds., Ben Jonson, *volume 6, 1938)*

Jonson's relations with Shakespeare seem to have been friendly though not close. In the *Discoveries* Jonson wrote, "I lov'd the man, and doe honour his memory (on this side Idolatry) as much as any." For the first folio collection of Shakespeare's plays (1623), Jonson composed a lengthy poem of praise. However, there was much in Shakespeare's writing that annoyed Jonson, and Jonson was never reluctant to criticize a perceived error. The famous remark in the *Conversations with Drummond,* "That Shaksperr wanted Arte," reappears in other guises elsewhere in Jonson's writing—in the induction to *Bartholomew Fair,* with its slighting references to "*Tales, Tempests,* and such like *Drolleries*"; in the prologue to *Every Man in His Humour,* which obliquely refers to Shakespeare's history plays as examples of

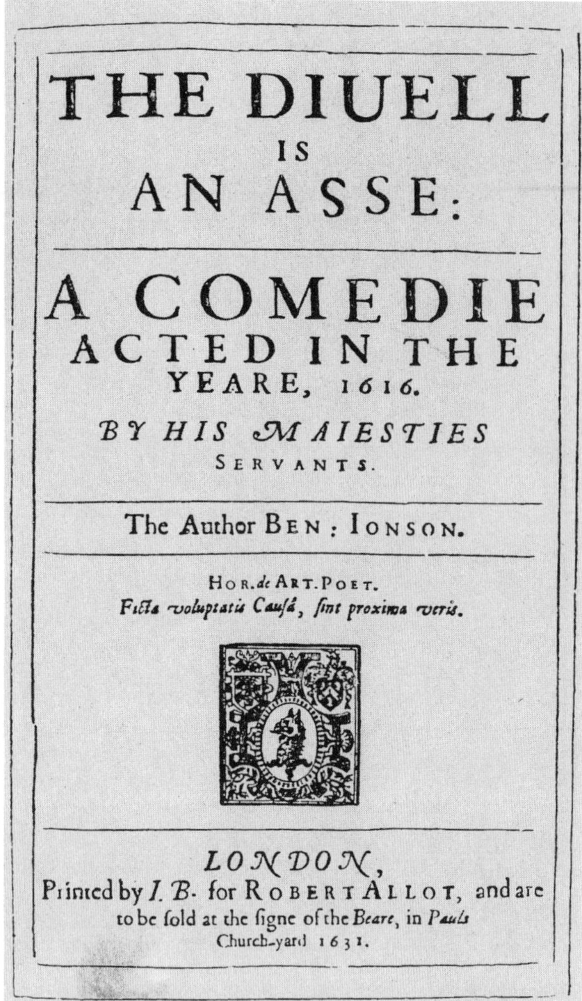

THE DIUELL
IS
AN ASSE:

A COMEDIE
ACTED IN THE
YEARE, 1616.

BY HIS MAIESTIES
SERVANTS.

The Author BEN: IONSON.

HOR. de ART. POET.
Ficta voluptatis Causâ, sint proxima veris.

LONDON,
Printed by *I. B.* for ROBERT ALLOT, and are
to be sold at the signe of the *Beare*, in *Pauls*
Church-yard 1631.

Interior title page, from the 1631 edition of volume 2 of Jonson's works, for the first printing of the play produced in 1616, after which Jonson was absent from the theater for nearly ten years (from C. H. Herford, Percy and Evelyn Simpson, eds., Ben Jonson, *volume 6, 1938)*

"th'ill customes of the age"; in the reference to "some mouldy tale, / Like *Pericles*" in the "Ode to Himselfe" on the failure of *The New Inn*; and in the observation in *Discoveries* that, "hee flow'd with that facility, that sometime it was necessary he should be stop'd: *Sufflaminandus erat.*"

Jonson's friends also included the poets John Donne, Francis Beaumont, and George Chapman. For Donne, Jonson held especially high regard. A letter has survived in which Jonson wrote to Donne, "You cannot but believe, how dear and reverend your friendship is to me." Jonson also respected greatly Donne's poetry. Although he criticized Donne's liberties with meter and his occasional obscurity, Jonson told Drummond that "he esteemeth John Done the first poet jn the World in some things." In an "Apologie" for *Bartholomew Fair,* which prefaced his translation of Horace's *Ars Poetica,* Jonson created a speaker named Criticus, who was intended to represent Donne. Unfortunately the preface was lost in the fire of 1623 that destroyed Jonson's library.

Jonson's friends were not all literary men. Among Jonson's closest friends were William Roe and his brother Sir John Roe. On one occasion, Sir John and Jonson were ejected from Whitehall by Lord Suffolk for boisterous behavior during the performance of a masque. In 1606 Sir John died of the plague in Jonson's arms, and Jonson paid the cost of his burial.

In late 1609 or early 1610 Jonson returned to the stage with the comedy *Epicoene,* performed by the Children of the Queen's Revels at Whitefriars. Ever since Dryden's discussion of the play in the *Essay of Dramatic Poesy, Epicoene* has been praised for the skill of its construction. But the play has also disturbed many readers by the heartlessness of the society it presents. None of the play's characters is ethically sound. Truewit and Dauphine, the comic heroes of the play, rise above their fellows in wit and breeding but are basically frivolous. And their treatment of Morose at the end of the play seems unnecessarily cruel.

The plot of the play, derived from two different classical sources, centers around the efforts of Dauphine, aided by his friend Truewit, to gain the inheritance of his uncle Morose, an old bachelor morbidly sensitive to noise of any kind. Morose is determined to disinherit his nephew, and thus decides to marry Epicoene, a woman remarkable for her silence. Truewit tries in many ways—each of which drives Morose to distraction—to dissuade him from marriage. However, Morose marries anyway, whereupon his bride immediately loses her silence. Dauphine then extracts from Morose a promise that he will make Dauphine his heir if Dauphine can find grounds to annul the marriage; when Dauphine reveals that Epicoene is not a woman but a boy in disguise, Morose is forced to keep his promise and is jeered off the stage.

In *Epicoene* Jonson's impulse to didacticism seems to have relaxed. This change is signaled in the play's prologue, which emphasizes entertainment rather than instruction. The poet is compared to a cook whose task is to please the palates of his guests—a striking contrast to the role of the poet in the comical satires, whose art is said to be "phisicke of the mind," good for the audience whether they like it or not.

However, not everyone was pleased by the feast which Jonson had prepared; in fact *Epicoene* involved Jonson in a new scandal, and by February the play was suppressed by the government. Some members of the audience detected a satirical reference to the king's cousin, Arabella Stuart, in a passage describing how Sir John Daw, a gull in the play, draws "maps of persons," including maps "of the Prince of *Moldauia,* and of his mistris, mistris EPICOENE." An imposter named Stephano Janiculo, who claimed to be the prince of Moldavia, had come to England in 1601 and in 1607, on the latter occasion receiving a grant of three thousand pounds from King James. In 1608 Janiculo was in Venice bruiting it about that he was engaged to be married to Lady Arabella. By this time Lady Arabella had become engaged to Sir William Seymour; however, because she was a close relative of the king, her marriage plans were a matter of importance to the state and were watched closely by observers both foreign and domestic. On 8 February 1610 the Venetian ambassador made the following report: "Lady Arabella is seldom seen outside her rooms and lives in greater dejection than ever. She complains that in a certain comedy the play-wright introduced an allusion to her person and the part played by the Prince of Moldavia. The play was suppressed." We know of no further consequences for Jonson from the affair.

At about the same time as the performance of *Epicoene,* Jonson's *The Speeches at Prince Henry's Barriers* was performed, on Twelfth Night 1610. The festivities marked a special occasion, the investiture of Prince Henry as Prince of Wales. The prince was portrayed as Meliadus, a knight destined to restore the lost glories of chivalry. By all accounts the royal entertainment was a success.

Later that year the King's Men produced Jonson's next play, *The Alchemist,* which was entirely successful in its own time and is regarded as one of his greatest works today. The tight construction seen in *Epicoene* is even more marked in this play; the action of the play takes place entirely within the two hours or so of the play's stage performance. The play centers around the desperate attempts of three rogues—Face the tricky butler, Subtle the alchemist, and Doll Common the whore—to swindle a variety of Londoners, all of whom are possessed by the dream of the philosophers' stone. Some of the dupes gulled by "the venter *tripartite*" are merely silly, like Dapper and Drugger. Sir Epicure Mammon, however, is a remarkable creation. For him the dream of infinite wealth is primarily a promise of infinite sensual variety; the dizzying speeches in which he describes his fantastic vision are among the most justly celebrated passages in Jonson's work.

Prominent among the victims of the alchemical conspiracy are the Puritans Ananias and Tribulation Wholesome. Jonson is unremittingly hostile toward the Puritans. They are depicted as entirely hypocritical, and their peculiar theological vocabulary as mere cant disguising their sordid greed. As early as *Every Man out of His Humour* Jonson had attacked those

> whose faces are all zeale,
> . . . that will not smell of sinne,
> But seeme as they were made of sanctitie!
> Religion in their garments, and their haire
> Cut shorter then their eye-browes!

In *Bartholomew Fair* he would continue his attack on the "Faction." It was not merely the Puritans' hostility toward the theater that earned Jonson's hostility, although that becomes a particular issue in *Bartholomew Fair.* Rather it is their rejection of the culture inherited from classical antiquity that earns Jonson's special contempt. "I hate *Traditions,*" says Ananias; in the context of Jonson's work that is a damning statement.

Having proved so successful in comedy, Jonson decided to return to classical tragedy. In 1611 *Catiline* was performed by the King's Men. Unfortunately the play was even more of a failure with the public than *Sejanus.* Although *Sejanus* had been rejected by the multitude, the intellectuals had rallied to its defense. *Catiline,* however, seems to have been rejected even by the educated. Jonson's response to the play's failure on the stage was to rush it into print within the year, with a dedication to the earl of Pembroke defending his "legitimate Poeme" from the censure of "these Iig-giuen times," and a contemptuous address "TO THE READER IN ORDINAIRIE." The Latin motto on the play's title page was carefully chosen to attack the nobles as well as the commons for their lack of judgment.

In the preface to *Sejanus,* Jonson had apologized for that play's failure to follow strictly the classical model of tragedy. *Catiline,* with its chorus, and its adherence to "the strict laws of time" was for Jonson a formal improvement, "a legitimate Poeme." And, as in *Sejanus,* Jonson again emphasized "truth of argument." Jonson followed

THE
WORKES
OF
Beniamin Jonson

—neque, me ut miretur turba, laboro:
Contentus paucis lectoribus.

LONDON
Printed by
William
Stansby.

An° D. 1616.

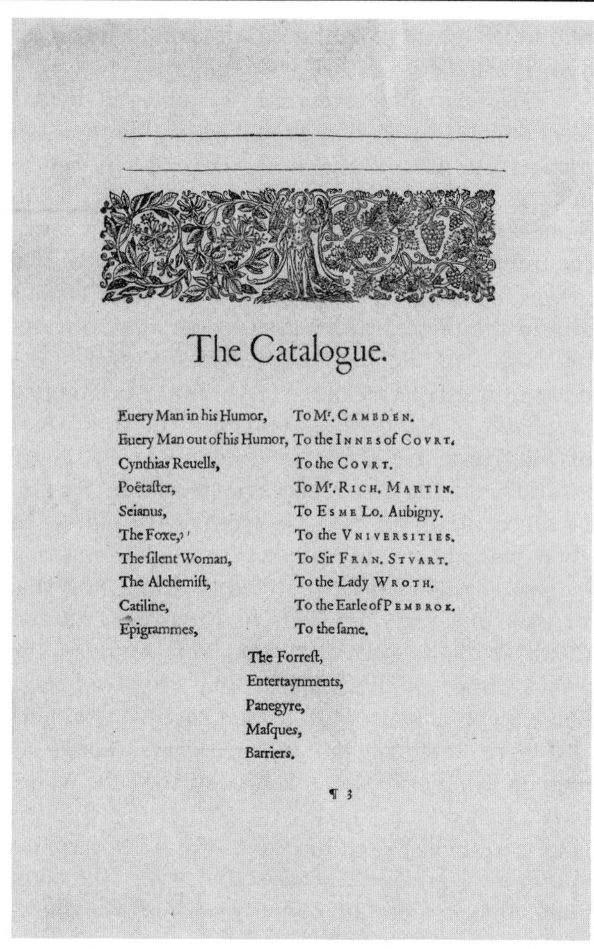
The Catalogue.

Euery Man in his Humor,	To Mr. CAMBDEN.
Euery Man out of his Humor,	To the INNES of COVRT.
Cynthias Reuells,	To the COVRT.
Poëtaster,	To Mr. RICH. MARTIN.
Seianus,	To ESME Lo. Aubigny.
The Foxe,	To the VNIVERSITIES.
The silent Woman,	To Sir FRAN. STVART.
The Alchemist,	To the Lady WROTH.
Catiline,	To the Earle of PEMBROK.
Epigrammes,	To the same.

The Forrest,
Entertaynments,
Panegyre,
Masques,
Barriers.

¶ 3

Title page and table of contents from a 1616 folio edition of the volume that provoked criticism of Jonson for his classifying plays as literary works (Bodleian Library)

his main source, Sallust, in making Catiline and his circle incarnations of evil. Thus the unmitigated malice, bloodlust, and delight in mischief expressed by the conspirators are melodramatic rather than tragic. That in itself would not have offended Jonson's audience, however. More damaging for the play's success was Jonson's treatment of the play's hero, Cicero. Cicero was one of the authors for whom Jonson felt a special affinity. Like Jonson he was a self-made man who had risen to prominence on the strength of his eloquence. And like Jonson he placed a premium on the moral function of eloquence. One of Jonson's most firmly held principles was the relation between sound language and sound morals. In the *Discoveries* he wrote, "Wheresoever, manners, and fashions are corrupted, Language is. It imitates the publicke riot." In the comedies he had repeatedly shown folly or vice expressed in degraded language—thus the uncouth style of Crispinus, the hollow oratory of Voltore, the glib prattle of Lady Would-be and the Collegiate ladies, and the cant of alchemy and Puritanism. In the character of Cicero, Jonson could emphasize the linguistic propriety of the well-settled soul.

Consequently *Catiline* places a good deal of emphasis on Cicero's oratory; in fact the plot hinges on the success of Cicero's famous oration denouncing Catiline, which Jonson translates into nearly three hundred lines of blank verse. As drama, however, the oration is tedious. The address "TO THE READER IN ORDINAIRIE" indicates that this long oration was the chief objection of the audience.

Meanwhile, for the court's celebration of Christmas 1610-1611, in which festivities the new Prince of Wales played a major role, Jonson had written two masques, *Oberon, the Fairy Prince,* performed on 1 January 1611, and *Love Freed from Ignorance and Folly,* scheduled for Twelfth Night but not performed until 3 February. For the next year's season he wrote *Love Restored,* performed

Page from a manuscript for Christmas, His Masque, *possibly in Jonson's hand (Maggs Bros. catalogue, number 569, 1932)*

on Twelfth Night 1612. Due to the king's severe financial difficulties at this time, little money could be spent on *Love Restored,* and the element of spectacle is drastically reduced in the masque, a circumstance to which Jonson refers wittily in the text.

By this time Jonson had returned to the Anglican church. Once again Drummond records an anecdote which vividly captures Jonson's personality: "after he was reconciled with the Church & left of to be a recusant at his first communion jn token of true Reconciliation, he drank out all the full cup of wyne."

In autumn 1612 Jonson traveled to France as the tutor of Sir Walter Ralegh's son. Ralegh had been imprisoned in the Tower of London since 1603; there he had written his *History of the World,* assisted, as Jonson told Drummond, by "the best wits of England. . . . Ben himselfe had written a peice to him of ye punick warre which he altered and set in his booke." Jonson may not have been the best choice for the position of tutor, however. His predilection to drink is well known; Drummond said it was "one of the Elements, jn which he liveth." One night in Paris the younger Ralegh got his tutor dead drunk and had him drawn through the streets stretched out on a cart, calling out at every corner that here was "a more Lively jmage of ye Crucifix then any they had." In seventeenth-century Catholic Paris, such blasphemy could have caused serious trouble. Fortunately nothing came of the incident.

We also know of other more edifying episodes during Jonson's stay in France. Records have survived showing that Jonson was present at a theological debate between a Catholic and a Protestant on the subject of the Real Presence. The topic was of great interest to Jonson, who had twice converted; given his scholarly interests he must have been familiar with both sides of the issue. (Drummond rather snidely records his opinion that Jonson was "for any religion as being versed jn both.") Jonson's interest in theological matters is also shown in the reference to the "humble Gleanings in Divinitie" listed among the poet's writings lost in the fire that destroyed his library in 1623.

While in France, Jonson also met the distinguished Cardinal Duperron, a powerful statesman who enjoyed a literary reputation in his own day. King James himself had expressed interest in Duperron's translations of Virgil. Jonson, however, was not impressed. When the cardinal showed his verses to Jonson, he was told that "they were naught."

Jonson was back in England by 29 June 1613; in the "Execration upon Vulcan" he mentions that he witnessed the burning of the Globe, which took place on that date. Jonson wrote two minor pieces, *The Irish Masque* and *A Challenge at Tilt,* for the next Christmas season at court, for which Campion wrote the principal masque. The annual festivities were dominated by another wedding—the notorious marriage of Frances Howard, Countess of Essex, to Robert Carr, Earl of Somerset.

By the fall of 1614 Jonson had written for the Lady Elizabeth's Men the last of his comedies that ranks among his best works: *Bartholomew Fair.* The play was first performed at the Hope, a bear-baiting pit that doubled as a theater, on 31 October, and then at Whitehall the next day.

Bartholomew Fair is remarkable among Jonson's comedies for its relaxation of censoriousness. The tension between the comic spirit of delight in misrule and the satirist's passion for punishing disorder is here resolved in favor of the comic spirit to an extent unmatched in any of the earlier comedies. Although *Bartholomew Fair* abounds in unsavory characters—thieves, whores, cheats, fools, and even poetasters—the play's punishments are mainly reserved for its authority figures, who foolishly try to correct the "enormities" of the fair without first learning self-control. Parallel to the humbling of authority that occurs in the action of the play is the more accommodating stance that Jonson takes toward his audience. The inflexible elitism of the address "TO THE READER IN ORDINAIRIE" preceding the 1611 quarto of *Catiline* is replaced by a much more obliging attitude in the induction to *Bartholomew Fair.* There the author propounds "certaine Articles" of agreement between his audience and himself, a covenant whereby each side undertakes to fulfill certain conditions for the common good. For his part Jonson promises to try to please everyone in the audience, including the "grounded Iudgements" of the pit, as well as the more refined and educated hearers.

Yet Jonson does not abandon his critical principles in the play. The induction emphasizes his continued realistic emphasis: "Hee is loth to make Nature afraid in his *Playes,* like those that beget *Tales, Tempests,* and such like *Drolleries.*" Jonson's impercipience to the glories of Shakespearean romance is sometimes embarrassing, but it derives from the same activity of ruthless critical judgment that is so essential to his artistic achievement. Jonson frequently invokes "truth to nature" as a criterion of his comedy, but Jonsonian "realism" is fundamentally satirical; the image reflected in the glass of Jonsonian comedy is never flattering. This is especially true in *Bartholomew Fair,* even though the would-be correctors of social mores, whose roles are analogous to those of the satirist figures in the comical satires, are singled out for particular abuse. The activities of the fair which the authority figures try unsuccessfully to curb are never sentimentalized in the play. On the contrary, the play's imagery and action unsparingly indicate the animality of human activity at the fair: eating, drinking, copulating, fighting, urinating, sweating, and vomiting—all the indignities of the body dominate the language of *Bartholomew Fair.*

The scene of the play is the annual fair held at Smithfield on St. Bartholomew's Day. Thither come people from every level of society, from the "Bartholomew-birds" hawking their shoddy wares and rotten gingerbread, selling roast pig and ale, stealing purses, and procuring whores, to the gentlefolks who come to eat, drink, and be amused. The plot involves a number of separate actions that interweave and crisscross; no one of

Costume designs by Inigo Jones for Welsh dancers in For the Honor of Wales, *the revised version of* Pleasure Reconciled to Virtue, *for which Jonson wrote a new antimasque set in Wales (from Stephen Orgel and Roy Strong,* Inigo Jones, *1973)*

them is dominant. The lack of focus on a single action might seem to be a relaxation of Jonson's critical standards; however, the management of the plot is exceptionally skillful. In fact the plot seems the least contrived of all Jonson's comedies.

Into the world of the play come two notable opponents of saturnalia, Adam Overdo, a justice of the peace whose zeal in correcting "enormities" is exceeded only by his incompetence; and Zeal-of-the-Land Busy, a Puritan "rabbi." The character of Busy continues the attack on the Puritans that Jonson began in *The Alchemist.* As in the earlier play, the Puritans are depicted as utter hypocrites. *Bartholomew Fair,* however, presents a kind of defense of the theater by Jonson when Busy tries to overthrow the puppet show, which he attacks in the same terms that the Puritans used in attacking the stage. Jonson does nothing to defend the dignity of the theater; the puppet show is a witless farce in doggerel verse. Busy is confuted simply by being made ridiculous in confronting a puppet. The Puritan attack on the stage, although dangerous in its factiousness, is shown as merely silly.

The action of the fair may be mindless, greedy, and even vicious, but those who attempt to suppress it are made to look more foolish than

Costume designs by Inigo Jones for masquers in Time Vindicated. *The figure at top left, wearing a cat mask, is the Curious personified while the other figures represent the Eyes (bottom left), the Ears (bottom right), and the Nose (top right) (from Stephen Orgel and Roy Strong,* Inigo Jones, *1973).*

those who come to enjoy it. The spirit of the play may be summed up in the rebuke addressed to Overdo at the close of the play: "remember you are but *Adam,* Flesh, and blood! you haue your frailty, forget your other name of Ouerdoo, and inuite vs all to supper." Yet Jonson does not encourage complacency in his audience. The frenetic animality that characterizes the fair is also associated with the larger world beyond the fair and beyond the playhouse in the last words of the play: "wee'll ha' the rest o' the *Play* at home."

The success of *Bartholomew Fair* was followed a few months later by the success of the masque *The Golden Age Restored,* which was performed at Court on Twelfth Night 1615 and again two days later. The next year Jonson produced another successful masque at Court, *Mercury Vindicated from the Alchemists,* first performed on 1 January and repeated on 6 January 1616 because of a quarrel over precedence among the foreign ambassadors in attendance.

Jonson's next play, *The Devil Is an Ass* (1616), was followed by Jonson's absence from the stage for almost ten years. Yet *The Devil Is an Ass* is more often grouped with the plays that followed it than with those that preceded it. Dryden characterized Jonson's late plays as "dotages," and it is undeniable that they display less rigor in the management of the plot, difficulty in maintaining a consistency of tone, and, in the last plays especially, a weakening of the author's imaginative powers betrayed by a blunting of the wit of Jonson's language and a tendency to recycle old conceits. Yet the late plays are of interest in their experimentation.

A notable feature of all the late plays, from *The Devil Is an Ass* to *A Tale of a Tub* (1633), is their employment of older conventions of the Elizabethan stage. Thus *The Devil Is an Ass* is a reworking of the Elizabethan devil play; *The Staple of News* (1626) employs some morality-play elements; *The New Inn* (1629) is a thoroughly romantic comedy; *A Tale of a Tub,* whether or not it is a revision of an early original, is a lighthearted rustic comedy; and the two fragments *The Sad Shepherd* and *The Fall of Mortimer* are a pastoral involving Robin Hood and an English history play. The only one of the late plays which is not marked by a revival of "un-Jonsonian" popular Elizabethan conventions is *The Magnetic Lady* (1632), which so consciously reworks the formulas of Jonson's middle period that it is almost a caricature of Jonsonian comedy.

It is interesting to note that this experimentation with older dramatic forms is often accompanied by a greater emphasis on love as a dramatic motive than in the earlier plays, and that romantic love becomes a more prominent theme in the later nondramatic poetry, as well. In the *Epigrams* and *The Forrest,* love as a theme was conspicuously absent, and Jonson had addressed this fact in *The Forrest* 1, "Why I Write Not of Love." In *The Underwood,* however, erotic love is a much more prominent theme than in the earlier verse collections.

The Devil Is an Ass shows Jonson's new interest both in earlier dramatic forms and in romantic love. The play inverts the conventions of the older devil plays as Jonson understood them. In the *Conversations with Drummond* Jonson told his host that "according to Comedia Vetus, jn England the divell was brought jn either w[t] one Vice or other, the Play done the divel caried away the Vice." In Jonson's play, however, a minor devil named Pug is shown to be no match for the shrewder wickedness of contemporary London. Thus Pug is returned to hell on the back of the Vice Iniquity, who delivers the moral in doggerel rhyme:

> The *Diuell* was wont to carry away the euill;
> But, now, the Euill out-carries the *Diuell.*

The villain who most notably "out-carries the devil" is Meercraft, a "projector" whose brain teems with insubstantial money-making schemes. Meercraft's plans especially appeal to the gull Fitzdottrel, who, like the gulls in *The Alchemist,* is utterly carried away by the prospect of infinite wealth. Fitzdottrel is especially attracted to a land-reclamation scheme which will make him the "Duke of Drownedland." Since there were actual land-reclamation projects in England at the time, and because Jonson's contemporaries were quick to identify characters satirized on the stage with actual men, he was accused of libel, and "the King desyred him to conceal" the offending passages. The discussion of this trouble in the *Conversations with Drummond* is vague, and there is no evidence that Jonson suppressed any part of the original play.

Besides being a gull like Sir Epicure Mammon in *The Alchemist,* Fitzdottrel is also a jealous but sordid husband, like Corvino in *Volpone.* Wittipol, a London gallant, becomes enamored of Mrs. Fitzdottrel and courts her with verses that also appear in *The Underwood* 2, "A Celebration of Charis." Although Wittipol's intentions are at first merely carnal, he comes to esteem Mrs. Fitzdottrel and at the end of the play places her honor ahead of his own desires.

Some scholars have speculated that the courtships dramatized in *The Devil Is an Ass* and "A Celebration of Charis" are based on an actual affair that Jonson engaged in at this time. The "Charis" lyrics especially seem to suggest a basis in fact, since the poet there describes himself, with comic detachment, as an aging lover:

> *Cupids* Statue with a Beard,
> Or else one that plaid his Ape,
> In a *Hercules*-his shape.

The year of *The Devil Is an Ass,* 1616, also saw two other important events in Jonson's career. The first was King James's grant to Jonson of a life pension of one hundred marks a year in recognition of his service to the king. Jonson thereby became the first poet laureate in English history. The second event was the publication of *The Workes of Benjamin Jonson,* a folio collection prepared for the press by the author himself. The collection contains nine plays (*Every Man in His Humour, Every Man out of His Humour, Cynthia's Revels, Poetaster, Sejanus, Volpone, Epicoene, The Alchemist,* and *Catiline*), the two verse collections *Epigrams* and *The Forrest,* and most of Jonson's masques and entertainments from 1604 to 1616. The absence of *Bartholomew Fair* is puzzling; otherwise it is clear that Jonson has selected his best works to date, those that most clearly present the image of himself and of his art that he wished to transmit to his contemporaries and to posterity.

Some of the works in the folio, such as the nondramatic poetry, were published for the first time in the collection. Others which had been previously printed were revised, revision being especially heavy in the earlier works. Thus *Every Man in His Humour* was wholly rewritten, with its scene transferred from Florence to London and the characters' Italianate names accordingly Anglicized. The references to the controversy surrounding the original ending to *Every Man out of His Humour* were tactfully suppressed. The "Apologeticall Dialogue" at the end of *Poetaster,* which had been suppressed by the government, was restored, as were several passages in *Cynthia's Revels* that were omitted from the quarto. Blasphemous oaths in the comedies were toned down, and the bad-tempered address "TO THE READER IN ORDINAIRIE" which had preceded *Catiline* was omitted from the folio.

The publication of plays from the professional stage in a folio collection with the haughty title "Works" was a bold move, and Jonson was ridiculed by some of his contemporaries for daring to call his plays works. However, the publication of the folio was the logical culmination of Jonson's career up to this point. Ever since the 1600 publication of *Every Man out of His Humour* in a quarto "Containing more than hath been Publikely Spoken or Acted," Jonson had welcomed the opportunity to present his plays to the reading public. The measure of control thus effected over his texts, their freedom from the vagaries of dramatic performance, the recognition of literate men—all of these seem to have appealed greatly to Jonson. For Jonson insisted that his plays be regarded as literature, as true "poems," and he liked to emphasize his own distance from the practice of most of his contemporaries in the theater. Jonson may have coined the word "playwright"; it is certain that he only uses it disparagingly. His preferred term for himself is "poet" and for his plays, "poems."

Jonson seems always to have harbored some ambivalence toward the theater as an artistic medium. The famous "Ode to Himself" prompted by the failure of *The New Inn* in 1629, which begins "Come leaue the lothed stage," is only the most extreme manifestation of this ambivalence. In 1616 when he was at the height of his success, Jonson withdrew from writing plays for almost ten years. In the folio he had called the *Epigrams* "the ripest of my studies." Now that he had the leisure and the opportunity, thanks to his pension from the king, he chose to devote himself mainly to nondramatic poetry. There is one possible exception to this trend, however. There is some evidence that in 1617 or thereabouts Jonson contributed a scene or two to a play by John Fletcher called *The Bloody Brother,* which was later revised by Philip Massinger and known by the title of *Rollo, Duke of Normandy.* No performance before 1630 is known, and the evidence of Jonson's involvement is hardly conclusive.

His work as a writer of court masques continued, however. The Christmas season of 1616-1617 brought two masques to write. *Christmas, His Masque,* a burlesque mumming, was the slighter of the two. For the Twelfth Night revels Jonson wrote the more elaborate *The Vision of Delight.* Among the guests attending the performance of *The Vision of Delight* was Pocahontas,

Costume designs by Inigo Jones for masquers in The Fortunate Isles and Their Union: *(left to right) Johphiel, the Airy Spirit; Scogan, based on poet Henry Scogan (1361?-1407); Skelton, based on poet John Skelton (1460?-1529); and Merefool, the Rosicrucian (from Stephen Orgel and Roy Strong,* Inigo Jones, *1973)*

who was visiting London at that time. The very next month brought the performance of yet another masque, *Lovers Made Men,* presented at the home of Lord James Hay for the entertainment of the French ambassador, and presided over by Jonson's longtime patron, the countess of Bedford.

The next year's Twelfth Night festivities marked an important occasion of state, the first appearance of Prince Charles, the new Prince of Wales, as a principal masquer. Jonson's offering for the occasion, *Pleasure Reconciled to Virtue,* is now recognized as one of his finest masques. However, the original performance was a disaster, so much so that King James lost his temper and shouted at the masquers. Illness had prevented Queen Anne from attending the Twelfth Night revels. For that reason and in order to try to make good the original failure of his debut, Prince Charles decided to repeat the masque on Shrovetide. Jonson revised the text, replacing the original antimasque with one set in the Welsh mountains, and giving the masque a new name, *For the Honor of Wales.* However, this performance, on 17 February, was hardly more pleasing than the first.

In the summer of 1618 Jonson set out on foot for Scotland, no small feat for the middle-aged and overweight poet. There he was received with great honor. John Taylor the "Water-Poet," who undertook a journey to Scotland on foot shortly after Jonson, met him in Leith in August and found him "amongst Noble-men and Gentlemen that knowes his true worth, and their owne honours, where with much respectiue loue he is worthily entertained." On 20 September Jonson was made a burgess and guild brother of the city of Edinburgh, and in October the city spent more than £221 on a banquet in his honor.

For a few weeks in late December 1618 or early January 1619 Jonson was the guest of the Scottish poet William Drummond of Hawthornden, whose record of his guest's remarks during the visit and of his own impressions of the man—"Certain Informations and maners of Ben Johnsons," which have come to be known to posterity as the *Conversations with Drummond*—are an invaluable source of information. Particularly interesting are the accounts of the works that Jonson was engaged in at that time, most of which have not survived (perhaps lost in the fire of 1623 that destroyed his library). These works include a pastoral called "The May Lord" in which noble ladies were to be represented allegorically, a description of his trip to Scotland, an apology for *Bartholomew Fair,* and a discourse written against Thomas Campion and Samuel Daniel defending couplets as "the bravest sort of Verses." We are also told "that he had ane jntention to perfect ane Epick Poeme jntitled Heroologia of the Worthies of [t]his Country, rowsed by fame, and was to dedicate it to his Country, it is all jn Couplets, for he detesteth all other Rimes."

Drummond described the character of his remarkable houseguest at the close of the *Conversations with Drummond,* revealing some annoyance with his proud and opinionated guest, whom he describes at times without any sympathy; yet the image of Jonson that emerges from the *Conversations with Drummond* is consistent with the view of him to be gained from his writing and the other known facts of his life: "he is passionately kynde and angry, carelesse either to gaine or keep, Vindicative, būt if he be well answered, at himself."

In July 1619 Jonson stayed at Christ Church College, Oxford, as the guest of his friend Richard Corbet, who became dean of Christ Church in 1620. During this stay the university granted him the honorary degree of master of arts in recognition of his learning.

The next few years saw a renewal of Jonson's activity as a masque writer after the hiatus occasioned by the trip to Scotland. On 7 January 1620 *News From the New World,* which anticipates *The Staple of News* in its satire of the fledgling news industry of Jacobean London, was performed at Court. In May the *Entertainment at Blackfriars* was performed at the house of William Cavendish, Earl of Newcastle, in celebration of the christening of Charles Cavendish, and in June *Pan's Anniversary* was performed at Court to celebrate the king's birthday.

In August and September 1621 *The Gypsies Metamorphosed* was produced. The original occasion of *The Gypsies Metamorphosed* was the entertainment of King James by his favorite, George Villiers, first Duke of Buckingham, and the masque is largely concerned with allusions to the Buckingham circle and the royal family, delivered through the dramatic device of a gypsy fortune-teller reading the palms of the distinguished members of the audience. The masque was a great success, and after its performance at the duke of Buckingham's residence on 3 September and at the home of his mother on 5 September, it was performed at Windsor in September, with minor revisions for the changed circumstances of production.

In October 1621 Jonson was nominated by warrant of reversion to the office of Master of the Revels. Under the provisions of the warrant the office would revert to Jonson upon the deaths of Sir George Buc and Sir John Astley, but Astley outlived Jonson, and nothing came of the nomination.

In January 1622 occurred the first performance of *The Masque of Augurs,* which was revised for another performance on 6 May of the same year. One of the most interesting features of this masque is the character of Vangoose, a "projector" like Meercraft, but a projector of masques. Vangoose's remarks about the masque form provide an inverse reflection of Jonson's own opinions. Thus his remarks about the antimasque—"de more absurd it be, and vrom de purpose, it be ever all de better"—emphasize Jonson's care to make his own antimasques contribute to the masque's main theme.

Time Vindicated to Himself and to His Honors, performed on 19 January 1623, shows Jonson once again venturing into personal satire, this time of the poet George Wither, who is lampooned in the figure of Chronomastix. Not all of the audience were pleased with the attack on Wither, but Jonson did not suffer for his boldness.

In October 1623 Jonson testified in court in connection with a dispute between Sir Walter Ralegh's widow and a London jeweller. At that time he gave Gresham College as his residence, which may indicate that he was a lecturer in rhetoric at that institution.

In the same month or possibly November, a fire broke out in Jonson's lodgings and destroyed his personal library. *The Underwood* 43, "An Execration upon Vulcan," lists a number of the items lost in the fire and thus provides valuable information about Jonson's literary activity in the years immediately preceding the fire. Thus we know that in addition to "twice-twelve-yeares stor'd up humanitie, / With humble Gleanings in Divinitie," Jonson had already composed his translation of

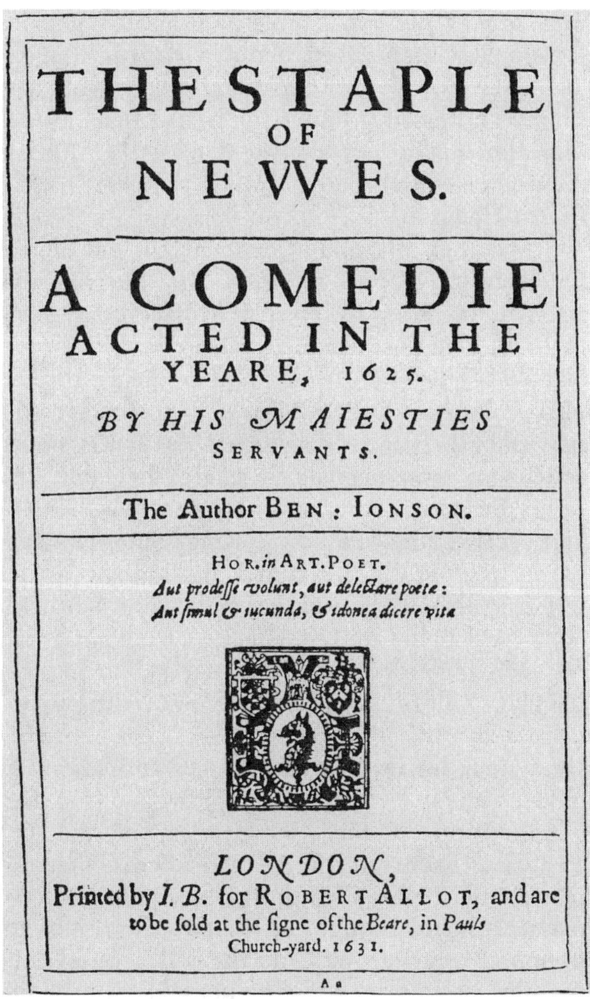

THE STAPLE
OF
NEWES.

A COMEDIE
ACTED IN THE
YEARE, 1625.

BY HIS MAIESTIES
SERVANTS.

The Author BEN: IONSON.

HOR. in ART. POET.
Aut prodesse volunt, aut delectare poetæ:
Aut simul & iucunda, & idonea dicere vitæ

LONDON,
Printed by *I. B.* for ROBERT ALLOT, and are
to be sold at the signe of the *Beare*, in *Pauls*
Church-yard. 1631.

A a

Interior title page, from the 1631 folio edition of volume 2 of Jonson's works, for the first printing of a play that was first produced by the King's Men in February 1626 (from C. H. Herford, Percy and Evelyn Simpson, eds., Ben Jonson, *volume 6, 1938)*

the *Ars Poetica,* including the apology for *Bartholomew Fair* mentioned in the *Conversations with Drummond*; a translation of John Barclay's *Argenis,* commissioned by the king; a verse account of his trip to Scotland; his English grammar; most of a history of the reign of Henry V, in which he was assisted by Richard Carew, Sir Robert Cotton, and Sir John Selden; and "parcels of a Play."

One of Jonson's best masques, *Neptune's Triumph for the Return of Albion,* was never performed due to a dispute between the French and Spanish ambassadors over precedence at the intended performance in January 1624. The masque celebrated the return of Prince Charles from his journey to Spain seeking the hand of the Infanta. By the next year Charles's return was old news and the prince was already betrothed to Henrietta Maria. Jonson salvaged what he could of the original composition and reworked it into *The Fortunate Isles and Their Union,* which was performed on 9 January 1625. Meanwhile a slighter piece, the *Masque of Owls,* was performed at Kenilworth on 19 August 1624.

The accession of Charles I to the throne in 1625 caused a six-year hiatus in Jonson's career as a masque writer. Jonson does not seem to have been as well liked by Charles as he had been by James. An undignified quarrel with Inigo Jones, who was admired by Charles, can only have worsened his situation at Court. Jonson would only receive two masque commissions from the new king. The loss of steady royal patronage may have contributed to Jonson's decision to return to the stage, although we know that he had already composed "parcels of a Play" in 1623. Whatever the motivating circumstances, *The Staple of News* was acted by the King's Men at the Blackfriars in February 1626.

The plot of *The Staple of News* centers around the efforts of Pennyboy junior, a prodigal heir, to gain the hand of the Lady Pecunia, the "*Infanta* of the *Mines,*" who during much of the play is a personification of wealth. Pennyboy junior hearkens back to Quicksilver in *Eastward Ho,* in that both characters are types of the prodigal-son figure so common in Tudor drama.

A prominent rival of Pennyboy's for the hand of Pecunia is Cymbal, the master of the Staple of News. The Staple is portrayed as "a weekly cheat to draw mony," much like the intrigues of Volpone and Mosca and of Subtle and Face. However, the satire of the Staple was highly topical; the publication of news sheets was a recent development, and Jonson's satire touches specific individuals, most notably Nathaniel Butter, who published a news sheet founded in 1622, and is alluded to in the figure of Nathaniel the stationer, as well as in the frequent references to the "buttering" of the news.

The play was not a great success with the public. In addition to the intended personal references, others were read into the play; for instance, Lady Pecunia was wrongly interpreted as a representation of the Infanta of Spain. Accordingly Jonson included a special address to the readers prefixed to act 3, in which he complained of the "sinister" interpretation put upon the play.

From this point on, the life of Jonson took a decidedly downward turn. In 1628 the poet suffered a paralytic stroke which rendered him "A *Bed-rid* Wit" for the rest of his life. Some solace

THE
NEVV INNE.
OR,
The light Heart.
A COMOEDY.
As it was neuer acted, but most negligently play'd, by some, the Kings Seruants.
And more squeamishly beheld, and censured by others, the Kings Subiects.
1629.
Now, at last, set at liberty to the Readers, his Maties Seruants, and Subiects, to be iudg'd.
1631.
By the Author, *B. Ionson.*
Hor. . . . . *me lectori credere mallem:*
Quam spectatoris fastidia ferre superbi.

LONDON,
Printed by *Thomas Harper*, for *Thomas Alchorne*, and are to be sold at his shop in Pauls Church-yeard, at the signe of the greene Dragon.
MDCXXXI.

The title page for the 1631 octavo edition of the Jonson comedy unsuccessfully performed by the King's Men in early 1629 expresses the playwright's anger at both the actors and the audience (Anderson Galleries auction catalogue, sale number 2077, 20-21 May 1926).

came in September of the same year with his appointment as "chronologer" or historian to the city of London, with a pension of one hundred nobles per year. There is no evidence that Jonson ever performed any services for the city in his capacity as chronologer, and in 1631 the city fathers ordered his wages frozen "vntill he shall have presented vnto this Court some fruits of his labours in that his place." Jonson's attitude toward the city's action is expressed in a letter to the earl of Newcastle: "Yesterday the barbarous Court of Aldermen haue withdrawne their Chander-ly Pension, for Veriuice, & Mustard." Eventually the king intervened on Jonson's behalf, and the pension was restored in 1634.

Less than four weeks after his appointment as chronologer, on 26 October 1628, Jonson was examined by the attorney-general, Sir Robert Heath, about his knowledge of some verses praising John Felton, who had assassinated the duke of Buckingham on 23 August. Jonson testified that he had seen the verses lying on a table in Sir Robert Cotton's house. He denied knowledge of their authorship but said that he had heard them attributed to Zouch Townly, a scholar and divine who later wrote two poems in praise of Jonson. Jonson was then asked about a dagger that he had given Townly. He explained that Townly had simply expressed a liking for it and that he had therefore made him a present of it. For Jonson the matter ended there. Townly, however, had to flee to Holland.

Another disappointment befell Jonson on the heels of his stroke when *The New Inn* was acted by the King's Men at the Blackfriars, early in 1629. The performance was a disaster. Jonson blamed the actors as well as the audience for the play's failure, and the title page of the octavo edition published in 1631 reads, "As it was neuer acted, but most negligently play'd, by some, the Kings Seruants. And more squeamishly beheld, and censured by others, the Kings Subiects." Apparently some kind of personal allusion was detected in the original name of the chambermaid, "Cis," which the author changed to "Prue." But no such busy deciphering is needed to explain the play's failure. Jonson's experiment with romantic comedy pushes the conventions of the genre beyond their limits. The last scene's revelations of hidden identity occur too rapidly and too frequently; indeed the awkwardness of the last scene has been interpreted as evidence that the play should be read ironically, as a parody of romantic comedy, though the evidence for this interpretation is not strong. And the collection of "humorous" characters who frequent the Inn of the Light Heart are drawn without much vitality; their dialogue is utterly void of the rapid fire that had enlivened the earlier comedies.

A more interesting feature of the play is the portrait of Lovel, the melancholy "Platonic" lover. In the earlier works love is not treated as a serious topic, and Jonson had scoffed at the conventional poses of unrequited love. In *The New Inn,* however, Lovel is treated with great sympathy for his dignified perseverance in what seems to be a hopeless passion, and Jonson makes him quite eloquent in defining and defending the existence of love in a "court of love" at which he makes his address to his mistress. Lovel also gives an eloquent defense of true valor, a subject that Jonson had addressed in some of the early plays and in his nondramatic verse as well, but which seems to have especially interested him at this time of his life; it is also a major theme in his next play, *The Magnetic Lady.*

The public's rejection of *The New Inn* infuriated Jonson, who vented his wrath in the "Ode to Himself" beginning, "Come leaue the lothed

Costume design by Inigo Jones for a "glorious boasting lover" in Love's Triumph through Callipolis

stage," appended to the 1631 octavo edition of the play. After mercilessly attacking the public for what he perceived as its degraded taste, Jonson promised to sing the glories of King Charles. For his part, Charles granted Jonson a gift of one hundred pounds, and upon Jonson's request increased his yearly pension from one hundred marks to one hundred pounds; in addition the king granted Jonson an annual tierce of canary wine.

Another welcome sign of royal favor was Jonson's commission to write a masque with the architect Inigo Jones for the 1630-1631 Christmas season. On 9 January 1631 *Love's Triumph through Callipolis* was performed, and on 22 February 1631 its companion piece, *Chloridia.* Collaboration between the two antipathetic artists was not easy. Although the two men had worked together harmoniously twenty-five years earlier, they had become estranged by the middle of James's reign. Thus in the *Conversations with Drummond* Jonson had several times expressed his dislike of Jones. Jones was now at the height of his career and of his powers, while Jonson was clearly on the decline, both artistically and in terms of his position at court. The texts of *Love's Triumph* and *Chloridia* suggest that Jonson was forced to relinquish much of the control over the masques that he had previously exercised. Spectacle clearly predominates over poetry in *Love's Triumph,* with its bare lists of names, and in *Chloridia,* with its elaborate antimasque containing eight separate "entries." The quarrel between Jones and Jonson came to a head in 1630 with the publication of *Love's Triumph.* Jonson included Jones's name on the title page but gave priority to his own, which angered Jones. Jonson's response was to attack Jones in verse with "An Expostulation with Inigo Jones," and two lesser pieces, "An Epigram of Inigo Jones" and "To Inigo Marquis Would-be." Jones's influence at court, however, worked against Jonson, and the poet was not commissioned to write a masque for the next Christmas season. In fact, Jonson would never write another court masque.

In 1631 Jonson decided to publish a second volume of his works. Three plays—*Bartholomew Fair, The Devil Is an Ass,* and *The Staple of News*—were printed before the project was abandoned. The printer, John Beale, treated the texts carelessly, and Jonson expressed his annoyance with "the lewd printer" in a letter to the duke of Newcastle: "My Printer, and I, shall afford subiect enough for a Tragi-Comoedy. for wth his delayes and vexation, I am almost become blind. . . ." The stock that was printed eventually was incorporated into the posthumous 1640 collected works.

By October 1632 Jonson had completed *The Magnetic Lady,* a play which consciously hearkens back to the triumphs of the early and middle comedies in its emphasis on "humours." The Boy who appears in the play's induction introduces the play with a speech emphasizing Jonson's consciousness that his career is almost at an end: "The *Author,* beginning his studies of this kind, with *every-man in his Humour,* and after, *every man out of his Humour:* and since, continuing in all his *Playes,* especially those of the *Comick* thred, whereof the *New-Inne* was the last, some recent humours still, or manners of men, that went along with the times, finding himselfe now neare the close, or shutting up of his Circle, hath phant'sied to himselfe, in *Idæa*, this *Magnetick Mistris*."

The play concerns the machinations of a number of suitors for the hand of the well-dowried Placentia, the niece of Lady Loadstone. Also present at the house is Polish, Lady Loadstone's parasite, and her daughter Pleasance, Lady Loadstone's waiting woman. Complications arise first when Placentia goes into labor and gives birth to a baby boy, and second when it is revealed to the audience, though not to all of the characters, that Pleasance is actually Placentia and vice versa, the two having been switched in their cradles when infants. Meanwhile a valiant captain, Ironside, displays the meaning of true valor by refusing to quarrel over an empty cause with Sir Diaphanous Silkworm, and Compass, the friend of Lady Loadstone and in many respects the hero of the play, struggles to thwart the villain of the piece, the usurer Sir Moth Interest, and his accomplice Bias, in their efforts to obtain Placentia's inheritance. The play ends with Compass married to "Pleasance," the real Placentia; Ironside betrothed to Lady Loadstone; and Needle, the father of the illegitimate child, betrothed to "Placentia," that is, the real Pleasance.

The character of Compass is akin to Crites in *Cynthia's Revels* and Horace in *Poetaster,* in that he is Jonson's spokesman and seems in some respects to be an idealized portrait of the author. Of himself he says,

> You know I am a Scholler,
> And part a Souldier; I have beene imployed,
> By some the greates States-men o' the kingdome,
> These many yeares: and in my time convers'd
> With sundry humors. . . .

His rule as spokesman is most clearly seen in his elaborate descriptions of the other characters in the play, which read like analogues in verse to the prose "characters" of *Every Man out of His Humour*.

Some trouble occurred during the play's first performance, when Sir Henry Herbert, the Master of the Revels, objected to profane oaths delivered on the stage. When Herbert accused the players, they at first blamed the script but eventually admitted that they had added the offending matter themselves.

Perhaps this episode, following upon what Jonson perceived as a negligent treatment of *The New Inn,* caused a rift between Jonson and the King's Men. Whatever the cause Jonson's next play, *A Tale of a Tub,* was performed by their rivals, Queen Henrietta's Men, at the Cockpit in May of 1633. On 14 January 1634 the play was presented at court, where it was "not likte," according to Sir Henry Herbert.

A Tale of a Tub presents unusual textual difficulties. Scholars are divided over the question of whether the play is Jonson's reworking of an original version composed in the 1590s or a composition of 1633 incorporating deliberate archaisms and possibly incorporating some passages composed earlier. The text of the play reveals striking stylistic differences, which seem to suggest different strata of composition. In addition the play is set in the reign of Queen Mary, and there are a number of references to figures from the early Tudor period. This may indicate a certain nostalgia for a much earlier period; much depends upon whether the allusions would be intelligible to an audience of 1633.

Whether the play is early or late, Jonson was conscious of its unusual position in the context of his work. The play is mainly a light-hearted rural comedy based on the crisscrossing intrigues of a number of homely suitors for the hand of a country maid, Audrey. The self-deprecating tone of the prologue and of the Latin motto printed on the title page are unusual for Jonson and suggest that he did not regard his experiment in the play with a great deal of confidence.

Into this rural comedy Jonson introduced some personal satire of Inigo Jones. Sir Henry Herbert's records show that originally the play had included "Vitruvius Hoop," a character clearly intended to represent Jones; his part and an earlier version of "the motion of the tubb," which must have been a more scathing attack on Jones's work than that which survives in the play, were struck out at the instigation of the lord chamberlain, to whom Jones had appealed for redress. However, Jonson continued his attack on Inigo Jones in the character of In-and-in Medlay, a cooper who is called upon to prepare a masque for a rustic wedding. The other characters sometimes call him a joiner, with pointed emphasis; Jones had begun his career as a joiner. Medlay's main device in the masque, the motion of the tub, is a parody of the *machina versatilis* that Jones had designed for the *Masque of Queens*.

In May 1633, the month in which *A Tale of a Tub* was originally performed, *The King's Entertainment at Welbeck* was performed at the house of Jonson's friend and patron the duke of Newcastle. The king was pleased with the performance,

Costume design by Inigo Jones for Chloris in Chloridia *(from Stephen Orgel and Roy Strong,* Inigo Jones, *1973)*

and Jonson was commissioned to write another entertainment, *Love's Welcome at Bolsover,* to celebrate the king's visit to another Newcastle estate in July 1634. Once again Jonson introduced satire of Inigo Jones into a work, this time in the figure of the surveyor Coronell Vitruvius. Although Jonson's satire of Jones in *A Tale of a Tub* had not pleased the court the previous January, no offense seems to have been taken by the king and queen on this occasion. Shortly afterward Charles intervened on Jonson's behalf with the City of London authorities to see that Jonson was paid his pension as city chronologer.

Thereafter little is heard of Jonson before his death. No new plays or masques appeared, though Jonson left incomplete a pastoral play, *The Sad Shepherd,* and a mere fragment of another play, *Mortimer his Fall.* We do know that to the end of his life Jonson remained a sociable man. Although the paralytic stroke had put an end to Jonson's reign at the Apollo room of the Devil Tavern, which had replaced the Mermaid as the chief gathering place for the poet's circle of friends and admirers, who now styled themselves "the Tribe of Ben" in his honor, his chamber in Westminster continued to draw admiring visitors. Among the friends of Jonson's later years were Sir Kenelm Digby, who served as Jonson's literary executor, and his wife, Lady Venetia Digby; Lucius Cary, second Viscount Falkland; and the writers Thomas Carew, James Howell, and Richard Brome.

Ben Jonson died in Westminster on 6 August 1637. Although he had earned a considerable pension, the poet died intestate; the total value of his property was estimated at eight pounds, eight shillings, and ten pence. Jonson was buried on 9 August in Westminster Abbey, accompanied to his grave by a great crowd of mourners. In 1638 a volume of undistinguished commemorative verse, *Jonsonus Virbius,* was published. In addition, a subscription was organized to raise money for a monument, but the outbreak of the Civil War caused the project to be abandoned. Jonson's grave was marked only by a square flagstone on which was later carved "O rare Ben Jonson." In 1640 the second folio edition of his works, containing some published for the first time, was published posthumously.

Today, as in the seventeenth century, Ben Jonson's status as a major dramatist and poet seems well established and unlikely to be shaken, but appreciation of his work has varied with the vicissitudes of critical fashion. Since the eighteenth century it has been Jonson's misfortune inevitably to be compared to his great contemporary, Shakespeare, and, because Jonson's artistic commitments are so frequently at odds with Shakespeare's, the comparison has often been an odious one for Jonson, whose (in-)famous strictures against the romantic drama of his contemporaries, which include a few shots at specific plays of Shakespeare, brought the wrath of bardolatry upon his head in the nineteenth century. The twentieth century has seen a renewal of critical appreciation of Jonson. The publication of the monumental Oxford *Ben Jonson* has been a great stimulus to Jonson scholarship, and there have also been excellent considerations of Jonson's use of language, his social and ethical ideals, and his use of classical and native English literary traditions. The nondramatic poetry and the masques as well as the plays have received critical attention. No longer is Jonson seen as the author of a handful of good comedies and a few pretty lyrics. We are now able to appreciate the diversity of Jonson's achievement and his continued willingness to experiment with new literary forms.

Bibliographies:

Samuel A. Tannenbaum, *Ben Jonson: A Concise Bibliography* (New York: Privately printed, 1938) and Samuel A. Tannenbaum and Dorothy R. Tannenbaum, *Supplement to a Concise Bibliography of Ben Jonson* (New York: Privately printed, 1947); both republished as volume 4 of *Elizabethan Bibliographies* (Port Washington, N.Y.: Kennikat Press, 1967);

D. Heyward Brock and James M. Welsh, *Ben Jonson: A Quadricentennial Bibliography, 1947-1972* (Metuchen, N.J.: Scarecrow Press, 1974);

James Hogg, *Recent Research on Ben Jonson* (Salzburg, Austria: Institut für Englische Sprache und Literatur, 1978);

Walter D. Lehrman, Dolores J. Sarafinski, and Elizabeth Savage, *The Plays of Ben Jonson: A Reference Guide* (Boston: G. K. Hall, 1980);

David C. Judkins, *The Nondramatic Works of Ben Jonson: A Reference Guide* (Boston: G. K. Hall, 1982).

Biographies:

Marchette Chute, *Ben Jonson of Westminster* (New York: Dutton, 1953);

Rosalind Miles, *Ben Jonson: His Life and Work* (London & New York: Routledge & Kegan Paul, 1986).

Engraved portrait of Jonson by Robert Vaughan with verses by Abraham Holland, circa 1625 (Hope Collection, Oxford). This engraving was later used as the frontispiece for the 1640 quarto edition of Ben: Jonson's Execration against Vulcan *and the first volume of the 1640 folio edition of Jonson's works.*

References:

Judd Arnold, *A Grace Peculiar: Ben Jonson's Cavalier Heroes,* Penn State University Studies, no. 35 (University Park: Pennsylvania State University Press, 1972);

J. B. Bamborough, *Ben Jonson* (London: Hutchinson, 1970);

Bamborough, "The Early Life of Ben Jonson," *Times Literary Supplement,* 8 April 1960, p. 225;

Jonas A. Barish, "*Bartholomew Fair* and Its Puppets," *Modern Language Quarterly,* 20 (March 1959): 3-17;

Barish, *Ben Jonson and the Language of Prose Comedy* (Cambridge, Mass.: Harvard University Press, 1960);

Barish, "The Double Plot in *Volpone,*" *Modern Philology,* 51 (November 1953): 83-92;

Barish, *"Volpone": A Casebook* (London: Macmillan, 1972);

Barish, ed., *Ben Jonson: A Collection of Critical Essays* (Englewood Cliffs, N.J.: Prentice-Hall, 1963);

Anne Barton, *Ben Jonson, Dramatist* (Cambridge & New York: Cambridge University Press, 1984);

C. R. Baskervill, *English Elements in Jonson's Early Comedy,* Bulletin of the University of Texas, no. 178, Humanistic Series, no. 12; Studies in English, no. 1 (Austin: University of Texas Press, 1911);

Helena Watts Baum, *The Satiric and the Didactic in Ben Jonson's Comedy* (Chapel Hill: University of North Carolina Press, 1947);

L. A. Beaurline, *Jonson and Elizabethan Comedy: Essays in Dramatic Rhetoric* (San Marino, Cal.: Huntington Library, 1978);

Beaurline, "Volpone and the Power of Gorgeous Speech," *Studies in the Literary Imagination,* 6 (April 1973): 61-76;

Gerald Eades Bentley, *Shakespeare and Jonson. Their Reputations in the Seventeenth Century Compared,* 2 volumes (Chicago: University of Chicago Press, 1945);

David Bergeron, "Harrison, Jonson and Dekker: The Magnificent Entertainment for King James (1604)," *Journal of the Warburg and Courtauld Institutes,* 31 (1968): 445-448;

Normand Berlin, "Ben Jonson," in his *The Base String: The Underworld in Elizabethan Drama* (Rutherford, N.J.: Fairleigh Dickinson University Press, 1968), pp. 130-171;

Ralph W. Berringer, "Jonson's *Cynthia's Revels* and the War of the Theatres," *Philological Quarterly,* 22 (January 1943): 1-22;

David Bevington, "Shakespeare vs. Jonson on Satire," in *Shakespeare 1971: Proceedings of the World Shakespeare Congress, Vancouver, August 1971,* edited by Clifford Leech and J. M. R. Margeson (Toronto: University of Toronto Press, 1972), pp. 107-122;

William A. Blissett, Julian Patrick, R. W. Van Fossen, eds., *A Celebration of Ben Jonson* (Toronto: University of Toronto Press, 1973);

Daniel C. Boughner, *The Devil's Disciple: Ben Jonson's Debt to Machiavelli* (New York: Philosophical Library, 1968);

Fredson T. Bowers, "Ben Jonson the Actor," *Studies in Philology,* 34 (July 1937): 392-406;

J. F. Bradley and J. Q. Adams, *The Jonson Allusion-Book, 1597-1700* (New Haven: Yale University Press, 1922);

D. Heyward Brock, *A Ben Jonson Companion* (Bloomington: Indiana University Press, 1983);

Joseph A. Bryant, Jr., "*Catiline* and the Nature of Jonson's Tragic Fable," *PMLA,* 69 (March 1954): 265-277;

Bryant, *The Compassionate Satirist: Ben Jonson and His Imperfect World* (Athens: University of Georgia Press, 1972);

Bryant, "Jonson's Revision of *Every Man in His Humour,*" *Studies in Philology,* 59 (October 1962): 641-650;

O. J. Campbell, *Comicall Satyre and Shakespeare's Troilus and Cressida* (San Marino, Cal.: Huntington Library, 1938);

M. Castelain, *Ben Jonson: l'Homme et l'Oeuvre* (Paris: Librairie Hachette, 1907);

Fran D. Chalfant, *Ben Jonson's London: A Jacobean Placename Dictionary* (Athens: University of Georgia Press, 1978);

Larry S. Champion, *Ben Jonson's "Dotages": A Reconsideration of the Late Plays* (Lexington: University of Kentucky Press, 1967);

Mary Chan, *Music in the Theatre of Ben Jonson* (Oxford: Clarendon Press, 1980);

John Creaser, "*Volpone:* The Mortifying of the Fox," *Essays in Criticism,* 25 (July 1975): 329-356;

Joe Lee Davis, *The Sons of Ben: Jonsonian Comedy in Caroline England* (Detroit: Wayne State University Press, 1967);

Barbara Nielson De Luna, *Jonson's Romish Plot: A Study of "Catiline" and Its Historical Context* (Oxford: Clarendon Press, 1967);

Alan C. Dessen, *Jonson's Moral Comedy* (Evanston, Ill.: Northwestern University Press, 1971);

Aliki L. Dick, *Paedeia Through Laughter: Jonson's Aristophanic Appeal to Human Intelligence* (The Hague: Mouton, 1974);

Ian Donaldson, "Jonson and the Moralists," in *Two Renaissance Mythmakers,* edited by Alvin Kernan (Baltimore: Johns Hopkins University Press, 1977), pp. 146-164;

Donaldson, "Language, Noise and Nonsense: *The Alchemist,*" in *Seventeenth-Century Imagery: Essays on Uses of Figurative Language from Donne to Farquhar,* edited by Earl Miner (Berkeley: University of California Press, 1971), pp. 69-82;

Donaldson, *The World Upside Down: Comedy from Jonson to Fielding* (London: Oxford University Press, 1970);

Kevin J. Donovan, "The Final Quires of the Jonson 1616 *Workes*: Headline Evidence," *Studies in Bibliography,* 40 (1987): 106-120;

Douglas J. M. Duncan, *Ben Jonson and the Lucianic Tradition* (Cambridge: Cambridge University Press, 1979);

Richard Dutton, *Ben Jonson: To the First Folio* (Cambridge & New York: Cambridge University Press, 1983);

Mark Eccles, "Jonson and the Spies," *Review of English Studies,* 13 (October 1937): 385-397;

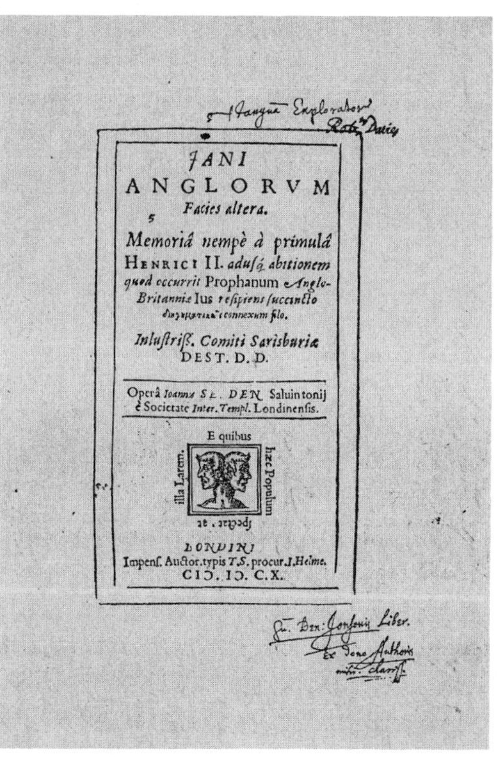
tanquam Explorator

JANI
ANGLORVM
Facies altera.

Memoriâ nempè à primulâ HENRICI II. adusq; abitionem quod occurrit Prophanum Anglo-Britannicæ Ius respiciens succinctò connexum filo.

Inlustriss. Comiti Sarisburiæ DEST. D.D.

Operâ Ioannis SELDENI Saluintonij è Societate Inter. Templ. Londinensis.

E quibus

illa Larem. hæc Populum spectat.

LONDINI
Impens. Auctor. typis T.S. procur. J. Helme.
CIϽ. IϽ. C.X.

Sum Ben: Jonsonij Liber. Ex dono Authoris amici clariss.

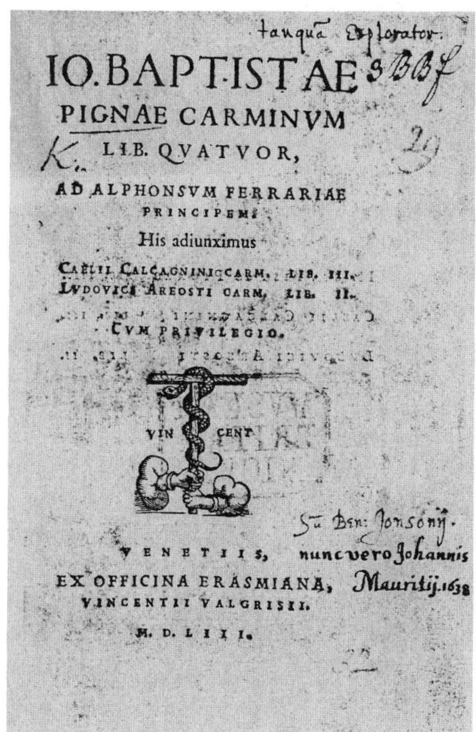
tanquã Explorator.

IO. BAPTISTAE PIGNAE CARMINVM LIB. QVATVOR,

AD ALPHONSVM FERRARIAE PRINCIPEM.

His adiunximus

CAELII CALCAGNINI CARM. LIB. III.
LVDOVICI AREOSTI CARM. LIB. II.

CVM PRIVILEGIO.

VIN CENT

Sum Ben: Jonsonij.

VENETIIS, nunc vero Johannis
EX OFFICINA ERASMIANA, Mauritij. 1638
VINCENTII VALGRISII.
M. D. LIII.

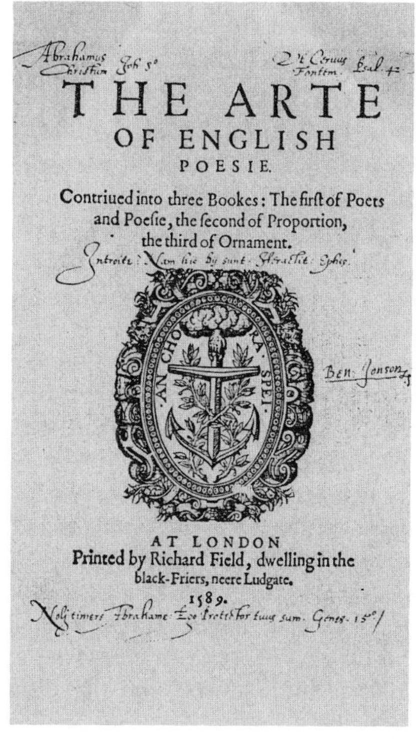
THE ARTE OF ENGLISH POESIE.

Contriued into three Bookes: The first of Poets and Poesie, the second of Proportion, the third of Ornament.

Ben: Jonson

AT LONDON
Printed by Richard Field, dwelling in the black-Friers, neere Ludgate.
1589.

Noli timere Abrahame Ego protector tuus sum. Genes. 15.

Title pages for three books from Jonson's library: (top) John Selden's Jani Anglorum Facies altera *(1610), later owned by Robert Davies, in which Jonson wrote his motto at top right ("as an explorer," from a line in Seneca's* Epistles *that may be translated as "I am accustomed as it were to go into the foreign camp not as a deserter to the enemy but as an explorer") and at bottom right Latin phrases that read "I am Ben Jonson's book. A gift from the author dear to me" (Anderson Galleries auction catalogue, sale number 1394, 29-30 January 1919); (bottom left) Giovanni Baptista Pigna's* Carminvm *(1553), with similar annotations by Jonson and note by a later owner (British Library); and George Puttenham's* The Arte of English Poesie *(1589), in which Jonson wrote quotations from John 8, Psalm 42, and Genesis 15 in the Latin Bible and from Hereclites of Ephesus (British Library)*

Eccles, "Jonson's Marriage," *Review of English Studies,* 12 (July 1936): 257-272;

T. S. Eliot, "Ben Jonson," in his *The Sacred Wood: Essay on Poetry and Criticism* (London: Methuen, 1920), pp. 95-111;

John J. Enck, *Jonson and the Comic Truth* (Madison: University of Wisconsin Press, 1957);

Willa McClung Evans, *Ben Jonson and Elizabethan Music* (Lancaster, Pa.: Lancaster Press, 1929);

R. A. Foakes and R. T. Rickert, eds., *Henslowe's Diary. Edited with Supplementary Material, Introduction and Notes* (Cambridge: Cambridge University Press, 1961);

Franz Fricker, *Ben Jonson's Plays in Performance and the Jacobean Theatre* (Bern: A. Francke, 1972);

W. Todd Furniss, "Ben Jonson's Masques," in *Three Studies in the Renaissance: Sidney, Jonson, Milton,* edited by B. C. Nangle (New Haven: Yale University Press, 1958), pp. 89-179;

Judith K. Gardiner, *Craftsmanship in Context: The Development of Ben Jonson's Poetry* (The Hague: Mouton, 1975);

Johann Gerritsen, "Stansby and Jonson Produce a Folio: A Preliminary Account," *English Studies,* 40 (1959): 52-55;

Brian Gibbons, *Jacobean City Comedy: A Study of Satiric Plays by Jonson, Marston, and Middleton* (Cambridge, Mass.: Harvard University Press, 1968);

Allan H. Gilbert, *The Symbolic Persons in the Masques of Ben Jonson* (Durham: Duke University Press, 1948);

D. J. Gordon, "Poet and Architect: The Intellectual Setting of the Quarrel Between Ben Jonson and Inigo Jones" and "*Hymenaei:* Ben Jonson's Masque of Union," in *The Renaissance Imagination,* edited by Stephen Orgel (Berkeley: University of California Press, 1975), pp. 77-101, 157-184;

Stephen J. Greenblatt, "The False Ending in *Volpone,*" *Journal of English and Germanic Philology,* 75 (January-April 1976): 90-104;

Thomas Greene, "Ben Jonson and the Centered Self," *Studies in English Literature,* 10 (Spring 1970): 325-348;

Sir W. W. Greg, "The Riddle of Jonson's Chronology," *Library,* 6 (March 1926): 340-347;

Greg, ed., *Jonson's "Masque of Gipsies" in the Burley, Belvoir and Windsor Versions: An Attempt at Reconstruction* (London: Oxford University Press, 1952);

Nicholas Grene, *Shakespeare, Jonson, Molière: The Comic Contract* (London: Macmillan, 1980);

Colburn Gum, *The Aristophanic Comedies of Ben Jonson: A Comparative Study of Jonson and Aristophanes* (The Hague: Mouton, 1969);

William Hazlitt, "On Shakespeare and Ben Jonson," in his *Lectures on the English Comic Writers* (London: Taylor & Hessey, 1819);

Ray L. Heffner, Jr., "Unifying Symbols in the Comedy of Ben Jonson," in *English Stage Comedy,* edited by W. K. Wimsatt, Jr., English Institute Essays, 1954 (New York: Columbia University Press, 1955), pp. 74-97;

G. R. Hibbard, ed., *The Elizabethan Theatre IV* (London & Basingstoke: Macmillan, 1974);

Peter Hyland, *Disguise and Role-Playing in Ben Jonson's Drama* (Salzburg, Austria: Institut für Englische Sprache und Literatur, 1977);

Gabriele B. Jackson, *Vision and Judgment in Ben Jonson's Drama* (New Haven: Yale University Press, 1968);

Bertil Johansson, *Religion and Superstition in the Plays of Ben Jonson and Thomas Middleton* (Cambridge, Mass.: Harvard University Press, 1950);

George Burke Johnston, *Ben Jonson: Poet.,* Columbia University Studies in English and Comparative Literature, no. 162 (New York: Columbia University Press, 1945);

Robert C. Jones, "The Satirist's Retirement in Jonson's 'Apologetical Dialogue,' " *ELH,* 34 (December 1967): 447-467;

Marie Thérèse Jones-Davies, *Inigo Jones, Ben Jonson et le Masque* (Paris: Didier, 1967);

R. J. Kaufman, ed., *Elizabethan Drama: Modern Essays in Criticism* (New York: Oxford University Press, 1961);

W. David Kay, "The Shaping of Ben Jonson's Career: A Re-examination of Facts and Problems," *Modern Philology,* 67 (February 1970): 224-237;

William R. Keast, ed., *Seventeenth-Century English Poetry: Modern Essays in Criticism,* revised edition (New York: Oxford University Press, 1971);

Alvin B. Kernan, *The Cankered Muse: Satire of the English Renaissance* (New Haven: Yale University Press, 1959);

Kernan, ed., *Two Renaissance Mythmakers: Christopher Marlowe and Ben Jonson,* Selected Papers from the English Institute, 1975-1976, new series 1 (Baltimore & London: Johns Hopkins University Press, 1977);

Arthur C. Kirsch, "Guarini and Jonson," in his *Jacobean Dramatic Perspectives* (Charlottesville: University Press of Virginia, 1972), pp. 7-24;

George Lyman Kittredge, "King James I and *The Devil Is an Ass*," *Modern Philology*, 9 (October 1911): 195-209;

David Klein, *The Elizabethan Dramatists as Critics* (New York: Philosophical Library, 1963);

L. C. Knights, *Drama and Society in the Age of Jonson* (London: Chatto & Windus, 1937);

Robert E. Knoll, *Ben Jonson's Plays: An Introduction* (Lincoln: University of Nebraska Press, 1964);

Louis Kronenberger, *The Thread of Laughter: Chapters on English Stage Comedy from Jonson to Maugham* (New York: Knopf, 1952);

Alexander Leggatt, *Ben Jonson: His Vision and His Art* (London: Methuen, 1981);

J. W. Lever, "Roman Tragedy: *Sejanus, Caesar and Pompey*," in his *The Tragedy of State* (London: Methuen, 1971), pp. 59-77;

Harry Levin, "Jonson's Metempsychosis," *Philological Quarterly*, 22 (July 1943): 231-239;

Eric Linklater, *Ben Jonson and King James: Biography and Portrait* (London: Cape, 1931);

Hugh Maclean, "Ben Jonson's Poems: Notes on the Ordered Society," in *Essays in English Literature from the Renaissance to the Victorian Age, Presented to A. S. P. Woodhouse*, edited by Millar MacLure and F. W. Watt (Toronto: University of Toronto Press, 1964), pp. 43-68;

Leah Marcus, "Present Occasions and the Shaping of Ben Jonson's Masques," *ELH*, 45 (June 1978): 201-225;

Arthur Marotti, "All About Jonson's Poetry," *ELH*, 39 (June 1972): 208-237;

Katherine Eisaman Maus, *Ben Jonson and the Roman Frame of Mind* (Princeton: Princeton University Press, 1984);

Scott McMillin, "Jonson's Early Entertainments: New Information from Hatfield House," *Renaissance Drama*, new series 1 (1968): 153-166;

John C. Meagher, *Method and Meaning in Jonson's Masques* (Notre Dame: University of Notre Dame Press, 1966);

Earl Miner, *The Cavalier Mode from Jonson to Cotton* (Princeton: Princeton University Press, 1971);

J. G. Nichols, *The Poetry of Ben Jonson* (New York: Barnes & Noble, 1969);

Allardyce Nicoll, *English Drama: A Modern Viewpoint* (New York: Barnes & Noble, 1968), pp. 56-74;

Robert Gale Noyes, *Ben Jonson on the English Stage, 1660-1776* (Cambridge, Mass.: Harvard University Press, 1935);

Stephen Orgel, *The Illusion of Power: Political Theater in the English Renaissance* (Berkeley: University of California Press, 1975);

Orgel, *The Jonsonian Masque* (Cambridge, Mass.: Harvard University Press, 1965);

Robert Ornstein, *The Moral Vision of Jacobean Tragedy* (Madison: University of Wisconsin Press, 1960);

John Palmer, *Ben Jonson* (New York: Viking, 1934);

George Parfitt, *Ben Jonson: Public Poet and Private Man* (New York: Barnes & Noble, 1977);

R. B. Parker, Introduction to *Volpone, or The Fox*, edited by Parker, The Revels Plays (Dover, N.H.: Manchester University Press, 1983);

Parker, "The Problem of Tone in Jonson's 'Comicall Satyrs,'" *Humanities Association Review*, 28 (Winter 1977): 43-64;

Edward B. Partridge, *The Broken Compass: A Study of the Major Comedies of Ben Jonson* (London: Chatto & Windus, 1958; New York: Columbia University Press, 1958);

Partridge, "The Symbolism of Clothes in Jonson's Last Plays," *Journal of English and Germanic Philology*, 56 (July 1957): 396-409;

Richard S. Peterson, *Imitation and Praise in the Poems of Ben Jonson* (New Haven & London: Yale University Press, 1981);

Norbert H. Platz, *Ethik und Rhetorik in Ben Jonsons Dramen* (Heidelberg: Winter, 1976);

Mario Praz, "Ben Jonson's Italy," in his *The Flaming Heart: Essays on Crashaw, Machiavelli, and Other Studies in the Relations Between Italian and English Literature from Chaucer to T. S. Eliot* (Garden City, N.Y.: Doubleday, 1958), pp. 168-185;

Dale B. Randall, *Jonson's Gypsies Unmasked: Background and Theme of "The Gypsies Metamorphos'd"* (Durham, N.C.: Duke University Press, 1975);

James D. Redwine, Jr., "Beyond Psychology: The Moral Basis of Jonson's Theory of Humour Characterization," *ELH*, 28 (December 1961): 316-334;

James A. Riddell, "Variant Title-Pages of the 1616 Jonson Folio," *Library*, series 6, 8 (June 1986): 152-156;

Andrew J. Sabol, ed., *A Score for "Lovers Made Men"* (Providence, R.I.: Brown University Press, 1963);

A. H. Sackton, *Rhetoric as a Dramatic Language in Ben Jonson* (New York: Columbia University Press, 1948);

Leo Salingar, "Comic Form in Ben Jonson: Volpone and the Philosopher's Stone," in *English Drama: Forms and Development: Essays in Honour of Muriel Clara Bradbrook,* edited by Marie Axton and Raymond Williams (Cambridge: Cambridge University Press, 1977), pp. 48-69;

James E. Savage, *Ben Jonson's Basic Comic Characters, and Other Essays* (Hattiesburg: University & College Press of Mississippi, 1973);

Evelyn Mary Simpson, "Jonson and Dickens: A Study in the Comic Genius of London," *Essays and Studies by Members of the English Association,* 22 (1944): 82-92;

C. J. Sisson, "Ben Jonson of Gresham College," *Times Literary Supplement,* 21 September 1951, p. 604;

Frederick W. Sternfeld, "Song in Jonson's Comedy: A Gloss on *Volpone,*" in *Studies in the English Renaissance Drama,* edited by Josephine W. Bennett, Oscar Cargill, and Vernon Hall, Jr. (New York: New York University Press, 1959), pp. 310-321;

Theodore A. Stroud, "Ben Jonson and Father Thomas Wright," *Journal of English Literary History,* 14 (December 1947): 274-282;

Claude J. Summers and Ted-Larry Pebworth, *Ben Jonson* (Boston: Twayne, 1979);

Summers and Pebworth, eds., *Classic and Cavalier: Essays on Jonson and the Sons of Ben* (Pittsburgh: University of Pittsburgh Press, 1982);

John Gordon Sweeney III, *Jonson and the Psychology of Public theater: "To Coin the Spirit, Spend the Soul"* (Princeton: Princeton University Press, 1985);

A. C. Swinburne, *A Study of Ben Jonson* (London: Chatto & Windus, 1889);

C. G. Thayer, *Ben Jonson: Studies in the Plays* (Norman: University of Oklahoma Press, 1963);

Mary Olive Thomas, ed., "Ben Jonson: Quadricentennial Essays," special issue of *Studies in the Literary Imagination,* 6 (April 1973);

Freda L. Townsend, *Apologie for Bartholomew Fayre: The Art of Jonson's Comedies* (New York: Modern Language Association of America, 1947);

Wesley Trimpi, *Ben Jonson's Poems: A Study of the Plain Style* (Palo Alto, Cal.: Stanford University Press, 1962);

Eugene M. Waith, "The Staging of *Bartholomew Fair,*" *Studies in English Literature,* 2 (Spring 1962): 181-195;

Geoffrey Walton, "The Tone of Ben Jonson's Poetry," in *Seventeenth-Century Poetry: Modern Essays in Criticism,* edited by William R. Keast (New York: Oxford University Press, 1962), pp. 193-214;

C. F. Wheeler, *Classical Mythology in the Plays, Masques, and Poems of Ben Jonson* (Princeton: Princeton University Press, 1938);

Glynne Wickham, "The Privy Council Order of 1597 for the Destruction of all London's Theatres," in *The Elizabethan Theatre I,* edited by David Galloway (Toronto: Macmillan of Canada, 1969), pp. 21-44.

Papers:

Several autograph manuscripts of Jonson have survived, including letters, inscriptions on books, a few poems, and the entire text of *The Masque of Queens.* These are located at the British Library; the Public Record Office, Kew; Dulwich College and Christ Church College, Oxford; Hatfield (among the Cecil papers); the Folger Shakespeare Library; Harvard; Princeton; and in private hands. They are listed in the Herford and Simpson edition of Jonson.

Sir Thomas Malory

(circa 1400-1410 - 14 March 1471)

Jeffrey Helterman
University of South Carolina

Works (1451-1470)

Manuscript: The only extant manuscript, a transcription in the hands of two scribes and dating from circa 1475, is the Winchester Manuscript in the British Library (Add. MS. 59678). Facsimile: *The Winchester Malory: A Facsimile*, edited by N. R. Ker, Early English Text Society, supplemental series no. 4 (London & New York: Oxford University Press, 1976).

First publication: *Thus endeth thys noble and Ioyous book entytled le morte Darthur* [colophon] (Westminster: Printed by William Caxton, 1485; facsimile, New York: Scolar Press, 1976).

Edition: *The Works of Sir Thomas Malory*, 3 volumes, edited by Eugène Vinaver (Oxford: Clarendon Press, 1947); third edition, revised by P. J. C. Field (Oxford: Clarendon Press, 1990).

The central issue of Malory scholarship and, therefore, of critical interpretation is whether the body of his work is a "hoole booke" or a collection of diverse tales centering in the Arthurian court. From the publication of William Caxton's edition in 1485 until this century, it was assumed that the body of work was a whole book that should be given the name of the last tale, "Le Morte Darthur." It was not until the discovery of the Winchester Manuscript of Malory by W. F. Oakeshott in 1934 that the unity of the work was seriously questioned. The manuscript, which predates Caxton, seems closer to Malory's original than does Caxton's printed text, based on another manuscript that is no longer extant. The Winchester Manuscript is a handwritten transcription, while the Caxton text, with a fulsome, rather moralistic preface, seems much more the *edition* of England's first printer. A study of the Winchester Manuscript by Eugène Vinaver, indicates that Caxton made changes in chapter rubrics and linkages that make more unity of these Arthurian tales than Malory intended. Vinaver's edition (1947), which has become the standard edition of the text, insists that the collection of tales be called *The Works of Sir Thomas Malory* and not be given *Le Morte Darthur* as an inclusive title. Criticism of Malory since Vinaver's edition, especially the collection of essays *Malory's Originality* (1964), has worked to reestablish the unity of Arthur's story, while making allowances for the anachronisms and inconsistencies (such as dead characters appearing in later tales). The resurfacing of the Winchester Manuscript reminds us that Malory's literary career ended right at the cusp that separated hand copying of manuscripts from printing. When Malory died (perhaps of the plague) in 1471, he could not have imagined any other transmission of his text than by the labor of hand copying. Given the length of the manuscript, one can imagine that very few such copies were made. Yet when, less than fourteen years later, Caxton set out to print the book, he guaranteed not only that Malory would be vilified for the so-called immorality of the popular book, but also, since Caxton set up as what we would now call a publisher rather than simply a printer, that the book would be launched by a preface that trumpeted the book's morality. "I . . . have doon sette it in enprynte to the entente that noble men may see and lerne the noble actes of chyvalrye. . . ."

Certainly the Winchester Manuscript is full of small inconsistencies which could well be explained by the checkered career of the author even if he were trying to write a unified book. Sir Thomas Malory, a knight of Warwickshire, was born between 1400 and 1410 to Sir John Malory and his wife, Philippa, and came into his father's holdings in 1433. He fought at Calais in 1436 and late in his life got involved on the side of Richard Neville, Earl of Warwick, in the Wars of the Roses. Warwick, as William Shakespeare records it in *Henry VI*, part 3 (circa 1590-1592), and *Richard III* (circa 1591-1592), was a traitor to Edward IV and went over to the Lancastrian side in 1468-1469, and, we may suppose, so did Malory. Malory was already a well-known ne'er-do-well, who had been accused of ambushing and at-

Sir John Malory and his wife, Philippa, the parents of Sir Thomas Malory. This sketch of a stained-glass window that was once in Grendon Church was first published in William Dugdale's Antiquities of Warwickshire Illustrated *(1656).*

tempting to murder Humphrey Stafford, Duke of Buckingham, in 1450, and of raping (or perhaps only seizing) the wife of another man *twice* in that same year, and of twice robbing the Cistercian Abbey of Blessed Mary Coombe in 1451. Over the years, beginning in 1451, Malory was jailed eight times, escaping twice by violent means. During this time Malory wrote most of what are now called his collected works. Prisoners then could use their own resources to fit themselves out well. Malory seems to have been fairly comfortable in prison, and while he was in Newgate (1460-1462) he had access to a nearby monastic library. In such turmoil, even if Malory intended to unify his works, it would seem unlikely that he could do it neatly. Even Shakespeare, only under the exigency of getting out a play in time, nodded often. He introduces Cassio as "a fellow damned in a fair wife," but in the text of *Othello* (1604), Cassio's wife disappears. So Malory, writing between brief bouts of freedom, is unlikely to be able to hold onto the details that would make the work seamless. It is also unlikely that the work, which comes to some nine hundred pages in the Oxford edition, was ever revised.

It is Malory who gave Arthur to England, who shaped the legend so that there could be Alfred, Lord Tennyson's *Idylls of the King* (1855-1885) and T. H. White's *Once and Future King* (1958). Arthur began as little more than a tribal chieftain. He was elevated by Geoffrey of Monmouth (who still claimed to be writing history) in his *Historia Regum Britanniae* (circa 1136) into a great and tragic hero whose queen is coveted by Mordred. The story grew to huge proportions through the vast prose romances, a "Holy Grail," a "Lancelot," a "Merlin," and a "Death of Arthur" written in France in the thirteenth century. Malory knew these French sources, but it is his vision that gives the Arthurian legend its mythic quality, as he tells of men (and women) who are doomed because they love each other too much. It is likely that Malory began his reworking of this material with a rather pedestrian handling of a story of Arthur at war, the book that turns up finally as book 5, the story of the war between Arthur and the Emperor Lucius. This book, different in kind and mood from the rest of Malory's output, is based on a native source, the fourteenth-century, alliterative *Morte Arthure*, rather than the French romances which support the rest of the work. In this tale Arthur and his knights seem much more warriors than courtiers, and there is little sense that Malory put his individual stamp on these characters.

From this handle into Arthurian story, Malory went back to the begetting of Arthur, and with the story of Uther Pendragon he began to explore the delicate lines that separate, and also link, love and hate. In a pattern that Arthur will follow with desperate results, Uther begets Arthur on Igrayne, the wife of his greatest enemy. It is by Merlin's sorcery that Uther is able to accomplish this act, and only by additional treachery is Arthur born in wedlock though conceived out of it. Such are the unpromising beginnings of a man who would be the greatest king in Christendom. Even as Arthur begins a pattern of virtuous activities, he also repeats his father's sin by begetting a child on Margawse, the wife of King Lot and also Arthur's half sister (she is Igrayne's daughter by her first husband), thereby adding incest to the stain of adultery. The product of this union, Mordred, will finally destroy Arthur and his kingdom.

Arthur, with the conspicuous aid of Merlin, becomes a victorious king and—in a theme that was picked up by Tennyson—the civilizer of the uncivilized. Arthur begins with a signal victory over the five kings, but Malory soon starts to pull at the threads that will destroy the fabric of knighthood everywhere. Arthur's early knights embrace chivalry with unbridled passion and rush off on a series of quests that lead to unmitigated disaster. Clearly, just having the right intentions is not enough. In one early episode three knights pursue three quests with the purpose of avenging the deaths of Gawain's dogs and Pellinor's horse. In the furious oneness of their determination to follow their quest, Pellinor ignores the needs of a wounded knight and his lady. When Pellinor returns from achieving his quest, only the knight's head remains, and the damsel ends up carrying it home. The unsuccored damsel turns out to be Pellinor's own daughter. Pellinor's son, Torre, ends up beheading a man through the ploy of the unexamined boon: the situation in which a knight pledges his word to an individual to do anything that person asks. Since a knight's word is an oath, to break it would be perjury. Under such constraints Arthur's knights commit many felonies because it is the honorable thing to do. The man whom Sir Torre kills is Abelleus, identified provisionally as the son of a cowherd. The third knight who rides out in this trio of quests is Sir Gawain, supposedly the best of the pre-Lancelotian knights. He beheads a lady by accident and is forced to carry the head with him when he returns from his quest. The toll for this vengeance over the deaths of some dogs and a horse is two beheaded men and one beheaded lady. Abelleus turns out to be the son of Pellinor, not the son of a cowherd but perhaps of a coward. Seeing these disastrous results, Arthur institutes a code of behavior which stresses always succoring ladies, damsels, gentlewomen, and widows—and never taking up battles in a wrongful cause. Now the real trouble starts. Up to this point mayhem is random and chaotic. Now it is institutionalized. From this point on, destructive and self-destructive acts will be carried out because they are the knightly thing to do.

By the time he gets to the story of Balin or "the Knight with Two Swords," Malory, a witness to, and probable participant in, the Wars of the Roses, finds his theme: divided loyalties, epitomized in the struggle of brother against brother. Balin, like Arthur, can draw a sword that no other man can, a sword that will go only to the best knight, but Balin is warned that with this sword he shall kill the man he loves most in the world. In the narrowest context (of the tale) the target of the sword is his brother Balan, who is slain in a mutual case of mistaken identity, but in one larger context Balin is also the one who will strike the Dolorous Stroke (of the Fisher-King legend) and so imperil all Western culture, and, on another backdrop, Balin's drawing this sword marks the beginning of the end of Arthur's world. Malory connects Balin's sword, which kills his brother Balan and delivers the Dolorous Stroke with the sword that Lancelot later uses to kill Gawain, a murder that does what not even the adultery of Lancelot and Guinevere can do: it separates Arthur and Lancelot. Malory uses a piece of syntactic maneuvering so that it appears that Lancelot will discover Balin's sword. In fact, it is Galahad who discovers Balin's sword, but the deliberate uncertainty of the locution (at various times—all in the future—Lancelot and Galahad will each be the Best Knight in the World) allows it to appear that Lancelot will have *this* sword and that with it he will kill Gawain: "there shall never man handyll thys swerde but the beste knyght of the worlde, and that shall be sir

Launcelot other ellis Galahad, hys sonne. And Launcelot with [t]hys swerde shall sle the man in the worlde that he lovith beste: that shall be sir Gawayne."

After the establishment of the code of courtesy and Arthur's signal victory over the Emperor Lucius, it appears that Arthur's world is headed for the order that is largely established in "The Tale of Sir Gareth." This tale of a youth growing into maturity—literally earning his spurs—is the kind of tale told of the two greatest knights, exclusive of Lancelot, of Arthurian legend. In the Middle High German romances, Parzifal and Tristram are polar opposites. Tristram is the prodigy, the child who knows everything—warfare, the code of the hunt, music, and love talk; and Parzifal is the bumpkin, a lad so benighted that he thinks knights in their armor are angels. Both are alike in one thing: they are the subjects of huge romances which record their upbringing. In "The Tale of Sir Gareth" we have the story of a young man growing up, but significantly, his hero/model, Lancelot, does not share the luxury of a Bildungsroman. Lancelot is, when we first see him, the best knight in the world, and he will continue to be plagued by this designation throughout Malory. Gareth, on the other hand, gets a chance to earn the right to use his name, Gareth, only when he gets to shed the mocking nickname, Bewmaines, given him by Sir Kay (Bewmaines, which means "fair hands," may refer to the fact that when Gareth is put to work as a kitchen knave he has fair, smooth hands rather than the red, rough hands of his supposed low-born origins). Though Gareth begins as a kitchen knave, he soon meets and defeats a series of different colored knights, one black, one blue, one red, and one green, and then a second red knight, the Red Knight of the Red Lands. It has been suggested that these defeated opponents make Gareth into an astrological hero who defeats the rainbow and then the sun (the Red Knight of the Red Lands, like the sun, grows stronger until noon) and then, in the conquest of the sisters Lyonette and Lyonesse, two representations of the moon (luna). There is no suggestion that Malory was aware of these origins in his sources, only that they are likely to be there.

Though it is not unlikely that the original of Gareth was some kind of conqueror of the heavens, a more satisfying explanation of the colored knights and the marriage with the moon is found in the language of alchemical lore, which would explain both the presence of the black knight and the existence of a second red knight. Medieval alchemical texts were usually allegorized so that metals and the reagents with which they were mixed were described as human beings, and the final act of the base metal/protagonist was a marriage. Each of the metals was identified with a heavenly body: copper was Venus, iron Mars, and silver the moon. The base metal would go through a series of struggles with the personified reagents. In such a system Gareth's meeting with the Black Knight would be the "mortifying" of the original reagent, and his confrontation with the Red Knight would be immersion into the "waters rubifying." In a pattern of alchemy, the defeat of the second red knight, the Red Knight of the Red Lands would signify "conclusion" of the alchemical process, the base metal becoming gold (in the Middle Ages gold was thought to be red, not yellow, in color).

Gareth's stint as a kitchen knave would increase the likelihood of this alchemical reading, since alchemical experiments were seen as literally "cooking things up," for which the Renaissance coined the term for the alchemical brew, *concoction*. Whether Malory would be aware of the alchemical imagery in his tale is uncertain, but it is worthy to note that early in his life, there was a flurry of interest in alchemy in England which led to the publication of English (in English, not merely Latin texts written in England) alchemical texts. What might have struck Malory about these texts was the inclusion of Chaucer, because of the Canon's Yeoman's Tale, as an alchemist. The alchemical reading of "The Tale of Sir Gareth" would reinforce the theme of the growth of the hero so that he can reclaim his name, earn his knighthood, and marry his bride. At the tournament which ends "The Tale of Sir Gareth," events are ordered so that all appears right in Arthur's world. On the three successive days of the tournament, the prize is won by the three best knights in the world with results that confirm both their greatness and their ranking. The third-best knight in the world, Lamerok, wins the first day, defeating thirty knights; the second-best knight in the world, Tristan, wins on the second, defeating forty knights; and, on the final day, the Best Knight in the World, Lancelot, wins, defeating fifty knights. All's right with Arthur's world, but we are only halfway through the book. At this point, Malory, a man living on the edge and a liegeman of the earl of Warwick, the real-life

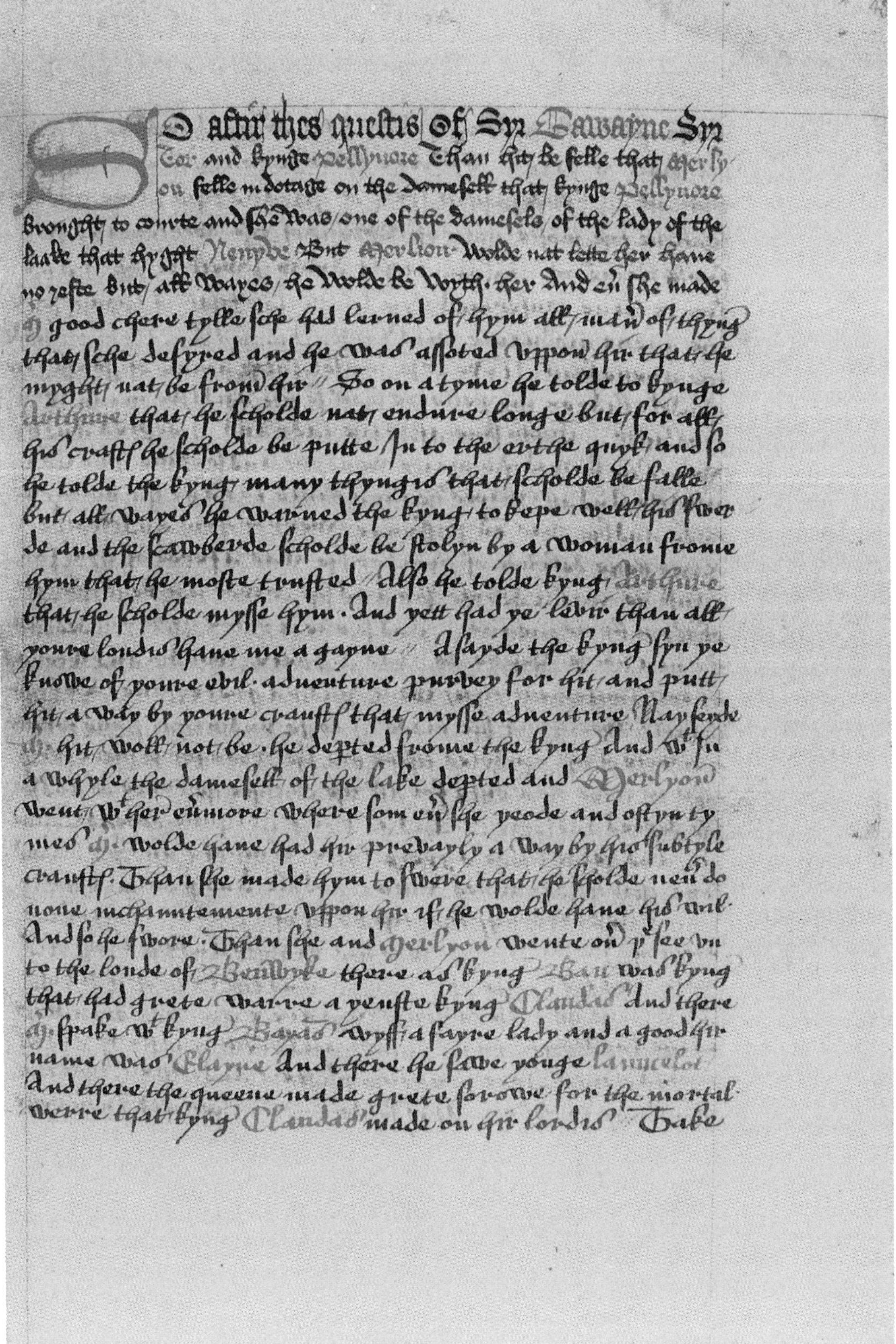
SO aftir thes questis of Syr Gawayne Syr
Tor and kynge Pellynore Than hit befelle that Merly
on felle in dotage on the damesell that kynge Pellynore
brought to courte and she was one of the damesels of the lady of the
lake that hyght Nenyve But Merlion wolde nat lette her have
no reste but all wayes he wolde be wyth her And ever she made
M. good chere tylle sche had lerned of hym all maner of thyng
that sche desyred and he was assoted uppon hir that he
myght nat be from hir // So on a tyme he tolde to kynge
Arthure that he scholde nat endure longe but for all
his craftes he scholde be putte in to the erthe quyk and so
he tolde the kyng many thyngis that scholde befalle
but all wayes he warned the kyng to kepe well his swer
de and the scawberde scholde be stolyn by a woman frome
hym that he moste trusted // Also he tolde kyng Arthure
that he scholde mysse hym. And yett had ye levir than all
youre londis have me a gayne // A sayde the kyng syn ye
knowe of youre evil adventure purvey for hit and putt
hit a way by youre craftes that mysse adventure Nay seyde
M. hit woll not be. he departed frome the kyng And within
a whyle the damesell of the lake departed and Merlyon
went with her evermore where som ever she yeode and oftyn ty
mes M. wolde have had hir prevayly a way by his subtyle
craftes. Than she made hym to swere that he sholde never do
none inchauntemente uppon hir if he wolde have his wil.
And so he swore. Than she and Merlyon wente over the see un
to the londe of Benwyke there as kyng Ban was kyng
that had grete warre a yenste kyng Claudas And there
M. spake with kyng Bayans wyff a fayre lady and a good hir
name was Elayne And there he sawe yonge Launcelot
And there the queene made grete sorowe for the mortal
werre that kyng Claudas made on hir londis Take

The first page of "The Death of Merlin" in the Winchester Manuscript of Malory's Works (Add. MS. 59678, f.45; British Library)

Best Knight in the World, knows where his book has to go.

After the tale of Gareth, Malory's book becomes Lancelot's, even though the next book is the huge, shapeless, and unfinished "Tale of Sir Tristram." From here on Lancelot wrestles with the irritating designation as the Best Knight in the World. A stranger meets Lancelot, hears his name, and says, Oh you are the Best Knight in the World. In this context appears the significance of Lancelot's not being accorded the Bildungsroman granted to his protégé, Gareth, as well as (in other texts) those two paragons Tristram and Parzifal. In a fiercely competitive world, perhaps best exemplified by Sir Palomides, knights pursue combat in the hope of gaining in the world's estimation or "worship." Therefore, if the sixth-best knight in the world defeats a better, that is, higher-ranking, knight, he moves up in the world's estimation. For Lancelot this is impossible; he begins—for us and for himself—as the Best Knight in the World, so that no victory will change anyone's estimation of him. In order to get beyond his designation, he has only two paths: transcendence or transgression, that is, going beyond the order of things or going below. In "The Tale of Sir Tristram," a vast confused work, Lancelot tries several petty transgressions as a way to cope with one of the inconveniences of being the Best Knight in the World: no one will joust with him once they know who he is. In order to get some competition he pretends to be the worst knight in the world, the craven coward Sir Kay. Throughout the tale, knights, especially Lancelot, refuse to acknowledge who they are and, perhaps worse, allow others to take on their identities. In order to get a combat out of the cowardly King Mark, Lamerok dresses as the even more cowardly Kay. Then, to mock Mark even further, Dagonet, the court fool, is dressed as Lancelot, which causes Mark shamefully to flee. But such confusions are made easy because Lancelot has taken to not acknowledging his name. He fights with covered shield, that is, with his coat of arms hidden. The reason for this begins from the pragmatic but soon becomes symbolic. Since the Knights of the Round Table are not supposed to joust against each other, and they include most of the best knights, the only challenge for a knight, such as Lancelot, who wants to be tested would be to fight against them anyway. For this reason Lancelot twice covers his shield and fights against Arthur's knights, but even this transgression pales against his decision to don a gown and fight in the guise of a woman. Even worse, with the gown over his armor, he defeats Sir Dinadan, the most decent of knights, and then Lancelot has his men dress Dinadan in the gown. This behavior makes him more mean-spirited than Sir Kay at his worst.

Yet the aggregate of such aberrant behavior does not begin to match his treatment of the mother of his son in the tale that became the favorite of Tennyson as well as of the Pre-Raphaelite painters. In "Lancelot and Elaine" Lancelot has a chance to shed officially the title of Best Knight in the World. In a reversal of Sir Gareth's Bildungsroman, he starts as a man with a proud name and ends with a nickname that epitomizes his opprobrium. For this reason, Malory chose to tell the story within the frame of his version of Tristram and Isode.

In "The Book of Sir Tristram" Malory describes the decline of Arthurian knighthood. Here it is revealed that the three greatest knights in the world are also the three greatest adulterers: Lancelot with Guinevere, Tristram with Isode, and Lamerok with Margawse. From the time of the medieval romance by Gottfried von Strassburg to the *Liebestod* of Richard Wagner's music drama, the tragic romance of Tristram and Isode was treated with sublimity. Not so in Malory, where it is little more than a pathedy of manners in which Tristram tries in vain to give a little dignity to the hapless Cornish knights of which he is one. Because Malory cuts off Tristram's tale before it ends, the tragic conclusion is simply not forthcoming. Instead, there are a lot of pointless jousting and pathetic outcomes, such as the great Sir Lamerok accidentally killing a man he has just saved and Tristram foolishly marrying the wrong woman because she is also named Isode. More and more both the quest and the joust seem pointless. The symbol of frustration in the book is a shield that the evil Morgan la Fay gives to Tristram to bring as a present to Arthur's court. The shield depicts a king and a queen on a red field with a knight standing above them with a foot on each of them. Morgan only says it represents Arthur and Guinevere and a knight who holds them in bondage. This shield turns out to be the public recognition of Lancelot and Guinevere's adultery, though not even Morgan yet knows Lancelot is guilty of it. Instead, she trusts in her philosophy of believing the worst of everyone, and in this case she is right. Tristram does not understand the message on the shield but carries it to Arthur anyway because he has given Morgan his word that he would. When Tristram reaches Arthur he has no name (a knight's family name should be represented on his shield). Instead, since he uses Morgan's shield, he unwittingly fights in the name of Lancelot's adultery. In this guise he defeats Arthur, who shatters his lance on the telltale shield. Arthur's impotence against the shield foreshadows the changes that will come to the court once the adultery is made public.

Another of Morgan's devices links the adultery in the two courts with the failure of the greatest knights. In order to embarrass Arthur and Guinevere, Morgan sends a bejewelled drinking horn to Camelot. No woman can drink wine from this horn without spilling it unless she is faithful to her husband. Morgan expects Guinevere to shame Arthur, but is intercepted by Lamerok (whose mistress, Margawse, would not be able to pass the horn test) and sent instead to Mark's Cornish court, where Isode is put to the test and fails. Unfortunately, so do ninety-six of the hundred ladies who try to drink from the horn. The Cornish court decides that either the horn does not work, or the results are too demeaning to accept.

The formal history of Lancelot's transgression reaches its peak in the story of Lancelot's begetting of Galahad upon Elaine. As with the begetting of Arthur, it is a matter of lust cooperating with deceit to produce goodness. This time Malory overlays the case with moral ambiguities. The avowed purpose of the tale is to tell of the begetting of the preeminent Grail Knight, Galahad. Even though Elaine is his mother, events are manipulated so that he is born out of the adulterous lust of Lancelot and Guinevere. Since the tale is a prelude to the Sankgreal (Holy Grail) episode, the grail appears to the two men, Bors and Percival, who will, in addition to Galahad, become Grail Knights. It is also declared that Galahad will become the primary achiever of the Grail. In an omen that tempts the reader into believing redemption is possible for Lancelot, the Grail also appears to Lancelot, the one man of these four who does not achieve it. Furthermore, Lancelot is told that if it were not for his carnal sin with Guinevere that he could be the Best Knight in the World in regard to spiritual as well as worldly matters.

Malory loves the ironies inherent in the begetting of Galahad, an event which will complete the Round Table because Galahad is the only knight who can fill the Siege Perilous; yet the moment of Galahad's completing the Round Table also marks the beginning of the end since his arrival marks the opening of the quest for the Grail, which will dismember the Round Table.

Lancelot's deflowering of Elaine is the first of a series of events which will stand moral certainties on their heads. Elaine knows she is fated to be the mother of Lancelot's child, and she is in love with him as well. Lancelot, however, is the faithful lover of another man's wife, so Elaine has to use sorcery to make herself look like Guinevere. Then she sends a message to Lancelot that she, "Guinevere" (really Elaine), wants him to come to her. Lancelot comes and begets Galahad on the transformed Elaine. In the morning the spell is broken, and Lancelot realizes he has slept with the wrong woman. Then he angrily accuses Elaine of treachery, so that we have the spectacle of a knight—who has just deflowered a maiden when in fact he intended to commit adultery against the best man in Christendom—indicting the deflowered virgin with whom he thought he was betraying his best friend. When Guinevere hears that Lancelot has had a son by another woman, she is outraged but forgives Lancelot when she discovers the circumstances of his betrayal.

This event could stand by itself as another of the rapes through transformation that bring about the most significant births in Camelot: Uther begetting Arthur on Igrayne and Arthur begetting Mordred on his half sister, Margawse. Instead, the act is repeated, this time with no genealogical significance so that the emotional impact alone is at issue. Elaine, her dynastic function completed, comes to Camelot, where she is acknowledged as the fairest woman, *not excluding Guinevere*, in the world. Guinevere, who knows of Elaine's relation to Lancelot, jealously indicates that she will send for him (mostly because she wants to make sure he is not sleeping with Elaine). Elaine's guardian sorceress anticipates the queen's message and goes to Lancelot to tell him "Guinevere" is waiting for him. Lancelot falls for the same trick again, goes to Elaine whose face is hidden in the dark, and spends the night with her. When Guinevere sends for Lancelot, her servant finds his bed is cold, but he can be found in the castle because of his habit of "clattering" in his sleep about Guinevere. This time perhaps because he thinks that he has just slept with Guinevere he jabbers louder than usual, and Guinevere finds him in Elaine's bed. This time he has no sorcery for an excuse, and he escapes from Guinevere's verbal abuse by leaping out the window. He strips off his clothes, and for two years he exists as a clownish (rustic) madman—thereby embodying all the playful transformations he had practiced in trying to escape his designation as the Best Knight in the World.

In his rustic madness, where he often fights naked and with bare fists, he takes on the appearance of a country bumpkin or villein; he has been transformed from heroic to "villeinous." When Lancelot finally recovers his sanity, he realizes what he has done. At this point, he gives up the name Lancelot and calls himself by a shameful epithet, "le shyvalere Mafete," the knight who has trespassed. In this, he reverses the history of two young knights, Gareth and Brewne le Noyre, who have, through their deeds, earned the right to give up their clownish nicknames, Beawmayns, and La Cote Male Tayle (the ill-fitting surcoat). Perhaps, if William Matthews is right when he says in *The Ill-Framed Knight* (1966) that Malory is not a surname but an epithet attesting to its owner's evil, then Sir Thomas is telling the story of a knight like himself, whose violent acts were always ill regarded.

The degradation born of confusion, even the official self-shaming of Lancelot, is nothing compared to the destruction brought about by the quest for the Holy Grail, which gives the court a purpose even as it tears at its very roots. Though Arthur's court is built on Christian ideals, Arthur realizes that the ideal of moral perfection that underlies the Grail quest will subvert the more worldly, yet noble, pursuits of the Round Table; so when the quest is taken up, Arthur laments the end of his enterprise in one of the most poignant speeches in English literature: "I am sure at this quest of the Sankegreall shall all ye of the Rownde Table departe, and nevyr shall I se you agayne holé togydirs, therefore ones shall I se you togydir in the medow [of Camelot], all holé togydirs. . . . To juste and to turney, that aftir youre dethe men may speke of hit that such good knyghtes were here, such a day, holé togydirs."

Though all of the Round Table pursues the Grail, Malory focuses on five knights to explain the options open to man. There are three Grail Knights, that is, those who will achieve the Grail: Galahad, Percival, and Bors. They are symbolized by a vision in which there are 150 bulls in a meadow; all are black except three; of these two are completely white, and one is white with a black spot. The two white bulls are Galahad and Percival, two virgin knights, and the spotted bull is Bors, who has lapsed once in his chastity. Lancelot's son, Galahad, temporarily takes the pressure off his father because now that he has achieved knighthood, he has also put on the mantle of the Best Knight in the World. After Galahad comes to Camelot, an old wise man chaffs Lancelot with the fact he does not have the name (of the Best Knight) that he had in the morning. The wise man does not realize that for Lancelot a great burden has been lifted. Galahad is the best not merely in prowess but in moral perfection as well. For this reason Galahad is also the most boring character in the book since he always does the right thing. Eventually he will take his perfection out of Arthur's worldly kingdom into the otherworld of the heavenly kingdom, leaving Lancelot with the possibility of being the Best Knight *in* the World.

Unlike the unerring Galahad, Percival does the right thing purely by chance throughout his quest for the Grail. For example, once he is about to be seduced by a demon who has taken the shape of a beautiful woman, but at the very moment of his yielding, he sees the crucifix in his sword hilt, crosses himself, and his naked, would-be paramour disappears in a cloud of black smoke. The accidental nature of his virtue suggests that no amount of reason will help in uncovering the mystery of the Grail. Bors is significant mostly for what his presence implies about the situation of Lancelot; that is, one can have been unchaste and still become a Grail Knight.

The other two knights who are significant in the book of the Holy Grail are Gawain and Lancelot. Gawain is the worldly knight who always makes the wrong choice almost the way Percival accidentally makes the right one. Gawain is also the first of the 147 worldly knights who elects to pursue the Grail, and his departure opens the floodgates for the "departition" of the Round Table. After he takes up the quest, all the other worldly knights decide to try also. Interestingly, Arthur calls Gawain a traitor for changing the Round Table's focus from knightly pursuits to those of Christian perfection. Arthur reprimands Gawain for seeking the truth, but Lancelot is not scolded for carrying on a twenty-four-year-long adulterous affair with Guinevere.

Gawain finds himself unable to maneuver through the arbitrary allegorical landscape of the Grail world. For example, he takes up for a group of white knights against a group of black

¶ Capitulum primum

Hit befel in the dayes of Uther pendragon when he was kynge of all Englond / and so regned that there was a myzty duke in Cornewaill that helde warre ageynst hym long tyme / And the duke was called the duke of Tyntagil / and so by meanes kynge Uther send for this duk / chargyng hym to brynge his wyf with hym / for she was called a fair lady / and a passynge wyse / and her name was called Igrayne / So whan the duke and his wyf were comyn unto the kynge by the meanes of grete lordes they were accorded bothe / the kynge lyked and loued this lady wel / and he made them grete chere oute of mesure / and desyred to haue lyen by her / But she was a passyng good woman / and wold not assente unto the kynge / And thenne she told the duke her husband and said I suppose that we were sente for that I shold be dishonoured Wherfor husband I councille yow that we departe from hens sodenly that we maye ryde all nyghte unto oure owne castell / and in lyke wyse as she saide so they departed / that neyther the kynge nor none of his councill were ware of their departyng Also soone as kyng Uther knewe of theire departyng soo sodenly / he was wonderly wrothe / Thenne he called to hym his pryuy councille / and told them of the sodeyne departyng of the duke and his wyf /

¶ Thenne they auysed the kynge to send for the duke and his wyf by a grete charge / And yf he wille not come at your somōs / thenne may ye do your best / thenne haue ye cause to make myghty werre upon hym / Soo that was done and the messagers hadde their ansuers / And that was thys shortly / that neyther he nor his wyf wold not come at hym /

Thenne was the kyng wonderly wroth / And thenne the kyng sente hym playne word ageyne / and badde hym be redy and stuffe hym and garnysshe hym / for within xl dayes he wold fetche hym oute of the byggest castell that he hath /

¶ Whanne the duke hadde thys warnynge / anone he wente and furnysshed and garnysshed two stronge Castels of his of the whiche the one hyght Tyntagil / & the other castel hyzt

a j

First page of text in the Pierpont Morgan Library copy of William Caxton's first edition of Le Morte Darthur. *The only other surviving copy of this edition, printed in 1485, is in the John Rylands Library in Manchester.*

knights. It turns out the white knights represent hypocrisy (as in "whited sepulchres"), so that he should have counterintuitively taken up for the black knights. If paths diverge in the allegorical landscape, Gawain always takes the wrong fork. He is the worldly knight who is destined to fail on a spiritual quest.

As usual, Lancelot has the most interesting story of all the knights in the book. He is the only one of the worldly knights who is capable of achieving the Grail, but he does not. The case of Sir Bors shows that Lancelot's past of indiscretion with Guinevere does not in itself prevent Lancelot from reaching the Grail. In fact, Lancelot confesses, then disavows, his love for Guinevere, and then he spends twenty-four hours in a steaming room: one hour for every year of the adultery. He emerges cleansed of his past sins and therefore capable of achieving the Grail. Lancelot knows that if he achieves the Grail and Galahad leaves the world, he would once again become the Best Knight in the World, an appellation he has worked so hard to erase. Unlike Gawain, Lancelot does see the Grail, but unlike the Grail Knights, he does not get to touch it or to share in its feast.

By the end of the Grail episode, Malory has embarked on a tragic story of transgression that will go far beyond the formal statement of trespass that ends "Lancelot and Elaine." There, Lancelot may have been wrong, but there was little emotional weight because the trespass was against the apparent form of things. He twice betrayed Guinevere only because he thought the woman he was sleeping with was Guinevere. Furthermore, since he was, in fact, sleeping with Elaine, he was not at those times technically guilty of the adultery that was in his heart.

All this changes after his unsuccessful quest for the Grail. The tale that follows Galahad's success begins with the striking fact that Lancelot's failure was not due to his past sin with Guinevere, but to the sin he would do with her in the future. Lancelot's sin takes on the dimension of Original Sin, by which mankind is punished with death not for the sin he has done but for the sin he will do. Lancelot tells Guinevere how much her love has cost him: "if that I had nat had my prevy thoughtis to returne to you[r]e love agayne as I do, I had sene as grete mysteryes as ever saw my sonne, sir Galahad, Percivale, other sir Bors." The history of the romance of Lancelot and Guinevere is now tightly plotted through interlocking incidents. Malory shows how this love brings down Arthur's court and how knightly behavior will destroy knighthood.

Lancelot's relation to Guinevere and Arthur is formulated and reformulated in a series of three trials in which Lancelot becomes the champion of Guinevere. In each trial the breach between the letter and the spirit of the law widens until finally Lancelot destroys the system of chivalry altogether.

The trials begin when Guinevere is falsely accused of poisoning one of the knights of the Round Table, a matter that has to be settled by judicial combat. Unfortunately, Guinevere has already sent Lancelot packing, mostly to quash the rumors of their affair. Arthur bawls her out for leaving herself without a champion. Fortunately, Lancelot returns in the nick of time to take his place as her defender. His success should cause no surprise, since she is innocent according to the letter and spirit of the law.

The second trial occurs when Malory tells a streamlined version of Chrétien de Troyes's romance "The Knight of the Cart" (circa 1177-1181). In Malory's version the evil Meleagaunt has captured Guinevere and some of Arthur's knights, who have been wounded. Guinevere is kept in the same donjon cell with the wounded knights, but in the night, Lancelot tears the bars off the window cutting his hand as he does, enters the donjon, sleeps with Guinevere, and leaves. In the morning, Meleagaunt sees the blood on Guinevere's sheets and accuses Guinevere of being unfaithful to her husband with one of the wounded knights. To shame Arthur's court, Meleagaunt decides to put Guinevere on trial. Lancelot comes forward to be her champion on this very specific charge. Meleagaunt, evil though he is, believes in the principle behind judicial combat: God will defend the Right. He, therefore, thinks that with the help of Divine Justice he can defeat Lancelot, especially when Lancelot agrees to fight with a quarter of his armor removed and, *literally*, with one hand tied behind his back, so he can neither hold a shield nor swing a broadsword properly. Nonetheless, Lancelot easily defeats Meleagaunt because Guinevere is innocent, even if it is only according to the letter of the law, and, therefore, in the eyes of God. What Malory, the greatest scofflaw in England, made of these proceedings is left unrecorded.

Meleagaunt's comeuppance is not lost on the most evil characters in Arthur's court: Arthur's son, Mordred, and Gawain's brother Aggravayne. They are determined to catch Guinevere in the act of adultery with Lancelot so that the long-rumored infidelity can be brought into the open and a trial can result in direct and deadly conflict between Lancelot and Arthur.

In these proceedings the disposition of Gawain's family is vital: there is one evil brother, Aggravayne, two good brothers, Gaheris and Lancelot's protégé, Gareth; the leader of the clan is Gawain, whose place as Arthur's nephew is insisted upon. In the later books Malory works to upgrade the character and reputation of Gawain. Throughout the Grail episode, Gawain is the epitome of the boorish worldly knight, often with more courage than sense, but in the later tales he becomes the fairest man in Camelot, Arthur's trusted counselor, and Lancelot's staunchest supporter, a man not given to wrath or rash action. Much of the last book is devoted to a single, simple question: what will it take to turn Gawain against Lancelot. He refuses to join his evil brother in the plot to entrap Lancelot, and even when Lancelot kills Aggravayne and two of Gawain's sons when they are trying to catch him in the act of adultery with Guinevere (we are never told if he is in the queen's chamber for *that* reason this time), Gawain defends Lancelot saying that his brother and his sons got what they were asking for.

Though the entrapment fails, Arthur is prevailed upon by his knights to put Guinevere to the stake for her adultery. When he is urged to put the issue of Guinevere's guilt up to a judicial combat, Arthur denies the whole point of knightly combat, all the jousting and tourneying for which his court is famous. Arthur's court has operated under the principle that Right makes Might, but Arthur now realizes that Lancelot will win no matter what side he is on, so that the operative principle is Might makes Right: "Lancelot trustyth so much uppon hys hondis and hys myght that he doutyth [fears] no man. And therefore for my quene he shall nevermore fyght, for she shall have the law."

Nonetheless, it is expected that Lancelot will try to rescue the queen, and a cordon of Knights of the Round Table is assigned to defend against her rescue. Among them are the brothers Gaheris and Gareth. They refuse to wear armor against Lancelot, the man who made Gareth knight, so they take their place in the cordon unarmed. Lancelot is troubled by the idea of going against Arthur, so he asks his cousins what he should do, and they invoke the original chivalric code: always defend ladies in distress, and so Lancelot goes "knightly" to rescue the queen. In riding to her rescue he unwittingly rides down Gaheris and Gareth, thereby committing the most dastardly of acts: killing unarmed knights. Before, in his rural madness, he was a "villein"; now he is a villain. This act is enough to set the long-suffering Gawain against Lancelot. In a wonderfully pathetic moment Gawain looks for his brothers immediately after declaring that Lancelot was only doing his knightly duty in rescuing the queen. Gawain's rage over the death of Gareth forces Lancelot to leave the court, and Gawain has him officially declared "false recreayed [recreant] knyght." Lancelot has now become, in a way he never expected, the Worst Knight in the World. In some of the coldest lines in literature, Arthur notes that he is brokenhearted not for Guinevere, but for the Round Table: "I am soryar for my good knyghtes losse than for the losse of my fayre quene; for of quenys I myght have inow, but such a felyship of good knyghtes shall never be togydirs in no company."

Lancelot's retreat from the court means that the king's strongest champion is away when Mordred comes to wound Arthur fatally and destroy the kingdom. As the Dolorous Day unfolds, Malory orchestrates events to a tragic conclusion. The fated end of Arthur and his Round Table is inherent in the New Testament message cited as early as "The Knight with the Two Swords": "And that knyght that hath encheved the swerde shall be destroyed thorow the swerde." Arthur, like Balin, is a knight who has achieved the sword, and, like Balin, his death is caused by a misunderstood sign. The sign that will break the fragile truce between the armies of Arthur and those of Mordred is the drawing of a sword. If the truce holds, then Lancelot will be able to come in time to succor the king. However, in an echo from Eden, an adder stings one of Arthur's knights, who "drew hys swerde to sle the addir, and thought none othir harme." With the flash of the sword the truce is broken, and Mordred and Arthur slay each other. Lancelot, who has always come in time to rescue the queen, comes too late to save the king. Malory closes his book at this point and asks the reader to pray for his deliverance (from prison we suspect). He calls this "the ende of the hoole book of kyng Arthur and of his noble knyghtes of the Rounde Table," and it is clear that Caxton made the book somewhat more whole than the manuscript he had.

The fact that Caxton would typeset a book as huge as Malory's testifies to the popularity of the Arthurian legend at the end of the fifteenth century. Arthur was the key to an important piece of political mythology. After ending the Wars of the Roses by defeating Richard III and marrying the daughter of the Yorkist line, Henry VII worked on establishing the Tudor myth, one of whose lynchpins was the claim that he was descended through his Welsh ancestors from King Arthur and, therefore, belonged to a royal line even older than the Norman Plantagenet one. To this end he named his eldest son (who did not survive) Arthur. Though it is likely that Caxton had a small circle of paying customers for a great Arthurian epic, he seems also to have expected to cash in on the popularity of the figure. Certainly since the great victory over the French at Agincourt (1415), there had been much interest in an authentic English hero. Malory was a boy when Henry V defeated the French in the greatest victory in English military history. His lifetime saw the aftermath of that victory, the bloody Wars of the Roses, in which brothers and cousins killed each other in the name of honor. It is out of this world that Malory wrote his tale of Arthur and the internecine struggle that destroyed the Round Table.

Bibliography:

Page West Life, *Sir Thomas Malory and the Morte Darthur: A Survey of Scholarship and Annotated Bibliography* (Charlottesville: Published for the Bibliographical Society of the University of Virginia by the University Press of Virginia, 1980).

Biography:

William Matthews, *The Ill-Framed Knight: A Skeptical Inquiry into the Identity of Sir Thomas Malory* (Berkeley: University of California Press, 1966).

References:

Stephen C. B. Atkinson, "Malory's 'Healing of Sir Urry' Lancelot, the Earthly Fellowship, and the World of the Grail," *Studies in Philology*, 78 (Fall 1981): 341-352;

J. A. W. Bennett, ed., *Essays on Malory* (Oxford: Clarendon Press, 1963);

Larry D. Benson, *Malory's Morte Darthur* (Cambridge, Mass.: Harvard University Press, 1976);

Muriel C. Bradbrook, *Sir Thomas Malory* (London & New York: Published for the British Council by Longmans, Green, 1958);

R. T. Davies, "Malory's Launcelot and the Noble Way of the World," *Review of English Studies*, 6 (November 1955): 356-364;

Bert Dillon, *A Malory Handbook* (Boston: G. K. Hall, 1978);

Murray J. Evans, "The Explicits and Narrative Division in the Winchester MS: A Critique of Vinaver's Malory," *Philological Quarterly*, 58 (Summer 1979): 263-281;

P. J. C. Field, *Romance and Chronicle: A Study of Malory's Prose Style* (London: Barrie & Jenkins, 1971; Bloomington: Indiana University Press, 1971);

Sandra Ness Ihle, *Malory's Grail Quest: Invention and Adaptation in Medieval Prose Romance* (Madison: University of Wisconsin Press, 1983);

Tomomi Kato, *A Concordance to the Works of Sir Thomas Malory* (Tokyo: University of Tokyo Press, 1974);

Beverly Kennedy, "Malory's Lancelot: 'Trewest Lover, of a Synful Man,' " *Viator*, 12 (1981): 409-456;

Edward D. Kennedy, "Malory's King Mark and King Arthur," *Mediaeval Studies*, 37 (1975): 190-234;

Mark Lambert, *Malory: Style and Vision in Le Morte Darthur* (New Haven: Yale University Press, 1975);

R. M. Lumiansky, ed., *Malory's Originality: A Critical Study of Le Morte Darthur* (Baltimore: Johns Hopkins Press, 1964);

Terence McCarthy, *An Introduction to Malory* (Cambridge, U.K.: D. S. Brewer, 1988; corrected edition, 1991);

Elizabeth Pochoda, *Arthurian Propaganda: Le Morte Darthur as an Historical Ideal of Life* (Chapel Hill: University of North Carolina Press, 1971);

Edmund Reiss, *Sir Thomas Malory* (New York: Twayne, 1966);

Felicity Riddy, *Sir Thomas Malory* (Leiden & New York: E. J. Brill, 1987);

Toshiyuki Takamiya and Derek Brewer, eds., *Aspects of Malory* (Cambridge, U.K.: D. S. Brewer, 1981);

Muriel A. Whitaker, *Arthur's Kingdom of Adventure: The World of Malory's Morte Darthur* (Cambridge, U.K.: D. S. Brewer, 1984);

Robert H. Wilson, "The Fair Unknown in Malory," *PMLA*, 58 (March 1943): 1-21.

Christopher Marlowe

(February 1564 - 30 May 1593)

This entry was updated by Roma Gill from her entry in DLB 62: Elizabethan Dramatists.

BOOKS: *Tamburlaine the Great. . . . Deuided into Two Tragicall Discourses* (London: Printed by R. Jhones, 1590);

The Tragedie of Dido Queene of Carthage (London: Printed by the Widdowe Orwin for T. Woodcocke, 1594);

The troublesome raigne and lamentable death of Edward the second, King of England (London: Printed by R. Robinson for W. Jones, 1594);

The Massacre at Paris: With the Death of the Duke of Guise (London: Printed by E. Allde for E. White, 1594?);

Certaine of Ouides Elegies, in *Epigrammes and Elegies*, by Marlowe and John Davies (Middleborugh [i.e., London], 1595?); enlarged as *All Ouids Elegies* (Middlebourgh [i.e., London], after 1602);

Hero and Leander (London: Printed by A. Islip for E. Blunt, 1598);

Lucans First Booke Translated Line for Line (London: Printed by P. Short, sold by W. Burre, 1600);

The Tragicall History of D. Faustus (London: Printed by V. Simmes for T. Bushell, 1604);

The Famous Tragedy of the Rich Jew of Malta, edited by Thomas Heywood (London: Printed by J. Beale for N. Vavasour, 1633).

Editions: *Christopher Marlowe: The Poems*, edited by Millar Maclure (London: Methuen / Manchester: Manchester University Press, 1968);

The Plays of Christopher Marlowe, edited by Roma Gill (Oxford: Oxford University Press, 1971);

Complete Plays and Poems, edited by E. D. Pendry and J. C. Maxwell (London: Dent, 1976);

The Complete Works of Christopher Marlowe, revised edition, 2 volumes, edited by Fredson Bowers (Cambridge: Cambridge University Press, 1981);

The Complete Works of Christopher Marlowe, 2 volumes to date, edited by Roma Gill (Oxford: Oxford University Press, 1987-).

PLAY PRODUCTIONS: *Dido Queen of Carthage*, Children of Her Majesty's Chapel, circa 1586;

Tamburlaine the Great, parts 1 and 2, London, Rose theater, 1587-1588;

The Jew of Malta, London, Rose theater, circa 1590;

The Massacre at Paris, London, Rose theater, circa 1590;

Edward II, Pembroke's Men, winter 1592-1593;

Dr. Faustus, London, Rose theater, 30 September 1594.

The achievement of Christopher Marlowe, poet and dramatist, was enormous—surpassed only by that of his exact contemporary William Shakespeare. A few months the elder, Marlowe was usually the leader, although Shakespeare was able to bring his art to a higher perfection. Most dramatic poets of the sixteenth century followed where Marlowe had led, especially in their use of language and the blank-verse line. The prologue to Marlowe's *Tamburlaine* (1587-1588) proclaims its author's contempt for the stage verse of the period, in which the "jygging vaines of riming mother wits" presented the "conceits [which] clownage keepes in pay"; instead the new play promised a barbaric foreign hero, the "Scythian Tamburlaine, Threatning the world with high astounding terms." English drama was never the same again.

The son of John and Catherine Marlowe, Christopher Marlowe was born in Canterbury, where his father was a shoemaker, in 1564. He received some of his early education at The King's School, Canterbury, and an Archbishop Parker scholarship took him from this school to Corpus Christi College, Cambridge. In 1584 he graduated as bachelor of arts. The terms of his scholarship allowed for a further three years' study if the holder intended to take holy orders, and Marlowe appears to have fulfilled this condition. But in 1587 the university at first refused to grant the appropriate degree of master of arts. The col-

Portrait of a young man found in 1953 when workmen were repairing the Master's Lodge at Corpus Christi College, Cambridge. Authenticated as a genuine painting from the Elizabethan period, it is possibly a portrait of Christopher Marlowe, who—like the young man in the painting—was twenty-one and enrolled at Corpus Christi in 1585 (Corpus Christi College).

lege records show that Marlowe was away from Cambridge for considerable periods during his second three years, and the university apparently had good reason to be suspicious of his whereabouts. Marlowe, however, was not without some influence by this time: John Whitgift, Archbishop of Canterbury; William Cecil, first Baron Burghley; and Sir Christopher Hatton were among members of Queen Elizabeth's Privy Council who signed a letter explaining, "Whereas it was reported that Christopher Morley was determined to have gone beyond the seas to Reames and there to remaine, Their Lordships thought good to certefie that he had no such intent, but that in all his accions he had behaved him selfe orderlie and discreetlie wherebie he had done her Majestie good service, & deserved to be rewarded for his faithfull dealinge. . . ." The reference to "Reames" makes everything clear. The Jesuit seminary at Reims was the refuge of many expatriate Roman Catholics, who were thought to be scheming to overthrow the English monarch: the Babington Conspiracy was plotted here—and its frustration in 1586 was achieved through the efforts of secret agents placed by Sir Francis Walsingham.

In 1587 Christopher Marlowe, M.A., went from Cambridge to London; and for the next six years he wrote plays and associated with other writers, among them the poet Thomas Watson and the dramatist Thomas Kyd. His friendship with Watson brought trouble: the two were arrested in 1589, charged with the homicide of William Bradley, and committed to Newgate Prison. Marlowe was released after a fortnight, and Watson (whose sword had killed Bradley) pleaded that he had acted "in self-defence" and "not by felony"; he was set free after five months in prison. The association with Kyd was also the cause of trouble some years later. In the spring of 1593 Kyd was arrested on a charge of inciting mob violence in riots against Flemish Protestants. His home was searched, and papers were found there containing "vile hereticall Conceiptes Denyinge the Deity of Jhesus Christ our Savior." Kyd denied that the document was his, asserting that the papers belonged to Marlowe and had been "shuffled with some of myne (unknown to me) by some occasion of our wrytinge in one chamber twoe yeares synce." Perhaps Kyd, a professional scrivener, had been transcribing the manuscript for Marlowe—who was not, however, the author (the ideas had been published in 1549 by John Proctor under the title *The Fal of the Late Arrian).* Riots combined with the plague made the spring of 1593 an unusually tense period; and the Privy Council (Archbishop Whitgift and Lord Burghley were still members, as they had been in 1587) acted quickly on Kyd's information and instructed a court messenger "to repaire to the house of Mr. Tho: Walsingham in Kent, or to anie other place where he shall understand Christofer Marlow to be remayning, and . . . to apprehend, and bring him to the Court in his Companie. And in case of need to require ayd." Marlowe—who had perhaps retreated to Kent in order to avoid the plague which had closed the London theaters—was commanded to report daily to the council. The treatment was proper for a gentlemen: a lesser person would have been imprisoned.

Attempting to exculpate himself from the charges of heresy and blasphemy, and to deny any continuing friendship with his former chamber mate, Kyd sent two letters to the lord chancellor, Sir John Puckering. In the first he affirmed Marlowe's ownership of the papers that had been "shuffled" with his own, declaring "That I shold love or be familiar frend, with one so irreligious, were very rare . . . besides he was intemperate & of a cruel hart." In the second he enlarged upon the subject of "marlowes monstruous opinions," offering examples of how Marlowe would "gybe at praiers, & stryve in argument to frustrate & confute what hath byn spoke or wrytt by prophets & such holie men."

Kyd was not alone in making such accusations at this time. Puckering also received a note from a certain Richard Baines, who may have been a government informer and had previously been arrested with Marlowe at Flushing in the Netherlands in 1592. On this occasion the governor of Flushing commented in a letter which he sent to Lord Burghley along with the prisoners, that "Bains and he [Marlowe] do also accuse one another of intent to goe to the Ennemy or to Rome, both as they say of malice one to another." In 1593 Baines denounced Marlowe for his "Damnable Judgement of Religion, and scorn of gods word." Marlowe, he said, had stated

> That the first beginning of Religioun was only to keep men in awe. . . .
>
> That Christ was a bastard and his mother dishonest. . . .
>
> That if there by any god or any good Religion, then it is in the papistes because the service of god is performed with more Cerimonies, as Elevation of the mass, organs, singing men, Shaven Crownes & cta. that all protestantes are Hypocriticall asses. . . .

It is perhaps understandable that the Elizabethans, fearful for their church and their state, should have given some credence to these wild statements, but it is astonishing to find that some readers of Marlowe's works—to the present day—are prepared to accept the slanders of Kyd and Baines and believe in Marlowe's "atheism."

Although such slanders have affected the dramatist's reputation, they did no harm to the man. By the time Puckering received Kyd's second letter and the note from Baines, Marlowe was probably already dead.

Marlowe's death and the events which immediately preceded it are fully documented in the report of the inquest (which was discovered by J. Leslie Hotson and published in *The Death of Christopher Marlowe*, 1925). The report tells of a meeting at the house of Mrs. Eleanor Bull in Deptford—not a tavern, but a house where meetings could be held and food supplied. On 30 May 1593 Marlowe spent the whole day there, talking and walking in the garden with three "gentlemen." In the evening there was a quarrel, ostensibly about who should pay the bill, "*le recknynge*"; in the ensuing scuffle Marlowe is said to have drawn his dagger and wounded one of his companions. The man, Ingram Frizer, snatched the weapon and "in defence of his life, with the dagger aforesaid of the value of 12d. gave the said Christopher then & there a mortal wound over his right eye of the depth of two inches & of the width of one inch; of which mortal wound the aforesaid Christopher Morley then & there instantly died." Ingram Frizer was granted a free pardon within one month, and returned to the

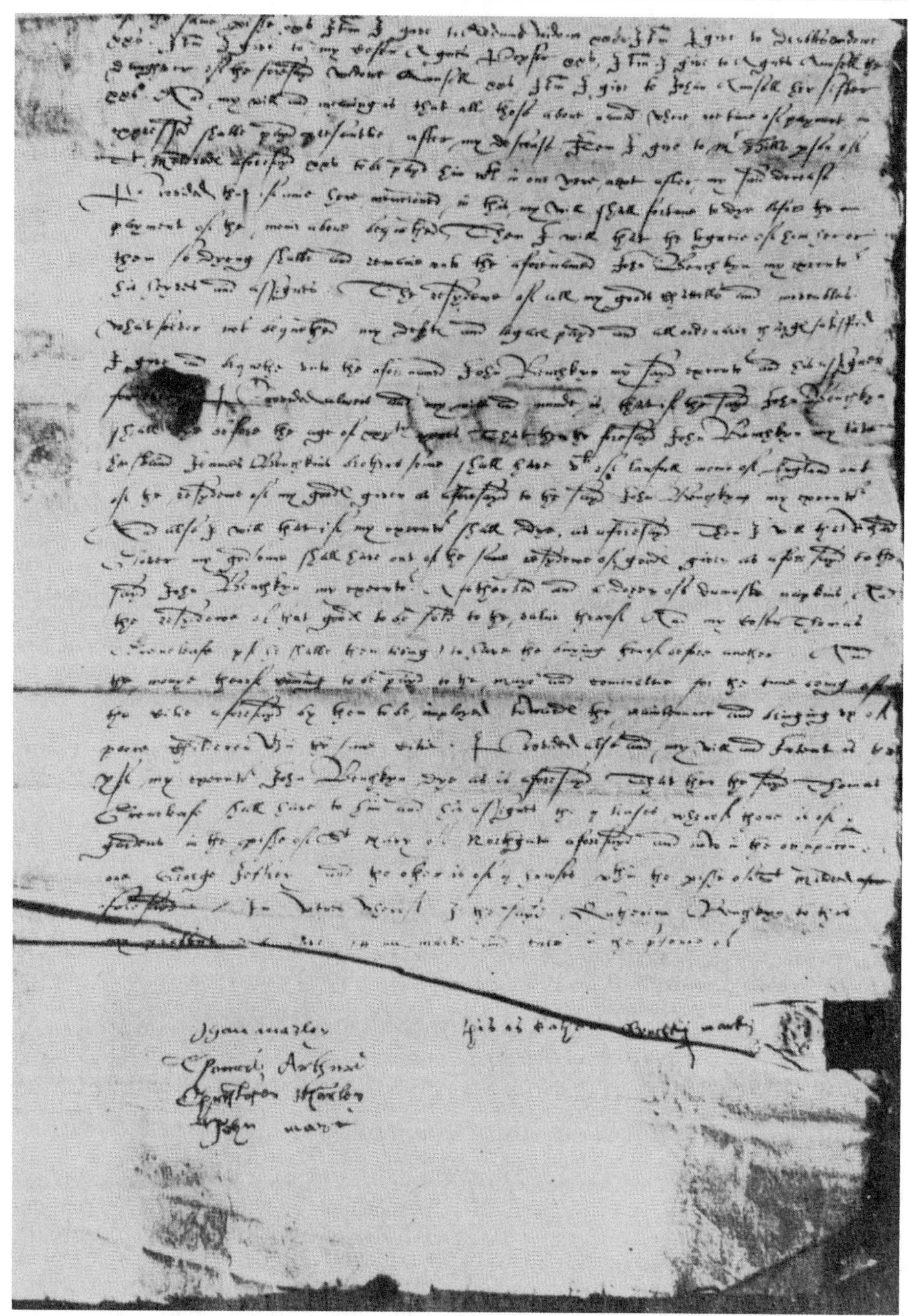

Last page of the will of Katherine Benchkyn, witnessed November 1585 by Christopher Marlowe (third signature, lower left) (Kent Record Office, Maidstone). The other witnesses were John Marlowe, Marlowe's father; Thomas Arthur, probably Marlowe's uncle; and John Moore, Marlowe's brother-in-law.

service of the Walsinghams. One of his accomplices was Robert Poley, the man largely responsible for the discovery of the Babington Conspiracy in 1586. The third man was Nicholas Skeres, who may have been the "Skyrres" who was with Poley and some of the conspirators shortly before the discovery. Such a combination of events and personalities makes it unlikely that this was a mere tavern brawl.

Some contemporary moralists seized on the story with an unholy glee; in 1597, for example, Thomas Beard recognized in it "a manifest signe of Gods judgement . . . in that hee compelled his owne hand which had written those blasphemies to be the instrument to punish him, and that in his braine, which had devised the same." The poets were more generous: Thomas Nash described Marlowe as "a diviner Muse" than Musaeus; George Peele called him "the Muses' darling"; and Michael Drayton observed in him "those brave translunary things That the first poets had." This early appreciation has extended over the years, so that now most critics—sharing the benefits of hindsight—would agree with Algernon Charles Swinburne that Marlowe was "the father of English tragedy and the creator of English blank verse." According to Havelock Ellis, "Marlowe's place is at the heart of English poetry"; and T. S. Eliot even predicted "the direction in which Marlowe's verse might have moved . . . [which was toward] . . . intense and serious and indubitably great poetry."

In his 1592 letter to Lord Burghley, the governor of Flushing described his prisoners and said that Marlowe was "by his profession a scholar." Marlowe's earliest writings are certainly those one would expect from a learned man—at the beginning of his career. Marlowe began writing verse by translating the Roman poets Ovid and Lucan. He could well have encountered Lucan while at grammar school; and at school too he would have read some of Ovid's verse—but not the *Amores*, which he chose to translate.

The Latin poems are written in the elegiac meter: a hexameter line followed by a pentameter. They show Ovid at his most sophisticated, writing of love in many different aspects with complete confidence in his linguistic brilliance. Marlowe's translations of these elegies are not uniformly successful; but they nevertheless form an impressive achievement. For the Latin elegiac couplet, Marlowe substituted the rhymed pentameter couplet—which John Donne later followed, imitating Marlowe with his own elegies. Instead of the polished artifice with which Ovid manipulated his inflective language, Marlowe wrote with the directness of the spoken voice, using the range and variety of speech tones to approach the "masculine perswasive force" for which Donne is so highly esteemed. The couplet and the speaking voice often combine to give a dramatic immediacy and wit to lines such as these from elegy 18 of book 2 of the *Amores*, where the poet makes his excuses for writing of love when he should be contemplating epic matters:

> Often at length, my wench depart, I bid,
> Shee in my lap sits still as earst she did.
> I sayd it irkes me: halfe to weping framed,
> Aye me she cries, to love, why art a shamed?
> Then wreathes about my necke her winding armes,
> And thousand kisses gives, that worke my harmes:
> I yeeld, and back my wit from battells bring,
> Domesticke acts, and mine owne warres to sing.

Here the closing of the couplet enacts the speaker's resignation as well as bringing to a close the first section of the poem.

There are forty-eight poems in the collection *All Ovids Elegies*, and many are less satisfying than this one. Sometimes Marlowe seems to be bored with his work and snatching at the most obvious English word without reflecting on its aptness ("admonisht" for *admonitus*); at other times the exigencies of rhyme force the English language to take new strange shapes ("forbod" to rhyme with "god"); and often the attractive circumlocutions of the Latin are rendered with a pedantry which assumes an ignorant readership (the worst example is the translation of Ovid's pretty reference to the birth of Bacchus in *Amores* III. iii.: *"non pater in Baccho matris haberet opus"* becomes "The fathers thigh should unborne *Bacchus* lacke"). More often, however, we see the praiseworthy attempts of a young poet to master the foreign language *and* his native tongue—and on occasion we see the genesis of a notion which is developed later in his career.

The translating of book 1 of Lucan's epic poem *Pharsalia* was in many ways less demanding than the translating of the *Amores*: the poem's narrative line and the medium (blank verse) were better guides to Marlowe—and when his comprehension of the Latin was inadequate, he had a copiously annotated commentary to help him. Neither this translation nor that of the *Amores* can be dated with any accuracy, but it seems likely that such academic—and apprentice—work would be undertaken at a time of (comparative) leisure

185

A note Containing the opinion of on Christopher
Marly Concerning his Damnable Judgment
of Religion, and scorn of gods word.

That the Indians and many Authors of antiquity have
assuredly writen of above 16 thousand yeares agone whereas
Adam is proved to have lived within 6 thowsand yeares.

He affirmeth that Moyses was but a Jugler, & that one
Heriots being Sir W Raleighs man Can do more then he.

That Moyses made the Jewes to travell xl yeares in the
wildernes, (which Jorney might have bin done in lesse then
one yeare) ere they Came to the promised land to thintent
that those who were privy to most of his subtilties might
perish and so an everlasting superstition Remain in the harts
of the people.

That the first beginning of Religioun was only to keep men
in awe.

That it was an easy matter for Moyses being brought vp in
all the artes of the Egiptians to abuse the Jewes being
a rude & grosse people.

That Christ was a bastard and his mother dishonest.

That he was the sonne of a Carpenter, and that if the
Jewes among whome he was borne did Crucify him theie
best knew him and whence he Came.

That Christ deserved better to dy then Barrabas and
that the Jewes made a good Choise, though Barrabas
were both a theif and a murtherer.

That if there be any god or any good Religion, then it
is in the papistes because the service of god is performed
with more Ceremonies, as Elevation of the mass, organs
singing men, Shaven Crownes, & cta. that all protestantes
are Hypocriticall asses.

That if he were put to write a new Religion, he would
undertake both a more Excellent and Admirable methode
and that all the new testament is filthily written.

That the woman of Samaria & her sister were whores
& that Christ knew them dishonestly.

Beginning of Richard Baines's 1593 letter denouncing Marlowe for his "Damnable Judgement of Religion, and scorn of gods word" (Harleian MS 6648, f. 185; British Library)

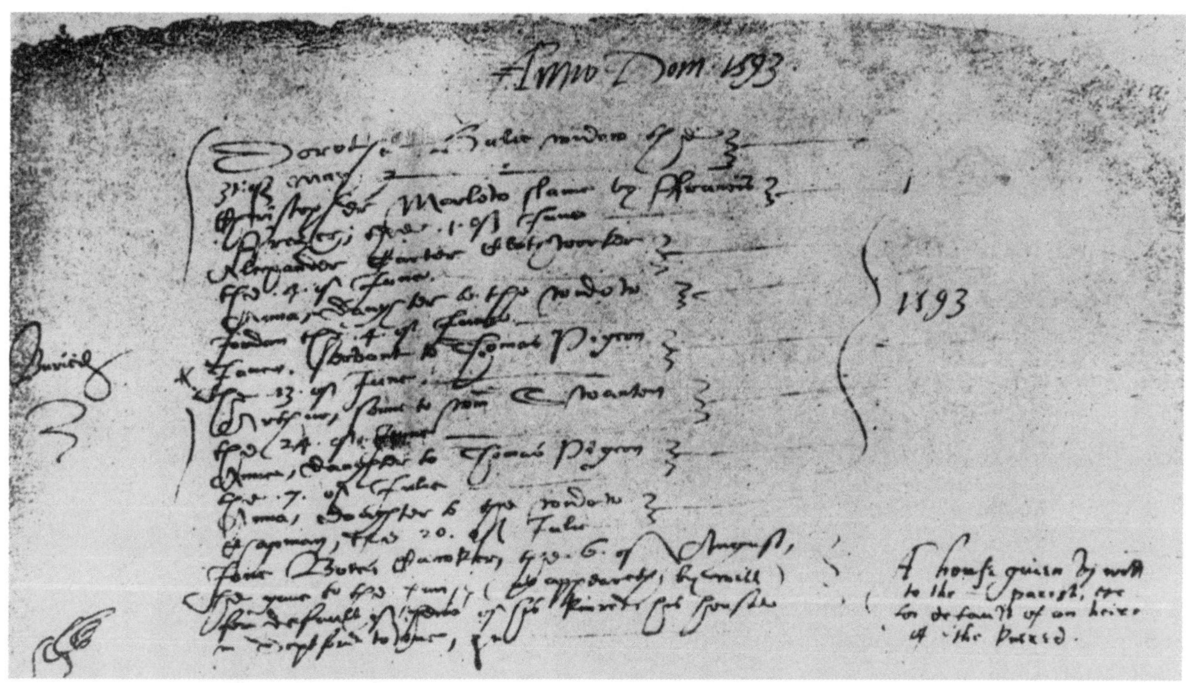

A portion of a page from the register of the Church of St. Nicholas, Deptford, listing the burial on 1 June 1593 of "Christopher Marlow slaine by ffrancis ffrezer" (Church of St. Nicholas, Deptford)

such as the Cambridge years. For the nation, these were times of political tension, with events such as the unmasking of the Babington Conspiracy, the execution of Mary, Queen of Scots, and the threat of the Spanish Armada. In literature the national unease manifested itself in works such as Thomas Lodge's play *The Wounds of Civil War* and Shakespeare's *Henry VI* trilogy. In this context book 1 of *Pharsalia* takes on a new dimension: it is not merely an academic and personal exercise but a warning of grim topicality against the horrors and dangers of civil butchery. Lucan's Centurion promises to wage war against his city at Ceasar's command, even if he should "Intombe my sword within my brothers bowels; / Or fathers throate . . . [.]" The lines may be compared with the stage direction which, for Shakespeare, indicated the greatest of civil (and natural) disorders: *"Enter a Sonne that hath kill'd his Father . . . and a Father that hath kill'd his Sone"* *(Henry VI*, part 3, II.v.).

In the preface to his translations of *Ovid's Epistles* (1680) John Dryden distinguished three kinds of translation, of which the first was "that of Metaphrase, or turning an Author word by word, and line by line, from one language into another." Marlowe's translations of Ovid and Lucan are of this kind—which is good reason to suppose that they are early works, where Marlowe might be reluctant to allow himself too much freedom because he lacked the confidence to use it. Dryden's second method offers greater scope: "Paraphrase, or Translation with Latitude," which is a useful term to describe Marlowe's handling of Virgil's *Aeneid* for what was probably his first play, *Dido Queen of Carthage* (1586).

Dryden explained "Paraphrase" by saying that in this kind of translation "the Author is kept in view by the Translator, so as never to be lost, but his Words are not so strictly followed as his Sense, and that too is admitted to be amplified, but not altered." Marlowe took the plot of his play from book 4 of Virgil's poem, but he moved easily around the epic, taking details from books one and two for his dramatic purposes. His translation changes the Latin into English, transforms epic narrative into stage action, and takes the part for the whole—the story of Dido occupies only one-twelfth of the *Aeneid*, so that the episode can be viewed sub specie aeternitatis.

Another difference—which is of great importance for the appreciation of the play—is that whereas Virgil's characters are superhuman, of proper epic proportions, Marlowe's are slightly less than human in size: they were meant to be acted by children. The title page of the first quarto edition advertises that the play was "Played by the Children of her Majesties

Chappell." The plays written for these highly professional children obeyed conventions different from those obtaining in plays written for adult performers: *Dido* is more appropriately compared—in respect of its technique—with the plays of Peele than with *Antony and Cleopatra* (whose subject matter is comparable).

Marlowe took from Virgil the account of Dido's passion for Aeneas, the Trojan hero shipwrecked on the Carthaginian coast after the destruction of Troy, and he added a subplot of the unrequited love of Anna, Dido's sister, for one of Dido's suitors, whose name—Iarbus—is mentioned only infrequently in the *Aeneid*. Virgil's hero is a man of destiny, ordained by the gods to sail to Italy and there establish the Roman race, the true descendants of the Trojans. The interlude with Dido is only a part of the divine plan, and Aeneas must not allow himself to be detained in Carthage, even though his departure is a tragic catastrophe for the Queen. Virgil's gods are always in control of the action.

Marlowe introduces the gods at the beginning of his play, daringly presenting them as a bunch of rather shabby immortals subject to very human emotions: Venus is anxious for the welfare of her shipwrecked son, Aeneas; Juno is jealous of Venus and irritated by her husband's infidelities; and Jupiter is besotted with a homosexual passion for Ganymede. This is a grotesquely "domestic" comedy, which might seem to endanger the tragic stature of the play's heroine and the epic status of its hero, since both Dido and Aeneas are at the mercy of such deities. The character of Aeneas has provoked varying reactions in critics of the play (one sees him as "an Elizabethan adventurer"; another adopts the medieval view in which he is the betrayer of Troy; and for yet another he is the unheroic "man-in-the-street" who has no desire for great actions). Dido, however, is unambiguously sympathetic. At first a majestic queen, she becomes almost inarticulate as she struggles with a passion that she does not understand; her grief at Aeneas's departure brings back her eloquence, and then, preparing for death, she achieves the isolated dignity of a tragic heroine. The inarticulateness was described by Virgil (*incipit effari, mediaque in voce resistit*), and Marlowe adds the immediacy of speech when in III.iv. Dido is overcome with love:

AENEAS. What ailes my Queene, is she falne sicke
of late?

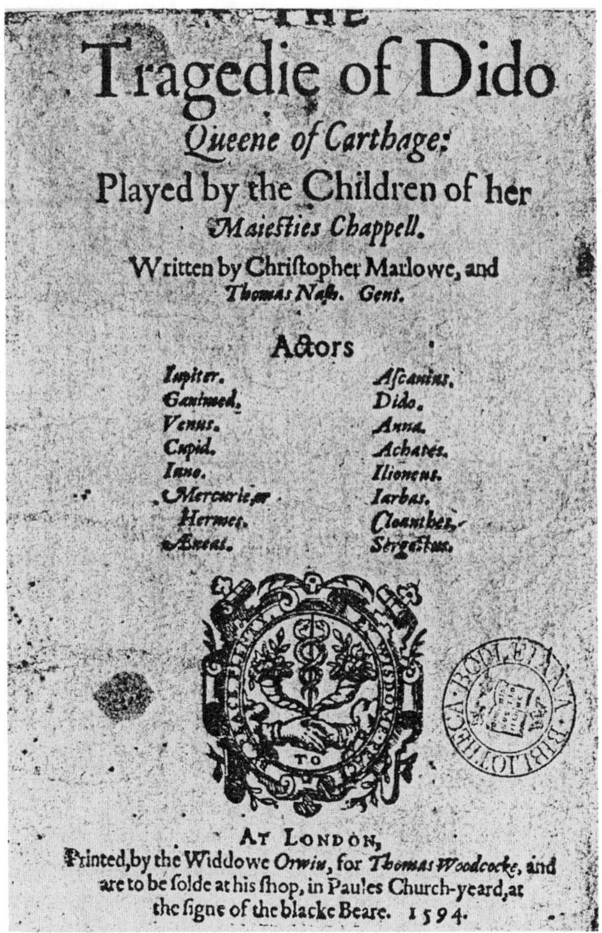
The Tragedie of Dido
Queene of Carthage:
Played by the Children of her
Maiesties Chappell.
Written by Christopher Marlowe, and
Thomas Nash. Gent.

Actors

Iupiter.	*Ascanius.*
Ganimed.	*Dido.*
Venus.	*Anna.*
Cupid.	*Achates.*
Iuno.	*Ilioneus.*
Mercurie, or Hermes.	*Iarbas.*
Aeneas.	*Cloanthes.*
	Sergestus.

AT LONDON,
Printed, by the Widdowe *Orwin*, for *Thomas Woodcocke*, and are to be solde at his shop, in Paules Church-yeard, at the signe of the blacke Beare. 1594.

Title page for the 1594 quarto edition of the play Marlowe based on the story of Dido in book 4 of Virgil's Aeneid *(Bodleian Library, Oxford). Thomas Nash may have prepared the manuscript for publication, but he is not believed to have had a hand in the play's composition.*

DIDO. Not sicke my love, but sicke:——I must
conceal
The torment, that it bootes me not reveale,
And yet Ile speake, and yet Ile hold my
peace,
Doe shame her worst, I will disclose my
griefe:——
Aeneas, thou art he, what did I say?
Something it was that now I have forgot.

At the end of the play Marlowe does not translate the Latin, and this has been called by Harry Levin "an evasion that smells of the university." Rather, it shows Marlowe's respect, both for his author and for his audience. The lines that he takes from Virgil are beautiful—and well known: he could not hope to equal them. When the stage Aeneas is adamant to Dido's entreaties, he utters the words of the epic hero (which include one of the best-known half lines in all poetry): *"Desine meque tuis incendere teque querelis, / Italiam non sponte sequor."* ("Cease to inflame both me and yourself within your lamentations. It is not of my own free will that I seek Italy.") And Dido's last words, as she curses Aeneas before her self-immolation, are the words of Virgil—but the dramatic moment is intensified by the interpolation of an English line:

> *Littora littoribus contraria, fluctibus undas*
> *Imprecor: arma armis: pugnent ipsíque nepotes:*
> Live false *Aeneas*, truest *Dido* dyes,
> *Sic sic juvat ire sub umbras.*

> ("I pray that coasts may be opposed to coasts, waves to waves, and arms to arms; may they and their descendants ever fight. . . . Thus, thus I rejoice to enter into the shades.")

Implicit tribute is paid in these lines not only to the verse of Virgil and the understanding of the audiences but also to the skills of the child actors, who were chosen from the (already highly selected) boys of the royal choirs and given special coaching for their theatrical roles. Writers in the sixteenth century such as Peele and John Lyly (and in the seventeenth century, Ben Jonson and Thomas Middleton) were proud to write for such companies, recognizing that special demands were made on them to exploit the assets and minimize the limitations of the child actors.

Immaturity was the most obvious limiting factor: verisimilitude was not to be looked for, and the presentation of "character" (in the modern sense of the word) was clearly impossible. Instead the productions compensated by offering spectacle, where the emphasis was always on artifice and where imitation was always ready to draw attention to itself qua imitation—expecting applause for the excellence of its craftsmanship in equaling (and, if possible, surpassing) nature. For example, an Oxford boys' production of an entertainment in 1583 was reported with wonder, for there was "a goodllie sight of hunters with full crie of a kennel of hounds . . . the tempest wherein it hailed small confects, rained rose water, and snew an artificial kind of snew, all strange, marvellous, and abundant" (in John Nichols, *The Progresses, and Public Processions, of Queen Elizabeth*, 1788-1807). The dramatists' choice of subject matter also emphasized the artificiality of the performances: boys with unbroken voices took the parts of the great figures from classical mythology—"Hercules and his load too," as Rosencrantz tells Hamlet.

The great strength of the children was their *elocution*, taught as part of the discipline of rhetoric in every Elizabethan grammar school. It included not only the training of the voice but practice in the appropriate accompanying gestures and facial expressions. And the child actors were, of course, far more accomplished than the average schoolboy. Marlowe's play calls for such talent—especially in Aeneas's account of the Fall of Troy, where more than sixty lines are punctuated only occasionally by comments from the other character, orchestrating pity and terror in fine narrative verse.

The play was published in 1594, and the title page claims Thomas Nash as part author—but there is no trace of his hand in the composition. Perhaps Nash secured, or even transcribed, the manuscript for publishers eager to take advantage of the notoriety of Marlowe's death and unable to obtain possession of the other plays since these were all the valued property of adult theatrical companies.

The earliest of these plays had, however, already been published: the two parts of *Tamburlaine the Great*, subtitled *Two Tragicall Discourses*, appeared in print in 1590, two or three years after the plays were performed by the Admiral's Men. The first of these "Discourses" appears to be complete in itself, leaving the eponymous hero triumphantly alive at the end of act 5, where he announces that now "*Tamburlaine* takes truce with al the world." The second "Discourse" opens with a prologue which testifies to the popularity of the first, explaining its own raison d'être:

> *The generall welcomes* Tamburlain *receiv'd,*
> *When he arrived last upon our stage,*
> *Hath made our Poet pen his second part*[.]

At the end of this play's act 5, "earth hath spent the pride of all her fruit": Tamburlaine is dead.

In outline, the action of *Tamburlaine* is simple. The hero of part 1, a Scythian shepherd of boundless aspiration, encounters no serious opposition in his rise to power and majesty. By force, either of rhetoric or of arms, he overcomes all resistance—winning allies, conquering kings and kingdoms, and captivating the beautiful Zenocrate. The play ends with amatory as well as martial triumph, anticipating the "celebrated rites of mariage." In part 2 the opposition grows and is not merely human in origin: Tamburlaine is dis-

Tamburlaine
the Great.
Who, from a Scythian Shepbearde,
by his rare and woonderfull Conquests,
became a most puissant and mighty tye Monarque.
And (for his tyranny, and terrour in Warre) was tearmed,
The Scourge of God.
Deuided into two Tragicall Dis-
courses, as they were sundrie times
shewed vpon Stages in the Citie
of London.
By the right honorable the Lord
Admyrall, his seruantes.
Now first, and newlie published.

LONDON.
Printed by Richard Ihones: at the signe
of the Rose and Crowne neere Holborne Bridge. 1590.

Title page for the 1590 octavo edition of the two-part tragedy whose "high astounding tearms" were both imitated and parodied by Marlowe's contemporaries (C. F. Tucker Brooke, ed., The Works of Christopher Marlowe, *1910)*

appointed in his sons; Zenocrate falls sick and dies; lastly Tamburlaine himself is forced to confess that "sicknesse proove[s] me now to be a man."

The play's style suits the character. In verses prefixed to the first folio edition of Shakespeare's plays (1623), Ben Jonson referred to "Marlowe's mighty line," and it is in part 1 of *Tamburlaine* that this line is evolved, especially when in II.vii. the hero enunciates his credo:

> Nature that fram'd us of foure Elements,
> Warring within our breasts for regiment,
> Doth teach us all to have aspyring minds:
> Our soules, whose faculties can comprehend
> The wondrous Architecture of the world:
> And measure every wandring plannets course:
> Still climing after knowledge infinite,
> And alwaies mooving as the restles Spheares,
> Wils us to weare our selves and never rest,
> Untill we reach the ripest fruit of all,
> That perfect blisse and sole felicitie,
> The sweet fruition of an earthly crowne.

The verse sweeps to its climax at the end of the paragraph, verbally enacting the speaker's breathless impetuousness and captivating audiences just as Tamburlaine's person vanquishes all resistance.

But the play does not ask for *uncritical* applause, either for the character or for the "high astounding tearms" of his utterances. Marlowe is well aware that both ambition and hyperbole are potentially ludicrous, and in the first scene he encourages laughter, thereby establishing criteria for the appreciation of his protagonist.

The very first lines of the play, spoken by Mycetes, King of Persia, make the proper association between personality and linguistic command:

> Brother *Cosroe*, I find my selfe agreev'd,
> Yet insufficient to expresse the same:
> For it requires a great and thundring speech[.]

Marlowe demonstrates the comic range of such "thundring speech" as soon as Mycetes attempts to speak as befits his dignity. His comedy includes the grimly incongruous—in the description of "milk-white steeds"

> All loden with the heads of killed men.
> And from their knees, even to their hoofes below,
> Besmer'd with blood, that makes a dainty show.

There is even one of the crude "conceits [which] clownage keeps in pay" which are scorned in the prologue:

> MYCETES. Well here I sweare by this my royal seate—
> COSROE. You may doe well to kisse it then.
> MYCETES. Embost with silke as best beseemes my state[.]

The folly and weakness of Mycetes justify Cosroe in his determination to overthrow his brother and wear the crown himself; and this act of usurpation serves to justify Tamburlaine in his subsequent decision.

Tamburlaine first appears in the company of Zenocrate, to whom he offers comfort and protection. Although he is dressed as a shepherd, his behavior is more like that of a knight in some medieval romance. Before our eyes, he seems to increase in stature as he sheds his humble garments ("weedes that I disdaine to weare") and exchanges them for "adjuncts more beseeming"—a "compleat armour" and a "curtle-axe." So accoutred, he is compared by his companions to a lion (the emblem of kingship), and he himself refers to "Empires"; but the first impassioned speech is made to Zenocrate—and Tamburlaine is thereby associated with beauty, jewels, love, and richness, rather than bloodthirsty conquests. The advance of the Persian horsemen also places Tamburlaine in a favorable position for winning the sympathy of the audience—he asks the Soldier to confirm the enemy numbers: "A thousand horsemen? We five hundred foote?" Undeterred he outlines a stratagem and declares his willingness to combat against far greater odds—"Weele fight five hundred men at armes to one"—and to face the foe himself—"My selfe will bide the danger of the brunt."

By the end of act 2, Tamburlaine is secure in his position of "super-man," because he has been seen to deserve it and to be morally as well as physically superior to those he has defeated. He reaches a pinnacle of success in act 3, when he fights against the Turkish Emperor Bajazeth.

The Turk's proud boasts overtop Tamburlaine's own claims, and Bajazeth is accompanied by apparently powerful allies—so that once again Tamburlaine's army seems to be heavily outnumbered. Furthermore, Tamburlaine is now presented as a defender of the faith, opposed to the infidel Turks and promising to

inlarge
Those Christian Captives, which you keep as slaves,
Burdening their bodies with your heavie chaines,
And feeding them with thin and slender fare,
That naked rowe about the Terrene sea.

The battle is splendidly managed. Fought offstage, its progress is commented on by Zabina and Zenocrate, who also wage a verbal battle which parallels the conflict of the warriors. But although Tamburlaine once again deserves victory, his treatment of the conquered Bajazeth gives rise to audience suspicion that he is beginning to overreach himself.

For the rest of part 1, and throughout most of part 2, Marlowe balances scenes of great brutality, performed with a ritual solemnity, against speeches of amazing beauty in praise of Zenocrate and in lament for her death. Themes of ambition, love, power, and justice are introduced in part 1 and developed further in part 2, so that the two parts form a symphonic unity.

Increasingly in part 1 and throughout the whole of part 2, Tamburlaine images himself as "the Scourge and Wrath of God," the instrument of some divine retribution; this must be accepted by the audience—who must also recognize (as an Elizabethan audience certainly would acknowledge) that the scourge itself must be scourged and destroyed. Even Tamburlaine seems sporadically aware of this fact—as when, at the death of Zenocrate, he inveighs in II.iv. against the

Proud furie and intollorable fit,
That dares torment the body of my Love,
And scourge the Scourge of the immortall God[.]

Thus admiration (for the valor) and horror (at the cruelty) are tempered with respectful anticipation of the inevitable catastrophe.

The style of *Tamburlaine* was immediately infectious: but imitation soon turned to parody and then to scorn. In *Timber* (1640) Ben Jonson warns his "true Artificer" that the language of his play should not "fly from all humanity, with the *Tamerlanes*, and *Tamer-Chams* of the late Age, which had nothing in them but the *scenicall* strutting, and furious vociferation, warrant them to the ignorant gapers." The actor responsible for the "*scenicall* strutting" was Edward Alleyn, the star performer of the Admiral's Men, for whom Marlowe wrote this play. For Alleyn, also, he created the role of Barabas in his next play, *The Jew of Malta* (1590).

Internal evidence (mainly stylistic) suggests that *The Jew of Malta* was written circa 1589; it was frequently performed by the Admiral's Men in the years immediately following Marlowe's death, and the recorded "box-office receipts" testify to its popularity. There was no printed text until 1633 when a quarto edition was published carrying new prologues and epilogues written by Thomas Heywood; it seems likely that Heywood was also responsible for a complete revision of the play—but the full extent of his revising cannot be ascertained. In both of his new prologues Heywood alludes to the play's antiquity: addressing the "Gracious and Great" in the "Prologue spoken at Court," he explains that *The Jew of Malta* was "writ many years agone," and he adds that it was "in that Age, thought second unto none."

The play has always been "second unto none" in the sense that nothing else in English drama is quite like it: it has no place in any recog-

Portrait of Edward Alleyn, who played the title role in Tamburlaine *and Barabas in* The Jew of Malta *(Dulwich College Picture Gallery, London)*

nizable dramatic tradition. Shakespeare's Shylock is a distant relation of Marlowe's Barabas, and Jonson's Volpone shares his interest: but these similarities only emphasize the differences between *The Jew of Malta* on the one hand, and *The Merchant of Venice* (circa 1596-1597) or *Volpone* (1606) on the other.

Marlowe's play has no obvious source. The action is set on the tiny Mediterranean island of Malta, which at the end of the sixteenth century was a Spanish possession occupied by the Knights Hospitaler after their expulsion from Rhodes in 1522. Marlowe's Knights (and audience) are reminded of this fact in II.ii.:

> Remember that to *Europ's* shame,
> The Christian Ile of *Rhodes*, from whence you came,
> Was lately lost, and you were stated here
> To be at deadly enmity with Turkes.

The Knights of the play, however, have a truce with the Turks, to whom they owe a tribute. In order to pay this tribute Ferneze, the Governor of Malta, determines to levy tax on the island's Jews, who must either pay one-half of their estates, or else be converted to Christianity. The wealthiest Jew, Barabas, rejects both alternatives. To punish him, Ferneze confiscates his entire property; the rest of the play shows Barabas's efforts to reinstate himself—he in fact becomes Governor of Malta—and to take revenge on those who have injured him. There follows a rapid succession of murders: Ferneze's son, who is in love with the Jew's daughter, fights a duel—in which both he and his rival are killed; Abigail, the object of their affections, is poisoned—and an entire convent of nuns dies with her; two suspicious friars quarrel—one is strangled and the other hanged; Ithamore, a villainous Turkish slave who has been Barabas's instrument, is poisoned before he can betray his master—a prostitute and her pimp die with him; a monastery housing the Turkish forces is blown up while their leader is preparing to banquet with Barabas—but the leader (the son of the Turkish emperor) is saved when Ferneze operates the mechanism which should have precipitated him into a cauldron of boiling water. It is Barabas who is boiled to death, caught in his own trap; and he dies with a fine, melodramatic defiance: "Dye life, flye soule, tongue curse thy fill and dye."

The speed with which these crimes are dispatched encourages in the spectator the detachment appropriate to comedy, precluding any sympathy with the victims. And only Abigail is presented as an attractive character—"The hopelesse daughter of a haplesse Jew." Her death is pathetic: in III.vi. she expires in the arms of the friar who converted her, with the laudable sentiment

ah gentle Fryar,
Convert my father that he may be sav'd,
And witnesse that I dye a Christian.

But pathos is immediately dissolved in laughter with the friar's response: "I [Aye], and a Virgin too, that grieves me most." None of the other murder victims emerges as more than a comic stereotype—the romantic lover, the avaricious friar (an anti-Catholic caricature), a slave whose curriculum vitae includes "setting Christian villages on fire, Chaining of Eunuches, binding gally-slaves," and a prostitute lamenting the decline of trade in Malta ("my gaine growes cold . . . now against my will I must be chast").

In contrast to all these Barabas is presented as a richly unique character. A "bottle-nos'd knave," he opens the play as a mercantile adven-

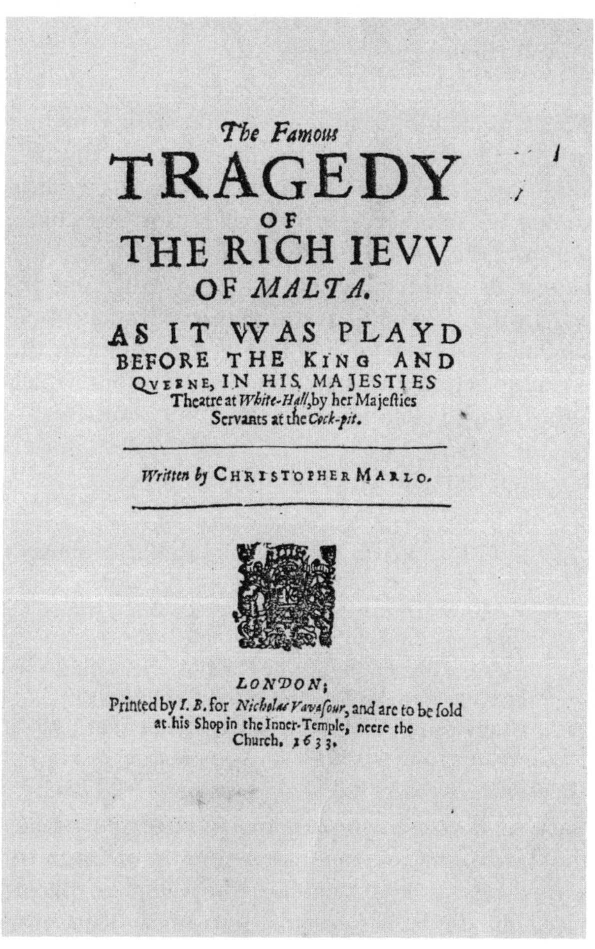
The Famous
TRAGEDY
OF
THE RICH IEVV
OF MALTA.
AS IT WAS PLAYD
BEFORE THE KING AND
QVEENE, IN HIS MAJESTIES
Theatre at White-Hall, by her Majesties
Servants at the Cock-pit.

Written by CHRISTOPHER MARLO.

LONDON;
Printed by I. B. for Nicholas Vavasour, and are to be sold
at his Shop in the Inner-Temple, neere the
Church, 1633.

Title page for the 1633 quarto edition of the play that—according to Thomas Heywood, who added new prologues and epilogues to this first printing of Marlowe's popular tragedy—was "writ many years agone" and was "in that Age, thought second unto none" (Anderson Galleries auction catalogue, sale number 2032, 15-16 February 1926)

turer, discovered *"in his Counting-house, with heapes of gold before him."* Absorbed in his enterprises, he is a businessman who keeps his accounts straight. In I.i. he says,

So that of thus much that returne was made:
And of the third part of the Persian ships,
There was the venture summ'd and satisfied.

But he soon shows frustration and envy:

Fye; what a trouble tis to count this trash.
Well fare the Arabians who so richly pay
The things they traffique for with wedge of gold[.]

Ambition turns him into a dreamer—a visionary lost in the admiration of

Bags of fiery *Opals*, *Saphires*, *Amatists*,
Jacints, hard *Topas*, grasse-greene *Emeraulds*,

> Beauteous *Rubyes*, sparkling *Diamonds*,
> And seildsene costly stones . . . [.]

The speech builds to a crescendo, rising to one of Marlowe's best-known lines when Barabas longs to "inclose / Infinite riches in a little roome." There are further revelations to come, but already we (as audience or readers) have begun to understand Barabas; we are more inward with him than any of the other dramatis personae. This sense of intimacy is developed in the ensuing action through the use of asides which allow us to feel superior to the other characters—to the Jews, for instance, when later in I.i. Barabas seems to be promising his support:

> 2. JEW. But there's a meeting in the Senate-house,
> And all the Jewes in *Malta* must be there.
> BARABAS. Umh; All the Jewes in *Malta* must be there?
> I [Aye], like enough, why then let every man
> Provide him, and be there for fashion-sake.
> If any thing shall there concerne our state
> Assure your selves I'le looke——*unto my selfe*.

Barabas is also a sympathetic character in that, at the beginning of the play, he is a man more sinned against than sinning: the victim of prejudice, his fault lies in his Jewishness—and the Knights of Malta are prepared to use religion as a cloak for theft when they take the Jews' property to pay the Turks. Barabas discloses their hypocrisy—"Preach me not out of my possessions."

In this confrontation of Jew and Roman Catholic, Marlowe is presenting two objects of fear, hatred, and suspicion to the Elizabethan Protestants who formed the play's contemporary audience. As Christians, the Elizabethans believed the Jews to be the race that betrayed and crucified their God; but as Englishmen they recognized in Roman Catholicism a threat to their church and their monarch. From the very beginning of the play there is a complexity of emotional response which is by no means reconciled at the end of act 5.

By overreaching himself in his villainy Barabas, like Tamburlaine in the earlier play, has alienated the audience; his ignominious death in the cauldron—standard Elizabethan punishment for the poisoner—is seen to be most appropriate. At the same time, it is impossible to share in the unctuous piety of Ferneze's closing couplet: "let due praise be given / Neither to Fate nor Fortune, but to Heaven." It is, perhaps, the last joke of this early "black comedy."

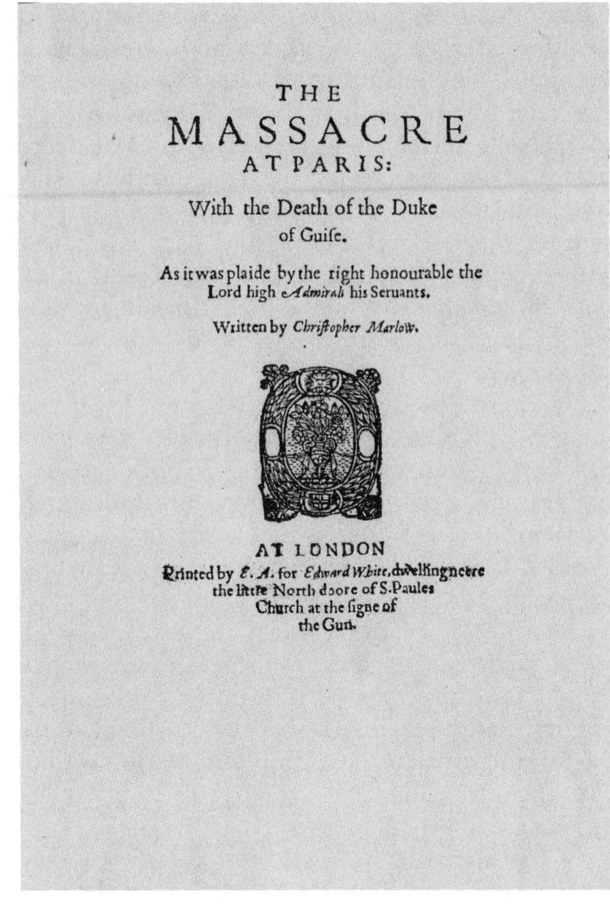
THE
MASSACRE
AT PARIS:
With the Death of the Duke of Guiſe.
As it was plaide by the right honourable the Lord high *Admirall* his Seruants.
Written by *Chriſtopher Marlow*.
AT LONDON
Printed by *E. A.* for *Edward White*, dwelling neere the little North doore of S. Paules Church at the ſigne of the Gun.

Title page for the 1594(?) octavo edition of the play that Marlowe must have written after the death of Henry III of France in August 1589 (Bodleian Library, Oxford)

Marlowe seems to be well acquainted with the history of Malta—whence Jews were expelled in 1422 unless they cared to purchase Christian baptism at the price of 45 percent of their individual estates. In the 1580s the island seems to have had a particular interest for the English. There were suspicions—still imperfectly understood—of conspiracies and espionage which might have been known to Marlowe, whose interest in politics and current events did not cease with his Cambridge career.

This interest is clearly evidenced by *The Massacre at Paris*, a play linked stylistically with *The Jew of Malta* by its grim humor. The date of *The Massacre at Paris* is unknown: it was performed circa 1590, and must have been written after the death, in August 1589, of Henry III of France. The first scenes of the play present the bloody violence of the French riots in 1572, when more than thirty thousand French Protestants were murdered at the hands of Roman Catholics led by Henri I de Lorraine, third Duke of Guise (drawing support from Catherine de Médicis). The play ends after Guise has been murdered (December 1588) at the instigation of Henry III, and when Henry himself is dying, passing the French crown to Henry of Navarre (Henry IV of France). Among the accusations made against Guise is the rhetorical reminder

> Did he not draw a sorte of English priestes
> From Doway to the Seminary at Remes,
> To hatch forth treason gainst their naturall
> Queene?
> Did he not cause the King of *Spaines* huge fleete,
> To threaten *England* . . . ?

Marlowe could, of course, have gained this information from the printed sources that he was using; but it must not be forgotten that he may well have been at Reims in the service of Walsingham and the Privy Council. Just before his death Henry III addresses the "Agent for *England,*" instructing him to "send thy mistres word, What this detested Jacobin [the Duke of Guise] hath done"; swearing to "ruinate that wicked Church of *Rome,*" he vows his loyalty to the Protestant cause, "And to the Queene of *England* specially, / Whom God hath blest for hating Papestry." The "Agent for *England*" at the time of Henry III of France was Walsingham himself.

Unfortunately, *The Massacre at Paris* survives only in a pitifully mangled form, and the undated octavo edition cannot offer adequate material for an assessment of Marlowe's work. There are the traces of a fine theatricality in the very first scene, where the religious tensions are shown at the wedding of the Protestant Navarre to the Catholic Margaret—a union which Catherine de Médicis threatens to "desolve with bloud and crueltie." The character of Guise is presented with typical Marlovian ambivalence: unquestionably a brutal, ruthless murderer, he nevertheless is possessed of aspiration and a high disdain which in themselves are praiseworthy:

> That like I best that flyes beyond my reach.
> Set me to scale the high Peramides,
> And thereon set the Diadem of *Fraunce,*
> Ile either rend it with my nayles to naught,
> Or mount the top with my aspiring winges,
> Although my downfall be the deepest hell.

And although Henry III's deeds are sanctioned by his Protestant sympathies, the character is not given uncritical approval: his hypocrisy is blatant, and we are clearly shown the weakness to which Queen Catherine draws attention: "His minde you see runnes on his minions." In this last respect, the character seems to adumbrate the protagonist of *Edward II* (1592-1593).

The eponymous hero of this play on the subject of English history is the only one of Marlowe's protagonists who is totally lacking in the charismatic energy with which the rest are driven, and which is voiced in the "high astounding tearmes" of *Tamburlaine.* This was not a part designed for Edward Alleyn.

According to the title page of the first edition (1594), *Edward II* was "sundrie times publiquely acted in the honourable citie of London, by the right honourable the Earle of Pembrooke his servants." Pembroke's Men seems to have been a scratch troupe of actors who toured the provinces in time of plague; in September 1593 they were penniless and forced to disband, pawning their costumes and selling their playbooks. Marlowe might have written his play especially for this company: it demands few elaborate costumes and asks for no multilevel staging, and in such respects it would suit a touring company. But it offers no roles comparable with those of Tamburlaine, Barabas, or Dr. Faustus—the parts played by Edward Alleyn for the Admiral's Men.

Most of the events of *Edward II* were taken from Raphael Holinshed's *Chronicles of England* (1597). The five acts of Marlowe's play span twenty-three years of English history, from the accession of Edward II in 1307 until the events of 1330 when Mortimer's treachery was discovered. Edward was a weak king, besotted by love for his "minion," Piers Gaveston. Neglecting—and even abusing—both his queen and the realm, he was imprisoned and cruelly murdered.

The play also shows the rise to power and "the tragicall fall of proud Mortimer." At first Mortimer is an impetuous patriot, resenting the honors which the King bestows on Gaveston because the country is thereby impoverished. But ambition leads him to rebel. He becomes the Queen's lover; forces Edward to resign the crown to his son; and takes upon himself the position of Protector to the young King. For a short time he can gloat over his power, saying in V.iv.:

> Now all is sure, the Queene and *Mortimer*
> Shall rule the realme, the king, and none rule us,
> Mine enemies will I plague, my friends advance,

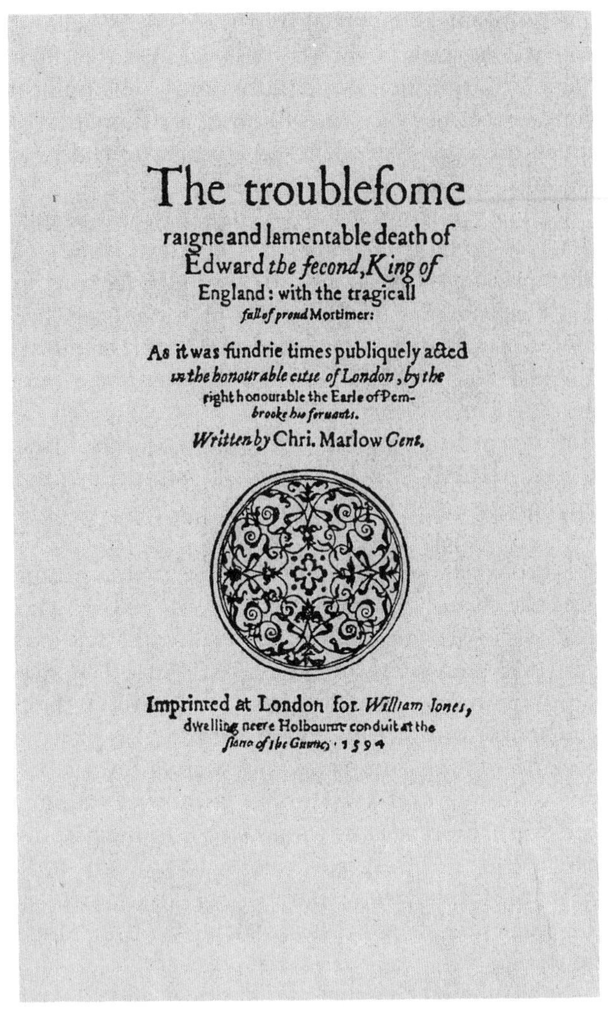
The troubleſome
raigne and lamentable death of
Edward the ſecond, King of
England: with the tragicall
fall of proud Mortimer:

As it was ſundrie times publiquely acted
in the honourable citie of London, by the
right honourable the Earle of Pembrooke his ſeruants.

Written by Chri. Marlow Gent.

Imprinted at London for William Iones,
dwelling neere Holbourne conduit at the
ſigne of the Gunne. 1594

Title page for the 1594 quarto edition of the play that Marlowe may have written for a provincial touring company (C. F. Tucker Brooke, ed., The Works of Christopher Marlowe, *1910)*

> And what I list commaund, who dare controwle?
> *Major sum quam cui possit fortuna nocere.*
> ("I am great beyond Fortune's harm.")

He has arranged the murder of Edward, who dies in agony; but the crime is discovered, and the new King condemns Mortimer to a traitor's death.

Sympathies in this play are never fixed, and the characters are usually complex. From a passionate patriot Mortimer becomes a Machiavellian usurper and a sadistic regicide. Isabella, the Queen, is at first (in II.iv.) a cruelly wronged wife, "Whose pining heart, her inward sighes have blasted, / And body with continuall moorning wasted." Love and obedience are eventually destroyed, and she finds comfort in Mortimer's gentle courtesy. Soon she is quite dominated by her lover: in IV.vi. we are told by the Earl of Kent (always a useful guide to the direction our sympathies should take) that *"Mortimer* And *Isabell* doe kisse while they conspire," and in V.ii. the Queen herself acknowledges her new love:

> Sweet *Mortimer*, the life of *Isabell*,
> Be thou perswaded, that I love thee well,
> And therefore so the prince my sonne be safe,
> Whome I esteeme as deare as these mine eyes,
> Conclude against his father what thou wilt,
> And I my selfe will willinglie subscribe.

Isabella's rival for her husband's attentions is the young Frenchman, Piers Gaveston. He too is a character who develops—or at least changes—during the course of the play's action. He opens the play with a soliloquy, outlining schemes he has devised to "draw the pliant king which way I please"; although he speaks of Edward with affection, it is certain that self-interest is a powerful motivating force. As the play progresses, however, it becomes equally certain his self-interest gives way to an unselfish love that overcomes the bitterness of captivity and the imminence of an ignoble death—in II.iv., for example, Gaveston looks forward to a final meeting with his lover: "Sweete soveraigne, yet I come To see thee ere I die."

Toward Edward II, Marlowe's attitude (and consequently *our* attitude) seems to be ambivalent. Edward is a danger to the country's stability in his free dispensation of offices and wealth to a commoner. Wailing over Gaveston's departure, or on tiptoe with excitement at his return, the King is ludicrous. And the husband who flaunts a lover before his wife, making her acceptance of Gaveston the condition for the continuance of their marriage, is utterly despicable. Against such charges Marlowe sets the solitary redeeming fact that Edward loves Gaveston:

> MORTIMER. Why should you love him, whome the world hates so?
> EDWARD. Because he loves me more then all the world.

Edward is a man of extremes, swerving violently from the blackest depression to carefree exuberance with no intervening stage of reasonable moderation. In his death he is the object of intense pity—and admiration.

Edward's death is a parody of the homosexual act. The details were supplied by history, and Marlowe accumulated them from various chronicle sources. The King is arrested at the Abbey of Neath, where he has tried to find sanctuary among friends and sympathizers; in IV.vii. Marlowe, the poet of striving and aspiration, becomes the poet of weariness and despondency:

good father on thy lap
Lay I this head, laden with mickle care,
O might I never open these eyes againe,
Never againe lift up this drooping head,
O never more lift up this dying hart!

It is the last comfort he will find. After his capture he is bundled "from place to place by night," shaved in puddle water, and finally imprisoned in a stinking cell—"the sincke, Wherein the filthe of all the castell falles" and where "One plaies continually upon a Drum." Edward recounts his pitiful story to Lightborn, a character of Marlowe's own imagination, who is in fact the murderer. Lightborn is subhuman, a machine for murder. He is the only character in the play who has no emotional response to Edward, and his heartless efficiency seems to intensify the King's muddled, suffering humanity. For one moment Edward becomes a king again as in V.v., where, with an almost habitual grace, he bestows his last jewel—"Know that I am a king. . . ."

Not until he lost his throne did Edward rise to kingship, and the sad eloquence of his final speeches is in contrast to the empty rhetoric that precedes them. The "mighty line" is subdued in this play, whose characteristic modes are irony and deflation: when in IV.iv. Isabella begins a peroration to justify the rebellion against Edward, she is abruptly silenced by Mortimer:

QUEENE..
Misgoverned kings are cause of all this wrack,
And *Edward* thou art one among them all,
Whose loosnes hath betrayed thy land to spoyle,
And made the channels overflow with blood,
Of thine own people patron shouldst hou be
But thou———
MORTIMER. Nay madam, if you be a warriar,
Ye must not grow so passionate in speeches[.]

Only Mortimer is allowed to hold up the play's action with a heroic parting speech, but the words of stoical courage are preceded and followed by references to Mortimer as "traitor" and "murderer" which effectively reduce the speech's impact.

Frustration and weakness are Marlowe's themes in *Edward II.* There is no superman hero—and the soaring splendor of the verse in *Tamburlaine* would be inappropiate here. In his next play, *Dr. Faustus* (1594), Marlowe sets the mighty lines of the hero's aspirations in a critical balance against the cool tones of experience, achieving thereby a tragedy which is still—in the twentieth century—able to startle and terrify with its thoughtful intensity.

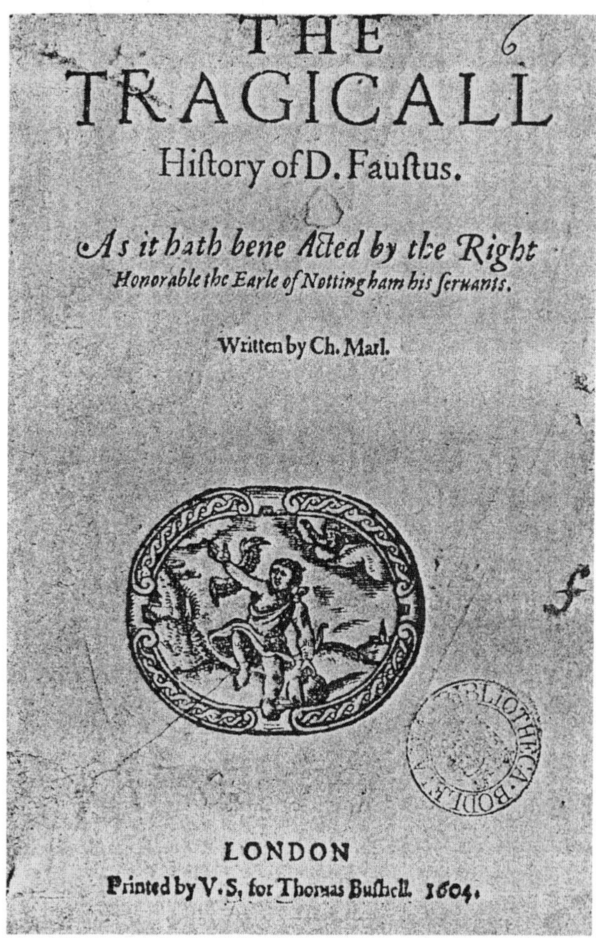

Title page for the unique copy of the 1604 quarto edition of the play that may have been left unfinished at Marlowe's death in May 1593 (Antiq.e E 1588[3]; Bodleian Library, Oxford)

At the beginning of the play Faustus, having excelled in all branches of human knowledge, finds his intellectual ambitions still unsatisfied: although as a physician, for instance, he has achieved renown in the treatment of a "thousand desperate maladies," he longs for greater power:

Couldst thou make men to live eternally,
Or being dead, raise them to life againe,
Then this profession were to be esteem'd.

At last he turns to Divinity, but upon opening the Bible he is confronted with an apparently insoluble dilemma when he juxtaposes two sentences: "The reward of sin is death" and "If we say that we have no sinne we deceive our selves, and there is no truth in us." From these two premises he proceeds to the syllogism's logical conclusion:

Why then belike
We must sinne, and so consequently die,
I [Aye], we must die, an everlasting death.

Throwing his books aside, he opts for the study of magic, resolving be this means "to get a Deity."

In I.iii., with his first invocation, he conjures up the devil, Mephostophilis, and makes a bargain with him: in exchange for twenty-four years of power and knowledge, when Mephostophilis will be his servant, Faustus will hazard his immortal soul. Mephostophilis, a surprisingly honest devil, tries to dissuade the eager conjurer by painting a bleak picture of the torments of the damned:

Think'st thou that I who saw the face of God,
And tasted the eternall Joyes of heaven,
Am not tormented with ten thousand hels,
In being depriv'd of everlasting blisse?
O *Faustus* leave these frivolous demandes,
Which strike a terror to my fainting soule.

Faustus is undeterred, refusing to believe "that after this life there is any paine." At the devil's request he writes a formal legal document in his own blood, which is "A Deed of Gift, of body and of soule."

For the next twenty-four years he pursues knowledge and pleasure, but finds only disappointment. All the time he is accompanied by two Angels, Good and Evil; the former urges him to turn to God in repentance and hope for mercy, while the Evil Angel persuades him that he cannot repent, that he can never be forgiven, and that "devils will teare [him] in peeces" if he attempts to break the promise he has made to the devil. In the last act of the play he twice conjures up the spirit of Helen of Troy—the first time for the benefit of his scholar friends, who have requested to see "the admirablest Lady that ever lived." The second conjuration is for his own delight and comfort; he asks for Helen as his "paramour,"

Whose sweet embraces may extinguish cleare,
Those thoughts that do disswade me from my vow,
And keepe mine oath I made to *Lucifer*.

The second appearance of Helen calls forth from Faustus the most famous lines that Marlowe ever wrote:

Was this the face that Launcht a thousand ships,
And burnt the toplesse Towers of *Ilium*?
Sweet *Hellen* make me immortall with a kisse:
Her lips sucke forth my soule, see where it flies.

Such hyperbole is by no means uncommon in the love poetry of the sixteenth century, but here there is a cruel irony. In Helen's embraces Faustus "from [his] soule exclud[es] the grace of heaven" (V.i.) and indeed assures himself of immortality—"in hell for ever" (V.ii.).

The final soliloquy enacts his last hour on earth and reverses the movement of the first soliloquy. The proud scholar, who had fretted at the restrictions imposed by the human condition and longed for the immortality of a god, now seeks to escape from an eternity of damnation. To be physically absorbed by the elements, to be "a creature wanting soule," "some brutish beast," even—at the last—to be "chang'd into little water drops": this is the final ambition of the man who had once tried "to get a Deity." Time is the dominant in this speech. The measured regularity of the opening gives way to a frantic tugging in two directions as Faustus is torn between Christ and the devil: "O I'le leape up to my God: who puls me downe?" The pace and passion increase as the clock strikes relentlessly, and the second half hour passes more quickly than the first. We are agonizingly aware of the last minutes of Faustus's life, trickling away like sand through the hourglass with what seems like ever-increasing speed. But as each grain falls, bringing Faustus closer to his terrible end, we become more and more conscious of the deserts of vast eternity and damnation that open up beyond death.

The critic Leo Kirschaum said in 1943 that "there is no more obvious Christian document in all Elizabethan drama than *Doctor Faustus*" (*Review of English Studies*). But its ideology is not simple. The form is, in some respects, that of the old morality plays—with two significant differences. Firstly, the central figure is not the generic Everyman: Dr. Faustus is an individual, with a history (born in Germany, "within a Towne cal'd *Rhode*," to parents "base of stocke") and an impressive curriculum vitae. And, in the second place, the fate of this individual is not that of the type character, whose fall into sin is condemned and then—before the end of the play—redeemed.

It is important to remember that Marlowe spent some time as a student of theology; and a close reading of *Dr. Faustus* reveals the dramatist's recollections of his study. Dr. Faustus sins willfully: he has full knowledge of the consequences of his deed (even though he does not believe in the reality of the threatened hell), and in II.i. he takes complete responsibility:

> MEPHOSTOPHILIS. Speake *Faustus*, do you deliver this as your Deed?
> FAUSTUS. I [Aye], take it, and the devill give the good of it.

Throughout the play there is a conflict in Faustus's mind, encouraged and expressed by the two Angels, as in these lines from II.ii.:

> GOOD ANGEL. *Faustus* repent, yet God will pitty thee.
> BAD ANGEL. Thou art a spirit, God cannot pity thee.

Orthodox theology taught that the devils—in this context "spirit" is a synonym—were by their very nature incapable of repentance and therefore of receiving divine forgiveness; and Faustus acknowledges this doctrine when he hears the two promptings and responds:

> FAUSTUS. Who buzzeth in mine eares I am a spirit?
> Be I a devill yet God may pitty me,
> Yea, God will pitty me if I repent.
> BAD ANGEL. I [Aye], but *Faustus* never shall repent.
> FAUSTUS. My heart is hardned, I cannot repent[.]

He confesses to despair—a "deepe despaire" which even prompts him to suicide, but which is overcome by "sweete pleasure."

The triviality in the central scenes of the play has often drawn attention away from its profound seriousness. Acts 3 and 4, where Faustus explores his magic powers, show scenes of slapstick farce and simple conjuring. Some suggestions for these scenes could have come from the prose narrative which was the main source of Marlowe's plot—*Das Faust-Buch* (1587) translated into English by 1592 as *The Historie of the Damnable Life and Deserved Death of Doctor John Faustus*. This prose work was a mixture of jestbook and moral fable, which offered also a guidebook to Europe and a tour of hell. But the storyteller's license was not available to the playwright, and the middle part of the dramatic *Dr. Faustus* is a disappointment.

But it is unlikely that Marlowe himself was responsible for this flaw. Perhaps the manuscript of the play, unfinished when Marlowe died in 1593, came into the hands of the impresario Philip Henslowe, who found other writers to complete the piece for performance in 1594. Eight years later Henslowe recorded in his diary a payment to two hack dramatists, Samuel Rowley and William Birde, for their "adicyones" to *Dr. Faustus*. The play in its earlier form was not published until 1604 (the A Text); the later edition, published in 1616 (the B Text), incorporates the 1602 "adicyones." These complications of writing and printing make *Dr. Faustus* one of the major bibliographical problems of English literature.

Before his death, Marlowe had returned to the writing of nondramatic verse and was again working on a form of translaion—the kind that Dryden describes as "imitation." In Dryden's sense, "imitation" does not seek to translate the words, or even the sense, of an author but "to set him as a pattern and to write as [the translator] supposes that author would have done, had he lived in our age and in our country." The "pattern" for Marlowe was Musaeus, a Greek poet of the fourth or fifth century A.D., whose narrative poem *Hero and Leander* earned him the title of "grammatikos"—which distinguished him as a scholarly writer, learned in the poetry, rhetoric, and philosophy of his own time and expert in the interpretation of the great authors of the past. Marlowe's poem (1598) is a worthy imitation; and to the necessary qualities of a "grammatikos" the English writer adds one more: wit.

The Greek poem briefly describes the first encounters of the two lovers and then narrates Leander's final attempt to swim the Hellespont on a winter's night; the youth is drowned, and his Hero dies by his side. Marlowe's poem, however, is a comedy, lavishing care on the meeting of Hero, "*Venus* Nun," with the stranger from Abydos. The two lovers are described in great detail. Hero is a masterpiece of art—her footwear, for example, is a technological tour de force:

> Buskins of shels all silvered, used she,
> And brancht with blushing corall to the knee;
> Where sparrowes pearcht, of hollow pearle and gold,
> Such as the world would woonder to behold:
> Those with sweet water oft her handmaid fils,

Which as shee went would cherupe throught the
bils.

The verse admires the elaborate luxury, while at the same time revealing its absurdity. In complete contrast to the description of Hero is Marlowe's portrait of Leander, which lingers erotically over the boy's naked body:

Even as delicious meat is to the tast,
So was his necke in touching, and surpast
The white of *Pelops* shoulder. I could tell ye,
How smooth his brest was, and how white his bellie,
And whose immortal fingers did imprint,
That heavenly path, with many a curious dint,
That runs along his backe . . . [.]

The admixture of comedy (especially through the rhymes) prevents the sensual and mythological richness from becoming self-indulgent.

Using persuasions taken from Ovid's *Amores*, Leander starts his seduction of Hero; he is at first a "bold sharpe Sophister," but quickly shows himself to be a "novice ... rude in love, and raw." Hero responds by protecting herself, initially, with her status as priestess, but instinctive attraction soon leads to unconscious encouragement as "unawares *(Come thither)* from her slipt." She shows her true innocence when she opens the door to Leander, who has just swum across the Hellespont, and "seeing a naked man, she sriecht for feare, / Such sights as this, to tender maids are rare." Marlowe's poem moves toward a climax as the poet slowly describes the encounter of the two lovers which leads to the consummation of their love. The passage is splendidly orchestrated. It begins with the human comedy of Leander's appeal to Hero's pity ("This head was beat with manie a churlish billow, / And therefore let it rest upon thy pillow"); a second movement is the sympathetic presentation of Hero's conflicting emotions as she halfheartedly tries to ward off Leander's assaulting hands; then, after a brief and "metaphysical" comparison of Hero's breasts to "a globe," we reach the moment of Leander's triumph, when he achieves the status of a superman and, "like Theban *Hercules*," accomplishes his mission.

Hero and Leander reveals qualities in its author which the plays seem to suppress or deny: tenderness, sympathy, and generous humor which can laugh without cruelty. The poem is not without flaws, of course; but the achievement is great in itself and suggests enormous potential for the future, which can only be lamented in the words of the epilogue to *Dr. Faustus*:

Cut is the branch that might have growne full
straight,
And burned is *Apollo's* Lawrell bough,
That sometime grew within this learned man[.]

But Marlowe's actual achievement (rather than his unfulfilled potential) is best summed up in the words of a contemporary: Shakespeare's reference to Marlowe's death (in *As You Like It*) serves as an epitaph on the writer's work—it was "A great reckoning in a little room."

References:

John E. Bakeless, *The Tragicall History of Christopher Marlowe* (Cambridge, Mass.: Harvard University Press, 1942);

J. Leslie Hotson, *The Death of Christopher Marlowe* (London: Nonesuch Press, 1925);

Paul H. Kocher, *Christopher Marlowe: A Study of His Thought, Learning, and Character* (Chapel Hill: University of North Carolina Press, 1946);

Constance Brown Kuriyama, *Hammer or Anvil: Psychological Patterns in Christopher Marlowe's Plays* (New Brunswick, N.J.: Rutgers University Press, 1980);

Clifford Leech, *Christopher Marlowe: Poet for the Stage* (New York: AMS Press, 1986);

Leech, ed., *Marlowe: A Collection of Critical Essays* (Englewood Cliffs, N.J.: Prentice-Hall, 1964);

Harry Levin, *The Overreacher: A Study of Christopher Marlowe* (Cambridge, Mass.: Harvard University Press, 1952);

J. B. Steane, *Marlowe: A Critical Study* (Cambridge: Cambridge University Press, 1964);

Judith Weil, *Christopher Marlowe: Merlin's Prophet* (Cambridge: Cambridge University Press, 1977).

Sir Walter Ralegh

(1554? - 29 October 1618)

Jerry Leath Mills
University of North Carolina at Chapel Hill

BOOKS: *A Report of the Truth of the Fight about the Iles of Acores, this last Sommer. Betwixt the Revenge, one of her Maiesties Shippes, And an Armada of the King of Spaine* (London: Printed for William Ponsonbie, 1591);

The Discoverie of the Large, Rich and Bewtiful Empire of Guiana, with a relation of the Great and Golden City of Manoa (which the spaniards call El Dorado) And the provinces of Emeria, Arromaia, Amapaia and other Countries, with their rivers, adjoyning. Performed in the yeare 1595 (London: Printed by Robert Robinson, 1596);

The History of the World (London: Printed for Walter Burre, 1614);

The Prerogative of Parliaments in England: Proved in a Dialogue (pro & contra) betweene a Councellour of State and a Justice of Peace. Written by the worthy (much lacked and lamented) Sir Walter Raleigh Knight, deceased. Dedicated to the Kings Maiestie, and to the House of Parliament now assembled (Midelburge [London: Printed by T. Cotes], 1628);

Sir Walter Raleighs Instructions to his Sonne and to Posterity. Whereunto is added a Religious and Dutifull Advice of a Loving Sonne to his Aged Father (London: Printed for Benjamin Fisher, 1632);

To day a man, To morrow none: or, Sir Walter Rawleighs Farewell to his Lady, The night before hee was beheaded: Together with his advice concerning Her, and her Sonne (London: Printed for R. H., 1644);

Sir Walter Rawleigh His Apologie For his Voyage To Guiana (London: Printed by T. W. for Humphrey Moseley, 1650);

A Discourse of the Originall and Fundamentall Cause of Naturall, Customary, Arbitrary, Voluntary and Necessary Warre. With the Mistery [sic] *of Invasive Warre. That Ecclesiasticall Prelates, have alwayes beene subject to Temporall Princes, And that the Pope had never any lawfull power in England, either in Civill or Eccesiasticall businesse, after such time, as Brittaine was won from the Roman Empire* (London: Printed by T. W. for Humphrey Moseley, 1650);

Excellent Observations and Notes, Concerning the Royall Navy and Sea-service. Written By Sir Walter Rawleigh and by him Dedicated to the Most noble and Illustrious Prince Henry Prince of Wales (London: Printed by T. W. for Humphrey Moseley, 1650);

Maxims of State (London: Printed by W. Bentley, 1651);

Remains of Sir Walter Raleigh; Viz. Maxims of State. Advice to his Son: his Sons Advice to his Father. His Sceptick. Observations concerning the causes of the Magnificency and Opulency of Cities. The Prerogative of Parliaments in England, proved in a Dialogue between a Councellour of State and a Justice of the Peace. His Letters to divers persons of quality (London: Printed for William Sheares, Junior, 1657; enlarged, 1661).

Editions and Collections: *The Works of Sir Walter Ralegh, Kt., Now First Collected: to Which Are Prefixed the Lives of the Author*, 8 volumes, edited by William Oldys and Thomas Birch (Oxford: Oxford University Press, 1829; New York: Franklin, 1965);

The Poems of Sir Walter Ralegh, edited by Agnes M. C. Latham (London: Constable, 1929; Boston & New York: Houghton Mifflin, 1929; revised edition, London: Routledge & Kegan Paul, 1951; Cambridge, Mass.: Harvard University Press/The Muses' Library, 1951);

Advice to a Son: Precepts of Lord Burghley, Sir Walter Ralegh, and Francis Osborne, edited by Louis B. Wright (Ithaca, N.Y.: Published for the Folger Shakespeare Library by Cornell University Press, 1962);

"The Poems of Sir Walter Ralegh: An Edition," edited by Michael Rudick, Ph.D. dissertation, University of Chicago, 1970;

The History of the World (selections), edited by C. A. Patrides (London: Macmillan, 1971; Philadelphia: Temple University Press, 1971);

Ralegh with his eldest son, Wat, in 1602; portrait by an unknown artist (National Portrait Gallery, London)

A Choice of Sir Walter Ralegh's Verse, edited by Robert Nye (London: Faber & Faber, 1972);

Sir Walter Ralegh: Selected Writings, edited by Gerald Hammond (Manchester, U.K.: Carcanet Press, 1984).

OTHER: George Gascoigne, *The Steele Glas* (London: Printed for Richard Smith, 1576)—includes prefatory poem, "Walter Rawely of the middle Temple, in commendation of the Steele Glasse";

Edmund Spenser, *The Faerie Queene*, Books I-III (London: Printed for William Ponsonbie, 1590)—includes Ralegh's sonnets "Methought I saw the grave where *Laura* lay" and "The prayse of meaner wits this worke like profit brings";

Nicholas Breton, *Brittons Bowre of Delights* (London: Printed by Richard Jhones, 1591)—includes Ralegh's poems "Like to a Hermite poore in place obscure" and "Hir face, Hir tong, Hir Wit";

The Phoenix Nest (London: Printed by John Jackson, 1593); edited by Hyder Edward Rollins (Cambridge, Mass.: Harvard University Press, 1931)—includes "Praisd be Dianas faire and harmles light" and other poems attributed to Ralegh;

Englands Helicon (London: Printed by J. R. for John Flasket, 1600; enlarged, 1614); edited by Hugh Macdonald (London: Etchells & Macdonald, 1925; Cambridge, Mass.: Harvard University Press, 1950)—includes "The Nimphs reply to the Sheepheard" and other poems attributed to Ralegh.

For all the opportunism, self-promotion, misjudgment, and personal failure that undeniably mark his long career, Sir Walter Ralegh remains the most credible embodiment that Tudor-Stuart England has to offer of the ideal of the Renaissance man. By turns a soldier, privateer, explorer, and projector for colonization, he was as well a courtier, poet, scientist, and historian. Almost all his own poetry was written for self-advancement at court, yet he promoted unselfishly the fortunes of Edmund Spenser and facilitated the publication of Spenser's epic, *The Faerie Queene* (1590, 1596). Though obviously cultivating a personal stake in his projects for colonization in the two Americas, he fixed those projects firmly in a larger perspective of advancing England's well-being in a world increasingly dominated by Spain; and his colonization plan, unlike the purely economic undertakings of the Spanish, included permanent settlement of families, the development of a nautical academy, and the learning of aboriginal languages, such as the Algonquian that his assistant, Thomas Harriot, remained on Roanoke Island for nearly a year to acquire. During his long imprisonment in the Tower of London his achievements included the production of a million-word history of the world (up to 131 B.C.) and the invention of a medical remedy ("Balsam of Guiana"), both of which sold vigorously for a hundred years.

Ralegh was born, probably in 1554, in Devonshire on the southern coast of England to a family long and intimately involved with the sea. The youngest son of Walter Ralegh of Budleigh and Katherine Champernown, he had two half-siblings by his father's first marriage to Joan Drake and four by his mother's to Otho Gilbert. The paternal name, like many in that age of extremely unstable orthography, is on record in a large number of variant spellings—including "Raleigh," "Rawleigh," "Rauleygh," "Rauley," "Raullygh," and "Raulligh"—but Sir Walter seems to have settled on "Ralegh" after his knighthood was conferred in 1585.

Ralegh's early education is nowhere described in any detail; but it may safely be assumed that it was Protestant, in keeping with the family religion, and classical in emphasis, in keeping with the expectations of boys of his class for eventual university training. By that time William Lyly's Latin grammar held sway in English grammar-school education; the book illustrated points of grammar and composition with quotations from the best Roman authors to insure that pupils not only learned the mechanics but also acquired an admiration for elegance of style. In prose, this style meant almost exclusively the balanced, oratorical style of Cicero, a personalized and flexible form of which Ralegh wrote, with considerable effect, for the rest of his life.

Judging from his lifelong intellectual curiosity and his quickness to master and digest information, Ralegh was no doubt an able student. Attraction to active pursuits must have outweighed the delights of study in his middle teens, however, for he set out to France, perhaps as early as 1569, to fight with Huguenot forces under his kinsman Henry Champernown. Such service was a popular but risky course of volunteer action for English Protestants, who could expect the tacit approval but not the overt support of a sovereign wary of applying too much pressure at any one point of the delicate interrelation of religious powers in Europe. Years later, in *The History of the World* (1614), Ralegh recalled in vivid detail some of the action he saw in France, including smoking enemy troops out of underground entrenchments with smoldering bales of hay.

On his return in 1572 he entered Oriel College, Oxford. Although based solidly on the Greek and Roman classics, humanistic education at Oxford was no ivory-tower experience but rather a course of preparation for public service in the military, clergy, law, or the governmental complex that had its center in the royal court. Since all these pursuits required facility in expression and persuasion, a rhetorical education was deemed appropriate. Students studied logic and rhetoric and other aspects of style on the premise that since we think in words, a balanced and elegant style was important in providing a framework for lucid and reasonable thought. The great Roman historians were studied not simply for historical and political principles but also in order to analyze and appreciate the orations they often attribute to generals and statesmen. Students put on dramatic performances to develop forensic skills, and school recitations involved a great deal of debate, often on paradoxes, ingenious dilemmas, and unanswerable questions, such as "Which is better, day or night?" (an exercise John Milton professionalized in a later age with his paired poems *L'Allegro* [circa 1631]) and *Il Penseroso* [circa 1631]. In debate the premium was on cleverness, wit, and rhetorical adroitness—excellent preparation for future careers in the web of clientage, patronage, and competition that made up the daily business of life at court.

Sixteenth-century universities also valued the study and composition of poetry. Students were required, as prescribed by the humanist "doctrine of imitation," to memorize long passages of Latin verse, analyze their grammatical and rhetorical structures, and then re-create them in English, with variations conceived by the young scholars themselves. Ralegh's remembrance of these exercises is probably attested in his lyric poem beginning "Now Serena bee not coy," an adaptive paraphrase and expansion of a Latin poem by Catullus. Contemporary poetry was not formally taught, but students were encouraged, by peer pressure as much as anything, to become knowledgeable about it, and it was an unmotivated pupil who could not quote extensively from French and Italian masters of recent ages.

Ralegh left Oxford in 1574 without a degree. In London he entered first Lyon's Inn and then the Middle Temple, institutions where one studied law and—more important for many of the aspirant courtiers who attended—formed contacts with people and institutions capable of furthering one's ambitions for public life. The latter, rather than preparation as a barrister, seems to have been Ralegh's intent (although—despite his protestation that he knew little of the law—he was to show considerable legal sophistication at his trial for treason in 1603). Probably the earliest extant example of his poetry, a set of commendatory verses written to his fellow Templar George Gascoigne on the publication of Gascoigne's satire *The Steele Glas* (1576) and published as a preface to that work, dates from this period. This poem reflects, as was no doubt intended, the aphoristic, generally nonmetaphorical Plain Style favored by Gascoigne himself. It is uncertain how well Ralegh knew the older poet; but he must have seen in him something of his own disposition, since Gascoigne too was a soldier as well as a poet and had served with Ralegh's half brother, Sir Humphrey Gilbert, in the Low Countries. Ralegh later adopted Gascoigne's motto *Tam marti quam mercutio* as one of his own, declaring a temperament as indebted to Mars for strength and vigor as to Mercury for intellectual and artistic powers.

After sea duty with Gilbert in an unsuccessful search for the Northwest Passage in 1578-1579 and a brief period of association with the entourage of Edward de Vere, seventeenth Earl of Oxford, Ralegh embarked on an important phase of his military career in 1580 when he took charge of a company of soldiers under Arthur, Lord Grey, in Ireland. He soon distinguished himself—dubiously so, in some modern eyes—as the leader, on Grey's orders, of a massacre of disarmed Spanish and Italian troops at Smerwick. It was in Ireland—although precisely when is not known—that he first met Spenser, who was Lord Grey's secretary, and there also that he defeated the ambush by Irish troops that Spenser was to turn into an episode in *The Faerie Queene*.

Soon after his return to England as something of a war hero in December 1581 Ralegh was called into personal consultation with the queen about affairs in Ireland. He thus began, through a combination of personal charm and astuteness of political and military opinion, his phenomenal rise in Elizabeth's favor and in prominence at her court. (The well-known story that Ralegh first attracted the queen's attention by spreading his cloak before her so that she could cross a puddle is almost certainly apocryphal.) By 1582 he was a well-established courtier, recipient of the lucrative privileges Elizabeth was disposed to grant her most cherished assistants. In 1583 he received a profitable commission to license the sale of wines. In 1584 Elizabeth granted him the customs receipts on imported woolens; he became warden of the stannaries and was admitted to Parliament in the same year. In 1585, the year he was knighted, he was appointed vice-admiral for his home region of Devon and Cornwall. The crown provided him lodgings at Durham House in London, and in 1587 he was appointed captain of the queen's personal guard.

During this period Ralegh exploited his standing with his sovereign to further his interests, first stimulated by Gilbert, in exploration and colonization. He sent settlers to a large area in Ireland, and with another Gilbert, his half brother Adrian, he obtained the letters patent necessary for the project on Roanoke Island in present-day North Carolina (Ralegh named the whole area Virginia, in honor of his Virgin Queen) that became famous as the Lost Colony. The product of a series of voyages beginning in 1584, the colony "planted" (to use the terminology of the time) on Roanoke in 1587 vanished mysteriously, probably through a combination of massacre and absorption into the Indian nation of Chief Powhatan in coastal regions to the north. Ralegh's plan to search for the colonists was stifled by the Spanish Armada's attempted invasion of England in 1588, when all English naval resources were required at home and Ralegh himself was put into service as a supervisor of preparations on the southern coast; he also contributed a ship, the *Bark Ralegh*, to the war effort. During 1589 his rivalry with Robert Devereux, Earl of Essex, who threatened to diminish Ralegh's influence with the queen, may have been a factor in his giving up his formal interests in North America, although he retained colonization rights to South America and was no doubt already contemplating the expedition to Guiana that he was to undertake personally in 1595. (Although Ralegh did not, as is often claimed, introduce American tobacco into England, he did popularize the smoking of it.)

To the years of Ralegh's association with the court can probably be attributed the majority of his poems. The word *probably* deserves special emphasis, however, because the poetry as a body, as Steven W. May observes in *The Elizabethan Courtier Poets* (1991), "presents one of the most difficult editorial problems of the English Renaissance." Although several of his verses circulated freely in manuscript during the 1580s, exact dating is in most cases impossible. The canon too remains quite unstable, because Ralegh made no apparent attempt to preserve his poems and because his name sometimes appears as an attention-getter in association with poems he almost surely did not write. In the various modern editions the number ascribed to him varies from forty-one (plus twelve others assigned conjecturally) in Agnes M. C. Latham's 1951 edition to a niggardly twenty-three (plus fragments of translation and seven "possible" works) in the conservative edition of Michael Rudick (1970). Detailed discussions of the problem of authenticity of individual poems are given in the apparatus in

Manuscript for a verse to "Cynthia," Ralegh's name for Queen Elizabeth I. These lines were written on the last leaf of a notebook that he kept while writing The History of the World *in the Tower of London (Add. 5755, f. 172v, British Library).*

Rudick's edition, in Pierre Lefranc's *Sir Walter Ralegh, écrivain* (1968), and in May's *Sir Walter Raleigh* (1989).

Many of Ralegh's court poems involved stylized descriptions of his relationship with Queen Elizabeth, and most of those involve his imaginative adaptation of themes and conventions from the literary mode established by the great Italian Francesco Petrarcha, or, as he was known in England, Francis Petrarch. Although Petrarch had lived and written in the Italy of two centuries earlier, Elizabethans of poetic inclination considered him a contemporary in spirit. His popularity during the Renaissance derived in large part from the formula he devised for a group of more than three hundred sonnets and other lyrical poems written to or about Laura, a lady whom he idealized as a paradigm of earthly beauty and spiritual inspiration during the twenty-one years between his first glimpse of her—an experience he claimed made him instantly a poet—and her death. In this formula, sex and spirituality find mutual accommodation and, indeed, interdependence. In its conventionalized form the Petrarchan experience takes something like the following pattern: the poet is overwhelmed at first sight of his lady with an admiration of her physical beauty that leads, in turn, to appreciation of her mind, then of her spiritual beauty, and finally to the realization that not only this beauty but also the poet's ability to appreciate it comes ultimately from the goodness of God.

For the Petrarchan, then, what begins as attraction to concrete, sensory phenomena ends in religious understanding. Laura's beauty eventually recedes into philosophical perspective as simply one stage in a continuum of increasingly refined levels of perspectivity, linking the sensual with the divine and thus reconciling the amatory and philosophical instincts within the personality of Renaissance man.

But for most workers in the Petrarchan literary vein, what proved of most frequent interest in this idealistic scheme was the midrange of the process, the stage at which the lover's burning desire and the lady's chaste refusal of his advances interact to create tension and stress. The posture of the despairing lover, who must suffer the agonies of his unrequited passion with fever, chills, and mental distraction before advancing to a higher stage of awareness, is a familiar one in Elizabethan literature. It occurs, for example, with great seriousness in Spenser's *Amoretti* (1595) sonnet sequence and, as the object of indulgent satire, in Shakespeare's *As You Like It* (circa 1600). With Ralegh its uses become complexly political.

If Ralegh did not actually invent what A. D. Cousins calls "political Petrarchism," he certainly developed it to new levels of self-serving appropriateness. Leonard Tennenhouse has argued that Ralegh exploits the fact that much of what was metaphorical in the imagined relationship between lover and lady in the sonnet tradition became, when transposed to the relationship between courtier and queen, literally true. The Petrarchan accorded his lady the power of life and death, banishment and acceptance, enchainment and freedom. Elizabeth—as Ralegh would be painfully reminded during his imprisonment in 1592—possessed these powers in a very real way. Her disdain could indeed be deadly, her approbation a shower of manna. "Praisd be Diana's faire and harmles light" (1593) provides a detailed example of the way in which Ralegh manipulated convention for results that are both flattering to the queen and assertive of his own material interest:

Praisd be Diana's faire and harmles light,
Praisd be the dewes, wherewith she moists the
  ground;
Praisd be hir beames, the glorie of the night,
Praisd be hir power, by which all powers abound.

Praisd be hir Nimphs, with whom she decks the
  woods,
Praisd be hir knights, in whom true honour lives,
Praisd be that force, by which she moves the floods,
Let that Diana shine, which all these gives.

In Heaven Queene she is among the spheares,
In ay she Mistres like makes all things pure;
Eternitie in hir oft change she beares,
She beautie is, by hir the faire endure.

Time weares hir not, she doth his chariot guide,
Mortalitie belowe hir orbe is plaste;
By hir the vertue of the starrs downe slide,
In hir is vertues perfect image cast.

  A knowledge pure it is hir worth to kno;
  With Circes let them dwell that thinke not so.

One can imagine how phrases such as "Time weares hir not" must have reverberated in the imagination of the notoriously vain Elizabeth, advanced in years when the poem was probably written and so conscious of the passage of time that she forbade any public discussion of her "grand climacteric," or sixty-third birthday, when it occurred in 1596. But there is also an elaborate subtext of petition and solicitation in the poem, established by allusion. Ralegh often addressed the Virgin Queen (as did Spenser, who follows his lead in this regard) with the names of goddesses associated with the virtue of chastity: Diana, Cynthia, or Phoebe (in Ralegh's poetic coinage, Belphoebe). All of these figures are connected in classical myth with the moon, as Diana is in Ralegh's poem. But the heavenly body most frequently used by poets and politicians alike as a symbol of kingship was the sun—partly because of its primacy in the sky and partly because of its traditional symbolism of the virtue of justice. These symbolic relations have biblical precedents: "For behold, the day cometh, that shall burn as an oven; and all the proud, yea, all that do wickedly, shall be stubble: and the day that cometh shall burn them up . . ." (Malachi 4:1-2). Ralegh draws on these precedents in the central section of "The Ocean to Scinthia," when he wants to represent the severity of Elizabeth's royal displeasure. But the moon, dominant in its own temporal sphere, is soft and feminine, a better vehicle for the image of monarchy that Ralegh wants to develop in his petitions to the queen. In contrast with the sun's evocation of justice, the moon evokes consolation, mercy, and love. By what Ralegh calls its "harmles" light, human failings are overlooked, and romance is allowed to flourish. Thus, a somewhat cynical but essentially accurate reading of the first line might be simply "Please keep on giving the honors and rewards to which your petitioner is joyfully accustomed."

"Like to a Hermite poore in place obscure" (1591) is another Petrarchan exercise, this time in the presentation of the lover in despair, seeking isolation and obscurity (situations that never appealed to Ralegh) as a response to his lady's neglect. Given Ralegh's propensity for sartorial splendidness and show, his contemporaries must have taken special note of the irony in his promise that "A gowne of graie, my bodie shall attire." But he knew what he was doing, and, presumably, so did the queen. Although to the modern ear these poems may sound overwrought or even fulsome (Henry David Thoreau thought Ralegh's genius was "warped by the frivolous society of the court"), it is possible to see them as part of a stylized, sophisticated discourse that brought grace and a measure of blitheness to the otherwise mundane power brokering that characterized the workings of the Tudor court.

Among the most memorable and possibly most successful of Ralegh's adaptations of the Petrarchan mode is the fine sonnet he contributed to the group of congratulatory verses printed with the first three books of *The Faerie Queene*, whose publication in 1590, if one is to believe Spenser's account in *Colin Clouts Come Home Againe* (1595), owed something to Ralegh's encouragement, as its favorable reception by Elizabeth owed something to Ralegh's recommendation. Ralegh, to whom Spenser's preface to *Colin Clouts Come Home Againe*, in the form of an epistle, is addressed, manages to eulogize the epic, flatter Elizabeth, and perhaps develop implications of his own feelings of neglect, all in fourteen lines:

> Methought I saw the grave, where *Laura* lay,
> Within that Temple, where the vestall flame
> Was wont to burne, and passing by that way,
> To see that buried dust of living fame,
> Whose tumbe faire love, and fairer vertue kept,
> All suddeinly I saw the Faery Queene:
> At whose approch the soule of *Petrarke* wept,
> And from thenceforth those graces were not seene.
> For they this Queene attended, in whose steed
> Oblivion laid him downe on *Lauras* herse:
> Hereat the hardest stones were seene to bleed,
> And grones of buried ghostes the hevens did perce.
> Where *Homers* spright did tremble all for griefe,
> And curst th' accesse of that celestiall thiefe.

Ralegh's ostensible purpose is to celebrate Spenser's achievement by holding that his poem will outgo all earlier accomplishments in verse—especially those of Petrarch, whose Laura will be dimmed in favor of Spenser's Gloriana, who by Spenser's own assertion represents Elizabeth. Homer and other poets of antiquity will lament in their afterlife to see Spenser stealing from them reputations once thought secure. Elizabeth, of course, whose virtues make the depiction possible, shares with the artist the glory that is now England's. But, as Peter Ure and A. D. Cousins have pointed out, most of the sonnet concentrates on the theme of displacement, on the abandonment and despair of those dislodged from former prominence. Ralegh's emotional identification with these figures may perhaps be explained by his anxieties throughout 1589 over competition for Elizabeth's favor with the young and powerful earl of Essex. Ralegh had, in fact, felt obliged literally to displace himself for a while to his Irish estates to avoid violent conflict and the royal anger that would have surely ensued (Ralegh and Essex had agreed on one occasion to a duel, but the queen's counselors prevented it). Being overshadowed, then, was more than merely a literary motif in Ralegh's mind at the time of composition.

In his sonnet on *The Faerie Queene* Ralegh has been seen as formulating an early literary statement of a theme that was also to figure largely in his historiographical musings in *The History of the World*: that all joy and all monuments lack permanence, and humanity is forever destined to watch its greatest achievements fade and die. An extremely poignant expression of this idea—among the most forceful expressions of it that the Elizabethan period has to offer—is Ralegh's "Nature that washt her hands in milke," a poem that turns again to the Petrarchan tradition, but this time with a clear-minded assertion of the way that time and mutability render futile the attempts of human beings, with their idealizing philosophies, to find permanence on earth. Ralegh begins with the poet idealizing his lady in good Petrarchan form, then moves on to the predictable lack of responsiveness of the proud and tyrannizing beauty, who plays the game with all the aloofness and stoniness of heart that the role of "cruel fair" requires. Yet Time is not impressed, nor tolerant of the self-deluding attitude of either party:

But Time which nature doth despise,
    And rudely gives her love the lye,
Makes hope a foole, and sorrow wise,
    His hands do neither wash, nor dry,
But being made of steele and rust,
Turnes snow, and silke, and milke to dust.

The Light, the Belly, lipps and breath
    He dimms, discolours, and destroyes;
With those he feedes, but fills not death,
    Which sometimes were the foode of Joyes;
Yea Time doth dull each lively witt,
And dryes all wantonnes with it.

Oh cruell Time which takes in trust
    Our youth, our Joyes and all we have,
And payes us but with age and dust;
    Who in the darke and silent grave,
When we have wandred all our wayes
Shutts up the story of our dayes.

Ralegh's notice of the human propensity for self-delusion is registered again, in a witty and sardonic vein, in his reply (1600) to Christopher Marlowe's poem of invitation, "The Passionate Shepherd to His Love" ("Come live with mee, and be my love," 1600). There Marlowe had indulged in a conventional pastoral escapist fantasy that the proper antidote to human problems is withdrawal from social complexity into a natural setting whose beauty transcends all the distractions of life in the city or court. To this attitude of neoprimitivism Ralegh does what he does to Petrarchism in "Nature that washt her hands in milke": he subjects it to the pressure of a rationalism based firmly on awareness of the power of time. To Marlowe's persuasive shepherd, Ralegh's "nimph" replies that the promise of a paradise requiring permanent youth and joy is a promise no mortal can fulfill:

Time drives the flocks from field to fold,
When Rivers rage, and Rocks grow cold,
And Philomell becommeth dombe,
The rest complaines of cares to come.

The skepticism evident in poems such as these has perhaps contributed to a tendency, once widespread but now generally discredited, to magnify some charges hinted at by Ralegh's enemies in his own time into a full-blown philosophical conspiracy, whereby Ralegh is seen as heading, throughout much of the 1590s, an antireligious and philosophically occult "School of Night" that included such men as George Chapman; Thomas Harriot; Sir Henry Percy, the "Wizard Earl" of Northumberland; and, in some accounts, Marlowe—all of whom are assumed to have been interested in such pursuits as occult science and necromancy and in defying conventional Christianity on every hand. These notions found full expression in two books published in 1936, M. C. Bradbrook's *The School of Night* and Frances Yates's *A Study of "Love's Labour's Lost."* These works differ in emphasis but find in William Shakespeare's play a satirical attack on Ralegh's group and a repudiation of its supposed premium on contemplation and abstract theory over active life. Although little factual evidence exists for these theories, they still come up occasionally in popular biographies. Ernest A. Strathmann's *Sir Walter Ralegh: A Study in Elizabethan Skepticism* (1951) and John W. Shirley's biography of Thomas Harriot (1983) provide authoritative rebuttals.

Had Ralegh ever entertained any delusions about the permanence of status and power, it is unlikely that they could have survived the events of 1592, a year that witnessed his precipitous decline from privilege and command to a cell in

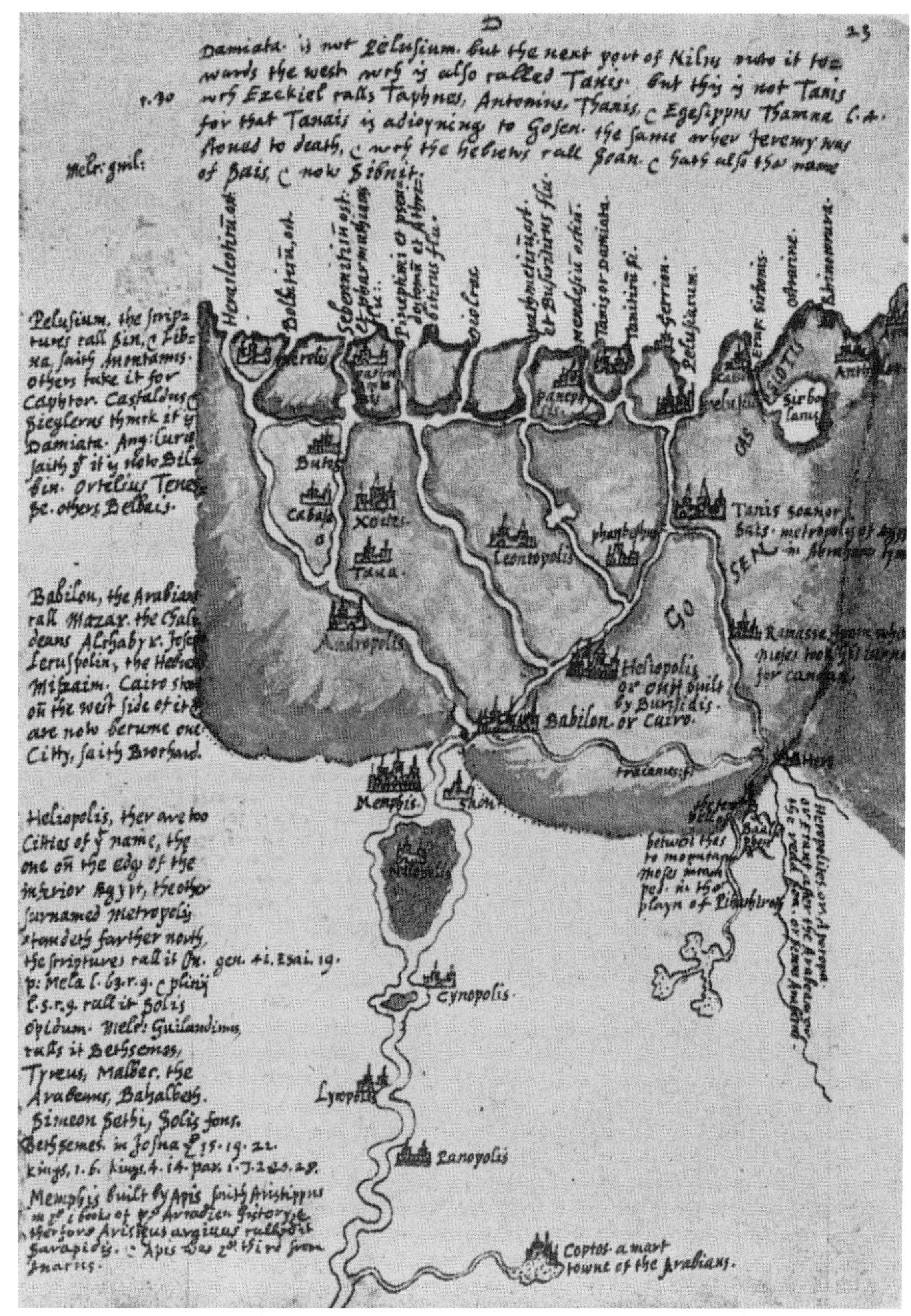

Page from Ralegh's notes for The History of the World *(British Library)*

the Tower of London. Chiefly through material from the diary of Ralegh's brother-in-law, published by A. L. Rowse in *Sir Walter Ralegh, His Family and Private Life* (1962), what seems to be the full story of his fall is now known. Possibly as early as 1588 Ralegh had married Elizabeth Throckmorton, an honorary attendant in the royal privy chamber. Because of the queen's well-known hostility to marriage on the part of her favorites, whose undivided loyalties her vanity required, the union had to be kept secret. A child, Damerei Ralegh, died soon after his birth on 26 March 1592, and although Elizabeth Ralegh returned to court in April as though nothing had happened, the queen discovered the true state of affairs and committed the couple to separate confinement in the Tower in July. In September, however, Ralegh was released to supervise the removal of captured Spanish goods from a ship whose crew could be kept in check only by the force of his personality and the respect in which they held him. Although she allowed him to keep Sherborne, the fine estate she had granted him only months before the scandal erupted, the queen removed Ralegh from his captainship of the guard and essentially exiled him from court. Lady Ralegh was never again admitted to the royal presence, even after her husband's restoration to favor in 1597.

Although these happenings were widely known and much talked about in their time, their chief literary consequences had to wait almost three hundred years for entry into public view. Discovered among some papers relating to Ralegh, in 1870 at Hatfield House, the family seat of Elizabeth's lord treasurer, William Cecil (Lord Burghley), are four poems that all but a few modern critics read as Ralegh's sustained lament to the queen during his imprisonment: a seven-line poem beginning "If Synthia be a Queene, a princes, and supreame"; a sonnet, "My boddy in the walls captived"; a 522-line poem in interlocking couplets, "The 21st: and last booke of the Ocean to Scinthia"; and a 22-line fragment, "The end of the bookes, of the Oceans love to Scinthia, and the beginninge of the 22nd Boock, entreatinge of Sorrow," which breaks off in the middle of a line. The last two poems, or parts of poems, are generally spoken of by critics collectively as "The Ocean to Cynthia." Some editors, Agnes M. C. Latham among them, read the numerals as "11th" and "12th"; but in 1985 Stacy M. Clanton confirmed in a detailed paleographic study of the manuscript (which is in Ralegh's own hand) the readings "21st" and "22nd."

Readers who appreciate neatness in literary history have found little comfort in the maze of problems surrounding these verses, problems involving the date, the exact nature of the events alluded to, and the possibility of a larger structure, either lost or unwritten, of which the surviving fragments may have been intended as parts. Because Spenser mentions in *Colin Clouts Come Home Againe* (written in some form in 1589 though not printed until 1595) that Ralegh, whom he calls the Shepherd of the Ocean, had written a "lamentable lay" about hard usage at the hands of his lady, Cynthia, many early critics assumed that the overall structure was at least conceived and partially executed prior to the exposure of Ralegh's marriage, then continued to include later events. And because of their fragmentary appearance, some writers have even assumed that they are parts of a vast epic, possibly planned for twelve books on the model of Virgil's *Aeneid*. The bulk of scholarly opinion, however, now is that the poems date from 1592 and were probably composed in the Tower, then transmitted to a member of the Cecil family with the hope that they would reach the queen (Katherine Duncan-Jones is in a distinct minority in her belief that "The Ocean to Cynthia" dates from Ralegh's second imprisonment, under King James, and that it mourns Elizabeth's death); and that what survives is almost surely all that was written, the unfinished appearance either resulting from Ralegh's release, which would have made further composition redundant, or constituting a literary effect in which the speaker's distracted state of mind is mirrored in the broken form of the poem itself.

That these poems exist as an intentionally unfinished structure may be argued on grounds of their possible organization in terms of "topomorphic composition," a compositional strategy common in the Renaissance. "Topomorphic composition" denotes the way in which poems achieve symmetrical or otherwise significant internal structures through repetition of motifs, images, numerical patterns, and even rhymes to achieve balance and internal cross-referencing related to the main ideas. Beginnings and ends of poems are frequently linked in this way, and the central idea or image often occurs in the exact center of the poem. (Spenser accomplishes such a structure in each of the first three books of *The Faerie Queene*.)

Regarded in light of topomorphic practice, "The Ocean to Cynthia" can be seen as possessing an internal completeness of structure that underlies the apparent fragmentation that first meets the eye. The "21st Book" begins and ends with the development of a winter pastoral scene (reminiscent of the setting in Thomas Sackville's induction to the 1563 edition of *A Mirror for Magistrates*), the landscape serving as a symbolic restatement of the motif of desolation and withering that exists inside the speaker's heart and mind. The first thirty-six and the last fifty-two lines develop this mood, echoing several central images—withered leaves, dryness, impending storms, sheep in the fields. The opening and closing lines share certain specific words, concepts, and rhyming sounds—*complain, again, mean* (pronounced "main")—to suggest a kind of circularity and closure:

Sufficeth it to yow my joyes interred,
In simpell wordes that I my woes cumplayne,
Yow that then died when first my fancy erred,
Joyes under dust, that never live agayne.
. . . .
To God I leve it, who first gave it me,
And I her gave, and she returnd agayne,
As it was herrs. So lett his mercies bee,
Of my last cumforts, the essentiall meane.
But be it so, or not, th' effects, ar past.
Her love had end; my woe must ever last.

"Woes" in the opening section is echoed in the "woe" of the closing; the "joyes" of line 4 corresponds to the "cumforts" of line 520; and the image of death dominates both sections.

Most of the poem consists of lament for a time when the speaker enjoyed the bounty of his sovereign and love, and for the fact that the gentle Belphoebe of former times (here, as usual, identified with the moon) has been supplanted by the blazing sun of justice, as the speaker's one thoughtless indiscretion has earned him perpetual grief. At the center of the poem falls a passage that contains the biblical image of justice burning away the stubble of a fallow field:

And as a feilde wherin the stubbell stands
Of harvest past, the plowmans eye offends,
Hee tills agayne or teares them up with hands,
And throwes to fire as foylde and frutless ends,

And takes delight another seed to sow. . . .
So douth the minde root up all wounted thought
And scornes the care of our remayning woes;
The sorrowes, which themsealvs for us have wrought,

Ar burnt to Cinders by new kyndled fiers,
The ashes ar dispeirsed into the ayre,
The sythes, the grones of all our past desires
Are clean outworne, as things that never weare. . . .

Other indications that the work is organized to achieve a subtext of significant form may be gleaned from the manuscript, which bears marks of Ralegh's plans for revision. The overall structure is a series of verse modules of varying lengths, developing the main ideas and related associationally, though not always in the sequence of a plot, with each other. Several such sections are written in lighter-colored ink than the rest of the manuscript and tick—marked to the left of each line. Since these passages are rhetorical exercises or elaborations of rhetorical topoi rather than advancements of the narrative, it seems reasonable to conclude that Ralegh left a certain number of lines uncomposed and places marked for later inclusion during the progress of the first draft but clearly knew how many lines or modular units he wanted in the completed poem: that is, that he was engaged in some form of numerical composition, working toward a predetermined proportionality which may or may not lie hidden in the work as it exists. Also to the point is that the "22nd Book" breaks off in the middle of its twenty-second line; the number twenty-two, in Spenser's works, usually symbolizes chastity, virginity, and self-denial, all qualities appropriate to the Virgin Queen who is the stimulus for Ralegh's poem.

It is not known whether Queen Elizabeth ever saw "The Ocean to Cynthia," or whether the remorse that Ralegh expresses there was a factor in her decision to free him from the Tower. But if she read Spenser's *The Faerie Queene* she must have recognized another, extended story of her relationship with Ralegh, continued allegorically through several books of Spenser's epic in the ongoing story of Arthur's squire, Timias, whom Spenser had created to represent Ralegh in Book III (published in 1590) and to whom he returned in Books IV and V (published in 1596). In Book III Timias falls in love with Belphoebe, one of several representations of the queen in Spenser's poem; but in the later section the story goes on to chronicle the complications of 1592. In Book IV, Canto 7, Timias's betrayal of the trust of Belphoebe by succumbing to the attractions of Amoret refers specifically to the Throckmorton

Engraved title page for the work Ralegh wrote to please Prince Henry, the young son of James I

marriage. A reconciliation begins in the following canto, as Spenser evidently hoped it would in real life; and the epic poet may be seen as taking Ralegh's part, although he does acknowledge the wrong done through human frailty. In Book VI Ralegh and his wife may be found again in the episodes with Timias and Serena (Serena is a name used by Ralegh in one of his lyric poems).

With characteristic resilience Ralegh took as active a part in national affairs as his fortunes permitted throughout 1593. Serving his third session in the House of Commons, he sponsored several measures favorable to the queen and continued his advocacy of an aggressive policy toward Spain. In the summer of that year he attended a dinner party with the Reverend Ralph Ironside, with whom he argued, evidently in a friendly way, some points of divinity. The exchange became the subject of much gossip and popular speculation, which attributed to Ralegh unorthodox, even heretical beliefs, and a commission was formed to investigate. Although Ralegh was cleared of the allegations and his case was dismissed without formal charges, the affair contributed to the perennial rumors about his atheistic and occult interests.

For some time Ralegh had been interested in a project of exploration and colonization in regions along the Orinoco River in Guiana, a part of what is today Venezuela, both for the wealth such a project might bring and for the hedge it might provide against Spanish power in the New World. Having obtained a measure of support from the crown, he set forth in February 1595 with hopes of finding El Dorado, the supposed interior capital of Guiana, a city rich beyond conception. He of course found no such city; but his explorations in Guiana provided, when he recorded them in *The Discoverie of the Large, Rich and Bewtiful Empire of Guiana* (1596), what one critic has termed one of the most fascinating adventure stories ever written.

Ralegh's talents as a prose stylist were great—in fact, up until the twentieth century his literary reputation rested chiefly on prose. In 1591 his rousing defense of Sir Richard Grenville's conduct in a naval encounter with Spanish forces, *A Report of the Truth of the Fight about the Iles of Acores, this last Sommer. Betwixt the Revenge, one of her Maiesties Shippes, And an Armada of the King of Spaine*, had been widely admired and had succeeded admirably in its intent. The Guiana tract embodies, with even greater skill, the combination of propagandistic sophistication and understanding of literary effect that invigorates most of Ralegh's prose. Ralegh always wrote with immediate purpose, with persuasion as his goal. In his main works he favors the first-person point of view, and his reader is consistently aware of a dominating personality behind the page. *The Discoverie of the Large, Rich and Bewtiful Empire of Guiana* is an example of Ralegh's prose at its best.

Having presumably been trained, like most Elizabethan pupils, on rhetorical principles deriving ultimately from Aristotle, Ralegh had learned the basic criteria of persuasive writing and oratory: the ethical, pathetic, and logical avenues of appeal. The ethical appeal, or the criterion of ethos, prescribes the speaker's establishment of his own authority to speak—his command of the facts and the legitimacy of his purposes. He must gain the audience's confidence in his character. Ralegh's attention to the narrator's persona is careful, because he is attempting to promote interest in further exploration and exploitation—managed, of course, by himself. Thus he is at pains to establish himself as a clear and practical thinker and planner, a man with a scientific mind and a capacity for retaining details—not some romantic visionary following the lead of idealism and an overactive imagination. Passages such as this establish practical authority: "The great river of *Orenoque* or *Baraquan* hath nine branches which fall out on the north side of his owne maine mouth: on the south side it hath seven other fallings into the sea, so it disemboketh by 16 armes in al, betweene Ilands and broken ground, but the Ilands are verie great, manie of them as bigge as the Isle of *Wight* and bigger, and many lesse. From the first branch on the north to the last of the south it is at lest 100 leagues, so as the rivers mouth is no lesse than 300 miles wide at his entrance into the sea. . . . al those that inhabite in the mouth of this river . . . are these *Tivitivas*, of which there are two chiefe Lords which have continuall warres one with the other. . . ."

The pathetic approach, or the criterion of pathos, requires appeal to the reader's emotions and capacity to imagine the sensory experience evoked by a scene such as one in which Ralegh draws on pastoral traditions in literature as well as on his own experience to depict Guiana as potentially an Eden of natural beauty and resources: "On both sides of this river, we passed the most beautifull countrie that ever mine eyes beheld: and whereas all that we had seen before was nothing but woods, prickles, bushes, and thornes, heere we beheld plaines of beauty miles in length, the grasse short and greene, and in divers parts groves of trees by themselves, as if they had been by all the art and labour in the world so made of purpose: and stil as we rowed, the Deere came downe feeding by the waters side, as if they had beene used to a keepers call."

The criterion of logos, the logical approach, gets to the purpose of it all. Having prepared his audience by building trust in the speaker and recreating the emotional context of his experience, Ralegh turns to the reasons and the means. Guiana, he argues, will be a source of national treasure as well as a defense against Spain in the very heart of its empire: "Nowe although these reportes may seeme straunge, yet if wee consider the many millions which are daily brought out of *Peru* into Spaine, wee may easely beleeve the same, for wee find that by the abundant treasure of that countrey, the Spanish King vexeth all the Princes of Europe, and is become in a fewe yeares from a poore king of *Castile* the greatest monarke of this part of the worlde, and likelie every day to increase, if other Princes forsloe the good occasions offered, and suffer him to adde this Empire to the rest, which by farre exceedeth all the rest: if his golde now indaunger us, hee will then be unresistable."

Ralegh's tract, for all the attention it elicited, succeeded more as a literary work than as an immediate incentive to investors or statesmen. It was not until twenty years later that he was able to go back to the Orinoco regions, and then it was on the final, calamitous expedition that precipitated his execution. Among the literary descendants of *The Discoverie of the Large, Rich and Bewtiful Empire of Guiana* can be counted such works as Shakespeare's *The Tempest* (circa 1611) and Daniel Defoe's *The Life and Strange Surprizing Adventures of Robinson Crusoe* (1719).

By 1597 Ralegh had regained the queen's favor and was reappointed captain of the guard. No small factor in his recovery of status was his participation in 1596 with Lord Admiral Thomas Howard and Ralegh's former antagonist, the earl of Essex, on a daring raid against the Spanish at Cadiz. In 1598 he spoke prominently in the House of Commons, and in 1600 he was appointed governor of the Isle of Jersey, a post whose duties he executed conscientiously, though chiefly in absentia. The following year he helped put down Essex's rebellion and attended, in his capacity as captain of the guard, the earl's execution, a function that earned him some accusations of callousness because he had supposedly smoked his pipe as Essex prepared to die.

During these years Ralegh wrote voluminously on many topics in prose—treatises on shipbuilding, agriculture and economics, the waging of war, the nature of the soul. Most of these works defy precise dating, and several, such as the Machiavellian political treatise "Cabinet-Council," have been convincingly banished from his canon. Most of his writings display the qualities of trenchancy, logical force, and a capacity for the startlingly apt phrase that led Thoreau to describe him as a man who gave the impression of writing with a pen in one hand and a sword in the other. The most impressive result of these abilities was *The History of the World*, another literary product of the Tower of London.

After the queen's death in 1603 Ralegh's lack of favor with the new monarch, James I, was readily apparent. James feared war with Spain, which Ralegh had long supported, and generally represented the opposite of Ralegh in most aspects of personality. Furthermore, his opinion of Ralegh had been soured by Lord Henry Howard and Sir Robert Cecil, both of whom feared Ralegh's ability to sway public opinion and wished to prevent him from obtaining the kind of influence he had enjoyed during Elizabeth's reign. James began dismantling Ralegh's major holdings almost immediately, removing him from the captaincy of the guard, lifting his patent to license wines, and evicting him from his London residence, Durham House. Then, on 17 November 1603, Ralegh was tried for high treason.

Specifically, Ralegh was charged with participation in the so-called Main Plot of Lord Cobham (Henry Brooke) and others, possibly with the assistance of Spain, to assassinate the royal family and place people of their own choosing in power. Ralegh seems to have had some inkling that schemes were afoot but shared no complicity in them. His conviction was guaranteed by James's desire and that of Ralegh's influential enemies; and despite his eloquent self-defense throughout the proceedings, he was sentenced to death, with execution scheduled for 9 December. In a last-minute reprieve the sentence was commuted to imprisonment at the pleasure of the king. Ralegh's confinement was to last for thirteen years.

In prison Ralegh was allowed regular visits from his wife and friends (his second son, Carew Ralegh, was begotten in the Tower) and allowed to develop interests in chemistry and other sciences, sometimes in the company of the earl of Northumberland, another prisoner of rank who was interested in the New Science. Among other achievements in the laboratory Ralegh produced his "Balsam of Guiana," a medicine that achieved considerable notice. Not long after his imprisonment began he apparently decided that his main hope for release lay in the young Prince Henry, his frequent visitor in the Tower. Prince Henry had selected Ralegh as a mentor or surrogate father, an attractive alternative to his own neglectful father. It was for Prince Henry that *The History of the World* was begun. When Henry died of typhoid fever in 1612 Ralegh gave up the project, writing a long, majestic preface before allowing the huge fragment to be printed in 1614.

In that preface his bitterness toward the king is everywhere apparent. Stressing the vanity of human pomp, the transitory nature of earthly rule, and the proposition that no monarch stands above the law of God, he thoroughly embarrassed James, who remarked that Ralegh was "too saucy in the censuring of princes" and ordered that Ralegh's name and portrait be excised from all copies before further distribution. Ralegh argued, according to a providential view of history common in Christian thought since it was formulated by Saint Augustine in the fifth century, that history is a map of God's will, that God intervenes in the course of history to punish and reward human rulers, either by immediate action or by consequences deferred to later generations in the same dynastic line. In history God is the First Cause, generating a plan decreed at the Creation and continuing to the Day of Judgment.

Portrait of Ralegh by an unknown artist, painted after his heroism in the Battle of Cadiz (1596). Because of injuries sustained during the raid, Ralegh limped and used a walking stick for the rest of his life (National Portrait Gallery, Ireland).

On the other hand, in the preface and throughout the body of the book Ralegh also shows an interest in the more recent, "politic" historians such as Jean Bodin, Niccolò Machiavelli, and Francis Bacon, who concentrated on the secondary causes constituted by human psychology, motives, and politics. These writers generally considered history and what is now called political science in a context apart from theology, believing that human beings to a large degree operate in a world of their own making and with consequences incurred or avoided by their own ability to plan and manipulate.

If Ralegh hoped to assimilate these two perspectives into a single coherent view, he was—in the opinion of most modern students of historiography—unsuccessful. But as a literary monument *The History of the World* retains its appeal. Ralegh illustrates points about ancient conflicts with vivid, concrete details from his own experiences at war, advising his reader how similar situations were handled when he met them during his service in France or Ireland or at sea. Biblical nations are compared in various respects with the native populations of Guiana and the North American Outer Banks. As a result of his own botanical study, he determines that the Tree of Life in Eden was a variety of *Ficus indica*, the Indian fig. On the whole, his history is less a map of God's will than a mirror of his own mind, in all its richness of imagination and its command of effect.

Ralegh seems ultimately to doubt that people are willing to learn much from history. Human pride and stubbornness probably insure that people will recommit the crimes and errors of their forebears. The sonorous conclusion to the preface, written after the death of Prince Henry and of Ralegh's best hopes, extols Death as the one superior teacher whom no one can ignore: "O eloquent, just and mighty Death! whom none could advise, thou hast persuaded; that none hath dared, thou hast done; and whom all the world hath flattered, thou only hast cast out of the world and despised: thou hast drawn together all the far stretched greatness, all the pride, cruelty, and ambition of man, and covered it all over with these two narrow words, *Hic jacet.*"

After two strokes, confiscation of his estate at Sherborne by the king, and other discommodities attendant upon being a perpetual prisoner, Ralegh at last persuaded James, who was short on funds, to accept his proposal to establish a gold industry with mines in Guiana, which he claimed gave almost certain promise of an abundance of precious metals. James may have been persuaded in part by his queen, Anne, who remained well disposed toward Sir Walter. It is not possible at this remove to know Ralegh's true intent, but many scholars believe that he knew quite well there was little hope of finding gold in Guiana but a good chance of taking lucrative Spanish prizes on the high seas in the old privateering style of Elizabethan days. Could enough Spanish gold be taken, Ralegh may have believed, James would find it impossible not to be appeased.

The expedition was a disaster. With more than a dozen ships and a thousand men, Ralegh left England in June 1617, unaware that the crown had covertly supplied his itinerary to the Spanish ambassador—either through fear of offending Spain or with direct intent to ruin Ralegh. Encountering Spanish troops near Santo Tomé in Guiana, Ralegh's forces attacked, and his eldest son was killed in battle. After some fruitless exploration the company returned to England, with Ralegh in grief and resignation to his fate. Captured after a half-hearted attempt to gain asylum in France, he was returned to the Tower for execution under the reinvoked sentence of 1603. He was beheaded, after a moving scaffold speech, on 29 October 1618, outside the Palace of Westminster.

Bibliographies:

T. N. Brushfield, *A Bibliography of Sir Walter Ralegh Knt. Second Edition with Notes Revised and Enlarged with Portraits and Facsimiles* (Exeter, U.K.: Commin, 1908; New York: Franklin, 1968);

Jerry Leath Mills, "Recent Studies in Ralegh," *English Literary Renaissance*, 15 (Spring 1985): 225-244;

Mills, *Sir Walter Ralegh: A Reference Guide* (Boston: G. K. Hall, 1986);

Christopher M. Armitage, *Sir Walter Ralegh: An Annotated Bibliography* (Chapel Hill: University of North Carolina Press, 1987).

Biographies:

Edward Edwards, *The Life of Sir Walter Ralegh*, 2 volumes (London: Macmillan, 1868);

Willard M. Wallace, *Sir Walter Ralegh* (Princeton: Princeton University Press, 1959; Oxford: Oxford University Press, 1959);

J. H. Adamson and H. F. Folland, *The Shepherd of the Ocean: An Account of Sir Walter Ralegh and His Times* (Boston: Gambit, 1969; London: Bodley Head, 1969).

References:

James P. Bednarz, "Ralegh in Spenser's Historical Allegory," *Spenser Studies*, 4 (1984): 49-70;

Stacy M. Clanton, "The 'Number' of Sir Walter Ralegh's *Booke of the Ocean to Scinthia*," *Studies in Philology*, 82 (Spring 1985): 200-211;

A. D. Cousins, "The Coming of Mannerism: The Later Ralegh and the Early Donne," *English Literary Renaissance*, 9 (Winter 1979): 86-107;

Cousins, "Ralegh's 'A Vision upon this Conceipt of The Faery Queen,'" *Explicator*, 41 (Spring 1983): 14-16;

Donald Davie, "A Reading of 'The Ocean's Love to Cynthia,'" in *Elizabethan Poetry*, edited by John Russell Brown and Bernard Harris (London: Arnold, 1960), pp. 71-89;

Katherine Duncan-Jones, "The Date of Ralegh's '21st: and Last Booke of the Ocean to Scinthia,'" *Review of English Studies*, new series 21 (May 1970): 143-158;

Philip Edwards, *Sir Walter Ralegh* (London: Longmans, Green, 1953);

Stephen J. Greenblatt, *Sir Walter Ralegh: The Renaissance Man and His Roles* (New Haven: Yale University Press, 1973);

Frank Wilson Cheney Hersey, "Sir Walter Ralegh as a Man of Letters," *Proceedings of the State Literary and Historical Association of North Carolina*, no. 25 (1918): 42-54;

Christopher Hill, "Ralegh—Science, History, and Politics," in his *The Intellectual Origins of the English Revolution* (Oxford: Clarendon Press, 1965), pp. 131-224;

Joyce Horner, "The Large Landscape: A Study of Certain Images in Ralegh," *Essays in Criticism*, 5 (July 1955): 197-213;

Michael L. Johnson, "Some Problems of Unity in Sir Walter Ralegh's *The Ocean's Love to Cynthia*," *Studies in English Literature*, 14 (Winter 1974): 17-30;

Pierre Lefranc, *Sir Walter Ralegh, écrivain* (Paris: Librairie Armand Colin, 1968);

F. J. Levy, *Tudor Historical Thought* (San Marino, Cal.: Huntington Library, 1967), pp. 286-294;

Steven W. May, *The Elizabethan Courtier Poets: The Poems and Their Contexts* (Columbia & London: University of Missouri Press, 1991);

May, *Sir Walter Raleigh* (Boston: Twayne, 1989);

Jerry Leath Mills, "Sir Walter Ralegh as a Man of Letters," in *Ralegh and Quinn: The Explorer and His Boswell*, edited by H. G. Jones (Chapel Hill: North Caroliniana Society, 1987), pp. 165-179;

Walker Oakeshott, *The Queen and the Poet* (London: Faber & Faber, 1960);

John Racin, *Sir Walter Ralegh as Historian: An Analysis of The History of the World* (Salzburg, Austria: Universität Salzburg, 1974);

A. L. Rowse, *Ralegh and the Throckmortons* (London: Macmillan, 1962); republished as *Sir Walter Ralegh, His Family and Private Life* (New York: Harper & Row, 1962);

John W. Shirley, *Thomas Hariot: A Biography* (Oxford: Clarendon Press, 1983);

Ernest A. Strathmann, *Sir Walter Ralegh: A Study in Elizabethan Skepticism* (New York: Columbia University Press, 1951);

Leonard Tennenhouse, "Sir Walter Ralegh and the Literature of Clientage," in *Patronage in the Renaissance*, edited by Guy Fitch Lytle and Stephen Orgel (Princeton: Princeton University Press, 1981), pp. 235-258;

Henry David Thoreau, *Sir Walter Raleigh*, edited by Henry Aiken Metcalf (Boston: Bibliophile Society, 1905; reprinted, New York: Gordon Press, 1976);

Peter Ure, "The Poetry of Sir Walter Ralegh," *Review of English Literature*, 1 (July 1960): 19-29;

Arnold Williams, *The Common Expositor: An Account of the Commentaries on Genesis, 1527-1633* (Chapel Hill: University of North Carolina Press, 1948);

J. W. Williamson, *The Myth of the Conqueror: Prince Henry Stuart. A Study of Seventeenth-Century Personation* (New York: AMS Press, 1978), pp. 56-60, 87-90.

Papers:

Ralegh's letters and other manuscripts are widely dispersed. The most important collection relating to his literary career is the material constituting the "Cynthia" poems in the Cecil Papers at Hatfield House. Many letters and other documents repose in the Bodleian Library, the British Museum, and the Carl H. Pforzheimer Library in New York. The most complete and useful guide to these materials is Pierre Lefranc, *Sir Walter Ralegh, écrivain* (cited above).

William Shakespeare

(on or about 23 April 1564 - 23 April 1616)

This entry was updated by John F. Andrews from his entry in DLB 62: Elizabethan Dramatists.

BOOKS: *Venus and Adonis* (London: Printed by Richard Field, sold by J. Harrison I, 1593);

The First Part of the Contention betwixt the two famous Houses of Yorke and Lancaster [abridged and corrupt text of *Henry VI,* part 2] (London: Printed by Thomas Creede for Thomas Millington, 1594);

Lucrece (London: Printed by Richard Field for John Harrison, 1594); republished as *The Rape of Lucrece. Newly Revised* (London: Printed by T. Snodham for R. Jackson, 1616);

The Most Lamentable Romaine Tragedie of Titus Andronicus (London: Printed by John Danter, sold by Edward White & Thomas Middleton, 1594);

A Pleasant Conceited Historie, Called The Taming of a Shrew [corrupt text] (London: Printed by Peter Short, sold by Cuthbert Burbie, 1594);

The True Tragedie of Richard Duke of Yorke, and the death of good King Henrie the Sixt [abridged and corrupt text of *Henry VI,* part 3] (London: Printed by Peter Short for Thomas Millington, 1595);

The Tragedy of King Richard the Third (London: Printed by Valentine Simmes & Peter Short for Andrew Wise, 1597);

The Tragedie of King Richard the second (London: Printed by Valentine Simmes for Andrew Wise, 1597);

An Excellent conceited Tragedie of Romeo and Juliet [corrupt text] (London: Printed by John Danter [& E. Allde?], 1597); *The Most Excellent and lamentable Tragedie of Romeo and Juliet. Newly Corrected, Augmented, and Amended* (London: Printed by Thomas Creede for Cuthbert Burby, 1599);

A Pleasant Conceited Comedie Called, Loues Labors Lost (London: Printed by William White for Cuthbert Burby, 1598);

The History of Henrie the Fourth [part 1] (London: Printed by Peter Short for Andrew Wise, 1598);

The Flower Portrait of Shakespeare, which came into the possession of Mrs. Charles Flower in 1895 (Royal Shakespeare Theatre, Stratford-upon-Avon, Picture Gallery). When the previous owner, H. C. Clements, acquired the portrait in 1840, he said he had seen it exhibited seventy years earlier, but his claim is unsubstantiated. Once thought to have been the original from which the engraving on the title page of the 1623 First Folio of Shakespeare's plays was copied, this portrait is now generally believed to have been based on that engraving.

A Midsommer nights dreame (London: Printed by R. Bradock for Thomas Fisher, 1600);

The most excellent Historie of the Merchant of Venice

(London: Printed by James Roberts for Thomas Heyes, 1600);

The Second part of Henrie the fourth, continuing to his death, and coronation of Henrie the fift (London: Printed by Valentine Simmes for Andrew Wise & William Aspley, 1600);

Much adoe about Nothing (London: Printed by Valentine Simmes for Andrew Wise & William Aspley, 1600);

The Cronicle History of Henry the fift [corrupt text] (London: Printed by Thomas Creede for Thomas Mullington & John Busby, 1600);

The Phoenix and Turtle, appended to *Loves Martyr: or, Rosalins Complaint,* by Robert Chester (London: Printed by Richard Field for E. Blount, 1601);

A Most pleasaunt and excellent conceited Comedie, of Syr John Falstaffe, and the merrie Wives of Windsor [corrupt text] (London: Printed by Thomas Creede for Arthur Johnson, 1602);

The Tragicall Historie of Hamlet Prince of Denmark [abridged and corrupt text] (London: Printed by Valentine Simmes for Nicholas Ling & John Trundell, 1603); *The Tragicall Historie of Hamlet, Prince of Denmarke. Newly Imprinted and Enlarged to Almost as Much Againe as It Was, According to the True and Perfect Coppie* (London: Printed by James Roberts for Nicholas Ling, 1604);

M. William Shak-speare: His True Chronicle Historie of the life and death of King Lear and his three daughters (London: Printed by N. Okes for Nathaniel Butter, 1608);

The Historie of Troylus and Cresseida (London: Printed by G. Eld for R. Bonian & H. Walley, 1609);

Shake-speares Sonnets (London: Printed by G. Eld for Thomas Thorpe, sold by W. Aspley, 1609);

The Late, and Much Admired Play, Called Pericles, Prince of Tyre (London: Printed by W. White for Henry Gosson, 1609);

The Tragœdy of Othello, The Moore of Venice (London: Printed by Nicholas Okes for Thomas Walkley, 1622);

Mr. William Shakespeares Comedies, Histories, & Tragedies. Published according to the True Originall Copies (London: Printed by Isaac Jaggard & Edward Blount, 1623)—comprises *The Tempest; The Two Gentlemen of Verona; The Merry Wives of Windsor; Measure for Measure; The Comedy of Errors; Much Ado About Nothing; Love's Labor's Lost; A Midsummer Night's Dream; The Merchant of Venice; As You Like It; The Taming of the Shrew; All's Well That Ends Well; Twelfth Night; The Winter's Tale; King John; Richard II; Henry IV,* parts 1 and 2;

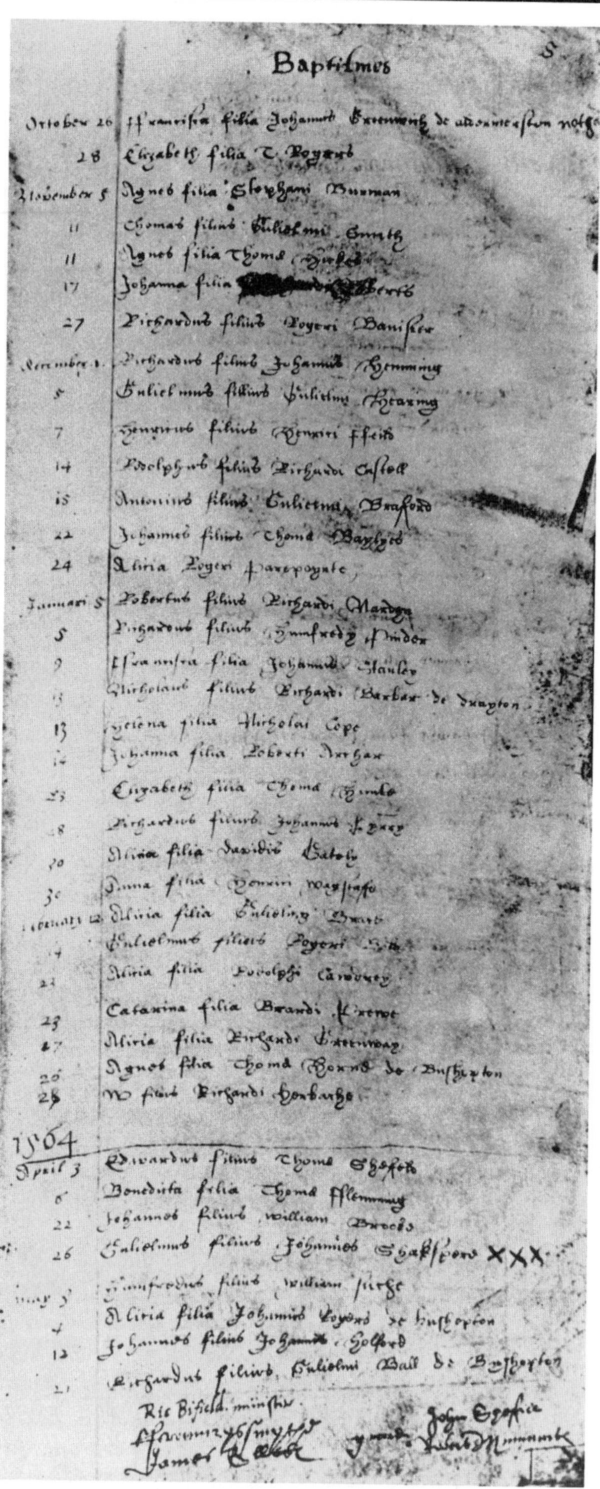

Page from the baptismal register of Holy Trinity Church, Stratford-upon-Avon, recording Shakespeare's christening on 26 April 1564 (Shakespeare's Birthplace Trust Records Office, Stratford-upon-Avon)

Henry V; Henry VI, parts 1-3; *Richard III; Henry VIII; Troilus and Cressida; Coriolanus; Titus Andronicus; Romeo and Juliet; Timon of Athens; Julius Caesar; Macbeth; Hamlet; King Lear; Othello; Antony and Cleopatra; Cymbeline;*

The Two Noble Kinsmen, by Shakespeare and John Fletcher (London: Printed by Thomas Cotes for John Waterson, 1634).

Editions: *A New Variorum Edition of Shakespeare,* 30 volumes to date, volumes 1-15, 18, edited by Horace Howard Furness; volumes 16-17, 19-20, edited by Horace Howard Furness, Jr. (Philadelphia & London: Lippincott, 1871-1928); volumes 1-25, general editor Joseph Quincey Adams; volumes 26-27, general editor Hyder Edward Rollins (Philadelphia & London: Lippincott for the Modern Language Association of America, 1936-1955); volumes 28- , general editors Robert K. Turner, Jr., and Richard Knowles (New York: Modern Language Association of America, 1977-);

The Works of Shakespeare, The New Shakespeare, 39 volumes, edited by J. Dover Wilson, Arthur Quiller-Couch, and others (Cambridge: Cambridge University Press, 1921-1967);

The Complete Works of Shakespeare, edited by George Lyman Kittredge (Boston: Ginn, 1936); revised by Irving Ribner (Waltham, Mass.: Ginn, 1971);

Shakespeare Quarto Facsimiles, 14 volumes, edited by W. W. Greg and Charlton Hinman (Oxford: Clarendon Press, 1939-1966);

William Shakespeare: The Complete Works, edited by Peter Alexander (London & Glasgow: Collins, 1951; New York: Random House, 1952);

The Arden Shakespeare, general editors Harold F. Brooks, Harold Jenkins, and others, now in its second major revision (London: Methuen, 1951-);

The Complete Works of Shakespeare, edited by Hardin Craig (Chicago: Scott Foresman, 1961); revised by David Bevington (Glenview, Ill.: Scott Foresman, 1973); revised again by Bevington (Glenview, Ill.: Scott Foresman, 1980);

The New Penguin Shakespeare, 33 volumes to date, general editor T. J. B. Spencer (Harmondsworth, U.K.: Penguin, 1967-);

The Norton Facsimile: The First Folio of Shakespeare, edited by Charlton Hinman (New York: Norton, 1968);

William Shakespeare: The Complete Works, The Complete Pelican Shakespeare, general editor Alfred Harbage (Baltimore: Penguin, 1969);

The Complete Signet Classic Shakespeare, general editor Sylvan Barnet (New York: Harcourt Brace Jovanovich, 1972; revised, 1989);

The Riverside Shakespeare, general editor G. Blakemore Evans (Boston: Houghton Mifflin, 1974);

Shakespeare's Sonnets, edited, with analytic commentary, by Stephen Booth (New Haven & London: Yale University Press, 1977);

Shakespeare's Plays in Quarto: A Facsimile Edition of Copies Primarily from the Henry E. Huntington Library, edited by Michael J. B. Allen and Kenneth Muir (Berkeley: University of California Press, 1982);

The Complete Works, general editors Stanley Wells and Gary Taylor (Oxford: Clarendon Press, 1986);

The Complete Works: Original-Spelling Edition, general editors Wells and Taylor (Oxford: Clarendon Press, 1986);

The Bantam Shakespeare, edited by Bevington (New York: Bantam Doubleday Dell, 1988);

The Guild Shakespeare, edited by John F. Andrews (New York: GuildAmerica Books, 1989-1992).

PLAY PRODUCTIONS: *Henry VI,* part 1, London, unknown theater (perhaps the Theater, the Rose, or the Newington Butts), circa 1589-1592 (performed 3 March 1592, according to Philip Henslowe's *Diary*);

Henry VI, part 2, London, unknown theater (perhaps the Theater, the Rose, or the Newington Butts), circa 1590-1592;

Henry VI, part 3, London, unknown theater (perhaps the Theater, the Rose, or the Newington Butts), circa 1590-1592;

Richard III, London, unknown theater (perhaps the Theater, the Rose, or the Newington Butts), circa 1591-1592;

The Comedy of Errors, London, unknown theater (perhaps the Theater, the Rose, or the Newington Butts), circa 1592-1594; London, Gray's Inn, 28 December 1594;

Titus Andronicus, London, unknown theater (perhaps the Rose, the Theater, or the Newington Butts), performed 24 January 1594 (Henslowe);

The Taming of the Shrew, London, unknown theater (perhaps the Theater, the Rose, or the

The earliest depiction of the house where Shakespeare spent his childhood, a watercolor painted by Richard Greene circa 1762 (Folger Shakespeare Library; Art Vol. d 75, no. 27c)

Newington Butts), performed 11 June 1594 (Henslowe);

The Two Gentlemen of Verona, London, unknown theater (perhaps the Theater, the Rose, or the Newington Butts), 1594;

Love's Labor's Lost, perhaps at the country house of a great lord, such as the Earl of Southampton, circa 1594-1595; London, at Court, Christmas 1597;

Sir Thomas More, probably by Anthony Munday, revised by Thomas Dekker, Henry Chettle, Shakespeare, and possibly Thomas Heywood; evidently never produced, circa 1594-1595;

King John, London, probably the Theater, circa 1594-1596;

Richard II, London, probably the Theater, circa 1595;

Romeo and Juliet, London, probably the Theater, circa 1595-1596;

A Midsummer Night's Dream, London, probably the Theater or the Curtain, circa 1595-1596;

The Merchant of Venice, London, probably the Theater or the Curtain, circa 1596-1597;

Henry IV, part 1, London, probably the Theater or the Curtain, circa 1596-1597;

Henry IV, part 2, London, probably the Theater or the Curtain, circa 1597;

The Merry Wives of Windsor, perhaps Windsor, Windsor Castle, 23 April 1597;

Much Ado About Nothing, London, probably the Curtain, circa 1598-1599;

Henry V, London, probably the Curtain or the Globe, between March and September 1599(?);

Julius Caesar, London, probably the Curtain or the Globe, 21 September 1599;

As You Like It, London, probably the Globe, circa 1599-1600;

Hamlet, London, probably the Globe, circa 1600-1601;

Twelfth Night, London, possibly at Court, no earlier than 6 January 1601; London, possibly the Globe, circa 1601-1602; London, Middle Temple, 2 February 1602;

Troilus and Cressida, London, possibly the Globe, circa 1601-1602;

All's Well That Ends Well, London, probably the Globe, circa 1602-1603;

Measure for Measure, London, possibly the Globe, 1604; London, at Court, 26 December 1604;

Othello, London, possibly the Globe, 1604; London, Whitehall, 1 November 1604;

King Lear, London, probably the Globe, by late 1605 or early 1606; London, at Court, 26 December 1606;

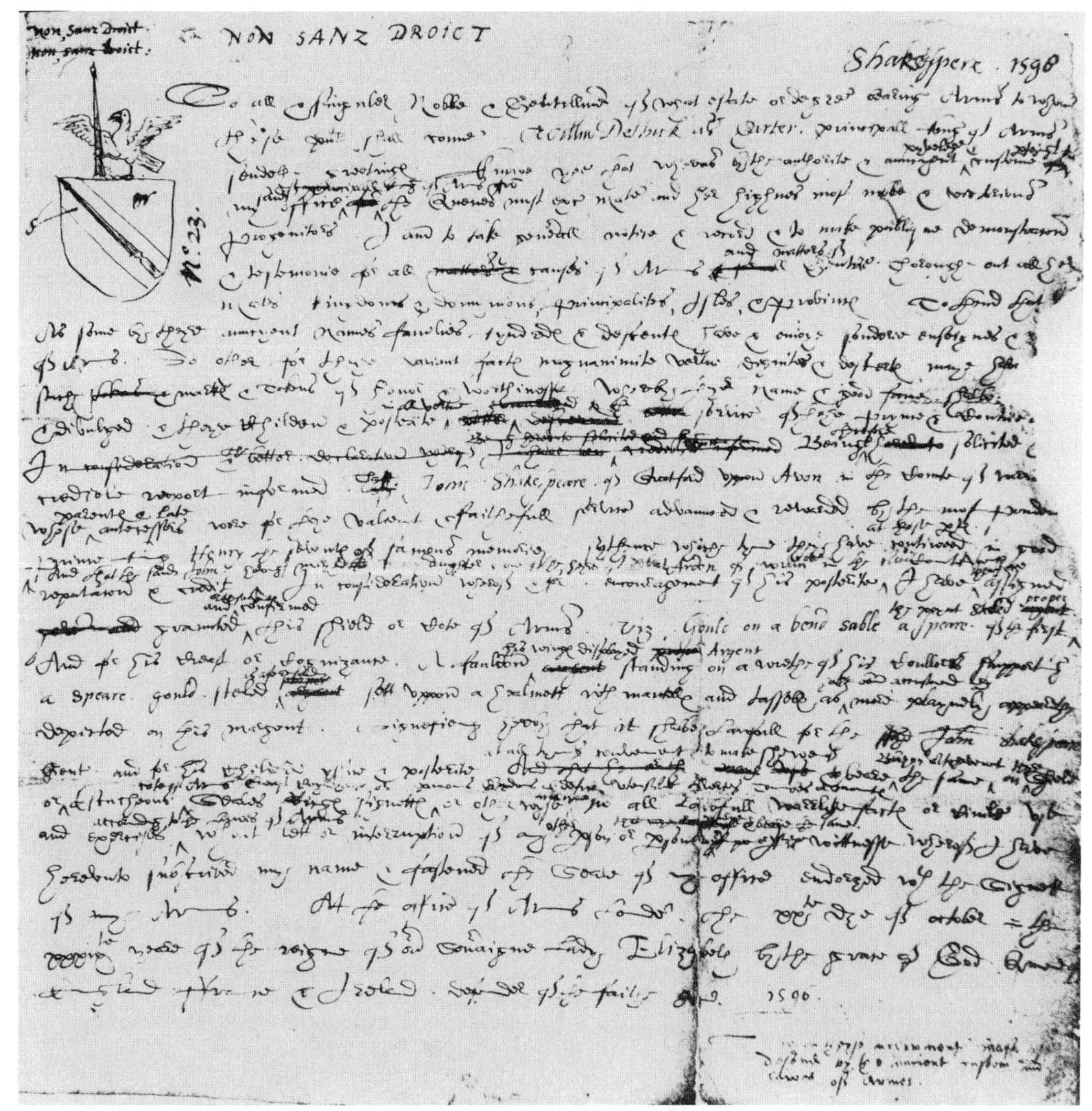

NON SANZ DROICT

Shakespere . 1596

Grant of Arms to John Shakespeare, the first of two rough drafts prepared by William Dethick, Garter King-of-Arms (College of Arms, MS Vincent. 157, art. 23)

Macbeth, possibly London, the Globe, 1606; London, at Court, probably 7 August 1606;

Antony and Cleopatra, probably London, the Globe, circa 1606-1607;

Pericles, possibly London, at Court, between May 1606 and November 1608; probably London, the Globe, circa 1607-1608;

Coriolanus, London, probably the Globe, circa 1607-1608;

Timon of Athens (possibly unperformed during Shakespeare's lifetime); possibly London, the Globe, circa 1608;

Cymbeline, London, probably both the Blackfriars and the Globe, 1609;

The Winter's Tale, London, the Globe, 15 May 1611 (probably the Blackfriars as well);

The Tempest, London, at Court, 1 November 1611 (probably the Globe and Blackfriars as well);

Cardenio, probably by Shakespeare and John Fletcher, London, probably the Globe, circa 1612-1613;

Henry VIII, London, the Globe, 29 June 1613;

The Two Noble Kinsmen, by Shakespeare and Fletcher, London, probably the Blackfriars (possibly the Globe as well), 1613.

The Guild Chapel and the Guild Hall with the schoolroom of the King's New School on the second floor (top) and the interior of the schoolroom (bottom). Shakespeare may have attended this grammar school.

"He was not of an age, but for all time." So wrote Ben Jonson in his dedicatory verses to the memory of William Shakespeare in 1623, and so we continue to affirm today. No other writer, in English or in any other language, can rival the appeal that Shakespeare has long enjoyed. And no one else in any artistic endeavor has projected a cultural influence as broad or as deep.

Shakespeare's words and phrases have become so familiar to us that it is sometimes with a start that we realize we have been speaking Shakespeare when we utter a cliché such as "one fell swoop" or "not a mouse stirring." Never mind that many of the expressions we hear most often—"to the manner born" or (from the same speech in *Hamlet*) "more honored in the breach than the observance"—are misapplied at least as frequently as they are employed with any awareness of their original context and implication. The fact remains that Shakespeare's vocabulary and Shakespeare's cadences are even more pervasive in our ordinary discourse today than the idiom of the King James Bible, which Bartlett's lists as only the second most plentiful source of *Familiar Quotations*.

And much the same could be said of those mirrors of our nature, Shakespeare's characters. From small delights such as Juliet's Nurse, or Flute the Bellows-mender, or Hamlet's Gravedigger, to such incomparable originals as Falstaff, King Lear, and Cleopatra, Shakespeare has enlarged our world by imitating it. It should not surprise us, therefore, that personalities as vivid as these have gone on, as it were, to lives of their own outside the dramatic settings in which they first thought and spoke and moved. In opera alone there are enough different renderings of characters and scenes from Shakespeare's plays to assure that the devotee of Charles-François Gounod, Giuseppe Verdi, Richard Wagner, and Benjamin Britten could attend a different performance every evening for six months and never hear the same aria twice. Which is not to suggest, of course, that the creators of other musical forms have been remiss: Franz Schubert, Felix Mendelssohn, Robert Schumann, Franz Liszt, Hector Berlioz, Pyotr Ilich Tchaikovsky, Claude Debussy, Jean Sibelius, Sergey Prokofiev, and Aaron Copland are but a few of the major figures who have given us songs, tone poems, ballets, symphonic scores, or other works based on the Shakespearean corpus. Cole Porter might well have been addressing his fellow composers when he punctuated *Kiss Me Kate* with the advice to "Brush Up Your Shakespeare."

Certainly the painters have never needed such exhortations. Artists of the stature of George Romney, William Blake, Henry Fuseli, Eugène Delacroix, John Constable, J. M. W. Turner, Pablo Picasso, and David Hockney have drawn inspiration from Shakespeare's dramatis personae; and thanks to such impresarios as the eighteenth-century dealer John Boydell, the rendering of scenes from Shakespeare has long been a significant subgenre of pictorial art. Illustrators of Shakespeare editions have often been notable figures in their own right: George Cruikshank, Arthur Rackham, Rockwell Kent, and Salvador Dalí. Meanwhile, the decorative arts have had their Wedgwood platters with motifs from the plays, their Shakespeare portraits on scrimshaw, their Anne Hathaway's Cottage tea cozies, and their Superbard T-shirts.

Every nation that has a theatrical tradition is indebted to Shakespeare, and in language after language he remains our greatest living playwright, not merely in terms of the hundreds of productions of his works in any given year either. No, one must also bear in mind the dozens of film and television versions of the plays, and the countless adaptations, parodies, and spinoffs that accent the repertory—from musicals such as *The Boys from Syracuse* (based on *The Comedy of Errors*) and *West Side Story* (Leonard Bernstein's New York ghetto version of the gang wars in *Romeo and Juliet*), to political lampoons such as *Macbird* (contra LBJ) and *Dick Deterred* (the doubly punning anti-Nixon polemic), not to mention more reflective dramatic treatments such as Edward Bond's *Bingo* (a "biographical drama" about Shakespeare the man) and Tom Stoppard's *Rosencrantz and Guildenstern Are Dead* (an absurdist re-enactment of *Hamlet* from the perspective of two innocents as bewildered by the court of Renaissance Elsinore as their twentieth-century counterparts would be by the bleak, unforgiving landscape in Samuel Beckett's *Waiting for Godot*).

When we broaden our survey to include the hundreds of novels, short stories, poems, critical appreciations, and other works of serious literature that derive in one way or another from Shakespeare, we command an even grander view of the playwright's literary and cultural primacy. Here in America, for example, we can look back to Ralph Waldo Emerson's awestruck response to the Stratford seer, his exclamation that Shakespeare was "inconceivably wise," all other great

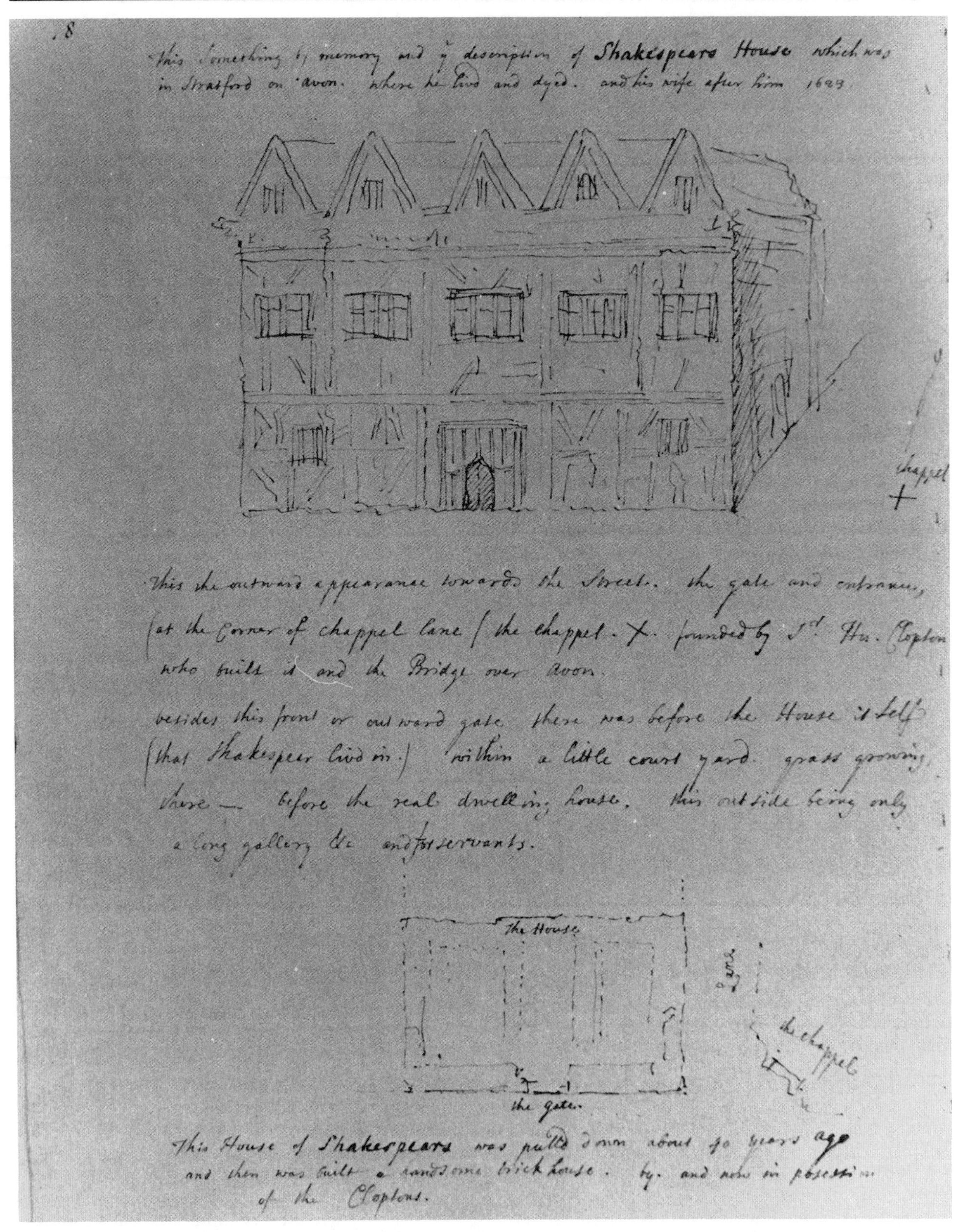

George Vertue's sketches and description of New Place, the house Shakespeare bought in 1597. The house was torn down in 1702, and Vertue, who visited Stratford-upon-Avon in autumn 1737, based his notes and drawings on the reminiscences of a local inhabitant, perhaps a descendant of Shakespeare's sister Joan Hart (British Library, MS Portland Loan 29/246, p. 18).

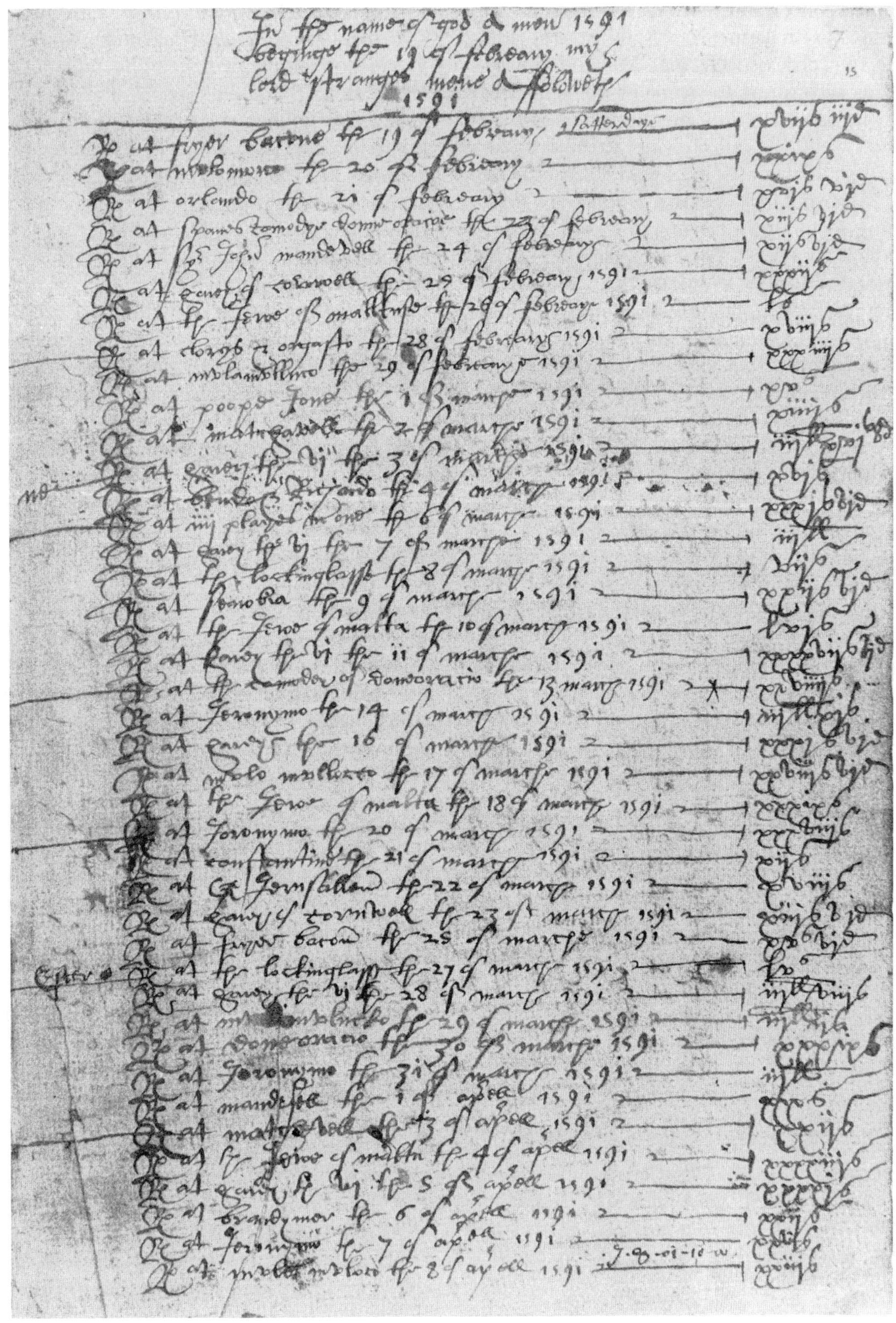

The first mention of a Shakespeare play in the diary of Philip Henslowe came on 3 March 1592 (1591 according to the calendar then in use) when the receipts for a performance of Henry VI *("harey the vj") by the Lord Strange's Men were recorded. The page shown above also records performances of the play on 7, 11, 16, and 28 March and 5 April. It was staged fourteen times between 3 March and 20 June of that year, earning large receipts (MSS VII, l. 7r; Dulwich College, London).*

writers only "conceivably." We can indulge in the speculation that Shakespeare was an aspect of the behemoth that obsessed Herman Melville's imagination, thus accounting for some of the echoes of *King Lear* in the form and rhetoric of *Moby-Dick.* In a lighter vein, we can chuckle at the frontier Bardolatry so hilariously exploited by the Duke and the King in Mark Twain's *Huckleberry Finn.* Or, moving to our own century, we can contemplate William Faulkner's *The Sound and the Fury* as an extended allusion to Macbeth's "tomorrow and tomorrow and tomorrow" soliloquy. Should we be disposed to cast our eye abroad, we can puzzle over "the riddle of Shakespeare" in the meditations of the Argentine novelist and essayist Jorge Luis Borges, or smile as the Nobel Prize-winning African poet and dramatist Wole Soyinka quips that "Sheikh Zpeir" must have had some Arabic blood in him, so faithfully did he capture the local color of Egypt in *Antony and Cleopatra.*

Implicit in all of these manifestations of Shakespeare's immortality is a perception best summed up, perhaps, in James Joyce's rendering of the charismatic name: "Shapesphere." For in showing "the very age and body of the time his form and pressure" (as Hamlet would put it), the playwright proved himself to be both the "soul" of the era his works reflected and adorned and the consummate symbol of the artist whose poetic visions transcend their local habitation and become, in some mysterious way, contemporaneous with "all time" (to return once more to Jonson's eulogy). If Jan Kott, a twentieth-century existentialist from Poland, can marvel that Shakespeare is "our contemporary," then his testimony is but one more instance of the tendency of every new period to claim the poet as its own. Whatever else we say about Shakespeare, in other words, we are impelled to acknowledge that, preeminent above all others, he has long stood and will no doubt long remain atop a pedestal (to recall a 1960s *New Yorker* cartoon) as "a very very very very very very important writer."

So important, indeed, that some of his most zealous admirers have paid him the backhand compliment of doubting that works of such surpassing genius could have been written by the same William Shakespeare who lies buried and memorialized in Stratford-upon-Avon. Plays such as the English histories would suggest in the writer an easy familiarity with the ways of kings, queens, and courtiers; hence their author must have been a member of the nobility, someone like Edward de Vere, the seventeenth Earl of Oxford. Plays such as *Julius Caesar,* with their impressive display of classical learning, would indicate an author with more than the "small Latin and less Greek" that Ben Jonson attributes to Shakespeare; hence the need to seek for their true begetter in the person of a university-trained scholar such as Francis Bacon. Or so would urge those skeptics (whose numbers have included such redoubtable figures as Henry James and Sigmund Freud) who find themselves in sympathy with the "anti-Stratfordians." Their ranks have never been especially numerous or disciplined, and they have often differed among themselves about which of the various "claimants"—the Earl of Derby, Christopher Marlowe, even Queen Elizabeth herself—should be upheld as the "true Shakespeare." But the anti-Stratfordians have at least kept us mindful of how little we can say for certain about the life of the author whose works have so enriched the lives of succeeding generations.

One thing we do know is that if Shakespeare was a man for the ages, he was also very much a product of his own epoch. Christened at Holy Trinity Church in Stratford-upon-Avon on 26 April 1564, he grew up as the eldest of five children reared by John Shakespeare, a tradesman who played an increasingly active role in the town's civic affairs as his business prospered, and Mary Arden Shakespeare, the daughter of a gentleman farmer from nearby Wilmcote. Whether William Shakespeare was born on 23 April, as tradition holds, is not known; but a birth date only a few days prior to the recorded baptism seems eminently probable, particularly in view of the fear his parents must have had that their first son, like two sisters who had preceded him and one who followed, might die in infancy. By the time the future playwright was old enough to begin attending school, he had a younger brother (Gilbert, born in 1566) and a baby sister (Joan, born in 1569). As he grew into adolescence, the youthful William found himself with two more brothers to help look after (Richard, born in 1574, and Edmund, born in 1580), the younger of whom eventually followed his by-then-prominent eldest sibling to London and the theater, where he had a brief career as an actor before his untimely death at twenty-seven.

The house where Shakespeare spent his childhood stood adjacent to the wool shop in which his father plied a successful trade as a glover and dealer in leather goods and other commodities. Before moving to Stratford sometime

Greenes

Sweet boy, might I aduise thee, be aduisde, and get not many enemies by bitter wordes: inueigh against vaine men, for thou canst do it, no man better, no man so well: thou hast a libertie to reprooue all, and name none; for one being spoken to, all are offended; none being blamed no man is iniured. Stop shallow water still running, it will rage, or tread on a worme and it will turne: then blame not Schollers vexed with sharpe lines, if they reproue thy too much liberty of reproofe.

And thou no lesse deseruing than the other two, in some things rarer, in nothing inferiour; driuen (as my selfe) to extreme shifts, a litle haue I to say to thee: and were it not an idolatrous oth, I would sweare by sweet S. George, thou art vnworthy better hap, sith thou dependest on so meane a stay. Base minded men all three of you, if by my miserie you be not warnd: for vnto none of you (like mee) sought those burres to cleaue: those Puppets (I meane) that spake from our mouths, those Anticks garnisht in our colours. Is it not strange, that I, to whom they all haue beene beholding: is it not like that you, to whome they all haue beene beholding, shall (were yee in that case as I am now) bee both at once of them forsaken? Yes trust them not: for there is an vpstart Crow, beautified with our feathers, that with his Tygers hart wrapt in a Players hyde, supposes he is as well able to bombast out a blanke verse as the best of you: and beeing an absolute Iohannes fac totum, is in his owne conceit the onely Shake-scene in a countrey. O that I might intreat your rare wits to be imploied in more profitable courses: & let those Apes imitate your past excellence, and neuer more acquaint them with your admired inuentions. I knowe the best husband of you

you

Robert Greene's attack on "Shake-scene" in Greene's Groatsworth of Wit *(1592; British Library). In saying that Shakespeare is a "Tygers hart wrapt in a Players hyde," Greene was alluding to a line in* Henry VI, *part 3, where the Duke of York calls Queen Margaret a "tiger's heart wrapped in a woman's hide."*

prior to 1552 (when the records show that he was fined for failing to remove a dunghill from outside his house to the location where refuse was normally to be deposited), John Shakespeare had been a farmer in the neighboring village of Snitterfield. Whether he was able to read and write is uncertain. He executed official documents, not with his name but with a cross signifying his glover's compasses. A few scholars interpret this as a signature that might have been considered more "authentic" than a full autograph; most have taken it to be an indication of illiteracy. But even if John Shakespeare was not one of the "learned," he was certainly a man of what a later age would call upward mobility. By marrying Mary Arden, the daughter of his father's landlord, he acquired the benefits of a better social standing and a lucrative inheritance, much of which he invested in property (he bought several houses). And by involving himself

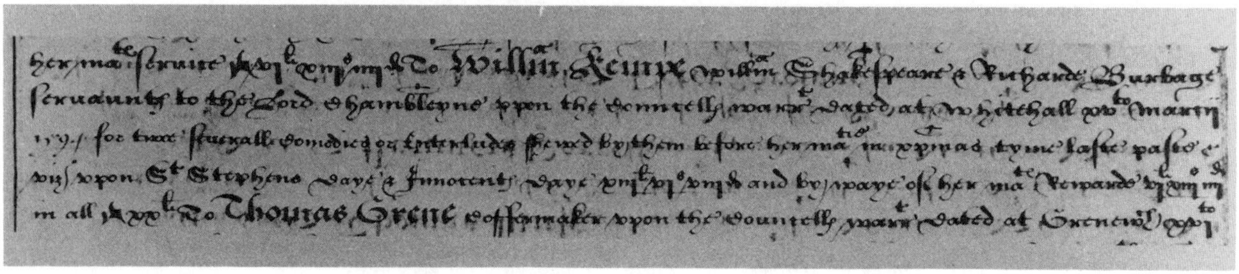

Anthony van Wyndgaerde's 1594 drawing of Greenwich Palace (top), where the Lord Chamberlain's Men performed during the Christmas season of 1594 (Ashmolean Museum, Oxford); and a portion of a page from the Accounts of the Treasurer of the Queen's Chamber (bottom) recording payment to Shakespeare, William Kempe, and Richard Burbage—all members of the Lord Chamberlain's company—for their part in those festivities. This entry is the earliest documentation of Shakespeare's membership in an acting company (Public Record Office, Exchequer, Pipe Office, Declared Accounts, E. 351/542, f. 107v).

in public service, he rose by sure degrees to the highest municipal positions Stratford had to offer: chamberlain (1561), alderman (1565), and bailiff (or mayor) and justice of the peace (1568). A few years later, probably around 1576, John Shakespeare approached the College of Heralds for armorial bearings and the right to call himself a gentleman. Before his application was acted upon, however, his fortunes seem to have taken a sudden turn for the worse, and it was not until 1596, when his eldest son had attained some status and renewed the petition, that a Shakespeare coat of arms was finally granted. This must have been a comfort to John Shakespeare in his declining years (he died in 1601), because by then he had borrowed money, disposed of property out of necessity, ceased to attend meetings of the town council, become involved in litigation and been assessed fines, and even stopped attending church services, for fear, it was said, "of process for debt." Just what happened to alter John Shakespeare's financial and social position after the mid 1570s is not clear. Some have seen his nonattendance at church as a sign that he had become a recusant, unwilling to conform to the practices of the newly established Church of England (his wife's family had remained loyal to Roman Catholicism despite the fact that the old faith was under vigorous attack in Warwickshire after 1577), but the surviving evidence is anything but definitive.

The records we have suggest that William's formative years were ones in which he enjoyed the advantages that would have accrued to the son of one of the most influential citizens of a bustling market town in the fertile Midlands. When he was taken to services at Holy Trinity Church, he would probably have sat with his family in the front pew, in accordance with his father's civic rank. There he would have heard and registered the words and rhythms of the Bible, the sonorous phrases of the 1559 Book of Common Prayer, and the admonitions of the official homilies on civic duty. In all likelihood, after spending a year or two at a "petty school" to learn the rudiments of reading and writing, William would have proceeded, at the age of seven, to "grammar school." Given his father's position, he would have been eligible to attend the King's New School, located above the Guild Hall and adjacent to the Guild Chapel (institutions that would both have been quite familiar to a man with the elder Shakespeare's municipal duties), a short walk from the family residence on Henley Street. Though no records survive to tell us who attended the Stratford grammar school during this period, we do know that it had well-qualified and comparatively well-paid masters; and, through the painstaking research of such scholars as T. W. Baldwin, we now recognize that a curriculum such as the one offered in the poet's hometown would have equipped its pupils with what by modern standards would be a formidable classical education.

During his lengthy school days there, young Shakespeare would have become thoroughly grounded in Latin, acquired some background in Greek, and developed enough linguistic facility to pick up whatever he may have wanted later from such modern languages as Italian, French, and Spanish. Along the way he would have become familiar with such authors as Aesop, Caesar, Cicero, Sallust, Livy, Virgil, Horace, Ovid, and Seneca. He would have studied logic and rhetoric as well as grammar, and he would have been taught the principles of composition and oratory from the writings of such masters as Quintilian and Erasmus. In all probability, he would even have received some training in speech and acting through the performance of plays by Plautus and Terence. If the mature dramatist's references to schooling and schoolmasters in the plays are a reliable index of how he viewed his own years as a student, we must conclude that the experience was more tedious than pleasurable. But it is difficult to imagine a more suitable mode of instruction for the formation of a Renaissance poet's intellectual and artistic sensibility.

Meanwhile, of course, the youthful Shakespeare would have learned a great deal from merely being alert to all that went on around him. He would have paid attention to the plant and animal life in the local woods that he would later immortalize, in *As You Like It,* as the Forest of Arden. He may have hunted from time to time; one legend, almost certainly apocryphal, has it that he eventually left Stratford because he had been caught poaching deer from the estate of a powerful squire, Sir Thomas Lucy, four miles upstream. He probably learned to swim as a youth, skinny-dipping in the river Avon. He may have participated in some of the athletic pursuits that were the basis of competition in the Elizabethan equivalent of the Olympics, the nearby Cotswold Games. He would undoubtedly have been adept at indoor recreations such as hazard (a popular dice game), or chess, or any of a number of card games. As he grew older, he would

The Workes of William Shakeſpeare, containing all his Comedies, Hiſtories, and Tragedies: Truely ſet forth, according to their firſt ORIGINALL.

The Names of the Principall Actors in all theſe Playes.

Illiam Shakeſpeare.
Richard Burbadge.
John Hemmings.
Auguſtine Phillips.
William Kempt.
Thomas Poope.
George Bryan.
Henry Condell.
William Slye.
Richard Cowly.
John Lowine.
Samuell Croſſe.
Alexander Cooke.

Samuel Gilburne.
Robert Armin.
William Oſtler.
Nathan Field.
John Underwood.
Nicholas Tooley.
William Eccleſtone.
Joſeph Taylor.
Robert Benfield.
Robert Goughe.
Richard Robinſon.
Iohn Shancke.
Iohn Rice.

List, from the First Folio edition of Shakespeare's works (1623; Folger Shakespeare Library), of the members of the company that Cuthbert and Richard Burbage formed as the Lord Chamberlain's Men in 1594. In 1603 the company came under the patronage of James I and was renamed the King's Men, or His Majesty's Servants.

have become accustomed to such vocations as farming, sheepherding, tailoring, and shopkeeping. He would have acquired skills such as fishing, gardening, and cooking. And he would have gathered information about the various professions: law, medicine, religion, and teaching. Judging from the encyclopedic range of daily life and human endeavor reflected in his poems and

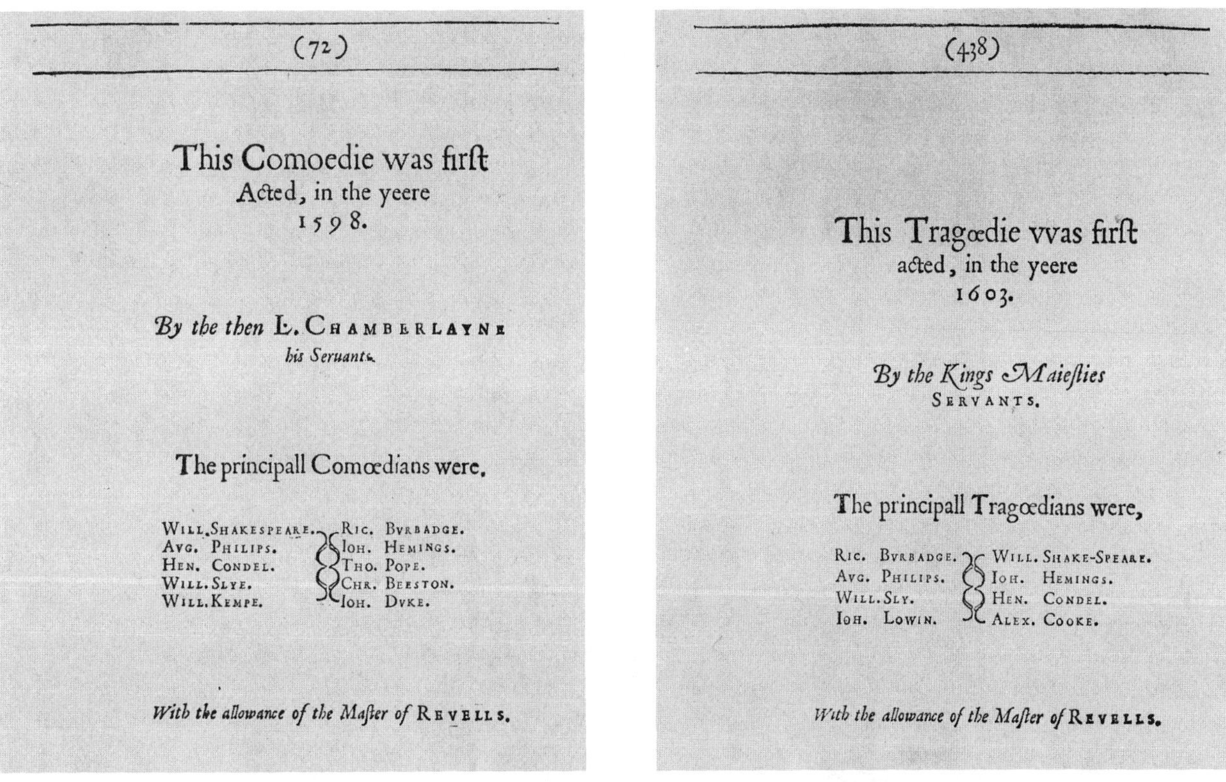

(72)

This Comoedie was firſt
Acted, in the yeere
1598.

By the then L. Chamberlayne
his Seruants.

The principall Comœdians were.

Will. Shakespeare.	Ric. Bvrbadge.
Avg. Philips.	Ioh. Hemings.
Hen. Condel.	Tho. Pope.
Will. Slye.	Chr. Beeston.
Will. Kempe.	Ioh. Dvke.

With the allowance of the Maſter of Revells.

(438)

This Tragœdie vvas firſt
acted, in the yeere
1603.

By the Kings Maieſties
Servants.

The principall Tragœdians were,

Ric. Bvrbadge.	Will. Shake-Speare.
Avg. Philips.	Ioh. Hemings.
Will. Sly.	Hen. Condel.
Ioh. Lowin.	Alex. Cooke.

With the allowance of the Maſter of Revells.

When the first volume of Ben Jonson's Works *was published in 1616, Shakespeare was listed as a cast member for the first performances of* Every Man in His Humour *(left) and* Sejanus *(right) (Bodleian Library).*

plays, we can only infer that Shakespeare was both a voracious reader and a keen observer, the sort of polymath Henry James might have been describing when he referred to a character in one of his novels as "a man on whom nothing was lost."

Once his school years ended, Shakespeare married, at eighteen, a woman who was eight years his senior. We presume that Anne Hathaway was pregnant when the marriage license was issued by the Bishop of Worcester on 27 November 1582, because a daughter, Susanna, was baptized in Holy Trinity six months later on 26 May 1583. We have good reason to believe that the marriage was hurriedly arranged: there was only one reading of the banns (a church announcement preceding a wedding that allowed time for any legal impediments against it to be brought forward before the ceremony took place), an indication of unusual haste. But whether the nuptials were in any way "forced" is impossible to determine. Some biographers (most notably Anthony Burgess) have made much of an apparent clerical error whereby the bride's name was entered as Anne Whateley of Temple Grafton in the Worcester court records; these writers speculate that William was originally planning to marry another Anne until Anne Hathaway of Shottery (a village a mile or so from Shakespeare's home in Stratford) produced her embarrassing evidence of a prior claim. To most scholars, including our foremost authority on Shakespeare's life, S. Schoenbaum, this explanation of the Anne Whateley court entry seems farfetched. Such hypotheses are inevitable, however, in the absence of fuller information about the domestic life of William and Anne Hathaway Shakespeare.

What we do have to go on is certainly compatible with the suspicion that William and his bride were somewhat less than ardent lovers. They had only two more children—the twins Hamnet and Judith, who were baptized on 2 February 1585—and they lived more than a hundred miles apart, so far as we can tell, for the better part of the twenty-year period during which Shakespeare was employed in the London theater. If we can give any credence to an amusing anecdote recorded in the 1602-1603 diary of a law student named John Manningham, there was at least one occasion during those years when the playwright, overhearing the actor Richard Burbage make an assignation, "went before, was entertained, and at

Self-portrait of Richard Burbage, who played roles such as Richard III, Othello, and King Lear (Dulwich College Picture Gallery, London)

his game before Burbage came; then, message being brought that Richard the Third was at the door, Shakespeare caused return to be made that William the Conqueror was before Richard the Third." If we read the sonnets as in any way autobiographical, moreover, we are shown a poet with at least one other significant female liaison: a "Dark Lady" to whom Will's lust impels him despite the self-disgust the affair arouses (and despite her infidelity with the fair "Young Man" to whom many of the poems are addressed and for whom the speaker reserves his deepest feelings).

But even if there is reason to speculate that Shakespeare may not have always been faithful to the marriage bed, there is much to suggest that he remained attached to Anne as the mother of his children. In 1597 he purchased one of the most imposing houses in Stratford—New Place, across the street from the Guild Chapel—presumably settling his family there as soon as the title to the property was clear. He himself retired to that Stratford residence, so far as we can determine, sometime between 1611 and 1613. And of course he remembered his wife in his will, bequeathing her the notorious "second-best bed"—which some modern biographers regard as a generous afterthought (since a third of a man's estate would have gone to his spouse by law even if her name never occurred in the document) rather than the slight that many interpreters have read into the phrasing.

Naturally we would like to know more about what Shakespeare was like as a husband and parent. But most of us would give just as much to learn what took place in his professional life between 1585 (when the parish register shows him to have become the father of twins) and 1592 (when we find the earliest surviving references to him as a rising star in the London theater). What did he do during these so-called dark years? Did he study law, as some have suspected? Did he travel on the Continent? Did he become an apprentice to a butcher, as one late-seventeenth-century account had it? Or—most plausibly, in the view of many modern biographers—did he teach school for a while? All we can say for certain is that by the time his children were making their own way to the classroom in bucolic Stratford, William Shakespeare had become an actor and writer in what was already the largest city in Europe.

The poet probably made his way to London by way of the spires of Oxford, as do most visitors returning from Stratford today. But why he went, or when, history does not tell us. It has been plausibly suggested that he joined an acting troupe (the Queen's Men) that was one player short when it toured Warwickshire in 1587. If so, he may have migrated by way of one or two intermediary companies to a position with the troupe that became the Lord Chamberlain's Men in 1594. The only thing we can assert with any assurance is that by 1592 Shakespeare had established himself as a performer and had written at least three plays. One of these—the third part of *Henry VI*—was alluded to in that year in a posthumously published testament by a once-prominent poet and playwright named Robert Greene, a member of the "University Wits" who had dominated the London theater in the late 1580s. Dissipated and on his deathbed, Greene warned his fellow playwrights to beware of an "upstart crow" who, not content with the lot of a mere player, was aspiring to a share of the livelihood that had previously been the exclusive province of professional writers such as himself. Whether *Greene's Groatsworth of Wit* accuses Shakespeare of plagiarism when it describes him as "beautified with our feathers" is not clear; some scholars have interpreted the phrase as a complaint that the younger writer had borrowed freely from the scripts of others (or had merely revised existing plays, a practice quite common in the Elizabethan theater). But there can be no doubt that Greene's anxieties signal the end of one era and the beginning of another: a glorious epoch, spanning two full decades, during which the dominant force on the London stage would be not Greene or Thomas Kyd or Marlowe or even (in the later years of that period) Jonson, but Shakespeare.

If we look at what the poet had written by the early 1590s, we see that he had already become thoroughly familiar with the daily round of one of the great capitals of the world. He knew

Robert Armin, who specialized in "wise fool" parts such as Touchstone in As You Like It, *Feste in* Twelfth Night, *and the Fool in* King Lear *(woodcut from the title page of the 1609 quarto edition of Armin's* The Two Maids of Moreclacke; *Anderson Galleries auction catalogue, sale number 2077, 20-21 May 1926)*

Saint Paul's Cathedral, famous not only as a house of worship but also as the marketplace where books and other goods were bought and sold. He knew the Inns of Court, where aspiring young lawyers studied for the bar. He knew the river Thames, spanned by the ever-busy, ever-fascinating London Bridge. He knew the Tower, where so many of the characters he would depict in his history plays had suffered or met their deaths, and where in his own lifetime such prominent noblemen as the Earl of Essex and Sir Walter Ralegh would be imprisoned prior to their executions. He knew Westminster, where Parliament met when summoned by the Queen, and where the monarch held court at Whitehall Palace. He knew the harbor, where English ships, having won control of the seas by defeating the "invincible" Spanish Armada in 1588, had begun in earnest to explore the New World.

In Shakespeare's day London was a vigorous city of somewhere between 150,000 and 200,000 inhabitants. If in its more majestic aspects it was dominated by the courts of Queen Elizabeth and (after 1603) King James, in its everyday affairs it was accented by the hustle and bustle of getting and spending. Its Royal Exchange was one of the forerunners of today's stock exchanges. Its many marketplaces offered a variety of merchandise for a variety of tastes. Its crowded streets presented a colorful pageant of Elizabethan modes of transport and dress, ranging from countrywomen in homespun to elegant ladies in apparel as decorative as their husbands' wealth—and the Crown's edicts on clothing—would allow. Its inns and taverns afforded a rich diversity of vivid personalities—eating, tippling, chatting, and enjoying games and pleasures of all kinds. It was, in short, an immensely stimulating social and cultural environment, and we can be sure that Shakespeare took full advantage of the opportunity it gave him to observe humanity in all its facets. Like Prince Hal, he must have learned "to drink with any tinker in his own language," and it was this as much as anything he was taught at school (or might have acquired by attendance at university) that equipped him to create such vibrant characters as Mistress Quickly, proud Hotspur, and the imperturbable Bottom.

Not that all was always well. Like any major city, London also had its problems. Preachers and moralists were constantly denouncing the excessive use of cosmetics. Thus, when Hamlet speaks out against "your paintings," telling Ophelia that "God hath given you one face, and you make yourselves another," he would have been sounding a note familiar to everyone in Shakespeare's audience. So also with the "furred gowns" so roundly cursed by Lear: courtiers and their ladies were accustomed to lavishing as much "pride" on a single article of bejeweled finery as a modern man or woman might pay for a very expensive automobile. But luxury was only one of the evils of the age. London's Puritan authorities, regarding the theaters as dens of iniquity, closed them down on any available pretext, particularly when the bubonic plague was rampant. Meanwhile, even without the plague or the theaters to concern them (and one gathers that some of the authorities were anything but sure about which was the greater peril), the city fathers had to contend with gambling, drunkenness, prostitution, and other vices, especially in the Bankside district south of the Thames and in the other "liberties" outside the city walls to the west, east, and north (such as Shoreditch, where James Burbage had erected the first permanent commercial playhouse, the Theater, when Shakespeare was only twelve, and where many of Shakespeare's plays prior to 1597 were probably first performed). Here most blatantly, but elsewhere as well, pickpockets, vagabonds, and other members of the fraternity of urban lowlife lay in wait for "conies," as they called their unsuspecting victims. Given so many "notorious villainies" for spokesmen like Thomas Dekker's "Belman of London" to bring to light, it is hardly surprising that among the most prolific literary genres of the period were the moralizing books and tracts that spewed forth from reformers incensed by the decadence of the early modern metropolis.

In such a setting did Shakespeare write and help perform the greatest dramatic works the world has ever experienced. And he did so in suburbs known primarily for amusements that might appear to be totally alien from the sweet Swan of Avon's poetic grace. For if Shoreditch and, later, Bankside were to blossom into the finest theatrical centers of that or any other age, they were also, for better or worse, the seedbeds for such brutal spectator sports as bearbaiting, bullbaiting, and cockfighting. This may help account for the blood and violence so frequently displayed on the Elizabethan and Jacobean stage, most notably in such early Shakespearean experiments as the *Henry VI* trilogy and *Titus Andronicus,* but also in mature achievements such as *Julius Caesar* and *King Lear.* But of course there was a good deal more than murder and mayhem in the "wooden O" that served as amphitheater for most of Shakespeare's works.

On a stage largely devoid of scenery but by no means lacking in spectacle, the playwright and his actors made efficient use of language, properties, and gesture to establish time, locale, situation, and atmosphere. In the process, through all the resources of rhetoric, symbolism, and what Hamlet in his advice to the players calls "action," the "artificial persons" of the drama (its dramatis personae) imitated humanity in such a way as to convey whatever "matter" an author and his company envisaged for a scene, an act, or a full theatrical sequence. By twentieth-century standards the means they used were relatively primitive—no spotlights, too few furnishings to achieve verisimilitude through setting and dress, only the crudest of "special effects," no curtains to raise and lower as a way of signaling the beginning and end of a

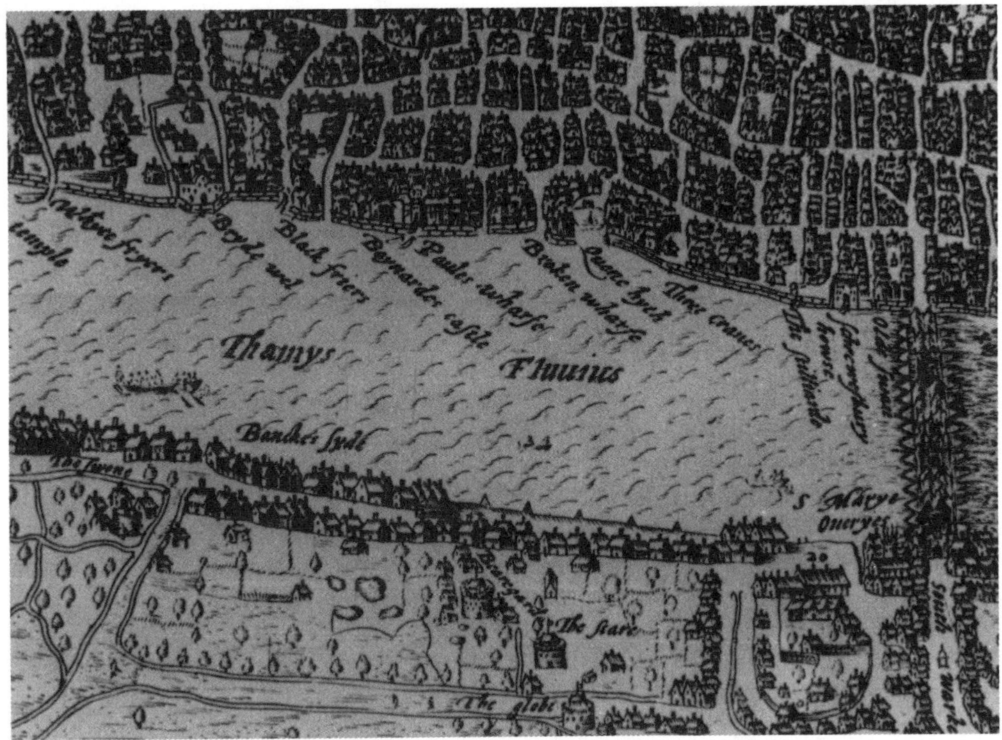

A portion of the inset John Norden prepared for the panorama of London he published in 1600 as Civitas Londini *(Royal Library, Kungliga Biblioteket, Stockholm). The first Globe theater, built from the timbers of the Theater in 1598-1599, is shown just south of the Rose theater (here mislabeled "The Stare").*

scene or act—but by any standards the results they achieved were brilliant. It has taken us nearly four centuries to rediscover what they seem to have understood intuitively: that in some things aesthetic, less is more.

Our best estimate is that approximately three thousand spectators could be crammed into a ninety-nine-foot-wide, polygonal structure such as the Theater (which opened in 1576 and was dismantled in 1598, after the owner of the land on which it stood refused to negotiate a lease acceptable to Shakespeare's acting company) or its successor the Globe (which opened in 1599, after the company transported the lumber from the Theater across the Thames and used it as the basis for an even more handsome playhouse on the Bankside). More than half of the audience stood in the yard (which measured about fifty-five feet in diameter); the remainder sat in the three galleries that encircled the yard and rose to a thatched roof some thirty-six feet above the ground.

The stage was probably about forty-three feet wide, and it thrust some twenty-seven feet into the yard from the "tiring house" (attiring room) at the rear of the building. It was covered by a pillar-supported superstructure—the "Heavens"—that protected the actors and their costumes from the elements and held the equipment Elizabethan companies used for ascents, descents, and other "flying" effects. In the floor of the stage platform (about five feet above the surrounding yard) was a trapdoor that could be opened for visitations from below or for access into what, depending on the context, might represent a grave or a pit or even hell itself. At the back of the stage in all likelihood, in the wall concealing the tiring house where the actors effected their wardrobe changes and awaited their cues to enter, were three doors. The two at the corners were probably used for most of the entrances and exits of the actors; the large middle one was capable of being employed as a shallow, draped "discovery space" that might be drawn open for tableaux (as when Ferdinand and Miranda are disclosed playing chess in *The Tempest*) or adapted to represent small spaces such as closets, studies, bedrooms, or shops like the Apothecary's cell in *Romeo and Juliet.* On the level above the tiring house, probably divided into five bays, was a balcony that accommodated a select number of the theater's highest-paying customers and functioned in many of the plays as the "upper stage" where brief scenes requiring a higher vantage point could be enacted. Sentinels on watch, lovers at a second-story bedroom window, seamen crying out from a ship's crow's nest: these and other situations called for the use of one or more of the upper-level enclosures (probably the central one in most instances) for characters to speak their lines and render the movements called for in the script.

Because the main playing area was surrounded on all four sides by spectators, the poet and the performer benefited from a more intimate relationship with the audience than is customary in present-day theaters fitted with a curtain and a proscenium arch. For Shakespeare, this meant that he could allow a character to confide in a nearby playgoer through asides, as does Iago in *Othello,* or to be overheard while he meditates in solitude, as does Brutus in the soliloquy in which he talks himself into joining the plot to assassinate Caesar. Such devices may strike a modern viewer as less refined than, say, the cinematic voice-over, but they proved eminently acceptable to a public that was willing to "piece out" a performance's "imperfections with [its] thoughts." And it says a great deal about the intelligence and sensitivity of Elizabethan theatergoers that they attended and were capable of appreciating dramatic works which, in many respects, were both responses to and sublimations of the coarser activities that competed for attention (and people's entertainment budgets) only a short distance away from the magic circle defined by the walls of a Theater or a Globe.

Just who composed the audiences of these and other popular playhouses is still a matter of debate (and we should remember that Shakespeare probably had associations at one time or another with such venues as the Rose, the Newington Butts, the Cross Keys Inn, and the Curtain, not to mention a variety of private halls), but recent research by Ann Jennalie Cook and Andrew Gurr suggests that they were a somewhat more affluent cross-section of Elizabethan society than earlier writings by such scholars as Alfred Harbage would have led us to believe. An examination of wages and prices during the period indicates, for example, that those who attended performances on weekday afternoons would have had to have more leisure, and more disposable income, than seems compatible with the view that even the groundlings (who paid the lowest admission, a penny to stand in the yard and risk getting soaked in the event of rain) were predominantly working-class people and illiterate apprentices. Because their position in the yard put their eyes on a level with the feet of the players, the commoners were sometimes satirized as "understanders"; it now begins to appear that a substantial percentage of these theatergoers must have been "understanders" in a more favorable sense. To be sure, some of them may at times have been a bit obstreperous, and their number may well have included an assortment of men and women (including prostitutes) preoccupied with extratheatrical pursuits. It may be, too, that the groundlings were more susceptible than other patrons (if merely because of their greater proximity to the stage) to manipulation by what we now call "naughty" actors, the overweening "clowns" whom Hamlet rebukes for their tendency to ply the crowd for inappropriate laughter, interrupting the flow of the action and causing spectators to miss "some necessary question of the play." But even if those who stood in the center of the amphitheater were not quite as cultivated, on the average, as those patrons who could afford to sit while they watched a play, it is difficult to reconcile the subtlety and indirection of Shakespeare's plotting and characterization, not to mention the complexity of his language and the incomparable music of his verse, with the assumption that an average audience at the public playhouses was unable to respond to anything more elevated than the broad humor of a Launce or a Dogberry. Even if we still find it valuable, then, to preserve something of the traditional distinction between the groundlings and the more "privileged" auditors who occupied the three-tiered galleries encircling the stage, we should now open our minds to the possibility that there were more of what Hamlet would call "judicious" viewers in every segment of the Elizabethan audience, including those who filled the yard, than we have tended to assume until recently in our analyses of Shakespearean drama.

Which is not to say, of course, that Shakespeare and his fellow dramatists were *completely* satisfied with *any* of their audiences (but then what writer ever is?). Hamlet bestows high praise on a play that he says "was never acted, or if it was, not above once," for "it pleased not the million, 'twas caviary to the general." He then instructs the players to disregard "a whole theater of others" if necessary, in order to please "those with judgments in such matters." Whether Hamlet's creator would himself have endorsed such extreme elitism is difficult to determine, but such a

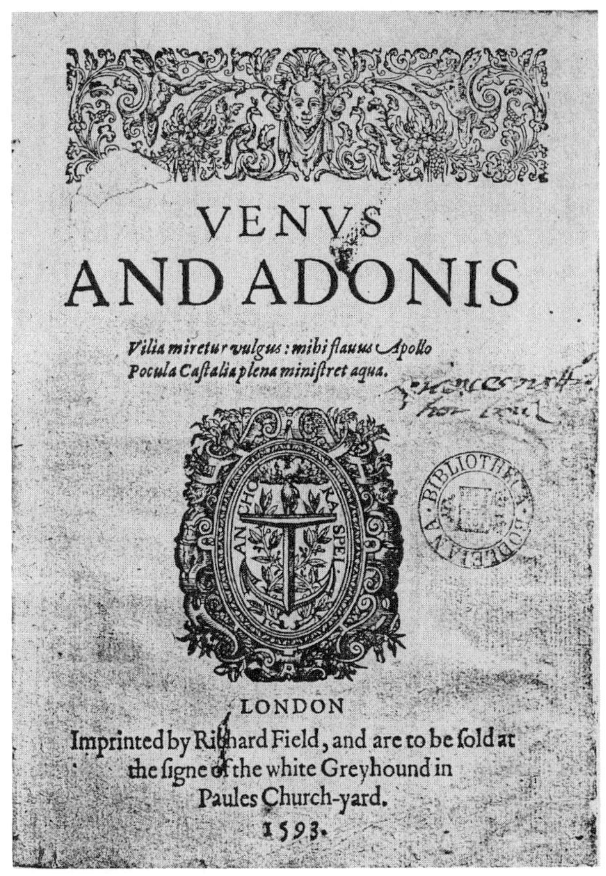

VENVS
AND ADONIS

Vilia miretur vulgus: mihi flauus Apollo
Pocula Castalia plena ministret aqua.

LONDON
Imprinted by Richard Field, and are to be sold at
the signe of the white Greyhound in
Paules Church-yard.
1593.

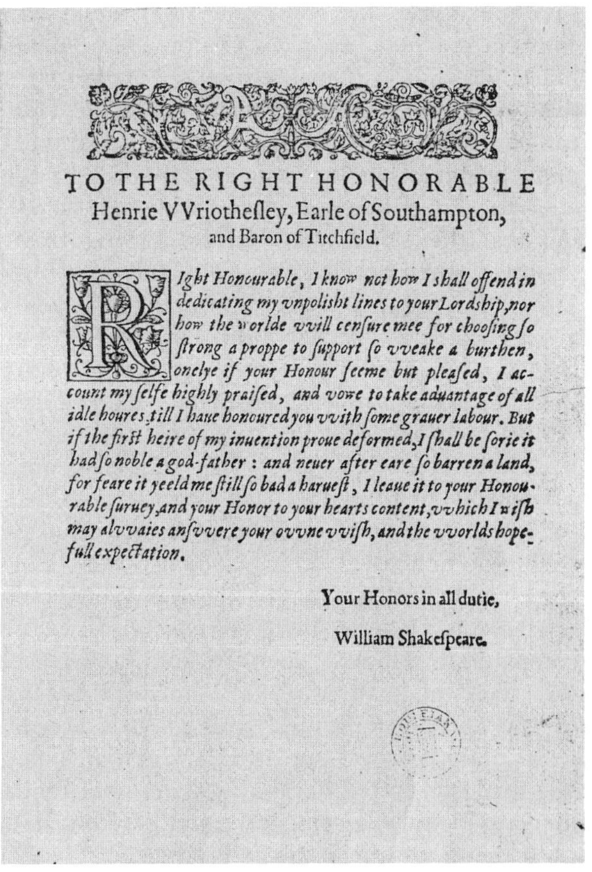

TO THE RIGHT HONORABLE
Henrie VVriothesley, Earle of Southampton,
and Baron of Titchfield.

RIght Honourable, I know not how I shall offend in dedicating my vnpolisht lines to your Lordship, nor how the worlde vvill censure mee for choosing so strong a proppe to support so vveake a burthen, onelye if your Honour seeme but pleased, I account my selfe highly praised, and vowe to take aduantage of all idle houres, till I haue honoured you vvith some grauer labour. But if the first heire of my inuention proue deformed, I shall be sorie it had so noble a god-father: and neuer after eare so barren a land, for feare it yeeld me still so bad a haruest, I leaue it to your Honourable suruey, and your Honor to your hearts content, vvhich I wish may alvvaies ansvvere your ovvne vvish, and the vvorlds hopefull expectation.

Your Honors in all dutie,
William Shakespeare.

Title page and dedication page from the 1593 quarto edition of Shakespeare's first publication, an erotic mythological poem based on Ovid's Metamorphoses *(Bodleian Library, Oxford)*

view is certainly consonant with the epistle to the reader that prefaced the revised 1609 first quarto edition of *Troilus and Cressida.* Here we are assured that we have "a new play, never staled with the stage, never clapper-clawed with the palms of the vulgar, and yet passing full of the palm comical"; and we are given to believe that it is to the credit rather than the discredit of the work that it has never been "sullied with the smoky breath of the multitude." Inasmuch as this foreword and the title page preceding it replaced an earlier title page advertising *Troilus and Cressida* "as it was acted by the King's Majesty's servants at the Globe," we are probably correct to assume that whoever wrote it had in mind the crowd who would have seen the play at one of the popular amphitheaters.

All of which is to acknowledge that even if the audiences who attended the public playhouses were sophisticated enough to support the vast majority of Shakespeare's dramatic efforts, they may nevertheless have proven deficient in their response to some of the extraordinary challenges he placed before them after he arrived at his artistic maturity. This should not surprise us, given Shakespeare's continual experimentation with inherited generic forms and his ever-more-complex approaches to traditional material. Nor should we assume that by terms such as "the million" and "the general" he and his fellow playwrights referred only to the groundlings. Writers of the period were equally acidulous in their criticism of the gallants who attended the theater to be "the observed of all observers"—the ostentatiously attired young men who sat not only in the galleries near the stage (where the admission price was thrice as much as for the places in the yard) and in the balconies above and behind the stage (which cost six times as much as the places in the yard), but even on the stage itself at some performances in the indoor "private" theaters (where the least expensive seat cost six times the price of general admission to the Theater or the Globe, and where some of the seats cost a full thirty times as much). It is difficult to believe that Shakespeare any more than Dekker (who derided such gallants in *The Gull's Hornbook*) would have considered these foppish Osrics even slightly more "judicious" than their fellow spectators at the lower end of the economic scale. And one can easily imagine that after 1609, when his company began using the exclusive Blackfriars theater as its primary venue during the colder months (the London authorities having finally dropped the restrictions that had prevented James Burbage from operating a commercial adult theater in the old monastery he had purchased and adapted in 1596), Shakespeare felt that he had simply exchanged one kind of less-than-perfect audience for another.

One gathers, nevertheless, that, like other playwrights of the period, Shakespeare was careful not to refer too overtly to inadequacies in the well-to-do members of his audiences, especially when such auditors might include the nobility or persons close to them. After all, an acting company's livelihood depended upon its securing and retaining favor at Court—not only because of the extra income and prestige that accrued from periodic royal performances commissioned by the Master of the Revels, but even more fundamentally because a company could perform in or near London only if it were licensed to do so by the Crown and enjoyed the protection of a noble or royal sponsor. A prudent playwright would not wish to jeopardize his company's standing with the monarch. And Shakespeare and his colleagues—the other "sharers" who owned stock in the company that was known as the Lord Chamberlain's Men from 1594 until 1603 (when Queen Elizabeth died and was succeeded by King James I) and the King's Men thereafter (having received a patent as his majesty's own players)—must have been prudent, because theirs was by far the most prosperous and the most frequently "preferred" theatrical organization in the land, from its inception in the mid 1590s until the triumph of Puritanism finally brought about the closing of the theaters half a century later in 1642.

Shakespeare's position with the Lord Chamberlain's Men was a source of professional stability that probably had a great deal to do with his growth and development as a writer. For one thing, it freed him from some of the uncertainties and frustrations that must have been the fate of other playwrights, virtually all of whom operated as free-lancers selling their wares to impresarios such as Philip Henslowe (often for as little as five pounds), and most of whom thus forfeited any real say about how their plays were to be produced and, in time (if a given acting company so wished or if chance provided), published. From at least 1594 on Shakespeare was a stockholder of the theatrical organization for which he wrote his plays. After 1598 (when the sons of the recently deceased James Burbage, Cuthbert and Richard, invited four of the principal actors in the Lord Chamberlain's Men to become their partners and put up half the capital needed to rebuild the Theater across the Thames as the Globe), Shakespeare was also a co-owner of the playhouse in which that troupe performed his works. As such, he benefited from all the profits the Lord Chamberlain's Men took in at the gate, and he was undoubtedly a participant in all of the major decisions affecting the company's welfare. We know from the surviving legal records of the playwright's various business transactions that he prospered financially by this arrangement: like his father, he invested wisely in real estate, purchasing properties in both Stratford and London. And we can infer from the evidence of his rapid progress as a dramatist that Shakespeare's membership in a close-knit group of theatrical entrepreneurs also helped him flourish artistically.

Henry Wriothesley, Earl of Southampton, to whom Shakespeare dedicated his first two books (miniature by Nicholas Hilliard, 1593 or 1594; Fitzwilliam Museum, Cambridge)

It meant, for example, that he could envisage and write his plays with particular performers in mind: Richard Burbage for leading roles such as Richard III, Othello, and King Lear; William Kempe for clowning parts such as Launce or Dogberry in the early years of the company, and thereafter (following Kempe's departure from the Lord Chamberlain's Men around 1599) Robert Armin, who seems to have specialized in "wise fools" such as Touchstone, Feste, and Lear's Fool; Shakespeare himself, perhaps, for "old men" such as Adam in *As You Like It*; "hired men" (adult actors who, not being shareholders in the troupe, were simply paid a sum of money for each job of work) for most of the lesser roles; and apprentice boy-actors for the youthful parts and many, if not all, of the female roles (there being no actresses on the English stage until the theaters reopened after the Restoration). Serving as the resident playwright for an organization in which he was both a player and a business partner meant that Shakespeare could revise and rewrite his works in rehearsal prior to a given title's initial presentation, and that he could adapt and further revise them later as differing circumstances required: as the company was called upon for performances requested by the Court during holiday seasons or on ceremonial occasions, or performances solicited by the great houses of the nobility, or (during sieges of plague when the London theaters were closed) performances on tour in the provinces, where, in all likelihood, the troupe was reduced to entertaining with fewer actors and was required to make do with provisional playing areas in guild halls, inn yards, and other makeshift theatrical spaces.

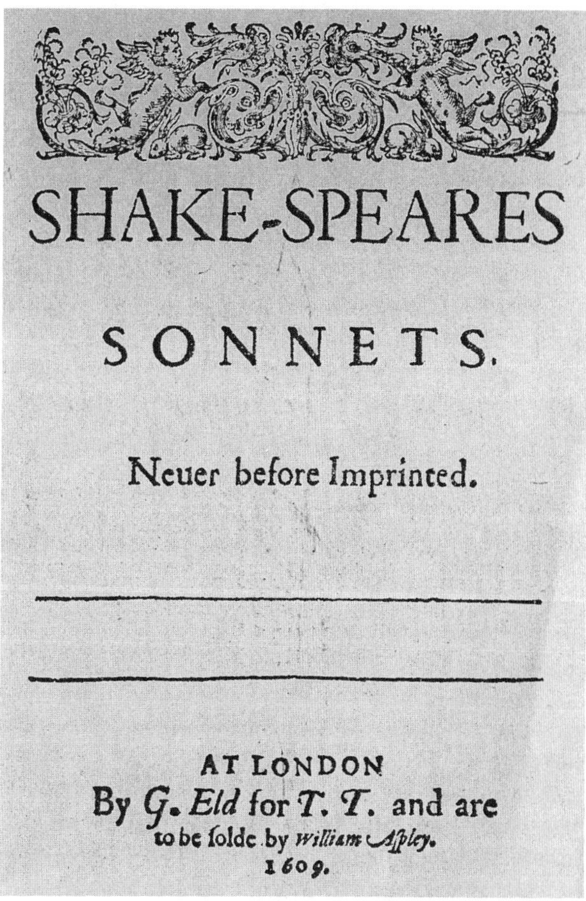

Title page for the 1609 quarto edition of the volume publisher Thomas Thorpe dedicated to "Mr. W. H.," fueling speculation about the identity of the young man in the sonnets (Anderson Galleries auction catalogue, sale number 1405, 4-5 March 1919)

Because the conditions under which Shakespeare worked required him, above all, to be pragmatic and flexible, we would probably be correct to infer that as he composed his plays he thought of them not as fixed "literary" texts but as provisional production notes—susceptible of lengthening or shortening or other modes of alteration as determined by the constraints of particular occasions and performance situations. He would have had to prepare each script with an eye to the number of actors available for speaking parts (most scholars believe that the majority of Shakespeare's plays were conceived with a cast of between thirteen and sixteen performers in mind), and he probably planned each scene with a view to the possibilities for "doubling" (a principle of theatrical economy whereby a given actor would alternate among two or more roles in the same play). It may well be that, in the absence of anyone else in the organization designated to function in that capacity, Shakespeare was the first "director" his plays had. If so, we can be sure that he approached the task with an awareness that the assembling of a production was a collaborative process and that the playscript, though normative, was never to be revered as a monument carved in stone. Shakespeare was, after all, a play*wright* (that is, a "maker" rather than merely a writer of plays), and he would have been the first to recognize that the final purpose of a dramatic text was a fully realized entertainment rather than a piece of literature to be contemplated in the privacy of a patron's parlor or pondered in the lamplight of a scholar's study.

If in his capacity as theater professional Shakespeare thought of himself primarily, then, as a deviser of "plays" (by definition ephemeral and "insubstantial" pageants, as Prospero observes in *The Tempest*) rather than as an author of literary "works" (the term that earned Ben Jonson the gibes of his fellow writers when he came out with a pretentiously titled folio volume of his collected texts in 1616), it is hardly surprising that we have little or no evidence of his involvement in the publication of his own dramatic scripts. Nor is it surprising that several of the titles that were published in the playwright's lifetime or shortly thereafter have come down to us in forms that vary from one printing to another.

Some of these variations probably result from authorial revisions or from theatrical modifications of different types. Others undoubtedly derive from the vicissitudes of textual transmission, with the extant state of a given play or passage dependent on whether it was typeset from the author's own manuscript (either in draft form or in a more polished version) or from a manuscript prepared by someone else (a scribe's "fair copy" of a manuscript owned by the author or the company, for example, or a rough compilation by one or more actors relying on faulty memories to patch together an abridged script for a reduced cast touring the provinces)—quite apart from any further complications that may have occurred in the printing house itself (where one copy editor, one compositor, or one proofreader differed from another in the fidelity with which he reproduced the manuscript before him). Whatever their origins, these variations are eloquent testimony to the difficulty—if not indeed the impossibility—of our ever arriving at an absolutely "final" version of a Shakespearean play. For if the conditions under which dramas were written, performed, and preserved make it clear that a "definitive" play text was rare, if not unknown, in Shakespeare's own time, we must recognize that any effort to produce an authoritative edition for our own day can aspire, at best, to reconstitute as accurately as possible the closest approximation to a given title at some point in its compositional or theatrical history.

And even this kind of edition will remain stubbornly "incomplete," for the simple reason that a Shakespearean script was originally intended for the use not of a reading audience but of a small company of theater professionals who would employ it as a "score" from which to orchestrate a complex, multidimensional performance. The texts that do survive are mostly dialogue, and a sensitive analysis of them can tell us a great deal about how the words were meant to be spoken, where the emphases were to be placed, and what character motivations were to be indicated at specific points in the action. But because we can no longer recover the context in

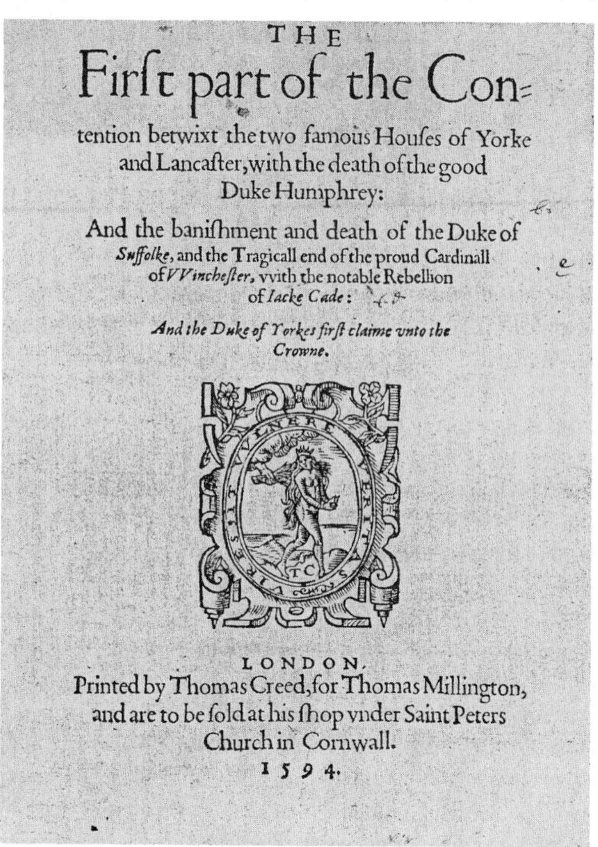
THE
Firſt part of the Con-
tention betwixt the two famous Houſes of Yorke
and Lancaſter, with the death of the good
Duke Humphrey:
And the baniſhment and death of the Duke of
Suffolke, and the Tragicall end of the proud Cardinall
of *VVincheſter*, vvith the notable Rebellion
of *Iacke Cade*:
And the Duke of Yorkes firſt claime vnto the Crowne.

LONDON.
Printed by Thomas Creed, for Thomas Millington,
and are to be ſold at his ſhop vnder Saint Peters
Church in Cornwall.
1594.

Title page for the 1594 quarto edition of an abridged and corrupt text of Henry VI, *part 2 (Folger Shakespeare Library)*

which these scripts were first realized—a context that would have included a good deal of oral communication about gesture, movement, blocking, and other stage business—we must content ourselves with renderings of the plays that will always be to some degree indeterminate. Perhaps this is just as well: it teases the director and the scholar with enough interpretive liberty to ensure that we will never be faced with a dearth of innovation in Shakespearean production and commentary.

We should bear in mind, of course, that a considerable investment of additional work would have been required to transform a theatrical score into a reading text for the public—not altogether unlike what is required nowadays to turn a screenplay into a coherent piece of narrative fiction—and that Shakespeare may never have had the time (even if we assume that he had the inclination) to effect such a generic adaptation. Still, those of us who would not object to a little more detail about some of the "matter" of Shakespeare's dramas may perhaps be pardoned for wishing that the playwright had been able to spare more thought for the morrow—for the afterlife that most (though who is to say all?) of his plays were eventually to have as a consequence of publication. Our sentiments are echoed in the address "To the Great Variety of Readers" at the beginning of the 1623 posthumous edition of Shakespeare's works known as the First Folio: "It had been a thing, we confess, worthy to have been wished, that the author himself had lived to have set forth and overseen his own writings." He did set forth and oversee some of his own writings, of course. But, perhaps significantly, these were not dramatic scripts.

In 1593 Shakespeare published a 1,194-line narrative poem that appears to have been intended as his opening bid for serious attention as an author of "literary works." Based on Ovid's *Metamorphoses* and capitalizing on a fashion for elegant romances that was being catered to by such writers as Thomas Lodge (whose *Scilla's Metamorphoses* had been published in 1589) and Christopher Marlowe (whose *Hero and Leander* may well have circulated in manuscript prior to his death in 1593 and certainly before it was published in 1598), Shakespeare's *Venus and Adonis* was an erotic mythological poem printed by fellow Stratfordian Richard Field and bearing a florid epistle to "the Right Honorable Henry Wriothesley, Earl of Southampton." Its six-line stanzas employed an *ababcc* rhyme scheme whose authority had been established by such contemporary Renaissance poets as Edmund Spenser, and its ornamented, "artificial" style solicited a favorable reception from the "wiser sort" of readers to be found in the Inns of Court, at the universities, and at Court. Although Shakespeare decorously apologized for the poem as "the first heir of my invention," he must have done so in full confidence that *Venus and Adonis* was an accomplishment worthy of his talent. It proved to be an immediate and sustained success, with nine reprints by 1616 and six more by 1640. The large number of references to it during the late 1590s and early 1600s suggests that it was the work for which the poet was most widely recognized during his own lifetime.

Within a year of the publication of *Venus and Adonis,* Shakespeare was back to press with another long narrative poem. This time he chose a seven-line stanza rhyming *ababbcc* (rhyme royal, a verse form whose tradition in English poetry extended all the way back to Geoffrey Chaucer), and once again he drew on Ovid for a second work dedicated (this time even more fervently) to the Earl of Southampton. If *Venus and Adonis* is most aptly viewed as a quasi-comic treatment of love (depicting the frustrations of an insatiate goddess who falls all over herself in her fumbling efforts to seduce an unresponsive youth), despite the fact that it ends with the death of the innocent young mortal, *Lucrece* is more properly described as a tragic "complaint," a stirring exploration of the personal and social consequences of a patrician Roman's surrender to lust, against his better nature and at the cost, ultimately, of both his victim's life and his own. In his foreword to *Venus and Adonis,* Shakespeare had promised the addressee "a graver labor" if his first offering pleased its would-be patron; in all likelihood, then, *Lucrece* was under way as a companion piece to *Venus and Adonis* at least a year before its eventual publication in 1594. It may be, as some have suggested, that Shakespeare's narrative of Tarquin's rape of Lucrece and her suicide was motivated by a desire to persuade anyone who might have considered the earlier work frivolous that the poet's muse was equally capable of a more serious subject. In any case it is clear that once again he struck a responsive chord: *Lucrece* went through eight editions prior to 1640, and it seems to have been exceeded in popularity only by *Venus and Adonis.*

Both poems were printed during what has been called Shakespeare's "apprenticeship"—the period preceding his emergence as a member of the Lord Chamberlain's Men in 1594—and they share stylistic characteristics with the plays that appear to have been completed during those same early years. As with such youthful dramatic efforts as the three parts of *Henry VI, Titus Andronicus, The Two Gentlemen of Verona, The Comedy of Errors,* and *The Taming of the Shrew,* the writing in *Venus and Adonis* and *Lucrece* is generically imitative (closely adhering to received poetic and dramatic forms), structurally and verbally derivative (echoing the poet's sources almost slavishly at times), and rhetorically formal (with a rigidly patterned verse containing far more rhymes, end-stopped lines, syntactic balances, and allusions to the classics than are to be observed in Shakespeare's writing after the mid 1590s). One feels immediately that *Venus and Adonis* and *Lucrece* are artistically of a piece with Shakespeare's first tentative experiments as a dramatist.

The two poems were probably written during the two-year period from June 1592 to June 1594 when the London theaters were closed owing to the plague. But whether they indicate

Quee. Welcome to *England*, my louing friends of *Frãce*,
And welcome *Summerſet*, and *Oxford* too.
Once more haue we ſpread our ſailes abroad,
And though our tackling be almoſt conſumde,
And *Warwike* as our maine maſt ouerthrowne,
Yet warlike Lords raiſe you that ſturdie poſt,
That beares the ſailes to bring vs vnto reſt,
And *Ned* and *I* as willing Pilots ſhould
For once with carefull mindes guide on the ſterne,
To beare vs through that dangerous gulfe
That heretofore hath ſwallowed vp our friends.
Prince. And if there be, as God forbid there ſhould,
Amongſt vs a timorous or fearefull man,
Let him depart before the battels ioine,
Leaſt he in time of need intiſe another,
And ſo withdraw the ſouldiers harts from vs.
I will not ſtand aloofe and bid you fight,
But with my ſword preſſe in the thickeſt thronges,
And ſingle *Edward* from his ſtrongeſt guard,
And hand to hand enforce him for to yeeld,
Or leaue my bodie as witneſſe of my thoughts.
Oxf. Women and children of ſo high reſolue,

And Warriors faint, why twere perpetuall
Shame? Oh braue yong Prince, thy
Noble grandfather doth liue againe in thee,
Long maieſt thou liue to beare his image,
And to renew his glories.

Qu. Great Lords, wiſe men ne'r ſit and waile their loſſe,
But chearely ſeeke how to redreſſe their harmes.
What though the Maſt be now blowne ouer-boord,
The Cable broke, the holding-Anchor loſt,
And halfe our Saylors ſwallow'd in the flood?
Yet liues our Pilot ſtill. Is't meet, that hee
Should leaue the Helme, and like a fearefull Lad,
With tearefull Eyes adde Water to the Sea,
And giue more ſtrength to that which hath too much,
Whiles in his moane, the Ship ſplits on the Rock,
Which Induſtrie and Courage might haue ſau'd?
Ah what a ſhame, ah what a fault were this.
Say *Warwicke* was our Anchor: what of that?

And *Mountague* our Top-Maſt: what of him?
Our ſlaught'red friends, the Tackles: what of theſe?
Why is not *Oxford* here, another Anchor?
And *Somerſet*, another goodly Maſt?
The friends of France our Shrowds and Tacklings?
And though vnskilfull, why not *Ned* and I,
For once allow'd the skilfull Pilots Charge?
We will not from the Helme, to ſit and weepe,
But keepe our Courſe (though the rough Winde ſay no)
From Shelues and Rocks, that threaten vs with Wrack,
As good to chide the Waues, as ſpeake them faire.
And what is *Edward*, but a ruthleſſe Sea?
What *Clarence*, but a Quick-ſand of Deceit?
And *Richard*, but a raged fatall Rocke?
All theſe, the Enemies to our poore Barke.
Say you can ſwim, alas 'tis but a while:
Tread on the Sand, why there you quickly ſinke,
Beſtride the Rock, the Tyde will waſh you off,
Or elſe you famiſh, that's a three-fold Death.
This ſpeake I (Lords) to let you vnderſtand,
If caſe ſome one of you would flye from vs,
That there's no hop'd-for Mercy with the Brothers,
More then with ruthleſſe Waues, with Sands and Rocks.
Why courage then, what cannot be auoided,
'Twere childiſh weakeneſſe to lament, or feare.

Queen Margaret's speech at the beginning of V.iv. of Henry VI, *part 3, as it appears in* The True Tragedie of Richard Duke of Yorke *(from the unique copy in the Bodleian Library; Arch G f1)—the 1595 octavo edition of an abridged and corrupt text of the play—and in the 1623 First Folio edition of Shakespeare's plays (Folger Shakespeare Library)*

an inclination to leave the theater altogether and essay a career as a traditional poet (as Shakespeare's quest for the patronage of the young Earl of Southampton might seem to imply), or merely demonstrate that Shakespeare was resourceful enough to turn his pen to other uses while he waited for the playhouses to reopen, is more than we can say. The only thing that seems beyond doubt is that Shakespeare regarded what he was doing when he wrote *Venus and Adonis* and *Lucrece* as something fundamentally different from what he was doing, prior to that and subsequent to it, in his capacity as a man of the theater.

Like his fellow playwrights when they donned personas as men of letters, Shakespeare was addressing his efforts, first of all, to a noble dedicatee and, second, to a cultivated readership. He was therefore concerned that his compositions be printed as he had written them, and he took pains to assure that they were accompanied by a graceful appeal for the approval of a society presumed to embody the highest standards of literary taste and judgment. It may be that during the same period when he was seeing *Venus and Adonis* and *Lucrece* through the press in carefully proofed editions he was also writing other nondramatic poetry. Many scholars believe that this was when he composed most if not all of the 154 sonnets that bear his name. And if he was in fact the author of *A Lover's Complaint* (a narrative poem in rhyme royal that was attributed to Shakespeare when it was published, along with the *Sonnets,* in what is usually regarded as an unauthorized edition in 1609), he probably wrote that labored lyric too during his years "in the workshop". But we have no evidence that he ever took any steps himself to print either *A Lover's Complaint* or the *Sonnets.* Apart from *Venus and Adonis* and *Lucrece,* the only other literary work that Shakespeare seems likely to have had anything to do with publishing on his own behalf was a curious poem called *The Phoenix and Turtle,* which appeared in 1601 as part of a collection "Shadowing the Truth of Love" and appended to Robert Chester's *Love's Martyr. The Phoenix and Turtle* is a sixty-seven-line lyric, probably allegorical, about one bird (the phoenix) legendary for its rarity and beauty and another (the turtledove) proverbial for its constancy. Its scholastic imagery—reminiscent in some ways of the highly technical language to be found in writing of the same literary climate by such "metaphysical" poets as John Donne—suggests that, if indeed it is by Shakespeare (which many have questioned), it was probably written expressly for the Chester volume at about the time the dramatist was at work on such philosophical plays as *Hamlet* and *Troilus and Cressida.*

If we except *The Phoenix and Turtle,* then, and assume that the *Sonnets* and *A Lover's Complaint* were published without Shakespeare's active participation, we are left with the conclusion that Shakespeare's "literary career," narrowly defined, was more or less limited to the two-year interruption in his activities as an actor and dramatist when the London playhouses were closed because of the plague. This does not require us to conclude, of course, that he ceased to have literary aspirations after 1594. He may have allowed his "sugared sonnets" to circulate in manuscript "among his private friends" (as Francis Meres asserted in *Palladis Tamia* in 1598, a year prior to Isaac Jaggard's publication of two of the sonnets in a volume called *The Passionate Pilgrim*) while he polished and augmented them in the expectation that he would publish an anthology at a later time. Nor is it inconceivable that he would have prepared a collected edition of his plays if he had lived (Jonson having braved the critical tempest that such audacity was bound to generate when he came out with his works in 1616, the year of Shakespeare's death). But the fact is that Shakespeare himself cannot be proven to have supervised the printing of any of the compositions we now value the most. We can only assume that doing so was of less urgency to him than what he did choose to devote his professional life to: the "wrighting" and producing of plays.

If so, he must at times have had his doubts about the choice he made. In Sonnet 110 (if we may be permitted to infer that the poet was either speaking in his own voice or echoing sentiments that he himself had felt), he allows that he has made himself "a motley to the view" and "sold cheap what is most dear." He then goes on in Sonnet 111 to lament that he "did not better for [his] life provide / Than public means which public manners breeds."

> Thence comes it that my name receives a brand,
> And almost thence my nature is subdu'd
> To what it works in, like the dyer's hand.

William Wordsworth believed the *Sonnets* to be the key whereby Shakespeare "unlocked his heart," and it may be that these intriguing poems are to some degree a spiritual testament—

imitating, as was traditional with lyric verse, the thought processes and shifts in sensibility of a person responding to the vicissitudes of private life. That granted, we may be correct to interpret Sonnets 110 and 111 as expressions of Shakespeare's own dissatisfaction with the career of a performer and playwright.

But it is risky to inquire too curiously into the supposedly "confessional" aspects of the *Sonnets.* Like Shakespeare's other writings, they employ the artifice of fictions, and they may have been but another form of story telling—different in kind from the dramas and narrative poems, to be sure, but similar to them in being "about" something other than, or in addition to, the poet's own experience. If we place them alongside earlier sonnet sequences—Petrarch's lyrics to Laura in fifteenth-century Italy, for instance, or such late-sixteenth-century English sequences as those by Philip Sidney, Edmund Spenser, Samuel Daniel, and Michael Drayton—we discover that they are quite conventional in many respects. They display the speaker's wit and attest to his originality; they imply a deeply felt personal situation and hint at a coherent narrative, but they usually stop short of connecting their emotional peaks and valleys into a fully textured autobiographical landscape; they assert the immortality of verse and claim its sovereignty over the ravages of time and change; and usually they deal with themes of truth and beauty in the context of love and friendship and all the circumstances that life arrays in opposition to such exalted values.

To a far greater degree than with most lyric sequences, Shakespeare's *Sonnets* have "the ring of truth." This is partly because, like all his works (from his earliest plays onward), they portray human nature so convincingly. But it is also a consequence of the extent to which they seem to go beyond, or even to disregard, tradition. Thus, instead of praising a woman by cataloguing all the attributes that make her lovely, Shakespeare turns Petrarchan convention on its head by denying his "dark lady" any of the expected beauties and virtues. "My mistress' eyes are nothing like the sun," he says in Sonnet 130; and far from being ethereal and inaccessible in her idealized spirituality, the dusky female described in Shakespeare's *Sonnets* is sensual, uncaring, and promiscuous. Petrarch's Laura may have inspired an earlier poet to Platonic transcendence, but Shakespeare's wanton leaves only the bitter aftertaste of "Th' expense of spirit in a waste of shame" (Sonnet 129). What is more, she comes between the poet and the fair young man to whom most of the first 126 sonnets in the sequence are addressed: the friend who occasions some of the deepest verses in English on such themes as fidelity, stewardship (Shakespeare seems to have been preoccupied with the Parable of the Talents, as rendered in Matthew 25: 14-30), and man's struggle against "never-resting time."

As one reads the sonnets directed to the handsome youth, one detects a descent from absolute devotion ("For thy sweet love rememb'red such wealth brings, / That then I scorn to change my state with kings"—Sonnet 29) to a fear that the older man's love may be unrequited, or at least taken for granted, by the young friend to whom he has given so much of himself ("For sweetest things turn sourest by their deeds; / Lilies that fester smell far worse than weeds"—Sonnet 94) to a noble but probably quixotic determination to remain true to his convictions despite his doubts about the gentleman's worthiness of such absolute faith ("love is not love / Which alters when it alteration finds / Or bends with the remover to remove"—Sonnet 116). The intensity of feeling expressed in these sonnets has led many interpreters to infer that they must have been based on a homoerotic passion. Sonnet 20 suggests that the relationship the poet describes is not physical. Nature, he says, has given the young man "one thing to my purpose nothing"; and "since she prick'd thee out for women's pleasure, / Mine be thy love, and thy love's use their treasure." But the sequence as a whole conveys the impression that the speaker, if not the object of the sonnets, seeks a union that is all-encompassing.

Several of the sonnets addressed to the friend refer to a "rival poet" who is also bidding for the youth's favors and affection (Sonnets 79, 80, 83, and 86, for example), and others (Sonnets 78, 82, 84, and 85) imply that the young aristocrat is the subject of praise by several poetic suitors. As he reflects upon his own position vis-à-vis his competitors for the loved one's affection, the narrator in Shakespeare's sonnets is subject to a depth of insecurity that sometimes borders on despair: "Wishing me like to one more rich in hope, / Featur'd like him, like him with friends possess'd, / Desiring this man's art, and that man's scope" (Sonnet 29). And many of the greatest lyrics in the sequence derive their peculiar power from what Robert Frost has termed a "sense of difficulty overcome"—the poet working through the tensions and conflicts described in

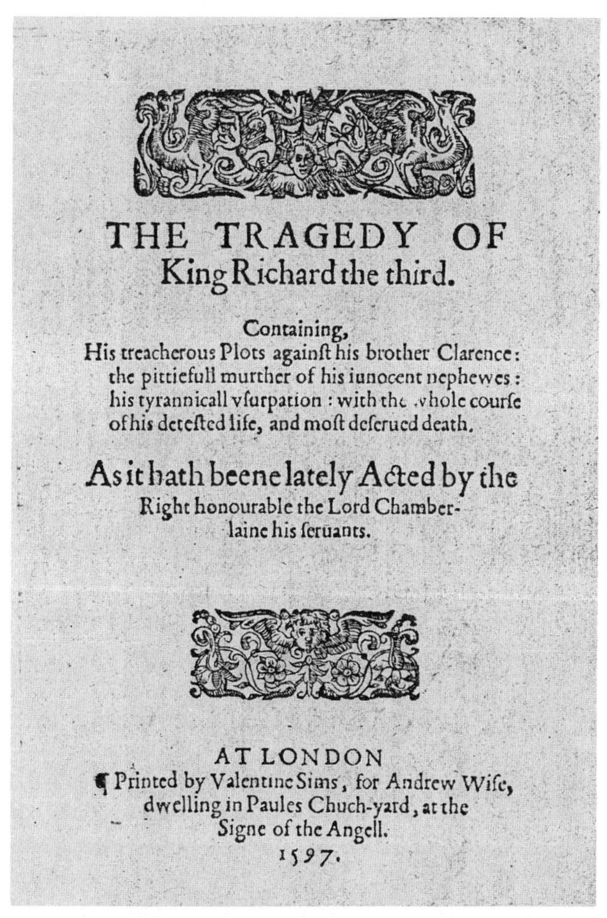

THE TRAGEDY OF
King Richard the third.

Containing,
His treacherous Plots against his brother Clarence:
the pittiefull murther of his iunocent nephewes:
his tyrannicall vsurpation: with the whole course
of his detested life, and most deserued death.

As it hath beene lately Acted by the
Right honourable the Lord Chamberlaine his seruants.

AT LONDON
Printed by Valentine Sims, for Andrew Wise,
dwelling in Paules Chuch-yard, at the
Signe of the Angell.
1597.

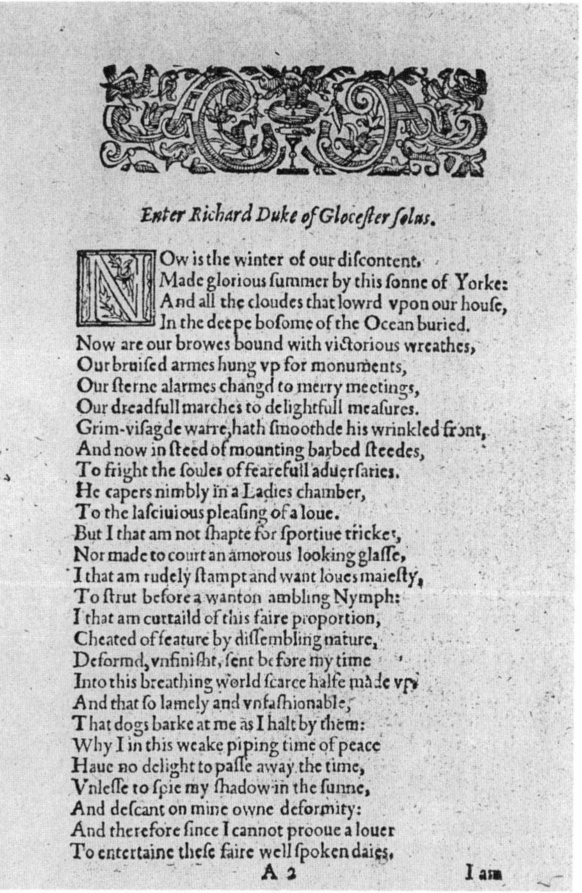

Enter Richard Duke of Glocester solus.

Now is the winter of our discontent,
Made glorious summer by this sonne of Yorke:
And all the cloudes that lowrd vpon our house,
In the deepe bosome of the Ocean buried.
Now are our browes bound with victorious wreathes,
Our bruised armes hung vp for monuments,
Our sterne alarmes changd to merry meetings,
Our dreadfull marches to delightfull measures.
Grim-visagde warre, hath smoothde his wrinkled front,
And now in steed of mounting barbed steedes,
To fright the soules of fearefull aduersaries.
He capers nimbly in a Ladies chamber,
To the lasciuious pleasing of a loue.
But I that am not shapte for sportiue trickes,
Nor made to court an amorous looking glasse,
I that am rudely stampt and want loues maiesty,
To strut before a wanton ambling Nymph:
I that am curtaild of this faire proportion,
Cheated of feature by dissembling nature,
Deformd, vnfinisht, sent before my time
Into this breathing world scarce halfe made vp,
And that so lamely and vnfashionable,
That dogs barke at me as I halt by them:
Why I in this weake piping time of peace
Haue no delight to passe away the time,
Vnlesse to spie my shadow in the sunne,
And descant on mine owne deformity:
And therefore since I cannot prooue a louer
To entertaine these faire well spoken daies,
A 2 I am

Title page and first page of text from the 1597 quarto edition of the fourth part of Shakespeare's "first tetralogy" of history plays (British Library)

the first three quatrains (linked by an *abab cdcd efef* rhyme scheme) to some kind of hard-won (though often not completely convincing) resolution in the concluding couplet (rhymed *gg*): "This thou perceiv'st, which makes thy love more strong, / To love that well, which thou must leave ere long" (Sonnet 73).

Because the other personalities who figure in the psychodrama of the *Sonnets* seem so vivid, at least as they impinge upon the emotions of the speaker, interpreters of the collection have been inexorably drawn toward speculation about real-life identities for the Dark Lady, the Young Man, and the Rival Poet. Some commentators (such as Oxford historian A. L. Rowse) have persuaded themselves, if not everyone else, that these characters can be positively linked with such contemporaries of Shakespeare as Emilia Bassano Lanier, the Earl of Southampton (or, alternatively, the Earl of Pembroke), and Christopher Marlowe (or possibly George Chapman). Unless further information should come to light, however, we are probably best advised to content ourselves with a position of agnosticism on such questions. Until we can be sure about how the *Sonnets* came to be published, and just what kind of debt the publisher Thomas Thorpe refers to when he dedicates the 1609 quarto to the "only begetter" of these poems "Never before Imprinted"—the elusive "Mr. W. H."—we are unlikely to be able to pin down the "real names" of any of the persons who inhabit the world of the *Sonnets*. Until then, indeed, we cannot even be certain that the *Sonnets* have any autobiographical basis in the first place.

Turning from Shakespeare's nondramatic poetry to the fruits of his two decades as a playwright, we should probably begin where many scholars now think he himself commenced: as the principal practitioner, if not in some ways the originator, of a new kind of drama that seems to have sprung from native patriotism. The most immediate "source" of the English history play appears to have been the heightened sense of national destiny that flowered in the wake of the

Richard III as portrayed by David Garrick in the eighteenth century (top; engraving by Thomas Cook from a painting by William Hogarth), Edmund Kean in the nineteenth century (bottom left; mezzotint by Charles Turner), and Laurence Olivier in 1949 (bottom right)

The hall in Gray's Inn, where The Comedy of Errors *was performed on 28 December 1594*

Royal Navy's seemingly providential victory over the Spanish Armada in 1588. Proud of the new eminence their nation had achieved, and immensely relieved that the threat of invasion by a Catholic power had been thwarted, many of Shakespeare's contemporaries were disposed to view England's deliverance as a sign of Heaven's favor. As such, it seemed to some to be a vindication of the reign of Queen Elizabeth and a substantiation of the Tudor order's claim to divine sanction—a claim that had been asserted by a succession of Renaissance chroniclers from Polydore Vergil (circa 1470-1555) through Edward Hall (circa 1498-1547) to Raphael Holinshed (circa 1529-1580), and a claim that was implicit in such government documents as the "Exhortation concerning Good Order and Obedience to Rulers and Magistrates," a 1547 homily read regularly in churches throughout England.

Given this context, it must have seemed entirely fitting that sometime in the late 1580s or early 1590s an enterprising young playwright began dramatizing a sequence of historical developments that were almost universally regarded as the "roots" of England's current greatness. Most of the material for the four history plays with which Shakespeare began his career as playwright he drew from Edward Hall's *Union of the Two Noble and Illustre Families of Lancaster and York* (1548) and Raphael Holinshed's *Chronicles of England, Scotland, and Ireland* (1587 edition). Here he found narratives of late-medieval English history that began with the reign of King Richard II (1377-1399), focused on Richard's deposition and execution by Henry Bullingbrook (Henry IV), detailed the Wars of the Roses (1455-1485) that were the eventual consequence of Bullingbrook's usurpation, and concluded with the restoration of right rule when Henry Richmond defeated the tyrannical Richard III (1483-1485) and acceded to the crown as Henry VII, inaugurating a Tudor dynasty that was to last until the death of Queen Elizabeth in 1603. Here the poet also found a theological reading of political history that treated England as a collective Everyman—falling into sin, undergoing a terrifyingly bloody punishment for its disobedience, and eventually finding its way back to redemption through the emergence of the Queen's grandfather.

There is evidence that as Shakespeare matured in his craft he came to view the "Tudor myth" (as E. M. W. Tillyard has termed this official dogma) with a degree of irony and detachment; but even so, he seems to have found in its clear, broad sweep a pattern that served quite well as a way of organizing the disparate materials he chose to dramatize. It gave him a theme of epic proportions, not altogether unlike the "matter" of Greece and Rome that had inspired such classical authors as Homer and Virgil in narrative genres and Aeschylus, Sophocles, Euripides, and Seneca in theatrical genres. It accorded with the biblical treatment of human destiny that Shakespeare's age had inherited from earlier generations, an approach to historical interpretation that had been embedded in such didactic entertainments as the Morality Play (allegorizing the sin, suffering, repentance, and salvation of a typical member of mankind) and the Mystery Play (broadening the cycle to a representation of the whole of human history, from man's fall in the Garden of Eden to man's redemption in the Garden of Gethsemane to man's bliss in the Paradise of the New Jerusalem). And it provided a rationale for Shakespeare's use of such powerful dramatic devices as the riddling prophecy and the curse—projecting retribution for present crimes, as the Old Testament would put it, to the third and fourth generations.

When we approach the four plays known as Shakespeare's "first tetralogy" (the three parts of *Henry VI* and *Richard III,* all written, so far as we can tell, by 1592) from the perspective of the author's "second tetralogy" (*Richard II, Henry IV,* parts 1 and 2, and *Henry V,* all of which appear to have been written between 1595 and 1597), the earlier plays seem comparatively naive. Like their sources, they place more emphasis on providential design and less on human agency. Their verse is more declamatory and less supple. And they provide less individuation of character. Still, they have their virtues, and in our time successful productions by the Royal Shakespeare Company, the British Broadcasting Corporation, and others have proven that they can be surprisingly effective in performance.

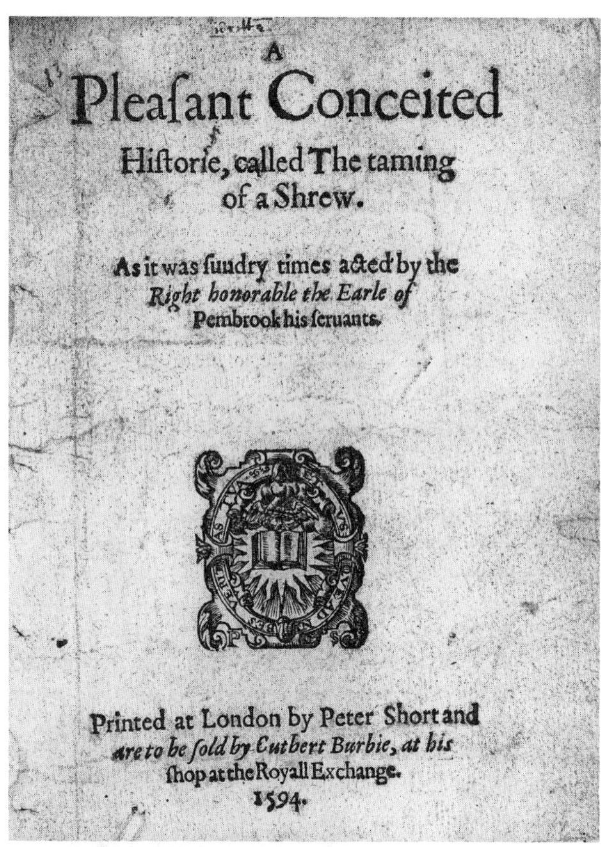
A Pleaſant Conceited Hiſtorie, called The taming of a Shrew.

As it was ſundry times acted by the Right honorable the Earle of Pembrook his ſeruants.

Printed at London by Peter Short and are to be ſold by Cutbert Burbie, at his ſhop at the Royall Exchange. 1594.

Title page for the 1594 quarto edition of what is generally believed to be a corrupt text of The Taming of the Shrew *(Henry E. Huntington Library and Art Gallery). The authoritative version of the play, first published in the 1623 First Folio, is significantly different from the text of this quarto.*

Henry VI, part 1, did not achieve print until the 1623 First Folio, but it is now generally thought to have been written prior to parts 2 and 3, which first appeared in corrupt texts, respectively, in a 1594 quarto edition titled *The First Part of the Contention betwixt the two famous Houses of Yorke and Lancaster* and in a 1595 octavo entitled *The True Tragedie of Richard Duke of Yorke. Henry VI,* part 1, begins with the funeral of King Henry V (which occurred in 1422), depicts the dissension at home and the loss of life and territory abroad that result from the accession of a new monarch too young and weak to rule, and concludes with King Henry VI's foolish decision to marry Margaret of Anjou. This step places the saintly King in the very unsaintly hands of an ambitious woman and a lustful nobleman (the Earl of Suffolk, who plans to enjoy Margaret as his own mistress and thereby "rule both her, the

King, and realm") and virtually assures the further degradation of a kingdom that has been in decline since the death of Henry VI's famous warrior-king father. *Henry VI,* part 2, covers a ten-year span from Margaret of Anjou's arrival in England (1445) to the Duke of York's victory over his Lancastrian enemies at Saint Albans in the first major battle of the Wars of the Roses (1455). The same kind of internecine strife that has left the noble Talbot exposed to the forces of the strumpet-witch Joan of Arc in *Henry VI,* part 1, works here to undo Henry VI's protector, Duke Humphrey of Gloucester, to topple two of the good Duke's enemies (Cardinal Beaufort and Suffolk), to unleash the anarchic rebellion of the peasant Jack Cade, and to divide further the warring factions (the Yorkists, who have chosen the white rose as their symbol in the famous Temple Garden scene, II.iv., of part 1, and the Lancastrians, who have rallied behind the red rose) that seem hell-bent to tear the kingdom asunder. In *Henry VI,* part 3, the war is at full pitch. As the feeble Henry VI withdraws into a private realm of pastoral longing, his fierce Queen and her allies exchange outrages with one Yorkist enemy after another, father killing son and son killing father in a nightmarish world that has degenerated into a spectacle of unmitigated cruelty. By the time the dust settles, Henry VI and other would-be claimants to the crown are dead or on their way to the grave, and the ominously crookbacked figure of Richard, Duke of Gloucester, is slouching his rough way to the throne he will occupy in the blood-drenched final movement of this hitherto unprecedented cycle of dramatized chronicles.

Richard III was first published in a 1597 quarto edition that many scholars believe to have been reconstructed from memory by actors plagued out of the London theaters between July and October of that year. The tragedy was evidently quite popular, because it went through at least five more printings before it appeared in a 1623 First Folio edition based largely on the third and sixth quartos. And it has remained popular ever since, with a stage tradition highlighted by Richard Burbage in Shakespeare's own theater, David Garrick in the eighteenth century, Edmund Kean in the nineteenth, and Laurence Olivier in the twentieth. Nor is the reason hard to find. For despite the bold strokes with which he is portrayed, Richard III is a character of sufficient complexity to sustain a great deal of audience interest. However much we find ourselves repelled by his ruthless treachery, we cannot help admiring the eloquence, resourcefulness, and virtuosity with which he confides and then proceeds to execute his wicked intentions. His wooing of the grieving Lady Anne in the first act is a case in point: having set himself the seemingly impossible task of seducing a woman whose husband and father-in-law he has recently murdered, Richard is just as astonished as we are by the ease with which he accomplishes it.

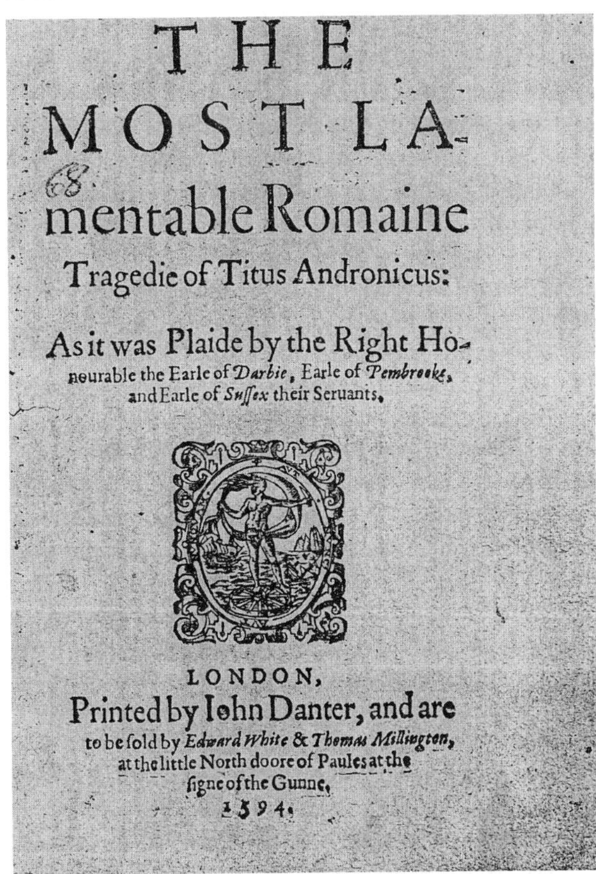
THE MOST LAmentable Romaine Tragedie of Titus Andronicus:

As it was Plaide by the Right Honourable the Earle of Darbie, Earle of Pembrooke, and Earle of Suffex their Seruants.

LONDON,
Printed by Iohn Danter, and are to be sold by Edward White & Thomas Millington, at the little North doore of Paules at the signe of the Gunne, 1594.

Title page for the only surviving copy of the 1594 quarto edition of Shakespeare's first experiment with revenge tragedy (Folger Shakespeare Library)

In many ways Richard seems, and would have seemed to Shakespeare's first playgoers, a conventional, even old-fashioned stage villain: the quick-witted, self-disclosing Vice of the late-medieval Morality Play, the dissimulating Devil familiar from the Scriptures. In other, more important, ways he seems, and would have seemed, disturbingly modern: the Machiavellian politician who acknowledges no law, human or divine, in restraint of his foxlike cunning and leonine rapacity; the totalitarian dictator who subverts every social and religious institution in pursuit of his psychopathic schemes; the cosmic rebel whose radical alienation is a challenge to every form of order. But if Richard seems in many ways a relentlessly twentieth-century figure, we learn by the end of the play that his "vaulting ambition" (so proleptic of Macbeth's) is ultimately but an instrument of the same providential design that he scorns and seeks to circumvent. Richard may be a "dreadful minister of Hell," as Lady Anne calls him, but members of Shakespeare's audience (familiar with the story through such earlier renderings of it as the portrait bequeathed by Thomas More) would have seen him simultaneously as a "scourge of God," unleashed to punish England for the sins of her fathers. Prophetic Margaret reminds us over and over that had there not been strife in the kingdom prior to the advent of Richard, there would have been no ripe occasion for "this poisonous bunch-backed toad" to ascend the throne in the first instance. As the play ends, an action that has drawn our attention again and again to the past looks with hope to the future. "By God's fair ordinance," the "bloody dog is dead," and Richmond and Elizabeth (the forebears of Shakespeare's sovereign Elizabeth) are ushering in "smooth-faced peace, / With smiling plenty, and fair prosperous days."

One other English history play is sometimes placed in Shakespeare's apprenticeship, though scholars differ about whether to date it in the early 1590s or (more probably, in the opinion of most) in the transition years 1594-1595. The earliest surviving text of *King John* is the version printed in the 1623 First Folio, and it offers a drama about a monarch of doubtful title whose reign (1199-1216) had been viewed in widely divergent ways. Medieval Catholics, focusing on King John's presumed complicity in the death of his nephew Arthur (whose claim to the throne was stronger than John's) and on his feud with Pope Innocent III (which had resulted in the King's excommunication before he finally capitulated five years later and "returned" his realm to the Church), had seen him as a usurper, a murderer, and a heretic. Sixteenth-century Protestants, on the other hand, had rehabilitated him as a proto-Tudor martyr and champion of English nationalism. In many respects, Shakespeare's own portrayal is ambiguous. He depicts John as a man who knows his position to be challengeable, and he has John plot to murder his saintly nephew. But through no fault of the King, the plot is not carried out. Meanwhile, John continues to receive the loyalty of characters who are presented sympathetically—most notably the bastard son of Richard the Lionhearted, Philip Faulconbridge—and by the end of the play it seems evident that a higher cause, the good of England, is to take precedence over such lesser concerns as John's weak title, his indirect responsibility for the accidental death of a potential rival, and his inadequacies as a leader. The Bastard, a political realist who seems quite Machiavellian at first—particularly in his analysis of the all-pervasiveness of "commodity" (self-interest) in human affairs—eventually becomes a virtual emblem of patriotism. He remains loyal to John despite the King's flaws; and to him is given a concluding speech that is frequently cited as Shakespeare's most eloquent summary of the moral implicit in all the poet's early history plays:

> This England never did, nor never shall,
> Lie at the proud foot of a conqueror
> But when it first did help to wound itself.
> . . . .
> . . . Naught shall make us rue
> If England to itself do rest but true.

If the playwright's initial efforts in the dramatization of history derived from his response to the political climate of his day, his first experiments in comedy seem to have evolved from his reading in school and from his familiarity with the works of such predecessors on the English stage as John Lyly, George Peele, Robert Greene, and Thomas Nash. Shakespeare's apprentice comedies are quite "inventive" in many respects, particularly in the degree to which they "overgo" the conventions and devices the young playwright drew upon. But because they have more precedent behind them than the English history plays, they strike us now as less stunningly "original"—though arguably more successfully executed—than the tetralogy on the Wars of the Roses.

Which of them came first we do not know, but many scholars now incline toward *The Comedy of Errors,* a play so openly scaffolded upon Plautus's *Menaechmi* and *Amphitruo* (two farces that Shakespeare probably knew in Latin from his days in grammar school) that one modern critic has summed it up as "a kind of diploma piece." Set, ostensibly, in the Mediterranean city familiar from Paul's Epistle to the Ephesians, the play begins with a sentence on the life of a luckless Syracusan merchant, Aegeon, who has stumbled into Ephesus in search of his son Antipholus. After narrating a tale of woe that wins the sympathy of Duke Solinus, Aegeon is given till five in the afternoon to come up with a seemingly impossible sum to ransom his breach

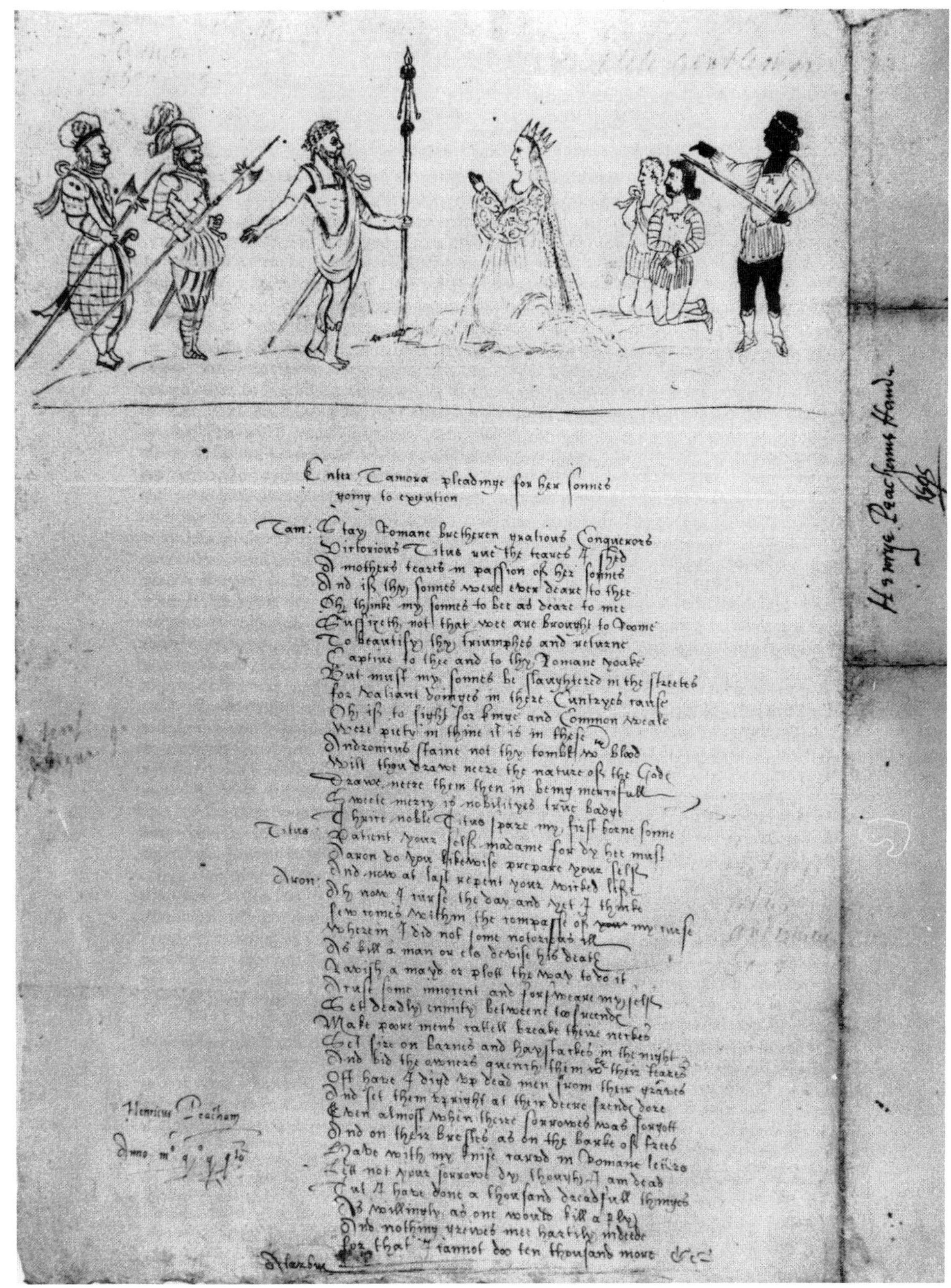

A 1595(?) transcription from memory of lines from a performance of Titus Andronicus, *with sketches of some of the characters. At center Tamora is shown begging Titus to spare her two sons, kneeling behind her. Aaron the Moor is at far right. Henry Peacham, whose name is at lower left, may have made the transcription and perhaps the drawing (Harley Papers, vol. i, f. 159ᵛ, Longleat).*

of an arbitrary law against Syracusans. Meanwhile, unknown to Aegeon, the object of his search is in Ephesus too, having arrived only hours before him; Antipholus had set out some two years earlier to find a twin brother by the same name who was separated from the rest of the family in a stormy shipwreck more than twenty years in the past. By fortuitous coincidence, the second Antipholus has long since settled in Ephesus, and so (without either's knowledge) has their mother, Aegeon's long-lost wife, Aemilia, who is now an abbess. To complicate matters further, both Antipholuses have slaves named Dromio, also twins long separated, and of course both sets of siblings are indistinguishably appareled. Into this mix Shakespeare throws a goldsmith, a set of merchants, a courtesan, a wife and a sister-in-law for the Ephesian Antipholus, and a conjuring schoolmaster. The result is a swirling brew of misunderstandings, accusations, and identity crises—all leading, finally, to a series of revelations that reunite a family, save Aegeon's life, and bring order to a city that had begun to seem bewitched by sorcerers.

We know that *The Comedy of Errors* was written prior to 28 December 1594, because there is record of a performance then at one of the four Inns of Court. Some scholars believe that the play was written for that holiday Gray's Inn presentation, but most tend to the view that it had been performed previously, possibly as early as 1589 but more likely in the years 1592-1594. Most critics now seem agreed, moreover, that for all its farcical elements, the play is a comedy of some sophistication and depth, with a sensitivity to love that anticipates Shakespeare's great festive comedies later in the decade: when Luciana advises her sister Adriana about how she should treat her husband Antipholus, for example, she echoes Paul's exhortations on Christian marriage in Ephesians. And with its use of the devices of literary romance (the frame story of Aegeon comes from fourteenth-century poet John Gower's treatment of the adventures of Apollonius of Tyre), *The Comedy of Errors* also looks forward to the wanderings, confusions of identity, and miraculous reunions so fundamental to the structure of "late plays" such as *Pericles* and *The Tempest.*

What may have been Shakespeare's next comedy has also been deprecated as farce, and it is frequently produced today with staging techniques that link it with the commedia dell'arte popular in Renaissance Italy. But for all its knockabout slapstick, *The Taming of the Shrew* is too penetrating in its psychology and too subtle in its handling of the nuances of courtship to be dismissed as a play deficient in feeling. Its main event is a battle of the sexes in which Petruchio, who has "come to wive it wealthily in Padua," takes on a dare that no other potential suitor would even consider: to win both dowry and docility from a sharp-tongued shrew avoided by everyone else as "Katherine the curst." Apparently recognizing that Katherine's willfulness is a product of the favoritism her father has long bestowed upon her younger sister, and having the further good sense to realize that the fiery Kate is capable of becoming a much more attractive wife than the much-sought-after but rather devious Bianca, Petruchio mounts a brilliant campaign to gain Kate's love and make her his. First, he insists that she is fair and gentle, notwithstanding all her efforts to disabuse him of that notion. Second, he "kills her in her own humour," with a display of arbitrary behavior—tantrums, scoldings, peremptory refusals—designed to wear her down and show her how unpleasant shrewishness can be. At the end of the play Petruchio shocks his skeptical fellow husbands by wagering that his bride will prove more compliant than theirs. When Kate not only heeds his commands but reproaches her sister and the other wives for "sullen, sour" rebellion against their husbands, it becomes manifest that Petruchio has succeeded in his quest: Kate freely and joyfully acknowledges him to be her "loving lord." If we have doubts about whether Katherine's transformation can be accepted as a "happy ending" today—and alterations of the final scene in many recent productions would suggest that it is too offensive to some sensibilities to be played straight in our own theater—we should perhaps ask ourselves whether the Kate who seems to be conspiring with Petruchio as she puts her hands beneath his foot to win a marital wager is any less spirited or fulfilled a woman than the Kate who drives all her would-be wooers away in the play's opening scene.

Whether or not *The Taming of the Shrew* is the mysterious *Love's Labor's Won* referred to by Francis Meres in 1598, it seems to have been written in the early 1590s, because what is now generally believed to be a corrupt quarto of it appeared in 1594. *The Taming of a Shrew* differs significantly from the version of Shakespeare's play that was first published in the 1623 Folio—most notably in the fact that the drunken tinker Christopher Sly, who appears only in the induc-

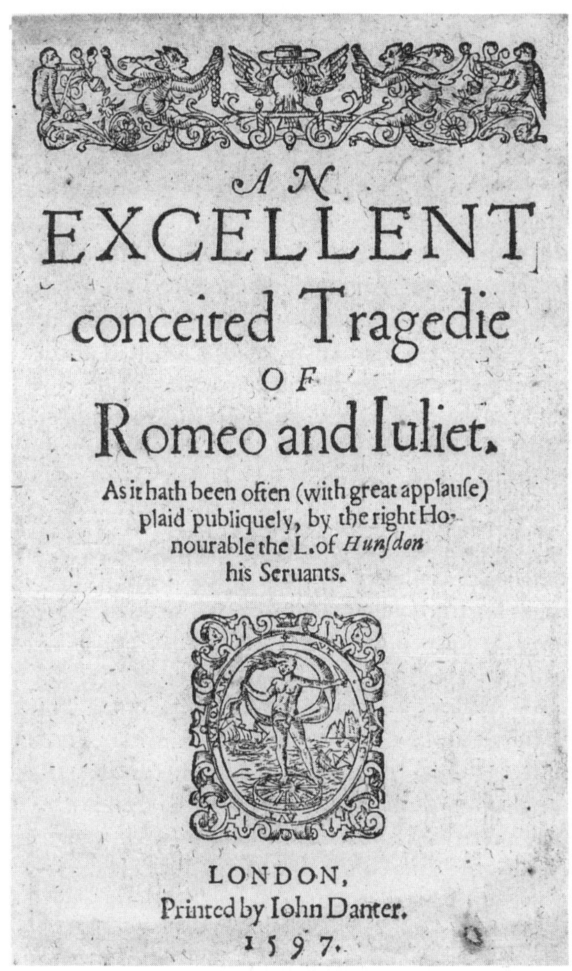
AN
EXCELLENT
conceited Tragedie
OF
Romeo and Iuliet.
As it hath been often (with great applause)
plaid publiquely, by the right Honourable the L. of *Hunsdon*
his Seruants.

LONDON,
Printed by Iohn Danter.
1597.

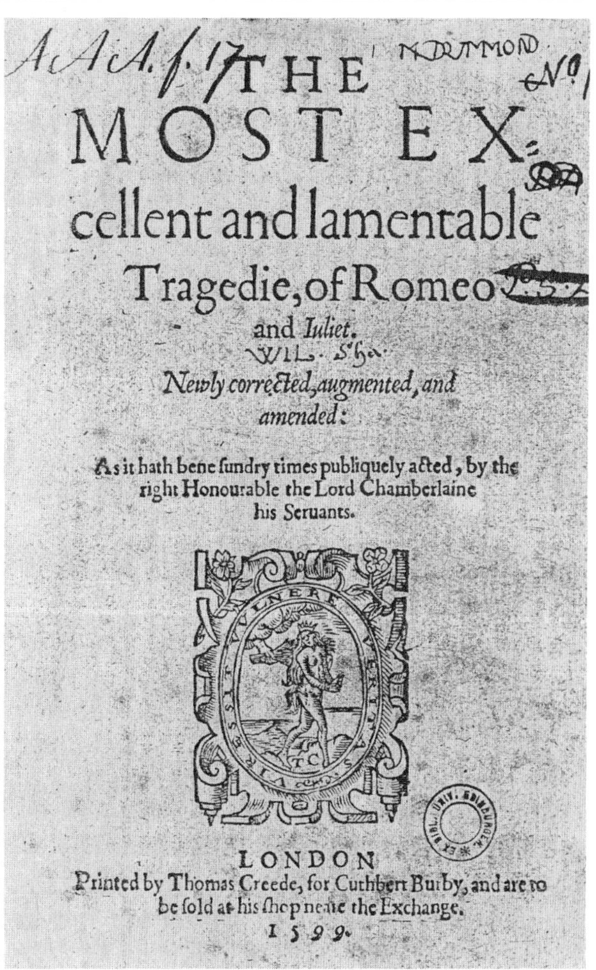
THE
MOST EX-
cellent and lamentable
Tragedie, of Romeo
and *Iuliet.*
Newly corrected, augmented, and amended:
As it hath bene sundry times publiquely acted, by the
right Honourable the Lord Chamberlaine
his Seruants.

LONDON
Printed by Thomas Creede, for Cuthbert Burby, and are to
be sold at his shop neare the Exchange.
1599.

Title pages for the 1597 corrupt quarto edition (Henry E. Huntington Library and Art Gallery) and the 1599 "corrected, augmented, and amended" quarto edition (University of Edinburgh) of the play for which Shakespeare drew on a didactic narrative poem of similar title by Arthur Brooke, first published in 1562. The copy of the second quarto shown here once belonged to William Drummond of Hawthornden, who wrote his name on the title page.

tion to the later printing of the work, remains onstage throughout *The Taming of a Shrew,* repeatedly interrupting the action of what is presented as a diversion for him and resolving at the end to go off and try Petruchio's wife-taming techniques on his own recalcitrant woman. Some directors retain the later Sly scenes, but no one seriously questions that the Folio text is in general the more authoritative of the two versions of the play.

The Folio provides the only surviving text of *The Two Gentlemen of Verona,* a comedy so tentative in its dramaturgy (for example, its comparative awkwardness in the few scenes where the playwright attempts to manage more than two characters on the stage at once), and so clumsy in its efforts to pit the claims of love and friendship against each other, that some now believe it to be the first play Shakespeare ever wrote. Based largely on a 1542 chivalric romance (*Diana Enamorada*) by Portuguese writer Jorge de Montemayor, *The Two Gentlemen of Verona* depicts a potential rivalry between two friends—Valentine and Protheus (Proteus)—who fall in love with the same Milanese woman (Silvia) despite the fact that Protheus has vowed his devotion to a woman (Julia) back home in Verona. Protheus engineers Valentine's banishment from Milan so that he can woo Silvia away from him. But Silvia remains faithful to Valentine, just as Julia (who has followed her loved one disguised as his page) holds true to Protheus, notwithstanding the protean character he discloses as a man who lives up to his name. In the concluding forest scene Valentine intervenes to save Silvia from being raped by Protheus; but, when Protheus exhibits remorse, Valentine offers him Silvia anyway, as a token of friendship restored. Fortunately, circumstances conspire to forestall such

A
PLEASANT
Conceited Comedie
CALLED,
Loues labors loſt.
As it vvas preſented before her Highnes
this laſt Chriſtmas.
Newly corrected and augmented
By W. Shakeſpere.
Imprinted at London by *W.W.*
for *Cutbert Burby*.
1598.

Title page for the 1598 quarto edition of a play that was performed before Elizabeth I during the 1597 Christmas season (British Library)

an unsatisfactory consummation, and the play ends with the two couples reunited in a wedding ceremony that features "One feast, one house, one mutual happiness."

Unlike *The Comedy of Errors* and *The Taming of the Shrew, The Two Gentlemen of Verona* has never been popular in the theater, even though it offers two resourceful women (whose promise will be fulfilled more amply in such later heroines as Rosalind and Viola), a pair of amusing clowns (Launce and Speed), and the most engaging dog (Crab) who ever stole a stage. In its mixture of prose and verse, nevertheless, and in its suggestion that the woods are where pretensions fall and would-be evildoers find their truer selves, *The Two Gentlemen of Verona* looks forward to the first fruits of Shakespeare's maturity: the festive "romantic comedies" of which it proves to be a prototype.

The one remaining play that most critics now locate in the period known as Shakespeare's apprenticeship is a Grand Guignol melodrama that seems to have been the young playwright's attempt to outdo Thomas Kyd's *Spanish Tragedy* (produced circa 1589) in its exploitation of the horrors of madness and revenge. The composition of *Titus Andronicus* is usually dated 1590-1592, and it seems to have been drawn from a ballad and *History of Titus Andronicus* that only survives today in an eighteenth-century reprint in the collection of the Folger Shakespeare Library. (The Folger also holds the sole extant copy of the 1594 first quarto of Shakespeare's play, the authoritative text for all but the one scene, III.ii., that initially appeared in the 1623 Folio.) If Shakespeare did take most of his plot from the *History of Titus Andronicus,* it is clear that he also went to Ovid's *Metamorphoses* (for the account of Tereus's rape of Philomela, to which the tongueless Lavinia points to explain what has been done to her) and to Seneca's *Thyestes* (for Titus's fiendish revenge on Tamora and her sons at the end of the drama).

Although *Titus Andronicus* is not a "history play," it does make an effort to evoke the social and political climate of fourth-century Rome; and in its depiction of a stern general who has just sacrificed more than twenty of his own sons to conquer the Goths, it anticipates certain characteristics of Shakespeare's later "Roman plays": *Julius Caesar, Antony and Cleopatra,* and *Coriolanus.* But it is primarily as a precursor to *Hamlet* (influenced, perhaps, by the lost *Hamlet* that seems to have been an antecedent to Shakespeare's play) that *Titus* holds interest for us today. Because whatever else it may be, *Titus Andronicus* is the playwright's first experiment with revenge tragedy. Its primary focus is the title character, whose political misjudgments and fiery temper put him at the mercy of the Queen of the Goths, Tamora, and her two sons (Demetrius and Chiron). They ravish and mutilate Titus's daughter Lavinia, manipulate the Emperor Saturninus into executing two of Titus's sons (Martius and Quintus) as perpetrators of the crime, and get Titus's third son (Lucius) banished for trying to rescue his brothers. Along the way, Tamora's Moorish lover Aaron tricks Titus into having his right hand chopped off in a futile gesture to save Martius and Quintus. After Lavinia writes the names of her assailants in the sand with her grotesque stumps, Titus works out the plan that yields him vengeance: he slits the throats of Demetrius and Chiron, invites Tamora to a banquet, and serves her the flesh of her sons baked in a pie. He then kills Tamora and dies at the hands of the Emperor.

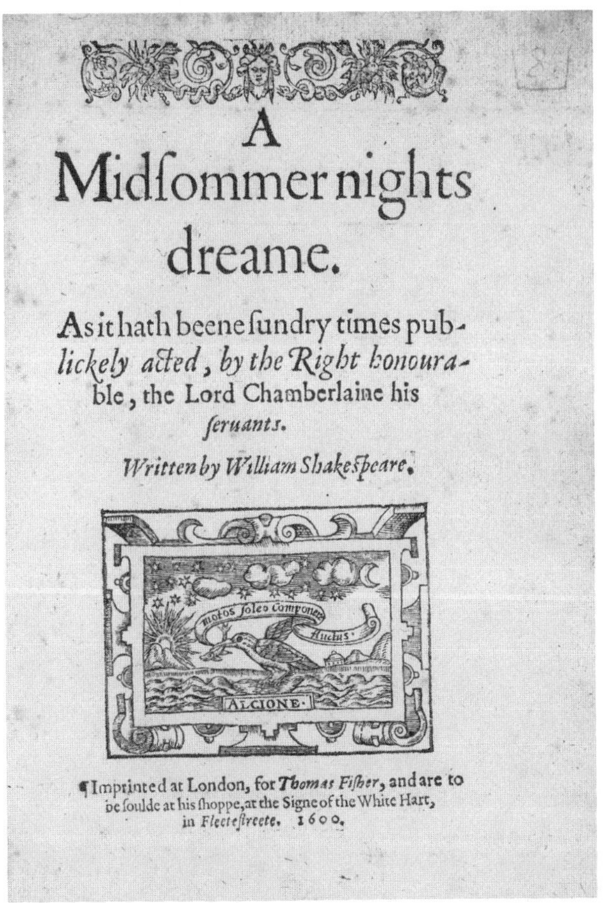
A Midsommer nights dreame.

As it hath beene sundry times publickely acted, by the Right honourable, the Lord Chamberlaine his seruants.

Written by William Shakespeare.

Imprinted at London, for Thomas Fisher, and are to be soulde at his shoppe, at the Signe of the White Hart, in Fleetestreete. 1600.

Title page for the 1600 quarto edition of a Shakespeare comedy that probably dates from 1595-1596, the same period as the tragedy Romeo and Juliet *(Henry E. Huntington Library and Art Gallery)*

At this point Lucius returns heading a Gothic army and takes over as the new Emperor, condemning Aaron to be half-buried and left to starve and throwing Tamora's corpse to the scavenging birds and beasts.

As Fredson Bowers has pointed out, *Titus Andronicus* incorporates devices characteristic of other revenge tragedies: the protagonist's feigned madness, his delay in the execution of his purpose, his awareness that in seeking vengeance he is taking on a judicial function that properly rests in Heaven's hands, and his death at the end in a bloody holocaust that leaves the throne open for seizure by the first opportunist to arrive upon the scene.

Revenge is also a significant motif in Shakespeare's other early tragedy, *Romeo and Juliet,* usually dated around 1595-1596. It is a blood feud between their two Veronese families that forces the lovers to woo and wed in secret, thereby creating the misunderstanding that leads Mercutio to defend Romeo's "honor" in act 3 when the just-married protagonist declines his new kinsman Tybalt's challenge to duel. And it is both to avenge Mercutio's death and to restore his own now-sullied name that Romeo then slays Tybalt and becomes "Fortune's fool"—initiating a falling action that leads eventually to a pair of suicides and a belated recognition by the Capulets and the Mountagues that their children have become "poor sacrifices of our enmity."

But it is not for its revenge elements that most of us remember *Romeo and Juliet.* No, it is for the lyricism with which Shakespeare portrays the beauty and idealism of love at first sight—all the more transcendent for the ways in which the playwright sets it off from the calculations of Juliet's parents (intent on arranging their daughter's marriage to advance their own status) and contrasts it with the earthy bawdiness of Juliet's Nurse and the worldly-wise cynicism of Romeo's friend Mercutio. The spontaneous sonnet of Romeo and Juliet's initial meeting at Capulet's ball, the lovers' betrothal vows in the balcony scene later that evening, the ominous parting that concludes their one night together and foreshadows their final meeting in the Capulet tomb—these are the moments we carry with us from a performance or a reading of history's most famous love story.

Romeo and Juliet may strike us as an "early" work in its formal versification and in its patterned structure. It has been faulted for its dependence on coincidence and on causes external to the protagonists for the conditions that bring about the eventual disaster—an emphasis implicit in the play's repeated references to Fortune and the stars. Critics have also encountered difficulty in their attempts to reconcile the purity of Romeo and Juliet's devotion to each other ("for earth too dear") with the play's insistence that their relationship is a form of idolatry—ultimately leading both lovers to acts of desperation that playgoers in Shakespeare's time would have considered consequential in a way that is lost on most modern audiences. But whatever its supposed limitations and interpretive problems, *Romeo and Juliet* seems likely to hold its position as one of the classics of the dramatic repertory.

The play's initial printing was a 1597 quarto edition that most scholars believe to derive from a text pieced together from memory. The version today's editors accept as the primary authority is the 1599 second quarto, "newly corrected, augmented, and amended," and apparently type-

A Midsummer Night's Dream: *(top)* Titania and Bottom, *painting by Henri Fuseli, circa 1780-1790; and (bottom) William Blake's watercolor,* Oberon, Titania and Puck with Fairies Dancing, *circa 1785-1787 (Tate Gallery, London)*

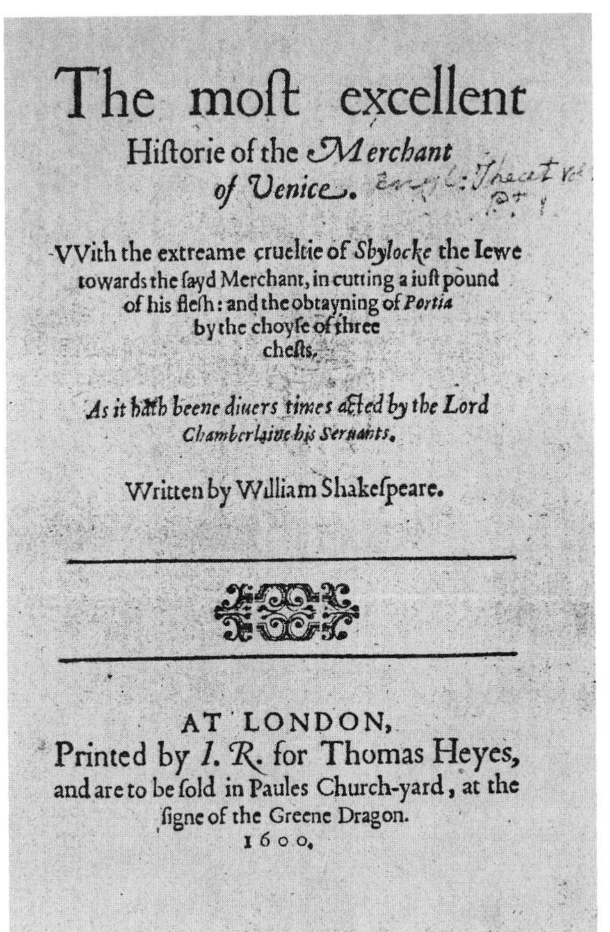

The most excellent
Historie of the *Merchant*
of Venice.

VVith the extreame crueltie of *Shylocke* the Iewe
towards the sayd Merchant, in cutting a iust pound
of his flesh: and the obtayning of *Portia*
by the choyse of three
chests.

As it hath beene diuers times acted by the Lord
Chamberlaine his Seruants.

Written by William Shakespeare.

AT LONDON,
Printed by *I. R.* for Thomas Heyes,
and are to be sold in Paules Church-yard, at the
signe of the Greene Dragon.
1600.

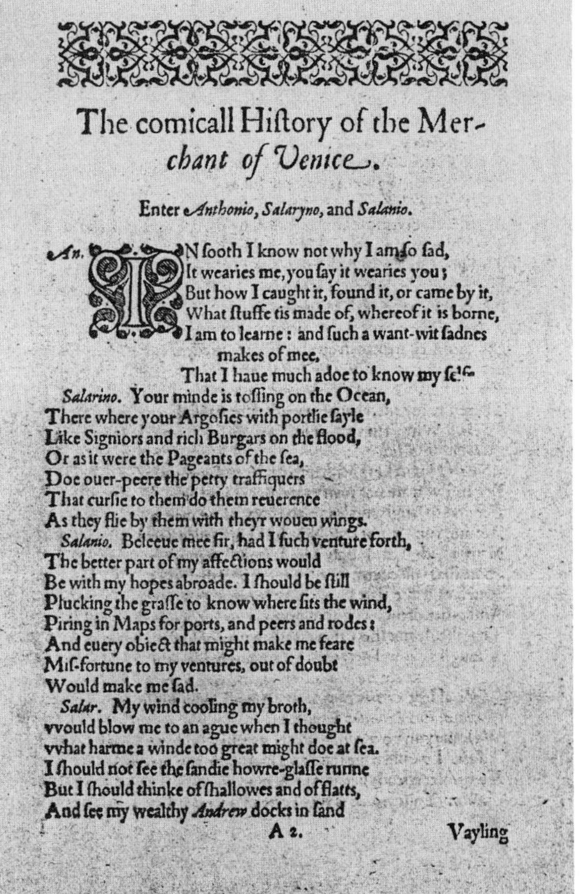

The comicall History of the Mer-
chant of Venice.

Enter *Anthonio, Salaryno,* and *Salanio.*

An. IN sooth I know not why I am so sad,
It wearies me, you say it wearies you;
But how I caught it, found it, or came by it,
What stuffe tis made of, whereof it is borne,
I am to learne: and such a want-wit sadnes
makes of mee,
That I haue much adoe to know my selfe.
Salarino. Your minde is tossing on the Ocean,
There where your Argosies with portlie sayle
Like Signiors and rich Burgars on the flood,
Or as it were the Pageants of the sea,
Doe ouer-peere the petty traffiquers
That cursie to them do them reuerence
As they flie by them with theyr wouen wings.
Salanio. Beleeue mee sir, had I such venture forth,
The better part of my affections would
Be with my hopes abroade. I should be still
Plucking the grasse to know where sits the wind,
Piring in Maps for ports, and peers and rodes:
And euery obiect that might make me feare
Mis-fortune to my ventures, out of doubt
Would make me sad.
Salar. My wind cooling my broth,
vvould blow me to an ague when I thought
vvhat harme a winde too great might doe at sea.
I should not see the sandie howre-glasse runne
But I should thinke of shallowes and of flatts,
And see my wealthy *Andrew* docks in sand
A 2. Vayling

Title page and first page of text from the 1600 quarto edition of the play that serves as a prototype for Shakespeare's later "problem comedies" (British Library)

set from Shakespeare's own "foul papers." Two more printings appeared before the 1623 Folio, whose rendering of the text—essentially a reprint of the third quarto edition (1609)—has no independent authority.

The principal source for the work was a 1562 narrative, *The Tragical History of Romeus and Juliet,* by Arthur Broke, a didactic poem urging children to be obedient to their parents. By telescoping three months into four days and by dramatizing the story in a manner more sympathetic to the young lovers, Shakespeare transformed a sermon into a tragedy whose urgency must have been just as moving in the Elizabethan theater as we know it to be in our own.

If *Romeo and Juliet* is a play that has lost none of its freshness in the four centuries since its first appearance, *Love's Labor's Lost* now strikes some as so thoroughly "Elizabethan" in its rhetoric and topicality as to be nearly inaccessible to modern audiences. Evidently another product of the "transition years" when Shakespeare was working his way back into the theater after a two-year hiatus due to the plague, *Love's Labor's Lost* appears to have been written in 1594-1595 for private performance and may well have been revised in 1597 for a presentation before the Queen during the Christmas revels. Its earliest extant printing was a 1598 quarto announcing itself as "newly corrected and augmented" and probably set from Shakespeare's "foul papers." The Folio text was essentially a reprint of this quarto, which has the distinction of being the first play to bear Shakespeare's name on its title page. Until recently no literary source had been found for the plot of *Love's Labor's Lost,* but Glynne Wickham has now turned up a 1581 analogue, *The Four Foster Children of Desire,* that helps account for much of its structure and several of its themes.

What emerges for a theatergoer or reader of the work today is a highly "artificial" comedy about a company of lords whose well-intended

King Richard the ſecond.

Peace ſhall go ſleepe with turkes and infidels,
And in this ſeate of peace, tumultuous warres,
Shall kin with kin, and kinde with kind confound:
Diſorder, horror, feare, and mutiny,
Shall heere inhabit, and this land be cald,
The field of Golgotha and dead mens ſculs.
Oh if yon raiſe this houſe againſt this houſe,
It will the wofulleſt diuiſion proue,
That euer fell vpon this curſed earth:
Preuent it, reſiſt it, let it not be ſo,
Leſt child, childs children, crie againſt you wo.
North. Well haue you argued ſir, and for your paines,
Of Capitall treaſon, we arreſt you heere:
My Lord of Weſtminſter, be it your charge,
To keepe him ſafely till his day of triall.
Bull. Let it be ſo, and loe on wedneſday next,
We ſolemnly proclaime our Coronation,
Lords be ready all. *Exeunt.*
Manent West. Caleil, Aumerle.
Abbot. A wofull Pageant haue we heere beheld.
Car. The woe's to come, the children yet vnborne,
Shall feele this day as ſharpe to them as thorne.
Aum. You holy Clergy men, is there no plot,
To ridde the realme of this pernitious blot?
Abbot. My Lo. before I freely ſpeake my mind heerein,
You ſhall not onely take the Sacrament,
To burie mine intents, but alſo to effect,
What euer I ſhall happen to deuiſe:
I ſee your browes are full of diſcontent,
Your harts of ſorrow, and your eies of teares:
Come home with me to ſupper, Ile lay a plot,
Shall ſhew vs all a merrie daie. *Exeunt.*
Enter the Queene with her attendants.
Quee. This way the King will come, this is the way,
To Iulius Cæſars ill erected Tower,
To whoſe flint boſome, my condemned Lord,
Is doomde a priſoner by proud Bullingbrooke.
H2 Heere

The Tragedie of

Oh if you rayſe this houſe againſt his houſe,
It will the wofulleſt diuiſion proue,
That euer fell vpon this curſed earth:
Preuent it, reſiſt it, and let it not be ſo,
Leaſt child, childes children crie againſt you woe.
North. Well haue you argued ſir, and for your paynes,
Of Capitall treaſon, we arreſt you here:
My Lord of Weſtminſter, be it your charge,
To keepe him ſafely till his day of triall.
May it pleaſe you Lords, to graunt the common ſuite,
Fetch hither *Richard*, that in common view
He may ſurrender, ſo we ſhall proceed without ſuſpition.
Yorke. I will be his conduct.
Bull. Lords, you that are heere, are vnder our areſt,
Procure your Sureties for your dayes of anſwere;
Litle are we beholding to your loue,
And litle looke for at your helping hands.
Enter king Richard.
Rich. Alacke why am I ſent for to a King,
Before I haue ſhooke off the regall thoughts
Wherewith I raignd; I hardly yet haue learnt
To inſinuate, flatter, bow, and bend my limbes?
Giue Sorrow leaue a while to tutor me to this ſubmiſsion:
Yet I well remember the fauours of theſe men,
Were they not mine? did they not ſometimes cry all hayle
To me? ſo *Iudas* did to *Chriſt*; but he in twelue,
Found trueth in all but one; I in twelue thouſand none:
God ſaue the King, will no man ſay Amen:
Am I both Prieſt and Clarke; well then, Amen,
God ſaue the King, although I be not hee,
And yet Amen, if heauen do thinke him mee:
To doe what ſeruice am I ſent for hither?
Yorke. To doe that office of thine owne good will,
Which tired maieſtie did make thee offer;
The reſignation of thy State and Crowne
To *Harry Bullingbrooke*.
Rich. Seaſe the Crowne.
Heere

King Richard the Second.

Heere Cooſin, on this ſide my hand, and on that ſide yours:
Now is this golden Crowne like a deepe Well,
That owes two Buckets filling one an other,
The emptier euer dauncing in the ayre,
The other downe vnſeene, and full of Water:
That Bucket downe, and full of teares, am I,
Drinking my griefe, whilſt you mount vp on high.
Bull. I thought you had been willing to reſigne?
Rich. My Crowne I am, but ſtill my Griefes are mine;
You may my Glories and my State depoſe,
But not my Griefes, ſtill am I King of thoſe.
Bul. Part of your Cares you giue me with your Crowne.
Rich. Your cares ſet vp, do not plucke my cares downe:
My care is loſſe of care, by old care don,
Your care is gaine of care by new care won:
The cares I giue, I haue, though giuen away,
They tend the Crowne, yet ſtill with me they ſtay.
Bull. Are you contented to reſigne the Crovvne?
Rich. I, no no I; for, I muſt nothing bee;
Therefore no no, for I reſigne to thee.
Now marke me how I will vndoe my ſelfe:
I giue this heauie waight from off my head,
And this vnweildie Scepter from my hand,
The pride of kingly ſway from out my heart:
With mine owne teares I waſh away my balme,
With mine owne hands I giue away my Crowne,
With mine owne tongue deny my ſacred ſtate,
With mine owne breath releaſe all duties rites,
All pompe and maieſtie I do forſweare,
My Manners, Rentes, Reuenewes I forgoe;
My Actes, Decrees, and Statutes I denie:
God pardon all Oathes that are broke to me;
God keepe all Vowes vnbroke that ſweare to thee:
Make me that nothing haue, with nothing grieud,
And thou with all pleaſd, that haſt all atchieud:
Long mayſt thou liue in *Richards* ſeat to ſit,
And ſoone lie *Richard* in an earthy pit:
H2 God

When the first quarto edition of Richard II *was printed in 1597 (top, Trinity College, Cambridge), its dethronement scene did not include the crucial passage in which the monarch surrenders his crown. But in the 1608 fourth quarto (bottom and next page, Bodleian Library) some 160 lines were added to stage Richard's transfer of the crown to Henry Bullingbrook. The new material was inserted after line 15 of the first quarto page shown above.*

The Tragedie of

God ſaue King *Harry*, vnkingd *Richard* ſayes,
And ſend him many yeeres of Sun-ſhine dayes.
What more remaines?
North. No more, but that you read
Theſe accuſations, and theſe greeuous crimes,
Committed by your perſon, and your followers,
Againſt the State and profit of this Land;
That by confeſsing them, the ſoules of men
May deeme that you are worthily depoſde.
Rich. Muſt I doe ſo? and muſt I rauell out
My weaud vp Folly, gentle *Northumberland?*
If thy offences were vpon record,
Would it not ſhame thee in ſo faire a troope,
To read a lecture of them, if thou wouldſt,
There ſhouldſt thou finde one haynous article,
Contayning the depoſing of a King,
And cracking the ſtrong warrant of an Oath,
Markt with a blot, damd in the booke of heauen:
Nay of you that ſtand and looke vpon,
Whilſt that my wretchedneſſe doth bate my ſelfe,
Though ſome of you (with *Pilat*) waſh your hands,
Shewing an outward pittie, yet you *Pilates*,
Haue heere deliuer me to my ſowre Croſſe,
And water can not waſh away your ſinne.
North. My Lord diſpatch, read ore theſe Articles.
Rich. Mine eyes are full of teares, I cannot ſee;
And yet ſalt water blindes them not ſo much,
But they can ſee a ſort of Traytors heere:
Nay, if I turne mine eyes vpon my ſelfe,
I find my ſelfe a Traytor with the reſt;
For I haue giuen heere my ſoules conſent
To vndecke the pompous body of a King;
Made Glory bace, and Soueraigntie a ſlaue;
Proud Maieſtie a ſubiect, State a peaſant.
North. My Lord.
Rich. No Lord of thine, thou haught inſulting man,
Nor no mans Lord; I haue no name, no title,

H No

King Richard the Second.

No not that name was giuen me at the Font,
But tis vſurpt; alacke the heauie day
That I haue worne ſo many Winters out,
And know not now, what name to call my ſelfe.
O that I were a mockerie King of Snow,
Standing before the ſunne of *Bullingbrooke*,
To melt my ſelfe away in water drops.
Good King, great King; and yet not greatly good;
And if my name be ſtarling, yet in Englang
Let it commaund a mirour hether ſtrayte
That it may ſhew me what a face I haue,
Since it is banckroût of his Maieſtie.
Bull. Goe ſome of you and fetch a Looking-glaſſe.
North. Read ore this paper while the Glaſſe doth come.
Rich. Feind, thou torments me ere I come to Hell.
Bull. Vrge it no more my Lord Northumberland.
North. The Commons will not then be ſatisfied.
Rich. They ſhall be ſatisfied, Ile read enough,
When I do ſee the very Booke indeed,
Where all my ſinnes are writ, and that's my ſelfe.
Giue me the Glaſſe: no deeper wrinckles yet?
Hath Sorrow ſtroke ſo many blowes vpon this
Face of mine, and made no deeper woundes?
Oh flattering Glaſſe, like to my followers in proſperitie!
Was this the face that euery day vnder his
Houſhould roofe did keepe ten thouſand men?
Was this the face that faaſt ſo many follies,
And was at laſt outfaaſt by *Bullingbrooke?*
A brittle Glorie ſhineth in this face,
As brittle as the Glorie is the face,
For there it is crackt in a hundred ſhiuers:
Marke ſilent King the morall of this ſport,
How ſoone my ſorrow hath deſtroyde my face.
Bull. The ſhadow of your ſorrow hath deſtroyd
The ſhadow of your face.
Rich. Say that againe: the ſhadow of my ſorrow;
Ha let's ſee; tis very true, my griefe

H 3. Lies

The Tragedie of

Lies all within, and theſe externall manners
Of laments are meerely ſhadowes to the vnſeene,
Griefe that ſwelles with ſilence in the tortured ſoule;
And I thanke thee King that not onely giueſt
Me cauſe to wayle, but teacheſt me the way
How to lament the cauſe; Ile begge one boone,
And then be gone, and trouble you no more.
Bull. Name it faire Cooſin.
Rich. Faire Cooſe, why? I am greater then a King:
For when I was a king, my flatterers were then but ſubiects;
Being now a ſubiect, I haue a King heere
To my flatterer; being ſo great, I haue no need to beg.
Bul. Yet aske.
Rich. And ſhall I haue it?
Bul. You ſhall.
Rich. Why then giue me leaue to goe.
Bull. Whither?
Rich. Whither you will, ſo I were from your ſights.
Bull. Goe ſome of you conuey him to the Tower.
Rich. O good conuey, conueyers are you all,
That riſe thus nimbly by a true Kings fall.
Bull. On Wedneſday next we ſolemnely ſet downe
Our Coronation; Lords prepare your ſelues.
Exeunt. Manet West. Carleill, Aumerle.
Abbot. A wofull Pageant haue we heere beheld.
Carl. The woe's to come, the children yet vnborne,
Shall feele this day as ſharpe to them as thorne.
Aum. You holy Clergie men, is there no plot,
To rid the Realme of this pernitious blot?
Abbot. Before I freely ſpeake my minde herein,
You ſhall not onely take the Sacrament,
To bury mine intentes, but alſo to effect,
What euer I ſhall happen to deuiſe:
I ſee your browes are full of diſcontent,
Your heart of ſorrow, and your eyes of teares;
Come home with me to ſupper, Ile lay a plot,
Shall ſhew vs all a merry day. *Exeunt.*

H Enter

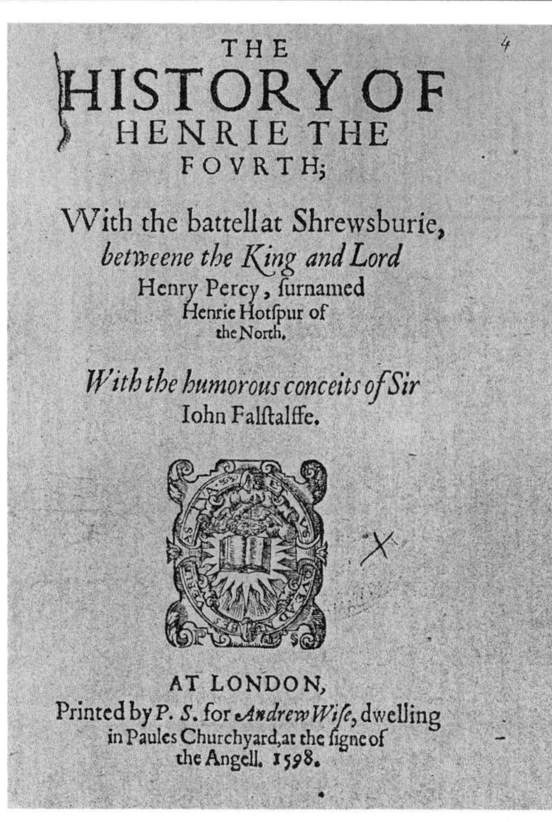

THE
HISTORY OF
HENRIE THE
FOVRTH;

With the battell at Shrewsburie,
betweene the King and Lord
Henry Percy, ſurnamed
Henrie Hotſpur of
the North.

With the humorous conceits of Sir
Iohn Falſtalffe.

AT LONDON,
Printed by *P. S.* for *Andrew Wiſe*, dwelling
in Paules Churchyard, at the ſigne of
the Angell. 1598.

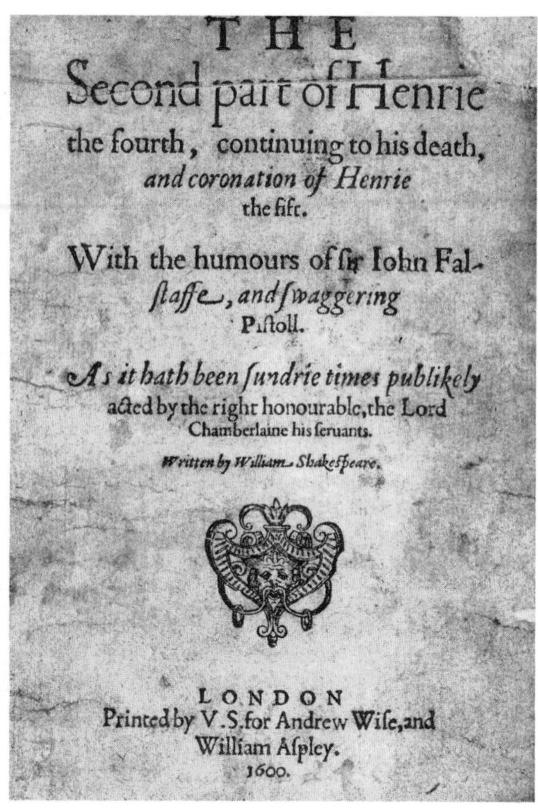

THE
Second part of Henrie
the fourth, continuing to his death,
and coronation of Henrie
the fift.

With the humours of ſir Iohn Fal-
ſtaffe, and ſwaggering
Piſtoll.

As it hath been ſundrie times publikely
acted by the right honourable, the Lord
Chamberlaine his ſeruants.

Written by William Shakeſpeare.

LONDON
Printed by V. S. for Andrew Wiſe, and
William Aſpley.
1600.

of Henry the fourth.

By heauen me thinkes it were an eaſie leape,
To plucke bright honor from the pale fac't moone,
Or diue into the bottome of the deepe,
Where fadome line could neuer touch the ground,
And plucke vp drowned honor by the locks,
So he that doth redeeme her thence might weare
Without corriuall all her dignities,
But out vpon this halfe fac't fellowſhip.
Wor. He apprehends a world of figures here,
But not the forme of what he ſhould attend,
Good cooſen giue me audience for a while.
Hot. I cry you mercy.
Wor. Thoſe ſame noble Scots that are your priſoners.
Hot. Ile keepe them all;
By God he ſhal not haue a Scot of them,
No, if a Scot would ſaue his ſoule he ſhal not,
Ile keepe them by this hand.
Wor. You, ſtart away,
And lend no eare vnto my purpoſes:
Thoſe priſoners you ſhal keepe.
Hot. Nay I wil, thats flat:
He ſaid he would not ranſome Mortimer,
Forbad my tongue to ſpeake of Mortimer,
But I wil find him when he lies aſleepe,
And in his eare ile hollow Mortimer:
Nay, ile haue a ſtarling ſhalbe taught to ſpeake
Nothing but Mortimer, and giue it him
To keepe his anger ſtil in motion.
Wor. Heare you coſen a word.
Hot. All ſtudies here I ſollemnly defie,
Saue how to gall and pinch this Bullingbrooke,
And that ſame ſword and buckler prince of Wales,
But that I thinke his father loues him not,
And would be glad he met with ſome miſchance:
I would haue him poiſoned with a pot of ale.
Wor. Farewel kinſman, ile talke to you
when you are better temperd to attend.
C.j. *North.*

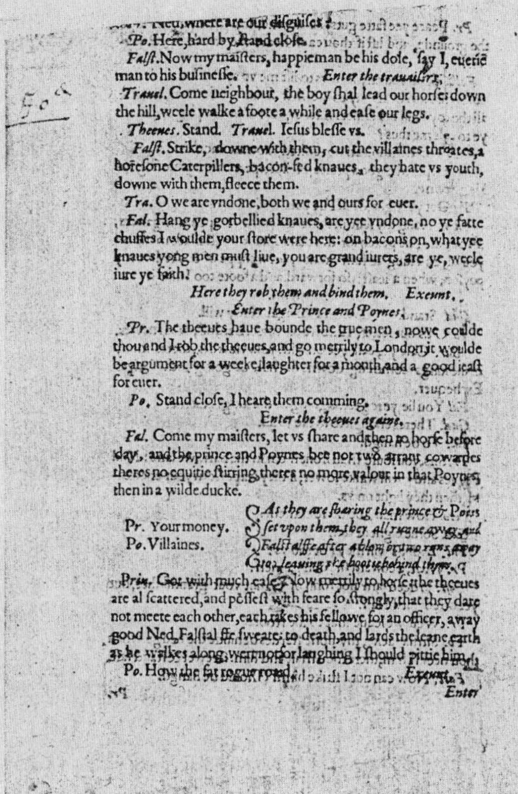

... Ned, where are our diſguiſes?
Po. Here, hard by, ſtand cloſe.
Falſt. Now my maiſters, happie man be his dole, ſay I, euerie man to his buſineſſe. *Enter the trauailers.*
Trauel. Come neighbour, the boy ſhal lead our horſes down the hill, weele walke a foote a while and eaſe our legs.
Theeues. Stand. *Trauel.* Ieſus bleſſe vs.
Falſt. Strike, downe with them, cut the villaines throates, a horeſone Caterpillers, bacon-fed knaues, they hate vs youth, downe with them, fleece them.
Tra. O we are vndone, both we and ours for euer.
Fal. Hang ye gorbellied knaues, are yee vndone, no ye fatte chuffes I woulde your ſtore were here: on bacons on, what yee knaues yong men muſt liue, you are grand iurers, are ye, weele iure ye faith.
Here they rob them and bind them. Exeunt.
Enter the Prince and Poynes.
Pr. The theeues haue bounde the true men, nowe coulde thou and I rob the theeues, and go merrily to London, it woulde be argument for a weeke, laughter for a month, and a good ieaſt for euer.
Po. Stand cloſe, I heare them comming.
Enter the theeues againe.
Fal. Come my maiſters, let vs ſhare and then to horſe before day, and the prince and Poynes bee not two arrant cowardes theres no equitie ſtirring, theres no more valour in that Poynes, then in a wilde ducke.
Pr. Your money. *As they are ſharing the prince & Poins ſet vpon them, they all runne away, and*
Po. Villaines. *Falſtalffe after a blow or two runs away too, leauing the bootie behind them.*
Prin. Got with much eaſe. Now merrily to horſe, the theeues are al ſcattered, and poſſeſt with feare ſo ſtrongly, that they dare not meete each other, each takes his fellowe for an officer, away good Ned, Falſtalffe ſweates to death, and lards the leane earth as he walkes along, wert not for laughing I ſhould pittie him.
Po. How the fat rogue road. *Exeunt.*
Enter

Title pages for 1598 and 1600 quarto editions of Shakespeare's examination of the reign of Henry Bullingbrook after he acquired the English crown (top left, Trinity College, Cambridge; top right, Henry E. Huntington Library and Art Gallery) and the first and last pages of an eight-leaf fragment from an earlier 1598 quarto edition, now preserved at the Folger Shakespeare Library

but ill-conceived attempt to outwit nature makes them all look foolish and lands them in a pickle. No sooner have King Ferdinand of Navarre and his friends Longaville, Dumaine, and Berowne—hoping to conquer the frailties of the flesh and find an antidote to "cormorant devouring Time"—forsworn the company of women and withdrawn to their quasi-monastic Academe than they find their fortress besieged by four beautiful ladies—the Princess of France and her attendants Maria, Katherine, and Rosaline—who camp in the park outside and watch with amusement as each of the "scholars" falls in love, forsakes his vows, and gets caught by the others. Eventually the men surrender and propose marriage, but by now it has become clear that they are so far gone in artifice that they need at least a year of penance—and time in real-world settings such as the hospital to which Berowne is consigned—before their protestations of devotion can be given any credit. Love's labor is "lost," then, in the sense that this is a comedy without the traditional conclusion in wedding, feasting, and dancing. The lyrics that serve as the play's epilogue move from spring ("When daisies pied") to winter ("When icicles hang"), and the year of penance to come is one that requires all of the men to reevaluate their aspirations with a renewed awareness of the omnipresence of disease and the inevitability of death.

Love's Labor's Lost is one of Shakespeare's most self-conscious plays generically, and it is also one of his most demanding works linguistically. Much is made of the pretentiousness of the four men's rhetoric, and it is shown to be detrimental to normal human feeling. It is also shown to be an infection that touches such lesser characters as the bombastic braggart soldier Don Adriano de Armado, the pedant schoolmaster Holofernes, and the clown Costard, and, like the poor curate Nathaniel in the Pageant of the Nine Worthies, all but the one who presents "Pompey the Huge" prove "a little o'erparted." One of the ironies of the play is that the four lords who laugh most cruelly at Armado and his companions also turn out to be "o'erparted" in the final reckoning. Such are the wages of affectation.

Affectation of another kind is depicted in a delightful scene from what many regard as Shakespeare's most charming comedy, *A Midsummer Night's Dream.* As the Athenian courtiers are quick to observe in their critiques of the "tragical mirth" of Pyramus and Thisby in V.i., the "mechanicals" who display their dramatic wares at the nuptial feast of Theseus and Hippolyta are even more fundamentally "o'erparted" than the inept supernumeraries of *Love's Labor's Lost.* But there is something deeply affectionate about Shakespeare's portrayal of the thespian aspirations of Bottom and his earnest company of "hempen homespuns," and the "simpleness and duty" with which they tender their devotion is the playwright's way of reminding us that out of the mouths of babes and fools can sometimes issue a loving wisdom that "hath no bottom." Like "Bottom's Dream," the playlet brings a refreshingly naive perspective to issues addressed more seriously elsewhere. And, by burlesquing the struggles and conflicts through which the lovers in the woods circumvent the arbitrariness of their elders, "Pyramus and Thisby" comments not only upon the fortunes of Demetrius and Helena, Lysander and Hermia, but also upon the misfortunes of Romeo and Juliet. Both plots derive ultimately from the same source in Ovid's *Metamorphoses,* and the playwright's parallel renderings of the "course of true love" in *Romeo and Juliet* and *A Midsummer Night's Dream* are so closely linked in time and treatment that it is tempting to regard the two plays as companion pieces—tragic and comic masks, as it were, for the same phase (1595-1596) of Shakespearean dramaturgy.

Whether or not *A Midsummer Night's Dream* was commissioned for a wedding ceremony at Court, as some scholars have speculated, the play is in fact a remarkable welding of disparate materials: the fairy lore of Oberon and Titania and their impish minister Puck, the classical narrative of Theseus's conquest of the Amazons and their queen Hippolyta, the confused comings and goings of the young Athenian lovers who must flee to the woods to evade their disapproving elders, and the rehearsals for a clumsy craft play by a band of well-meaning tradesmen. It is in some ways the most original work in the entire Shakespearean canon, and one is anything but surprised that its "something of great constancy" has inspired the best efforts of such later artists as composer Felix Mendelssohn, painters Henry Fuseli and William Blake, director Peter Brook, and filmmakers Max Reinhardt and Woody Allen.

A Midsummer Night's Dream is in many respects the epitome of "festive comedy," an evocation of the folk rituals associated with such occasions as May Day and Midsummer Eve, and its culminating mood is one of unalloyed romantic fulfillment. Romance is also a key ingredient in the concluding arias of Shakespeare's next comedy, *The Merchant of Venice,* where Bassanio and Portia, Lorenzo and Jessica, and Gratiano and Nerissa celebrate the happy consummation of three love quests and contemplate the music of the spheres from a magical estate whose name means "beautiful mountain." But the "sweet harmony" the lovers have achieved by the end of *The Merchant of Venice* has been purchased very dearly, and it is hard for a modern audience to accept the serenity of Belmont without at least a twinge of pain over what has happened in far-off Venice to bring it about.

Whether *The Merchant of Venice* is best categorized as an anti-Semitic play (capitalizing on prejudices that contemporaries such as Marlowe had catered to in works such as *The Jew of Malta*) or as a play about the evils of anti-Semitism (a work as critical of the Christian society that has persecuted the Jew as it is of the vengeance he vents in response), its central trial scene is profoundly disturbing for an audience that has difficulty viewing the moneylender's forced conversion as a manifestation of mercy. Shylock's "hath not a Jew eyes" speech impels even the most bigoted of viewers to see him as a fellow human being, notwithstanding the rapacious demand for "justice" that all but yields him Antonio's life before Portia's clever manipulations of the law strip the usurer of half his fortune. Even if we feel that Shylock's punishment is less severe than what strict "justice" might have meted out to him, his grim exit nevertheless casts a pall over the festivities of the play's final act.

By contrast with *A Midsummer Night's Dream,* a work in which the disparate components of the action are resolved in a brilliantly satisfying synthesis, *The Merchant of Venice* remains, for many of us, a forerunner of those later Shakespearean experiments that twentieth-century critics have labeled "problem comedies." Even its fairy-tale elements, such as the casket scenes in which three would-be husbands try to divine the "will" of Portia's father, seem discordant to a modern playgoer who hears the heroine dismiss one of her suitors with a slur on his Moroccan "complexion." Though it seems to have been written in late 1596 or early 1597 and, like *A Midsummer Night's Dream,* was first published in a good quarto in 1600, *The Merchant of Venice* feels closer in mood to *Measure for Measure*—which also pivots on a conflict between justice and mercy—than to most of the other "romantic comedies" of the mid to late 1590s.

THE
CRONICLE
Hiſtory of Henry the fift,
With his battell fought at *Agin Court* in *France.* Togither with *Auntient Piſtoll.*

As it hath bene ſundry times playd by the Right honorable the Lord Chamberlaine his ſeruants.

LONDON
Printed by *Thomas Creede,* for Tho. Millington, and Iohn Busby. And are to be ſold at his houſe in Carter Lane, next the Powle head. 1600.

Title page for one of the first, if not the first, of Shakespeare's plays to be performed at the Globe theater, which opened in 1599 (Anderson Galleries auction catalogue, sale number 1405, 4-5 March 1919)

But if *The Merchant of Venice* strikes us now as a play that looks forward to a later phase of Shakespearean dramaturgy, the works the author produced next were a return to his beginnings. Possibly as early as 1595, Shakespeare began a fresh exploration of the "matter" of English history with a drama focusing on the events that precipitated the Wars of the Roses. It is impossible to say whether the playwright knew, when he began composing *Richard II,* that he would go on to write the two parts of *Henry IV* and the treatment of *Henry V* that would furnish the link between *Richard II* and the *Henry VI* trilogy with which he had begun his dramatization of the Wars of the Roses. But complete the cycle he did, and the four English history plays Shakespeare wrote between 1595 and 1599 were even more impressive in their epic sweep than the four he had completed prior to the theatrical hiatus of 1592-1594.

Richard II was, among other things, a major advance in Shakespeare's evolution as a poetic dramatist. Not only does the play contain the dying John of Gaunt's paean to "This royal throne of kings, this sceptred isle, . . . This other Eden, demi-paradise"; it also affords us a telling contrast between the laconic bluntness of Henry Bullingbrook, a man of action who is not quick to speak, and the self-indulgent lyricism of Richard II, a man of words who is, finally and fatally, not quick to act.

At the beginning of the action Richard's security in his presumption that God's deputy is above the law leads him to disregard the principles of primogeniture that are the basis of the King's own position as head of state. He dismisses the counsel of his elders, seizes the estates of the Duke of Lancaster and other nobles, banishes in Bullingbrook a cousin who has maintained a discreet silence about crimes that implicate the monarch himself, and sets in motion the uprising that will eventually render his title untenable. By the climax of the play Richard is forced to surrender his crown in a Parliament scene that neatly counterpoises the declining King's complicity for his own downfall with the rising King's usurpation of a throne to which he has no legitimate right. And by the end of the drama Richard's pastoral musings in the Tower transform him into a quasi-martyr whose meditations on his failure to use time fruitfully are as deeply moving as anything that Shakespeare had written up to this point in his career. As the expiring Richard prophesies, his murder at the hands of Henry IV's henchmen releases a tide of bloodshed that will not be stemmed until a Tudor monarch ascends the throne nearly a century in the future.

When *Richard II* was published in a good quarto in 1597, it lacked any staging of Richard's surrender of the crown, owing almost certainly to the fact that even without such a scene the play could be construed as threatening to the aging Queen Elizabeth. That such apprehensions were justified was borne out four years later when a performance of the work was commissioned by followers of the Earl of Essex on the eve of the Earl's abortive attempt at a coup. The dramatized deposition first appeared in print in the fourth quarto of 1608, five years after the Queen's death.

As with the earlier English history plays, *Richard II* and the three *Henry* plays that followed it derived in large measure from the 1587 second edition of Holinshed's *Chronicles*. But in all likelihood the tetralogy was also influenced, and possibly even inspired, by the 1595 publication of Samuel Daniel's *Civil Wars*.

Within a year of his completion of *Richard II* Shakespeare probably began work on its sequel, the first part of *Henry IV*. Taken together, parts 1 and 2 of *Henry IV* focus our attention on the immediate consequences of Henry Bullingbrook's seizure of the crown. Of these, the first is signaled by the opening lines of the first part, where the new King, "shaken" and "wan with care," announces his desire to lead a crusade to the Holy Land, both as a means of expiating his guilt and as a means of unifying a "giddy-minded" nation that is now divided into volatile factions. Unfortunately, rest is not to be attained by this tainted monarch. His claim to the title is immediately challenged by his former allies, the Percies, and thereafter his reign is disturbed by one threat after another until he expires. The King does eventually arrive at "Jerusalem" near the end of *Henry IV*, part 2, but ironically this destination turns out to be a room in the castle, and the setting for his deathbed scene, rather than the city he had hoped to wrest from pagan occupation at the birthplace of Christendom.

The price that Henry IV pays for his usurpation turns out to be a nagging consciousness that "uneasy lies the head that wears the crown." And as poignant as any other cause of the King's anxiety is his fear that God has chosen to punish him with a wayward son whose "loose behavior" will forfeit the throne his father has expended so much effort to mount and maintain. For all the King and his rivals can tell, the "nimble-footed madcap Prince of Wales" is squandering his royal inheritance in the dissolute company of "that villainous abominable misleader of youth, Falstaff," and a low-life lot of tavern keepers, thieves, and prostitutes. But as we learn early in *Henry IV*, part 1, Prince Hal is actually "redeeming time" in ways that surpass the political sagacity of even so Machiavellian a ruler as his father. The heir apparent is acquiring firsthand knowledge of his nation's ordinary citizens, and the benefit he anticipates is that once he is King of England he will be able to "command all the good lads in Eastcheap." As he prepares himself for the military trials with which he must be tested, moreover, he does so in the expectation that once he throws off the "base contagious clouds" that "smother up his beauty from the world," he will be accepted as England's true "sun," not distrusted as the flawed monarch everyone knows his father to be.

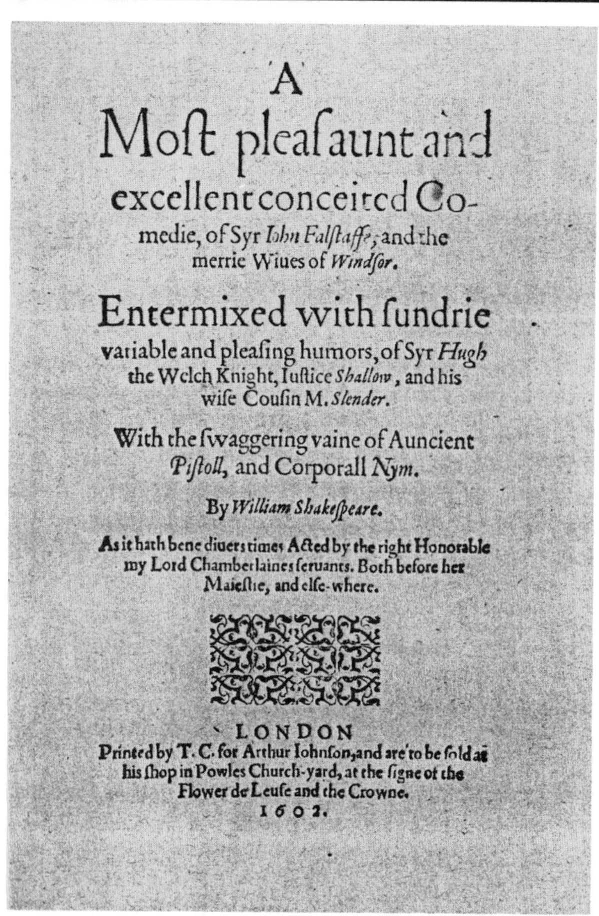

A
Moſt pleaſaunt and
excellent conceited Co-
medie, of Syr *Iohn Falſtaffe*, and the
merrie Wiues of *Windſor*.
Entermixed with ſundrie
variable and pleaſing humors, of Syr *Hugh*
the Welch Knight, Iuſtice *Shallow*, and his
wiſe Couſin M. *Slender*.
With the ſwaggering vaine of Auncient
Piſtoll, and Corporall *Nym*.
By *William Shakeſpeare*.
As it hath bene diuers times Acted by the right Honorable
my Lord Chamberlaines ſeruants. Both before her
Maieſtie, and elſe-where.
LONDON
Printed by T. C. for Arthur Iohnſon, and are to be ſold at
his ſhop in Powles Church-yard, at the ſigne of the
Flower de Leuſe and the Crowne.
1602.

Title page for the 1602 quarto edition of the play that was probably first produced before Queen Elizabeth and George Carey, Lord Hunsdon, patron of the Lord Chamberlain's Men, at Windsor Castle on 23 April 1597, in honor of the awarding of the Order of the Garter to Hunsdon (British Library)

And so he is. In the battle of Shrewsbury at the end of *Henry IV,* part 1, the valiant Hal defeats the fiery warrior the King would have preferred for an heir. By winning Hotspur's honors, the Prince finally earns, at least for a moment, the respect and gratitude of a father whose life and kingdom he has rescued. But it is not enough for Hal to have demonstrated the courage and prudence required of a future monarch. In part 2 Shakespeare has him back at the Boar's Head tavern once again, and it is only after he has demonstrated the remaining kingly virtues of temperance and justice—by casting off the influence of Falstaff and claiming as his second surrogate father the Lord Chief Justice—that Hal is finally granted the crown for which he has been educating himself.

His epic reaches its apogee in *Henry V,* a play described by its Chorus as a pageant in honor of "the mirror of all Christian kings." Whether or not we are to feel that the new King has discarded some of his humanity in his rejection of the "old fat man" at his coronation, and whether or not we are to regard with suspicion the ambiguous "Salic Law" that the Bishops invoke to justify England's invasion of France, and whether or not we are to see the monarch as cruel in his threat to allow the maidens and children of Harfleur to be raped and slaughtered if the town refuses to surrender, the impression that *Henry V* has made on most readers and producers is one dominated by heroic exaltation. The King proves firm and resourceful in battle, mingling with his men in disguise on the eve of the engagement and then inspiring them to noble valor in his famous St. Crispin's Day address. And once his "happy few," his "band of brothers," have triumphed against all odds and won the day, the leader of Britain's united forces gives all the glory to God. He thus illustrates those qualities of the nurturing mother pelican—self-sacrifice, humility, and magnanimity—that pious kings were to display in addition to the monarchial attributes that Machiavelli and other political theorists had long associated with the lion and the fox. Later, in his wooing of his French bride Katherine at the end of the play, the King also exhibits the wit and charm that had endeared the historical Henry V to his adoring countrymen.

It is possible that the "wooden O" referred to in the Chorus's opening prologue was the Globe, newly opened on Bankside in 1599, and hence that *Henry V* was one of the first, if not *the* first, of Shakespeare's works to be performed in that now-famous playhouse. Be that as it may, the drama was evidently completed in 1599, a year after *Henry IV,* part 2, and two years after *Henry IV,* part 1. All three plays made their first appearances in print by 1600, the two parts of *Henry IV* in good quartos and *Henry V* in a corrupt quarto. The first reliable text of *Henry V* was that published in the First Folio in 1623.

The first sound text of a related work, *The Merry Wives of Windsor,* also appeared in the Folio, but it too was initially published in a flawed quarto, this one in 1602. Just when *Merry Wives* was written, and why, has been vigorously debated. According to one legend, questionable but not totally lacking in plausibility, Shakespeare was urged to write the comedy because the Queen wanted to see Falstaff in love. If so, it seems likely that the entertainment was also de-

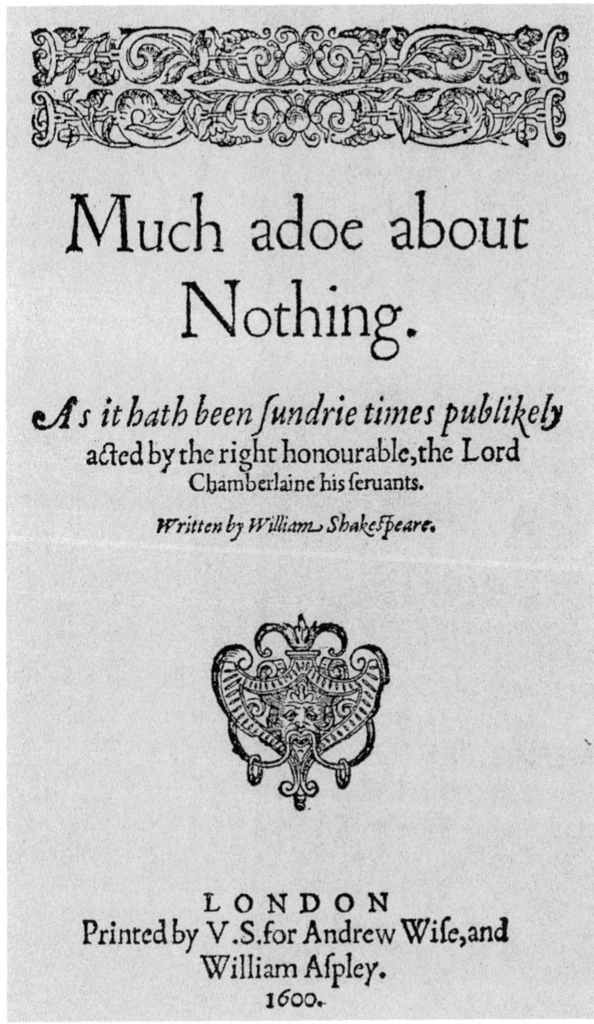

Much adoe about Nothing.

As it hath been ſundrie times publikely acted by the right honourable, the Lord Chamberlaine his ſeruants.

Written by William Shakeſpeare.

LONDON
Printed by V.S. for Andrew Wiſe, and William Aſpley.
1600.

Title page for the 1600 quarto edition of one of Shakespeare's most popular comedies (Anderson Galleries auction catalogue, sale number 2078, 24-25 May 1926)

signed to honor George Carey, Lord Hunsdon, the patron of the Lord Chamberlain's Men, who was awarded the Order of the Garter on 23 April 1597. There are references to a Garter ceremony in *The Merry Wives of Windsor,* and Leslie Hotson has argued that even though the play may well have been performed later at the Globe, its first presentation was before Queen Elizabeth and Lord Hunsdon at Windsor Castle on St. George's Day 1597.

The Merry Wives of Windsor is unique among Shakespeare's comedies in having an English town for its setting. Its bourgeois characters have delighted audiences not only in the playhouse but also on the operatic stage, in what many consider the most successful of Verdi's notable achievements in Shakespearean opera. Despite its obvious virtues, however, the play has never been a favorite among Shakespeare's readers and scholarly interpreters. The reason is that the Falstaff we see in *The Merry Wives of Windsor* is a character largely lacking in the vitality and appeal of the knight who wins our hearts in the first part of *Henry IV*. Without Prince Hal and the wit combats afforded by his jokes at Falstaff's expense, the protagonist of *Merry Wives* is merely conniving and crude. We may laugh at the comeuppances he receives at the hands of the merry wives he tries to seduce—the buck-basket baptism he gets as his reward for the first encounter, the beatings and pinchings he suffers in his later encounters—but we see nothing of the inventiveness that makes Falstaff such a supreme escape artist in part 1 of *Henry IV*. So debased is the Falstaff of *The Merry Wives of Windsor* that many commentators have argued that it is simply a mistake to approach him as the same character. In any case, we never see him in love. His is a profit motive without honor, and it is much more difficult for us to feel any pity for his plight in *Merry Wives* than it is in the three history plays that depict the pratfalls, decline, and demise of the Prince's genial lord of misrule.

The comedy does have the clever Mistress Ford and Mistress Page. And in the jealous Master Ford it also has a gull whose sufferings can be amusing and instructive in the theater. But it is doubtful that *The Merry Wives of Windsor* will ever be our favorite Shakespearean play, particularly when we set it alongside such contemporaneous delights as *Much Ado About Nothing* and *As You Like It*.

These works were probably written in late 1598 and 1599, respectively, with the former first published in a good quarto in 1600 and the latter making its initial appearance in the 1623 First Folio. Both are mature treatments of love, and both have enjoyed considerable success in performance.

"Nothing" is a word of potent ambiguity in Shakespeare (the playwright was later to explore its potential most profoundly in the "nothing will come of nothing" that constitutes the essence of *King Lear*), and in *Much Ado About Nothing* its implications include the possibilities inherent in the wordplay on the Elizabethan homonym "noting." Through the machinations of the surly Don John, who dupes the superficial Claudio into believing that he notes his betrothed Hero in the act of giving herself to another lover, an innocent maiden is rejected at the altar by a young man who believes himself to have been dishon-

This portrait of Shakespeare was once attributed to Richard Burbage and said to have belonged to Sir William Davenant, but it is now believed to have been painted in the eighteenth century (National Portrait Gallery, London).

ored. Fortunately, Don John and his companions have themselves been noted by the most incompetent watch who ever policed a city; and, despite their asinine constable, Dogberry, these well-intended but clownish servants of the Governor of Messina succeed in bringing the crafty villains to justice. In so doing, they set in motion a process whereby Hero's chastity is eventually vindicated and she reappears as if resurrected from the grave. Meanwhile, another pair of notings have been stage-managed by the friends of Benedick and Beatrice, with the result that these two sarcastic enemies to love and to each other are each tricked into believing (as it turns out, correctly) that the other is secretly infatuated. Much ado is made of Benedick and Beatrice's notings, and by the time the play ends these wry critics of amorous folly, grudgingly acknowledging that "the world must be peopled," have been persuaded to join Claudio and Hero for a double wedding that will draw the action to a close with feasting, dancing, and merriment.

Shakespeare could have gone to several antecedents for the story of Hero and Claudio, among them cantos from Ariosto's *Orlando Furioso* and Spenser's *Faerie Queene.* But the nearest thing to a "source" for Beatrice and Benedick may well have been the playwright's own *Taming of the Shrew,* where another pair of unconventional would-be lovers skirmish their way to a relationship that is all the more vital for the resistance that has to be channeled into concord to bring it about. In any event, if there is some doubt about where Benedick and Beatrice came from, there is none about where they point—to such gallant and witty Restoration lovers as Mirabell and Millamant in William Congreve's *The Way of the World.*

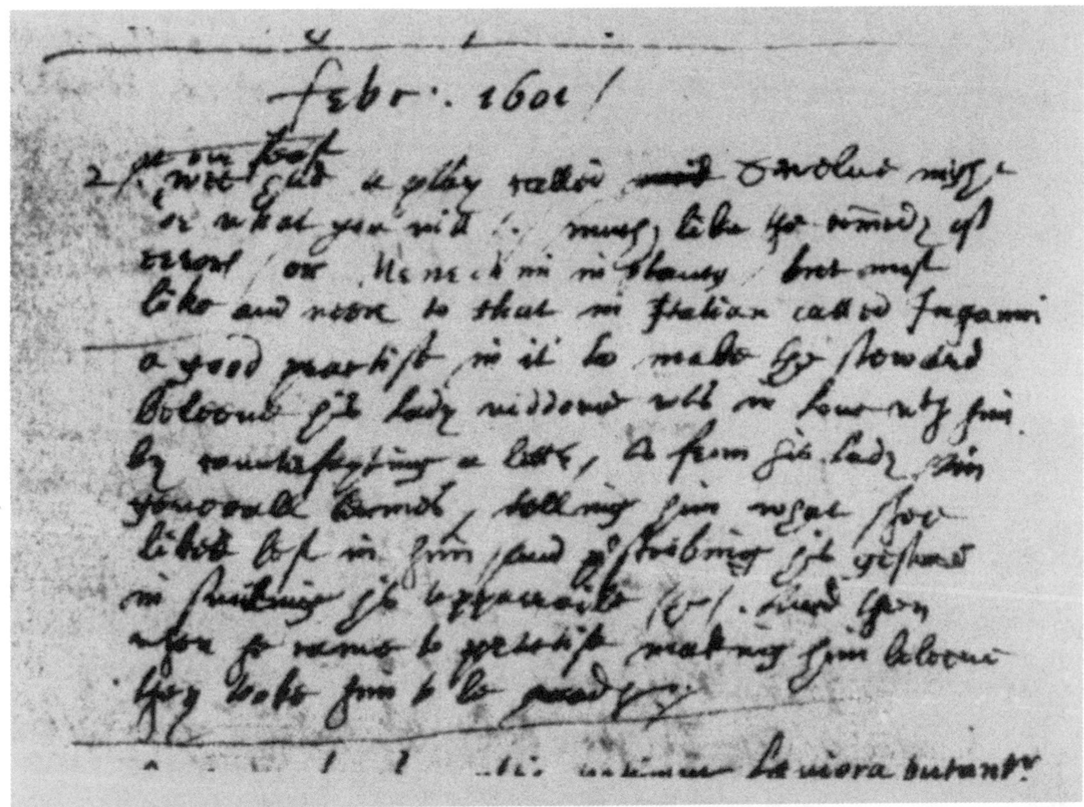

Top: passage from the diary of law student John Manningham, who reports having seen a performance of Twelfth Night *on 2 February 1602 (1601 according to the calendar then in use) at a feast in the hall of the Middle Temple (British Library, MS. Harley 5353, f. 12ᵛ). Bottom: the hall in which the play was performed. Manningham compares the play to* The Comedy of Errors, *Plautus's* Menaechmi, *and the Italian comedy "called 'Ingannati'"* (Gl'Ingannati, *which may in fact have been one of Shakespeare's sources for* Twelfth Night), *and he praises the scene in which Malvolio the steward, having been tricked into thinking the Countess Olivia loves him, dresses and acts in a way that convinces the lady he is mad.*

With *As You Like It* Shakespeare achieved what many commentators consider to be the finest exemplar of a mode of romantic comedy based on escape to and return from what Northrop Frye has termed the "green world." As in *A Midsummer Night's Dream* (where the young lovers flee to the woods to evade an Athens ruled by the edicts of tyrannical fathers) and *The Merchant of Venice* (where Belmont serves as the antidote to all the venom that threatens life on the Rialto), in *As You Like It* the well-disposed characters who find themselves in the Forest of Arden think of it as an environment where even "adversity" is "sweet" and restorative.

Duke Senior has been banished from his dukedom by a usurping younger brother, Duke Frederick. Shortly after the play opens, Duke Senior and his party are joined by Orlando and his aged servant Adam (who are running away from Orlando's cruel older brother Oliver), and later they in turn are joined by Duke Senior's daughter Rosalind and her cousin Celia (who have come to the forest, disguised as men, because the wicked Duke Frederick can no longer bear to have Rosalind in his daughter's company at Court). The sylvan scenes are punctuated by reflections on the relative merits of courtly pomp and pastoral simplicity, with the cynical Touchstone and the melancholy Jaques countering any sentimental suggestion that the Forest of Arden is a "golden world" of Edenic perfection. Meanwhile, her sojourn in the forest allows the wise and resourceful Rosalind to use her usurped masculinity as a means of testing the affections of her lovesick wooer Orlando. Eventually Orlando proves a worthy match for his lady, in large measure because he shows himself to be his brother's keeper. By driving off a lioness poised to devour the sleeping Oliver, Orlando incurs a wound that prevents him from appearing for an appointment with the disguised "Ganymede"; but his act of unmerited self-sacrifice transforms his brother into a "new man" who arrives on the scene in Orlando's stead and eventually emerges as a suitable match for Celia. As the drama nears its end, we learn that a visit to the forest has had a similarly regenerative effect on Duke Frederick, who enters a monastery and resigns the dukedom to its rightful ruler, Duke Senior.

The plot of *As You Like It* derives in large measure from Thomas Lodge's *Rosalynde or Euphues' Golden Legacy*, a prose classic dating from 1590. But in his treatment of the "strange events" that draw the play to a conclusion presided over by Hymen, the god of marriage, Shakespeare hints at the kind of miraculous transformation that will be given major emphasis in his late plays.

The last of the great romantic comedies of Shakespeare's mid career, probably composed and performed in 1601 though not published until the 1623 First Folio, was *Twelfth Night.* Based, in part, on an Italian comedy of the 1530s called *Gl'Inganniati, Twelfth Night* is another work with implicit theological overtones. Its title comes from the holiday traditionally associated with Epiphany (6 January, the twelfth day of the Christmas season), and much of its roistering would have seemed appropriate to an occasion when Folly was allowed to reign supreme under the guise of a Feast of Fools presided over by a Lord of Misrule. In Shakespeare's play, the character who most openly represents Misrule is Sir Toby Belch, the carousing uncle of a beautiful countess named Olivia. Together with such companions as the witless Sir Andrew Aguecheek, the jester Feste, and a clever gentlewoman named Maria, Sir Toby makes life difficult not only for Olivia but also for her puritan steward Malvolio, whose name means "bad will" and whose function in the play, ultimately, is to be ostracized so that "good will" may prevail. In what many consider to be the most hilarious gulling scene in all of Shakespeare, Malvolio is beguiled into thinking that his Lady is in love with him and persuaded to wear cross-gartered yellow stockings in her presence—attire that he believes will allure her, but attire that persuades her instead that he is deranged. The "treatment" that follows is a mock exercise in exorcism, and when Malvolio is finally released from his tormentors at the end of the action, the play's real Lord of Misrule exits vowing revenge "on the whole pack" of them.

As with the dismissal of Shylock in *The Merchant of Venice,* the punishment of Malvolio's presumption in *Twelfth Night* has seemed too harsh to many viewers and readers. But that should not prevent us from seeing that *Twelfth Night* is also a play about other forms of self-indulgence (Count Orsino's affection for the pose of a courtly lover, and Olivia's excessively long period of mourning for her deceased brother), and about the means by which characters "sick of self-love" or self-deception are eventually restored to mental and emotional sanity. Through the ministrations of the wise fool, Feste, and the patient Viola, who arrives in Illyria after a shipwreck in which she mistakenly believes her brother Sebastian to have died, we witness a sequence of coincidences and in-

THE

Tragicall Hiſtorie of

HAMLET

Prince of Denmarke

By William Shake-ſpeare.

As it hath beene diuerſe times acted by his Highneſſe ſeruants in the Cittie of London : as alſo in the two Vniuerſities of Cambridge and Oxford, and elſe-where

At London printed for N.L. and Iohn Trundell. 1603.

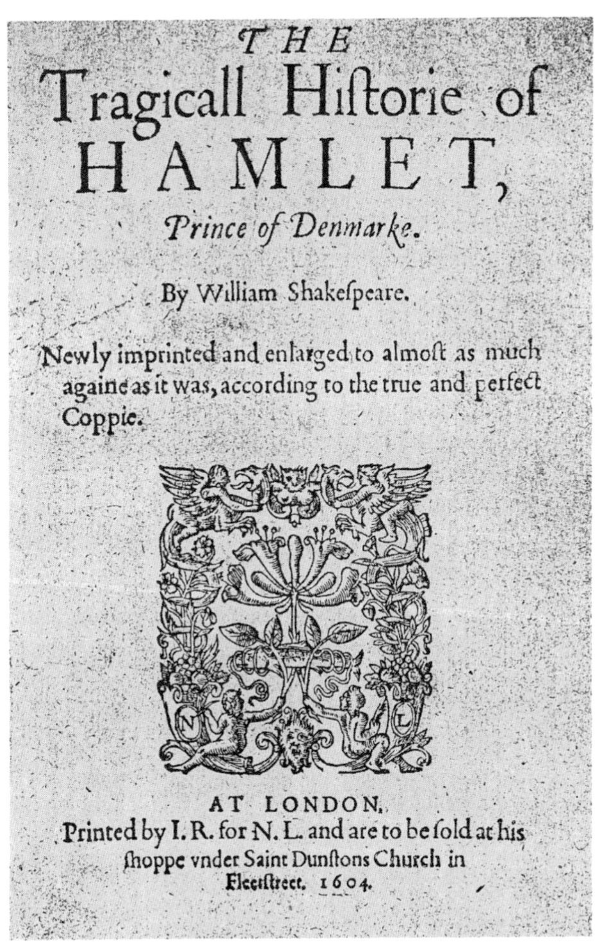

THE

Tragicall Hiſtorie of

HAMLET,

Prince of Denmarke.

By William Shakeſpeare.

Newly imprinted and enlarged to almoſt as much againe as it was, according to the true and perfect Coppie.

AT LONDON,

Printed by I. R. for N. L. and are to be ſold at his ſhoppe vnder Saint Dunſtons Church in Fleetſtreet. 1604.

Title pages for the 1603 corrupt quarto edition (Henry E. Huntington Library and Art Gallery) and the 1604 good quarto edition (Library of the Earl of Verulam) of Shakespeare's first major tragedy

terventions that seems too providential to have been brought about by blind chance. By taking another series of potentially tragic situations and turning them to comic ends, Shakespeare reminds us once again that rescue and reconciliation are at the root of what Northrop Frye calls the "argument of comedy."

If Shakespeare's middle years are notable for sophisticated achievements in the genre we now refer to as romantic or festive comedy, they are equally notable for the playwright's unprecedented strides in the development of two other genres: tragedy and tragicomedy. In 1599, probably at the Globe, the Lord Chamberlain's Men offered the earliest recorded performance of *Julius Caesar* (the first of three mature tragedies, now grouped as "the Roman Plays," which all saw print for the first time in the 1623 Folio). Two years later, in late 1600 or early 1601, the company probably added to its repertory *Hamlet* (a drama whose immediate and sustained popularity was attested to by its 1603 publication in an unauthorized corrupt quarto, succeeded a year later by a good quarto that most textual scholars still rely upon for all but a few passages, in preference to the slightly revised text in the 1623 Folio, which appears to have been set principally from a copy of the promptbook). Then in late 1601 or early 1602—once again drawing on the "classical" matter that had been the basis for the action of *Julius Caesar* and for many of the allusions in *Hamlet*—Shakespeare completed *Troilus and Cressida,* a drama so uncompromisingly "intellectual" in its insistence that the audience "by indirections find directions out" that readers from the seventeenth century to the present have found it difficult to interpret and all but impossible to classify. If *Troilus and Cressida* is a comedy, as the epistle prefacing the second issue of the 1609 First Quarto would indicate, it is at best a specimen of black humor very different in tone and treatment from Shakespeare's other efforts in tragi-

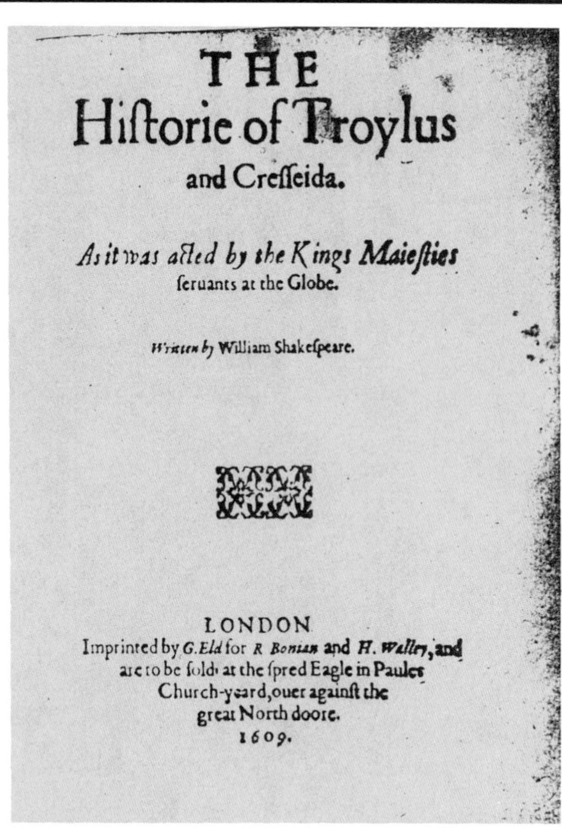

THE
Hiſtorie of Troylus
and Creſſeida.

As it was acted by the Kings Maieſties ſeruants at the Globe.

Written by William Shakeſpeare.

LONDON
Imprinted by *G.Eld* for *R. Bonian* and *H. Walley*, and are to be ſold at the ſpred Eagle in Paules Church-yeard, ouer againſt the great North doore.
1609.

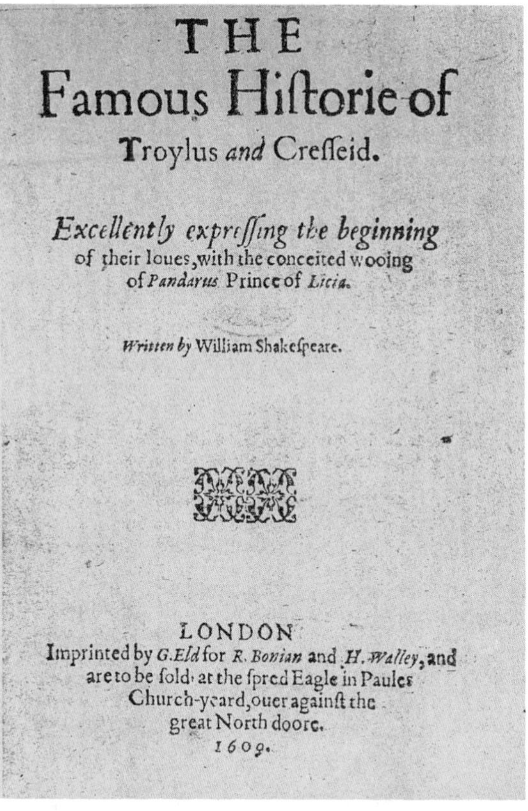

THE
Famous Hiſtorie of
Troylus *and* Creſſeid.

Excellently expreſſing the beginning of their loues, with the conceited wooing of *Pandarus* Prince of *Licia*.

Written by William Shakeſpeare.

LONDON
Imprinted by *G.Eld* for *R. Bonian* and *H. Walley*, and are to be ſold at the ſpred Eagle in Paules Church-yeard, ouer againſt the great North doore.
1609.

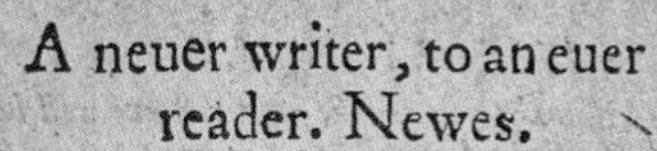

A neuer writer, to an euer reader. Newes.

Ternall reader, you haue heere a new play, neuer ſtal'd with the Stage, neuer clapper-clawd with the palmes of the vulger, and yet paſſing full of the palme comicall; for it is a birth of your braine, that neuer vnder-tooke any thing commicall, vainely: And were but the vaine names of commedies changde for the titles of Commodities, or of Playes for Pleas; you ſhould ſee all thoſe grand cenſors, that now ſtile them ſuch vanities, flock to them for the maine grace of their grauities: eſpecially this authors Commedies, that are ſo fram'd to the life, that they ſerue for the moſt common Commentaries, of all the actions of our liues. ſhewing ſuch a dexteritie, and power of witte, that the moſt diſpleaſed with Playes, are pleaſd with his Commedies. And all ſuch dull and heauy-witted worldlings, as were neuer capable of the witte of a Commedie, comming by report of them to his repreſentations, haue found that witte there, that they neuer found in them-ſelues, and haue parted better wittied then they came: feeling an edge of witte ſet vpon them, more then euer they dreamd they had braine to grinde it on. So much and ſuch ſauored ſalt of witte is in his Commedies, that they ſeeme (for their height of pleaſure) to be borne in that ſea that brought forth Venus. *Amongſt all there is none more witty then this: And had I time I would comment vpon it, though I know it needs not, (for ſo*

¶ 2 *much*

THE EPISTLE.

much as will make you thinke your teſterne well beſtowd) but for ſo much worth, as euen poore I know to be ſtuft in it. It deſerues ſuch a labour, as well as the beſt Commedy in Terence *or* Plautus. *And beleeue this, that when hee is gone, and his Commedies out of ſale, you will ſcramble for them, and ſet vp a new Engliſh Inquiſition. Take this for a warning, and at the perrill of your pleaſures loſſe, and Iudgements, refuſe not, nor like this the leſſe, for not being ſullied, with the ſmoaky breath of the multitude; but thanke fortune for the ſcape it hath made amongſt you. Since by the grand poſſeſſors wills I beleeue you ſhould haue prayd for them rather then beene prayd. And ſo I leaue all ſuch to bee prayd for (for the ſtates of their wits healths) that will not praiſe it.*

Vale.

Variant title pages for the 1609 quarto edition of a play that has been variously classified as comedy, tragedy, and tragicomedy; and the epistle to the reader in the second state, which contradicts the statement on the title page of the first that the play had been performed (top left: Elizabethan Club, Yale University; top right and bottom: British Library)

comedy. If it is a tragedy, as its equivocal placement (occupying a no-man's-land between the Histories and the Tragedies) in the First Folio has led some to argue, it is unique to the genre in the way its language and action undercut the dignity of its heroic protagonists. *Troilus and Cressida* was followed, in 1602-1603 and 1604 respectively, by two other plays, again ambiguous in tone, that, like it, are frequently discussed today as "problem plays." *All's Well That Ends Well* and *Measure for Measure* (both of which made their initial appearances in print in the First Folio) are tragicomedies that turn on "bed tricks," and in their preoccupation with the seamier aspects of sexuality they can be viewed as links between *Hamlet,* the first of Shakespeare's "great tragedies," and *Othello,* the second (which seems to have been composed in 1604, when there is a record of performance at Court).

Julius Caesar—a play that may owe something to sources as seemingly remote as Saint Augustine's *City of God* and Erasmus's *Praise of Folly,* in addition to such obvious classical antecedents as Plutarch's parallel *Lives of the Noble Grecians and Romans* (in the 1579 translation by Sir Thomas North) and Tacitus's *Annals*—is now regarded as a dramatic work of considerable complexity. On the one hand, the play captures with remarkable fidelity the ethos and rhetorical style of late-republican Rome—so much so, indeed, that it may be said that Shakespeare's portraits of Caesar and his contemporaries have largely molded our own impressions of how the ancient Romans thought and talked and conducted their civic affairs. Recent studies of the play's references to "philosophy" indicate, moreover, that Shakespeare knew a good deal about Roman Stoicism and perceived it as one of the characterizing traits that differentiated Brutus from Cassius, an Epicurean continually nonplussed by his companion's mental rigidity and emotional aloofness.

But if Shakespeare brought to his dramatic art a historical imagination capable of reconstructing a self-consistent Roman world—and one that was distinct in significant ways from his own Elizabethan England—he was also capable of embodying in his representation of that world a perspective that amounted, in effect, to a Renaissance humanist critique of pre-Christian classical civilization. Thus it was quite possible for Shakespeare to portray the conspirators and their cause, as it were, "sympathetically"—so much so, indeed, that a nineteenth-century New World audience, unwittingly misreading the play, found it almost impossible not to hear in such exclamations as "peace, freedom, and liberty!" the precursors of America's own founding fathers. At the same time, however, Shakespeare would have known that he could rely on most of his Elizabethan contemporaries to regard as foredoomed any attempt to achieve social harmony through an act that they would have seen as savage butchery. The playwright could encourage viewers to "identify" with Brutus through participation in his soliloquies, while simultaneously assuming that alert members of the audience would recognize that the protagonist's thought processes are often misguided, self-deceptive, and self-defeating.

In the late 1930s Mark Van Doren observed that, whatever Brutus's positive qualities as a high-minded patriot, he tends to come across in the play as a self-righteous, almost pharisaical prig, particularly in the quarrel scene with Cassius. In recent years scholars have reinforced Van Doren's perception by showing that it is consistent with the hypothesis that in his portrayal of Brutus, Shakespeare was drawing on a widely held Christian tradition that regarded Stoicism as a philosophy that rendered its adherents hard-hearted, arrogant, and so assured of their own virtue as to be largely incapable of recognizing or repenting of their faults. If this reading of Brutus is closer to Shakespeare's intention than the more sentimental view that approaches everything in the play from the retrospective vantage point of Mark Antony's eulogy for "the noblest Roman of them all," it tends to cast much of *Julius Caesar* in an ironic light—and by implication to require a playgoer alert to clues that are not always so self-evident as a twentieth-century reader or viewer might expect.

An attentive audience seems called for by *Hamlet* as well, at least if we are going to take seriously the Prince's admonition that the players direct their performance to "the judicious," to those who are capable of viewing all the action, including that involving the most engaging of protagonists, with a critical eye. This is difficult for us, because we have long been accustomed to thinking of Hamlet as the "sweet Prince" who epitomizes the ideal Renaissance courtier.

There is no danger, to be sure, that Hamlet will ever lose his appeal as an articulate and ardent existentialist—as the prototype of modern man in spiritual crisis. But recent critical studies and productions of the tragedy have raised questions about the "matter" of *Hamlet* that suggest a somewhat less admirable protagonist than most

Shakespeare's company becomes the King's Men: Letters Patent under the Great Seal, 19 May 1603 (Public Record Office, Chancery, Patent Rolls, C.66/1608, m. 4)

of us would like to believe the work presents. It is no longer universally assumed, for example, that the play within the play, by proving the Ghost reliable in his testimony about Claudius's guilt, is sufficient to prove the Ghost "honest" in Hamlet's more fundamental sense. Enough evidence remains to suggest that the Ghost may yet be a "devil" intent on "abusing" the melancholic Hamlet by exhorting him to the kind of vengeance that Elizabethan Christians believed to belong solely to God or to his deputed magistrates. And Hamlet's disinclination to "try" the spirit earlier in the action is but one of many indications that he fails to put to proper use what he elsewhere describes as "godlike reason." A close examination of many of Hamlet's reflective speeches, including his famed "To be or not to be" soliloquy, will show that they serve functions similar to those of Brutus in *Julius Caesar.* By bringing the audience into the protagonist's confidence, they endear him to us and incline us to see everything and everyone else in the action through his eyes. But if we pay careful attention to the nuances of thought and feeling in these meditations, we will notice that many of them tend to be illogical—peppered with non sequiturs and disclosing the kind of emotional stress that renders a person prone to error.

A dispassionate scrutiny of the roles of Rosencrantz and Guildenstern will reveal that, however conventionally ambitious these young courtiers may be, they seem to mean Hamlet well and cannot be shown to be the "adders fanged" that the Prince regards them as having become. The play provides no evidence that they deserve the "sudden death, not shriving time allowed" that Hamlet gleefully bequeaths them; and it is arguable that Shakespeare expected his audience to feel that they *should* be near the Prince's "conscience" when he assures Horatio that they are not. And near the end of the play, when Hamlet disregards the "gaingiving" that warns him not to accept the "wager" proffered by the treacherous Claudius—when he dismisses Horatio's caution and disdains the kind of premonition that "would perhaps trouble a woman"—he allows himself to be seduced (and in a way that parallels Julius Caesar's being led to the Capitol) into a trap that means almost certain death. Far from allowing himself to be guided by Providence, as his New Testament allusions would suggest at this point in the action, Hamlet is being lured by his own pride into an ambush that he might have avoided by heeding his well-founded doubts. As Claudius had predicted, the Prince shows himself to be "remiss."

None of which in any way diminishes the attractiveness of Hamlet's wit and fervor, or suggests that he is not infinitely to be preferred to the "mighty opposite" whose regicide and usurpation he puts to scourge. No, there is no doubt that the Prince uncovers and "sets right" much that is "rotten in the state of Denmark." The only question is whether the play invites us to consider a set of "might have beens" that would have permitted us to approve of the protagonist even more unreservedly than we do. It would seem likely that our identification with Hamlet's cause is meant to be qualified by an awareness that he did not completely find the way "rightly to be great." On the positive side of the ledger, Hamlet's exchange of forgiveness with Laertes goes a long way toward mitigating our sense of the title character's "purposes mistook." And what tragic figure ever received a more touching benediction than "Good night, sweet Prince, / And flights of angels sing thee to thy rest"?

"The whole argument is a whore and a cuckold." So the acid-tongued Thersites sums up the "matter of Troy" and the occasion of *Troilus and Cressida.* We may not wish to see our legendary forebears reduced so unceremoniously to the base matter of lust and dishonor, but there is little in the plot or dialogue of Shakespeare's play to cite in refutation of Thersites' contention. The Trojan War as the dramatist depicts it is in fact a conflict over the ravishingly beautiful but thoughtless Helen (the "whore" whom Paris has stolen away from the "cuckold" Menelaus), and one would have to search hard to find anything to admire in most of the principals who figure in the inconsequential council scenes, squalid intrigues, and interrupted combats that dominate such action as the work affords. Because what *Troilus and Cressida* is largely "about" is a ludicrously unheroic siege to determine whether the Trojans return Helen to the Greeks or see their city fall in defense of a "bad cause" that Troy's own champion considers ethically and politically irresponsible.

As Hector points out, the Trojans can appeal to neither justice nor reason in support of their resolve to keep Helen; the best that anyone can say of her is that, quite apart from what she may be in and of herself, "she is a theme of honor and renown, / A spur to valiant and magnanimous deeds." But when we look for such deeds in the play, what we find on both sides are acts of questionable valor at best (as when Hec-

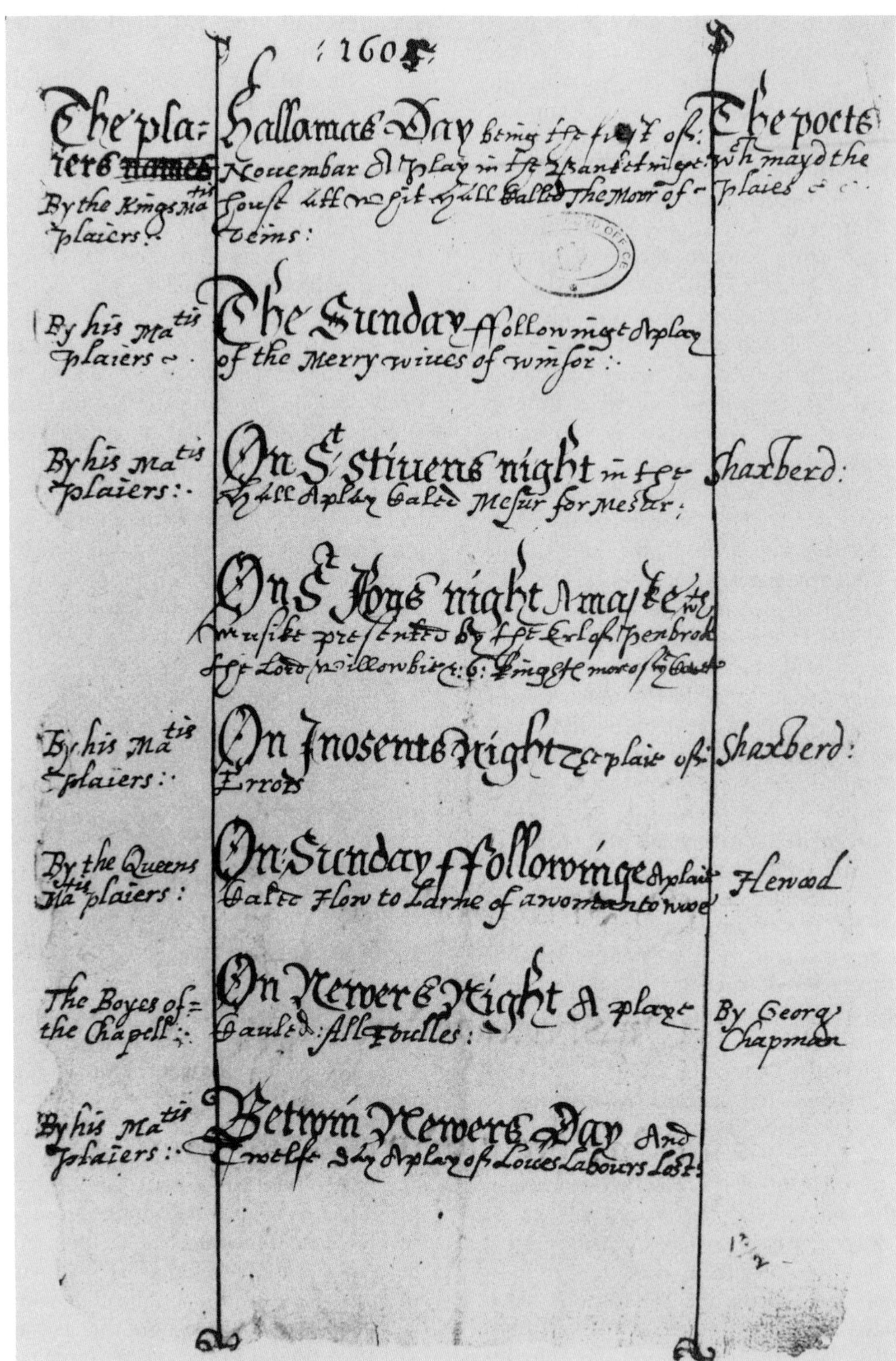

1605

The plaiers		The poets wch mayd the plaies
By the Kings Matis plaiers:	Hallamas Day being the first of Nouembar A play in the Banketinge house att Whithall Called The Moor of Venis:	
By his Matis plaiers	The Sunday ffollowinge A play of the Merry wiues of winsor:	
By his Matis plaiers:	On St Stiuens night in the hall A play Caled Mesur for Mesur:	Shaxberd:
	On St Jons night A maske wth musike presented by the Erl of Penbrok the Lord Willowbie & 6 Knightes more of the Court	
By his Matis plaiers:	On Inosents night the plaie of Errors	Shaxberd:
By the Queens Matis plaiers:	On Sunday ffollowinge A plaie Called How to Larne of a woman to wooe	Hewood
The Boyes of the Chapell:	On Newers Night A playe Caulled: All ffoulles:	By George Chapman
By his Matis plaiers:	Betwin Newers Day And Twelfe day A play of Loues Labours Lost:	

Pages from the account book of Sir Edmund Tilney, Master of the Revels, in which a scribe listed eleven court performances by the King's Men from 1 November 1604 to 31 October 1605. Seven of the plays were by Shakespeare: Othello *(first recorded performance),* The Merry Wives of Windsor, Measure for Measure *(first recorded performance),* The Comedy of Errors, Love's Labor's Lost, Henry V, *and* The Merchant of Venice, *which was performed on two occasions. Though the authenticity of these records was once challenged, they are now generally accepted as genuine (Public Record Office, Audit Office, Accounts, Various, A.O. 3/908/13).*

The plaiers		The poets
	On Twelfe Night The Queens Ma[tie] Maske of Moures wth Aleven Ladies of honnor to Accupayney her ma[tie] wch cam in great showes of devises wch thay satt in wth exselent musike	
By his Ma[tis] plaiers:	On the 7 of January was played the play of Henry the fift:	
By his Ma[tis] plaiers:	The 8 of January A play Cauled Every on out of his umor	
By his Ma[tis] plaiers:	On Candelmas night A playe Every one In his umor	
	The Sunday ffollowing A playe provided And discharged	
By his Ma[tis] plaiers:	On Shrousunday A play of the Marthant of Venis	Shaxberd
By his Ma[tis] plaiers:	On Shroumonday A Tragidye of the Spanishe Maz:	
By his Ma[tis] players:	On Shroutusday A play Cauled The Martchant of Venis Againe Comanded By the Kings Ma[tie]:	Shaxberd:

THE
Tragœdy of Othello,
The Moore of Venice.

As it hath beene diuerſe times acted at the Globe, and at the Black-Friers, by *his Maieſties* Seruants.

Written by VVilliam Shakeſpeare.

LONDON,
Printed by *N. O.* for *Thomas Walkley*, and are to be ſold at his ſhop, at the Eagle and Child, in Brittans Burſſe.
1622.

Title page for the 1622 quarto edition of the second of Shakespeare's four major tragedies (Elizabethan Club, Yale University)

tor, having challenged the Greeks to find a combatant to uphold their honor as lovers, breaks off a hand-to-hand duel with Ajax on the grounds that they are cousins) and downright cowardice at worst (as when Achilles, having come upon the imprudent Hector at a moment when he has removed his armor to rest, cynically summons his Myrmidons to slaughter the pride of the Trojans). Along the way we are treated to the voyeurism of Pandarus, an impotent and diseased bawd whose only pleasure in life is to serve as go-between for Troilus and Cressida, and the homosexual indulgence of Achilles and Patroclus, who have withdrawn from combat because of a slight the prima donna Achilles believes he has suffered at the hands of his general, Agamemnon. Small wonder that Ulysses should observe that "degree is shak'd." And how apt that director Jonathan Miller, in his 1982 BBC television production of *Troilus and Cressida,* should hit upon *M*A*S*H* as the most telling twentieth-century analogue for a satiric seventeenth-century depiction of war as the triumph of irrationality, ennui, and depravity.

There is, to be sure, some momentary relief in the scenes depicting the wooing of Troilus and Cressida. And when the heroine is eventually delivered to the Greek camp at the request of her father, one feels that her submission to Diomede is more a result of her feminine helplessness in a male-controlled world than a manifestation of some prior proclivity to infidelity. But despite the lyricism of Troilus and Cressida's lovemaking, and the agony both lovers feel upon parting, one comes away from this play moved less by the pathos of the love story than by Shakespeare's presentation of what T. S. Eliot, writing three centuries later about another literary work deriving ultimately from Homer, described as a reflection of "the immense panorama of futility and anarchy which is contemporary history." *Troilus and Cressida* must have seemed just as puzzling and "modern" (if not what we now term "post-modern") in the early seventeenth century as James Joyce's *Ulysses* did when it appeared in the early twentieth.

Modern in another sense may be a good way to describe *All's Well That Ends Well.* After a long history of neglect, this tragicomedy has recently enjoyed considerable success in the theater and on television, and one of the explanations is that it features a heroine who, refusing to accept a preordained place in a corrupt patriarchal society, does what she has to do to win her own way.

Orphaned at an early age and reared as a waiting-gentlewoman to the elegant and sensitive Countess of Rossillion, Helena has the audacity to fall in love with the Countess's snobbish son Bertram. Using a cure she learned from her dead father, who had been a renowned physician, Helena saves the life of the ailing King of France, whereupon she is rewarded with marriage to the man of her choice among all the eligible bachelors at the French court. She astonishes Bertram by selecting him. Reluctantly, the young lord consents to matrimony, but before the marriage can be consummated he leaves the country with his disreputable friend Parolles, telling Helena in a letter that he will be hers only when she has fulfilled two presumably impossible conditions: won back the ring he wears upon his finger, and borne a child to him. Disguised as a pilgrim, Helena follows Bertram to Florence. There

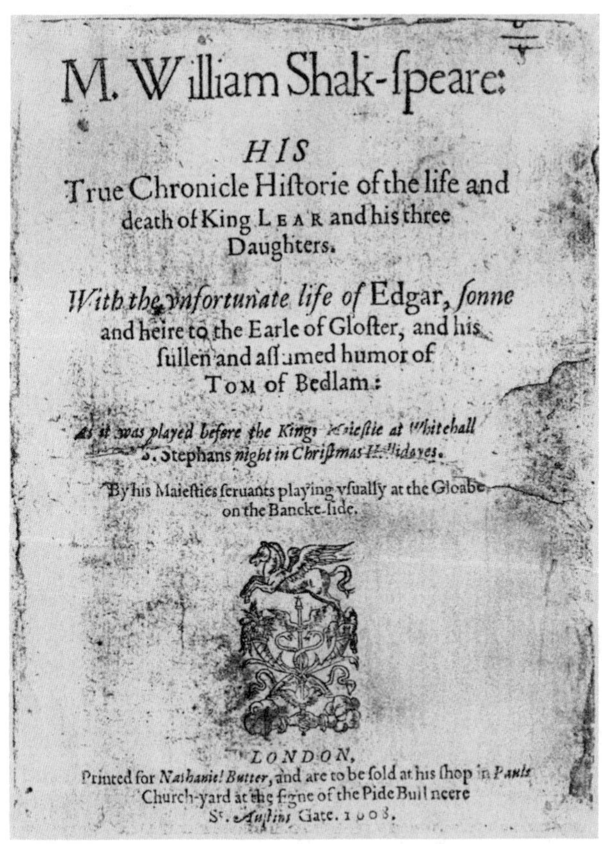

M. William Shak-ſpeare:
HIS
True Chronicle Hiſtorie of the life and death of King LEAR and his three Daughters.
With the vnfortunate life of Edgar, ſonne and heire to the Earle of Gloſter, and his ſullen and aſſumed humor of TOM of Bedlam:
As it was played before the Kings Maieſtie at Whitehall vpon S. Stephans night in Chriſtmas Hollidayes.
By his Maieſties ſeruants playing vſually at the Gloabe on the Bancke-ſide.
LONDON,
Printed for Nathaniel Butter, and are to be ſold at his ſhop in Pauls Church-yard at the ſigne of the Pide Bull neere St. Auſtins Gate. 1608.

Title page for the 1608 quarto edition of what many scholars now regard as a reconstruction based on an earlier version of King Lear *(Bodleian Library)*

she substitutes herself for a maiden named Diana, with whom Bertram has sought an assignation, and satisfies her despicable husband's demands.

One of the "problems" that have troubled critics of *All's Well That Ends Well* is the heroine's "bed trick." We know that Shakespeare had biblical precedent for such a device (Genesis 35), and that it was associated in the Old Testament with divine intervention. But that explanation carries little weight today. Then there are the play's other issues. Why should Helena want so vain and selfish a man as Bertram in the first place? And how can we accept at face value his vow of reformation at the end?

Everything depends upon what Samuel Taylor Coleridge called "poetic faith." If we are willing to suspend our disbelief enough to grant the fairy-tale premises of the plot (which derived from a story in Giovanni Boccaccio's *Decameron*), we should be able to grant as well that in a providentially ordered world, the end may not only justify the means but sanctify them. And if the end that Helena has in view is not only to win Bertram but to make him "love her dearly ever, ever dearly," we must grant the playwright the final marvel of a Bertram who can be brought to see his evil ways for what they are and genuinely repent of them.

A similar metamorphosis would seem to be the final cause of *Measure for Measure.* At the beginning of the play, Duke Vincentio, noting that he has been too lenient in his administration of the laws of Venice, appoints as deputy an icy-veined puritan named Angelo, whom he expects to enforce justice rigorously for a season of much-needed civic discipline. Almost immediately upon the Duke's departure, the naive Angelo finds himself confronted with a novitiate, Isabella, who, in pleading for the life of a brother condemned for fornication, unwittingly arouses the new deputy's lust. Angelo offers her an exchange: her brother's life for her chastity. Astonished by the magistrate's disrespect for both God's laws and man's, Isabella refuses. Later, as she tries to prepare her brother for his death, she discovers that Claudio is less shocked by the deputy's proposition than his sister had been. The disillusioned Isabella upbraids him, too, as a reprobate.

At this point the Duke, who has disguised himself as a friar, persuades Isabella to "accept" Angelo's offer on the understanding that the deputy's former betrothed, Mariana, will meet him instead. Once again the bed trick proves effectual and restorative. In the "trial" that takes place at the entrance to the city upon the Duke's return, Isabella accuses Angelo of perverting his office and executing her brother despite an agreement to pardon him (unknown to Isabella, Claudio's death sentence has been forestalled by the "friar"). But then, in response to Mariana's pleas for her assistance, Isabella decides not to press her claim for justice. Instead she kneels before the Duke to beg that Angelo's life be spared. The Duke grants her request, but only after it is clear that Angelo—illustrating Mariana's statement that "best men are molded out of faults"—has shown himself to be transformed by his discovery of his own frailty.

Measure for Measure qualifies as a tragicomedy because the questions it raises are serious (how to balance law and grace, justice and mercy, in human society) and the issue (whether or not Angelo will be required to pay for his evil intentions) is in doubt until the moment when Isabella does her part to prevent what might have been a kind of revenge tragedy. (The Duke tells Mari-

Macbeth and the Witches, *from the first illustrated edition of Shakespeare's works, edited by Nicholas Rowe in 1709 (Maggs Bros. catalogue, number 550, 1931)*

ana, "Against all sense you do importune her./ Should she kneel down in mercy of this fact, / Her brother's ghost his paved bed would break, / And take her hence in horror.") Justice is tempered with mercy, and characters who might have died in self-deception or guilt are given a second chance. As for Isabella, she too gains insight and compassion as a consequence of her travails. At the conclusion of the play she receives a marriage proposal from her previously disguised counselor, the Duke. Whether she accepts it, and if so how, has become one of the chief "problems" to be solved by directors and actors in productions for today's audiences.

After *Measure for Measure,* so far as we can tell, Shakespeare turned his attention entirely to tragedy for three or four years. By 1604, apparently, he finished *Othello,* the second of the four major tragedies. By 1605 he seems to have completed *King Lear,* the third and, in the estimation of many, the greatest of the group. And by 1606 he had evidently written the last of the "big four," *Macbeth.* During the next two to three years the playwright appears to have turned once more to classical sources, completing *Antony and Cleopatra* and *Coriolanus,* respectively, in 1606-1607 and 1607-1608, and *Timon of Athens* sometime around 1607 or 1608. Only two of these

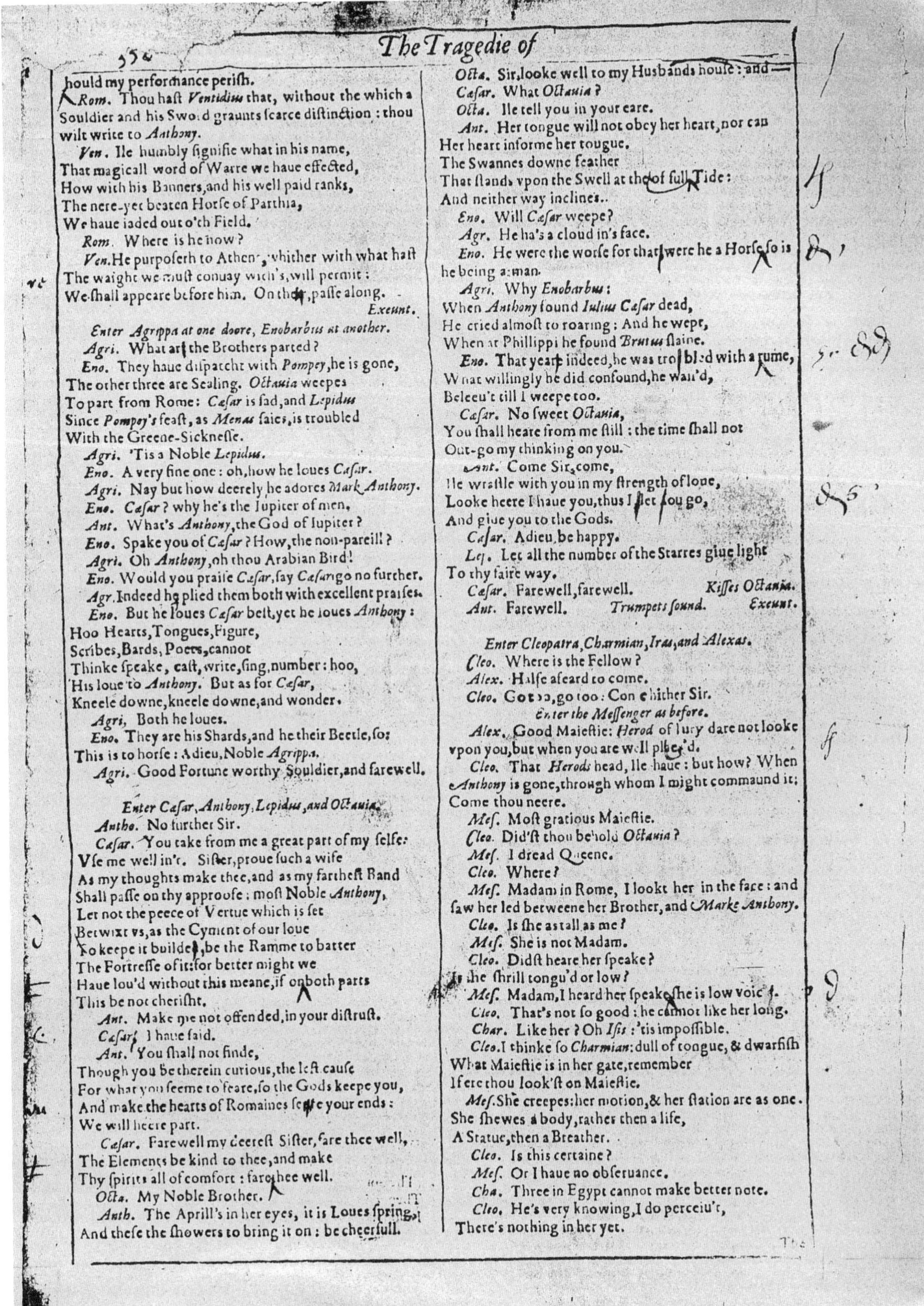

The Tragedie of

hould my performance periſh.
Rom. Thou haſt Ventidius that, without the which a Souldier and his Sword graunts ſcarce diſtinction: thou wilt write to Anthony.
Ven. Ile humbly ſignifie what in his name,
That magicall word of Warre we haue effected,
How with his Banners, and his well paid ranks,
The nere-yet beaten Horſe of Parthia,
We haue iaded out o'th Field.
Rom. Where is he now?
Ven. He purpoſeth to Athens, whither with what haſt
The waight we muſt conuay with's, will permit:
We ſhall appeare before him. On there, paſſe along.
Exeunt.

Enter Agrippa at one doore, Enobarbus at another.

Agri. What are the Brothers parted?
Eno. They haue diſpatcht with Pompey, he is gone,
The other three are Sealing. Octauia weepes
To part from Rome: Cæſar is ſad, and Lepidus
Since Pompey's feaſt, as Menas ſaies, is troubled
With the Greene-Sickneſſe.
Agri. 'Tis a Noble Lepidus.
Eno. A very fine one: oh, how he loues Cæſar.
Agri. Nay but how deerely he adores Mark Anthony.
Eno. Cæſar? why he's the Iupiter of men.
Ant. What's Anthony, the God of Iupiter?
Eno. Spake you of Cæſar? How, the non-pareill?
Agri. Oh Anthony, oh thou Arabian Bird!
Eno. Would you praiſe Cæſar, ſay Cæſar go no further.
Agr. Indeed he plied them both with excellent praiſes.
Eno. But he loues Cæſar beſt, yet he loues Anthony:
Hoo Hearts, Tongues, Figure,
Scribes, Bards, Poets, cannot
Thinke ſpeake, caſt, write, ſing, number: hoo,
His loue to Anthony. But as for Cæſar,
Kneele downe, kneele downe, and wonder.
Agri. Both he loues.
Eno. They are his Shards, and he their Beetle, ſo:
This is to horſe: Adieu, Noble Agrippa.
Agri. Good Fortune worthy Souldier, and farewell.

Enter Cæſar, Anthony, Lepidus, and Octauia.

Antho. No further Sir.
Cæſar. You take from me a great part of my ſelfe:
Vſe me well in't. Siſter, proue ſuch a wife
As my thoughts make thee, and as my fartheſt Band
Shall paſſe on thy approofe: moſt Noble Anthony,
Let not the peece of Vertue which is ſet
Betwixt vs, as the Cyment of our loue
To keepe it builded, be the Ramme to batter
The Fortreſſe of it: for better might we
Haue lou'd without this meane, if on both parts
This be not cheriſht.
Ant. Make me not offended, in your diſtruſt.
Cæſar. I haue ſaid.
Ant. You ſhall not finde,
Though you be therein curious, the leſt cauſe
For what you ſeeme to feare, ſo the Gods keepe you,
And make the hearts of Romaines ſerue your ends:
We will heere part.
Cæſar. Farewell my deereſt Siſter, fare thee well,
The Elements be kind to thee, and make
Thy ſpirits all of comfort: fare thee well.
Octa. My Noble Brother.
Anth. The Aprill's in her eyes, it is Loues ſpring,
And theſe the ſhowers to bring it on: be cheerfull.

Octa. Sir, looke well to my Husbands houſe: and —
Cæſar. What Octauia?
Octa. Ile tell you in your eare.
Ant. Her tongue will not obey her heart, nor can
Her heart informe her tougue.
The Swannes downe feather
That ſtands vpon the Swell at the of full Tide:
And neither way inclines.
Eno. Will Cæſar weepe?
Agr. He ha's a cloud in's face.
Eno. He were the worſe for that were he a Horſe, ſo is he being a man.
Agri. Why Enobarbus:
When Anthony found Iulius Cæſar dead,
He cried almoſt to roaring: And he wept,
When at Phillippi he found Brutus ſlaine.
Eno. That yeare indeed, he was trobled with a rume,
What willingly he did confound, he wail'd,
Beleeu't till I weepe too.
Cæſar. No ſweet Octauia,
You ſhall heare from me ſtill: the time ſhall not
Out-go my thinking on you.
Ant. Come Sir, come,
Ile wraſtle with you in my ſtrength of loue,
Looke heere I haue you, thus I let you go,
And giue you to the Gods.
Cæſar. Adieu, be happy.
Lep. Let all the number of the Starres giue light
To thy faire way.
Cæſar. Farewell, farewell. Kiſſes Octauia.
Ant. Farewell. Trumpets ſound. Exeunt.

Enter Cleopatra, Charmian, Iras, and Alexas.

Cleo. Where is the Fellow?
Alex. Halfe afeard to come.
Cleo. Go to, go too: Come hither Sir.

Enter the Meſſenger as before.

Alex. Good Maieſtie: Herod of Iury dare not looke vpon you, but when you are well pleas'd.
Cleo. That Herods head, Ile haue: but how? When Anthony is gone, through whom I might commaund it:
Come thou neere.
Meſ. Moſt gratious Maieſtie.
Cleo. Did'ſt thou behold Octauia?
Meſ. I dread Queene.
Cleo. Where?
Meſ. Madam in Rome, I lookt her in the face: and ſaw her led betweene her Brother, and Marke Anthony.
Cleo. Is ſhe as tall as me?
Meſ. She is not Madam.
Cleo. Didſt heare her ſpeake?
Is ſhe ſhrill tongu'd or low?
Meſ. Madam, I heard her ſpeake, ſhe is low voic'd.
Cleo. That's not ſo good: he cannot like her long.
Char. Like her? Oh Iſis: 'tis impoſſible.
Cleo. I thinke ſo Charmian: dull of tongue, & dwarfiſh
What Maieſtie is in her gate, remember
If ere thou look'ſt on Maieſtie.
Meſ. She creepes: her motion, & her ſtation are as one.
She ſhewes a body, rather then a life,
A Statue, then a Breather.
Cleo. Is this certaine?
Meſ. Or I haue no obſeruance.
Cha. Three in Egypt cannot make better note.
Cleo. He's very knowing, I do perceiu't,
There's nothing in her yet.

Proof, with corrections in an unknown hand, for Antony and Cleopatra *in the 1623 First Folio (Folger Shakespeare Library)*

plays appeared in quarto printings, *King Lear* in 1608 in what many scholars now regard as a text deriving from an early version of the play, and *Othello* in 1622 in a text of uncertain provenance. Modern editions of *King Lear* and *Othello* generally follow the First Folio printings as their prime authorities, supplementing those renderings where appropriate with readings or passages from the quartos (although, particularly with *King Lear,* where the two printings of the play are thought by many to derive from discrete and self-consistent earlier and later scripts of the play, there is now a school of thought that opposes any conflation of the Folio and quarto versions). The other three tragedies all appeared for the first time in the 1623 Folio.

When we come to *Othello* fresh from a reading of either *Hamlet* or *Measure for Measure*, we can see links with the earlier works in the play's treatment of sexual love and in its preoccupation with ethical questions that turn, ultimately, on retaliation or reconciliation. For whatever else *Othello* is, it is a species of revenge tragedy. To the extent that Iago is impelled by something more specific than what Coleridge termed "motiveless malignity," he is driven by a determination to prove Othello "egregiously an ass" for promoting Michael Cassio rather than Iago to the lieutenancy. By convincing the Moor that his new wife has slept with Cassio, Iago transforms Othello into the principal tool as well as the prime object of his vengeance.

Iago's "poison" is administered in two doses. First he provides enough circumstantial "proof" to make plausible his insinuation that Desdemona has been unfaithful to the Moor. Then, second and far more crucial, he works Othello into such a frenzy that the General is unable to give serious consideration to any response to his "knowledge" other than revenge against both his wife and her supposed lover. Once the Moor becomes persuaded that Desdemona is indeed guilty of infidelity, his instinctive reaction is to exclaim, "But yet the pity of it, Iago! O Iago, the pity of it, Iago!" To which Iago replies, "If you are so fond over her iniquity, give her patent to offend, for if it touch not you, it comes near nobody." Here as elsewhere Iago's method is to get his victim to focus not on Desdemona but on himself. By constantly reiterating such terms as "reputation," "good name," and "honor," he plays upon Othello's insecurity as a dark-skinned alien and implies that his wife's behavior will make him the laughingstock of a refined Venetian society.

It is a mark of his worthiness as a tragic hero that, to the end, Othello retains the "free and open nature" that made him vulnerable to Iago at the outset. Iago may manipulate the Moor into committing a rash and terrible murder, but he cannot reduce Othello entirely to a blunt instrument of the Ensign's hatred. Before the General can bring himself to suffocate Desdemona, he must first delude himself into believing that he is an agent of divine justice. And even in that role his innate compassion leads him to offer his wife a moment to prepare her soul for Heaven. It is true that Othello waxes angry again when Desdemona fails to confess to a crime that would have been inconceivable to her, but one of the things that makes the Moor's deeds pathetic rather than malicious is the fact that he continues to express devotion for his beloved even as he forces himself to snuff out her life. In that as well as in Iago's more cynical sense, then, Othello becomes "an honorable murderer." And no matter how we judge the Moor's final speech and "bloody period," we have to agree with Cassio's assessment that "he was great of heart."

With *King Lear* we come to a work whose pattern is without parallel in the Shakespearean canon. In all the other tragedies, despite the eloquence of the eulogies that convey the protagonists to their eternal destinies, we are left at the end with a nagging sense of misunderstandings and misdeeds that might have been averted or deflected. The basic movement of the plot has been downward, and we come away feeling that we have perceived something that the central characters themselves have been unable or unwilling to see. In those tragedies in which heroes or heroines have committed suicide, we are shown that in so doing they are knowingly or unknowingly admitting failure or submitting to despair, notwithstanding their best efforts to keep their spirits up and evade the full implications of the choices that have brought them to their dismal pass. But this is not the trajectory we find in *King Lear.* Here the spiritual movement (as distinguished from the protagonists' outward fortunes) is essentially upward. To be sure, there are terrible errors and terrifying consequences; in this play, however, we are led to believe that at least some of the pain is purgative. There can be little doubt that both Lear and Gloucester are in some sense "better" men at the end of their lives than they were at the beginning of the action. And if the play is performed in such a way as to emphasize the degree to which two "lust-dieted" old men have been able to learn and grow through the endurance of suffering, the audience is likely to leave the play with a sense of uplift rather than with the weight of unmitigated pity and fear.

This is not to suggest, of course, that there is any less agony and tragic loss in *King Lear* than in Shakespeare's other works in the same genre. Indeed, given the play's cosmic resonance—the honored place it now holds in the tradition represented by such theodicies as the Book of Job, *Paradise Lost,* and *The Brothers Karamazov*—*King Lear* has been thought by many to evoke more philosophical angst than all of Shakespeare's other tragedies combined.

Lear eventually comes to the realization that in the love-test that begins the play he has been "a foolish fond old man." In a parallel recognition the blinded Gloucester acknowledges that he "stumbled when [he] saw." But first both fathers must feel the brunt of the brutality their earlier misdeeds have unleashed upon the world. Having abdicated his throne and divided his kingdom, Lear discovers that he is powerless to prevent his "pelican daughters" from joining with Gloucester's bastard son in an all-out effort to devour it—and each other. The King's faithful Fool wastes away. The loyal Kent and Gloucester's legitimate son Edgar are both reduced to "wretches." And, most insupportable of all, at the end of the play the innocent Cordelia is hanged. For Lear, as he enters cradling his cherished daughter in his arms, her fate is the ultimate punishment for the arrogance and folly that drove him initially to spurn and disinherit "this little seeming substance."

But as heartrending as the play's concluding pietà is for a sensitive playgoer, it can represent "a chance which does redeem all sorrows" if it is staged in keeping with the psychological and spiritual undulations of Lear's dying moments. Just before he says "Pray you undo this button," Lear believes that, as Kent puts it, "all's cheerless, dark, and deadly." After he says "Thank you, sir," however, the King utters what can be read as an exclamation that by some miracle Cordelia yet lives: "Do you see this? Look on her! Look, her lips, / Look there, look there!" In our time these words have most often been treated as expressions of bleak despair. But an interpretation that is at least equally consonant with the rest of the play is that Lear, like Gloucester, " 'Twixt two extremes of passion, joy and grief, / [Bursts] smilingly."

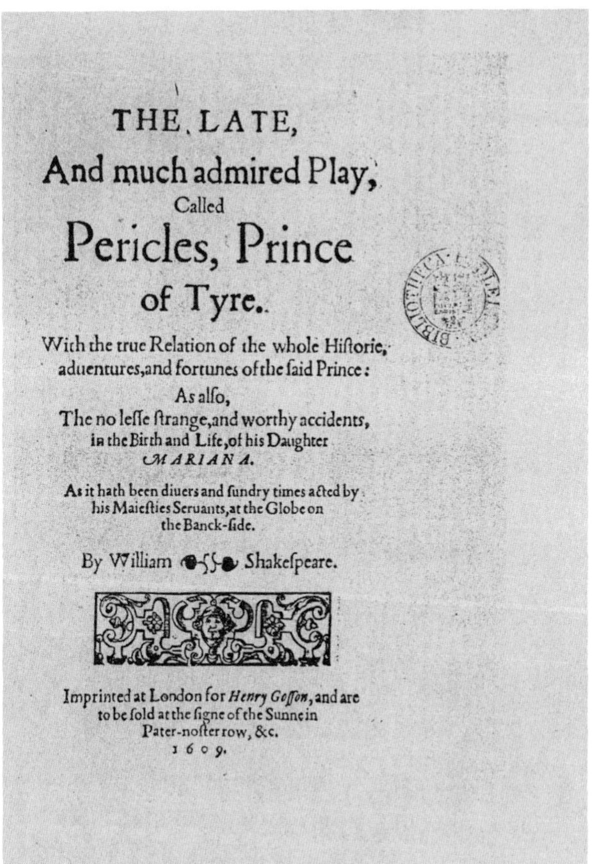

THE LATE,
And much admired Play,
Called
Pericles, Prince
of Tyre.
With the true Relation of the whole Hiſtorie, aduentures, and fortunes of the ſaid Prince:
As alſo,
The no leſſe ſtrange, and worthy accidents, in the Birth and Life, of his Daughter
MARIANA.
As it hath been diuers and ſundry times acted by his Maieſties Seruants, at the Globe on the Banck-ſide.
By William Shakeſpeare.
Imprinted at London for *Henry Goſſon*, and are to be ſold at the ſigne of the Sunne in Pater-noſter row, &c.
1609.

Title page for the 1609 quarto edition of a late romance that was omitted from the 1623 First Folio and not included in a collection of Shakespeare's works until 1664 (Bodleian Library)

We know, of course, that Cordelia is "dead as earth." But it seems fitting that as Lear expires he should see her as alive. If so, it may be nothing more than a merciful hallucination. It may be a desperate man's last grasp at something to sustain a flicker of faith. But it may also register an experience comparable to that of another long-suffering king, the protagonist in Sophocles' *Oedipus at Colonus.* In short, it is conceivable that Lear is here granted a last epiphany that takes him out of this "tough world" to a glimpse of something more benign beyond. Because by the end of his long pilgrimage, in the words of T. S. Eliot's *Little Gidding,* it would seem that the spent King has finally arrived at the ultimate meaning of "nothing": "a condition of complete simplicity, costing not less than everything."

Near the conclusion of Macbeth's bloody reign, as he braces for the closing in of his adversaries, he too would like to achieve a kind of simplicity: "I gin to be aweary of the sun," he says, "And wish th' estate o' th' world were now undone." But in Macbeth's situation the goal to be ob-

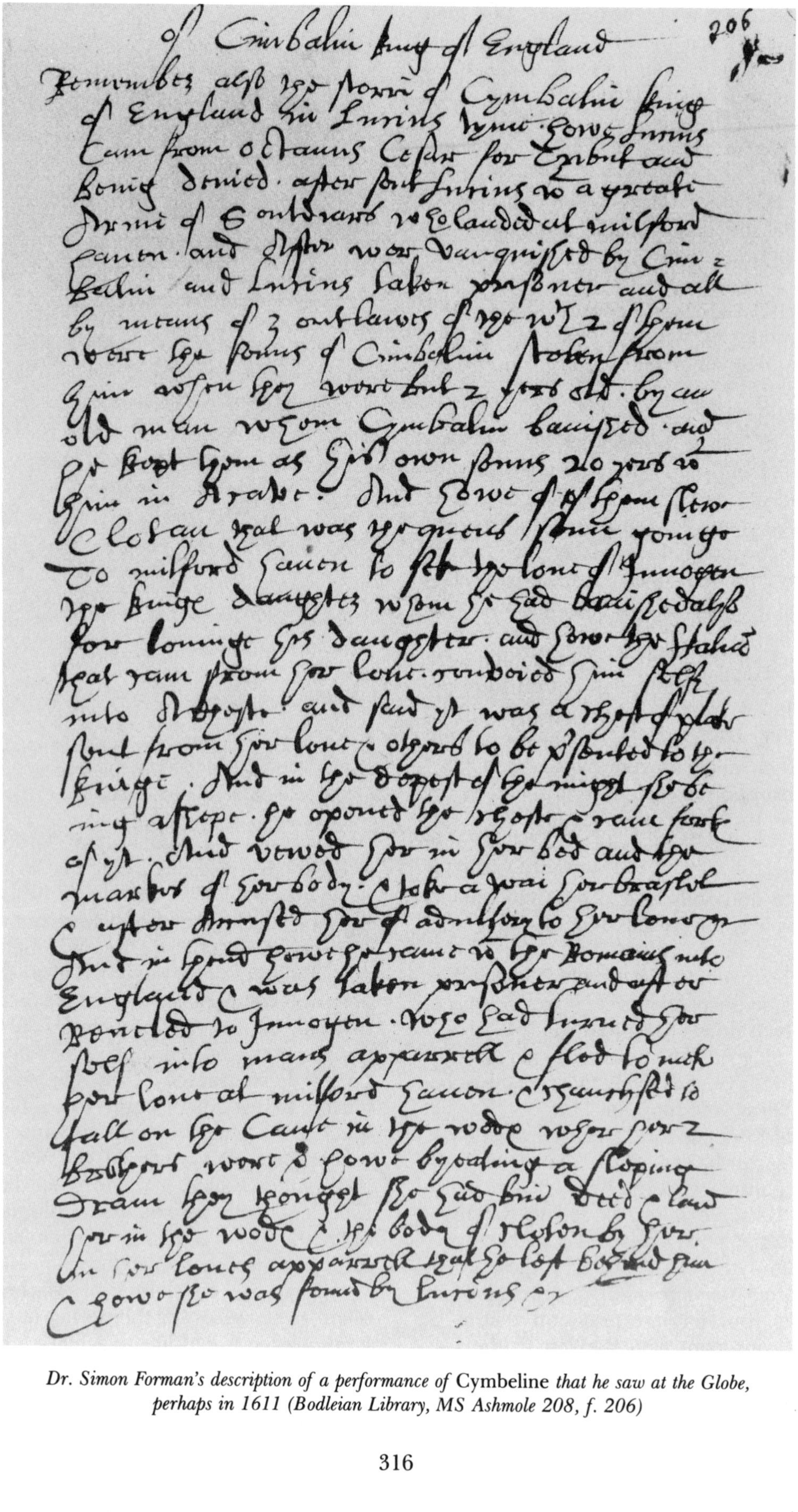

206

Of Cimbalin king of England

Remember also the storri of Cymbalin king
of England in Lucius tyme. howe Lucius
cam from Octavus Cesar for Tribut and
being denied. after sent Lucius wt a greate
Armi of Souldiars who landed at milford
haven. and after wer vanquished by Cimbalin and Lucius taken prisoner and all
by means of 3 outlawes of the which 2 of them
were the sonns of Cimbalim stolen from
him when they were but 2 yers old by an
old man whom Cymbalin banished. and
he kept them as his own sonns 20 yers wt
him in A cave. And howe of of them slewe
Clotan that was the quens sonne goinge
to Milford haven to sek the love of Innogen
the kinge daughter whom he had banished also
for lovinge his daughter. and howe the Italian
that cam from her love conveied him selfe
into A Cheste. and said yt was a chest of plate
sent from her love & others to be presented to the
kinge. And in the depest of the night she beinge aslepe. he opened the cheste & came forth
of yt. And vewed her in her bed and the
markes of her body. & toke awai her braslet
& after Accused her of adultery to her love &c
And in thend howe he came wt the Romains into
England & was taken prisoner and after
Reveled to Innogen. Who had turned her
self into mans apparrell & fled to mete
her love at milford haven. & chanchsed to
fall on the Caue in the wodes wher her 2
brothers were & howe by eating a sleping
Dram they thought she had bin deed & laid
her in the wodes & the body of Cloten by her
in her loves apparrell that he left behind him
& howe she was found by Lucius &c.

Dr. Simon Forman's description of a performance of Cymbeline *that he saw at the Globe, perhaps in 1611 (Bodleian Library, MS Ashmole 208, f. 206)*

tained is "mere oblivion," not the brief but beatific vision of a broken old man for whom at last something has come of the outbursts with which his agonizing pilgrimage commenced. For, unlike Lear, Macbeth has charted a downward course, from the magnificently heroic warrior whom Duncan has greeted as "valiant cousin! worthy gentleman!" to the frenzied tyrant whose acts of regicide and wanton slaughter have "tied [him] to a stake" as the "fiend" who must be executed if the time is ever to be set "free."

As a tragic action, *Macbeth* is almost the polar opposite of *King Lear*. Whereas in *Lear* we may be inclined to feel that in some cases "death is swallowed up in victory," in *Macbeth* we focus on a protagonist whose defeat is merely the prelude to final judgment and damnation. Lear's is a "fortunate fall" that results from miscalculations bred of habitual self-indulgence; it forces the King to contemplate "unaccommodated man" in all his impotence, and it subjects him to a refining "wheel of fire" that purifies him spiritually. Macbeth's is the kind of downfall that springs from premeditated murder in the service of "vaulting ambition." As the usurper himself acknowledges, there are no extenuating circumstances behind which he can shield his crime, and the only change it brings about in Macbeth is to rob him of sleep and security until, "supp'd full with horrors," he eventually loses all capacity for "the taste of fears" or for any other humanizing emotion or sensation. By the final act, life for Macbeth is "but a walking shadow," "a tale / Told by an idiot, full of sound and fury, / Signifying nothing."

And yet, despite his infamy, we still find it possible to participate in, and even in some fashion to identify with, Macbeth's descent into hell. In part this derives from our awareness of his auspicious beginnings—our recollection of that period at the outset when we see the noble Thane tempted but nevertheless resisting the promptings of the Witches and of his ambitious Lady. Because Macbeth himself is aware of the heinousness of the deed he is on the verge of committing, we can empathize with him as a man like one of us. Once he has taken the fatal plunge, moreover, we become parties to his inner turmoil. By means of the soliloquies and meditations that Shakespeare allows us to "overhear," we share Macbeth's torment and anxiety, his feverish desire to put out of mind that which he cannot bear to dwell upon. And thus, even though what he and his wife do is beyond the pale of thinkable human behavior, we can still bring pity and fear to both their plights—recalling, in the words of a famous prayer, that "there, but for the grace of God, go I."

Moving from the Scotland of *Macbeth* to the Mediterranean ambience of *Antony and Cleopatra* is a culture shock so disorienting as almost to make us lose our bearings. Can the same author who gave us Macbeth and Lady Macbeth, two potent personalities who seize power and then degenerate into tremulous tyrants, so soon thereafter have created Antony and Cleopatra, two mercurial characters who seem, at least in their grandiloquent gestures, to become increasingly engaging as their fortunes wane and they throw their power away? And how do we graph the movement of the action in a drama where at least part of the problem is to assess the relative merits of a "Roman" way of looking at things (which judges both lovers as failures because they have declined to elevate civic and military duty above all other human concerns) as opposed to an "Egyptian" way of looking at things (which is based on the premise that one should be willing, in John Dryden's later phrase, to sacrifice "all for love")? Is it likely that Shakespeare expected his audience to bring a coherent "Elizabethan" perspective to bear on both ancient cultures? And if so, what would a person viewing the play from that vantage have thought about Antony and Cleopatra?

These are the kinds of questions a reading of *Antony and Cleopatra* elicits, and the majority of its interpreters during the last three centuries have answered them in a manner that places this work in a category largely its own. Noting that the "Roman" characters are bloodless and coldly calculating—particularly Octavius, who marries his sister Octavia to Antony, ostensibly in an effort to resolve the political differences he has been having with his slothful counterpart in Egypt, but more probably in the expectation that Antony's failures as a husband will provide Octavius a pretext for all-out war—most critics and theater professionals have found them much less appealing than they do the two lovers. The consequence has been that readers and viewers have tended to see Antony and Cleopatra as the protagonists see themselves and thus to regard the play primarily as a dramatization of what John Donne termed "the canonization of love."

The main difficulty with this approach to the action is that it requires us to ignore the many indications that the title characters are im-

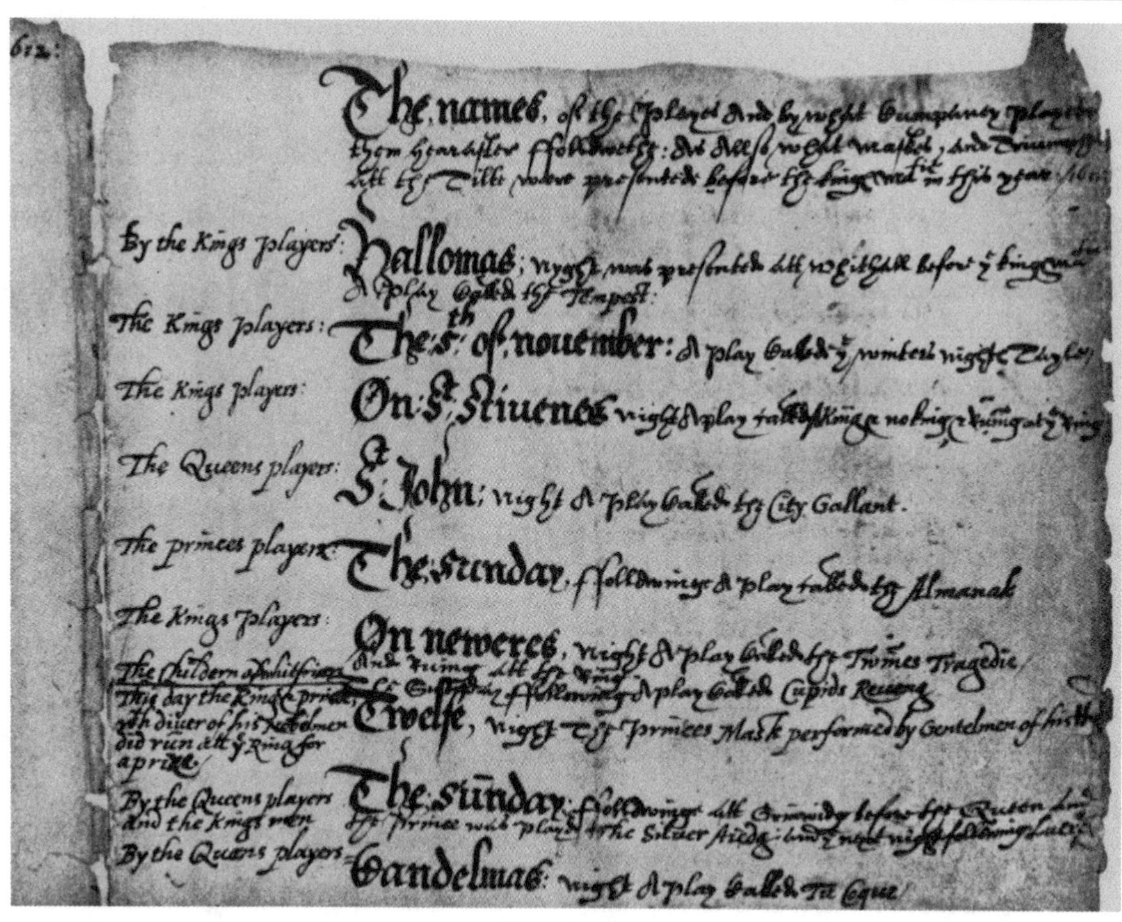

A portion of a page for 1611-1612 from the account book of Sir George Buc, Master of the Revels, in which a scribe listed a performance of The Tempest *at Court on Hallomas (1 November) 1611 (Public Record Office, Audit Office, Accounts, Various)*

pulsive and escapist. A sentimental appraisal of *Antony and Cleopatra* blinds us to clues that the "new Heaven and new Earth" to which the lovers orient their suicides is little more than a fantasyland that they have created as a way of palliating their defeat and impending capture. We may be stirred by Enobarbus's description of the Queen's "infinite variety," and we cannot help admiring the eloquence with which the protagonists prepare themselves for death. But we should remember that it is easy to count the world well lost if through neglect one has already handed it over to one's rivals. An apt Elizabethan gloss on the careers of the central figures might well be borrowed from Shakespeare's Sonnet 129: "All this the world well knows, yet none knows well / To shun the Heaven that leads men to this Hell." The realm inherited by the victorious Octavius will achieve fame for the *pax Romana* into which another "Prince of Peace" is born. But if Shakespeare does little to make us applaud the political folly of Antony and Cleopatra, he does even less to suggest that there is anything endearing in the Caesar whose political efficiency will earn him the title "Augustus."

Because of the vividness of its title characters and the exoticism and luxuriance of its language, *Antony and Cleopatra* has long been one of Shakespeare's most popular plays. But nothing could be farther from the case with its successor. *Coriolanus,* the last of Shakespeare's "Roman plays," is sparing and harsh in much of its diction and spartan in its spectacle. And only rarely—but usually with distinction—has it been performed, even in our own production-rich century.

The hero of the play is one of the least engaging of Shakespeare's major characters. Godlike in battle, where his feats of valor and leadership are so extraordinary as to seem Herculean, Caius Martius Coriolanus becomes a veritable beast when called upon to play a role in the civic affairs of early republican Rome. His contempt for the populace is exceeded only by his hatred of the Tribunes, Sicinius and Brutus, who play

John Lowin, who joined Shakespeare's company in 1603 and became shareholder in the King's Men in 1604 (Dulwich College). By tradition Lowin was the first actor to play Henry VIII and took over the role of Falstaff in the Henry IV plays.

the soldier-general and the common people off against one another. Coriolanus refuses to flatter anyone for any reason, and he lashes out at the hypocrisy required of him when he is told that he must bare his wounds and beg for the "voices" of the plebeians in order to be elected Consul, an office he would not have sought without prompting and a responsibility for which he has little relish. Eventually his intransigence makes Martius so unpopular that he gets himself banished from Rome, to which he offers an arch retort that is perfectly in character: "I banish you!"

Confident that "there is a world elsewhere," Coriolanus departs from the city as "a lonely dragon." But soon, to the astonishment and terror of his native countrymen, he joins forces with Rome's archenemies, the Volscians. In the final movement of the drama he leads an army to the gates of Rome and threatens to abort the nascent Empire. At this point Martius's mother, Volumnia, intervenes and pleads with the hero to spare his birthplace and negotiate a lasting peace between the Romans and the Volscians. Reluctantly, and with a premonition that his decision will prove fatal to him, Coriolanus accedes to his mother's request.

Now Martius finds himself in the unfamiliar role of a diplomat. He has metamorphosed into an infant butterfly, and he proves defenseless against a cunning rival who welcomes an occasion to destroy him. Almost as soon as Coriolanus begins speaking to the Volscian lords, the foxlike Aufidius accuses him of treason and calls him a "boy of tears." Predictably, this arouses Coriolanus to one last intemperate eruption, and Aufidius's thugs rise up and slaughter him.

Just what *Coriolanus* is "about" has been much debated. But critics as varied as T. S. Eliot

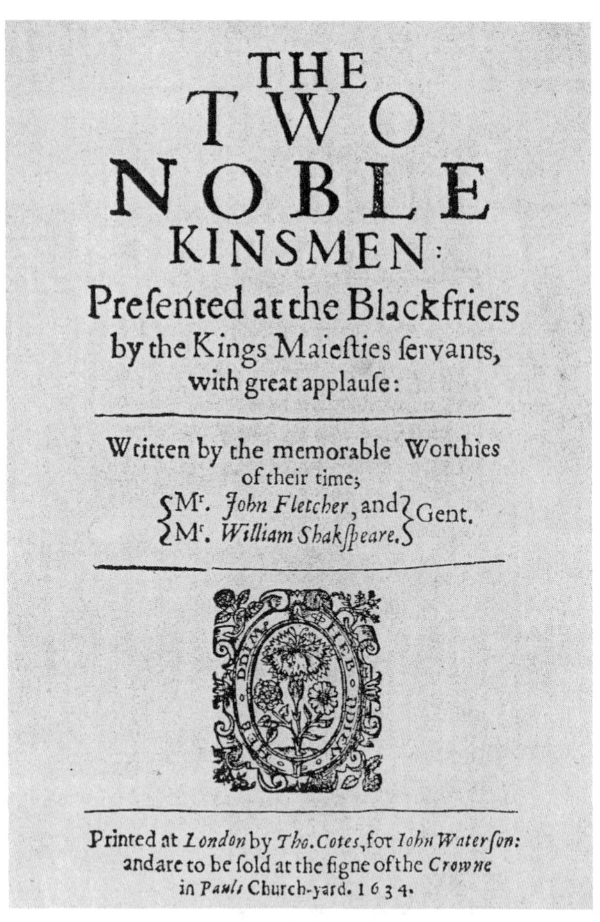

THE
TWO
NOBLE
KINSMEN:
Preſented at the Blackfriers
by the Kings Maieſties ſervants,
with great applauſe:

Written by the memorable Worthies
of their time;
Mr. *John Fletcher*, and Mr. *William Shakſpeare.* Gent.

Printed at *London* by *Tho. Cotes*, for *Iohn Waterſon*:
and are to be ſold at the ſigne of the *Crowne*
in *Pauls* Church-yard. 1634.

Title page for the 1634 quarto edition of a play that Shakespeare wrote with the playwright who succeeded him as chief dramatist for the King's Men (Maggs Bros. catalogue, number 493, 1927)

and Frank Kermode, and actors as distinguished as Laurence Olivier and Alan Howard, have shown that it can be a challenging and at times a thrilling drama. In all likelihood it will receive more attention—and admiration—in the future than it has tended to receive in the past.

Whether this will be true of Shakespeare's final experiment in tragedy, *Timon of Athens,* is less certain. Derived, like the three mature Roman plays, primarily from Plutarch's *Lives, Timon of Athens* is generally regarded as a work that the author abandoned before he had completed its finishing touches. This may or may not be true, but there is no indication that the play was ever performed in Shakespeare's lifetime, and it has only appeared sporadically (and seldom notably) in the centuries since.

As a character, Timon has affinities with Lear and Coriolanus. Like Lear, he comes to think of himself as a victim of ingratitude, a man "more sinned against than sinning." And, like Coriolanus, he responds to his mistreatment by "banishing" all society from his presence. Unlike either character, however, Timon is incapable of growth or compromise. Once he has spurned the "friends" who have refused to help him with the creditors his excessive generosity has brought to the door, Timon retreats to a cave and scorns every entreaty to concern himself with his fellowman. His foil, the banished Alcibiades, can forgive Athens its injustices and spare the city he has returned to annihilate. But Timon elects to spend the rest of his life in exile, cursing all of humanity and bestowing gold, which he now sees as the root of all evil, the plague of civilization, on the whores who come to seek him out.

Critics such as G. Wilson Knight and Rolf Soellner have argued valiantly for the poetic, philosophical, and theatrical merits of *Timon of Athens.* But its acerbic tough-mindedness makes even more demands upon an audience than does *Troilus and Cressida* and few have given it the careful study it requires for proper appreciation.

After *Coriolanus* and *Timon of Athens,* Shakespeare seems to have shifted his focus once again. He wrote no more tragedies, so far as we know, and the single "history play" that appeared at the end of his career was so different from the dramatist's previous efforts in that genre that it seems to belong to the realm of romance rather than to the world of ordinary political and social interaction. Indeed "romance" is now the generic term most frequently applied to the mature tragicomedies that are usually referred to, somewhat loosely, as "the late plays." If we include *Henry VIII* in their number, there are six surviving works that qualify as late romances. One of them, *The Two Noble Kinsmen,* we know to have been written by Shakespeare in collaboration with his fellow dramatist John Fletcher. Two others, *Pericles* and *Henry VIII,* are also regarded by many scholars as likely to have resulted from joint authorship—as was evidently the case, too, with the lost *Cardenio,* attributed to Shakespeare and Fletcher in a Stationers' Register entry of 1753. This leaves us with three plays—*Cymbeline, The Winter's Tale,* and *The Tempest*—that are unanimously accepted as works entirely by Shakespeare.

Since all but one of the late plays (*Pericles,* which seems to have been completed in 1606-1608) appeared after Shakespeare's company added the Blackfriars as a venue for performance—and since even that work may have been written with indoor staging in view (we

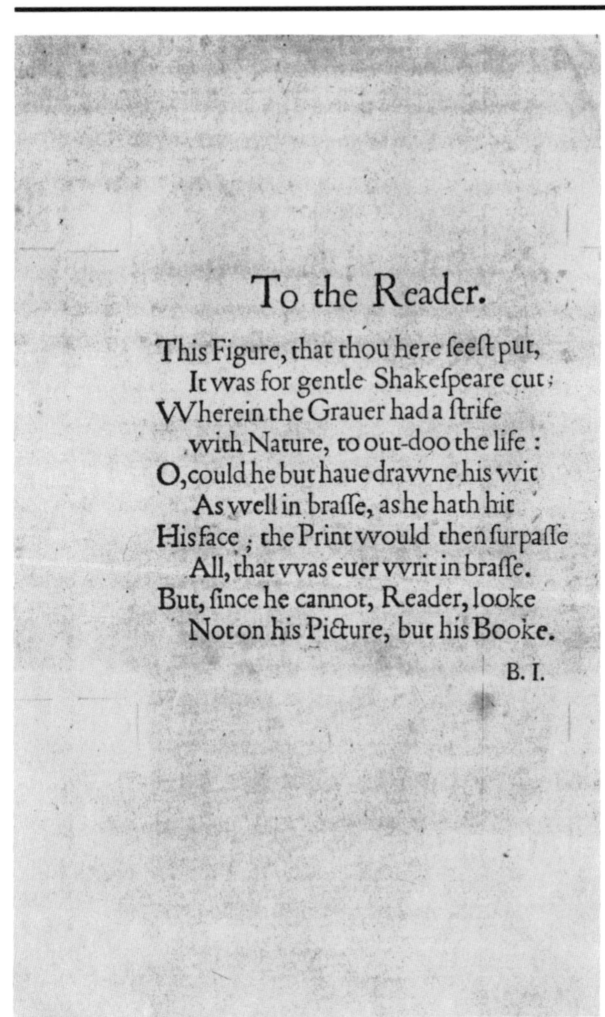
To the Reader.

This Figure, that thou here ſeeſt put,
It was for gentle Shakeſpeare cut;
Wherein the Grauer had a ſtrife
with Nature, to out-doo the life :
O, could he but haue drawne his wit
As well in braſſe, as he hath hit
His face ; the Print would then ſurpaſſe
All, that was euer writ in braſſe.
But, ſince he cannot, Reader, looke
Not on his Picture, but his Booke.

B. I.

MR. WILLIAM
SHAKESPEARES
COMEDIES,
HISTORIES, &
TRAGEDIES.
Publiſhed according to the True Originall Copies.

LONDON
Printed by Iſaac Iaggard, and Ed. Blount. 1623.

Note to the reader by Ben Jonson and title page for the First Folio (Folger Shakespeare Library). The engraved portrait is generally thought to be by Martin Droeshout the younger, who was fifteen when Shakespeare died and twenty-two when this volume was published. Droeshout is unlikely to have drawn Shakespeare from life and probably worked from a drawing or painting given to him. It has been pointed out that the volume's editors, John Heminge and Henry Condell—both shareholders in Shakespeare's company—accepted the portrait for inclusion in the volume, though the fact that it was twice revised during the printing of the First Folio indicates that it was considered to be less than perfect.

know that *Pericles* was presented at Court sometime between May 1606 and November 1608)—it seems eminently possible, as Gerald Eades Bentley has suggested, that the author's modifications in dramaturgical style resulted, at least in part, from changes in emphasis by the King's Men. If the playwright and his colleagues were easing away from total dependence on the comparatively broad-based audiences they had long attracted to the Globe and were beginning to cast their fortunes more confidently with the aristocratic clientele they served at Court or would be able to cultivate at the more elegant Blackfriars theater, they may well have begun to rethink their dramatic repertory. Under these circumstances, the poet and his fellow shareholders could readily have arrived at a determination to concentrate on the kinds of offerings their more well-to-do audiences enjoyed: masquelike entertainments of the sort that Court patronage encouraged, and mythological and fanciful diversions of the type that the children's companies had made their specialty in indoor halls like the Blackfriars.

In any event, the dramatic works initiated by *Pericles* are strikingly different in many respects from the sequence that preceded them. Relying as most of them do on such devices as a choral "presenter" (Gower in *Pericles,* or Time in *The Winter's Tale*) to narrate background incidents, the romances tend to be rambling and panoramic by comparison with the earlier plays (the salient exception being *The Tempest,* which is unusually fo-

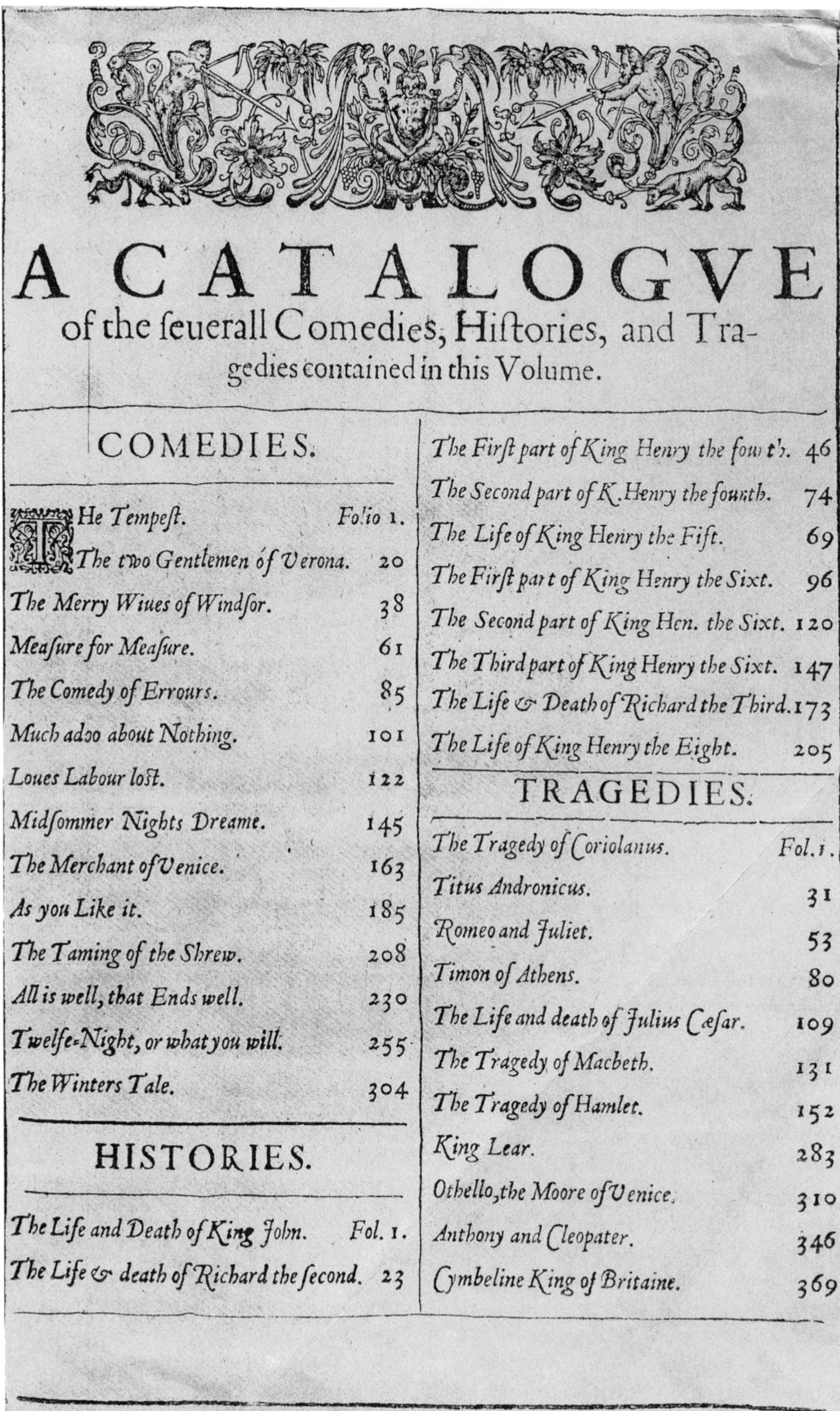

A CATALOGVE
of the ſeuerall Comedies, Hiſtories, and Tragedies contained in this Volume.

COMEDIES.

The Tempeſt. Folio 1.
The two Gentlemen of Verona. 20
The Merry Wiues of Windſor. 38
Meaſure for Meaſure. 61
The Comedy of Errours. 85
Much adoo about Nothing. 101
Loues Labour loſt. 122
Midſommer Nights Dreame. 145
The Merchant of Venice. 163
As you Like it. 185
The Taming of the Shrew. 208
All is well, that Ends well. 230
Twelfe-Night, or what you will. 255
The Winters Tale. 304

HISTORIES.

The Life and Death of King John. Fol. 1.
The Life & death of Richard the ſecond. 23
The Firſt part of King Henry the fourth. 46
The Second part of K. Henry the fourth. 74
The Life of King Henry the Fift. 69
The Firſt part of King Henry the Sixt. 96
The Second part of King Hen. the Sixt. 120
The Third part of King Henry the Sixt. 147
The Life & Death of Richard the Third. 173
The Life of King Henry the Eight. 205

TRAGEDIES.

The Tragedy of Coriolanus. Fol. 1.
Titus Andronicus. 31
Romeo and Juliet. 53
Timon of Athens. 80
The Life and death of Julius Cæſar. 109
The Tragedy of Macbeth. 131
The Tragedy of Hamlet. 152
King Lear. 283
Othello, the Moore of Venice. 310
Anthony and Cleopater. 346
Cymbeline King of Britaine. 369

Table of contents for the First Folio (Folger Shakespeare Library). In addition to the plays listed here, the volume contains Troilus and Cressida.

cused in time, place, and action). Frequently they contain incidents that are wildly implausible (as when Antigonus exits "pursued by a bear" in *The Winter's Tale*), and most of them draw heavily on storms, shipwrecks, and other violently disruptive "acts of God" to move the action forward. Families are separated at sea, left to wander for years in adversity, and then miraculously reunited at the close. Symbolically named children (Marina in *Pericles,* Perdita in *The Winter's Tale,* Miranda in *The Tempest*) function dramatically as instruments of special grace, restoring faith and vision to parents who have temporarily lost their way. Terrible calamities are but narrowly averted, and then only because of sudden reversals that depend either upon some character's astonishing change of heart or upon an inexplicable visitation from above. Rather than conceal their artifice, the romances tend to display it openly, on the one hand reminding the audience that what it is witnessing is only make-believe, on the other hand manipulating viewers' responses so as to prepare the theater for a climactic "wonder" that will turn out to have been the purpose behind all the preceding action.

The first three acts of *Pericles* seem so naive dramaturgically that many scholars consider them, rightly or wrongly, to be by a playwright other than Shakespeare. Among the contemporaries whose names have been proposed for the dubious honor of coauthor in accordance with this hypothesis is George Wilkins, whose novel *The Painful Adventures of Pericles Prince of Tyre* appeared in the same year (1608) as the entry for *Pericles* in the Stationers' Register. All we know for certain is that the play was first published in 1609 in a relatively crude quarto that was reprinted several times before *Pericles* made its initial folio entry in the second issue of the Third Folio in 1664. Just why *Pericles* was not included in the First Folio has never been determined. Its omission may have had something to do with the poor condition of the only available text. It may have resulted from difficulties in obtaining publication rights to the work. Or it may have stemmed from the compilers' knowledge that the play was not completely by Shakespeare. The third of these hypotheses would also account for the exclusion of *The Two Noble Kinsmen* (though of course it would not account for the *in*clusion of *Henry VIII* if, as many scholars believe, that too was a work that Shakespeare wrote in collaboration with another playwright).

Whatever the case, *Pericles* is immediately recognizable as a point of departure. Drawing from a fifth-century narrative about a prince named Apollonius of Tyre, as retold in the *Confessio Amantis* of the fourteenth-century English poet John Gower, the play is studiously "antique" in its apparently unsophisticated presentational style. Old Gower himself is resurrected to serve as the barnacled chorus, and the singsong tetrameters that serve as the metrical vehicle for his medieval diction remove the play's events from the present to a dreamlike past more suited to legend than to realistic fiction. In such an atmosphere the audience is induced to suspend its habitual expectations, with the consequence that playgoers become vicarious participants in episode after strange episode as the hero's adventures convey him from youth (when he solves the riddle of Antiochus and is immediately forced to flee for his life upon disclosing the wicked King's incestuous relationship with his daughter) through old age (when, having been reduced almost to despair by decades of wandering and loss, he is miraculously rejoined with his radiant daughter, Marina). As we allow ourselves to be hypnotized into accepting the premises of such a fairy-tale universe, we fall under the spell of a "moldy tale" peopled by such characters as a wicked stepmother (Dionyza), a Bawd, and a Governor (Lysimachus) who becomes so enraptured by Marina's innocence that he extracts her from the brothel into which she has been sold and makes her his wife.

Pericles' final "awakening" has often been compared to Lear's reunion with Cordelia. And a lovely lyric ("Marina") by T. S. Eliot is eloquent testimony that twentieth-century audiences can still be moved by a beloved child's power to regenerate her father and renew his will to live. Until recently *Pericles* has rarely been performed, but as the magic of its marvels becomes more widely known, it may one day find a secure footing in the repertory.

Such may also be the case with *Cymbeline.* First printed in the 1623 Folio, it probably enjoyed its initial performances in 1609-1610, either at Blackfriars or at the Globe (where the physician Dr. Simon Forman saw it, evidently in 1611). Its historical framework, featuring a pre-Christian British monarch from approximately the same era as King Lear, derives primarily from Holinshed's *Chronicles.* In this portion of the play, wherein Cymbeline at first refuses and then later volunteers his kingdom's annual tribute to Emperor Augustus Caesar, Shakespeare alludes to the commingling of British and Roman traits that Renaissance Englishmen believed to be the source of their nation's greatness. Within this political context the playwright develops other motifs, his sources varying from Boccaccio's *Decameron* to a pair of anonymous plays of the 1580s, *The Rare Triumphs of Love and Fortune* and *Sir Clyomon and Sir Clamydes.* The result is a romantic tragicomedy unusually episodic in structure and so breathtaking in the rapidity and complexity of its concluding disclosures as to leave an audience wondering how any agency other than Providence could possibly have tangled and untangled the strands of so intricate a web.

At the heart of the play is Imogen, a princess of exemplary chastity whose husband Posthumus allows himself to be tricked into a foolhardy wager that leads to his conviction that she has been seduced by a braggart named Iachimo. Like the brave heroines in Shakespeare's earlier tragicomedies, Imogen assumes a male disguise in her efforts to preserve herself in a perilous world. In time her circumstances bring her to the cave where Cymbeline's long-lost sons, Guiderius and Arviragus, have been reared in rustic exile by an old lord, Belarius, whom the King has unjustly banished. She casts her lot with them and eventually becomes a page in the service of the general who conducts Rome's invasion of Britain. Once the Romans are repulsed, she is reunited with her father, Cymbeline, and her penitent husband. In the same denouement the King learns that his long-lost sons are still alive. Then in a reconciliation that carries overtones of the Augustan *pax Romana* under which Christ was born, Cymbeline announces that "Pardon's the word to all." Evil has been exorcised (the King's "bad angels," his wicked Queen and her doltish son Cloten, have died); Belarius, Iachimo, and Posthumus have been forgiven; and the wayward characters who survive have all experienced contrition and enlightenment.

Contrition and enlightenment are prerequisite to the happy ending of *The Winter's Tale* too. Here again a husband falls victim to vengeful jealousy, and here again the plot builds up to the moment when he can finally be freed from the folly that, so far as he knows, has brought about his innocent wife's death. Based primarily on Robert Greene's *Pandosto: The Triumph of Time,* a prose romance first published in 1588 and reprinted under a new title in 1607, *The Winter's Tale* was probably completed in 1610 or 1611. Its initial appearance in print was in the 1623 Folio.

The action begins when Leontes, King of Sicilia, is seized with the "humour" that his wife Hermione has committed adultery with his childhood friend Polixenes. It is abundantly clear to everyone else, most notably Leontes' faithful steward Camillo and Hermione's lady-in-waiting Paulina, that Leontes' suspicions are irrational. But he refuses to listen either to the counsel of his advisers or to the oracle at Delphi—persisting with his "trial" of Hermione until he has largely devastated his court. He drives Polixenes away, and with him the virtuous Camillo, who has warned the Bohemian king that his life is in danger; he frightens to death his son Mamilius; and he pursues Hermione so relentlessly that she finally wilts into what Paulina declares to be a fatal swoon. At this point, suddenly recognizing that he has been acting like a madman, Leontes vows to do penance for the remainder of his life.

Years later, after Perdita (the "lost" child whom the raging Leontes has instructed Paulina's husband Antigonus to expose to the elements) has grown up, supposedly as an old shepherd's daughter, and fallen in love with Florizel, the heir to Polixenes' throne in Bohemia, the major characters are providentially regathered in Leontes' court. The joyous King is reunited with his daughter. And then, in one of the most stirring and unexpected moments in all of Shakespeare's works, a statue of Hermione that Paulina unveils turns out to be the living—and forgiving—Queen whom Leontes had "killed" some sixteen years previously. In a speech that might well serve to epitomize the import of all the late romances, Paulina tells the King, "It is requir'd / You do awake your faith." Like a latter-day Pygmalion, the regenerated Leontes embraces his long-lamented wife, bestows the widowed Paulina on the newly returned Camillo, and blesses the forthcoming marriage of Perdita to the son of his old friend Polixenes, the object of the jealousy with which the whole agonizing story began.

The circle that is completed in *The Winter's Tale* has its counterpart in *The Tempest,* which culminates in the marriage of Prospero's daughter Miranda to Ferdinand, the son of the Neapolitan king who had helped Prospero's wicked brother Antonio remove Prospero from his dukedom in Milan a dozen years previously.

Like *The Winter's Tale, The Tempest* was completed by 1611 and printed for the first time in the 1623 Folio. Because it refers to the "still-vext Bermoothes" and derives in part from several accounts of the 1609 wreck of a Virginia-bound

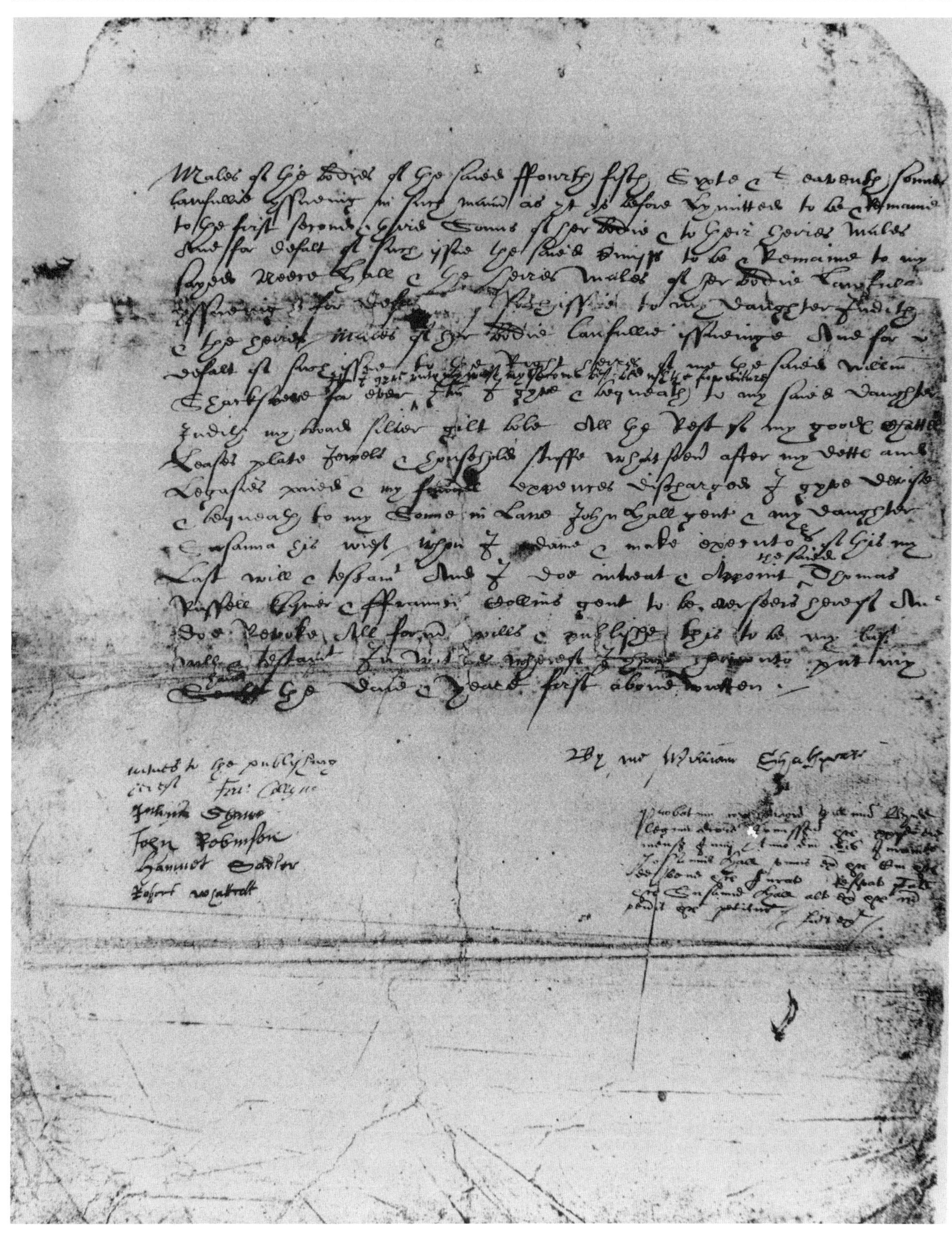

The last page of Shakespeare's will, written by lawyer Francis Collins or his scribe in January 1616 and revised in March, when Shakespeare signed each of the three pages (Public Record Office, Principal Probate Registry, Selected Wills, Prob. 1/4)

ship called the *Sea Adventure,* the play has long been scrutinized for its supposed commentary on the colonial exploitation of the New World.

Nothwithstanding the details that Shakespeare drew from accounts of Bermuda and the Caribbean tropics, Prospero's isle is probably to be thought of as a Mediterranean locale. But there can be no doubt that under Prospero's ministrations the setting of *The Tempest* becomes a locale whose features transcend our normal understanding of geographical boundaries.

At times, when he is recalling the usurpation that has placed him and his daughter on the island they have shared with Caliban for a dozen lonely years, the aging Duke is reminiscent of Lear; despite his earlier indiscretions, the Duke has cause to feel like a victim of ingratitude. At other times, when he is ordering the spirit Ariel to manipulate the comings and goings of the enemies he has brought aground in a violent storm, Prospero reminds us of the Duke of Vienna in *Measure for Measure.* But though his influence on the lives of others turns out in the end to have been "providential," Prospero arrives at his beneficence only through a psychological and spiritual process that turns upon his forswearing "vengeance" in favor of the "rarer action" of forgiveness. Such dramatic tension as the play possesses is to be found in the audience's suspense over whether the protagonist will finally use his Neoplatonic magic for good or for ill. And once Prospero has brought the "men of sin" to a point where they must confront themselves for what they are and beg for mercy, it is paradoxically Ariel who first notes that to be truly human is ultimately to be humane.

Uniquely among the late tragicomic romances, *The Tempest* has long been a favorite with both readers and playgoers. Its ardent young lovers have always held their charm, as has the effervescent Ariel, and its treatment of the temptations afforded by access to absolute power gives it a political and religious resonance commensurate with the profundity of its exploration of the depths of poetic and dramatic art. In the final analysis its burden seems to be that an acknowledgment of the limits imposed by mortality is the beginning of wisdom.

Significantly, these limits apply to an "insubstantial pageant" such as *The Tempest,* and even to "the great globe itself." The epilogue makes it clear that the "isle" from which Prospero seeks help to set sail is, among other things, the theater that a player and a playwright share with an audience they hope will be gracious and compassionate.

The last of the plays attributed wholly to the dramatist by its inclusion in the First Folio, where it first achieved print, is *Henry VIII.* Modern stylistic analyses have called Shakespeare's sole authorship into question, but since the case for collaboration has never been definitively proven we may be forgiven if, for this play as for *Pericles,* we proceed on the assumption that it was mostly if not entirely a work for which the playwright was responsible. Its theatrical history has had more ups and downs than is true of many of Shakespeare's plays (the most notable occurrence on the downside being the accident during its earliest recorded performance, on 29 June 1613, that burned the Globe to the ground, leaving "not a rack behind"), and its critical reception, like that of *Troilus and Cressida,* has been complicated by debates about its genre.

In many respects *Henry VIII* seems to be the capstone to Shakespeare's nine earlier English history plays. It focuses on responsible monarchy as the key to a nation's political and social stability, and it glorifies the Tudor dynasty as God's means of bringing peace, prosperity, and empire to an England whose greatness had reached new heights during the reigns of the two rulers under whom Shakespeare had served. Fittingly, the drama's "final cause" is the birth of Elizabeth, the "royal infant" whose advent, according to the prophecy uttered by Archbishop Cranmer at the end of the action, "promises / Upon this land a thousand thousand blessings." Meanwhile, as is so often true in Shakespeare, the play also offers a topical glance at an event of contemporary significance, in this instance the February 1613 wedding of Princess Elizabeth, daughter of King James I and his Queen, to Frederick, the Elector of Palatine.

Like the earlier English history plays, *Henry VIII* is epic in scope and in its patriotic impulse. And like them, it manifests the author's interest in the grand themes of English historiography, as reflected not only in the 1587 second edition of Holinshed's *Chronicles* but also in other sources as varied as John Foxe's *Acts and Monuments* (1563) and John Speed's *History of Great Britain* (1611). In its earliest performances *Henry VIII* even seems to have had an alternate title, *All is True,* to assert its fidelity to the essence of its subject matter. But a close examination of its way of treating that material will indicate that, far more than the history plays that preceded it, *Henry VIII* presents the events it dramatizes almost solely in the light of eternity.

Though the King is not without his faults, he is portrayed more positively by Shakespeare than he had usually been by the chroniclers the playwright drew upon. During the first half of the play the bluff Henry may be misled by his "bad angel" Cardinal Wolsey; but the King's intentions come across as noble, and after Wolsey's discomfiture he evolves into a creditable exemplar of God's deputy. Meanwhile, there is an unmistakable emphasis on Heaven's mysterious ways. The action is structured around a succession of "trials," each of which serves to test a character's mettle and to induce in him or her a new degree of self-knowledge, humility, faith, and compassion. In the early going Buckingham is framed by Wolsey's machinations, but as he proceeds to his execution he forgives his enemies and blesses the monarch who has condemned him. Katherine, another of Wolsey's victims, pleads eloquently and forcibly in her own defense; but once her fate is settled, she resigns herself with patience to the destiny prepared for her and even expresses pity for her archenemy Wolsey. As for Wolsey, once he recognizes that there is no escape from the noose he has unwittingly prepared for himself, he himself dies penitent and "never so happy." In each instance death is swallowed up in a victory of sorts, and the sequence as a whole implies that even in the often-brutal arena of English history all's well that ends well.

Perhaps the best way to describe *Henry VIII* is to call it a tragicomic historical romance. Whatever it is generically, it is a play that offers a plenitude of majestic pageantry. As the 1979 BBC television production reminded us, it is what Shakespeare would have written if his day had had *Masterpiece Theatre.*

Whether or not it is the last work in which Shakespeare had a hand, *The Two Noble Kinsmen* is probably the last surviving instance of the playwright's dramaturgy. With but a handful of exceptions, modern scholars regard the play as a collaborative effort in which the guiding hand was John Fletcher's rather than that of his older colleague. It was probably completed in 1613, and its first appearance in print was in a quarto edition of 1634 that attributed it to both authors. It was reprinted in the Beaumont and Fletcher second folio of 1679, but it never appeared in any of the seventeenth-century folios of Shakespeare's dramatic works.

The play is a dramatization of Geoffrey Chaucer's "Knight's Tale" about two cousins, Palamon and Arcite, who come to blows as a consequence of their both having fallen in love with the same damsel, Emilia. Like the other late romances of Shakespeare, it has a remote Mediterranean setting (ancient Thebes and Athens), it invokes the gods for intervention in human affairs, and it depends for its effects on scenes of grand spectacle such as the wedding procession of Theseus and Hippolyta. It is not a great work, but it has probably received less notice than it merits.

Tradition holds that Shakespeare returned to Stratford for his declining years, and three years after the burning of the Globe his own flame went out. Following his death on 23 April 1616, he was laid to rest where fifty-two years earlier he had been christened. Shortly thereafter, a monument to his memory was erected above the tomb in Holy Trinity, and that monument is still in place for Shakespeare admirers to see today. But the greatest testament to his immortality appeared seven years later, when his theatrical colleagues John Heminge and Henry Condell (both of whom had been mentioned in the playwright's will) assembled their collection of his plays. The 1623 First Folio was a labor of love, compiled as "an office to the dead, to procure his orphans guardians" and "to keep the memory of so worthy a friend and fellow alive as was our Shakespeare."

Our Shakespeare. It is not without exaggeration that the book that preserves what is probably his most reliable portrait and the most authoritative versions of the majority of his dramatic texts (indeed the *only* surviving versions of roughly half of them) has been called "incomparably the most important work in the English language."

In the words and actions that fill his poems and plays, in the performances that enrich our theaters and silver screens, in the countless offshoots to be found in other works of art, and in the influence the playwright continues to have on virtually every aspect of popular culture throughout the world, now as much as in the age of Elizabeth and James, Shakespeare lives.

Bibliographies:

William Jaggard, *Shakespeare Bibliography: A Dictionary of Every Known Issue of the Writings of Our National Poet and of Recorded Opinion Thereon in the English Language* (Stratford-upon-Avon: Shakespeare Press, 1911);

The Shakespeare Monument (top) and grave (bottom) in Holy Trinity Church, Stratford-upon-Avon. The monument was made by Gheerart Janssen, a stonemason from Amsterdam whose name was anglicized to Gerard Johnson and who may have been acquainted with Shakespeare.

Walter Ebish and Levin L. Schucking, *A Shakespeare Bibliography* (Oxford: Clarendon Press, 1931);

Gordon Ross Smith, *A Classified Shakespeare Bibliography, 1936-1958* (University Park: Pennsylvania State University Press, 1963);

Ronald Berman, *A Reader's Guide to Shakespeare's Plays,* revised edition (Glenview, Ill.: Scott Foresman, 1973);

David Bevington, *Shakespeare* (Arlington Heights, Ill.: AHM Publishing, 1978);

Larry S. Champion, *The Essential Shakespeare: An Annotated Bibliography of Major Modern Studies* (Boston: G. K. Hall, 1986).

See also the annual bibliographies in *Shakespeare Quarterly,* plus the reviews of current scholarship, criticism, and performance in two annuals, *Shakespeare Survey* and *The Year's Work in English Studies.*

Handbooks and Study Guides:

Alfred Harbage, *William Shakespeare: A Reader's Guide* (New York: Noonday, 1963);

F. E. Halliday, *A Shakespeare Companion, 1564-1964* (London: Duckworth / Harmondsworth, U.K.: Penguin, 1964);

O. J. Campbell and Edward G. Quinn, *The Reader's Encyclopedia of Shakespeare* (New York: Crowell, 1966);

John W. Velz, *Shakespeare and the Classical Tradition: A Critical Guide to Commentary, 1660-1960* (Minneapolis: University of Minnesota Press, 1968);

Kenneth Muir and S. Schoenbaum, eds., *A New Companion to Shakespeare Studies* (Cambridge: Cambridge University Press, 1971);

David M. Bergeron, *Shakespeare: A Study and Research Guide* (New York: St. Martin's Press, 1975);

David M. Zesmer, *Guide to Shakespeare* (New York: Barnes & Noble, 1976);

Stanley Wells, *The Cambridge Companion to Shakespeare Studies* (Cambridge: Cambridge University Press, 1986);

Wells and Gary Taylor, *William Shakespeare: A Textual Companion* [to the Complete Oxford Shakespeare] (Oxford: Clarendon Press, 1987);

Levi Fox, ed., *The Shakespeare Handbook* (New York: G. K. Hall, 1987);

S. Schoenbaum, *Shakespeare: His Life, His Language, His Theater* (New York: Signet, 1990).

Biographical Studies:

E. K. Chambers, *William Shakespeare: A Study of Facts and Problems,* 2 volumes (Oxford: Clarendon Press, 1930);

M. M. Reese, *Shakespeare: His World and His Work* (London: Arnold, 1953);

Gerald Eades Bentley, *Shakespeare: A Biographical Handbook* (New Haven: Yale University Press, 1961);

A. L. Rowse, *William Shakespeare: A Biography* (London: Macmillan, 1963);

Anthony Burgess, *Shakespeare* (Harmondsworth, U.K.: Penguin, 1970);

S. Schoenbaum, *Shakespeare's Lives* (New York: Oxford University Press, 1970; revised, 1991);

Schoenbaum, *William Shakespeare: A Documentary Life* (London: Oxford University Press/Scolar Press, 1975);

Schoenbaum, *William Shakespeare: Records and Images* (London: Oxford University Press/ Scolar Press, 1981);

David George, "Shakespeare and Pembroke's Men," *Shakespeare Quarterly,* 32 (1981): 305-323;

Mary Edmonds, "It Was for Gentle Shakespeare Cut," *Shakespeare Quarterly,* 42 (1991): 3301-3344.

Periodicals:

Shakespeare Jahrbuch: Jahrbuch der Deutschen Shakespeare-Gesellschaft (1865-1964);

Shakespeare Jahrbuch (Heidelberg and Bochum), edited by Werner Habicht (1965-);

Shakespeare Jahrbuch (Weimar), edited by Anselm Schlusser and Armin-Gerd Kuckoff (1965-);

Shakespeare Newsletter, edited by Louis Marder (1951-);

Shakespeare Quarterly, edited by James G. McManaway, Richard J. Schoeck, John F. Andrews, Barbara A. Mowat (1950-);

Shakespeare Studies, edited by J. Leeds Barroll (1965-);

Shakespeare Studies (Tokyo), edited by Jiro Ozu (1962-);

Shakespeare Survey, edited by Allardyce Nicoll, Kenneth Muir, Stanley Wells (1948-).

References:

BACKGROUND, MILIEU, SOURCE, AND INFLUENCE STUDIES

E. A. Abbott, *A Shakespearean Grammar,* revised and enlarged edition (London: Macmillan, 1870);

John Cranford Adams, *The Globe Playhouse* (Cambridge, Mass.: Harvard University Press, 1942);

John F. Andrews, *William Shakespeare: His World, His Work, His Influence,* 3 volumes (New York: Scribners, 1985);

T. W. Baldwin, *William Shakspere's Small Latine & Lesse Greeke* (Urbana: University of Illinois Press, 1943);

Bernard Beckerman, *Shakespeare at the Globe, 1599-1609* (New York: Macmillan, 1962);

Gerald Eades Bentley, *The Profession of Dramatist in Shakespeare's Time, 1590-1642* (Princeton: Princeton University Press, 1971);

Bentley, *The Profession of Player in Shakespeare's Time* (Princeton: Princeton University Press, 1984);

Bentley, "Shakespeare and the Blackfriars Theatre," *Shakespeare Survey,* 1 (1948): 38-50;

Herbert Berry, *Shakespeare's Playhouses* (New York: AMS Press, 1987);

Fredson Bowers, *Bibliography and Textual Criticism* (Oxford: Clarendon Press, 1964);

Bowers, *On Editing Shakespeare* (Charlottesville: University Press of Virginia, 1966);

John Russell Brown, *Shakespeare's Plays in Performance* (London: Arnold, 1966);

Geoffrey Bullough, ed., *Narrative and Dramatic Sources of Shakespeare,* 8 volumes (London: Routledge & Kegan Paul, 1957-1975);

Fausto Cercignani, *Shakespeare's Works and Elizabethan Pronunciation* (Oxford: Clarendon Press, 1981);

E. K. Chambers, *The Elizabethan Stage,* 4 volumes (Oxford: Clarendon Press, 1923), III: 479-490;

Wolfgang Clemen, *The Development of Shakespeare's Imagery* (Cambridge, Mass.: Harvard University Press, 1951);

Ruby Cohn, *Modern Shakespeare Offshoots* (Princeton: Princeton University Press, 1976);

Ann Jennalie Cook, *The Privileged Playgoers of Shakespeare's London: 1576-1642* (Princeton: Princeton University Press, 1981);

Richard David, *Shakespeare in the Theatre* (Cambridge: Cambridge University Press, 1978);

Madeleine Doran, *Endeavors of Art: A Study of Form in Elizabethan Drama* (Madison: University of Wisconsin Press, 1954);

G. R. Elton, *The Tudor Revolution in Government* (Cambridge: Cambridge University Press, 1953);

Roland M. Frye, *Shakespeare and Christian Doctrine* (Princeton: Princeton University Press, 1963);

W. W. Greg, *The Editorial Problem in Shakespeare: A Survey of the Foundations of the Text* (Oxford: Clarendon Press, 1954);

Greg, ed., *Dramatic Documents from the Elizabethan Playhouses: Stage Plots; Actors' Parts; Prompt Books,* 2 volumes (Oxford: Clarendon Press, 1931);

Andrew Gurr, *Playgoing in Shakespeare's London* (Cambridge: Cambridge University Press, 1987);

Gurr, *The Shakespearean Stage, 1574-1642* (Cambridge: Cambridge University Press, 1970);

Alfred Harbage, *Shakespeare's Audience* (New York: Columbia University Press, 1941);

Christopher Hill, *The Century of Revolution, 1603-1714* (New York: Norton, 1961);

Charlton Hinman, *The Printing and Proof-Reading of the First Folio of Shakespeare,* 2 volumes (Oxford: Clarendon Press, 1963);

C. Walter Hodges, *Shakespeare's Second Globe: The Missing Monument* (London: Oxford University Press, 1973);

Richard Hosley, "The Discovery-Space in Shakespeare's Globe," *Shakespeare Survey,* 12 (1959): 35-46;

Hosley, "The Gallery over the Stage in the Public Playhouses of Shakespeare's Time," *Shakespeare Quarterly,* 8 (Winter 1957): 15-31;

Hosley, ed., *Shakespeare's Holinshed* (New York: Putnam's, 1968);

Jack Jorgens, *Shakespeare on Film* (Bloomington: Indiana University Press, 1977);

Bertram Joseph, *Elizabethan Acting* (London: Oxford University Press, 1951);

George R. Kernodle, *From Art to Theatre: Form and Convention in the Renaissance* (Chicago: University of Chicago Press, 1944);

Helge Kökeritz, *Shakespeare's Pronunciation* (New Haven: Yale University Press, 1953);

Wallace T. MacCaffrey, *The Shaping of the Elizabethan Regime* (Princeton: Princeton University Press, 1968);

Scott McMillin, *The Elizabethan Theatre &* The Book of Sir Thomas More (Ithaca, N.Y.: Cornell University Press, 1987);

W. Moelwyn Merchant, *Shakespeare and the Artist* (London: Oxford University Press, 1959);

Sister Miriam Joseph, *Shakespeare's Use of the Arts of Language* (New York: Columbia University Press, 1947);

Kenneth Muir, *Shakespeare's Sources,* 2 volumes (London: Methuen, 1961);

Richmond Noble, *Shakespeare's Biblical Knowledge and Use of the Book of Common Prayer* (New York: Macmillan, 1935);

C. T. Onions, *A Shakespeare Glossary*, revised edition (Oxford: Clarendon Press, 1919);

John Orrell, *The Quest for Shakespeare's Globe* (Cambridge: Cambridge University Press, 1983);

Eric Partridge, *Shakespeare's Bawdy*, revised edition (London: Routledge & Kegan Paul, 1969);

Alfred W. Pollard, *Shakespeare's Folios and Quartos: A Study in the Bibliography of Shakespeare's Plays, 1594-1685* (London: Methuen, 1909);

Alexander Schmidt, *Shakespeare-Lexicon*, 2 volumes, revised and enlarged by Gregor Sarrazin (Berlin: de Gruyter, 1962);

S. Schoenbaum, *Shakespeare: The Globe and the World* (New York: Oxford University Press, 1979);

Peter J. Seng, *The Vocal Songs in the Plays of Shakespeare: A Critical History* (London: Oxford University Press, 1967);

Charles H. Shattuck, *Shakespeare on the American Stage: From the Hallams to Edwin Booth* (Washington, D.C.: Folger Shakespeare Library, 1976);

Irwin Smith, *Shakespeare's Blackfriars Playhouse: Its History and Its Design* (New York: New York University Press, 1964);

Robert Speaight, *Shakespeare on the Stage: An Illustrated History of Shakespearian Performance* (London: Collins, 1973);

T. J. B. Spencer, ed., *Shakespeare's Plutarch* (Harmondsworth, U.K.: Penguin, 1964);

Marvin Spevack, *The Harvard Concordance to Shakespeare* (Cambridge, Mass.: Harvard University Press, 1973);

Arthur Colby Sprague, *Shakespearian Players and Performances* (Cambridge, Mass.: Harvard University Press, 1954);

Lawrence Stone, *The Crisis of the Aristocracy, 1558-1641* (Oxford: Oxford University Press, 1965);

Stone, *The Family, Sex, and Marriage in England, 1500-1800* (New York: Harper & Row, 1977);

J. L. Styan, *The Shakespeare Revolution: Criticism and Performance in the Twentieth Century* (Cambridge: Cambridge University Press, 1979);

J. A. K. Thomson, *Shakespeare and the Classics* (London: Allen & Unwin, 1952);

E. M. W. Tillyard, *The Elizabethan World Picture* (London: Chatto & Windus, 1943);

J. C. Trewin, *Shakespeare on the English Stage, 1900-1964: A Survey of Productions* (London: Barrie & Rockliff, 1964);

Virgil K. Whitaker, *Shakespeare's Use of Learning* (San Marino, Cal.: Huntington Library, 1953);

Glynne Wickham, *Early English Stages, 1300-1600*, 2 volumes (London: Routledge & Kegan Paul, 1959-1972).

GENERAL CRITICAL STUDIES

W. H. Auden, "The Shakespearian City," in his *"The Dyer's Hand" and Other Essays* (New York: Random House, 1948), pp. 171-172;

Gerald Eades Bentley, *Shakespeare and Jonson: Their Reputations in the Seventeenth Century Compared*, 2 volumes (Chicago: University of Chicago Press, 1945);

David Bevington and Jay L. Halio, eds., *Shakespeare: Pattern of Excelling Nature*, essays from the 1976 Washington Congress of the International Shakespeare Association (Newark: University of Delaware Press, 1978);

M. C. Bradbrook, *The Living Monument: Shakespeare and the Theatre of His Time* (New York: Barnes & Noble, 1969);

Philip Brockbank, ed., *Players of Shakespeare* (Cambridge: Cambridge University Press, 1985);

Sigurd Burkhardt, *Shakespearean Meanings* (Princeton: Princeton University Press, 1968);

James L. Calderwood, *Shakespearean Metadrama* (Minneapolis: University of Minnesota Press, 1971);

Nevill Coghill, *Shakespeare's Professional Skills* (Cambridge: Cambridge University Press, 1964);

Walter Clyde Curry, *Shakespeare's Philosophical Patterns* (Baton Rouge: Louisiana State University Press, 1937);

Leonard F. Dean, ed., *Shakespeare: Modern Essays in Criticism*, revised edition (New York: Oxford University Press, 1967);

Alan C. Dessen, *Elizabethan Drama and the Viewer's Eye* (Chapel Hill: University of North Carolina Press, 1977);

Dessen, *Elizabethan Stage Conventions and Modern Interpreters* (Cambridge: Cambridge University Press, 1984);

John Drakakis, *Alternative Shakespeares* (London: Methuen, 1985);

Juliet Dusinberre, *Shakespeare and the Nature of Women* (London: Macmillan, 1975);

Arthur M. Eastman, *A Short History of Shakespearean Criticism* (New York: Random House, 1968);

Philip Edwards, *Shakespeare and the Confines of Art* (London: Methuen, 1968);

G. Blakemore Evans, *Shakespeare: Aspects of Influence* (Cambridge, Mass.: Harvard University Press, 1976);

Michael Goldman, *Shakespeare and the Energies of Drama* (Princeton: Princeton University Press, 1972);

Harley Granville-Barker, *Prefaces to Shakespeare,* 2 volumes (Princeton: Princeton University Press, 1946-1947);

Alfred Harbage, *Shakespeare and the Rival Traditions* (New York: Macmillan, 1952);

Terence Hawkes, *That Shakespeaherean Rag* (London: Methuen, 1986);

Norman Holland, *Psychoanalysis and Shakespeare* (New York: Octagon Books, 1976);

Robert G. Hunter, *Shakespeare and the Mystery of God's Judgments* (Athens: University of Georgia Press, 1976);

Emrys Jones, *The Origins of Shakespeare* (Oxford: Clarendon Press, 1977);

Jones, *Scenic Form in Shakespeare* (Oxford: Clarendon Press, 1971);

Coppelia Kahn, *Man's Estate: Masculine Identity in Shakespeare* (Berkeley: University of California Press, 1981);

Alvin B. Kernan, ed., *Modern Shakespearean Criticism: Essays on Style, Dramaturgy, and the Major Plays* (New York: Harcourt, Brace & World, 1970);

Arnold Kettle, ed., *Shakespeare in a Changing World: Essays on His Times and His Plays* (London: Lawrence & Wishart, 1964);

Arthur C. Kirsch, *Shakespeare and the Experience of Love* (Cambridge: Cambridge University Press, 1981);

G. Wilson Knight, *Shakespeare and Religion: Essays of Forty Years* (London: Routledge & Kegan Paul, 1967);

L. C. Knights, *Some Shakespearean Themes* (London: Chatto & Windus, 1959);

Jan Kott, *Shakespeare Our Contemporary,* translated by Boleslaw Taborski (Garden City, N.Y.: Doubleday, 1964);

Clifford Leech and J. M. R. Margeson, eds., *Shakespeare 1971: Proceedings of the World Shakespeare Congress, Vancouver, August 1971* (Toronto: University of Toronto Press, 1972);

Harry Levin, "The Primacy of Shakespeare," *Shakespeare Quarterly,* 26 (Spring 1975): 99-112;

Richard Levin, *New Readings vs. Old Plays: Recent Trends in the Reinterpretation of English Renaissance Drama* (Chicago: University of Chicago Press, 1979);

James G. McManaway, ed., *Shakespeare 400: Essays by American Scholars on the Anniversary of the Poet's Birth* (New York: Holt, Rinehart & Winston, 1964);

John Munro, ed., *The Shakespeare Allusion Book: A Collection of Allusions to Shakespeare from 1591 to 1700,* 2 volumes (London: Chatto & Windus, 1909);

Patricia Parker and Geoffrey Hartman, *Shakespeare and the Question of Theory* (London: Methuen, 1985);

Hereward T. Price, *Construction in Shakespeare* (Ann Arbor: University of Michigan Press, 1951);

Norman Rabkin, *Shakespeare and the Common Understanding* (New York: Free Press, 1967);

Rabkin, *Shakespeare and the Problem of Meaning* (Chicago: University of Chicago Press, 1981);

Rabkin, ed., *Approaches to Shakespeare* (New York: McGraw-Hill, 1964);

Thomas M. Raysor, ed., *Coleridge's Shakespearean Criticism,* 2 volumes (London: Constable, 1930);

Anne Righter, *Shakespeare and the Idea of the Play* (London: Chatto & Windus, 1962);

A. P. Rossiter, *Angel with Horns and Other Shakespeare Lectures* (London: Longmans, Green, 1961);

Wilbur Sanders, *The Dramatist and the Received Idea* (Cambridge: Cambridge University Press, 1968);

Murray M. Schwartz and Coppelia Kahn, eds., *Representing Shakespeare: New Psychoanalytic Essays* (Baltimore: Johns Hopkins University Press, 1980);

Arthur Sherbo, ed., *Johnson on Shakespeare,* volumes 7 and 8 of *The Yale Edition of the Works of Samuel Johnson* (New Haven: Yale University Press, 1968);

Theodore Spencer, *Shakespeare and the Nature of Man* (New York: Macmillan, 1942);

Derek Traversi, *An Approach to Shakespeare,* revised and enlarged edition (Garden City, N.Y.: Doubleday, 1956);

Robert Y. Turner, *Shakespeare's Apprenticeship* (Chicago: University of Chicago Press, 1974);

Mark Van Doren, *Shakespeare* (New York: Holt, 1939);

Brian Vickers, ed., *Shakespeare: The Critical Heritage,* 6 volumes (London: Routledge & Kegan Paul, 1973-1981);

Enid Welsford, *The Fool: His Social and Literary History* (London: Faber & Faber, 1935);

Robert H. West, *Shakespeare and the Outer Mystery* (Lexington: University of Kentucky Press, 1968).

STUDIES OF THE NONDRAMATIC POEMS

Stephen Booth, *An Essay on Shakespeare's Sonnets* (New Haven: Yale University Press, 1969);

Herbert Dubrow, *Captive Victors: Shakespeare's Narrative Poems and the Sonnets* (Ithaca, N.Y.: Cornell University Press, 1987);

Edward Hubler, *The Sense of Shakespeare's Sonnets* (Princeton: Princeton University Press, 1952);

Hubler, Northrop Frye, Stephen Spender, and R. P. Blackmur, *The Riddle of Shakespeare's Sonnets* (New York: Basic Books, 1962);

Murray Krieger, *A Window to Criticism: Shakespeare's "Sonnets" and Modern Poetics* (Princeton: Princeton University Press, 1964);

J. B. Leishman, *Themes and Variations in Shakespeare's Sonnets* (London: Hutchinson, 1961);

J. W. Lever, *The Elizabethan Love Sonnet* (London: Methuen, 1956);

Giorgio Melchiori, *Shakespeare's Dramatic Meditations: An Experiment in Criticism* (Oxford: Clarendon Press, 1976);

Hallett Smith, *Elizabethan Poetry* (Cambridge, Mass.: Harvard University Press, 1952).

STUDIES OF THE COMEDIES, TRAGICOMEDIES, AND ROMANCES

Robert M. Adams, *Shakespeare: The Four Romances* (New York: Norton, 1989);

C. L. Barber, *Shakespeare's Festive Comedy: A Study of Dramatic Form and Its Relation to Social Custom* (Princeton: Princeton University Press, 1959);

Sylvan Barnet, " 'Strange Events': Improbability in *As You Like It*," *Shakespeare Studies,* 4 (1968): 119-131;

Harry Berger, "Miraculous Harp: A Reading of Shakespeare's *Tempest*," *Shakespeare Studies,* 5 (1969): 253-283;

Ralph Berry, *Shakespeare's Comedies: Explorations in Form* (Princeton: Princeton University Press, 1972);

M. C. Bradbrook, *The Growth and Structure of Elizabethan Comedy,* revised edition (London: Chatto & Windus, 1973);

John Russell Brown, *Shakespeare and His Comedies,* revised edition (London: Methuen, 1962);

O. J. Campbell, *Comicall Satyre and Shakespeare's "Troilus and Cressida"* (San Marino, Cal.: Huntington Library, 1938);

H. B. Charlton, *Shakespearian Comedy* (London: Methuen, 1938);

Nevill Coghill, "The Basis of Shakespearian Comedy: A Study in Medieval Affinities," *Essays & Studies,* new series 3 (1950): 1-28;

Jackson I. Cope, *The Theater and the Dream: From Metaphor to Form in Renaissance Drama* (Baltimore: Johns Hopkins University Press, 1973);

Bertrand Evans, *Shakespeare's Comedies* (Oxford: Clarendon Press, 1960);

Howard Felperin, *Shakespearean Romance* (Princeton: Princeton University Press, 1972);

Northrop Frye, "The Argument of Comedy," in *English Institute Essays 1948* (New York: Columbia University Press, 1949), pp. 58-73;

Frye, *A Natural Perspective: The Development of Shakespearean Comedy and Romance* (New York: Columbia University Press, 1965);

Frye, *The Secular Scripture: A Study of the Structure of Romance* (Cambridge, Mass.: Harvard University Press, 1976);

Darryl J. Gless, *"Measure for Measure," the Law, and the Covenant* (Princeton: Princeton University Press, 1979);

William Green, *Shakespeare's "Merry Wives of Windsor"* (Princeton: Princeton University Press, 1962);

Joan Hartwig, *Shakespeare's Tragicomic Vision* (Baton Rouge: Louisiana State University Press, 1972);

Sherman H. Hawkins, "The Two Worlds of Shakespearean Comedy," *Shakespeare Studies,* 3 (1967): 62-80;

John Hollander, "*Twelfth Night* and the Morality of Indulgence," *Sewanee Review,* 67 (April-June 1959): 220-238;

G. K. Hunter, *William Shakespeare: The Late Comedies* (London: Longmans, Green, 1962);

Robert G. Hunter, *Shakespeare and the Comedy of Forgiveness* (New York: Columbia University Press, 1965);

Frank Kermode, "What is Shakespeare's *Henry VIII* About?," *Durham University Journal,* 40 (Spring 1948): 48-55;

Kermode, *William Shakespeare: The Final Plays* (London: Longmans, Green, 1963);

Alvin B. Kernan, *The Cankered Muse: Satire of the English Renaissance* (New Haven: Yale University Press, 1959);

Arthur C. Kirsch, "The Integrity of *Measure for Measure*," *Shakespeare Survey,* 28 (1975): 89-105;

G. Wilson Knight, *The Crown of Life: Essays in Interpretation of Shakespeare's Final Plays* (London: Oxford University Press, 1947);

W. W. Lawrence, *Shakespeare's Problem Comedies* (New York: Macmillan, 1931);

Clifford Leech, *"Twelfth Night" and Shakespearian Comedy* (Toronto: University of Toronto Press, 1965);

Alexander Leggatt, *Citizen Comedy in the Age of Shakespeare* (Toronto: University of Toronto Press, 1973);

Leggatt, *Shakespeare's Comedy of Love* (London: Methuen, 1974);

Barbara Lewalski, "Biblical Allusion and Allegory in *The Merchant of Venice,*" *Shakespeare Quarterly,* 13 (Summer 1962): 327-343;

Barbara Mowat, *The Dramaturgy of Shakespeare's Romances* (Athens: University of Georgia Press, 1976);

Kenneth Muir, ed., *Shakespeare, The Comedies: A Collection of Critical Essays* (Englewood Cliffs, N.J.: Prentice-Hall, 1965);

A. D. Nuttall, *Two Concepts of Allegory: A Study of Shakespeare's "The Tempest" and the Logic of Allegorical Expression* (London: Routledge & Kegan Paul, 1967);

Stephen Orgel, *The Illusion of Power: Political Theater in the English Renaissance* (Berkeley: University of California Press, 1975);

Douglas L. Peterson, *Time, Tide, and Tempest: A Study of Shakespeare's Romances* (San Marino, Cal.: Huntington Library, 1973);

E. C. Pettet, *Shakespeare and the Romance Tradition* (London: Staples, 1949);

Hugh M. Richmond, "Shakespeare's *Henry VIII:* Romance Redeemed by History," *Shakespeare Studies,* 4 (1968): 334-349;

Jeanne Addison Roberts, *Shakespeare's English Comedy: "The Merry Wives of Windsor" in Context* (Lincoln: University of Nebraska Press, 1979);

Leo Salinger, *Shakespeare and the Traditions of Comedy* (Cambridge: Cambridge University Press, 1974);

Ernest Schanzer, *The Problem Plays of Shakespeare: A Study of "Julius Caesar," "Measure for Measure," and "Antony and Cleopatra"* (London: Routledge & Kegan Paul, 1963);

Meredith Skura, "Discourse and the Individual: The Case of Colonialism in *The Tempest,*" *Shakespeare Quarterly,* 40 (1989): 42-69;

David L. Stevenson, *The Achievement of Shakespeare's "Measure for Measure"* (Ithaca, N.Y.: Cornell University Press, 1966);

Joseph H. Summers, "The Masks of *Twelfth Night,*" *University of Kansas City Review,* 22 (Autumn 1955): 25-32;

E. M. W. Tillyard, *Shakespeare's Last Plays* (London: Chatto & Windus, 1938);

Tillyard, *Shakespeare's Problem Plays* (Toronto: University of Toronto Press, 1949);

Derek Traversi, *Shakespeare: The Last Phase* (London: Hollis & Carter, 1954);

Glynne Wickham, *"Love's Labor's Lost* and *The Four Foster Children of Desire,* 1581," *Shakespeare Quarterly,* 36 (Spring 1985): 49-55;

David Young, *The Heart's Forest: A Study of Shakespeare's Pastoral Plays* (New Haven: Yale University Press, 1972);

Young, *Something of Great Constancy: The Art of "A Midsummer Night's Dream"* (New Haven: Yale University Press, 1966).

STUDIES OF THE ENGLISH HISTORY PLAYS

Edward I. Berry, *Patterns of Decay: Shakespeare's Early Histories* (Charlottesville: University Press of Virginia, 1975);

Lily B. Campbell, *Shakespeare's "Histories": Mirrors of Elizabethan Policy* (San Marino, Cal.: Huntington Library, 1947);

Larry S. Champion, "The Function of Mowbray: Shakespeare's Maturing Artistry in *Richard II,*" *Shakespeare Quarterly,* 26 (Winter 1975): 3-7;

Alan C. Dessen, "The Intemperate Knight and the Politic Prince: Late Morality Structure in *1 Henry IV,*" *Shakespeare Studies,* 7 (1974): 147-171;

Donna B. Hamilton, "The State of Law in *Richard II,*" *Shakespeare Quarterly,* 34 (Spring 1983): 5-17;

Sherman H. Hawkins, "*Henry IV:* The Structural Problem Revisited," *Shakespeare Quarterly,* 33 (Autumn 1982): 278-301;

Hawkins, "Virtue and Kingship in Shakespeare's *Henry IV,*" *English Literary Renaissance,* 5 (Autumn 1975): 313-343;

G. K. Hunter, "Shakespeare's Politics and the Rejection of Falstaff," *Critical Quarterly,* 1 (Autumn 1959): 229-236;

Harold Jenkins, *The Structural Problem in Shakespeare's "Henry the Fourth"* (London: Methuen, 1956);

Ernst H. Kantorowicz, *The King's Two Bodies: A Study in Mediaeval Political Theology* (Princeton: Princeton University Press, 1957);

Alexander Leggatt, *Shakespeare's Political Drama: The History Plays and the Roman Plays* (London: Routledge, 1988);

Robert Ornstein, *A Kingdom for a Stage: The Achievement of Shakespeare's History Plays* (Cambridge, Mass.: Harvard University Press, 1972);

Robert B. Pierce, *Shakespeare's History Plays: The Family and the State* (Columbus: Ohio State University Press, 1971);

Moody E. Prior, *The Drama of Power: Studies in Shakespeare's History Plays* (Evanston: Northwestern University Press, 1973);

Phyllis Rackin, *Stages of History: Shakespeare's English Chronicles* (Ithaca, N.Y.: Cornell University Press, 1990);

M. M. Reese, *The Cease of Majesty: A Study of Shakespeare's History Plays* (London: Arnold, 1961);

Irving Ribner, *The English History Play in the Age of Shakespeare* (Princeton: Princeton University Press, 1965);

David Riggs, *Shakespeare's Heroical Histories: "Henry VI" and Its Literary Tradition* (Cambridge, Mass.: Harvard University Press, 1971);

Peter Saccio, *Shakespeare's English Kings: History, Chronicle, and Drama* (New York: Oxford University Press, 1977);

E. M. W. Tillyard, *Shakespeare's History Plays* (London: Chatto & Windus, 1944);

Harold E. Toliver, "Falstaff, the Prince, and the History Play," *Shakespeare Quarterly,* 16 (Winter 1965): 63-80;

Eugene M. Waith, ed., *Shakespeare, The Histories: A Collection of Critical Essays* (Englewood Cliffs, N.J.: Prentice-Hall, 1965);

Karl P. Wentersdorf, "The Conspiracy of Silence in *Henry V,*" *Shakespeare Quarterly,* 27 (Summer 1976): 264-287;

Richard P. Wheeler, *Shakespeare's Development and the Problem Comedies* (Berkeley: University of California Press, 1979);

J. Dover Wilson, *The Fortunes of Falstaff* (Cambridge: Cambridge University Press, 1943).

STUDIES OF THE TRAGEDIES, INCLUDING THE ROMAN PLAYS

Janet Adelman, *The Common Liar: An Essay on "Antony and Cleopatra"* (New Haven: Yale University Press, 1973);

John F. Andrews, " 'Dearly Bought Revenge,': *Hamlet, Samson Agonistes,* and Elizabethan Revenge Tragedy," *Milton Studies,* 13 (1979): 81-108;

John S. Anson, "*Julius Caesar:* The Politics of the Hardened Heart," *Shakespeare Studies,* 2 (1966): 11-33;

Howard Baker, *Induction to Tragedy: A Study in a Development of Form in "Gorboduc," "The Spanish Tragedy," and "Titus Andronicus"* (Baton Rouge: Louisiana State University Press, 1939);

J. Leeds Barroll, *Artificial Persons: The Formation of Character in the Tragedies of Shakespeare* (Columbia: University of South Carolina Press, 1974);

Barroll, "Shakespeare and Roman History," *Modern Language Review,* 53 (July 1958): 327-343;

Roy W. Battenhouse, *Shakespearean Tragedy: Its Art and Its Christian Premises* (Bloomington: Indiana University Press, 1969);

Adrien Bonjour, *The Structure of "Julius Caesar"* (Liverpool: Liverpool University Press, 1958);

Stephen Booth, *"King Lear," "Macbeth," Indefinition, and Tragedy* (New Haven: Yale University Press, 1983);

Fredson Bowers, *Elizabethan Revenge Tragedy, 1587-1642* (Princeton: Princeton University Press, 1940);

Bowers, "Hamlet as Minister and Scourge," *PMLA,* 70 (September 1955): 740-749;

M. C. Bradbrook, *Themes and Conventions of Elizabethan Tragedy* (Cambridge: Cambridge University Press, 1935);

A. C. Bradley, *Shakespearean Tragedy: Lectures on "Hamlet," "Othello," "King Lear," and "Macbeth"* (London: Macmillan, 1904);

Nicholas Brooke, *Shakespeare's Early Tragedies* (London: Methuen, 1968);

Cleanth Brooks, "The Naked Babe and the Cloak of Manliness," in his *The Well-Wrought Urn* (New York: Reynal & Hitchcock, 1947), pp. 21-46;

Reuben A. Brower, *Hero and Saint: Shakespeare and the Graeco-Roman Heroic Tradition* (New York: Oxford University Press, 1971);

Lily B. Campbell, *Shakespeare's Tragic Heroes: Slaves of Passion* (Cambridge: Cambridge University Press, 1930);

Paul A. Cantor, *Shakespeare's Rome: Republic and Empire* (Ithaca, N.Y.: Cornell University Press, 1976);

Larry S. Champion, *Shakespeare's Tragic Perspective: The Development of His Dramatic Technique* (Athens: University of Georgia Press, 1976);

H. B. Charlton, *Shakespearian Tragedy* (Cambridge: Cambridge University Press, 1948);

Maurice Charney, *Shakespeare's Roman Plays: The Function of Imagery in the Drama* (Cambridge, Mass.: Harvard University Press, 1961);

Charney, *Style in "Hamlet"* (Princeton: Princeton University Press, 1969);

Dolora G. Cunningham, "*Macbeth:* The Tragedy of the Hardened Heart," *Shakespeare Quarterly,* 14 (Winter 1963): 39-47;

J. V. Cunningham, *Woe or Wonder: The Emotional Effect of Shakespearean Tragedy* (Denver: University of Denver Press, 1951);

John F. Danby, *Shakespeare's Doctrine of Nature: A Study of "King Lear"* (London: Faber & Faber, 1949);

Alan C. Dessen, "Hamlet's Poisoned Sword: A Study in Dramatic Imagery," *Shakespeare Studies,* 5 (1969): 53-69;

Franklin M. Dickey, *Not Wisely But Too Well: Shakespeare's Love Tragedies* (San Marino, Cal.: Huntington Library, 1957);

T. S. Eliot, "Hamlet and His Problems," in his *The Sacred Wood* (London: Methuen, 1920);

William R. Elton, *"King Lear" and the Gods* (San Marino, Cal.: Huntington Library, 1966);

Willard Farnham, *The Medieval Heritage of Elizabethan Tragedy* (Berkeley: University of California Press, 1936);

Farnham, *Shakespeare's Tragic Frontier: The World of His Final Tragedies* (Berkeley: University of California Press, 1950);

Francis Fergusson, "*Macbeth* as the Imitation of an Action," in *English Institute Essays 1951,* edited by A. S. Downer (New York: Columbia University Press, 1952), pp. 31-43;

Northrop Frye, *Fools of Time: Studies in Shakespearean Tragedy* (Toronto: University of Toronto Press, 1967);

S. L. Goldberg, *An Essay on "King Lear"* (Cambridge: Cambridge University Press, 1974);

O. B. Hardison, Jr., "Myth and History in *King Lear,*" *Shakespeare Quarterly,* 26 (Summer 1975): 227-242;

Robert B. Heilman, *Magic in the Web: Action and Language in "Othello"* (Lexington: University of Kentucky Press, 1956);

Heilman, *This Great Stage: Image and Structure in "King Lear"* (Baton Rouge: Louisiana State University Press, 1948);

Heilman, " 'Twere Best Not Know Myself: *Othello, Lear, Macbeth,*" *Shakespeare Quarterly,* 15 (Spring 1964): 89-98;

John Holloway, *The Story of the Night: Studies in Shakespeare's Major Tragedies* (London: Routledge & Kegan Paul, 1961);

David L. Jeffrey and Patrick Grant, "Reputation in *Othello,*" *Shakespeare Studies,* 6 (1970): 197-208;

Paul A. Jorgensen, *Lear's Self-Discovery* (Berkeley: University of California Press, 1967);

Jorgensen, *Our Naked Frailties: Sensational Art and Meaning in "Macbeth"* (Berkeley: University of California Press, 1971);

G. Wilson Knight, *The Wheel of Fire: Interpretation of Shakespeare's Tragedy* (London: Methuen, 1949);

L. C. Knights, "How Many Children Had Lady Macbeth?," in his *Explorations: Essays in Criticism* (London: Chatto & Windus, 1946);

Clifford Leech, ed., *Shakespeare, The Tragedies: A Collection of Critical Essays* (Chicago: University of Chicago Press, 1965);

Harry Levin, *The Question of "Hamlet"* (New York: Oxford University Press, 1959);

Maynard Mack, "The Jacobean Shakespeare: Some Observations on the Construction of the Tragedies," in *Jacobean Theatre,* edited by John Russell Brown and Bernard Harris, Stratford-upon-Avon Studies, 1 (London: Arnold, 1960);

Mack, *"King Lear" in Our Time* (Berkeley: University of California Press, 1965);

Mack, "The World of *Hamlet,*" *Yale Review,* 41 (June 1952): 502-523;

J. M. R. Margeson, *The Origins of English Tragedy* (Oxford: Clarendon Press, 1967);

Bernard McElroy, *Shakespeare's Mature Tragedies* (Princeton: Princeton University Press, 1973);

Kenneth Muir, *Shakespeare's Tragic Sequence* (London: Hutchinson, 1972);

Matthew N. Proser, *The Heroic Image in Five Shakespearean Tragedies* (Princeton: Princeton University Press, 1965);

Eleanor Prosser, *Hamlet and Revenge,* revised edition (Stanford: Stanford University Press, 1971);

William Rosen, *Shakespeare and the Craft of Tragedy* (Cambridge, Mass.: Harvard University Press, 1960);

Marvin Rosenberg, *The Masks of "King Lear"* (Berkeley: University of California Press, 1972);

J. L. Simmons, *Shakespeare's Pagan World: The Roman Tragedies* (Charlottesville: University Press of Virginia, 1973);

Susan Snyder, *The Comic Matrix of Shakespeare's Tragedies* (Princeton: Princeton University Press, 1979);

Snyder, "*King Lear* and the Psychology of Dying," *Shakespeare Quarterly,* 33 (Winter 1982): 449-460;

Rolf Soellner, *"Timon of Athens," Shakespeare's Pessimistic Tragedy, With a Stage History by Gary Jay Williams* (Columbus: Ohio State University Press, 1979);

Robert Speaight, *Nature in Shakespearian Tragedy* (London: Hollis & Carter, 1955);

Bernard Spivack, *Shakespeare and the Allegory of Evil: The History of a Metaphor in Relation to His Major Villains* (New York: Columbia University Press, 1958);

Brents Stirling, *Unity in Shakespearian Tragedy: The Interplay of Theme and Character* (New York: Columbia University Press, 1956);

Elmer E. Stoll, *Art and Artifice in Shakespeare* (Cambridge: Cambridge University Press, 1933);

Gary Taylor and Michael Warren, *The Division of the Kingdoms: Shakespeare's Two Versions of "King Lear"* (Oxford: Clarendon Press, 1983);

Marvin L. Vawter, " 'Division 'tween Our Souls': Shakespeare's Stoic Brutus," *Shakespeare Studies,* 7 (1974): 173-195;

Eugene M. Waith, *The Herculean Hero in Marlowe, Chapman, Shakespeare, and Dryden* (New York: Columbia University Press, 1962);

Waith, "The Metamorphosis of Violence in *Titus Andronicus,*" *Shakespeare Survey,* 10 (1957): 39-49;

Virgil K. Whitaker, *The Mirror up to Nature: The Technique of Shakespeare's Tragedies* (San Marino, Cal.: Huntington Library, 1965);

Harold S. Wilson, *On the Design of Shakespearian Tragedy* (Toronto: University of Toronto Press, 1957);

David Young, *The Action to the Word: Structure and Style in Shakespearean Tragedy* (New Haven: Yale University Press, 1990).

Papers:

The Booke of Sir Thomas More (a play probably written principally by Anthony Munday, with revisions by Thomas Dekker, Henry Chettle, William Shakespeare, and possibly Thomas Heywood) survives in a manuscript now at the British Library (Harleian MS. 7368). Most scholars now believe that two brief passages are Shakespeare's work, circa 1594-1595, and that one of them represents the only surviving example of a literary or dramatic manuscript in Shakespeare's own hand. For a convenient summary of *Sir Thomas More* and the evidence linking it with Shakespeare, see G. Blakemore Evans's discussion of the play in *The Riverside Shakespeare* (Boston: Houghton Mifflin, 1974), pp. 1683-1700; and Scott McMillin's *The Elizabethan Theatre & *The Book of Sir Thomas More.

Sir Philip Sidney

(30 November 1554 - 17 October 1586)

Marvin Hunt
Campbell University

BOOKS: *The Countess of Pembroke's Arcadia* [*The New Arcadia*] (London: Printed for William Ponsonbie, 1590);

Astrophil and Stella (London: Printed for T. Newman, 1591);

The Countess of Pembroke's Arcadia [composite version of the New and Old *Arcadias*] (London: Printed by T. Creede for William Ponsonbie, 1593);

An Apologie for Poetry (London: Printed by J. Roberts for Henry Olney, 1595);

The Defence of Poesie (London: Printed for William Ponsonby, 1595);

The Countess of Pembroke's Arcadia [containing *The Lady of May* and *Certain Sonnets*] (London: Printed by R. Field for William Ponsonby, 1598);

The Countess of Pembroke's Arcadia [*The Old Arcadia*], edited by Albert Feuillerat (Cambridge: Cambridge University Press, 1926).

Editions and Collections: *The Correspondence of Sir Philip Sidney and Hubert Languet*, translated and edited by Steuart A. Pears (London, W. Pickering 1845);

The Complete Works of Sir Philip Sidney, 4 volumes, edited by Albert Feuillerat (Cambridge: Cambridge University Press, 1912-1926);

The Poems of Sir Philip Sidney, edited by William A. Ringler, Jr. (Oxford: Clarendon Press, 1962);

An Apology for Poetry; or, The Defence of Poetry, edited by Geoffrey Shepherd (London: Thomas Nelson, 1965);

Miscellaneous Prose of Sir Philip Sidney, edited by Katherine Duncan-Jones and Jan van Dorsten (Oxford: Clarendon Press, 1973);

The Countess of Pembroke's Arcadia—The Old Arcadia, edited by Jean Robertson (Oxford: Clarendon Press, 1973);

The Countess of Pembroke's Arcadia, edited by Maurice Evans (Harmondsworth, U.K.: Penguin, 1973);

The Countess of Pembroke's Arcadia [*The New Arcadia*], edited by Victor Skretkowicz (Oxford: Clarendon Press, 1987).

TRANSLATION: *The Psalmes of David* (Chiswick, U.K.: C. Whittingham for R. Triphook, 1823).

Grandson of the duke of Northumberland and heir presumptive to the earls of Leicester and Warwick, Sir Philip Sidney was not himself a nobleman. Today he is closely associated in the popular imagination with the court of Elizabeth I, though he spent relatively little time at the English court, and until his appointment as governor of Flushing in 1585 received little preferment from Elizabeth. Viewed in his own age as the best hope for the establishment of a Protestant League in Europe, he was nevertheless a godson of Philip II of Spain, spent nearly a year in Italy, and sought out the company of such eminent Catholics as the Jesuit martyr Edmund Campion. Widely regarded, in the words of his late editor William A. Ringler, Jr., as "the model of perfect courtesy," Sidney was in fact hot-tempered and could be surprisingly impetuous. Considered the epitome of the English gentleman-soldier, he saw relatively little military action before a wound in the left thigh, received 23 September 1586 during an ill-conceived and insignificant skirmish in the Netherlands outside Zutphen, led to his death on 17 October, at Arnhem. Even his literary career bears the stamp of paradox: Sidney did not think of himself as primarily a writer, and surprisingly little of his life was devoted to writing.

Philip, the first child of Sir Henry Sidney and his wife, Mary, née Dudley, was born in 1554 at Penshurst in Kent, "on Friday the last of November, being St. Andrews day, a quarter before five in the morning." Present at the birth were his royal Spanish godfather and his maternal grandmother, whose husband, John Dudley, Duke of Northumberland, and son Guildford

Sir Philip Sidney; portrait by an unknown artist (National Portrait Gallery, London)

had been beheaded in 1553 following the failure of the Northumberland plan to place Guildford's wife, Lady Jane Grey, on the throne.

It was an auspicious beginning to an often fatherless childhood. In 1559 Queen Elizabeth appointed Sir Henry lord president of the Marches of Wales, a post that required him to spend months on end away from home. As painful as his absence from family must have been to Sir Henry, his absence from Penshurst itself could only have compounded his distress. In the 1590 *Arcadia* Sidney recalled in the character Kalander's house the warmth, serviceability, and understated grace of the Sidney home:

> The house itself was built of fair and strong stone, not affecting so much any extraordinary kind of fineness, as an honorable representing of firm stateliness; the lights, doors and stairs, rather directed to the use of the guest than to the eye of the artificer, and yet, as the one chiefly heeded, so the other not neglected; each place handsome without curiosity, and homely without loathsomeness, not so dainty as not to be trod on, nor yet slubbered up with good fellowship—all more lasting than beautiful (but that the consideration of the exceeding lastingness made the eye believe it was exceeding beautiful).

The dominance of women in the poet's early life was doubtless formative. Sidney's skill in portraying female characters, from the bewitching, multifarious Stella of *Astrophil and Stella* to Philoclea and Pamela, the bold, beautiful, and articulate princesses of the two *Arcadias*, is, as C. S. Lewis noted, without equal before William Shakespeare. The two versions of the *Arcadia*, his most ambitious works, were written under the guiding spirit and often in the presence of Mary, his "dear Lady and sister, the Countess of Pembroke," herself a great patron of writers, to whom the *Arcadias* are dedicated. Mary went on to serve as Sidney's literary executor after his death.

The benevolent influence of Sidney's mother, Lady Mary, also cannot be doubted. Lady-in-waiting to the queen, she contracted the pox in October 1562 while caring for Elizabeth during her bout with the sickness. Her face severely disfigured, she thereafter avoided appearing at court. Sir Fulke Greville recalled that "she rather chose to hide herself from the curious eyes of a delicate time, than come up on the stage of the world with any manner of disparagement, the mischance of sickness having cast such a kind of veil over her excellent beauty." According to Ben Jonson in the *Conversations with Drummond*, when Lady Mary could not avoid appearing in public she wore a mask. Four of Sidney's *Certain Sonnets* (8-11) that lament the damage done to a beautiful face by the pox may owe something to his memory of his mother's ordeal. And his portrait of the long-suffering Parthenia in the *New Arcadia*, whose lover Argalus marries her despite her ruined beauty, clearly echoes his mother's plight and his father's continuing devotion.

On 17 October 1564 Sir Henry enrolled the ten-year-old Philip in Shrewsbury school, the same day as Philip's lifelong friend and biographer, Sir Fulke Greville, was enrolled. Although far from Penshurst, Shrewsbury was a logical choice for Sidney's early education. The town was under Sir Henry's jurisdiction and boasted a fine grammar school under the direction of its headmaster, Thomas Ashton. The rigors of Elizabethan education—in winter students were at their studies from six o'clock in the morning until four-thirty in the afternoon—suited Sidney's precocity and his extraordinary self-discipline. The curriculum was almost entirely in Latin, though modern languages seem to have had some place at Shrewsbury. An account of Philip's expenses at school includes an entry "for two quires of paper, for example books, phrases and sentences in Latin and French." Another account records expenditures for a book of Virgil and a catechism of Calvin, testifying to the school's mix of classical and Puritan values. Philip may even have developed his taste and love for drama by acting in the didactic plays that were a staple of many Elizabethan grammar schools, including Shrewsbury.

At school he demonstrated a remarkable mastery of academic subjects. "His talk [was] ever of knowledge," reports Greville, "so as even his teachers found something in him to observe, and learn, above that which they had usually read, or taught." Greville may have appraised Sidney's accomplishments fairly accurately. The physician Thomas Moffett, a friend of the Sidneys and another early biographer of Philip, notes his mastery of grammar, rhetoric, mathematics, Latin, French, and some Greek. But the remarkable and very important trait of Sidney's mind was that he saw the aim of human life to be, as he said of poetry in *The Defence of Poetry*, "well-doing, and not of well-knowing only." Though Moffett comments that he treated games and sports "negligently," forsaking them "for the sake of literary studies," he developed into a handsome young man with a natural grace and considerable athletic prowess. His excellent horsemanship would later make him, despite delicate health, a champion in tiltyards and tournaments. Greville's observation that Philip's "very play tend[ed] to enrich his mind" seems close to the mark. A similar desire to make all experience educational distinguishes the childhood of Pyrocles and Musidorus, the precocious hero-princes of the *Arcadias*.

Twice during his school days at Shrewsbury, Sidney traveled to Oxford for ceremonies presided over by Queen Elizabeth. On the first trip, in August 1566, he resided at Lincoln College and must have enjoyed a privileged view of the queen's activities, as he was in the company of his uncle, Robert Dudley, first Earl of Leicester, Chancellor of the University. Sidney's servant, Thomas Marshall, recorded that on the return trip to Shrewsbury, Philip gave twelvepence to a blind harper at Chipping Norton—a moment he may have recalled years later in *The Defence of Poetry*, when he reflected on the pleasures of lyric: "I never heard the old song of Percy and Douglas that I found not my heart moved more than with a trumpet; and yet is it sung but by some blind crowder, with no rougher voice than rude style." The second trip to Oxford came early in 1568, just before he completed his studies at Shrewsbury. On that occasion, according to his horoscope, he "delivered an oration before her most serene Highness that was both eloquent and elegant."

Shortly after his 1568 visit, Sidney returned to Oxford as a student at Christ Church, where it seems he studied for three years. He soon established a reputation for excellence in public debate. Richard Carew recalls in his *Survey of Cornwall* (1602) an incident when "being a scholar in Oxford of fourteen years age, and three years standing, upon a wrong conceived opinion touching my sufficiency I was . . . called to dispute *ex tempore (impar congressus Achilli)* with the matchless Sir Philip Sidney, in presence of the Earls Leicester, Warwick, and other great personages."

During his Oxford years a marriage was proposed between Philip and Anne, daughter of Sir William Cecil, that would have linked the Sidneys to one of the most powerful families of the realm. But when Sir William's investigations revealed that the Sidneys were rather poor, his enthusiasm waned, and relations between the two families cooled. Anne later married Edward de Vere, seventeenth Earl of Oxford.

Like most men of his rank Sidney left Oxford without taking a degree. After recovering from the plague in the spring of 1572, he may have spent a term at Cambridge. During this time his family was busy with preparations for his first tour of the Continent. A peace treaty between England and France, concluded in April, provided the opportunity. Late the following month he was given permission to travel to Paris as one of the delegation accompanying Lord High Admiral Edward de Fiennes, ninth Earl of Lincoln, with a license from Elizabeth for "her trusty and well-beloved Philip Sidney, Esquire, to go out of England into parts beyond the seas" for a period of two years. By her instructions he was to attain "the knowledge of foreign languages." Leicester commended his nephew to Elizabeth's ambassador in Paris, Sir Francis Walsingham, who would become Sidney's friend, adviser, and father-in-law. Sidney was not yet eighteen years old.

Such trips were rare among Englishmen of Sidney's day. For him it was to be most fateful, contributing deeply to his education and preparing him for a career in the service of the state. Traveling with Griffin Madox, his Welsh servant, and Lodowick Bryskett, a London-born gentleman of Italian parents, Sidney arrived in Paris in early June. There he participated in official ceremonies marking the Treaty of Blois. He and his companions remained in Paris for the summer, where Sidney cultivated the friendship—and earned the admiration—of an extraordinary variety of people. These included Walsingham, the rhetorician Peter Ramus, the printer Andrew Wechel, and perhaps even the distinguished Huguenot Hubert Languet, his future mentor, whose friendship he cultivated later in Strasbourg. But Sidney impressed not only Protestant intellectuals. In early August 1572, King Charles IX created him "Baron de Sidenay"—partly in recognition of his unusual personal appeal and partly in an effort to cultivate powerful English Protestants. Because Elizabeth disliked foreign titles, Sidney did not sign himself "Baron Sidney" in England, though his friends on the Continent regularly addressed him by that title.

This successful summer ended in horror. The marriage of Charles IX's sister Margaret de Valois to the Huguenot King Henry of Navarre, in late August, was designed to end a decade of bloodshed between French Catholics and Protestants. Over the summer soberly dressed Huguenots from the provinces and splendidly attired Catholics of King Charles's family and the French nobility had flocked to Paris for the wedding. Rumor swelled that the Huguenots would attempt a coup d'état after the wedding. On the Catholic side, even before the wedding, Henri I de Lorraine, Duke of Guise (with the assent of Catherine de Médicis), had been plotting the assassination of Admiral Gaspard de Coligny, the most able and powerful of Navarre's advisers.

Sidney witnessed many of the events of the week of 17-23 August 1572: secular and religious wedding ceremonies, important state meetings, and lavish evening entertainments. Festivities ended abruptly on Friday morning, when a sniper's bullet wounded Admiral de Coligny in the arm and finger. The Guise plot had been irrevocably launched. After a day of well-coordinated planning, the Saint Bartholomew's Day Massacre began in earnest just after midnight on Sunday, 23 August. All over Paris, Huguenot men, women, and children were rounded up and killed. The recuperating Coligny was murdered and his body thrown into the street. Peter Ramus was ambushed and butchered, his corpse was hurled from a window, and its entrails were dragged through the city. Languet himself barely escaped a gang of assassins. News of the violence spread beyond the city, and thousands more Protestants were dispatched in Lyons, Orléans, Bordeaux, and other regions.

How much of the slaughter Sidney witnessed in Paris is not known. Perhaps he was among the Englishmen who found refuge with Walsingham at the English embassy outside the city walls. Perhaps he was part of an English group taken to view the mutilated corpse of Coligny. He seems to have been in little danger; there is evidence that influential Catholics were careful to protect their English visitors. Nevertheless, when word of the violence reached England, the Queen's Council commanded Walsingham to secure Sidney's safe passage back to England. These instructions arrived too late, for Walsingham had already spirited Sidney away toward Germany. He never returned to France.

Arriving in Frankfurt via Strasbourg, Sidney had the leisure over the following winter to establish his friendship with the fifty-four-year-old bachelor Hubert Languet, envoy of the elector of Saxony, with whom he was to exchange a voluminous and invaluable correspondence in Latin for more than a decade. The stately and erudite Languet, one of the leading Huguenot figures of Europe, took what now seems a more-than-fatherly interest in Sidney's personal well-being, the development of his scholarship, and the friendships he established on the Continent. He saw in the brilliant young Englishman a potential leader in an effort he himself regarded as essential: to interest England in an alliance for the protection of European Protestants.

After visiting Vienna for several months in 1573, Sidney set out in late August or early September on a brief trip into Hungary that extended into a three-month stay. His experience there is fondly remembered in *The Defence of Poetry* in a passage praising lyric songs: "In Hungary I have seen it the manner at all feasts, and other such meetings, to have the songs of their ancestors' valor, which that right soldierlike nation think one of the chiefest kindlers of brave courage." In his first letter to Sidney, dated September 1573, Languet chided him for not having revealed his plans: "When you left [Vienna] you said that you would not be gone for more than three days. But now, like a little bird that has forced its way through the bars of its cage, your delight makes you restless, flitting hither and yon, perhaps without a thought for your friends."

When Sidney announced his intention to visit Italy, Languet, envisioning an even longer and more dangerous separation from his protégé, could win from him only a promise that he would not visit Rome. Some of this anxiety was quite practical: the more tolerant cities of northern Italy were reasonably safe for Protestant travelers, but this was not so farther south, where the Inquisition held sway. But Languet's letters reveal that he also feared that Sidney's youth and tolerant disposition would make him, despite events of the previous summer, susceptible to the persuasion of Catholics.

Because of their reputation for religious and intellectual tolerance, Venice and the university city of Padua were natural destinations for Englishmen who wanted to see Italy. Again traveling with Bryskett and Madox, Sidney reached Venice in early November 1573. He spent most of the following year there and in Padua, with excursions to Genoa and Florence. In letters to Languet from Venice and Padua he recounted meeting his distant cousin Richard Shelley (an ancestor of the Romantic poet Percy Bysshe Shelley, and a longtime resident of the city), an erudite man who was, in Sidney's phrase, "sadly addicted to Popery." In Venice he also met a variety of important Europeans.

Sidney immersed himself in Italian culture—so much so that in one letter Languet addressed him as "you Italians," and Walsingham began to be concerned that the young man was wavering in his faith. The philosopher Giordano Bruno, who later traveled to Oxford under Sidney's auspices and dedicated verses to him, recorded that Sidney enjoyed an excellent reputation during this visit. Yet one of Languet's replies to a now-missing letter suggests that Sidney was not overly smitten with Venice's fabled charms, and in a 1578 letter to his brother Robert, Sidney roundly criticized the "tyrannous oppression" and "counterfeit learning" he observed in Italy, though he admitted to admiring Italian arms and horsemanship.

By February 1574 Sidney was sufficiently prominent in Venice to sit for a portrait (now lost) by the Venetian master Paolo Veronese. Languet seems to have found it indifferently pleasing. There are now extant only two primary likenesses of Sidney, neither painted *ad vivum*: the youthful Longleat portrait, dated 1578; and the Penshurst portrait executed for his brother, Robert, probably in the 1590s.

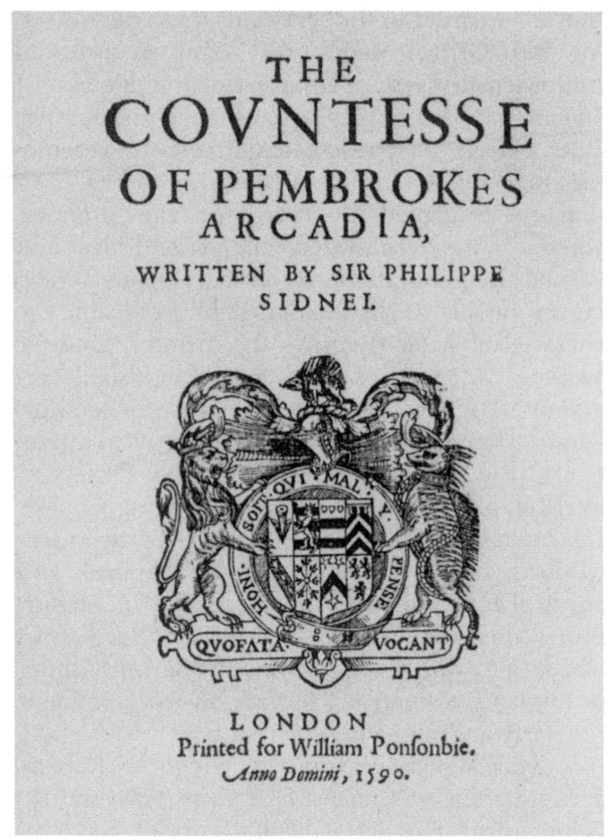

Title page, with Sidney's coat of arms, for the first published version of his best-known work

The renowned university at Padua, to which Sidney repaired in January 1574, provided a focus for his voluminous reading and improved his mastery of languages, particularly Latin. At Languet's suggestion he translated "Cicero into French, then from French into English, and then back into Latin again by an uninterrupted process." But he demurred at Languet's recommendation that he study German: "Of the German language I quite despair, for it has a certain harshness about it." He complained that at his age he had no hope of mastering it, "even so as to understand it." He seems also to have studied astronomy and geometry—the latter because he had "always had the impression that it is closely related to military science." His reading included a vast range of subjects. According to John Buxton, he read works on Venetian government (considered the model of European nations), world history, a book on the Council of Trent, and collections of letters by Paolo Manzio, Bernardo Tasso, Pietro Bembo, and Lorenzo de'

Medici—as well as several books on *imprese*, the emblematic devices that he would put to great creative use in his life and writings.

Sidney also read widely in Italian poetry and criticism, which he chose not to mention to Languet. Like many of his contemporaries he held Italian literature in high esteem, and his work was significantly shaped by Italian influences. His reference in *The Defence of Poetry* to Dante's Beatrice (in the *Paradiso* rather than the *Vita nuova*) is the first by an Englishman. Jacopo Sannazaro, twice mentioned as an authority in *The Defence of Poetry*, through his *Arcadia* (1504) contributed to Sidney's understanding of pastoral romance. The valiant hero of Torquato Tasso's *Orlando Furioso*, also twice mentioned in the *Defence*, helped shape the characters of Pyrocles and Musidorus in the *Arcadias*. And though he resists the influence of Petrarch and his followers in *Astrophil and Stella*, Sidney's awareness of Petrarchism is everywhere apparent.

In August 1574, after ten months in Italy, Sidney left Venice for Languet's house in Vienna, where he fell seriously ill. Nursed back to health by Languet, he spent the winter of 1574-1575 enjoying the friendship of that city's important men. His most intimate friend at the time was Edward Wotton, whom Walsingham had appointed to a post in Vienna. The friendship would last until Sidney's death. At the beginning of *The Defence of Poetry* he recalls how during his stay in Vienna he and "the right virtuous Edward Wotton" studied horsemanship under the famed John Pietro Pugliano, the Italian maestro of the emperor Maximilian II's stables:

> according to the fertileness of the Italian wit, [Pugliano] did not only afford us the demonstration of his practice, but sought to enrich our minds with the contemplations therein, which he thought most precious.... Nay, to so unbelieved a point he proceeded as that no earthly thing bred such wonder to a prince as to be a good horseman—skill of government was but a *pedanteria* in comparison. Then would he add certain praises, by telling what a peerless beast the horse was . . . that if I had not been a piece of a logician before I came to him, I think he would have persuaded me to have wished myself a horse.

Beneath the levity of this passage—part of the fun is that in its original Greek the name *Philip* (*phil-*, *hippos*) denotes love of horses—is a tribute to an art that Sidney, like Wotton, practiced to excellence. That he chose to discourse upon the exercise of the "peerless beast" as an introduction to his work about the "peerless poet" may seem peculiar unless we realize how highly he regarded horsemanship as an art of "well-doing" and not of "well-knowing" only. In sonnet 41 of *Astrophil and Stella* he recalls the satisfaction of "Having this day my horse, my hand, my lance / Guided so well that I obtained the prize." In the *Arcadia* he explores the elements of horsemanship in greater detail, portraying the dynamics of control, the unspoken trust and communication between horse and rider, that makes of the two a single composite being.

Instructions from Leicester to hasten his return to England in the spring of 1575 altered Sidney's planned route through Burgundy and Paris. He followed Languet to Prague in early March, then joined Wotton in Dresden; after stops in Strasbourg and Frankfurt the company reached Antwerp at the beginning of May and arrived in England on the last day of the month—almost exactly three years after his departure.

He found the Sidney family well, though still mourning the death, in February 1574, of Philip's youngest sister, Ambrosia, at the age of ten. This had prompted from the queen a letter of uncharacteristically intimate condolence, in view of her usually aloof and ambivalent treatment of the Sidneys. The same letter commanded Philip's sister Mary, not yet fourteen, to court. Sir Henry, who had resigned his post as lord deputy of Ireland in 1571, was happily employed as president of the Marches of Wales, but his wife was seriously depressed through bad health, bereavement, and financial problems.

Philip Sidney had left England "young and raw," in the words of his uncle Leicester; he returned in full manhood, having acquired a vast store of new experience and learning, a network of important Continental friends, and a knowledge of European political affairs that few Englishmen could match. Eager to enter the service of his country, he spent the next eighteen months in England, awaiting assignment. During his first summer at home he and his family witnessed the spectacular entertainments—pageants, speeches, hunts, tilts, games, animal baitings, and more—presented daily to the queen during her three-week visit to Kenilworth, Leicester's estate near Warwick.

Later that summer Sidney saw his father off to Ireland, where—much to Sir Henry's regret—he had been reappointed lord deputy. Neglecting his correspondence with his European friends, Philip spent the autumn and winter in London, where he gave himself over to the pleasures at court; Elizabeth made him her Cup-Bearer. Letters from Languet and other friends on the Continent were addressed to him at Leicester House, and an edition of Ramus's *Commentaries* was dedicated to him. During this period Sidney enjoyed a deepening friendship with Walter Devereux, first Earl of Essex, Sir Henry's comrade in Ireland. The following summer he accompanied Essex back to Ireland and was reunited with Sir Henry.

Essex soon fell victim to a plague of dysentery that swept Ireland and died on 22 September 1576, in Dublin. Sidney, who had received a letter summoning him to the earl's bedside, arrived too late. There he found a touching message, written during the earl's last days, in which he left Philip nothing except the wish that "if God do move both their hearts . . . he might match with my daughter." "I call him son," the earl continued, "he is so wise, so virtuous, so goodly; and if he go on in the course that he hath begun, he will be as famous and worthy a gentleman as ever England bred." This daughter, Penelope Devereux, would become the "Stella" of Sidney's *Astrophil and Stella.*

Although Essex's agent, Edward Waterhouse, repeated the hope that Philip and Penelope would marry, it is unlikely that Philip, much less his father or any of his mother's Dudley family, took this proposal seriously at the time. He was a man of twenty-one, Penelope a girl of twelve. Moreover, he longed for a political commission that would allow him to employ the knowledge and skills he had acquired during his three years on the Continent. If Astrophil is naively read as an undeflected representation of Sidney himself, he can be forgiven for his neglect of Penelope, though it is a neglect that he later regretted when she married Lord Robert Rich in 1581. In the second sonnet of *Astrophil and Stella*, Astrophil explains that his love for Stella was the result of a gradual process, growing "by degrees." In the thirty-third he blames himself for not having taken advantage of opportunity when it presented itself:

> But to myself myself did give the blow,
> While too much wit (forsooth) so troubled me,
> That I respects for both our sakes must show:
> And yet could not by rising Morn foresee
> How fair a day was near, o punished eyes,
> That I had been more foolish or more wise.

When news of the death of Maximilian II of Austria reached England in late October 1576, Sidney seemed to Elizabeth's advisers the logical choice to lead a special embassy to extend her condolences to the emperor's family. Ostensibly, Sidney's mission would be strictly formal; its informal purpose was entirely political. Hard upon this news came the death of the staunch Calvinist Frederick III, elector of the Palatinate. Political uncertainty deepened when Spanish mercenaries in the Low Countries sacked and burned Antwerp as well as other smaller towns. While Sidney and his entourage visited the courts of Europe, he would use his audiences with heads of state to enlist their support for the creation of a Protestant League—a mission that seemed now more urgent and propitious than ever before.

After two months of preparations, Sidney's instructions were delivered on 7 February 1577, and he left for the Continent at the end of the month. Accompanying him were two experienced statesmen, Sir Henry Lee and Sir Jerome Bowes, among other career diplomats, and his personal friends Fulke Greville and Edward Dyer, both of whom figure importantly in Sidney's literary career. At Louvain he charmed the Spanish governor, Don John, who (abetted by a group of English and Scottish exiles) was plotting to overthrow Elizabeth, free Mary, Queen of Scots, and marry her. From Brussels, Sidney's party traveled up the Rhine to Heidelberg, where he greeted Prince John Casimir, and from thence to Prague, where he accomplished his official mission of extending the queen's condolences to the family of Maximilian II.

In Prague he also visited Edmund Campion, whom he must have known, if only casually, from their days at Oxford. To his tutor in Rome, Campion described Sidney, mistakenly, as "a poor wavering soul" who might be amenable to conversion to the Roman Church. It is clear that his interest in Sidney was opportunistic. Yet Campion's words provide no basis for saying, as John Buxton has, that Sidney was cynically "using all his tact and charm to learn from Campion's own lips how far conversion had led him on the path of disloyalty." Rather, though Sidney held Campion to be in "a full wrong divinity"—as he said of Orpheus, Amphion, and Homer in the *Defence*—he probably admired the gifted and accomplished Jesuit, as many others did. Sidney genuinely sought "the prayers of all good men" and was happy to assist even Catholics who would ease the suffering of the poor. The catalogue of the long-dispersed library at Penshurst, recently discovered by Germaine Warkentin, lists an edition of the *Conference in the Tower with Campion*, published in 1581, shortly after Campion's execution. If in fact this book belonged to Philip Sidney, perhaps he hoped to find in it evidence that Campion had discovered the true religion in the hours before his death.

On the return trip to England Sidney met with William I of Orange and discussed plans for a Protestant League. It is a testament to his growing international status—which S. K. Heninger, Jr., believes was so great as to unsettle Elizabeth herself—that William offered him his daughter's hand in marriage. The promised dowry included the provinces of Holland and Zeeland.

In Ireland, Sidney had witnessed firsthand Sir Henry's vigorous prosecution of the campaign against the Irish rebels. Returned from the Continent in the fall of 1577, he found himself obliged to defend his father's policies. To maintain the English garrison Sir Henry had ordered the imposition of a cess or land tax against certain lords living within the Pale. The Irish lords resisted the tax and through their effective spokesman, Thomas Butler, tenth Earl of Ormonde, argued their case before Elizabeth and the Queen's Council. Sidney entered the debate with his "Discourse on Irish Affairs," which survives only in a holograph fragment. To the modern reader his reasoning seems shockingly brutal, yet the repression he advocates is typical of English attitudes toward the Irish during Elizabeth's reign. He does argue that a tax that exempted no one would ease the suffering of the many, who had traditionally borne the brunt of taxation: "this touches the privileged . . . persons [who] be all the rich men of the Pale, the burden only lying upon the poor, who may groan, for their cry cannot be heard." But this seems ingenuous, for further on he advocates a policy of complete subjugation, saying that "severe means" are more justified in Ireland than "lenity." In the end Sir Henry's fortunes in Ireland worsened, and he was recalled as lord deputy in February 1578.

In the years after 1577 Sidney's political career was frustrated by Elizabeth's interest in balancing the power of Spain against that of France, a balance she feared would be upset by the creation of a Protestant League. Thwarted in his political ambition, Sidney turned his attention briefly to exploration, investing in three New World voyages by Martin Frobisher. He also began, perhaps as early as 1578, what soon became an intensive writing career.

Among his first literary projects Sidney experimented with a type of drama that would reach its most sophisticated form in the seventeenth-century court masque. In 1578 or 1579, for the queen's visit to his uncle Leicester's new estate at Wanstead, he wrote the pastoral entertainment known as *The Lady of May*. The only published version, of 1598, is not a text, but rather a detailed transcription of the production, perhaps done at Sidney's request. Ostensibly a tribute to Elizabeth, it is a work of some literary merit and considerable political and propagandistic import.

The Lady of May, a young and beautiful maiden much pursued by country bachelors, faces an emblematic choice of marriage between two men she likes but does not love: the wealthy shepherd Espilus, a man "of very small deserts and no faults," and the pleasing but sometimes violent forester Theron, a man of "many deserts and many faults." The drama combines several elements that were to figure prominently as themes and issues in Sidney's later writings, especially *Astrophil and Stella* and the *Arcadias*: the Petrarchan stance of stylized veneration of a lady by her lover, the pastoral mode of setting and plot, and some dramatized speculations about the uses and abuses of rhetoric. But like many of his contemporaries, Sidney adapts convention to topicality; and Elizabeth's own unmarried status, together with her apparent pleasure at the courtship of François Alençon, Duke of Anjou, are deeply implicated in this superficially innocuous entertainment. The action was designed to favor Theron the forester over Espilus the shepherd, in whose country blandness Sidney intended to reflect Alençon. But "it pleased her Majesty to judge that Espilus did the better deserve [the Lady of May]." Although Sidney left open the way to such a resolution—the final verses of Espilus and Theron allow for either choice—Elizabeth's selection of Espilus over Theron illustrates the degree to which Sidney and his queen saw things differently.

Late in 1579 Sidney made his opposition to Alençon's suit explicit in an open letter to the queen. By that time the issue had focused the divided loyalties of English Protestants and Catholics. The queen had been considering Alençon's proposal of marriage for some time. Her childlessness invited a bitter struggle over succession, and many English Protestants feared a Catholic con-

Sir Philip Sidney; miniature by Isaac Oliver at Windsor Castle (Collection of Her Majesty the Queen)

sort. Sidney's faction, which included his father and his powerful uncle Leicester, believed that a French marriage might lead to civil war.

To the modern reader this letter, "Written . . . to Queen Elizabeth, Touching Her Marriage with Monsieur," seems remarkably frank and fearless of the displeasure it might bring. Sidney addresses the queen forthrightly as a courtier whose function it is to advise his monarch. He reminds her that the peace of the land, no less than her own power, depends upon the confidence of her subjects, a confidence likely to be eroded by an unpopular marriage. Although he does not mention Alençon's famed ugliness, as others did, he does rehearse much about her prospective husband that she already knew and did not need to hear from one of her subjects: that Alençon was "a Frenchman, and a papist"; that his mother was the notorious Catherine de Médicis, "the Jezebel of our age" (though he does not directly say that she had engineered the massacre of Huguenots in 1572); that Alençon himself had sacked La Charité and Issoire "with fire and sword"; and that his race was afflicted with congenital "unhealthfulness." Sidney concludes with the warning that "if he do come hither, he must live here in far meaner reputation than his mind will well brook, having no other royalty to countenance himself with; or else you must deliver him the keys of your kingdom, and live at his discretion."

There is no evidence that Elizabeth took umbrage at the letter, but it is difficult to imagine that it did anything to smooth the troubled relationship that persisted between the Sidney family and the queen throughout Philip's lifetime. Perhaps his tone in the letter owes something to a liminal resentment he felt because of her niggardly treatment of his father, who, as president of the Marches of Wales and twice as her lord deputy of Ireland, had been among her ablest subjects. Perhaps too it reflects on an incident that embroiled Sidney's politics with his personal dignity. Greville reports that sometime in 1579 Edward de Vere, Earl of Oxford, a staunch supporter of Alençon's suit, had ordered Sidney off a tennis court in the presence of the French delegation. Sidney issued a challenge the next day, but the queen herself intervened to prevent the duel and reminded him of his inferior status—a rebuke that may have recalled to him as well that de Vere had married Anne Cecil after her father had found the Sidney family unworthy. Sidney was absent from the court the next year and probably spent much of the time at Wilton, his sister's home, composing the *Old Arcadia*. When he returned to court after a year in seclusion, Sidney presented Elizabeth with a 1581 New Year's gift of a "whip garnished with diamonds," signifying by this astonishing Petrarchan gesture his complete submission to the queen's will in the Alençon affair. That summer his personal fortunes received a blow when the countess of Leicester bore the earl a son, thereby depriving Sidney of both lands and title that he stood to inherit as Leicester's heir presumptive. On the following tilt day, Sidney bore the device—~~*SPERAVI*~~ "hope"—dashed through.

Sidney had begun writing poetry probably in 1578. This was an "unelected vocation," as he says in *The Defence of Poetry*, "in these my not old years and idlest times having slipped into the title of a poet." But exactly when he became a poet we do not know. None of his works was published before 1590, four years after his death. This fact, together with the brevity and intensity of Sidney's writing career—no more than seven or eight years, during which he worked simultaneously on different texts—only complicates the problem of determining when his works were composed.

Among Sidney's earliest ventures in this unelected vocation were attempts, undertaken with his friends Greville and Dyer, at writing a new kind of English poetry grounded not in accentual stress but in duration of syllables, work that was in progress by October 1579, when Edmund Spenser reported it in letters to Gabriel Harvey. These experiments in quantitative verse, examples of which Sidney incorporated into the *Old Arcadia*, were efforts to make English verse conform to the rules of Latin prosody. Although they never exerted a significant influence upon English metrics, they have long interested scholars and critics. The dactylic hexameters of *Old Arcadia* 13 are an example of what Sidney achieved:

> Lady, reserved by the heav'ns to do pastors' company honor
> Joining your sweet voice to the rural muse of a desert,
> Here you fully do find this strange operation of love,
> How to the woods love runs as well as rides to the palace.

In his correspondence with Harvey, Spenser also claimed that Sidney, Greville, and Dyer had formed an English Academy or Areopagus to advance the cause of the new metrics, a claim that has been investigated many times and is at present widely doubted.

The years 1579 through 1584 represent the peak of Sidney's literary activity. The winter of 1579-1580 seems the best conjectural date for *The Defence of Poetry*, written probably in response to Stephen Gosson's *School of Abuse*, which was printed in the summer of 1579 and dedicated to Sidney without permission. The connection with Gosson's work, along with a reference to Spenser's *Shepheardes Calender*, also published in 1579 and dedicated to Sidney, indicate that Sidney began *The Defence of Poetry* in that year, whereas the sustained intensity of his argument would seem to make it equally likely that he completed the work in a relatively short time. It did not appear in print, however, until 1595, which saw two editions by different printers. William Ponsonby, the established printer for the Sidney family, entered *The Defence of Poetry* in the Stationer's Register on 29 November 1594 but seems to have delayed publication until the next year. Before Ponsonby's text appeared, another edition was published by Henry Olney, titled *An Apology for Poetry*, of which a now unknown number of copies was sold before Ponsonby, claiming precedence, interceded and halted further sales. Ponsonby's edition was then printed and sold, and the title page of his edition was also fixed to some liberated copies of the Olney edition. The Ponsonby text and the De L'Isle manuscript at Penshurst form the basis of Jan van Dorsten's definitive modern edition.

The Defence of Poetry is undoubtedly the most important critical treatise on poetry written by an Englishman during the Elizabethan period. It has achieved the status of a classical text. Although it reflects Sidney's Protestantism, it is nevertheless a very worldly work. Drawing on an extraordinary range of classical and Continental texts, Sidney sets out to defend "poor poetry" against its attackers and to argue positively that poetry, whose "final end is to lead and draw us to as high a perfection as our degenerate souls, made worse by their clayey lodgings, can be capable of," is the best vehicle for the "purifying of wit." He disposes his argument according to a traditional seven-part classical structure, beginning with an introduction or exordium and moving through the stages of proposition, division, examination and refutation to a final peroration, and including, as custom permitted, a *digressio* on a related issue.

Sidney opens his argument by claiming that poetry gave rise to every other kind and division of learning. For this reason the Romans called the poet *vates*, "which is as much as a diviner, foreseer, or prophet," such as David revealed himself to be in his Psalms. With equal reverence the Greeks called the poet a "maker," as do the English (from the Greek verb *poiein*, "to make"). In all cases true poetry makes things "either better than nature bringeth forth, or, quite anew, forms such as never were in nature." Nature's "world is brazen," Sidney argues; only the poets "deliver a golden [one]."

Sidney explains that the poet is able to create this heightened fictive world by coupling an idea with an image: "the skill of each artificer standeth in that *idea* or fore-conceit of the work, and not in the work itself. And that the poet hath that *idea* is manifest, by delivering them forth in such excellency as he had imagined them." The union of fore-conceit and image results in a poetic event which has extraordinary "energaic" capacity, that is, the power to move the human will and thus to motivate its own reproduction. Xenophon's Cyrus is a poetic creation so forceful that if readers comprehend the character, they will be prompted to reproduce its virtues in their own medium: "so far substantially it worketh, not only to make a Cyrus, which had been but a particular excellency as nature might have done, but to bestow a Cyrus upon the world to make many Cyruses, if [readers] will learn why and how that maker made him." It is the replicability of the poetic image among those who understand why and how it was created that distinguishes poetry from nature. The ongoing replication of poetic images is what enables our "erected wit" to mitigate against the effects of our "infected wills."

Sidney then presents the crucial definition of the process of encoding fore-conceits in images to create energaic poetic constructs: "Poesy therefore is an art of imitation, for so Aristotle termeth it in the word *mimesis*—that is to say, a representing, counterfeiting, or figuring forth—to speak metaphorically, a speaking picture—with this end, to teach and delight." This definition—a tightly composed amalgam of ideas lifted from Aristotle (*mimesis*), Plutarch ("speaking picture"), and Horace ("teach and delight")—with its emphasis upon activity, informs all the theoretical matter of *The Defence of Poetry.*

Of mimetic poets Sidney conceives three kinds: divine poets who imitate the "inconceivable excellencies of God," of whom David, Solomon, and pagan poets—Orpheus, Amphion, and Homer, "though in a full wrong divinity"—are cited as examples; poets who imitate "matter philosophical," of which there are four subtypes (moral, natural, astronomical, and historical); and "right poets." Sidney is primarily concerned with the right poets: "these third be they which most properly do imitate to teach and delight, and to imitate borrow nothing of what is, has been, or shall be; but range, only reined with learned discretion, into the divine consideration of what may be and should be." They are arrayed in a hierarchy from "the most notable" heroic poets down to pastoral poets "and certain others, some of these being termed according to the matter they deal with, some by the sorts of verses they liked best to write in." But Sidney is quick to point out that verse is but "an ornament and no cause to poetry." Rather, the "feigning" of "notable images of virtues, vices, or what else, with that delightful teaching . . . must be the right describing note to know a poet by."

The right poet is then set off against other masters of "earthly learning" who claim to lead men to "virtuous action," an ancient contest developed at length in Aristotle's *Poetics.* The poet's principal competitors are two: the moral philosopher, a figure of "sullen gravity . . . rudely clothed . . . casting largess of definitions, divisions and distinctions" before him; and the historian, "laden with old mouse-eaten records," who knows more about the past than his own age, who is "a wonder to young folks and a tyrant in table talk." The philosopher maintains that there is no better guide to virtue than he who "teacheth what virtue is; and teach it not only by delivering forth his very being, his causes and effects, but also by making known his enemy, vice, which much be destroyed, and his cumbersome servant, passion, which must be mastered." For his part the historian claims a significant advantage over the philosopher in that he teaches an "active" virtue rather than a "disputative" one. The philosopher delivers virtue "excellent in the dangerless Academy of Plato," but the historian "showeth forth [Virtue's] honorable face in . . . battles." "[The philosopher] teacheth virtue by certain abstractions," adds the historian, "but I only bid you follow the footing of them that have gone before you." Sidney can see no end to this tedious dispute and so interrupts it by noting only "that the one giveth the precept, the other the example."

The poet, of course, "standeth for the highest form in the school of learning" because he is the "moderator" between the philosopher and the historian. Through the art of mimesis the poet unites in one event the philosopher's "precept" and the historian's "example." Rephrasing his earlier argument on "fore-conceit" and "image," Sidney proclaims that "the peerless poet . . . giveth a perfect picture" of something, "so as he coupleth the general notion with the particular example." He then lists exemplary precepts that poets encode in speaking pictures: anger, wisdom, temperance, valor, friendship, remorse, pride, cruelty, and ambition. But the greatest of these is "the most excellent determination of goodness," as in Xenophon's "feigning" of the prince in Cyrus, in Virgil's fashioning of a virtuous man in Aeneas and in Sir Thomas More's representation of an entire commonwealth in his *Utopia.* The reference to the Catholic More prompts a brief digression in which Sidney states a general tenet of mimesis he has not made before: if the poetic artifact is flawed, the fault lies with the poet, not with poetry. Having made this point, he caps his list by citing the practice of Jesus, who couched his teachings in lively stories.

Because of its forcefulness, the poet's "feigned example" has as much capacity as the "true example" for teaching what is to be shunned or followed. Moreover, Sidney remarks wryly, by reading a representation of, rather than actually duplicating, the strategy of Darius's faithful servant Zopyrus, who severed his own nose and ears to persuade the Babylonians that he was a traitor, "you shall save your nose by the bargain." Conversely, the poet's "moving is of a higher degree than [the philosopher's] teaching," for which he cites as his authority Aristotle's comments on *gnosis* (knowing) and *praxis* (acting, doing) in the *Ethics*.

The poet emerges from this comparison transformed from "moderator" to "monarch." "Either accompanied with, or prepared for, the well-enchanting skill of music," poetry has the capacity to transmute even horrors—"cruel battles, unnatural monsters"—into delightful experience. The "strange effects of . . . poetical invention" are such that orators and prophets have employed it for their several purposes. Menenius Agrippa, Livy tells us, calmed the mutinous population of Rome not with "figurative speeches or cunning insinuations" but with a tale of the rebellious body attempting to starve the stomach and so hurting itself. Similarly, the prophet Nathan revealed to David a precept "most divinely true" by means of a feigned discourse.

Sidney turns next to an examination of the various subgenres in which poetry is arrayed, with a cautionary comment about overly rigid distinctions. At the very outset he warns against overdetermining such matters, noting that "some poesies have coupled together two or three kinds, as the tragical and comical, whereupon is risen the tragicomical." Anticipating the design of his own *Arcadia*s, he recommends Sannazaro and Boethius, who "mingled prose and verse," and others who "mingled matters heroical and pastoral." "If severed [genres] be good," he concludes, "the conjunction cannot be hurtful."

Sidney moves up the hierarchy of genres from the lowest to the highest, discussing pastoral, elegy, comedy, lyric, and epic or heroic, "whose very name (I think) should daunt all backbiters." Characteristically, he reserves his highest praise for the epic, whose champions—Achilles, Cyrus, Aeneas, Turnus, Tydeus, and Rinaldo—"not only teach and move to a truth, but teacheth and moveth to the most high and excellent truth." Epic is, in short, "the best and most accomplished kind of poetry." He concludes this section of *The Defence of Poetry* with a summary of his major points: that poetry deals with universal considerations; that (unlike the historian and the philosopher) the poet is not confined to already delimited parameters of inquiry but brings his own "stuff" to the act of mimesis, so that he "doth not learn a conceit out of a matter, but maketh a matter out of a conceit"; that poetry teaches goodness and delight; and that the Scriptures—indeed Christ himself—employed poetry. All this indicates that "the laurel crown appointed for triumphant captain doth worthily (of all other learnings) honor the poet's triumph."

Yet such reasoning is not likely to dissuade the *misomousoi*, the poet-haters, who wrongly identify poetry with rhyming and versifying, although, Sidney concedes, poetry often employs verse because "verse far exceedeth prose in the knitting up of memory." But laying this complaint aside, poetry and "poor [that is, maligned] poets" stand accused of four principal crimes: that they divert men from the pursuit of "other more fruitful knowledges"; that poetry "is the mother of lies"; that poetry "is the nurse of abuse, infecting us with many pestilent desires"; and that Plato banished poets from his ideal commonwealth in the *Republic*. These charges are, of course, made by straw men whom Sidney will easily hew down. The first charge he has already demonstrated to be spurious, since of all learning poetry alone "teacheth and moveth to virtue." "I still and utterly deny," he writes, "that there is sprung out of the earth a more fruitful knowledge." The second charge, that poetry fosters lies, occasions a spirited rebuttal that anticipates several hallmark concepts of structuralist and poststructuralist assumptions about language, such as arbitrariness and difference. The confidence with which he addresses the third charge, that poetry fosters "not only love, but lust, but vanity, but (if they list) scurrility," would seem to belie Astrophil's failed attempt to transmute his desire into spirituality. Nevertheless Sidney maintains that if love poetry leads man astray, we "need not say that poetry abuseth man's wit, but that man's wit abuseth poetry." Moreover, rather than enervating the spirit of warriors, implicit in the charge that it is the nurse of abuse, poetry is often "the companion of camps." Thus, Plutarch tells us, when Alexander went to war he left his

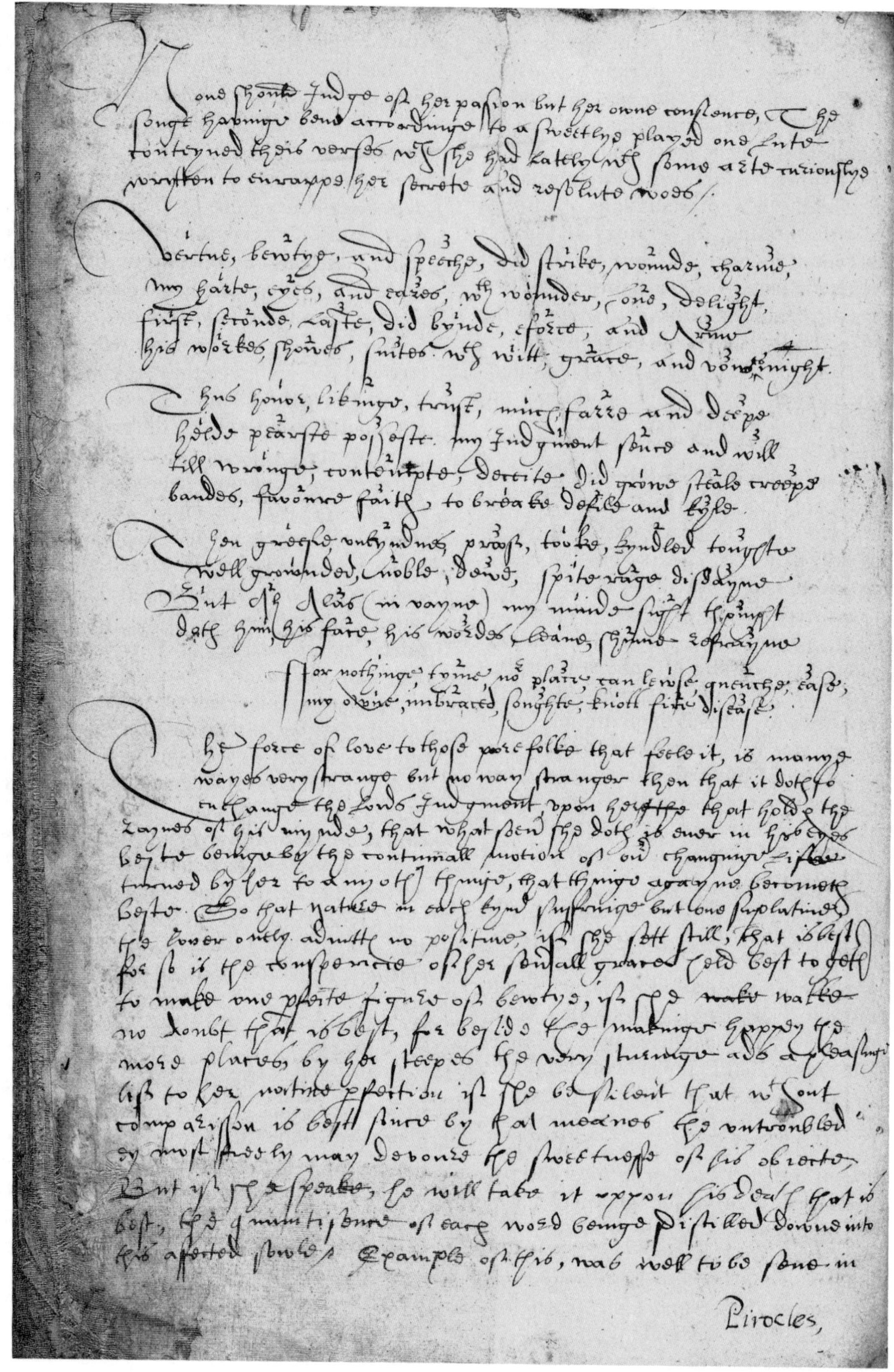

Pages from a manuscript for The Old Arcadia, *transcribed circa 1580 in as many as five hands (HM 162; 116v and 154r; Henry E. Huntington Library and Art Gallery)*

263 154

And thou poore earth, whom fortune doth attaint
in natures name, to suffer such a harme,
as for to lose thy gemme, our earthly saynte,
Upon thy face, lett coaly ravens swarme,
Lett all the sea, thy teares accompted be,
thy bowells wth all killing mettalles arme,
Lett gold nowe ruste, lett diamondes waste in the,
Lett pearles be wanne wth woe, ther damme doth beare,
thy self henceforth, the light do never see
And you O flowers, wch sometimes princes were
(till these strange altringe you did hap to try)
of princes losse, your selves for tokens reare.
Lylly, in mourning black, thy whitenes dye,
O, hiacinthe lett ai, be on thee still
your dolefull tunes sweete muses nowe apply
O, Echo, all these woodes, wth roaring fyll
sounde of my greves: and lett it never end
till yt yt all woodes and waters past,
Nay to the heavens your just complayninge send
and stay the starres inconst constant race,
till yt they do unto your dolours bende,
And aske the reason of that speciall grace,
yt they wch have no lives, should lyve so longe:
and vertuous soules, so sone should lose ther place
Aske if in greate men, good men so do ~~thee~~ thronge
that he for want of elbow roome must dye
or if that they be skante, if this be wronge,
Dyd wisdome, this our wretched tyme espie,
in one true chest, to robb all vertues treasure?
your dolefull tunes sweete Muses nowe applye,
And if that any counsaile, you to measure,
your dolefull tunes, to them still playning saye,
to well felt greif, plaint is the only pleasure.
O, light of sonne wch is intitled daye
O, well thou doest, that thou no longer byedest,
for mourning night; her black weedes may displaye
O phebus, wth good cause, thy face thou hidest,
rather than have thy all beholding eye,
foulde wth this sight, while thou thy chariott guydest,
And well me thinkes, becomes this vaultye skye,
a stately tombe, to cover him deceassed,
your dolefull tunes sweete muses nowe applye
O Philomela, wth

teacher Aristotle behind but took Homer with him.

Of the four charges against poets issued by the poet-haters, Sidney devotes the most space to refuting the final one, that Plato banned poets from his ideal republic. "But now indeed," he begins, "my burden is great; now Plato's name is laid upon me, whom, I confess, of all philosophers I have ever esteemed most worthy of reverence," for Plato "is the most poetical." Yet if Plato would "defile the fountain out of which his flowing streams have proceeded," Sidney says, "let us boldly examine with what reasons he did it." He claims that "a man might maliciously object" that Plato, a philosopher, "was the natural enemy of poets." For philosophers have made a "school-art" out of the matter that poets have conveyed "by a divine delightfulness," and then cast off their "guides, like ungrateful apprentices." Yet as Cicero noted, though many cities rejected philosophers, seven cities wished to claim Homer as a citizen. Simonides and Pindar made of the tyrant Hiero I a just king while, and here again Sidney follows Cicero, Plato was made the slave of Dionysius. For a clinching rhetorical effect Sidney, whose debt to Plato is everywhere apparent in the *Defence*, reminds his readers that both Plato (in the *Symposium* and the *Phaedrus*) and Plutarch condoned the "abominable filthiness" of homosexuality.

Having thus exposed in Plato crimes far exceeding those of poets, Sidney rehabilitates his straw man. When he claims that in banning the poet from his republic Plato places the onus "upon the abuse, not upon poetry," we should remember that he began this passage by confessing that Plato was the most poetical of philosophers. Plato's strictures were directed toward practitioners of mimesis rather than mimesis itself: "Plato therefore . . . meant not in general of poets . . . but only meant to drive out those wrong opinions of the Deity (whereof now, without further law, Christianity hath taken away all the hurtful belief) nourished by the then-esteemed poets"—as can be seen in the *Ion*, where Plato "giveth high and rightly divine commendation unto poetry." Indeed Plato, who "attributeth unto poesy more than myself do, namely, to be a very inspiring of a divine force," has been misread: witness Plato's mentor Socrates, who spent his old age turning Aesop's fables into verse, and Plato's student Aristotle, who wrote the *Poetics*—"and why, if it should not be written?" And let us not forget Plutarch, who in writing philosophy and history "trimmeth both their garments with the guards of poesy."

Following this stirring refutation—actually a set piece with unanticipated ramifications for his own later work—Sidney considers, in a relevant digression, the lamentable condition of poetry in England, directing his criticism, characteristically, at poets rather than poetry. "Sweet poesy," he begins, "that hath anciently [claimed] kings, emperors, senators, great captains," and which had heretofore flourished in Britain, is in "idle England" now little more than flim-flam, poets having "almost . . . the good reputation as the mountebanks at Venice." "Base men," he asserts, "with servile wits undertake it . . . as if all the Muses were got with child to bring forth bastard poets." Feigning as burdensome the task of defending poets and their work, only to be "overmastered by some thoughts" and thus yielding "an inky tribute to them," he defers authority in the matter of poetry to those who practice it. Restating the hugely problematic conditions of mimesis he had already presented in the Cyrus passage, he concludes that "they that delight in poesy itself should seek to know *what* they do, and *how* they do and especially look in the unflattering glass of reason" (emphasis added). For poetry must be led gently—or rather it must lead, as it cannot be acquired by "human skill." "A poet no industry can make," Sidney claims in a reaffirmation of the poet as *vates* (compare Spenser's "October Eclogue" in *The Shepheardes Calender*), "if his own genius be not carried into it."

Yet there are English poets who warrant commendation. Sidney is typical of his age in praising Chaucer's *Troilus and Criseyde* but exceptional in acknowledging that Englishmen of his time had not mastered Chaucerian metrics: "I know not whether to marvel more, either that he in that misty time could see so clearly, or that we in this age go so stumblingly after him." He also approves of the brief tragedies gathered in Thomas Sackville and others' *Mirror for Magistrates* (1563) and commends the lyrics of Henry Howard, Earl of Surrey, who regularized the English sonnet form.

None of this is controversial. However, Sidney's subsequent discussion of *The Shepheardes Calender* raises the question of how well, if at all, Sidney and Spenser were acquainted. He acknowledges that Spenser, who dedicated the *Calender* to him in 1579, "hath much poetry in his eclogues, indeed worthy of reading, if I be not deceived." In his correspondence with Gabriel Harvey, Spenser claimed to have had Sidney "in some use of familiarity." The two poets may have met at Leicester House, where Spenser was employed and where Sidney was a frequent guest at the time. Yet they were of vastly different social rank, Sidney being the earl's nephew and Spenser the earl's secretary. And Sidney does not mention Spenser by name in his discussion of the *Calender* in *The Defence of Poetry*. Indeed, after praising its poetry, Sidney criticizes its author for the "framing of his style to an old rustic language." After his death in 1586, Sidney's influence upon Spenser was pervasive. Yet his only comments upon Spenser's work do not suggest the intimacy between them that Spenser claimed to enjoy.

It is noteworthy that Sidney devotes more of his survey of English literature to drama than to poetry. He possessed an instinctive sense of dramatic structure, as *The Lady of May* demonstrates. Readers since Thomas Nash have been impressed by the dramatic character of *Astrophil and Stella*, and the first version of *Arcadia* is divided into acts. Yet although he offers here the first example of sustained dramatic criticism in English, Sidney's discussion utterly fails to anticipate the maverick forms of English theater that were to explode with such brilliance in the decade after his death. Except for Thomas Sackville and Thomas Norton's *Gorboduc* (1561), the first English tragedy in blank verse, which he endorses with qualifications, and the tragedies of his friend George Buchanan, Sidney dismisses the rest of English drama he has seen as "observing rules neither of honest civility nor skillful poetry." He criticizes English playwrights for failing to observe the rigid program of unities (time, place, and action), a prescription generally attributed to Aristotle, and he praises ancient exemplars such as Terence (*Eunuchus*), Plautus (*Captivi* and *Amphitruo*), and Euripides (*Hecuba*). Though he has already claimed to see no harm in mixed poetic genres per se, he is especially harsh in his comments on English tragicomedy, which, he remarks, is guilty of promiscuously "mingling kings and clowns" and "hornpipes and funerals." English comedy also fails to make the necessary distinction between delight and laughter, a distinction he develops in considerable detail. He concludes that he has spent too much time on plays because "they are excelling parts of poesy" and because "none [other poetry is] so much used in England, and none can be more pitifully abused."

Just before his peroration Sidney returns to the subject of lyric poetry, "songs and sonnets," which poets should direct toward the Platonic end of "singing the praises of immortal beauty: the immortal goodness of that God who giveth us hands to write and wits to conceive." In a passage rife with implications for *Astrophil and Stella*, he complains of the wooden language of so many love poets who, "if I were a mistress, would never persuade me they were in love." He attacks pseudo-Ciceronianism at some length, allowing himself to stray "from poetry to oratory." But he finally excuses the slip because it allows him to include penultimately a tribute to the ease, grace, and beauty of the English language, which "for the uttering sweetly and properly [of] the conceits of the mind . . . hath not its equal with any other tongue in the world."

Apparently Sidney was serious in his private, concurrent hopes of introducing a quantitative metrics into English poetry, for here he writes that of the two methods of versifying, by quantity and stress, "the English, before any vulgar language I know, is fit for both." Of other poetic qualities loosely grouped under the heading of rhyme, he argues that English is superior to other modern languages in its use of the caesura and in its ability to rhyme with masculine, feminine, and medial formations.

The brilliant peroration to *The Defence of Poetry* is a masterly composite of summary, exhortation, and admonition. Every praiseworthy poesy is full of "virtue-breeding delightfulness" and possesses all traits of learning; the charges against it are "false or feeble," and bad poetry is produced by "poet-apes, not poets." The English language is "most fit to honor poesy, and to be honored by poesy." Then, in the name of the Nine Muses, Sidney enjoins the reader of his "ink-wasting toy" to believe with Aristotle that poets were the keepers of the Greek divinities; with Pietro Bembo that poets first brought civility to mankind; with Joseph Justus Scaliger that poetry will sooner make an honest man than philosophy, with the German Conrad Clauser that in fables poets communicated "all knowledge, logic, rhetoric, philosophy natural and moral, and *quid non*"; with Sidney himself "that there are many mysteries contained in poetry, which of purpose were written darkly"; and with Cristoforo Landino that poets are so loved by the gods that "whatsoever they write proceeds of a divine fury." Alluding wryly to the often fulsome tone of dedications and patron-seeking prefaces, he reminds potential defenders of poetry that poets will make them "immortal by their verses," that their names "shall flourish in the printers' shops," and that poets shall make laymen "most fair, most rich, most wise," so that their souls shall dwell with Dante's Beatrice and Virgil's Anchises.

His concluding admonition, directed to anyone who might have "so earth-creeping a mind that it cannot lift itself up to look to the sky of poetry," is a masterpiece of tone, combining the witty with the deadly serious for an audience that knew both the triviality of much fashionable rhetoric and the crucial role of literature and language in resisting the monument-destroying power of mutability and relentless time. As for those who refuse to value poetry, in the name of all poets Sidney offers the malediction that "while you live, [may] you live in love, and never get favor for lacking skill of a sonnet; and when you die, your memory die from the earth for want of an epitaph."

The Defence of Poetry emerges today, in the hindsight of literary history, as a fulcrum in Sidney's career, gathering, organizing, and clarifying the critical energies developed in his early work (such as *The Lady of May* and the experiments in quantitative verse) and discharging these energies into the mature creations of the 1580s, *Astrophil and Stella* and the revised *Arcadia*. Sidney's attractiveness as a critic, like that of John Dryden in a later age, derives partly from his authority as a practicing poet who speaks as much from experience with what works and what does not as from familiarity with abstract notions of art. This is not to say, however, that his later works simply actualize conceptual blueprints from *The Defence of Poetry*. Rather, the mature writings are empirical tests whose results do not always confirm his theory. Indeed the sunny optimism of *The Defence of Poetry*, the blind faith in the ability of mimesis to overcome the obstacles presented by a realistic test of theory, is the first casualty of Sidney's praxis.

Astrophil and Stella provides a case in point. Written probably between 1581 and 1583, and circulated during Sidney's lifetime but not published until 1591, the 108 sonnets and eleven songs of this great sequence are freely experimental in technique and mark, according to William A. Ringler, Jr., "an innovation in English poetry and in Sidney's own practice." Sidney employs Italian rather than English rhyme schemes and in six of the songs introduces a trochaic rhythm unknown in English before him. Descended from Dante through Petrarch and his imitators, the sonnet tradition, with its opposition of desire and reason, body and mind, heart and soul, offered the opportunity to experiment with a fictional lover-poet challenged with the task of transmuting, through the activity of mimesis, physical love into spiritual love. Thus he might, as Sidney wrote in *The Defence of Poetry*, sing "the praises of immortal beauty" which is synonymous with the goodness of God.

Of course Astrophil is a refracted version of Sidney himself; as the poems that pun on the word *rich* (sonnets 24 and 37, for example) make clear, Stella is just as certainly a refracted version of Penelope Devereux, who married Lord Rich in 1581. The autobiographical dimensions of *Astrophil and Stella* remain of interest to scholars and critics. Yet it is as literary constructs that the lover and his beloved offer the most rewarding context for investigation. Both Astrophil and Stella are engaged in reading mimetic representations of each other. Stella, Astrophil hopes, will become a reader of his poetry in which his own painful love is written. He sketches this character-as-text metaphor in the opening sonnet:

> Loving in truth, and fain in verse my love to
> show,
> That the dear She might take some pleasure of
> my pain:
> Pleasure might cause her read, reading might
> make her know,
> Knowledge might pity win, and pity grace ob-
> tain,
> I sought fit words to paint the blackest face of
> love.

This paradigm of persuasion, in which Stella is urged to read representations of Astrophil's suffering, reappears throughout the sequence (compare sonnets 45, 57, 61, 93). In sonnet 66 Astrophil observes that "Stella's eyes sent to me the beams of bliss, / Looking on me, while I looked other way." Belief that his woe has elicited Stella's pity fosters the hope celebrated in sonnet 67, which erupts into wild joy with the announcement in sonnet 69 that "Stella hath with words where faith doth shine, / Of her high heart given me the monarchy." He relishes the mere illusion of conquest: "I, I, oh I may say, that she is mine." Forgetting Stella's earlier caveats—that true love is not the slave of desire (61) and that she loves but with "a love not blind" (62)—Astrophil here scarcely pauses over the acknowledgment that Stella gives her heart "conditionally."

Astrophil is thus poised for a fall. The condition that Stella attaches to her love precludes expression of physical desire and points up the misguided nature of Astrophil's attempt to persuade her to read him. Properly construed, the character-as-text metaphor, a metaphor dictated by the terms of mimesis presented in *The Defence of Poetry*, requires that Stella rather than Astrophil stand as the text to be read. Though he is blinded by desire, this necessity is not lost on Astrophil. In sonnet 71, at the structural center of the work, he reverses the paradigm, construing himself as the reader of Stella and so begins an ascent toward the "immortal beauty" that is synonymous with the "immortal goodness of God":

Who will in fairest book of Nature know
How Virtue may best lodged in beauty be,
Let him but learn of Love to read in thee,
Stella, those fair lines, which true goodness show.

Perceived as a representation of virtue, Stella's beauty has the capacity to rid Astrophil of tormenting desire that threatens to trap him in images of the flesh rather than free him in the reality of the spirit:

There shall he find all vice's overthrow,
Not by rude force, but sweetest soveraignty
Of reason, from whose light those night-birds fly;
That inward sun in thine eyes shineth so.

As Sidney repeatedly emphasizes in *The Defence of Poetry*, abstract knowledge is not the ultimate goal of mimesis but only an intermediate, preparatory condition that must yield action. Mimetic and didactic impulses properly complement each other when the literary creation serves to alter and improve the personality of the person exposed to it—in this case exposed both as reader and as author. Spenser discusses this in his letter to Sir Walter Ralegh prefatory to *The Faerie Queene* of 1590, when he implies that a central purpose of the poem is to fashion its reader as well as its characters in "gentle and virtuous discipline." Thus Sidney continues:

And not content to be Perfection's heir
Thyself, dost strive all minds that way to move,
Who mark in thee what is in thee most fair.
So while thy beauty draws the heart to love,
As fast thy Virtue draws that love to good.

But this is theory, not practice; the way things should be, not the way they are. In a single assertion of unconquerable appetite, the wrenching reversal of the ultimate line—" 'But ah,' Desire still cries, 'give me some food' "—collapses the elegant ascent of the previous thirteen lines. Alimentary, gustatory, and instinctive, Desire devours Theory in sonnet 71 and so presages the stolen kiss of the Second Song, when Astrophil's failure to love properly, which is a precondition of mimetic poetry, becomes manifest.

Sidney's final creation, the work still in progress at his death, was the revised *Arcadia*. Among the earliest examples of prose fiction in English, the two substantial versions of the *Arcadia* present an extraordinarily complex textual history. The original or *Old Arcadia* has five books or acts with poetic eclogues following books 1 through 4. Sidney seems to have worked on this version at intervals from 1577 to 1582 (especially during his retirement at Wilton and Ivy Church from March to August 1580), composing the work "in loose sheets of paper" in the presence of his sister—and, Greville reports, at times on horseback. Probably in 1582 he undertook an extensive revision of the original work, which he broke off in mid sentence, midway through book 3 in 1584, the date of the Cambridge manuscript of the revised or *New Arcadia*. The first version to appear in print was the incomplete *New Arcadia*, titled *The Countess of Pembroke's Arcadia*, in 1590. Three years later there appeared a second *Countess of Pembroke's Arcadia*, consisting of a reprint of the 1590 version, a lengthy addition to book 3, and the final two books of the *Old Arcadia*. This composite *Arcadia* of 1593 was the only version of the work read for the next three hundred years. Long suspected to exist, manuscripts of the original *Arcadia* were discovered by Bertram Dobell early in the present century and first published by Albert Feuillerat in his edition of 1912-1926.

Both versions develop the same principal characters in a plot dictated by the terms of an oracle. Sidney models his work upon four Continental sources: the *Ethiopian History* of Heliodorus, a Greek romance of the third century A.D.; Sannazaro's sixteenth-century pastoral *Arcadia*; Jorge de Montemayor's Spanish romance *Diana Enamorada*; and a medieval book of chivalry, *Amadis of Gaul*. In the *Old Arcadia* the princes Pyrocles and Musidorus travel to Arcadia, where they fall in love with Philoclea and Pamela, daughters of the Arcadian king Basilius and his queen, Gynecia. To gain access to the princesses, Pyrocles and Musidorus disguise themselves as, respectively, a woman and a simple shepherd. The plot is complicated when both Basilius and Gynecia fall in love with Pyrocles, who is posing as an Amazon warrior under a nom de guerre (Cleophila in the *Old Arcadia*, Zelmane in the *New Arcadia*). Pyrocles pursues Philoclea while Basilius and Gynecia pursue him. Confusion reaches a crisis when Basilius is mistakenly given a sleeping potion. The plot to wed Philoclea and Pamela is discovered, and the princes are implicated in the apparent murder of the sleeping king. The judge at their trial is Euarchus, father of Musidorus and uncle to Pyrocles. Just before Euarchus delivers his verdict, the princes' true identity is revealed, and Euarchus faces the heavy responsibility of condemning his son and nephew to death. But Basilius miraculously rises from his slumber, and the princes are absolved. Contrite, the king confesses his role in the plot and gives his daughters in marriage to Pyrocles and Musidorus. In a finale characteristic of pastoral romance, the *Old Arcadia* closes with the reconciliation of Basilius and Gynecia and the anticipated double wedding of their daughters and the princes.

More than twice as long, the unfinished *New Arcadia* covers less than half of the original plot. It contains substantial blocks of narrative transferred outright from the first two books of the old version, yet introduces entirely new adventures for the princes, with and against many new characters. Sidney also shifts emphasis significantly, from pastoral romance to epic, opening his revision in medias res, disrupting the straightforward narrative of the original with many digressive episodes, placing a new emphasis upon the political dimension of represented experience, and, by reducing the role of his signature character, Philisides, shifting the narrative from first-person to third-person point of view. Although the governing oracle, which remains essentially unchanged, implies that Sidney would have concluded the new version in basically the same fashion as the old, the *New Arcadia* is altogether a more ambitious work. As such, it offers complex implications for the theoretical program laid out in *The Defence of Poetry*.

Until recently, however, critics and scholars found the *Arcadias* of less interest than *Astrophil and Stella*, which has always been highly appreciated. Yet among Sidney's contemporaries the *Arcadia* was remarkably influential. Puritans denounced its eroticism, but even in its cobbled-together composite form the work nevertheless quickly achieved the status of a manual of decorum and high sentiment. Abraham Fraunce pilfered from it many of the examples for his important *Arcadian Rhetoric* (1588), and numerous imitations, sequels, and expansions appeared through the middle of the next century. Jonson mentioned the *Arcadia* in his *Every Man out of His Humor* (1600), Shakespeare took the Gloucester subplot of *King Lear* (circa 1606) from it, and it provided the material for *Mucedorus* (1598), the most popular play of the age. In the seventeenth century the *Arcadia* was translated into French, Dutch, Italian, and German. Except for a translation or metaphrase of forty-three of the Psalms, undertaken with his sister in 1584 or 1585, Sidney's writing career ended with the incomplete revision of the *Arcadia*.

Sidney's public career resumed in July 1585, when he was made master of the ordnance. In September he attempted to join the Sir Francis Drake expedition at Plymouth but was called back by the queen. In November 1585 Elizabeth compensated him with the governorship of Flushing, where, under his uncle Leicester, he served as second-in-command of the English expeditionary forces in the Low Countries. The brief remainder of Sidney's life was marked by struggle, loss, disaster, and death. Greatly respected by the Dutch, he maintained the Flushing garrison admirably but with much difficulty. Elizabeth, employing the same penurious strategy she had used with his father in Ireland, kept the garrison's finances at a barely minimal level. To add to his trials, his father died in the following May and his mother in August.

On 23 September 1586, Sidney participated with his uncle in an ill-advised ambush of Spanish troops near Zutphen; entering the skirmish without leg armor, he was fatally wounded in the thigh. Greville, who was not present, reported that as he was coming from the field Sidney offered his water bottle to a dying soldier with the words "Thy necessity is yet greater than mine." He was removed from Zutphen to Arnhem, where he was joined by his wife, Frances (née Walsingham, whom he had married only the year before), his brother, other friends, and surgeons. For some days he seemed to recover. On 30 September he was sufficiently well to compose a will of several thousand words, so excessively generous that it bankrupted his father-in-law and delayed his burial for five months. But the wound became septic, and Sidney's condition deteriorated rapidly. He died on 17 October. The physician George Gifford, a dubious source, reports that

Scene from Sidney's funeral procession, 17 February 1587 (engraving by Derick Theodor de Bris after a drawing by Thomas Lant). Members of Sidney's household walked before the bier while noblemen rode behind it.

in his last hours Sidney spoke of Penelope Devereux, Lady Rich.

The legend of Sir Philip Sidney as the model of the Renaissance chivalric knight was conceived even before his writings appeared in print. After months of public mourning, his body was accorded what was tantamount to a state funeral on 17 February 1587. The procession was led by thirty-two poor people, signifying his thirty-two years, followed by his household, then two riderless horses, and the bier, carried by Thomas Dudley, Dyer, Greville, and Wotton. Then on horseback came high noblemen—Leicester, Huntingdon, Pembroke, and Essex—and a contingency of Dutch officials. The Lord Mayor and the Aldermen, Sheriffs, and Civic Guard of London closed the somber march up Ludgate Hill to the burial site in St. Paul's Cathedral.

Cherished to overripeness by nostalgic Victorians, the idealized portrait of Sidney the gentleman-warrior, a fulfillment of mythic aspirations, continued to obscure his merits as a poet and theorist well into the twentieth century. Like many legends, his betrays some evidence of having been concocted at its origin. Sidney's sumptuous funeral followed by less than ten days the execution of Mary, Queen of Scots, and thus served to distract attention from that problematic event. Four years later, when the earl of Essex (the son of Philip's old friend), who had married Sidney's widow, appeared at the Ascension Day tilt carrying Sidney's best sword, the myth of Philisides the Shepherd Knight was being actively exploited. Jonson, who denied Sidney's fabled good looks in the *Conversations with Drummond*, attempted to correct the legend, as did the seventeenth-century biographer John Aubrey, who claimed that Sidney had died because he would not forgo sexual relations with his wife after being wounded. But counterlegend made little impact on a life destined for emblematic status. Only in the last half-century, and especially since 1970, as the armor of myth has been stripped away, has the more authentic and compelling figure emerged.

Bibliographies:

William L. Godshalk, "Bibliography of Sidney Studies Since 1935," in *Sir Philip Sidney as a Literary Craftsman*, by Kenneth Orne Myrick

(Lincoln: University of Nebraska Press, 1965), pp. 352-358;

Godshalk, "Recent Studies in Sidney, 1945-1969," *English Literary Renaissance*, 2 (1972): 148-164;

Godshalk and A. J. Colaianne, "Recent Studies in Sidney (1970-1977)," *English Literary Renaissance*, 8 (1978): 212-233;

Donald V. Stump, Jerome S. Dees, and C. Stuart Hunter, eds., *Sir Philip Sidney: A Reference Guide* (New York: G. K. Hall, forthcoming, 1992).

Biographies:

Fulke Greville, *The Life of Sir Philip Sidney* [1652], edited by Nowell Smith (Oxford: Clarendon, 1907);

Thomas Moffett, *Nobilis, or A View of the Life and Death of a Sidney and Lessus Lugubris* [1592], edited by Virgil B. Heltzel and Hoyt H. Hudson (San Marino, Cal.: The Huntington Library, 1940);

Frederick S. Boas, *Sir Philip Sidney, Representative Elizabethan: His Life and Writings* (London: Staples Press, 1955);

James M. Osborn, *Young Philip Sidney 1572-1577*, published for the Elizabethan Club, series 5 (New Haven: Yale University Press, 1972);

A. C. Hamilton, *Sir Philip Sidney: A Study of His Life and Works* (Cambridge: Cambridge University Press, 1977);

John Buxton, *Sir Philip Sidney, and the English Renaissance* (New York: Macmillan, 1987).

References:

Michael J. B. Allen, et al., eds., *Sir Philip Sidney's Achievements* (New York: AMS Press, 1990);

John Aubrey, *Brief Lives*, edited by Oliver L. Dick (London: Secker, 1949);

Lorna Challis, "The Use of Oratory in Sidney's *Arcadia*," *Studies in Philology*, 62 (July 1965): 561-576;

Dorothy Connell, *Sir Philip Sidney: The Maker's Mind* (Oxford: Clarendon, 1977);

Walter R. Davis, "A Map of Arcadia: Sidney's Romance in Its Tradition," *Yale Studies in English*, 158 (1965): 1-179;

Jan van Dorsten, Dominic Baker-Smith, and Arthur F. Kinney, eds., *Sir Philip Sidney: 1586 and the Creation of a Legend* (Leiden: Leiden University Press, 1986);

Nona Fienberg, "The Emergence of Stella in *Astrophil and Stella*," *Studies in English Literature 1500-1900*, 25 (Winter 1985): 5-19;

John A. Galm, *Sidney's Arcadian Poems* (Salzburg: Institute for English Speech and Literature, 1973);

Stephen Greenblatt, "Sidney's *Arcadia* and the Mixed Mode," *Studies in Philology*, 70 (July 1973): 269-278;

Thelma Greenfield, *The Eye of Judgement: Reading the New Arcadia* (Lewisburg, Pa.: Bucknell University Press, 1982);

A. C. Hamilton, "Sidney's *Arcadia* as Prose Fiction: Its Relation to Its Sources," *English Literary Renaissance*, 2 (Winter 1972): 29-60;

S. K. Heninger, Jr., *Sidney and Spenser: The Poet as Maker* (University Park: Pennsylvania State University Press, 1989);

Marvin Hunt, " 'Of Lovers' Ruine some sad Tragedie': The *Hamartema* of *Astrophil and Stella*," *Renaissance Papers* (Durham, N.C.: Southeastern Renaissance Conference, 1989), pp. 51-63;

Ben Jonson, *Timber: or, Discoveries (1641) and Conversations with William Drummond of Hawthornden (1619), Elizabethan and Jacobean Quartos*, edited by G. B. Harrison (New York: Barnes & Noble, 1966);

Dennis Kay, ed., *Sir Philip Sidney: An Anthology of Modern Criticism* (Oxford: Clarendon, 1987);

C. S. Lewis, *English Literature in the Sixteenth Century, Excluding Drama* (Oxford: Clarendon, 1954);

Nancy Lindheim, *The Structures of Sidney's "Arcadia"* (Toronto & Buffalo: University of Toronto Press, 1982);

Michael McCanles, *The Text of Sidney's Arcadian World* (Durham, N.C.: Duke University Press, 1989);

Richard C. McCoy, *Sir Philip Sidney: Rebellion in Arcadia* (New Brunswick, N.J.: Rutgers University Press, 1979);

Louis Adrian Montrose, "Celebration and Insinuation: Sir Philip Sidney and the Motives of Elizabethan Courtship," *Renaissance Drama*, new series 8 (1977): 3-35;

Morriss H. Partee, "Anti-Platonism in Sidney's *Defence*," *English Miscellany*, 22 (1971): 7-29;

James J. Scanlon, "Sidney's *Astrophil and Stella*: 'See what it is to Love' Sensually!," *Studies in English Literature 1500-1900*, 16 (Winter 1976): 65-74;

Alan Sinfield, "Sidney and Astrophil," *Studies in English Literature 1500-1900*, 20 (Winter 1980): 25-41;

Edmund Spenser, *Poetical Works*, edited by J. C. Smith and E. de Selincourt (London: Oxford University Press, 1912);

Robert E. Stillman, *Sidney's Poetic Justice: The Old Arcadia, Its Eclogues, and Renaissance Pastoral Traditions* (Lewisburg, Pa.: Bucknell University Press, 1986);

Andrew D. Weiner, *Sir Philip Sidney and the Poetics of Protestantism: A Study of Contexts* (Minneapolis: University of Minnesota Press, 1978).

Papers:

There are no extant holographs of Sidney's literary works; manuscript copies are widely dispersed. Copies of the *Old Arcadia* are reposed at Jesus and Queens colleges, Oxford; at the Bodleian Library and British Museum; and at the Huntington and Folger libraries in the United States. Manuscripts of the *New Arcadia* are housed at Cambridge University Library and Penshurst Place; manuscripts of *Astrophil and Stella* are at the British Museum and the University of Edinburgh. The unique manuscript of *The Defence of Poetry* is part of the De L'Isle Collection at Penshurst Place.

Edmund Spenser

(circa 1552 - 13 January 1599)

Donald Stump
University of Notre Dame

BOOKS: *The Visions of Petrarch* and *The Visions of Bellay*. In *A Theatre wherein be represented as wel the miseries & calamities that follow the voluptuous Worldlings, As also the greate ioyes and plesures which the faithfull do enioy. . . . Deuised by S. Iohn van-der Noodt* (London: Imprinted by Henry Bynneman, 1569);

The Shepheardes Calender Conteyning twelue Æglogues proportionable to the twelue monethes. Entitled to the Noble and Vertvous Gentleman most worthy of all titles both of learning and cheualrie M. Philip Sidney (London: Printed by Hugh Singleton, 1579);

Three Proper and wittie familiar Letters: lately passed between two V-niversity men: touching the Earthquake in April last, and our English refourmed Versifying and *Two other very commendable Letters of the same mens writing: both touching the foresaid Artificial Versifying, and certain other Particulars* (London: H. Bynneman, 1580);

The Faerie Qveene. Disposed into twelue bookes, Fashioning XII. Morall vertues (London: Printed for William Ponsonbie, 1590) [contains Books I-III];

Complaints. Containing Sundrie Small Poemes of the Worlds Vanitie. . . . By Ed. Sp. (London: Imprinted for William Ponsonbie, 1591) [contains *The Rvines of Time, The Teares of the Mvses, Virgils Gnat, Prosopopoia Or Mother Hubberds Tale, Rvines of Rome: by Bellay, Mviopotmos, Or The Fate of the Bvtterflie, Visions of the Worlds Vanitie, The Visions of Bellay,* and *The Visions of Petrarch*];

Daphnaïda. An Elegie vpon the death of the noble and vertuous Douglas Howard, Daughter and heire of Henry Lord Howard, Viscount Byndon, and Wife of Arthure Gorges Esquier. Dedicated to the Right honorable the Lady Helena, Marquesse of Northampton. By Ed. Sp. (London: Printed for William Ponsonby, 1591);

Colin Clovts Come home againe. By Ed. Spencer (London: Printed for William Ponsonbie, 1595) [also contains *Astrophel. A Pastorall Elegie vpon the death of the most Noble and valorovs Knight, Sir Philip Sidney*];

Amoretti and Epithalamion. Written not long since by Edmunde Spenser ([London]: Printed for William Ponsonby, 1595);

The Faerie Qveene. Disposed into twelue bookes, Fashioning XII. Morall vertues (London: Printed for William Ponsonbie, 1596) [contains Books I-VI, with revised ending to Book III];

Fowre Hymnes, Made by Edm. Spenser (London: Printed for William Ponsonby, 1596);

Painting by an unknown artist widely believed to be a portrait of Edmund Spenser, discovered at Dupplin Castle, Perthshire, the seat of the Earl of Kinnoull in the eighteenth century (British Museum). No likeness of Spenser can be entirely authenticated.

Prothalamion Or A Spousall Verse made by Edm. Spenser. In Honovr of the Dovble mariage of the two Honorable & vertuous Ladies, the Ladie Elizabeth and the Ladie Katherine Somerset, Daughters to the Right Honourable the Earle of Worcester and espoused to the two worthie Gentlemen M. Henry Gilford, and M. William Peter Esquyers (London: Printed for William Ponsonby, 1596);

The Faerie Qveene, Disposed Into XII. Bookes, Fashioning twelue Morall Vertues, 2 volumes (London: Printed by H[enry] L[ownes] for Mathew Lownes, 1609-1613) [contains Books I-VI and *Two Cantos of Mutabilitie* from Book VII];

A Vewe of the Present State of Ireland, in *The Historie of Ireland, collected by Three Learned Avthors, viz. Meredith Hanmer . . . Edmvnd Campion . . . and Edmvnd Spenser, esq.*, edited by Sir James Ware (Dublin: Printed by the Society of Stationers, 1633).

Editions and Collections: *Spenser: Poetical Works*, edited by J. C. Smith and Ernest de Selincourt (Oxford: Clarendon Press, 1912);

The Works of Edmund Spenser: A Variorum Edition, 11 volumes, edited by Edwin Greenlaw, Charles Grosvenor Osgood, Frederick Morgan Padelford, and Ray Heffner (Baltimore: Johns Hopkins University Press, 1932-1957);

Books I and II of The Faerie Queene, The Mutability Cantos, and Selections from The Minor Poetry, edited by Robert Kellogg and Oliver Steele (Indianapolis: Bobbs-Merrill, 1965);

The Faerie Qveene, edited by A. C. Hamilton (London & New York: Longmans, 1977);

The Faerie Queene, edited by Thomas P. Roche, Jr. (Harmondsworth, U.K.: Penguin, 1978);

Edmund Spenser's Poetry, in Norton Critical Edition Series, revised edition, edited by Hugh Maclean (New York: Norton, 1982);

The Yale Edition of the Shorter Poems of Edmund Spenser, edited by William A. Oram, Elinar Bjorvand, Ronald Bond, Thomas H. Cain, Alexander Dunlop, and Richard Schell (New Haven & London: Yale University Press, 1989).

To understand Edmund Spenser's place in the extraordinary literary renaissance that took place in England during the last two decades of Queen Elizabeth I's reign, it is helpful to begin with the remarks of the foremost literary critic of the age, Sir Philip Sidney. In *The Defence of Poetry*, written in the early 1580s, Sidney looked back on the history of English literature and saw little to admire. He mentions the works of Geoffrey Chaucer and a few sonnets by Henry Howard, Earl of Surrey; occasional tragedies such as those printed in the 1560s in *A Mirror for Magistrates*; and just one book of contemporary poetry, Spenser's *Shepheardes Calender* (1579). Although France and Italy and even lesser nations such as Scotland had their notable poets and held them in esteem, England, according to Sidney, had recently brought forth only "bastard poets" and "poet-apes," and, consequently, the art itself had "fallen to be the laughing-stock of children." Though one might quarrel with Sidney over his list of the best native writers, it is certainly true that England could boast of no early poet other than Chaucer comparable in stature to Dante, Petrarch, or Giovanni Boccaccio. At the time Sidney was writing, moreover, England lacked altogether the sort of thriving literary culture that was so visible across the Channel in France. Sidney himself set out to repair this deficiency, and with him the other most important writer of his generation, Edmund Spenser.

A glimpse of Spenser's audacious plan to help provide England with a great national literature appears in an appendix printed in the 1590 edition of the first three books of his most important work, *The Faerie Queene*. In a letter addressed to his neighbor Sir Walter Ralegh, Spenser sets out to explain the "general intention and meaning" of his richly elaborated epic. It is "an historicall fiction," written to glorify Queen Elizabeth and "to fashion a gentleman or noble person in vertuous and gentle discipline." In pursuing this latter aim, the poet explains that he has followed the example of the greatest epic writers of the ancient and the modern worlds: Homer and Virgil, Ludovico Ariosto and Torquato Tasso. Now, to set out to depict the queen herself and to "fashion" members of her nobility in virtuous and well-bred discipline was certainly a bold undertaking for the son of a London weaver. For him to compare his work with the most exalted poetry of Italy, the glittering center of European culture in this period, must have seemed to many of his readers mere bravado or self-delusion.

The very attempt to write a neoclassical epic in English was without precedent—unless, perhaps, we include Sidney's *Arcadia* (1590), which was begun at about the same time. Among those named in Spenser's *Letter to Ralegh* as worthy practitioners of the form, Virgil was generally regarded as the greatest, and Spenser, like Dante and Petrarch before him, seems to have taken Virgil as his personal mentor and guide. From the Proem to Book I of *The Faerie Queene*, we may infer that he sometimes thought of his entire career as a recapitulation of that of his illustrious Roman counterpart. He began, as Virgil had begun in his *Ecloques*, with pastoral poetry, which Spenser published in his first major work, *The Shepheardes Calender* (1579). A decade later, in *The Faerie Queene*, he graduated to poetry on martial and political subjects, as Virgil had done when he wrote his great epic the *Aeneid* for the court of Caesar Augustus. Spenser's opening lines, which echo verses prefixed to the *Aeneid*, announce his intention to exchange his "Oaten reeds" (or shepherd's pipes) for "trumpets sterne." Although he transformed the traditional epic introduction to include an invocation to Cupid, god of love, along with the more traditional address to the Muses, and although the poem actually resembles the quasi-medieval romance epics of Ariosto and Tasso more closely than it does classical epics, the poet's claim to follow in the great line established by Homer and passed down by Virgil was altogether serious.

Conscious self-fashioning according to the practices of ancient poets, and also of more recent ones on the Continent, was an essential part of Spenser's project—but only a part. With his eye frequently turned to Chaucer and other English authors, he set out to create poetry that was distinctively English—in religion and politics, in history and custom, in setting and language. For example, he mentions in the *Letter to Ralegh* that he designed his epic to depict "twelve private morall vertues, as Aristotle hath devised." In reality, however, just three of the six books that he lived to complete revolve around virtues that Aristotle would have recognized, and even those three—temperance, friendship, and justice—were greatly altered by Spenser's Anglo-Protestant form of Christianity and by other elements in his English background. The other three—holiness, chastity, and courtesy—have little to do with Aristotle but much to do with England in the high Middle Ages. In the best sense Spenser's art is syncretistic, drawing together elements from many traditions. Its aim, however, was to enrich the culture of his native land.

The process by which he realized this aim was neither rapid nor predictable. As C. S. Lewis has written in comparing him with Sidney, he was "a more ordinary man, less clever, less easily articulate," and he succeeded with more work. For that very reason, perhaps—along with his understated humor, his deep understanding of human psychology, and his easy humanity and good sense—he has been closer than Sidney to the hearts of many of his countrymen.

He was born into the family of an obscure cloth maker named John Spenser, who belonged to the Merchant Taylors' Company and was married to a woman named Elizabeth, about whom almost nothing is known. Since parish records for the area of London where the poet grew up were destroyed in the Great Fire of 1666, his birth date is uncertain, though the dates of his schooling and a remark in one of his sonnets (*Amoretti* 60) lend credence to the date traditionally assigned, which is around 1552. Just which John Spenser was his father is also uncertain, since there were at least three men of that name working in London as weavers at this time. If the poet took his lineage from John Spenser of Hurstwood, then he derived from a well-established family that had lived in Lancashire since the thirteenth century. If Edmund was the son of the John Spenser mentioned in John Stow's *Survey of London* (1603), then his father became a man of some prominence who in later years bought a house that had once belonged to Humphrey, Duke of Gloucester, and who was knighted in 1594 by Queen Elizabeth upon his election as lord mayor of London. From the poem *Prothalamion* (1596), we do know that Spenser thought of himself as a descendant of "An house of auncient fame," namely the family of the Despencers, but there is no evidence that he could claim to be a gentleman, and that fact alone made his rise to prominence more difficult in a class-conscious age.

His parents took what may have been the most important step in advancing their son's fortunes by enrolling him in the Merchant Taylors' School in London. During the early 1560s, when Spenser began his studies there, it was under the able direction of a prominent humanist educator named Richard Mulcaster, who believed in thoroughly grounding his students in the classics and in Protestant Christianity, and who seems to have encouraged such extracurricular activities as musical and dramatic performances. Mulcaster was also important to Spenser's career for purely pragmatic reasons, since he had good connections with the universities and sent students of modest means such as Spenser on to them with some regularity. The poet later expressed his gratitude to Mulcaster by depicting him as "A good olde shephearde, *Wrenock*" in the *December* eclogue of *The Shepheardes Calender* and by naming his first two children, Sylvanus and Katherine, after those of his master.

The only glimpse of the young poet at school comes from financial records indicating that in 1569, when he was in his last year, he was one of six boys given a shilling and a new gown to attend the funeral of Robert Nowell, a prominent lawyer connected with the school. This connection with Nowell was to prove important to Spenser's later development, for the lawyer's estate helped support his subsequent education.

In 1569, at the usual age of sixteen or seventeen, Spenser left the Merchant Taylors' School for Cambridge, where he enrolled at Pembroke Hall. Even before he arrived, however, he was already composing poetry and attracting the attention of other writers. Perhaps with the help of Mulcaster, who had friends in the Dutch immigrant community, he had recently arranged to publish thematically linked sets of epigrams and sonnets entitled *The Visions of Petrarch* and *The Visions of Bellay*, which appeared in the collection *A Theatre for Worldlings* (1569) by the Dutch poet Jan van der Noot. Even in his maturity Spenser seems to have thought well of these early translations of French and Italian poetry, for he revised and reprinted them among his *Complaints* in 1591. Although not original, they nonetheless shed light on Spenser's interests at the time, which were directed toward poets of the Continent and had already settled on themes that would surface again and again in his later poetry, namely the tragic precariousness of life and the impermanence of things in the material world.

Such scraps of reliable information that are known about Spenser during his university days suggest that he served as a sizar (a scholar of limited means who does chores in return for room and board) and that he received his B.A. in 1573 and his M.A. in 1576 with no official marks of distinction as a scholar, but that he regarded the experience as vital to his development, as can be seen in his later reference to the university as "my mother Cambridge" (*The Faerie Queene* IV.xi.34). Little is known of his friendships at Pembroke. He must have been acquainted with Lancelot Andrewes, two years his junior, who later became a bishop and was well known for his sermons and for his part in translating the King James Version of the Bible. Clearly, Spenser had also gained the confidence of the master of Pembroke, John Young, who later became bishop of Rochester and gave the poet his first post as a personal secretary. Most important for Spenser's literary career, however, was his close friendship with Gabriel Harvey, a professor of rhetoric who served initially as his mentor and ultimately as his literary promoter. Spenser later celebrated their friendship in *The Shepheardes Calender*, in which he appears as Colin Clout and Harvey is represented as the wise shepherd Hobbinoll.

Though a lackluster poet himself, Harvey seems to have encouraged Spenser in many of the aspirations that later shaped his career. Harvey was characteristically effusive, for example, about the need to ground English poetry on the great models of Greco-Roman antiquity, both by shaping its versification on Latin principles and by undertaking classical genres that had not yet been attempted in English. In the late 1570s he composed a vernacular epic (now lost) and a work on the ancient Muses of poetry that is simi-

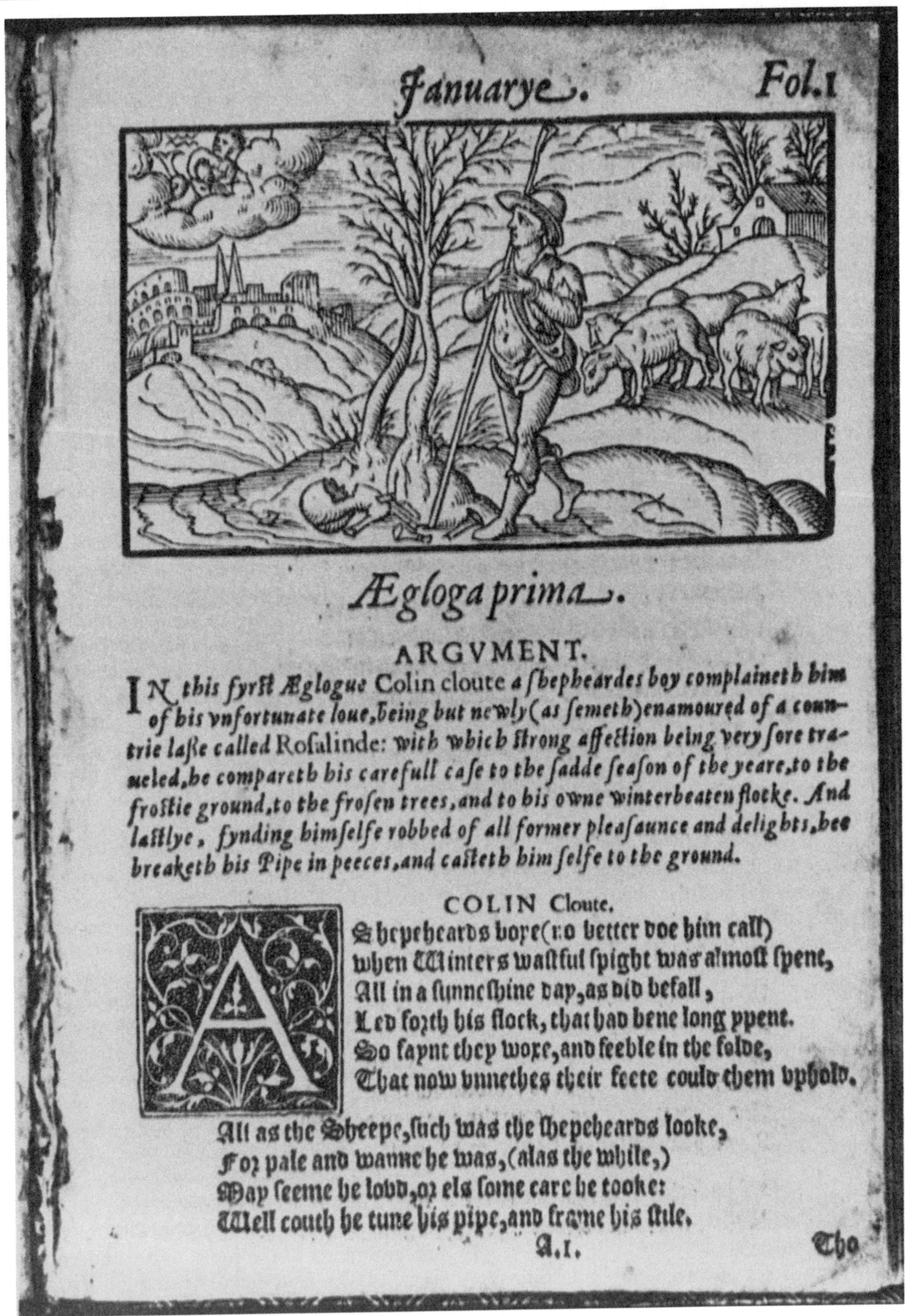
Januarye. Fol.1

Ægloga prima.

ARGVMENT.

IN this fyrst Æglogue Colin cloute a shepheardes boy complaineth him of his vnfortunate loue, being but newly (as semeth) enamoured of a countrie lasse called Rosalinde: with which strong affection being very sore traueled, he compareth his carefull case to the sadde season of the yeare, to the frostie ground, to the frosen trees, and to his owne winterbeaten flocke. And lastlye, fynding himselfe robbed of all former pleasaunce and delights, hee breaketh his Pipe in peeces, and casteth him selfe to the ground.

COLIN Cloute.

A Shepeheards boye (no better doe him call)
when Winters wastful spight was almost spent,
All in a sunneshine day, as did befall,
Led forth his flock, that had bene long ypent.
So faynt they woxe, and feeble in the folde,
That now vnnethes their feete could them vphold.

All as the Sheepe, such was the Shepeheards looke,
For pale and wanne he was, (alas the while,)
May seeme he lovd, or els some care he tooke:
Well couth he tune his pipe, and frame his stile.

A.1. Tho

First page of the January *eclogue from the first edition of* The Shepheardes Calender. *The illustration depicts Colin Clout, the shepherd boy.*

lar in outline to Spenser's *Teares of the Muses* (1591). At about the same time, he may have played a part in introducing Spenser to Sidney and in securing for his friend a position in the London household of Robert Dudley, Earl of Leicester, who was a favorite of Queen Elizabeth as well as a key figure in the radical Protestant faction at court and one of the most powerful noblemen in the realm. The connections with Leicester and Sidney helped to launch Spenser's career, both as a poet and as a government official. Finally, in 1580, just before circumstances forced a separation between the two friends, Harvey gave Spenser's prominence as a writer a boost by publishing a set of five high-spirited letters that had passed between them, which helped to establish his friend's public image as England's "new poet."

In the letters Spenser and Harvey natter on happily about their contacts with great men and their various works in progress, including Spenser's *Faerie Queene* and a surprising array of his other early works that were later lost—or perhaps silently incorporated into those that were published. These included ten Latin comedies, several dream visions, an epithalamium celebrating the "marriage" of the rivers of England, and a work of literary criticism entitled *The English Poete*. The letters are even more interesting for their revelation that Spenser and Harvey had recently become involved in a literary circle gathered around Sidney. The group, which called itself the "Areopagus," was short-lived, and though it may have been formed with playful reference to the great literary academies of France and Italy, it seems to have been better known for its high spirits and good conversation than for its high seriousness. The writers involved—including the learned diplomat Daniel Rogers, Sidney's friends Sir Edward Dyer and Fulke Greville, and the academician Thomas Drant—seem to have occupied themselves primarily with experiments in Latin prosody, attempts at various genres of "new poetry" based on classical models, and the promotion of English as a literary language. Rogers, however, also mentions grand discussions "of the law, of God and of the good," and these may have had some effect on the heroic works that occupied Sidney and Spenser in the years that followed.

Spenser's direct involvement with Sidney and his circle in 1579-1580 set him on a literary course that he would pursue for the rest of his life. Though the two men never saw one another again, they adopted remarkably similar literary agendas, writing mainly in genres that Sidney had encountered among prominent neoclassical and religious poets on the Continent. Both men, for example, wrote works of literary criticism addressing the current state of poetry in England, and both devoted most of their creative energies to pastoral poetry and romance epic, to sonnets and epithalamiums, and to religious hymns or psalms. Both also wrote political tracts about Ireland, where Sidney's father served for more than two decades and Spenser was soon to become a government official. Expressions of admiration for the Sidneys and the Dudleys appear repeatedly in his works, from early poems such as his *Stemmata Dudleiana* (now lost) to later ones such as *The Ruines of Time* (1591), *Colin Clouts Come home againe* (1595), and *Astrophel* (1595).

Through his contact with men such as Sidney and Leicester, who were deeply involved in affairs of state, Spenser may have been emboldened to publish his *Shepeardes Calender*, which was dedicated to Sidney and dealt with sensitive political controversies of the day. Appearing in six editions before the end of the century, it became a milestone in the English literary renaissance because it was the first major published work of "new poetry" written along the neoclassical lines advocated by nationalistic poets such as those of the Areopagus. With a flair for self-promotion reminiscent of Harvey, Spenser—or perhaps his publisher—arranged to bring out the volume as if it were a venerable and ancient text. The archaic language of the poems, which Sidney disliked, may have been adopted in part to heighten this effect. Beautifully illustrated with woodcuts, the poems appeared from the outset already encrusted with learned prefatory matter and a running gloss by an unidentified scholar designated only as "E. K." Most likely, this was Spenser's friend Edward Kirke, whom he had known since their days together at Pembroke Hall in the early 1570s. Whoever he was, however, he shared Spenser's views that English poetry was in disarray and that it should be reestablished on "an eternall image of antiquitie"—an argument that is repeated in the eclogue for October. In his prefatory epistle to the volume, E. K. lauds Spenser as "this our new Poete," who will be "beloved of all, embraced of the most, and wondred at of the best." If he had been writing of Virgil or Petrarch, rather than an obscure English poet, he could hardly have said more.

Spenser's skillful literary borrowings contributed to the volume's impressive effect. From the

Italian poets Petrarch and Mantuan he adopted a variety of pastoral that conceals beneath its surface biting political allegories and topical allusions to prominent figures in the church and the state. From the more traditional *Eclogues* of Virgil and from ancient writers such as Theocritus, Bion, and Moschus, he took other features, such as the curiously static sense of time characteristic of classical pastoral. His rustics debate and sing, love and despair, but there is no real narrative progression in the *Calender* and very little action. Variety is introduced in the subjects that the shepherds contemplate and in the poetic forms that they employ, which include amorous complaints, fables, singing matches and debates, an encomium, a funeral elegy, and a hymn to the god Pan.

Spenser also drew upon the visual arts of his day, particularly works known as "emblem books." These typically brought together three disparate elements: a series of pictures of a figurative or symbolic kind, "mottos" or pithy sayings related to the pictures but phrased in enigmatic terms, and explanations in prose or verse that interpret the mottos and pictures and draw a moral. Each of Spenser's twelve eclogues follows a more complicated version of this pattern. First comes a woodcut, which typically depicts the shepherd(s) in the eclogue and something from their songs or their situations, with the sign of the zodiac appropriate to the month in question represented at the top. Then comes the poem itself, preceded by a brief "argument" or summary, which may have been added by E. K. After the eclogue comes one or more verbal "emblems" or mottoes in various languages, which briefly sum up the nature or situation of the speakers and the themes of their songs, but which often tease the imagination with alternative interpretations. And finally there is E. K.'s gloss, serving some of the same functions as the explanation beneath a conventional emblem.

Spenser also added important innovations to the traditional elements in the *Calender*. One involved poetic technique. In sheer variety of meter and form, his eclogues are without precedent in earlier pastoral poetry and provided an ample showcase for the experiments in prosody that so fascinated the poets of the Areopagus. Another conspicuous innovation was his organization of the poems into a seasonal progression. By following the cycle of the year, Spenser was able to employ the outer world of pasture and sheepfold as a way to depict the inner world of the young shepherd Colin Clout, whose unrequited love of Rosalind provides a thread of unity through the entire volume. In the first poem, *January*, Colin despairs, breaking his shepherd's pipe and, with it, the last source of pleasure that remains to him. In his eyes the land, the trees, and the flocks around him have themselves become emblems for the state of his soul. He complains, "Thou barrein ground, whome winters wrath hath wasted, / Art made a myrrhour, to behold my plight." Though not present or even mentioned in several of the eclogues, Colin provides a melancholy bass line over which all the other shepherds sing, setting their higher notes of anger and joy, debate and reflection, in poignant contrast to his listless desolation.

The emotional counterpoint is never more moving than in *April*, where his good friend Hobbinoll sings one of Colin's old songs, written to celebrate the shepherdess Eliza in the springtime of an earlier and happier year. The inner world of the song continues to match the outward season in which it is sung, as all the songs in the *Calender* do; but it also heightens our sense of the dark winter of the soul in which Colin continues to suffer. At the midpoint of the cycle, in *June*, he laments that Rosalind has left him for another shepherd named Menalcas. In the final poem, he sings weary complaints to the god Pan and feels premonitions of his imminent death, thus returning the sequence to a point resembling the one at which it began, though even more desolate.

Besides the revolving of the seasons, other cycles are involved in the work. As E. K.'s headnote to *December* reminds us, the passing of the year has traditionally served as an emblem for the stages of life. From the springtime of childhood to the summer of desire and love to the winter of loneliness and old age, Colin's life becomes an emblem for everyone's experience in this world. Interpreted in this way, the *Calender* returns to the themes of tragic uncertainty and relentless mutability expressed ten years earlier in Spenser's contributions to *A Theatre for Worldlings*.

These larger themes are, in turn, related to the political allegory that often lurks just below the surface of the poems. One of the implications of this allegory is that states, too, have their cycles of springtime and autumn. The celebration of "her Majestie" Eliza in *April*, which is a thinly veiled encomium addressed to Queen Elizabeth, suggests that England is in the full flower of a new age. *Maye*, *July*, and *September*, however, all turn on the controversy between Protestant reformers and Elizabeth's more conservative Catholic subjects, which was the greatest single threat to her ability to rule. The topical allegory in these eclogues suggests that in 1579 strains in the body politic were a matter of particular concern to Spenser. The cause for his alarm was undoubtedly the marriage negotiations being carried out between Queen Elizabeth and a French Catholic prince, François, Duke of Anjou. The staunchly Protestant faction surrounding Leicester and Sidney took every opportunity to oppose such a marriage as a grave threat to the religious and political independence of England. If, as some critics suppose, Rosalind is a figure for Queen Elizabeth, and Colin for Spenser and his Protestant cause, then Rosalind's rejection of Colin for Menalcas may have to do with Queen Elizabeth's rejection of the Protestant faction in favor of the Catholic Anjou.

If this is so, then Colin's dejection at the end of the *Calender* may reflect Spenser's low political fortunes in late 1579 and early 1580, when the queen took harsh measures to silence critics of her plan for a French marriage. Sidney, for instance, was dismissed from court, most likely for addressing a letter to her on the subject. Spenser, too, seems to have feared the queen's displeasure, for he published his *Calender* under the pseudonym "Immeritô" and prefaced it with a poem to Sidney in which he speaks to the *Calender* itself, saying "when thou are past jeopardee, / Come tell me, what was sayd of mee: / And I will send more after thee." It may be that the young poet's representation of delicate affairs of state had left him with few defenders and fewer prospects for advancement at court.

In any case, in July 1580 he accepted a post as a private secretary to Arthur Grey, the new lord deputy of Ireland. There is some evidence that when he set out for Dublin, he took with him a new wife named Machabyas Chylde, about whom little is known except that she married one "Edmounde Spenser" on 27 October 1579, that she apparently bore him two children named Sylvanus and Katherine, and that she died sometime before 1594. Most of the next twenty years of the poet's life were spent in Ireland, where he served in various governmental posts, from clerk of the Privy Council in Dublin in the early years to queen's justice and sheriff-designate for county Cork at the end of his life. His positions allowed him to acquire a considerable list of landholdings, including most prominently Kilcolman Castle with three thousand acres in county Cork, which served as his principal residence from 1588 until the year before his death in 1599. Such holdings were important, for they gave him the status of a landed gentleman, and this eased his way in society, enabling him, for example, to make friends with Sir Walter Ralegh and to marry his second wife, Elizabeth Boyle, who came from an important landed family in Herefordshire.

References to Ireland appear frequently in Spenser's later poetry, and some of them reveal a good deal of gentle affection for the land and its people. Most memorable, perhaps, are the country wedding captured with such rustic beauty in his *Epithalamion* (1595) and the great judgment scene on Arlo Hill, a mountain near Kilcolman Castle, which occupies much of the *Mutability Cantos* in Book VII of *The Faerie Queene*. Most of the poet's descriptions of Ireland, however, are colored by sorrow or disgust at the destitute state of its people or by resolute hostility toward its wily and elusive rebels, who harassed the English occupiers throughout the period. Spenser portrays the darker side of his experiences in Ireland, for example, in the attacks on the House of Alma in Book II of *The Faerie Queene* and in the savagery of the scurrilous, long-haired rebel Malengin in Book V.

The less submissive among the Irish had no reason to be any fonder of Spenser than he of them. In 1580, as a new official in the colonial administration, he was present when the English slaughtered papal troops at Smerwick, and he also witnessed the terrible famine in Munster that darkened the end of Desmond's Rebellion. In fact, he wrote the official report on the battle of Smerwick and later described it and other incidents during the turbulent years of his colonial service in his only prose work, *A Vewe of the Present State of Ireland* (1633). This was written sometime before 1598 as a proposal for ways to establish a just and stable colonial regime in the country, and parts of it were incorporated into an official report that he presented in London in 1598 as *A Brief Note on Ireland*. In the late 1580s he had been responsible for settling English immigrants at Kilcolman on lands confiscated from the rebel Gerald Fitzgerald, fifteenth Earl of Desmond, and some of Spenser's other landholdings had come from the forced dissolution of Catholic monasteries in Ireland. It is not surprising, then, that his last years in Cork were ones of conflict, tumult, and loss.

Until the late 1590s, however, Ireland provided a living, a place to write, and even literary friends for whom to write. During his years there, Spenser may have become acquainted with Barnaby Rich and Barnaby Googe, and he knew Sidney's close friend and occasional fellow poet Lodowick Bryskett, who turned two posts over to him before moving on. Most important, however, was Spenser's friendship with Ralegh, who was his neighbor on the former Desmond estates and who, in the summer and fall of 1589, came to see him at Kilcolman and took a personal interest in his poetry. Spenser later revealed the importance of his relationship with Ralegh by preserving a poetic account of it in *Colin Clouts Come home againe* and by writing the *Letter to Ralegh* and a dedicatory sonnet to him in *The Faerie Queene*. According to *Colin Clout*, it was Ralegh who arranged for Spenser to travel to London in 1590 to publish the first three books of his epic and to present them in person to Queen Elizabeth, who was pleased and expressed a desire to hear it read to her "at timely houres." So pleased was she, in fact, that she granted the poet a pension of fifty pounds a year, which was more than the parsimonious queen granted to any other poet of the period. Spenser expressed his gratitude for Ralegh's patronage by writing a sympathetic allegory of the adventurer's often turbulent and romantically tinged relationship with the queen, which appears in the story of Timias and Belphoebe in Books III, IV, and VI of *The Faerie Queene*.

The best way to begin an examination of Spenser's epic is, perhaps, to come to it as Ralegh did, with Spenser's prefatory letter in hand—though, admittedly, some of its intentions do not match the poem as the author actually wrote it. As the letter reveals, the six books (and two cantos of a seventh) that were ultimately published represent but a fraction of the plan, which was to extend to the traditional twelve books of an epic, one devoted to each of "the twelve private morall vertues." Another section of the poem, perhaps of equal length but never written, was to cover the public or "pollliticke" virtues. Each book in this vast structure was to concentrate on a single habit of character, represented by one or more exemplary knights such as Britomart, the Knight of Chastity in Book III, and Sir Artegall, the Knight of Justice in Book V. It may be that, as time went on and Spenser realized the magnitude of the undertaking, he changed his mind and began to incorporate political virtues among the moral virtues of the first section. Certainly Book V, the Legend of Justice, involves a good deal of political allegory. In any case, the six books that he completed begin with virtues in a person's relations with God and self (holiness and temperance) and proceed to those involving relations with other people (chastity, friendship, justice, and courtesy). The entire scheme accords with the two great commandments of Christian tradition: "Thou shalt love the Lord thy God with all thy heart, and with all thy soul, and all thy mind" and "Thou shalt love thy neighbor as thyself" (Matt. 22:36-39).

The first twelve books were to be united by the presence of two dominant characters: Prince Arthur, mythical founder of the Round Table, who was to appear as a wandering knight in each of the books, and Gloriana, the Faerie Queene, who was to frame the action of the poem by holding an annual feast of twelve days, on which she assigned her knights twelve quests, each described in one book of the epic. At the end of the poem, it seems, Prince Arthur was to marry Gloriana, and since the poet postponed the wedding of other heroes in the individual books, there were doubtless to be other marriages in Book XII as well. Since Arthur represents the virtue of Magnificence, which comprehends within itself all the other active virtues, and since the Faerie Queene represents glory, which was for Spenser the end of all earthly action, there is a tidy philosophy behind the entire structure.

As the poet concedes, the main difficulty for readers lies not in grasping the grand organization of the poem, but in knowing how to interpret its allegory. He offers a clue, however, by calling the work a "continued" allegory or "darke conceit." In his day, the term "conceit" could have carried at least two senses in this context, both of them helpful. First, it could have meant simply a thought or, in certain philosophical contexts, a form or Idea in something very like the Platonic sense. Second, the term could have denoted an extended metaphor, that is, an implied comparison between the primary subject of the author's thought and something more easily visualized or grasped, which acts as a "figure" for that subject.

In interpreting Book I as such an extended metaphor, one might concentrate on the heroine, Una, the daughter of the "King of *Eden*," who sets out from her home to save her parents from a great dragon. To this end she travels to the court of the Faerie Queene and gains the help of the Red Crosse Knight, who, after various trials and wanderings, returns with her to her parents' city. There he defeats the dragon, is honored as a victor, and offers to marry Una once he has served his queen for six more years. Taking a clue from the Book of Revelation, which identifies Satan as a dragon who has enslaved human beings (the fallen descendants of Adam and Eve) and is the great enemy of the Church, we might take Una as a "conceit" for the universal body of believers as it has acted through history. This, then, would be the metaphor "continued" through the whole of Book I. On this assumption, we might conclude that the meaning of the allegory is something like this: the Church, which is descended from sinful human beings, sets out to redeem them by releasing them from bondage to Satan. In this it requires the help of the individual Christian, who may lose his way for a time but, through the aid of the Church, will ultimately find the straight and narrow way again, and will go on to defeat the forces of evil around him. Once he lives out his "six days" of life on earth, he will be united with the Church forever on the seventh, at rest on God's Sabbath day in heaven (see VII.viii.2).

Now such a reading, based on the assumption that the poem is a kind of code to be deciphered character by character, has something to be said for it. It reveals a point that is probably central to Spenser's attempt to "fashion a gentleman in vertuous and noble discipline," namely that Christians tend to respond to the call of the Church enthusiastically enough in the beginning, but often lose their zeal or fall away. Each stage in the wanderings of the Red Crosse Knight—his initial acceptance of lies about Una, his departure from her and his affair with another woman named Duessa, his drifting into the broad path of worldly fame and pleasure represented by the Palace of Pride, and finally his removal of his Christian armor, his defeat, and his overwhelming sense of failure at the Castle of Orgoglio and the Cave of Despair—represents a stage in the process by which an immature believer might fall away. A period of humility, instruction, and hard discipline (represented in the House of Holiness) is required before a young man like this can be of much use in helping others.

There are, however, problems with attempts to "decode" the poem in such a simplistic fashion. The most invidious, perhaps, is that once one has worked the puzzle, it loses its interest. In an 1831 issue of the *Edinburgh Review*, Thomas Macaulay, who must have read the poem in something like this way, complains that "Even Spencer himself . . . could not succeed in the attempt to make allegory interesting. . . . One unpardonable fault, the fault of tediousness, pervades the whole of the Fairy Queen. We become sick of Cardinal Virtues and Deadly sins, and long for the society of plain men and women." One wonders whether an attempt to decipher characters merely as clever signs for abstractions may not have been behind the tendency, notable throughout the nineteenth century, to discount Spenser's allegory and to concentrate instead on the beauties of his verse and imagery.

THE FAERIE QVEENE.

Diſpoſed into twelue books,

Faſhioning

XII. Morall vertues.

VBIQVE FLORET

LONDON

Printed for William Ponſonbie.

1590.

Title page for Spenser's attempt to write a neoclassical epic in English, part of his plan to establish a great national literature

The fault here lies more with Spenser's readers, however, than with the poet himself. There is nothing simple or boring about the allegory, which frequently manages to juggle several different meanings simultaneously. Along with "darke conceits" of a moral, political, and religious kind, Spenser also undertakes at least three other varieties. There are psychological allegories, which probe the faculties of the mind and their working in both normal and abnormal states. There are also topical allegories, which glorify or satirize the actions of rulers and other prominent figures of Spenser's day, and there are historical allegories involving their personal or national pasts. Only by resolutely ignoring crucial details can one read the poem as a "continued" metaphor with a single pat "meaning."

Una, for instance, is not only the one true Church but also (as her name suggests) "oneness" itself. Spenser calls her simply "truth" and seems to have in mind the sense of oneness expounded by Renaissance Neoplatonic philosophers, who saw the world as a sometimes discordant multiplicity that emanates from the perfect unity and simplicity of the divine mind. To depart from Una is to lose sight of the truth apprehended by contemplating the eternal Ideas that inform everything in the material world. To take up with Duessa (duality, duplicity) is to depart from truth and break one's union with the one source of all that is good.

"Una" is also a name applied in this period to Queen Elizabeth, the one supreme governor of the Church of England, and Spenser's maiden lady is clearly one of many figures for her in the poem. Elizabeth lived under constant threat of military attack or assassination by the great Catholic princes on the Continent, who wanted to reverse the Protestant Reformation in England and to return the nation to the Catholic fold. In the historical allegory of the poem Duessa represents Mary, Queen of Scots, who had legal claims to the English crown and who vied with Elizabeth for the allegiance of the English people. In polemics of the day, Mary was sometimes pictured as the "whore of Babylon" mentioned in the Book of Revelation, who rides on a beast with seven heads and is associated with Rome. In Canto viii Spenser employs this imagery when Duessa rides out on a "manyheaded beast" to attack the heroic representative of England, Prince Arthur, who defeats her and forces her to cast away her "golden cup" and "crowned mitre," which are symbols associated with the wealth and pride of the papacy.

Even the three quite different interpretations of Una discussed here may not exhaust the allegorical possibilities. Spenser was a master of compression and deep implication who recognized the multiplicity of meanings inherent in certain primal concepts and images, such as oneness and duality, and it is that multiplicity that lies at the heart of the fascination that *The Faerie Queene* has exerted over many of its readers. Rather than interpret the poet's "darke conceit" simply as an extended metaphor, one does better, particularly in analyzing the plots of the poem, to take it more broadly as a governing thought or form. Spenser's patron Sidney wrote in *The Defence of Poetry* (1595) that the poet begins with an "Idea, or fore-conceit," which he embodies in the matter of the poem—its stories, characters, and images. The reader then uses that matter as an "imaginative ground-plot of a profitable invention," comprehending the author's "conceit" by an act of mental re-creation. The richer the author's initial idea and the clearer the matter of his creation, the richer and more profitable the reader's own act of "invention" will be. So long as one remains true to the details of the matter, the possibilities for meaning are limited only to the extent that the primal forms or ideas are limited in their inherent implications.

In relation to Una, the Red Crosse Knight becomes an extraordinarily rich creation. As one learns in Canto x, he is Saint George, the patron saint of England. In many ways he is also the Everyman of medieval Christian tradition, who, after his fall into sin and his recovery in the House of Holiness, imitates the life of Christ by fighting the dragon, falling in the battle, and being resurrected in victory on the morning of the third day. He also represents the English people at the time of the Protestant Reformation, defending the "one true church" against the late-medieval corruption of Roman Catholicism. More particularly, he may represent Christian writers and intellectuals in sixteenth-century England who were prone to certain errors and were in need of firmer doctrinal foundations. The knight begins his quest in Canto i with a battle against a lesser dragon named "Errour," which is associated with religious books and pamphlets, and only after he has been rescued from doctrinal error himself, represented in the false philosophy of Despair, can he fulfill his quest. After a period with the hermit Contemplation and other teachers in the House of Holiness, he fights a second and greater dragon, and this time, with God's grace, he prevails.

Even in the passages of Book I devoted to philosophical abstractions, such as the virtues and vices that bored Thomas Macaulay, Spenser invites more from his readers than a dry process of "decoding." His stories and pictorial descriptions are not simply means to convey philosophical insights. They are themselves the ends of the poet's labors, figures capable of transforming barren philosophy into what Sidney's friend Fulke Greville once called "pregnant images of life." It is one thing to know the definition of a particular vice, but quite another to know how people afflicted with it might talk or act and to see how their sinful dispositions might harm them over a period of time. It is these latter points that most interested Spenser. In Canto iv of Book I, for example, Queen Lucifera and her "six wisards old" are readily identified as the Seven Deadly Sins of medieval Christian tradition. Yet it is the extraordinary detail with which the poet depicts them that matters, not simply what they represent. In a series of exquisitely painted miniatures, Spenser depicts each of the six counselors on one of the beasts that draw Lucifera's coach: Idleness on an ass, Gluttony on a pig, Lechery on a goat, Avarice on a camel, Envy on a wolf, and Wrath on a lion. Each detail in the imagery of coach and team—from the animals themselves to the clothing and behavior of their riders and the things that they bear in their hands—serves to characterize the six vices and Pride, their queen. Even the order of the riders is significant, for Spenser has dramatically altered the traditional Catholic sequence in order to place Idleness first as the "nourse of sin." Since Idleness is dressed "Like to an holy Monck," the change in order doubtless has to do with what we now call the Protestant "work ethic" and with common complaints in the Renaissance that the Catholic monasteries were bastions of laziness and corruption.

It would, of course, be a mistake to suppose that every passage in the poem is as rich in meaning as the description of the Palace of Pride and its inhabitants, or that readers need understand everything that is lurking under the surface of the poem in order to enjoy it. Much of its appeal lies in plain sight, in its strange and marvelous stories and its colorful pageantry. In probing its deeper implications, however, it helps to begin with what are sometimes called the allegorical "cores" or "shrines" of the poem. In the great temples, palaces, noble houses, gardens, and caves that dominate the landscape, Spenser provides the main distinctions needed to comprehend the philosophical concepts that he is exploring, often revealing key points in the names of the characters and in the details of their appearance or their surroundings. Along with the Palace of Pride and the House of Holiness in Book I, major "cores" include Mammon's Cave, the House of Alma, and the Bower of Bliss in Book II; the Garden of Adonis and the House of Busirane in Book III; the Temple of Venus in Book IV; the Temple of Isis and the Palace of Mercilla in Book V; Mount Acidale in Book VI; and Arlo Hill in the fragment of Book VII that Spenser wrote just before his death. In the narratives that lead the main characters to and from such places of instruction, the poet often provides less concentrated allegories in their actions, as in Una's wanderings after she is separated from the Red Crosse Knight. And finally, in the peripheral stories and episodes constantly woven into the main lines of plot in each book, Spenser provides moral examples that further illustrate his main themes. An instance of such a tale in Book I is the story of Fraelissa and Fradubio, two lovers who are parted by Duessa in much the same way that the Red Crosse Knight is lured away from Una.

In the sequence of allegorical "cores" within each book, Spenser tends to move from the simple to the complex, arriving only late in the action at a full picture of the virtue required of the hero. In Book II, the first "core" leaves the impression that temperance is a "natural" virtue, that is, one that can be grasped without the divinely revealed truths of Scripture. Spenser offers portraits of three sisters: Elissa ("excess"), Perissa ("deficiency"), and Medina (the "golden mean"), and the Latin roots of their names call to mind the philosophy of Aristotle. One who is temperate, in Aristotle's view, has formed the habit of taking the mean between extremes such as squandering and miserliness, foolhardiness and cowardice. The suitors courting Elissa and Perissa illustrate this point in a colorful way. Huddibras represents a "froward" nature that tends to draw back from others in arrogance or anger, and Sansloy represents a "forward" nature that draws toward others in uncontrolled desire. A temperate person would restrain impulses toward either of these extremes.

The House of Medina suggests that in Book II we have come into a new region of Spenser's fairyland, one different from the quasi-medieval religious landscape of Book I and more like the plain humanist schoolrooms of the Merchant Taylors' School that Spenser attended as a boy. To take its classical philosophy as his final word on temperance, however, would be a mistake. Guyon's attempt to put into practice the rational ideal embodied in Medina is successful, but only for a time. To be sure, he avoids the corruption inherent in characters such as Pyrochles and Cymochles, who allow themselves to be governed by excesses of the bodily fluids (or "humours") of choler and phlegm. The brothers provide emblems of the two great temptations of the book: irascibility (which is seen in the hotheaded characters of the early cantos) and concupiscence (which appears in lazy and self-indulgent figures later in the book). Guyon avoids both. Yet, as early as Canto iii, he makes a crucial blunder, allowing a buffoon named Braggadocchio to steal his horse and so becoming the only pedestrian hero in the poem. At the midpoint of the book, in Canto vi, he makes a second mistake in parting from his Christian counselor and friend, the Palmer. By accepting a boat ride from a languid and sensuous lady named Phaedria at Idle Lake and allowing the Palmer to go on by foot, Guyon needlessly subjects himself to temptation. He does so again in the next episode by voluntarily undertaking a traditional epic descent into the underworld, where he is tempted with every imaginable form of worldly excess. These are represented in three subterranean chambers: the treasure house of Mammon, god of money and possessions; the temple of Philotime, the goddess of honor and ambition; and the garden of Proserpina, the goddess of worldly pleasure and rest. The very sense of his own self-sufficiency that prompts the hero's needless descent into hell is a sign of danger, for, in Spenser's view, no one can long stand out against the corruptions of fallen human nature without the grace of God.

This point comes home in Canto vii, where, having emerged from Mammon's Cave, Sir Guyon faints from exhaustion, falling prey to several of the enemies that he had earlier avoided, including Pyrochles and Cymochles. An angel is required to save him, and does so by fetching the Palmer, who stays with Guyon until Prince Arthur arrives to beat back the figures of intemperance attempting to despoil the hero of his armor. A stay in the House of Alma, which is the second important locus of instruction in the book, educates Guyon in the limits of his strength, presenting in the very structure of the house an emblem of the human body and the human psyche for his instruction. It is a place besieged by assaults on the senses, which are represented in the attacks of lawless rebels outside the castle. Their leader, Maleger (who represents appetite and passion), has the ability to regain his strength simply by touching his mother, the earth. As Prince Arthur later discovers, Maleger can be defeated only when he is cast into water.

This last point reveals the very Christian conception of temperance that underlies the entire book. The water in which Maleger drowns is an emblem of baptism, and his defeat is related to the episode that first set Guyon forth on his quest. In Cantos i-ii he and the Palmer had come upon the body of a knight, Sir Mortdant, who had been lured to his destruction by a false enchantress named Acrasia (whose name means both "badly mixed," referring perhaps to the bodily humours, and "incontinent," implying an inability to contain her desires). The knight's wife, Amavia, had stabbed herself in grief at his loss, and their baby, Ruddymane, had stained his hands in her blood. When Guyon had attempted to wash the child's hands in an enchanted spring—one associated with pagan mythology and the goddess Nature—the stain would not wash away. It had remained as an emblem of Original Sin, which can only be cleansed by the Christian sacrament of Holy Baptism. At the time, Guyon had not understood the meaning of this incident, but in the battle against Maleger the point comes home.

With his temperance now "fast settled on firm foundation," the hero departs on the last stage of his quest to avenge the death of Ruddymane's parents upon Acrasia. After a sea voyage on which he encounters fresh allegorical representations of the Seven Deadly Sins, he ruthlessly destroys Acrasia's Bower of Bliss, releasing the many men whom she has transformed to beasts and binding the witch herself.

From the analysis of inward psychological states in Book II, Spenser next turns to outward social relations in Book III. At the outset he pauses, as he often does, to show the relation between the central virtues of adjoining books by having their heroes meet briefly in conversation and in feats of strength. Here, the superiority of the social virtue of chastity, represented by the heroine Britomart, over the personal virtue of temperance appears clearly in Britomart's defeat of Guyon in a joust. Other episodes suggest further contrasts between the books. In comparison with Acrasia's Bower of Bliss in Book II, Spenser portrays another garden in Book III that is also concerned with the fulfillment of bodily desires, but in healthier ways. Whereas the Bower had been a false Paradise, apparently natural but actually created by self-indulgent art (see II.xii.58-59), the Garden of Adonis is a true Eden, where "All things, as they created were, doe grow" and obey God's first command "to increase and multiply" (III.vi.34). The two passages are linked by the classical myth of Adonis, presented first in a bad form in Acrasia's Bower and then in a good form in the Garden of Adonis. Though the healthy garden embodies a philosophy of divine generation that is as rich and enigmatic as any other conceptual scheme in the poem, the place of the passage in the unfolding narrative is fairly straightforward. The chaotic inner forces of the psyche explored in Book II are here presented in ordered and temperate manifestations, with particular stress on healthy sexual desire. Whereas Acrasia was governed by an insatiable appetite for young men, the characters Amoret and Belphoebe, who were born and raised in the Garden of Adonis, seek higher goods. Amoret takes as her goals marriage and family, whereas Belphoebe chooses lifelong virginity and an active life outside the home.

The classical myths woven into these and other episodes in Book III do much to illuminate the characters. The myth of Cupid and Psyche, which is retold in the episode at the Garden of Adonis, shows the human mind brought into proper and fruitful union with the divine power of erotic love. Britomart, the heroine of the book, best fulfills this ideal. She is not like the delicately beautiful Florimell, who is timid and inclined to flee from men. She is not like Belphoebe, who seems contemptuous of affairs of the heart. Nor is she like Amoret, who lives for such experiences. Britomart combines the best qualities of all three women, drawing them toward a golden mean. She shares, for example, Florimell's determination to leave the comforts of courtly life and seek through the world for the man whom she is destined to marry. She matches Belphoebe in mental prowess, courage, and skill in manly pursuits such as hunting and jousting. Yet she also shares Amoret's capacity for warmth and nurturing.

It is tempting to take Britomart as a figure for Queen Elizabeth, but it seems likely that she is something far more complex. The *Letter to Ralegh*, which identifies major figures for the queen in the poem, makes no mention of Britomart in this regard. As the wise magician Merlin reveals in Canto iii, she is actually an ancestor of the English queen, though one who displays a close family resemblance. Britomart is, in fact, a far more glorious figure than either of the other main embodiments of Elizabeth: the noble but somewhat icy Belphoebe, who represents the queen in her private life, and the magnificent but absent Gloriana, who represents Elizabeth in her public role as a ruler but who appears only in the dreams of Prince Arthur (I.vii) and in brief references in the proems and elsewhere, but never in the action itself. Some see Britomart's quest for her future husband, Artegall—which begins with a vision of him in a crystal ball and is destined to end in marriage, joint rule over England, and a long line of glorious offspring—as a reference to Elizabeth's often stated desire to marry no suitor but England itself. This way of reading the poem makes a good deal of sense of later passages in Book V, where the character Radigund represents Mary, Queen of Scots; Britomart resembles Elizabeth; and Artegall suggests some of Elizabeth's most powerful noblemen at court, who were torn in their allegiances between the two queens. When Britomart rescues Artegall from captivity in Radigund's city of Amazons, there is reason to believe that the incident represents Elizabeth's salvation of England from the threat of Catholic domination under Mary. Yet the potentially fruitful Britomart stands in notable contrast to the virginal and childless Belphoebe, and it may be that one of Spenser's points in the poem was to criticize Elizabeth for not marrying and providing England with a proper heir.

In any case, Britomart stands in glorious contrast to two degraded types of womanhood in Book III, both defined once again with the help of classical mythology. The first is Malecasta in Canto i, who represents the tradition of Courtly Love. She leads men on by the gradual stages of courtship represented in the six knights who fight on her behalf: Gardante ("brief glances"), Parlante ("enticing words"), Iocante ("courtly play"), Basciante ("kissing"), Bacchante ("wine drinking"), and Noctante ("spending the night"). Once Malecasta has conquered a man, she makes him a slave to her whims and desires. She represents woman as predator. The tapestries depicting Venus and Adonis that hang in her castle link her with the more classical figure of Acrasia in Book II. The second example of unchastity in Book III is Hellenore, who represents the tradition of Ovidian love. Like Helen of Troy, she yields to the seductions of a guest (named, appropriately, Paridell) and allows herself to be carried away from her aged and jealous husband Malbecco, only to be discarded by her new lover

George Gower's Armada Portrait *of Queen Elizabeth I (Bedford Estates), who was Spenser's inspiration for Gloriana in* The Faerie Queene

and left to satisfy the lusts of forest satyrs. She represents woman as prey.

Both she and Malecasta are medieval embodiments of ancient types, and their presence helps to extend the moral allegory of the poem to include glimpses of the history of Western culture. For Spenser, lines of dynastic descent are important, as they had been for earlier epic poets such as those mentioned in his *Letter to Ralegh.* Here, he glorifies Britain through the ancestry of its representative Britomart. Like Paridell (and Virgil's Aeneas), she traces her ancestry back to the old stock of Troy. Unlike Paridell, however, she descends from the worthy hero Brutus, the founder of Troynovant (or England), not from the lustful and irresponsible Paris (III. ix.32-46). Through passages such as this—along with depictions of legendary English heroes throughout the poem and accounts of early English history, such as those that Arthur reads at Alma's castle and Britomart hears in Merlin's cave—Spenser establishes himself as a writer of "an historicall fiction" on which England may establish a sense of its national heritage.

In the climactic episode of Book III, when Britomart rescues Amoret from the evil enchanter Busirane, Spenser briefly sketches the history of relations between the sexes in Western culture, tying his account to the current difficulties that Amoret has suffered in marrying the aggressive young knight Scudamour. As we subsequently learn in Canto i of Book IV, she was kidnapped by Busirane during a ribald entertainment or "masque" performed on the night of her wedding, and clues in various rooms of the enchanter's house suggest that he represents the power of poetry and the visual arts to shape the attitudes of one gender toward the other. At least one of Amoret's problems on that night was a clash of cultural expectations.

In the first room, rich tapestries illustrate the dominance of men over women that characterized the myths of ancient Greece and Rome. In the second room, golden ornaments suggest the dominance of women over men found in the tradition of Courtly Love in the late Middle Ages. In the third room, where Amoret herself appears, we find what seems to be a Renaissance confusion of masculine and feminine dominance, fostered by an attempt to combine classical and medieval erotic ideals. As we learn in Book IV, Amoret's husband Scudamour sees himself as a domineering male of the classical sort, who bears the sign of triumphant Cupid on his shield (see III.xi.7 and IV.x). Amoret, however, sees herself as a "recluse virgin," whose education at the Temple of Venus has elevated her to a station much like that enjoyed by women in the medieval tradition of Courtly Love (see IV.x). If we may assume that Amoret's mental state following the night of her marriage is represented in the nightmarish procession known as the Masque of Cupid that appears in Busirane's third room, then the lady is not only suffering from a virgin's fears of the bridal night but also from confusion over her proper role as a wife. The allegorical figures surrounding her in the masque represent the course of her relationship with Scudamour. It began happily enough with Ease, Fancy, and Desire, but eventually graduated to more turbulent emotions such as Fear and Hope, Grief and Fury, and ended with feelings of Cruelty and Despight. Following these personifications comes the cause of her distress, depicted as Cupid riding on a lion. This figure reminds us of Scudamour's shield and probably represents his aggressive desire to dominate. Although Scudamour has attempted to release his bride from Busirane, only a third party such as Britomart, who understands the problem from a woman's point of view, can subdue the enchanter and dispel Amoret's fears.

In the second edition of the poem, which was printed in 1596, the problem of Scudamour and Amoret is never satisfactorily resolved. In Book IV she transfers her affections to her new friend Britomart, is captured by a lustful giant and rescued by Timias, and passes through a series of painful adventures ending in the Castle of Corflambo (or "burning heart"), from which she can only be saved by the intervention of Prince Arthur himself. Meanwhile, Scudamour mistakes the armed Britomart for a man, and after she goes off with Amoret, he suffers a fit of jealousy in the Cave of Care. Not until Canto vi, in which he attacks Britomart, does he discover her gender and his own folly. After these incidents, we hear little more of him or of Amoret. In the first edition of the poem published in 1590, however, Spenser fully resolved the tensions between the newlyweds. Upon Amoret's release from captivity to Busirane, she and Scudamour embrace and fuse with one another in a single hermaphroditic form, which seems to symbolize not only sexual union but also a golden mean between masculine and feminine forms of dominance and the consummation of an ideal Christian marriage.

By now it should be obvious that, as Spenser moved from the inward virtues of holiness and temperance in Books I and II to the more outward ones of chastity and friendship in Books III and IV, he adopted a far more complicated method of plotting. The first two books had followed a fairly straightforward and self-contained pattern: the hero had set forth on his quest, suffered a disastrous fall, been rescued by Arthur in Canto viii, joined forces with the Prince for a time, undergone a process of reeducation, and finally completed his quest with a victory in Canto xii. In Books III and IV, however, events are far more chaotic. This may be the case because the god Cupid has come into the picture. Among the epic invocations at the beginning of the poem, Spenser added something not found in Virgil or Homer, a prayer to the "most dreaded impe of highest *Jove*, / Faire *Venus* sonne," and Cupid's enormous power over earthly events is manifested in the social disorder of Books III and IV.

In the opening canto of Book III, for example, Spenser demonstrates love's power by drawing together all the major heroes of the poem so far, only to have Cupid divide and scatter them. Arthur appears with his squire Timias, Guyon with the Palmer, Britomart with her nurse, Glauce—and, not far away from them, the women also encounter the Red Crosse Knight. Almost as soon as the heroes meet, however, Florimell rides by, fleeing a forester who intends to rape her, and the men in the party ride off in hot pursuit. Guyon and Arthur pursue the lady more, it seems, for her beauty than for her safety, and they soon become separated and lost. Timias nobly rides off to subdue the forester, but afterward falls in love with Belphoebe, forgetting about Arthur and eventually becoming entangled in a romantic scandal involving Belphoebe and Amoret that drives him to despair and turns him into a hermit. Even the Red Crosse Knight loses his head in Book III, requiring assistance from

Britomart in turning back Malecasta's six knights. Thereafter, hardly a male in the poem can guide his own affairs sensibly until a semblance of order has been restored in Book V. The point seems to be that, in matters of love and friendship, women do better than men, and no one does very well. The beauty of a woman such as Florimell is like a comet, an astrological sign that "importunes death and dolefull drerihed" (V.i.16).

One of the governing aims of Books III and IV is to harmonize love with friendship. In the Renaissance many took from antiquity the view that bonds between two men were nobler than those between a man and a woman or between two women. Spenser undercuts this view by exalting marriage over friendship and also by idealizing amicable relationships between women and between members of the opposite sexes. In the first episode of Book IV, Britomart and Amoret arrive at a castle where no knight may enter without a lady. Britomart's solution is to exploit her disguise as a knight in order to enter as Amoret's champion, thus raising interesting issues of homoerotic attraction between the two ladies but also exalting the importance of their friendship. Later, Prince Arthur saves Amoret at the Castle of Corflambo, acting magnanimously as her male friend rather than as a potential lover.

Spenser's emblem of the social ideal is a foursome of two men and two women, all bound in complex interrelationships of erotic attraction and friendship. This pattern is seen most clearly in the main heroes of the book, Campbell and Triamond, and in the ladies whom they love. Before Campbell would allow anyone to marry his sister Canacee, he required that they first defeat him in battle. Triamond's two brothers, Priamond and Diamond, tried and failed. Because, however, their mother, Agape (or "love"), had made a pact with the Destinies that Triamond should inherit the spirits and the strengths of his brothers, he was able to succeed where they had failed. Later, Campbell married Triamond's sister Cambina, and the four became fast friends.

A second foursome, that of Paridell and Blandamour and their ladies Duessa and Ate, acts as a false parody of the first. Since the men are altogether faithless to one another and to their ladies, they quarrel over a third woman, a demonic copy of Florimell created by a witch in Book III. Once they have gone after this new "comet" of beauty in Canto ii, discord erupts among all four members of the group.

The primary destructive force in Book IV is represented in the hag Ate, the "mother of debate / And all dissention which doth dayly grow / Amongst fraile men" (IV.i.19). Her power can be seen most dramatically in the central incident of the book, the Tournament of Satyrane. There, ladies compete for the "glorie vaine" of owning a magic girdle of "chast love / And wivehood true" that once belonged to Florimell. This prize is to be given to the most beautiful among them, and the knights are to do battle for the hand of the winner. Ironically, at the end of the violent turmoil and strife represented in the tournament, the girdle is awarded to the false Florimell, who represents the beautiful but cruel mistress idealized in Petrarchan love sonnets of the period. Victory on the field is awarded to Satyrane, one of the Knights of Maidenhead (who, in the historical allegory of the episode, are associated with the virgin queen Elizabeth). The false Florimell, however, insists on choosing a mate to her own liking and selects one as shallow as she is, namely the impostor Braggadocchio. The folly of Petrarchan love conventions, which Spenser will take up again in the episode of Serena among the cannibals in Book VI and in his sonnet sequence *Amoretti*, is amusingly satirized in this outcome.

Yet even amid the discord and delusions of Book IV, the "fatall purpose of divine foresight" is nonetheless at work, guiding lovers to mates destined to them by higher powers from the foundation of the world (see III.iii.1-2). At Satyrane's tournament, Britomart encounters and defeats her long-sought future husband Artegall, though without recognizing him in his disguise as the Salvage Knight. In Canto vi he attempts to avenge this dishonor on her, but when her helmet falls off in battle, he falls in love with her instead. After a brief period of courtship, he plights his troth to marry her. Similarly, the true Florimell, who had been taken captive by the sea-god Proteus in Book III, finds her Marinell in the closing cantos of Book IV and is subsequently betrothed to him, as prophecies had foretold. Though confusion still reigns late in the book—as the brawl in Canto ix involving Britomart and Scudamour, Blandamour and Paridell, Prince Arthur and others reveals—images of harmony begin to appear, like sunlight after a storm. Most notable is the image of Concord celebrated in the Temple of Venus. Spenser says of her, "Of litle much, of foes she maketh frends, / And to afflicted minds sweet rest and quiet sends" (IV.x.34).

Many of the discords of Book IV are resolved in Book V, which recounts the Legend of Justice. Florimell marries Marinell at another great tournament, and in this contest the outcome is more just. Braggadocchio is revealed as a coward and a fraud; the false Florimell is revealed as a demonic illusion; and Guyon, who had long ago lost his horse to Braggadocchio, reclaims it again. Yet both the proem and the opening canto of the book remind us of the deeply fallen state of the world, where even the stars and planets no longer follow their ancient courses, and the goddess of justice, Astraea, has departed from the earth. Spenser here invokes Ovid's myth of the Four Ages of Mankind, which began with the Golden Age of Saturn and has since declined from the Age of Silver toward those of Brass and Stone.

The allegory of Book V focuses on the last period in this decline, stressing the corruption and injustice of England's enemies in Spenser's own day. Nearly everything in the main plot is related to Queen Elizabeth's struggle to preserve the independence of the English church and state against the Catholic forces arrayed against her in Scotland and Ireland, France and Spain. The main quest of the book is Artegall's attempt to rescue Irena from the tyrant Grantorto, which represents the English attempt to free Ireland from Catholic domination in the 1580s and 1590s. The incident in which Artegall encounters the Amazons and Queen Radigund is an account of the actions of Mary, Queen of Scots, beginning in 1558 and ending in 1571, when Elizabeth imprisoned her in England. Her execution in 1587 is later portrayed in the death of Duessa in Canto ix. The incident in which Prince Arthur and Artegall defeat the Souldan in Canto viii represents England's repulse of the sea invasion mounted by the Spanish Armada in 1588, and Arthur's rescue of Belgae from Geryoneo in Cantos x-xi represents England's intervention to free the Netherlands from Spanish forces in the 1580s, in which Sidney died and Leicester came to grief.

Against these forces, the hero of the book proves—like the Red Crosse Knight and Guyon before him—an inexperienced and sometimes inadequate hero. When we first see Artegall in Satyrane's Tournament in Book IV, he is armed as the Salvage Knight, and some of his untamed roughness carries over into Book V. Although he is successful in the early episodes, overthrowing Munera (or "bribery") and settling property disputes between the likes of Amidas and Bracidas, he seems incapable of conceiving of justice in any but legalistic terms, and he is also harsh and inflexible. His limitations appear most clearly in the brutality of his servant Talus and in his own submission to the Amazonian tyrant Radigund, who manages to lure him into agreeing to a foolish contract with her concerning their private combat in Canto v. What Artegall requires is a sounder philosophy of justice that will allow him to avoid such errors and to moderate his severity, and Spenser provides him with one in the figure of his future wife, Britomart, who rescues him from Radigund.

Britomart represents a form of justice known as "equity," which allows a judge or public official to mitigate the severity of punishments or to adjust the application of the law whenever the case involves unusual circumstances that could not have been foreseen when the written legal code was drafted. In following normal procedures of equity, the judge returns to the philosophical principles on which the code was originally based and infers the proper way to handle the case at hand. Such moderating procedures are allegorized at the Temple of Isis in Canto vii, where Britomart learns to temper Artegall's sternness with clemency, and his rigid adherence to the legal code with wisdom. After she has rescued him from Radigund, he serves an apprenticeship under Prince Arthur and receives his final education in the Palace of Mercilla.

The queen of that house represents the Christian virtue of mercy, which is different from the equitable justice allegorized in Britomart. Whereas equity returns to philosophical principles in order to ensure that the defendant receives his proper due, mercy offers freely to redeem offenders who sincerely repent their crimes. Artegall's education thus leads him from legal justice through classical equity to Christian mercy, symbolized respectively in the iron man Talus, the mostly silver idol of Isis, and the gold-bedecked queen Mercilla. By this progression the poet seems to point the way to reclaim Ovid's lost Age of Gold, and indeed, with Artegall's liberation of Belgae in Canto xii, nearly all the disorders of Books III-V have been resolved.

As often happens in *The Faerie Queene*, however, moments of victory and harmony prove short-lived. At the end of Book V, Artegall encounters a new threat, the Blatant Beast, whose name means both "prattling" or "babbling" and "hurtful." The monster, which Spenser describes as a "hellish Dog," represents slander, backbiting, and other forms of verbal abuse that tend to disrupt in private the social harmony that Artegall has been working so hard to establish in public. The monster may seem a minor threat in comparison with the more imposing enemies of justice in Book V—such as the Giant with Scales in Canto ii, who advocates the overthrow of the aristocracy in favor of an egalitarian form of government, or Grantorto in Canto xii, who represents political and religious tyranny. Yet because of the widespread and covert nature of its abuses, the Blatant Beast is more difficult to subdue. Throughout Book VI it appears unexpectedly, attacking with poisoned teeth and "thousand tongues," and then disappearing again before anyone can bring it to bay. It is first set on by Envy and Detraction (V.xii.35-37) and is later employed by Despetto ("malice"), Decetto ("deceit"), and Defetto ("detraction"), who succeed in provoking the Beast to wound Timias, a figure identified by his name with "honor" (VI.v). The two major strands of plot in Book VI—those involving Calidore's quest to bind the Beast and Calepine's search for Serena—both include episodes illustrating the power of the tongue.

The line of plot in which Serena (or "tranquillity") is ravaged by the Blatant Beast suggests the loss of reputation and the subsequent shunning and abuse that aristocratic women of Spenser's day sometimes suffered because of rumors that they had been unchaste. In Serena's case, the Beast attacks soon after she is discovered in a secluded forest glade with her lover, Calepine, who has violated the social conventions of aristocratic courtship by removing his armor "to solace with his Lady in delight" (VI.iii.20). The inward torments that she suffers in consequence of this tryst appear in her gradual decline into illness, which is brought on by the festering bites of the Beast (Cantos v-vi). The social degradations to which she is subjected are allegorized in her subsequent capture by the "Salvage Nation," a band of cannibals who are prevented from sacrificing her naked body on a forest altar only by the timely arrival of Calepine (Canto viii). The threat of similarly violent social repercussions hangs over Priscilla and her less nobly born lover Aladine in Canto ii, where they are also found dallying in the woods and are immediately attacked by a lustful knight.

The story of Serena among the cannibals involves more, however, than issues of reputation and the abuse of young lovers who overstep the bounds of custom. The language of the episode suggests the Petrarchan love poetry of Spenser's day, in which the woman was depicted as alluringly beautiful but cold and unattainable, and her lover was expected to vacillate endlessly between abject adoration and frustrated erotic desire. That such poetry should degrade an entire "Nation" to the level of savages, worshiping feminine beauty in a leering and cannibalistic religion of love, raises serious questions about the proper role of literature in shaping the social order. The more refined and pragmatic lover Calepine, whose name means "gracious speech," offers a contrasting ideal, in which love is mutual and courtship progresses naturally toward "solace" and "delight."

The chivalric code of the Middle Ages—in which men have a duty to honor and protect women, and women have an obligation to provide patterns of morality and images of "grace" to temper masculine aggressiveness—lies behind much of Spenser's thought about love and courtesy in Book VI. The opening episode, for example, involves an inversion of this ideal. In it the proud knight Crudor entices the lady Briana to serve him by forcing knights and ladies who pass her castle to shave their beards or their hair. By this means she hopes to win Crudor's love by lining a mantle with hair, as he has demanded. The true ideal of chivalry appears when Calidor intervenes on behalf of Briana, forcing her cruel knight to marry her. Crudor must also promise to behave better toward errant knights and to assist ladies "in every stead and stound" (VI.i.42). The Knight of Courtesy later confronts ethical dilemmas posed by this chivalric ideal. In Canto iii, for example, he violates his knightly duty to tell the truth in order to conceal Priscilla's secret meetings with Aladine from her father. In Cantos ix-xi the Knight of Courtesy is tempted to discard his armor and to abandon his quest altogether in order to court the shepherdess Pastorella.

This last incident reveals a conflict between personal fulfillment and social responsibility that is an underlying theme of Book VI. Spenser identifies the virtue responsible for maintaining a proper balance between the two as courtesy, which he sees broadly as "the ground, / And roote of civill conversation" (VI.i.1). In its original sense, courtesy was simply the pattern of con-

George Vertue's 1727 engraving based on the Chesterfield portrait of a subject believed to be Spenser. The original painting once hung in the library of Chesterfield House, London, the home of Philip Dormer Stanhope, fourth Earl of Chesterfield.

duct acceptable at a prince's court. By Spenser's day, however, it had come to imply a rather lengthy list of personal traits and abilities: noble birth and elegant manners, comely appearance and cultivated speech, athletic skill and martial prowess. All these traits were combined in a man such as Sir Philip Sidney, who is sometimes regarded as the Elizabethan knight on whom Sir Calidore was modeled. In the initial description of the Knight of Courtesy, Spenser depicts him as a marvel of courtly refinement. He is one

> In whom it seemes, that gentlenesse of spright
> And manners mylde were planted naturall;
> To which he adding comely guize withall,
> And gracious speach, did steale mens hearts away.
> Nathlesse thereto he was full stout and tall,
> And well approv'd in batteilous affray" (VI.i.2).

Only certain parts of this description, however, actually involve things that Calidore has "added" at court. The first qualities mentioned are the "naturall" elements of courtesy: "gentlenesse of spright" and "manners mylde," and these subsequently receive special attention.

Perhaps because Spenser was distressed by the extravagant artificialities and corruptions common in the royal courts of his day, he laid his greatest stress on the natural roots of courtesy. His most idealized depictions of the virtue are set in the partly civilized yet predominantly natural settings of the pastoral countryside. The sheepfolds of Pastorella and her foster father, Meliboe, in Cantos ix-xi provide a refuge both from the savagery of uncivilized nature (represented by the brigands who live in nearby forests and caves) and from the follies and extravagances of aristocratic life (depicted at the castles of Briana and Aldus). The fruitful interplay between the natural and the cultivated, the wild and the civilized is depicted emblematically in Calepine's rescue of an infant from a wild bear in Canto iv. Afterward, he gives the orphan to the barren Lady Matilde and her husband Sir Bruin so that their aristocratic house may have a suitable heir.

In the central episode involving Turpine (or "baseness") and his wife Blandina (or "flattery") in Cantos vi-vii, Spenser explores the two extremes represented in the symbolic forests and castles of the book. Both characters have the trappings, but not the substance, of true civility. When Calepine attempts to find shelter for the wounded Serena in Turpine's castle, he is repulsed and forced to spend the night with his lady in the forest, where he is gravely wounded by Turpine on the next day. From the forest, however, comes a wild and apparently "Salvage" man, who is actually more courteous than Turpine and his wife. That the wild man risks his life to rescue Calepine and his lady and carefully tends the knight's wounds suggests something of the inherent goodness of human nature. That he succeeds in curing only Calepine's injuries and not those of Serena, however, suggests the limitations of that nature when it is not cultivated by civil custom and informed by religion. A pious hermit who had once been a great knight is the only one who can save Serena.

In Calidor's quest to subdue the Blatant Beast, Spenser presents a further exploration of the relationship between the civil and the natural. The knight first finds the Beast in Gloriana's city of Cleopolis, which in one of its allegorical senses stands for Elizabethan London. The knight then pursues the monster from smaller towns past outlying castles to the sheepfolds of Pastorella and Meliboe, which are associated with Spenser's own rural home in Ireland. So much more courteous are the simple shepherd and his daughter than those whom Calidore has left behind in "civil" society that he abandons his life as a knight and takes up that of a shepherd, hoping to win the heart of Pastorella. His most exalted moment comes in Canto x, when he is immersed in the beauties of nature, far from the court of his queen. Walking on Mount Acidale, he comes upon the shepherd Colin Clout, whose name associates him with Spenser and *The Shepheardes Calender*. Colin is playing his pipes, and all before him are "An hundred naked maidens lilly white," dancing in a ring about the three Graces of classical mythology, who in turn are dancing about Colin's beloved, who represents Spenser's second wife, Elizabeth Boyle. Though the poet might have placed Queen Elizabeth in the midst of the rings, portraying her as the central emblem of grace and courtesy in Book VI, he pointedly avoids doing so, beseeching his monarch to give him leave to place his own Elizabeth there instead. His own natural bonds with his wife take precedence over his civil bonds with his queen.

This curious detail is sometimes interpreted as a sign that Spenser, like his hero Calidore, had turned away from Gloriana's court, abandoning in disillusionment his great project of glorifying Queen Elizabeth in *The Faerie Queene*. Certainly, he composed very little more of the poem after he finished the pastoral cantos of Book VI, which were the last episodes published in his own lifetime. Yet the poet's gesture toward his wife need not be taken as a slight to the queen. After all, he had only recently remarried and therefore had special reason to request leave of his monarch "To make one [brief passage] of thy poore handmayd, / And underneath thy feete to place her prayse" (VI.x.28). It seems clear, moreover, that he did not entirely endorse Calidore's "truancy" among the shepherds. By adopting their life of pleasure and contemplation, the knight has acted irresponsibly, as subsequent events reveal. Not only has he left the Blatant Beast free to do further harm, which is described in Canto xii, but he has also left Pastorella and her father undefended from other evils in the surrounding forest. A band of brigands soon sweeps down on them, killing Meliboe and several other shepherds and binding Pastorella in a cave in hopes of selling her into slavery. To rescue her, Calidore is forced to rearm himself, and after he has scattered the brigands, he is compelled to seek shelter for his beloved at a nearby castle. In a fallen world, the natural life divorced from the civil is no more sustainable than the civil divorced from the natural.

Even Calidore's idealization of the shepherds has been based partly on a mistake, for as he discovers in Canto xii, Pastorella is actually a child of the aristocracy, born to Sir Bellamour and Lady Claribell in a secret love affair like those examined elsewhere in Book VI. She was abandoned among the shepherds to conceal her parents' shame. At the climax of the book, this noble child raised by common shepherds returns in joy to her parents as an emblem of the ideal union of the natural with the civilized. Whatever Spenser's personal attitudes toward Elizabeth and her court may have been when he wrote this part of the poem, it hardly endorses a radical reappraisal of the prevailing social order or a renunciation of the poet's lifelong project. At the end of Book VI, Calidore resumes his quest, captures the Blatant Beast, and leads it captive through Faerie Land.

When Books I-III of *The Faerie Queene* were first published in 1590, Queen Elizabeth was not the only one to admire them, and by 1596, when Books IV-VI appeared, her grant of a royal pension was not the only reward that its author had received. The poem won immediate recognition as the finest poetic achievement of its generation, and further works by the poet were evidently in demand. In 1591 he returned to London to print two other works, *Daphnaïda* and the *Complaints*. Just four years later, three more of his works were published: *Colin Clouts Come home againe*, the sonnet sequence entitled *Amoretti*, and his widely admired *Epithalamion*. These were followed in 1596 by the last of the works published during his own lifetime, the *Fowre Hymnes* and the *Prothalamion*.

Daphnaïda is a dreary and somewhat overly expansive pastoral lament written soon after the death of the wife of Spenser's friend Arthur Gorges, a minor poet and translator. Based on Chaucer's *Book of the Duchess*, it is partly an experiment in patterning poetry according to symbolic numbers (here multiples of seven, the number associated with divine judgment and rest from sorrows), and it may have helped to prepare the way for the wonderfully detailed and suggestive number symbolism of the *Epithalamion*.

More successful were the *Complaints*, nine lengthy poems on the general themes of mutability and the vanity of earthly desires. The volume looks back to Spenser's earliest work, reprinting revised versions of his two dream visions from the 1569 volume *A Theatre for Worldlings* and adding a similar poem entitled *Visions of the Worlds Vanitie*. These three show a side of Spenser that would later appeal to writers of the Romantic period, namely his sense of the poet as a prophet, speaking inspired truths against the follies of his age. The volume also includes an imitation of the French poet Joachim du Bellay's *Antiquitez de Rome* (1558), which is a meditation on the tragic impermanence of even the greatest works of human ambition, epitomized in the ancient city of Rome.

The *Complaints* continue the experiments in poetic technique characteristic of *The Shepheardes Calender*, and they explore some of the same literary forms and themes. Like *October*, for example, *The Teares of the Muses* laments the current low esteem of poets in England. Like *February*, *Muiopotmos* employs a beast fable to expound a moral point. It is a mock epic about a vain butterfly caught by an envious spider, and may have been written as a light interlude in the serious business of composing *The Faerie Queene*. Like *Maye* and *September*, the poem *Mother Hubberds Tale* employs another beast fable for satirical purposes, presenting four stories about a fox and an ape that warn of abuses among the three traditional "estates" of English society: the commoners, the clergy, and the nobility. The dedication preceding the poem calls it "the raw conceipt" of the poet's youth, and since topical allusions tie it to political affairs in the years 1579-1580, it is probably work of the same period as *The Shepheardes Calender*.

As a counterweight to the dominant theme of mutability, the *Complaints* offer poetry as one of the few means to resist the depredations of time. The volume begins with *The Ruines of Time*, a poem that contrasts a depiction of the great but forgotten city of Verulame with an elegy for Sidney, who had died of wounds suffered in battle in the Netherlands in 1586. By means of this contrast Spenser celebrates the power of poetry to confer on Sidney a kind of glory that will outlast empires. The pastoral poem *Astrophel* and the six elegies and epitaphs for Sidney by other authors that Spenser gathered four years later at the end of *Colin Clouts Come home againe* reiterate this theme and offer a belated though impressive tribute to Spenser's early patron.

Sidney's impact on Spenser did not end with the tributes printed in the *Complaints* and *Colin Clout*. Along with the mingling of pastoral and epic in Book VI of *The Faerie Queene*, which resembles the same blending in Sidney's *Arcadia*, the dead poet's influence also appears in the *Amoretti*, a series of sonnets published with the *Epithalamion* in 1595. Spenser's volume reads as if it were designed as a reply to Sidney's dazzling sonnet sequence, *Astrophil and Stella*, which was printed in London in 1591 by Spenser's own publisher, William Ponsonby, and which began a vogue for English sonnets that lasted for more than a decade.

The contrasts between the two sequences are illuminating. Whereas Sidney's poems had followed Continental models in depicting the love of a distant and unattainable woman, Spenser's sonnets went against this widespread Petrarchan convention by celebrating a successful courtship, which culminates in the joyous wedding ceremony depicted in the *Epithalamion*. Both sequences seem to have been, at least in part, autobiographical, with Sidney's reflecting his love of Lady Penelope Rich and Spenser's his courtship of his second wife, Elizabeth Boyle, who later bore him a son named Peregrine. Yet, whereas Sidney had been in love with another man's wife and had described a gradual process by which passion had conquered reason and religious principle, Spenser moved from such passion early in his sequence toward an eventual restoration of Christian piety and self-control. His address to the *Amoretti* themselves in Sonnet 1 sets a tone for the entire sequence that is lighter and less turbulent than that of *Astrophil and Stella*: "Happy ye leaves when as those lilly hands, / . . . / shall handle you." Though the poems that follow show the influence of various earlier sonneteers—including Petrarch and Philippe Desportes, Tasso and du Bellay—Spenser never departs from his own vision of healthy courtship, which progresses from the follies and excesses of infatuation toward the stability and fruitfulness of Christian marriage.

The organizing principle of the *Amoretti* and the *Epithalamion* is, as in *The Shepheardes Calender*, the passage of time. The poet's wooing of Elizabeth Boyle initially seems an endless endeavor. Like Petrarch's love of Laura, it drives the poet to exclaim in Sonnet 25, "How long shall this lyke dying lyfe endure"? Yet, even as he says this, an important phase in the courtship has already begun that will eventually lead to the resolution that he desires. As scholars have pointed out, in Sonnet 22 he mentions the beginning of Lent, "This holy season fit to fast and pray." If one sonnet is counted for each day between Ash Wednesday and Easter, then the celebration of Christ's Resurrection would be expected in Sonnet 68, and that is where it appears. Sonnet 67 announces the end of the lover's "hunt" for his "gentle deare," in which the lady has been "fyrmely tyde" and "goodly wonne." In Sonnet 68 the poet prays to Christ: "This joyous day, deare Lord, with joy begin, / and grant that we for whom thou diddest dye / being with thy deare blood clene washt from sin, / may live for ever in felicity." Before the Lenten section there had been twenty-one sonnets of preparation, and after the Easter sonnet there are again twenty-one in the denouement. These eighty-nine, plus the four short mythological poems known as anacreontics that come between the *Amoretti* and the *Epithalamion*, make a total of ninety-three, which is the number of days in the season of spring. That the central sonnets of the sequence are meant to be read as a depiction of springtime courtship is suggested in Sonnets 19 and 70, which fall just before and after the Lenten sonnets.

The *Epithalamion* continues this elaborately patterned sequence of symbolic seasons and times. Spenser's wedding took place on St. Barnabas's Day, 11 June 1594, which was, by Elizabethan reckoning, the longest day of the year. As A. Kent Hieatt has shown, the twenty-four stanzas of the poem represent the hours of that particular day, beginning with the groom's preparations before dawn and ending at the same hushed hour on the following morning. So precise is the temporal sequence that the coming of night is announced in the fourth line of stanza 17, just as Irish almanacs of the period set the hour of sunset at sixteen and a fraction hours after sunrise. All the stanzas leading up to this long-awaited moment contain a refrain that rejoices in the happy sounds of the day, from the singing of the birds at the bride's awakening to the joyous ringing of the church bells after the ceremony is over. All the stanzas after nightfall, however, call for silence: "Ne let the woods us answere, nor our Eccho ring."

As in *The Shepheardes Calender*, where the passing of the months becomes a metaphor for the entire span of Colin's life, so here the hours are connected with the larger cycles of the year and of life itself. Perhaps to magnify the significance of the wedding day, it is represented as if it had lasted a year, as we can see from the fact that the poem contains 365 long lines. At the end, as Spenser and his bride lie in bed in the darkness before the dawn, he thinks of the whole course of their coming life together, looking forward to their final rest and that of their children in "heavenly tabernacles." Along with this God-given way to escape from time, the wedding poem itself provides another, becoming, as the last line suggests, "for short time an endless monument."

Throughout the *Epithalamion*, Spenser maintains a delicate balance between the heavenly and the earthly, the classical and the Christian. The poem begins with invocations to the Muses and to the forest, river, and sea nymphs of antiquity, who, along with Hymen and the Graces and the greater gods Bacchus and Venus, Cynthia and Juno, rule over mundane affairs in the poem. The poet, acting as a genial (though sometimes fretful) master of ceremonies, seems to invite the entire creation to join in celebrating his wedding day. He begins by depicting the sun as it rises, proceeds through the fish in the river and the beasts and birds in the forest, and continues up the Great Chain of Being to village children and the musicians hired to play for the wedding. This progression leads finally to his bride, who comes forth like a goddess among less comely "merchants daughters." At the beginning of stanza 12, which is the midpoint of the poem, the poet sings, "Open the temple gates unto my love," and this turns our attention from the world outside the church to the Christian ceremony of Holy Matrimony that is to be celebrated within. The musicians then raise a great crescendo to heaven, and the priest unites the couple before the altar, invoking the authority of a God who stands far above the pagan deities in the natural world of the poem. Afterward, the music and the bells that follow the service fade away, and the wedding party gradually disperses, leaving the poet alone with his bride. The final image of the poem is of him lying awake beside her in the silence just before dawn, thinking of children to come and the joys of heaven. This image is perhaps Spenser's most telling response to the fruitless idolatry and the frustrated earthly desire that are the subjects of Sidney's *Astrophil and Stella*.

A similar, though more puzzling, blend of the classical with the Christian appears in Spenser's next volume, the *Fowre Hymnes*. The first two hymns, which are meditations on earthly love and beauty, invoke the pagan gods Cupid and Venus as their reigning deities. The second two, which deal with heavenly love and heavenly beauty, are addressed to Christ and Sapience (or Christian wisdom). Though hymns modeled on the work of Pindar and other pagan poets of antiquity had recently been revived on the Continent, Spenser's book is unusual in setting such poems side by side with more traditional Christian material. To be sure, the pagan hymns follow a Platonic "ladder of love" in which the speaker progresses from love of the body to love of the soul, but there is no way to reconcile their essentially worldly and self-centered philosophy with that depicted in the second pair of poems. Whereas the pagan hymns celebrate an altogether human form of love that aims to conquer and possess the beloved for its own self-fulfillment, the Christian hymns celebrate a divine love that aims to free others from bondage to sin by undertaking selfless acts of personal sacrifice.

The difficulty in resolving such contradictions has led some critics to accept at face value comments in the poet's letter of dedication to the volume, which suggest that the first pair was written "in the greener times of my youth" and the second was offered by way of a retraction. Other scholars have noted, however, internal evidence suggesting that the pagan hymns were written—or at least revised—in the same period as the Christian ones and therefore that they are not likely to represent the mere errors of Spenser's youth. Perhaps the most likely explanation is that the poet was simply repeating a pedagogical device employed frequently in *The Faerie Queene*. First, he presented a widely respected view from antiquity, and then he offered a far richer Christian view of the same subject, leaving his readers to puzzle out the differences and choose for themselves.

The *Prothalamion*, which was the last of Spenser's poems to be published during his lifetime, also involves unresolved tensions, though of a darker sort than those found in the *Fowre Hymnes*. The poem was written to celebrate a double betrothal ceremony for the two daughters of Edward Somerset, Earl of Worcester, which took place during Spenser's journey to London in the latter half of 1596, which he apparently undertook in order to seek a government position in England. Like *The Shepheardes Calender*, the poem begins with notes of weariness and despair. As the poet wanders along the bank of the river Thames, thinking about his own "long fruitlesse stay / In Princes Court" and seeking to ease his "payne," he sees two lovely swans floating on the water, with river nymphs gathering about them. These, of course, represent the prospective brides and their attendants. The counterpoint between the poet's sadness and the rising tones of joy in the betrothal ceremony is caught most movingly in a song of blessing sung to the swans by one of the nymphs. Only two years earlier, Spenser had sung a wedding song of his own, but sorrows have since crowded in upon him. In coming from a turbulent world beyond the security of London, he cannot see the peaceful scene before him without thinking of faraway wars, glimpsed briefly at the end of the poem in a stanza glorifying the recent English burning of the Spanish fleet at Cadiz under the direction of Elizabeth's young favorite, Robert Devereux, second Earl of Essex. The refrain in the poem, which invokes the river to "runne softly till I end my Song," suggests that the river may not always run softly, and the lingering impression of the poem is one of fragile beauty and transient joy.

The tone of dejection in Spenser's *Prothalamion* appears in other of his works published in 1596. It may reflect the worsening situation in Ireland, where Tyrone's Rebellion would soon uproot the English colonists and, with them, Spenser's family. It may also have arisen from Spenser's belief that he was being slandered at the English court and that old enemies were preventing him from gaining a better and safer position there. Both concerns stand out prominently in the last three cantos of Book VI of *The Faerie Queene*. There, shepherds associated with Spenser's literary persona, Colin Clout, are attacked by lawless brigands, and the poet's final words are a complaint that the Blatant Beast has escaped once again and "raungeth through the world againe / . . . / Ne spareth he the gentle Poets rime, / But rends without regard of person or of time." This passage probably refers to William Cecil, Baron Burghley, Elizabeth's powerful counselor, who had censured Spenser's epic for dealing too much with themes of erotic love (see *The Faerie Queene* IV. Proem). In any case, the poet's last work, the *Mutabilitie Cantos*, published posthumously in 1609, reflects once again on the old themes of time and the sorrows and uncertainties of life.

The cantos were apparently written as the main allegorical "core" for an otherwise unfinished book of *The Faerie Queene*, which a headnote by the printer identifies as "the legend of *Constancie*." Appropriately set amid the turbulence of the Irish countryside, the cantos place the local and the immediate problems threatening Spenser and his family within a universal context, reflecting on the role of mutability in God's creation. Once again using classical myth to explore issues that deeply touched his Christian view of the world, Spenser tells the story of the goddess Mutability, a daughter of the Titans who long ago rebelled against Jove. Longing to be admired like her sisters Hecate and Bellona, Mutability sets out in the world's first innocence to ravage "all which Nature had establisht first" and all the laws of civil society, thereby bringing death into the world. She then mounts up to the circle of the moon, attempting to drag from her throne the goddess Cynthia (who, in one of her allegorical references, stands for Queen Elizabeth). Ascending higher, Mutability then challenges Jove himself, putting forth her case that she is the rightful ruler of the universe. In order to resolve her dispute with Jove, she appeals to the highest judge of all, Dame Nature, who assembles all the gods on Arlo Hill to hear her judgment.

Within this larger framework Spenser tells the story of Faunus, who bribes the Irish river nymph Molanna to place him near Diana's favored haunts on Arlo Hill, where he may see the goddess bathing. When the satyr betrays himself by laughing, he is captured by Diana's nymphs, covered with a deer skin, and set upon by hounds. He manages to escape, but Diana thereafter abandons Arlo Hill, cursing it as a haunt for wolves and thieves. Through the Irish setting of the story and its depiction of a humiliation offered to the moon goddess Diana, the poet links the account of Faunus to Mutability's attack on Cynthia and her subsequent trial by Dame Nature. The inner story raises, however, an important issue not so clearly presented in the outer story, namely the role of erotic desire in bringing discord into the world.

The *Mutability Cantos* represent the highest perfection of Spenser's art, combining almost effortlessly the strains of moral, psychological, and historical allegory that run through the entire poem. The poet's description of the great trial on Arlo Hill brings forth all his poetic powers, providing opportunities for dramatic word paintings of Mutability's effects upon the heavens and the earth, but also for more delicate passages, such as the colorful miniatures of the seasons, months, and hours that parade before Dame Nature as evidence of endless change. Many of the dominant themes and images of Spenser's other works, from the earliest vision poems and *The Shepheardes Calender* to the *Complaints* and the *Prothalamion*, come together here.

The closing stanzas of the *Mutability Cantos* offer Spenser's last word on the problem that had preoccupied him throughout his life, and, like the mottoes in the *Calender*, that word is enigmatic. Addressing Mutability, Dame Nature says only,

> I well consider all that ye have sayd,
> And find that all things stedfastnes doe hate
> And changed be: yet being rightly wayd
> They are not changed from their first estate;
> But by their change their being doe dilate:
> And turning to themselves at length againe,
> Doe work their owne perfection so by fate:
> Then over them Change doth not rule and raigne;
> But they raigne over change, and doe their states
> maintaine.

Characteristically, Spenser leaves his reader to bring light to this "darke conceit," offering afterward only another equally mysterious solution to the problem of mutability, a Christian one that lies beyond the earthly wisdom of Dame Nature:

> . . . all that moveth, doth in *Change* delight:
> But thence-forth all shall rest eternally
> With Him that is the God of Sabbaoth hight:
> O that great Sabbaoth God, graunt me that
> Sabbaoths sight.

It may be that this prayer for rest in another world was the last line of poetry that Spenser ever wrote, for after it the fragmentary third canto of *Mutability* breaks off. Certainly, the last two years of his life allowed him little leisure to write. In 1598 rebels attacked and burned Kilcolman Castle, forcing Spenser and his family to flee to Cork. In December he returned to England, where he delivered a report on the Irish crisis at Whitehall on Christmas Eve. Three weeks later, on 13 January 1599, he died, perhaps of illness brought on by exhaustion. He was buried soon after in the south transept of Westminster Abbey in the Poets' Corner.

Twenty years after his death, Anne Clifford, Countess of Dorset, erected at his tomb a monument on which was engraved, "Heare lyes (expecting the Second comminge of our Saviour Christ Jesus) the body of Edmond Spencer, the Prince of Poets in his tyme. . . ." If there is partiality here, shown in the surprising preference of Spenser over Shakespeare, the inscription is for that very reason revealing because it suggests the strong devotion that the poet has so often aroused in his readers. Although his impact in our own century has not been great by the standards of Chaucer, Shakespeare, or Milton, in earlier periods he exerted an influence on English culture that rivaled that of any poet in the language. Much of this influence was exerted through other poets, who have frequently turned to him as a teacher, incorporating his thought or his poetic methods into their own works. It is not without reason that Spenser is called the "poet's poet."

This may, in some measure, have been true even during Spenser's own lifetime. In describing his funeral, the contemporary historian William Camden records that his body was placed "neere *Chawcer*, . . . all Poets carrying his body to Church, and casting their dolefull Verses, and Pens too into his grave." Already, contemporaries such as Michael Drayton, Samuel Daniel, and Thomas Lodge were beginning to imitate *The Faerie Queene* and *The Shepheardes Calender*. His influence continued to grow among writers of the seventeenth century, including William Browne, Giles and Phineas Fletcher, and William Davenant. Ben Jonson, who once remarked about *The Faerie Queene* that "Spencers stanzaes pleased him not, nor the matter," elsewhere calls the poem "*Spenser's* noble booke" and lists him, sometimes rather grumpily, among the great writers in the language. Milton was more consistent in his praise, depicting Spenser in the masque *Comus* (1637) as the wise shepherd Meliboeus and calling him "our sage and serious poet *Spencer*, whom I dare be known to think a better teacher than *Scotus* or *Aquinas*." Dryden confirms the autobiographical importance of this statement, reporting in *Fables, Ancient and Modern* (1700) that "*Milton* has acknowledg'd to me, that *Spencer* was his Original."

Even more striking, however, is the response of writers in the eighteenth century, when scores of poets produced literally hundreds of imitations, adaptations, and continuations of Spenser's works. No other English poet except Milton can claim a greater following among the writers of that period. So pervasive was his influence, in fact, that Samuel Johnson felt obliged to write an essay in the *Rambler* opposing the publication of any more imitations, remarking with some exasperation that "they appeal not to reason or passion, but to memory, and pre-suppose an accidental or artificial state of mind." Johnson was right, of course; most of these imitations have since been forgotten. Yet some—by writers of ability such as James Thomson, James Beattie, Samuel Croxall, Moses Mendez, and Robert Burns—retain much of their original force, if not their original popularity.

By the nineteenth century the flood of imitations in England had narrowed, but it had also grown deeper. Along with Chaucer, Shakespeare, and Milton, Spenser stood as one of the great English sources of inspiration for the Romantic age, providing in *The Faerie Queene* the quasi-medieval setting, the romance form, the stanzaic and metrical patterns, the archaic language, and the mingling of the natural with the artful and the supernatural that became the very stuff of romanticism. Every one of the major Romantic poets was a serious reader of his works. William Wordsworth, who had memorized long swatches of his poetry as a boy and who frequently adapted and imitated his poetic effects, describes him in *The Prelude* (1850) as "Sweet Spenser, moving through his clouded heaven / With the moon's beauty and the moon's soft pace." Samuel Taylor Coleridge revealed his indebtedness in such things as the archaic language of the *Rime of the Ancient Mariner* (1798) and the forested realms of chivalry and enchantment in *Christabel* (1816). John Keats, in turn, was so delighted by Spenser's language and prosody (and by *Christabel*) that he composed his *Eve of Saint Agnes* (1820) and four other poems in Spenserian stanzas. During his last illness he passed the time marking favorite passages in Spenser for the young Fanny Brawne, whom he had hoped to marry. Percy Bysshe Shelley looked to his Renaissance predecessor for models of multifaceted allegory, attempting in *Laon and Cythna* (1818) the longest of the Romantic poems in the Spenserian stanza and composing *Adonais* (1821) in response to Spenser's funeral elegy *Astrophel*. Even George Gordon, Lord Byron, was affected, fashioning his Childe Harold after the knights of *The Faerie Queene* and composing much of his early poetry in Spenserian stanzas, which he called "the measure most after my own heart."

Though most writers of the nineteenth century looked to Spenser for his metrical forms and his language, for his settings and his "atmospherics," there were some who admired him for the thought embodied in his poetry. William Butler Yeats incorporated something of Spenser's Platonism in his early Rose Poems and pondered, in his own edition of the *Poems of Spenser*, the moving interplay between the delights of the senses and the stern moral allegories of *The Faerie Queene*. Widespread reaction against such allegory throughout the century, however, inevitably meant that influential writers other than practicing poets gradually came to read him less and less. There were, however, notable exceptions. In England prose writers such as Sir Walter Scott, Charles Lamb, and George MacDonald were deeply touched by his work, and in America, where religious sympathies were perhaps closer to Spenser's own devout brand of Anglo-Protestantism, Nathaniel Hawthorne and Herman Melville turned to *The Faerie Queene* for its moral allegory and for its rich abundance of narrative models.

The extraordinary strength of Spenser's appeal over the centuries can perhaps be most clearly revealed by comparing him with Sidney. Initially, the poet of *Astrophil and Stella* and *Arcadia* was far more important than Spenser, exerting an influence on the Renaissance that was arguably broader and greater than that of any other author of the Elizabethan period. By the time Milton had published the final version of *Paradise Lost* (1674), however, Sidney's impact upon the world of letters was diminishing rapidly, and his reputation as a poet did not rebound to any great extent until the late nineteenth century.

Spenser, on the other hand, grew in importance during the very periods when Sidney suffered his greatest decline. Only in the twentieth century has his influence on the culture of the English-speaking world diminished. The very qualities in his work that earlier ages valued—his fondness for things timeworn and venerable, his deeply religious cast of mind, his subordination of his own delicate appreciation of the delights of the senses to the nobler aims of ethical and political action, and his endless fascination with the complexities of literary form—all these have proved liabilities in a culture shaped by spare and skeptical modernism and by forms of entertainment more immediately striking to the senses than poetry. His decline as a major force among contemporary writers, however, has not necessarily meant a decline in the size of his audience, since he probably delights more readers today in college and university classrooms throughout the world than he ever did in the middle- and upper-class parlors of England during the periods of his greatest influence.

Bibliographies:

Spenser Newsletter (1970-) [prints reviews and annotated bibliographies three times yearly];

Waldo F. McNeir and Foster Provost, *Edmund Spenser: An Annotated Bibliography 1937-72* (Pittsburgh: Duquesne University Press, 1975);

William L. Sipple and Bernard J. Vondersmith, *Edmund Spenser 1900-1936: A Reference Guide* (Boston: G. K. Hall, 1984).

Biography:

Alexander C. Judson, *The Life of Edmund Spenser* (Baltimore: Johns Hopkins University Press, 1945).

Study Guide:

A. C. Hamilton, Donald Cheney, W. F. Blissett, David A. Richardson, and William Barker, eds., *The Spenser Encyclopedia* (Toronto: University of Toronto Press / London: Routledge, 1990).

References:

Paul J. Alpers, *The Poetry of "The Faerie Queene"* (Princeton: Princeton University Press, 1967);

Alpers, "Spenser's Late Pastorals," *English Literary History*, 56 (Winter 1989): 797-816;

Peter Bayley, ed., *Spenser: "The Faerie Queene," A Casebook* (London: Macmillan, 1977);

Harry Berger, Jr., *The Allegorical Temper: Vision and Reality in Book II of Spenser's "Faerie Queene"* (New Haven: Yale University Press, 1957);

Berger, *Revisionary Play: Studies in the Spenserian Dynamics* (Berkeley & Los Angeles: University of California Press, 1988);

John D. Bernard, *Ceremonies of Innocence: Pastoralism in the Poetry of Edmund Spenser* (Cambridge & New York: Cambridge University Press, 1989);

Douglas Brooks-Davies, *Spenser's "Faerie Queene": A Critical Commentary on Books I and II* (Manchester, U.K.: Manchester University Press, 1977);

Donald Cheney, *Spenser's Image of Nature: Wild Man and Shepherd in "The Faerie Queene"* (New Haven: Yale University Press, 1965);

Terry Comito, "A Dialectic of Images in Spenser's *Fowre Hymnes*," *Studies in Philology*, 74 (1977): 301-321;

Alexander Dunlop, "The Unity of Spenser's *Amoretti*," in *Silent Poetry: Essays in Numerological Analysis*, edited by Alastair Fowler (London:

Routledge & Kegan Paul, 1970), pp. 153-169;

Maurice Evans, *Spenser's Anatomy of Heroism: A Commentary on "The Faerie Queene"* (Cambridge: Cambridge University Press, 1970);

A. Bartlett Giamatti, *Play of Double Senses: Spenser's "Faerie Queene"* (Englewood Cliffs, N.J.: Prentice-Hall, 1975);

Jonathan Goldberg, *Endlesse Worke: Spenser and the Structures of Discourse* (Baltimore & London: Johns Hopkins University Press, 1981);

Stephen Greenblatt, *Renaissance Self-Fashioning: From More to Shakespeare* (Chicago & London: University of Chicago Press, 1980), pp. 157-192;

A. C. Hamilton, " 'Like Race to Runne': The Parallel Structure of *The Faerie Queene*, Books I and II," *PMLA*, 73 (1958): 327-334;

Hamilton, ed., *Essential Articles for the Study of Edmund Spenser* (Hamden, Conn.: Archon, 1972);

Richard Helgerson, *Self-Crowned Laureates: Spenser, Jonson, Milton and the Literary System* (Berkeley: University of California Press, 1983);

S. K. Heninger, Jr., *Sidney and Spenser: The Poet as Maker* (University Park & London: Pennsylvania State University Press, 1989);

A. Kent Hieatt, *Short Time's Endless Monument: The Symbolism of the Numbers in Edmund Spenser's "Epithalamion"* (New York: Columbia University Press, 1960);

Robert Hoopes, " 'God Guide Thee, Guyon': Nature and Grace Reconciled in *The Faerie Queene*, Book II," *Review of English Studies*, 5 (1954): 14-24;

Graham Hough, *A Preface to "The Faerie Queene"* (London: Duckworth, 1962);

Lynn Staley Johnson, *The Shepheardes Calender: An Introduction* (University Park: Pennsylvania State University Press, 1990);

Carol V. Kaske, "Spenser's *Amoretti* and *Epithalamion* of 1595: Structure, Genre, and Numerology," *English Literary Renaissance*, 8 (1978): 271-295;

Judith M. Kennedy and James A. Reither, eds., *A Theatre for Spenserians* (Toronto: University of Toronto Press, 1973);

John N. King, *Spenser's Poetry and the Reformation Tradition* (Princeton: Princeton University Press, 1990);

C. S. Lewis, *The Allegory of Love* (Oxford: Clarendon Press, 1936), pp. 297-360;

Lewis, "Sidney and Spenser," in *English Literature in the Sixteenth Century Excluding Drama* (Oxford: Clarendon Press, 1954), pp. 318-393;

David Lee Miller, *The Poem's Two Bodies: The Poetics of the 1590 "Faerie Queene"* (Princeton: Princeton University Press, 1988);

Montrose, "The Elizabethan Subject and the Spenserian Text," in *Literary Theory/Renaissance Texts*, edited by Patricia Parker and David Quint (Baltimore: Johns Hopkins University Press, 1986), pp. 303-340;

William Nelson, *The Poetry of Edmund Spenser: A Study* (New York: Columbia University Press, 1963);

Richard Neuse, "Book VI as Conclusion to *The Faerie Queene*," *English Literary History*, 35 (1968): 329-353;

Michael O'Connell, *Mirror and Veil: The Historical Dimension of Spenser's "Faerie Queene"* (Chapel Hill: University of North Carolina Press, 1977);

Charles Grosvenor Osgood, *A Concordance to the Poems of Edmund Spenser* (Washington, D.C.: Carnegie Institution of Washington, 1915);

Thomas P. Roche, Jr., *The Kindly Flame: A Study of the Third and Fourth Books of Spenser's "Faerie Queene"* (Princeton: Princeton University Press, 1964);

Mark Rose, *Spenser's Art: A Companion to Book I of "The Faerie Queene"* (Cambridge, Mass.: Harvard University Press, 1975);

Naseeb Shaheen, *Biblical References in "The Faerie Queene"* (Memphis, Tenn.: Memphis State University Press, 1976);

David R. Shore, *Spenser and the Poetics of Pastoral: A Study of the World of Colin Clout* (Kingston & Montreal: McGill-Queen's University Press, 1985);

Donald V. Stump, "Isis Versus Mercilla: The Allegorical Shrines in Spenser's Legend of Justice," *Spenser Studies*, 3 (1982): 87-98;

Humphrey Tonkin, *The Faerie Queene* (London: Unwin Hyman, 1989);

Tonkin, *Spenser's Courteous Pastoral: Book VI of "The Faerie Queene"* (Oxford: Clarendon Press, 1972);

Robin Headlam Wells, *Spenser's "Faerie Queene" and the Cult of Elizabeth* (London & Canberra: Croom Helm / Totowa, N.J.: Barnes & Noble, 1983);

Kathleen Williams, *Spenser's "Faerie Queene": The World of Glass* (Berkeley: University of California Press, 1966);

Susanne Woods, "Spenser and the Problem of Women's Rule," *Huntington Library Quarterly*, 48 (Spring 1985): 141-158.

Papers:

More than a hundred autograph items by Spenser survive. Unfortunately, however, none are of his literary or political works. The majority are official letters and documents that he prepared as secretary to Lord Arthur Grey and later to Sir John Norris in Ireland, and the rest are addresses, endorsements, receipts, and legal documents relating to his landholdings and other matters. The only literary items are his transcriptions of two Latin poems by Lotichius and a Latin letter on poetry by Erhardus Stibarus. Most of his papers are among the State Papers Ireland in the Public Record Office, the Additional and Cotton Manuscripts in the British Library, and the Cecil Papers at Hatfield House. A complete listing may be found in Anthony G. Petti's article on Spenser's handwriting in *The Spenser Encyclopedia.*

Izaak Walton

(9 August 1593 ? - 15 December 1683)

Clayton D. Lein
Purdue University

BOOKS: *The Life and Death of Dr Donne, Late Deane of St Pauls London* in *LXXX Sermons Preached by that Learned and Reverend Divine, John Donne, D^r^ in Divinity, Late Deane of the Cathedrall Church of S. Pauls London* (London: Printed for Richard Royston . . . and Richard Marriot, 1640);

The Life of Sir Henry Wotton in *Reliquiae Wottonianae* (London: Printed by Thomas Maxey, for R. Marriot, 1651);

The Compleat Angler or the Contemplative Man's Recreation (London: Printed by T. Maxey for Rich. Marriot, 1653);

The Life of Mr. Rich. Hooker (London: Printed by J. G. for Rich. Marriot, 1665);

The Life of Mr. George Herbert (London: Printed by Tho. Newcomb, for Richard Marriot, 1670);

The Lives of Dr John Donne, Sir Henry Wotton, Mr Richard Hooker, Mr George Herbert (London: Printed by Tho. Newcomb for Richard Marriot, 1670);

The Life of Dr. Sanderson, Late Bishop of Lincoln (London: Printed for Richard Marriot, 1678).

Editions and Collections: *The Lives of Dr. John Donne, Sir Henry Wotton, Mr. Richard Hooker, Mr. George Herbert,* edited by Thomas Zouch (York: Printed by Wilson, Spence, and Mawman, 1796);

The Complete Angler, edited by Sir Harris Nicolas (London: William Pickering, 1836);

The Complete Angler, edited by George Washington Bethune (New York & London: Wiley & Putnam, 1847);

Waltoniana: Inedited Remains in Verse and Prose of Izaak Walton (London: Pickering & Co., 1878);

The Compleat Angler, 2 volumes, edited by R. B. Marston (London: Sampson Low, Marston, Searle & Rivington, 1888);

The Compleat Angler, edited by George A. B. Dewar (London: Freemantle & Company, 1902);

The Lives of Dr. John Donne, Sir Henry Wotton, Mr. Richard Hooker, Mr. George Herbert, edited by George Saintsbury (London: Oxford University Press, 1927);

The Compleat Walton, edited by Geoffrey Keynes (Bloomsbury: Nonesuch, 1929);

The Lives of Dr. John Donne, Sir Henry Wotton, Mr. Richard Hooker, Mr. George Herbert, edited by S. B. Carter (London: Falcon Educational Books, 1951);

The Compleat Angler, 1653-1676, edited by Jonquil Bevan (Oxford: Clarendon Press, 1983).

Few authors, as George Saintsbury has observed, have acquired fame through such differ-

Izaak Walton; portrait by Jacob Huysmans (National Portrait Gallery, London)

ent volumes as Izaak Walton's *The Compleat Angler* and his collected *Lives of Dr. John Donne, Sir Henry Wotton, Mr. Richard Hooker, Mr. George Herbert.* Walton, it must be added, did not anticipate a serious career as a man of letters. Any account of his life must accordingly trace both his evolution into a writer and the influences and experiences that led to such diverse masterpieces.

Walton's fascination with nature, which finds exuberant expression throughout *The Compleat Angler*, may perhaps be attributed at least in part to a childhood spent (like Shakespeare's) in the Midlands. Walton was christened on 21 September 1593 in Stafford, to which his father, Gervase Walton, an alehouse-keeper, had migrated shortly before. He lost his father at the age of three. In 1598 his mother, Anne, married an innkeeper who later became a burgess of the town. Walton presumably spent his childhood in Stafford, where he probably received his only formal education: instruction in Latin at the Edward VI Grammar School. That education was sufficient to enable Walton to read simple Latin prose, but Latin composition or versification of any complexity confused him throughout his adult life.

Walton's immediate future, however, lay in business. Izaak was apprenticed to Thomas Grinsell, a member of the Ironmongers' Company, who had married his sister around 1605. Grinsell pursued a career as a cloth merchant in the parish of St. Dunstan's-in-the-West. Walton himself became free of the Ironmongers' Company on 12 November 1618. He moved to London where, he, too, prospered in the cloth trade. Grinsell's retirement and the advent of civil war, during which the Parliamentary party gained control of his company, brought this phase of Walton's life to a close.

Walton's evolution into a man of letters doubtless had something to do with the decline of his business career, yet that evolution was protracted. Somehow Walton acquired a taste for poetry, in which he dabbled all his life; that interest was undoubtedly stirred and heightened by the presence of booksellers in St. Dunstan's. By 1613 Walton was sufficiently accomplished for a friend, S. P., to refer to his poetic abilities in prefatory verses to *The Love of Amos and Laura*, published by Grinsell's neighbor Richard Hawkins. Walton had thus demonstrated literary talent by the age of twenty. His earliest literary mentor may have been Michael Drayton, whom he termed his "honest old friend" in *The Compleat Angler*. Drayton lived near Stafford during Walton's childhood, and he later resided not far from Walton in London. Walton may have sought out Drayton to advance such literary interests, as he did Ben Jonson.

Walton became known, in turn, to John Donne, Henry King, and Sir Henry Wotton. Donne, then dean of St. Paul's Cathedral, became Walton's pastor at St. Dunstan's in 1624. Walton claimed to be his "Convert"; consequently, Donne must have played some critical role in his development, and evidence increasingly suggests that Walton was probably more in Donne's acquaintance than certain critics allow. Since Wotton and King were Donne's intimates, Donne may have provided introductions. Both men regarded Walton as Donne's friend, and King, in a famous letter, placed Walton at Donne's deathbed.

After Donne and his circle, the crucial associations in Walton's early life derive from his marriage to Rachel Floud in 1626. Rachel's mother was a descendant of the family of Thomas Cranmer, archbishop of Canterbury. Her brother, William Cranmer, was a prominent member of the Merchant Adventurers' Company. Since Cranmer was also in the cloth trade, Walton's association with William and his family probably began as a trade connection. Walton was fond of Rachel's family and remained in contact with her relatives until his death. William and his sisters had received part of their education from the theologian Richard Hooker, with whom their brother George had been intimate. Through them Walton gleaned invaluable details about Hooker's person, career, and family.

Walton's public career is bound to Donne and his circle of friends. Neither *The Compleat Angler* nor the *Lives* are conceivable apart from that group, and Walton's first publication was an elegy on the death of Donne, which appeared in the 1633 first edition of Donne's poems. Some argue that Walton may have been involved with this edition; a stronger case has been made for his involvement with the 1635 edition of Donne's poems, for which he revised his elegy, wrote a new poem on Donne's portrait, and edited a series of Donne's letters. Even at the height of his business career, then, Walton engaged in literary pursuits, notably projects concerning Donne. These led to Walton's association with the publisher John Marriot, whose son Richard became Walton's lifelong friend, patron, and publisher.

Walton became better friends in the 1630s, too, with Sir Henry Wotton, the provost of Eton. During the middle of that decade, Wotton shared with Walton his intention to provide a biography of Donne for an edition of Donne's sermons from Marriot's press. Walton had previously delved into Donne's life; he now undertook additional biographical research on Wotton's behalf. Walton's visits to Eton—one of which he preserved in *The Compleat Angler*—may have had as much to do with biography as with angling. Wotton, in fact, probably became Walton's mentor in both, and at Eton, Walton may have found historical sources to which he later refers and which do not appear to have formed part of his personal library.

The genial atmosphere of the 1630s ended with Wotton's death in December 1639. Marriot was impatient, and when he discovered that Wotton had failed to produce a narrative, Marriot rushed ahead with the edition. The publisher's impatience was fueled in part by the intervention of John Donne, Jr., who busied himself without principle to gain control of his father's work, displacing the chief sponsor, Henry King, who vented his frustration years later in a letter to Walton. Donne's son acted unconscionably, but he managed to persuade a reluctant Walton to perform the task left unfinished by Wotton. Walton reviewed the notes he had made for Wotton and completed the original version of his biography on 15 February 1640.

Walton was thus shoved into the literary limelight against his wishes, but to great acclaim. His effort was riddled with flaws, all of which have been exhaustively analyzed. Yet Walton's narrative was based on personal accounts by those well acquainted with the dean, and he had at his disposal records long since lost. This material allowed him to convey the fundamental sequences of Donne's life, and he recovered priceless details. Furthermore, Walton recognized the outstanding problems in his own work and attempted to rectify them in various revisions. Donne's mature character is memorably captured in Walton's account, one of the best biographies of its time and one justly admired by Walton's contemporaries, among them Thomas Fuller, John Hales, and King Charles I.

Walton happened upon literary success, then, just as his civic career was waning. He continued, however, to advance in his parish. In February 1640 he was elected to the vestry, but the outbreak of civil war shattered Walton's parish community. The same period witnessed the breakup of Walton's family. He lost his wife in 1640; in 1641 William Cranmer transported his family abroad; and in 1642 Walton lost his seventh and final child by Rachel. Events may have forced Walton to flee temporarily at the end of 1643, but he was back at St. Dunstan's in early 1644.

From 1644 until 1647 Walton's movements are obscure, but he had not (as is often reported) retired to Staffordshire. If he bore arms, nothing is known of it, but he is associated with many Royalists, and he refers obliquely to losses. He may have been absent from London for most of 1644, but he was regularly in the vicinity of London thereafter, performing services for kinsmen, friends, and fellow Royalists.

Some of Walton's travel in this period must have been concerned with investigations into the life and work of Wotton, and it seems likely that Walton was at Oxford, as well as at Eton, in the early years of the decade. His friend George Morley became a canon of Christ Church College, Oxford, in 1642. Walton had known Morley since 1630 and also claimed another Christ Church figure, William Cartwright, as a "Dear Friend." Walton was demonstrably influenced by their mode of thought (a mode shared by John Hales, another member of that circle), and he was no doubt often found in Morley's company, for by 1647 he "knew Dr. *Morley* well."

In 1647 Walton remarried at St. James, Clerkenwell. His wife, Anne Ken, was a lawyer's daughter; her brother Thomas (who may have received some education in Walton's household) later became bishop of Bath and Wells. Walton's children by Anne were all baptized at Clerkenwell, which became his chief residence. Two, Izaak and Anne, survived their parents. Around 1653 Walton retired to Staffordshire, migrating periodically between there and London during the remainder of the interregnum.

The years between his marriage and his retirement were of extraordinary importance for Walton's literary career, and he grew closer to a wide range of figures within Royalist literary and religious circles. King spoke warmly of "the constant experience of [Walton's] Love, even in the worst of the late sad times." There seems little doubt that Walton was highly regarded, and this partially accounts for his celebrated exploit in 1651, when he transported part of the Garter Regalia—lost by King Charles I at Worcester—from Staffordshire to the Tower of London. It is unlikely Walton would have been entrusted with the task had he not been well known to Royalists about London.

Walton's publications of the 1650s hark back to the early years of his second marriage. These include three major works: *The Life of Sir Henry Wotton* (1651), *The Compleat Angler* (1653), and a major revision of the *Life of Donne* (1658). These works are so tightly interrelated that it is impossible to unravel their precise genesis. Walton may have determined to revise the *Life of Donne* shortly after its initial publication in 1640; he clearly collected material for such a revision throughout the 1640s, obtaining information from Arthur Woodnoth prior to 1645 and from Bishop Thomas Morton prior to 1648. Marriot, meanwhile, engaged Walton to edit the works of Sir Henry Wotton. New evidence suggests that Walton may have begun that project as early as 1640, and the chief materials for that edition had been collected by 1648, so Walton must have largely completed his research by that point. *The Compleat Angler* was clearly an outgrowth of the work on Wotton, who, Walton says, had proposed such a project for himself. Walton's work on Wotton assures us that he was regularly at Eton, to consult Wotton's manuscripts and to confer with Wotton's colleagues. Certain references in *The Compleat Angler* that later became problematic for Walton have led to speculation that Walton may have used Hales's library at Eton, a library lost to Walton after 1649, when Hales was expelled from his fellowship.

Walton, therefore, was engaged throughout the 1640s in three projects involving Wotton in one way or another, and it seems likely that he worked on all three simultaneously. Interrelationships continue in the final productions. *The Life of Wotton*, the most secular and urbane of Walton's biographies (although it makes much of Wotton's becoming a deacon), is composed in the fashion of Plutarch's parallel lives, with strong echoes in the *Life of Donne*, a relationship strengthened in successive revisions. *The Compleat Angler* acts as a biographical supplement to *The Life of Wot-*

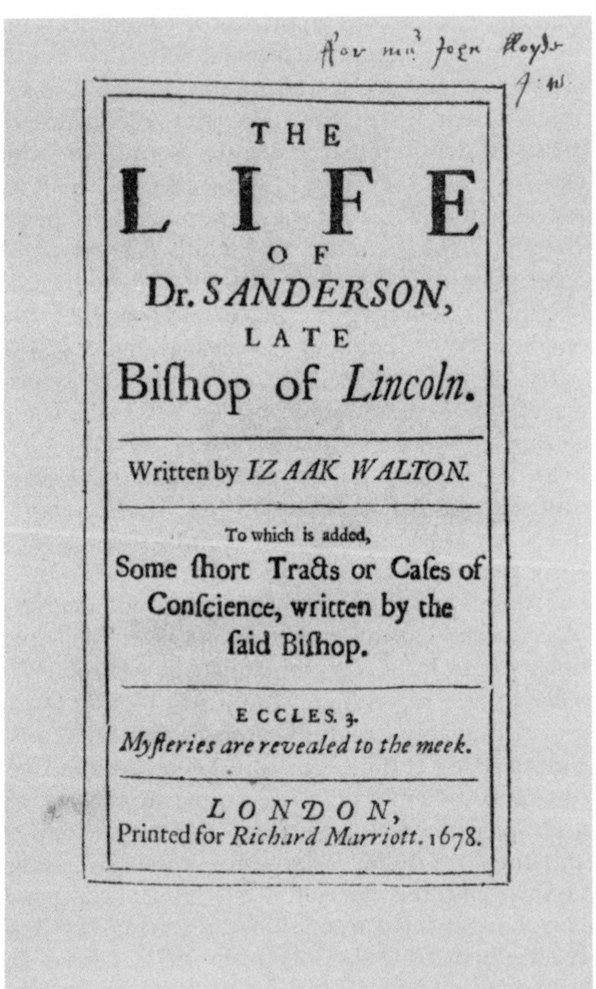

THE

LIFE

OF

Dr. *SANDERSON*,

LATE

Biſhop of *Lincoln*.

Written by *IZAAK WALTON*.

To which is added,

Some ſhort Tracts or Caſes of Conſcience, written by the ſaid Biſhop.

ECCLES. 3.

Myſteries are revealed to the meek.

LONDON,

Printed for *Richard Marriott*. 1678.

Title page for Walton's last, and most methodically researched, biographical work

ton. Sir Henry appears in it in less formal, more convivial terms than in the official biography. The three works also serve as Royalist tracts. *The Life of Wotton* is the portrait of a resourceful royal servant; *The Compleat Angler* is a subtle work directed to the sequestered Anglican clergy, several of whom (among them Gilbert Sheldon) are mentioned indirectly in the 1655 edition; and the revised *Life of Donne* is a powerful portrait of a restless spirit bent to its proper spiritual calling by kingly influence, and also serves as an affirmation of the old Anglican order. Walton's political leanings were thus much in evidence in these as well as other writings throughout the period.

Morley's return from exile in 1660 drew Walton's life into new spheres of activity. The author had returned to London by May 1660, at which time he wrote an eclogue on the return of King Charles II. Shortly thereafter Morley was made dean of Christ Church College, and by autumn 1660 Walton was acting as Morley's agent there. Walton remained in Morley's service until the final years of his life. When Morley became bishop of Worcester in 1660, Walton became his steward, moving his family to Worcester, where records exist of his activities. Anne Walton died in April 1662 and was buried in Worcester Cathedral.

In 1662 Morley became bishop of Winchester. Walton lived thereafter in the bishop's establishments until very near the end of his life. His personal ties to Morley and Sheldon led to new friendships with the Restoration bishops, among them Humphrey Henchman, Seth Ward, and Thomas Barlow, and he was well known to other leaders in the Anglican establishment.

Work for Morley did not inhibit literary activity. A third edition of *The Compleat Angler* came forth in 1661, the first version to include the Laws of Angling. The following year Sheldon proposed that he undertake a biography of Richard Hooker. The Restoration bishops were eager to appropriate Hooker as their champion. That task had first fallen to John Gauden, bishop of Exeter, who published the first full edition of Hooker's *Laws of Ecclesiastical Polity* in 1662, along with an account of his life. Walton was offended by the biography, which was grossly inaccurate. Sheldon and his associates were offended by the edition, for Gauden published sections of the *Polity* revealing that Hooker was at odds with their positions. Sheldon, eager to correct both embarrassments, commissioned Walton to address them. For his labors Walton received a lease to lucrative property in Paternoster Row.

Walton's *Life of Mr. Rich. Hooker* is incomparably superior to Gauden's, and it stood forth as his best-researched biography up to that time. It is Walton's first life-and-times biography, and his talent for historical writing is displayed to advantage. Walton's relation to the Cranmer family also permitted him to produce a better picture of Hooker as a person. Had Walton not been persuaded to compose this life, it is unlikely that many of his details would have survived to our time. He also provided a more informed account of Hooker's academic and ecclesiastical career than that supplied by Gauden; in this, undoubtedly under the sponsorship of Sheldon and Morley, he was much aided by Oxford antiquaries. Yet, if Walton could rely upon privileged information, he was too prone to trust gossip, and he seriously maligned the family of Hooker's wife. His account of the genesis of Hooker's *Polity* is also incorrect, although his remarks denying the authenticity of the final books were unquestionably to the liking of Sheldon and his friends. Walton was doubtless guided by their opinions and did not possess the requisite skills to challenge their authority. In this, as in other biographies, Walton's approach committed him to serious errors.

The Life of Hooker appeared in 1665, about which time Walton's daughter married Dr. William Hawkins, a prebendary of Winchester Cathedral. Thomas Ken lived near him as a fellow at Winchester College. Walton's friendships with figures in Hampshire and, in particular, about Winchester, by and large date from this time.

The period from 1665 to 1670 was marked by disaster for Walton and his friends. Marriot lost badly in the Great Fire of London (1666) and was ultimately compelled to relocate his business. Edward Hyde, first Earl of Clarendon's fall from power in 1667 also brought Morley and Sheldon into disgrace, pushing Walton and Morley into retreat. They resided at Farnham Castle in Surrey, where Walton became better acquainted with figures in that region, particularly Samuel Woodforde, who later supplied prefatory verses for two of his *Lives*.

The startling result of this retirement was Walton's *Life of Mr. George Herbert* and the *Lives*—a collected edition of Walton's first four biographies—both of which appeared in 1670. Walton's books are all works of attenuated genesis, and *The Life of Herbert* is no exception. Walton's professional interest in Herbert dated back to the 1640s, and Walton's works throughout the 1650s demonstrate that interest. He had seen Herbert at least once, at the funeral of the poet's mother, Magdalen Herbert, where he had heard Donne preach. He knew, therefore, of Donne's association with Herbert and his mother, and he most likely began to gather information about the Herberts in anticipation of his revision of Donne's biography.

Consequently, Walton may have begun planning *The Life of Herbert* in 1658, being forced to abandon the project by the advent of the Restoration and by his commissioned work on *The Life of Hooker*. We can be grateful for the delay, for the *Lives* all benefited from the machinery devised to assist Walton with that project. Through the Restoration bishops, Walton enjoyed, in effect, a living biographical college, and he relied on them heavily for his final biographies. Walton also had access to clerics such as Robert Creighton, Edmund Duncon, and James Duport, all of whom presumably supplied him with information. The bench of bishops may also have supported Walton in archival research, for the *Lives* of 1670 bears evidence of fresh research in the records of both Oxford and Cambridge. Now nearing eighty, Walton also found his artistic powers at their peak. *The Life of Herbert* is the most subtly crafted of his biographies, an elegantly patterned hagiographic narrative celebrating the beauty of holiness in an Anglican saint, hence an implicit defense of the party in disfavor. It likewise served as propaganda for the Sheldonian project of encouraging sons of the nobility to enter orders. And the *Lives* boasted a dedication to Bishop Morley, generously attributing the excellencies of the biographies to Morley's benevolent influence over a forty-year period.

Publication of the *Lives* secured Walton's place as England's premier biographer. He does not seem to have contemplated a new project for some time, spending his time instead with friends, notably Charles Cotton, whose celebrated fishing house at the edge of the Dove, built by Cotton to commemorate their friendship, bears an arch piece containing their interwoven initials and the date 1674. Walton also regularly visited Oxford in this period. His son Izaak was launched on his career there, receiving his B.A. from Christ Church College in 1672. Izaak's attendance at Oxford brought Walton into increasing contact with figures there, chief among them Anthony à Wood and William Fulman, both of whom became good acquaintances.

Even in this period Walton could not dampen the desire to write. In 1672 he brought out a further edition of Wotton's works with an improved biographical narrative. In 1673 he undertook research for Fulman for a life of John Hales. Walton subsequently made alterations in *The Life of Herbert* for its inclusion with an edition of Herbert's *The Temple* in 1674. Then in 1675 the biographer brought out a revised edition of the collected *Lives*, one boasting new celebratory verses by James Duport and Charles Cotton. The following year saw the publication of the final version of *The Compleat Angler*, accompanied by the famous sequel by Cotton, who, with Duport, also supplied new verses for Walton's portion.

Walton was cleaning house, bringing his literary career to an elegant close. He consequently strove to put his works into the best shape possible. For this final edition of the *Lives*, he reviewed all his notes, incorporating material he had previously left dormant, including the notorious description of Donne's vision of his wife with a stillborn child. Other additions in the 1675 *Lives* demonstrate that Walton had undertaken further research, aiming to perfect these biographies in every respect. Walton may have simultaneously worked on the final versions of *The Compleat Angler* and the *Lives*, which may account for their striking coherence of style and perspective. He viewed his writing canonically and made subtle adjustments in phrasing that brought his works closer together.

Walton's labors in revision apparently reawakened his creative energies, for he must have begun work on *The Life of Dr. Sanderson, Late Bishop of Lincoln* by 1676. He had written lives of a worldly deacon (Wotton), a saintly poet-priest in a country cure (Herbert), a metropolitan preacher (Donne), and a renowned theologian (Hooker); it remained to write the life of a bishop. Robert Sanderson was a natural choice: Walton had known him personally, and he was the dearly admired friend of Sheldon and Morley, both of whom offered Walton personal testimony and doubtless provided him with introductions to aid in documentary research. The result, published in 1678, is in many ways Walton's most professional biography. Walton received assistance from Bishop William Barlow as well as from Dr. Thomas Pierce, theologians he had known for some time. They led him astray, however, and Walton's account of Sanderson's works is flawed. *The Life of Sanderson* is nonetheless one of the great achievements of seventeenth-century biography. Anthony à Wood relied upon it himself.

It is not clear when Walton left Morley's service, but it does not seem to have been prior to 1674. After the appearance of *The Life of Sanderson*, however, he spent more time in Hampshire. Despite his great age, however, Walton's literary activities continued unabated; he clearly could not tolerate idleness. He dated a tract he composed against nonconformity 12 September 1679 and published it the following year as *Love and Truth* with another letter dated 18 February 1668. The tract appeared anonymously, but scholars have established that Walton was indeed the author; and the publisher, Henry Brome, had produced work for Cotton and Morley. Walton adopted the pose of a "Quiet and Comformable Citizen of London," addressing it to "Factious Shopkeepers" in Coventry, a notorious haven for nonconformists.

That same year he sent a celebrated letter to John Aubrey, sharing Morley's reminiscences about Ben Jonson and disclosing the otherwise unknown fact that he, too, had known the great poet. And during the last year of his life, Walton published *Thealma and Clearchus*, a "pastoral history" for which he supplied a preface. Once attributed to Walton himself, the work is in fact by John Chalkhill, a kinsman of his second wife, who had also contributed verses to *The Compleat Angler*. The preface is dated 7 May 1678, indicating that Walton prepared the edition for press while putting the final touches on *The Life of Sanderson*. It is not known what delayed the publication, perhaps something to do with Marriot's retirement.

Walton likewise continued to pursue biographical interests. When the *Life of Sanderson* was republished in 1681, it contained some revisions. New evidence indicates that during his final years Walton had commenced work on a biography of Archbishop Sheldon. However, he did not live to bring the project to conclusion.

Walton's publications assure us that even toward the close of his life he was regularly in London, and he was often with Morley, for two of Walton's surviving letters are dated from Farnham Castle in 1678 and 1683. But he spent more and more time during these years with his daughter and her husband at Winchester and at Hawkins's country cure in Droxford. Men and women from these communities are noticed in his will. The tradition that Walton was living with his daughter at the end of his life is likely true, for cathedral records contain notices of Hawkins's enlargement of his premises in 1682; and in his will, which Walton began on 9 August 1683, then in his "neintyeth yeare of age," he describes himself as "of Winchester." He died four months later and was buried in Prior Silkstede's Chapel in Winchester Cathedral. Walton doubtless chose the location with Morley's approval. Prior Silkstede had been a great lay benefactor of the cathedral, and Walton wished to be remembered in similar terms: the final decades of his life had been devoted to the church he held dear.

Two portraits of Walton, both done in the closing years of his life, survive, and they complement each other well. The larger of the two, by Jacob Huysmans, now in the National Portrait Gallery, is a portrait in oils showing Walton with gloves and sword; it presents the merchant and country gentleman known to dignitaries. The second portrait, a head and shoulders in colored chalk by Edmund Ashfield, displays Walton in plain old-fashioned clothing and with penetrating eyes, the man cherished as a companion.

Of Walton's major works, *The Compleat Angler*, a guide to freshwater fishing in dialogue form, has proved to be the one of broadest and most enduring fame. Walton apparently began to fish seriously about 1630, and he was inspired to compose his masterpiece in part because he found no useful, comprehensive guides to the art of angling in English. Walton was himself a master of older methods of angling, to such an extent that his method and information were derided by some, such as Richard Franck, even in his own time, and by many others since. However, Walton's scientific interests and his flair for writing about nature have been deftly defended; and some fishermen, most notably the expert angler R. B. Marston, have borne personal witness to the enduring value of Walton's details.

The Compleat Angler, however, is anything but the customary manual. It is instead an exceedingly artful book, a fine example of seventeenth-century *genera mixta*, fusing the practical treatise with literary and contemplative material drawn from the various traditions of the georgic, the pastoral, pastoral drama, spiritual autobiography, the philosophic dialogue, and tracts for the times. It is indeed a volume for the contemplative man (as the title page professes), and one packed with a surprising range of observations. It is also a work of recreation, of "innocent Mirth" for those able to afford it ("if they be not needy"), offering a tidy anthology of poems and songs, including a composition by Henry Lawes to be sung around a table.

Walton's brotherhood of anglers, furthermore, behaves like a spiritual community, one manifesting patterns of conversion and communion, and one devoted to the practice of charity, much like the communities of primitive Christians to which Walton makes repeated allusions. In his successive revisions Walton principally expanded the practical and technical dimensions of the work, a development frequently deplored but one thereby fulfilling the promise of the title. And his attention to all of his revisions reveals that Walton continued to strengthen the meditative and literary aspects of the work as well. The resulting compound is utterly idiosyncratic.

The Compleat Angler is a work of decidedly personal character. Walton's larger importance to English literature lies in his evolution into the

Title page for Walton's most enduring work, a guide to freshwater fishing that also includes poems, songs, and philosophical writing

first professional biographer of undeniable stature in English letters. The course of his development can be charted quickly. Walton's initial biography filled a mere seventeen folio pages in a large volume of sermons. Walton's final biography was a freestanding work of nearly three hundred pages, with a few tracts appended by way of supplement. That development reflects the changing attitude toward biography itself, for the greater dignity accorded the freestanding work reflects the mounting importance accorded biography as a literary form during the seventeenth century. The publication of the collected *Lives* in 1670 was a sign of Walton's mature stature, and the publication and republication of that volume did much to advance claims for the artistry of biography.

Walton alludes to Plutarch's *Life of Pompey* in his first biography, a reference suggesting that some study of the Greek biographer (perhaps under Wotton's tutelage) may have preceded Walton's work as a biographer. That influence may also account for Walton's conservative theory of biography. Life writing, he maintained, was chiefly commemorative—"an honour due to the dead, and a generous debt due to those that shall live, and succeed us." Such a view did not lead him at first to cultivate dates and historical records, and Walton's fledgling effort displays surprisingly little documentation. The discipline of rendering life histories, however, and the abundance of materials made available to him by his unique connections gradually led Walton to pioneering efforts in the use of the materials of modern biography—primary sources, public records, and abundant dates established by public and private documents.

Walton introduced all of these into biographical narrative, and his final efforts reveal extensive use of ecclesiastical, university, and private archives. More noteworthy is Walton's elaborate use of his subjects' personal records—their correspondence, accounts books, autobiographical statements in prefaces to their works, and (more problematic) their poetry. Walton has been accused of misusing his subjects' subjective works to establish life records, and such may occasionally be the case. Nevertheless, his responsiveness to such material led to a greater sensitivity to the inner conflicts and dilemmas of his subjects and enabled him to render their personalities dramatically. Whatever his errors, he was ahead of his time in recognizing the significance of such material for biography.

If he was a pioneer in modern methods, however, Walton falls short of modern scruples. Like virtually all of his contemporaries, he penned his biographies in relation to a preconceived thesis, deeply influenced by his personal knowledge of his biographical subjects. The impressive unity of tone and effect in his biographies is one consequence of that approach. To advance his governing paradigm, however, Walton was not above tampering with the evidence—suppressing some dates, inventing others, conflating documents, and altering texts. Nor did he subject his evidence to the severe tests demanded by contemporary scholarship.

Walton, by nature, trusted those in authority, particularly clerics, many of whom were his informants. He rarely tested their anecdotes against documentary evidence, and when he became aware of discrepancies, he tended to trust the anecdote, particularly if it corroborated the conception to which he was committed. Walton also lacked the educational resources for exhaustive research, which would have led him to complicating material and could have provided him with a more skeptical temperament. Yet, for all these flaws, Walton manages to capture fundamental features of his biographical subjects: if he is not wholly right about them, he is quite right about certain aspects of their lives.

Walton is redeemed from his transgressions by his artistry. He often deprecated his talent, yet he is an eminent (if labored) stylist in biography, the worthy predecessor of Samuel Johnson, who much enjoyed his contributions. Walton is a master of structure, which he controls obsessively, as well as of the individual touch, ever alert to the implications of the facts he reports, coordinating and shaping them accordingly. Walton also displays an enviable ability to compose brisk historical summaries, an ability particularly evident in the lives of Wotton, Hooker, and Sanderson. Like Boswell, Walton has an insatiable appetite for telling anecdotes, which reveals a benign delight in human failures and inconsistencies. His zeal in sharing such material rescues the biographies from his constricting structural paradigms and raises them far above the commemorative biographies written by his contemporaries.

Walton is, in sum, a most curious writer. He professes to be "artlesse," claims to be a mere medium, wielding only a pen "guided by the hand of Truth." In reality he is an exceedingly calculating writer who perfected his various narratives through elaborate, painstaking revisions. He wrote no works of pure literature, apart from a few poems in *The Compleat Angler*, but succeeded, through craft and imaginative reach, in raising works of utilitarian concern and of historical cast to the realm of literature.

His collective achievements gained the approval of an impressive list of his more learned contemporaries. He viewed his evolution into an artist with wonder and constantly gave credit to others for his achievements. He was widely admired as much for his person as for his works, leaving behind irreplaceable accounts of leading personalities of his age and, in William Hazlitt's judgment, the finest pastoral in the English language. Walton would unquestionably be confounded by his subsequent reputation.

Bibliographies:

Peter Oliver, *A New Chronicle of The Compleat Angler* (New York: Paisley, 1936);

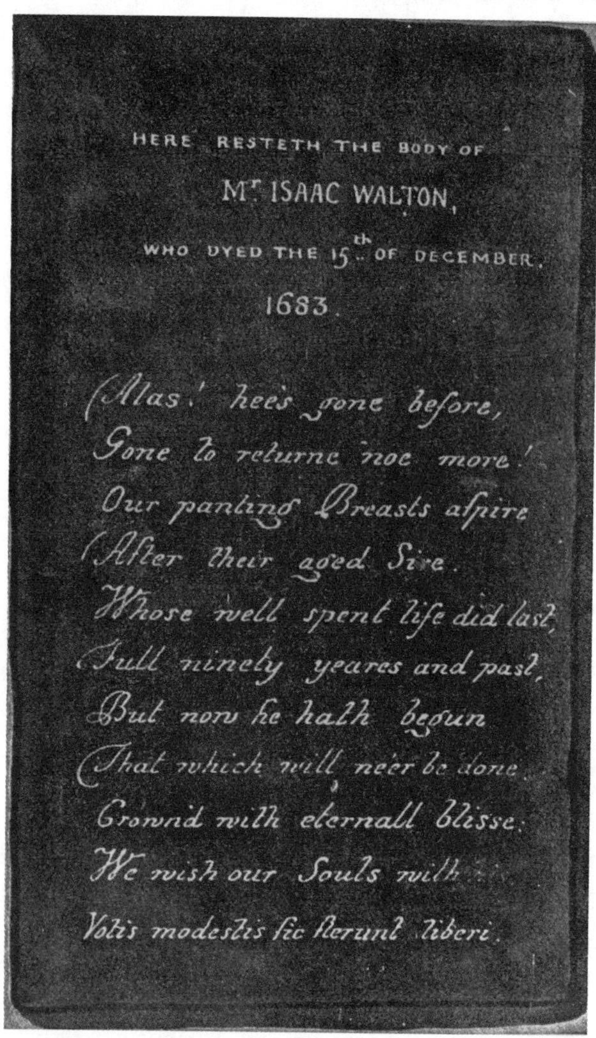

Walton's grave in Winchester Cathedral

Bernard S. Horne, *The Compleat Angler, 1653-1967: A New Bibliography* (Pittsburgh: University of Pittsburgh Press, 1970).

References:

Judith H. Anderson, *Biographical Truth: The Representation of Historical Persons in Tudor-Stuart Writing* (New Haven: Yale University Press, 1984);

Jonquil Bevan, "Henry Valentine, John Donne, and Izaak Walton," *Review of English Studies*, 40 (1989): 179-201;

Bevan, "Izaak Walton and his Publisher," *Library*, 32 (1977): 344-359;

Bevan, "Izaak Walton's Collections for Fulman's Life of John Hales: The Walker Part," *Bodleian Library Record*, 13 (1989): 160-171;

Bevan, *Izaak Walton's The Compleat Angler: The Art of Recreation* (New York: St. Martin's Press, 1988);

Bevan, "Some Books from Izaak Walton's Library," *Library*, 2 (1980): 259-263;

Bevan and I. A. Shapiro, "Donne and the Walton Forgeries: A Correspondence," *Library*, 4 (1982): 329-339;

Tucker Brooke, "The Lambert Walton-Cotton Collection," *Yale University Library Gazette*, 17 (1942-1943): 61-65;

John Butt, *Biography in the Hands of Walton, Johnson, and Boswell* (Los Angeles: University of California Press, 1966);

Butt, "Izaak Walton as Biographer," in *Pope, Dickens and Others* (Edinburgh: Edinburgh University Press, 1969);

Butt, "Izaak Walton's Collections for Fulman's Life of John Hales," *Modern Language Review*, 29 (1934): 267-273;

Butt, "Izaak Walton's Methods in Biography," *Essays and Studies*, 19 (1933): 67-84;

Arthur M. Coon, "The Family of Izaak Walton," *Times Literary Supplement*, 15 May 1937, p. 380;

Coon, "Izaak Walton and Edmund Carew," *Notes and Queries*, 178 (1940): 298;

Coon, "Izaak Walton, *Prochein Amy*," *Modern Language Notes*, 54 (1939): 589-592;

Coon, "Izaak Walton's Birthday," *Notes and Queries*, 176 (1939): 424;

Coon, "Izaak Walton's Mother," *Times Literary Supplement*, 19 December 1939, p. 980;

Coon, "Izaak Walton's Occupation and Residence," *Notes and Queries*, 176 (1939): 110-112;

Coon, "Izaak Walton's Second Marriage," *Notes and Queries*, 176 (1939): 299;

Coon, "The Life of Izaak Walton," Ph.D. dissertation, Cornell University, 1938;

John R. Cooper, *The Art of The Compleat Angler* (Durham, N.C.: Duke University Press, 1968);

Francisque Costa, "The Ashmolean Museum and *The Angler*," *Caliban*, 5 (1968): 31-34;

P. J. Croft, "Izaak Walton's John Chalkhill," *Times Literary Supplement*, 27 June 1958, p. 365;

Richard B. Croft, *Izaak Walton and the River Lee* (Ware, U.K.: Privately printed, 1907);

William H. Epstein, *Recognizing Biography* (Philadelphia: University of Pennsylvania Press, 1987);

Richard E. Fehner, "Izaak Walton's *Life of Sir Henry Wotton*, 1651, 1654, 1670, 1672, 1675: A Study of Sources, Revisions, and Chronology," Ph.D. dissertation, University of Minnesota, 1961;

Helen Gardner, "Dean Donne's Monument in St. Paul's," in *Evidence in Literary Scholarship: Essays in Memory of James Marshall Osborn*, edited by René Wellek and Alvaro Ribeiro (Oxford: Oxford University Press, 1979);

Marcus Selden Goldman, "Izaak Walton and *The Arte of Angling*, 1577," in *Studies in Honor of T. W. Baldwin*, edited by Don Cameron Allen (Urbana: University of Illinois Press, 1958), pp. 185-204;

Irvine Gray, "An Unknown Record of Izaak Walton," *Country Life*, 30 August 1973, pp. 546-547;

B. D. Greenslade, "*The Compleat Angler* and the Sequestered Clergy," *Review of English Studies*, 5 (1954): 361-366;

Jim Hayes, "Izaak Walton's Secret Stream," *Outdoor Life*, 127 (1961): 42-43, 96-98;

F. G. P. Kellendonk, "Izaak Walton and Sir Henry Wotton's Panegyrick of King Charles," *Neophilologus*, 61 (1977): 316-320;

Lionel Lambert, *Izaak Walton and the Royal Deanery of Stafford* (Stafford, U.K.: J. & C. Mort, 1926);

Clayton D. Lein, "Art and Structure in Walton's *Life of Mr. George Herbert*," *University of Toronto Quarterly*, 46 (1976-1977): 162-176;

Lein, *Izaak Walton: Angler and Biographer* (forthcoming);

Anna K. Nardo, " 'A recreation of a recreation': Reading *The Compleat Angler*," *South Atlantic Quarterly*, 79 (1980): 302-311;

David Novarr, "Izaak Walton, Bishop Morley, and *Love and Truth*," *Review of English Studies*, 2 (1951): 30-39;

Novarr, *The Making of Walton's Lives* (Ithaca, N.Y.: Cornell University Press, 1958);

H. J. Oliver, "The Composition and Revisions of 'The Compleat Angler,' " *Modern Language Review*, 42 (1947): 295-313;

Oliver, "Izaak Walton as Author of *Love and Truth* and *Thealma and Clearchus*," *Review of English Studies*, 25 (1949): 24-37;

Oliver, "Izaak Walton's Prose Style," *Review of English Studies*, 21 (1945): 280-288;

Clement Price, "Izaak Walton," *Times Literary Supplement*, 14 August 1919, p. 437;

Michael P. Rewa, *Reborn as Meaning: Panegyrical Biography from Isocrates to Walton* (Washington, D.C.: University Press of America, 1983);

Herbert Rothschild, Jr., "The 'Higher Hand' in Walton's 'Life of John Donne,' " *Notes and Queries*, 25 (1978): 506-508;

I. A. Shapiro, "Donne and Walton Forgeries," *Library*, 3 (1981): 232;

C. J. Sisson, *The Judicious Marriage of Mr. Hooker and the Birth of The Laws of Ecclesiastical Polity* (Cambridge: Cambridge University Press, 1940; reprinted, New York: Octagon, 1974);

Donald A. Stauffer, *English Biography Before 1700* (Cambridge, Mass.: Harvard University Press, 1930);

John Vaughan, "Izaak Walton at Droxford," in *The Wild-Flowers of Selborne and Other Papers* (London: John Lane, 1906), pp. 157-171;

Vaughan, "The Plant-Lore of 'The Compleat Angler,' " *Scribner's Magazine*, 70 (1921): 720-728;

Vaughan, "Where Izaak Walton Died," *Cornhill Magazine*, 47 (1919): 595-607;

Richard Wendorf, *The Elements of Life* (Oxford: Clarendon Press, 1990).

Papers:

Few documents have survived in Walton's hand, and those few are found in widely scattered locations, including the British Library and the Public Record Office in London, the Bodleian Library and Corpus Christi College Library in Oxford, and Harvard University Library.

John Webster

(1579 or 1580 - 1634?)

This entry was written by Antony Hammond (McMaster University) for DLB 58: Jacobean and Caroline Dramatists.

BOOKS: *The Famous History of Sir T. Wyat*, by Webster, Thomas Dekker, Henry Chettle, Thomas Heywood, and Wentworth Smith (London: Printed by E. Allde for Thomas Archer, 1607);

West-ward Hoe, by Webster and Dekker (London: Printed by W. Jaggard, sold by John Hodges, 1607);

North-ward Hoe, by Webster and Dekker (London: Printed by G. Eld, 1607);

The White Divel (London: Printed by N. Okes for Thomas Archer, 1612);

A Monumental Columne, Erected to the Memory of Henry, Late Prince of Wales (London: Printed by N. Okes for William Welby, 1613);

The Tragedy of the Dutchesse of Malfy (London: Printed by Nicholas Okes for John Waterson, 1623);

The Devils Law-Case (London: Printed by A. Mathewes for John Grismand, 1623);

Monuments of Honor. Derived from Remarkable Antiquity, and Celebrated in London. At the Confirmation of John Gore (London: Printed by Nicholas Okes, 1624);

The Fair Maid of the Inn, by John Fletcher, Philip Massinger, and perhaps Webster and John Ford, in *Comedies and Tragedies Written by Francis Beaumont and John Fletcher, Gentlemen* (London: Printed for Humphrey Robinson & Humphrey Moseley, 1647);

Appius and Virginia, by Webster and Heywood (London: Printed for Richard Marriot, 1654);

A Cure for a Cuckold, by Webster and William Rowley (London: Printed by Thomas Johnson, sold by Francis Kirkman, 1661);

Anything for a Quiet Life, by Thomas Middleton, perhaps with Webster (London: Printed by Thomas Johnson for Francis Kirkman & H. Marsh, 1662).

Editions: *The Complete Works of John Webster*, 4 volumes, edited by F. L. Lucas (London: Chatto & Windus, 1927)—comprises *The White Devil, The Duchess of Malfi, The Devil's Law-Case, Cure for a Cuckold, Appius and Virginia, Shorter Poems, A Monumental Column*, Induction to *The Malcontent, Monuments of Honour, Characters, Anything for a Quiet Life*, and *The Fair Maid of the Inn*;

The Famous History of Sir Thomas Wyat, in *The Dramatic Works of Thomas Dekker*, edited by Fredson Bowers, volume 1 (Cambridge: Cambridge University Press, 1953);

Westward Ho and *Northward Ho*, in *The Dramatic Works of Thomas Dekker*, edited by Bowers, vol-

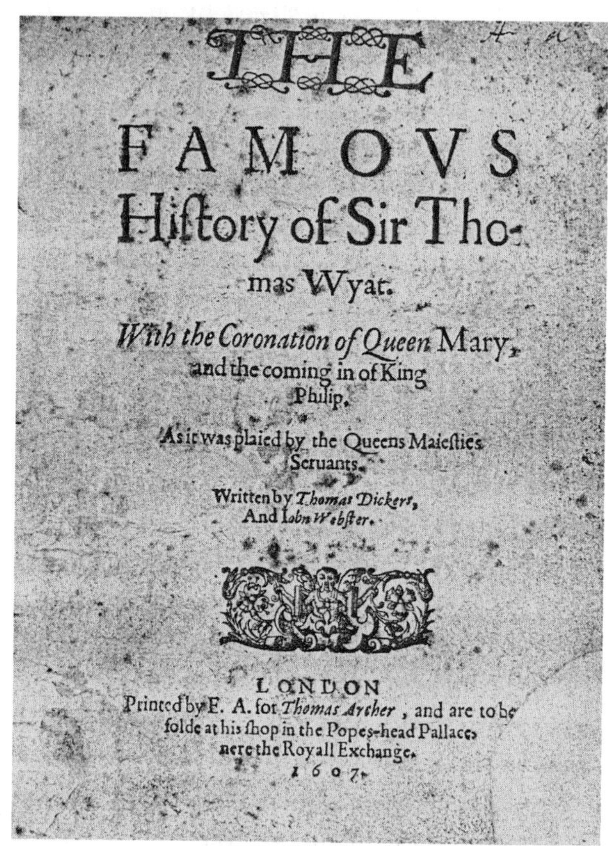
THE FAMOVS History of Sir Thomas Wyat.

With the Coronation of Queen Mary, and the coming in of King Philip.

As it was plaied by the Queens Maiesties Seruants.

Written by Thomas Dickers, And Iohn Webster.

LONDON Printed by E. A. for Thomas Archer, and are to be solde at his shop in the Popes-head Pallace, nere the Royall Exchange. 1607.

Title page for the 1607 quarto edition of the play that is probably an abridgment of the two-part play Lady Jane, *on which Webster collaborated with Thomas Dekker, Henry Chettle, Thomas Heywood, and Wentworth Smith (British Library)*

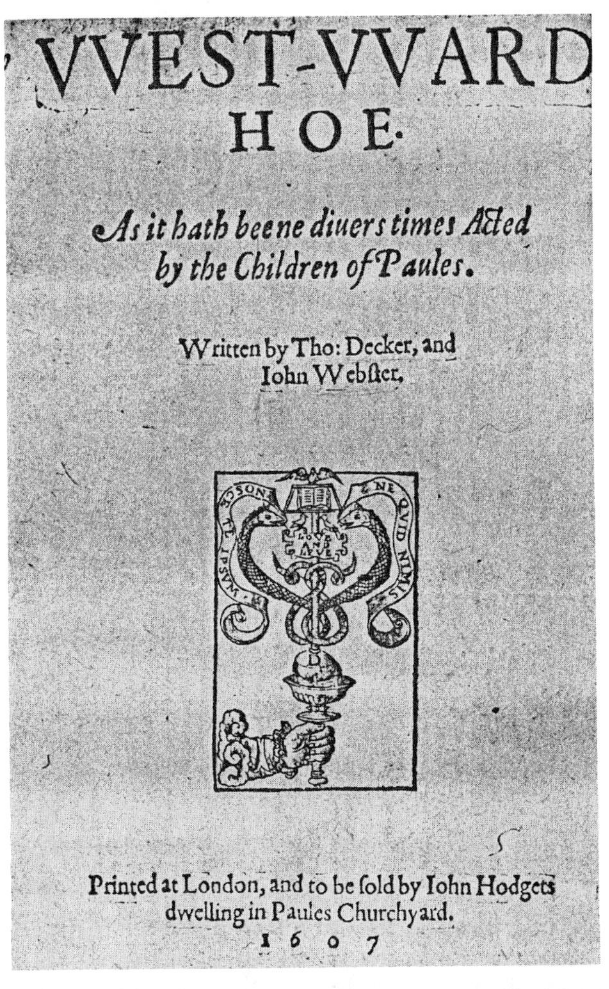

VVEST-VVARD HOE.

As it hath beene diuers times Acted by the Children of Paules.

Written by Tho: Decker, and Iohn Webster.

Printed at London, and to be sold by Iohn Hodgets dwelling in Paules Churchyard.

1607

NORTH-VVARD HOE.

Sundry times Acted by the Children of Paules.

By Thomas Decker, and Iohn Webster.

Imprinted at London by G. Eld.

1607.

Title pages for the 1607 quarto editions of Webster and Dekker's controversial city comedies (British Library)

ume 2 (Cambridge: Cambridge University Press, 1955);

The White Devil, edited by John Russell Brown (London: Methuen, 1960);

The Duchess of Malfi, edited by Brown (London: Methuen, 1964);

The Devil's Law-Case, edited by Elizabeth M. Brennan (London: Benn, 1975).

PLAY PRODUCTIONS: *Caesar's Fall or The Two Shapes*, by Webster, Anthony Munday, Michael Drayton, Thomas Middleton, and Thomas Dekker, London, Fortune theater, May 1602;

Sir Thomas Wyatt (presumably the same play as *Lady Jane*), by Webster, Henry Chettle, Dekker, Thomas Heywood, and Wentworth Smith, London, Boar's Head or Rose theater, October 1602;

Christmas Comes But Once a Year, by Webster, Heywood, Chettle, and Dekker, London, Boar's Head or Rose theater, November 1602;

Westward Ho, by Webster and Dekker, London, Paul's theater, late 1604;

Northward Ho, by Webster and Dekker, London, Paul's theater, late 1604;

The White Devil, London, Red Bull theater, January-March 1612;

The Duchess of Malfi, London, Blackfriars theater, 1614;

Guise, unknown theater and date;

The Devil's Law-Case, London, Cockpit theater, circa 1619-1622;

Anything for a Quiet Life, by Middleton and perhaps Webster, London, Globe theater, 1621(?);

The Late Murder of the Son upon the Mother, or Keep the Widow Waking, by Webster, Dekker, John Ford, and William Rowley, London, Red Bull theater, September 1624;

A Cure for a Cuckold, by Webster and Rowley, London, Cockpit or Curtain theater, circa 1624-1625;

The Fair Maid of the Inn, by John Fletcher, Philip Massinger, and perhaps Webster and Ford, London, Blackfriars theater, licensed 22 January 1626;

Appius and Virginia, by Webster and perhaps Heywood, London, Phoenix theater, 1634.

OTHER: Anthony Munday, trans., *The Third and Last Part of Palmerin of England*, includes prefatory verses by Webster (London: Printed by J. Roberts for W. Leake, 1602);

Samuel Harrison, *The Arch's of Triumph Erected in Honor of James, the First at His Entrance and Passage Through London*, includes an ode by Webster (London: Printed by J. Windet, 1604);

John Marston, *The Malcontent*, augmented edition, includes an induction by Webster (London: Printed by V. Simmes for William Aspley, 1604);

Thomas Heywood, *An Apology for Actors*, includes prefatory verses by Webster (London: Printed by N. Okes, 1612);

Sir Thomas Overbury, *New and Choise Characters, of Several Authors . . . Sixt Impression*, includes thirty-two "New Characters" attributed to Webster (London: Printed by Thomas Creede for Laurence L'Isle, 1615);

Henry Cockeram, *The English Dictionarie*, includes prefatory verses by Webster (London: Printed for N. Butter, 1623).

Despite his seminal importance in Jacobean drama (most critics rank him as second only to William Shakespeare as a tragedian), very little was known about John Webster's life until recently. However, the researches of Mary Edmond and the discovery in 1985 of a fragment of a manuscript play which may be in Webster's hand have materially changed the information available about him. Webster has been the subject of much critical enthusiasm this century, and his two tragedies, *The White Devil* and *The Duchess of Malfi*, are more frequently revived than any Jacobean plays other than Shakespeare's. Yet most of this critical and theatrical attention is paid to only a small portion of Webster's output. Part of the reason for this is that beyond reasonable question *The White Devil* and *The Duchess of Malfi* are his finest surviving achievements. But these masterpieces need to be seen in context.

Edmond established that Webster was the son of a prosperous coach maker, John Webster the elder, who was a member of the prestigious Company of Merchant Taylors (coach making was a relatively new trade, which did not have its own livery company). The Websters lived in London at the corner of Hosier Lane and Smithfield Street (then called Cow Lane), right next to what is now the Central Smithfield Meat Markets, and was in Webster's day the location of the famous St. Bartholomew's Fair, as well as a great horse fair, and center for other dealings in livestock. Webster's father married in 1577, and it is a reasonable inference that the baby who was to become the dramatist was born shortly afterward. (Webster had a brother, Edward, who was presumably younger.) Unfortunately, the parish records of St. Sepulchre, Holborn, were destroyed in the Great Fire of London, so it is not possible to obtain precise dates of birth, marriage, and death for Webster's family. Even so, documentary items survive, and it is possible to draw some reasonable inferences.

It seems probable that Webster was sent to the Merchant Taylors' School, probably in about 1587. Certainly his father had the right to send him there and, as a prosperous man, was in a position to do so. In *John Webster, Citizen and Dramatist* (1980) Muriel C. Bradbrook comments, "It would have been an act not merely of eccentricity but of ostracism for a member of the company to send his child anywhere else." The point is of importance, for the Merchant Taylors' School was an important educational institution, whose high master from 1561 to 1586 was the influential Richard Mulcaster. (It is interesting that Thomas Jenkins, the Stratford schoolmaster who taught the young William Shakespeare, was probably a product of Mulcaster's teaching, so that Mulcaster's influence may have extended to Shakespeare as well as to Webster.) Mulcaster was succeeded by Henry Wilkinson, who continued the tradition Mulcaster had established; as boys could be admitted to the school at the age of nine, Webster probably arrived there shortly after Wilkinson's tenure began. Mulcaster's curriculum was unusual in several ways: he believed in teaching in English rather than exclusively in Latin, and he encouraged the performance of music and plays to encourage discipline and self-confidence in his students. Earlier, the boys had performed even at court, but after the opening of the Theatre in 1576 their main outlets were in City of London pageants and other civic events, in some of which Webster must surely have participated.

A John Webster was entered at the Middle Temple in 1598. The evidence that this was the playwright is not positive, but it does seem likely. Certainly there is more than a suggestion of legal training in Webster's plays: there are centrally important trial scenes in *The White Devil*, *The Devil's Law-Case*, and *Appius and Virginia*; a point of law is the focus of the comic subplot of *A Cure for a Cuckold*; and a vein of legal imagery runs in the other works besides. Webster had connections with Templars, such as Sir Thomas Overbury, and the dramatists John Marston and John Ford. Certainly, if Webster did attend the Temple, this would not only account for his preoccupation with legal matters, but this great legal university also would have acquainted him with its lively inmates, his fellow students. He would have met such writers as John Davies, and participated in such events as the Revels, with their satirical sports. The Inns of Court were celebrated for their connections with the literary life of the times, and there can be no question, from the quantity of borrowings detected in Webster's work, that he was alert to the writings of his contemporaries. But one must not hypothesize beyond the facts, and there were certainly other John Websters in Elizabethan London.

Whatever his training, his practical career in the theater began with collaborative work for Philip Henslowe. If we discount *The Weakest Goeth to the Wall* (no one has made an even remotely convincing case for Webster's authorship of this play), the earliest reference to his work as a professional author comes in May 1602, when Henslowe paid an advance to a group of authors, Anthony Munday, Michael Drayton, Webster, and Thomas Middleton, for a play titled *Caesar's Fall* (or, in Henslowe's spelling, "sesers ffale"); a few days later Henslowe made "fulle paymente" to the same group (with the addition of Thomas Dekker), but now the play is called "too shapes" (the inserted title in the diary is not in Henslowe's hand). It seems unlikely that the same consortium was working on two plays at once, so, odd as the name seems, *Caesar's Fall or The Two Shapes* is generally accepted as the title of the lost play in question.

In October of the same year Henslowe paid Henry Chettle, Dekker, Thomas Heywood, Wentworth Smith, and Webster two amounts for a play called "Ladey Jane"; he also paid Dekker an advance on a second part of it later in November. The other dramatists are not mentioned, and it may be that not all of them were engaged in the second part: Webster was already working on another play. *Lady Jane* survives only as a bad quarto, printed in 1607 and titled *The Famous History of Sir T. Wyat*. According to Cyrus Hoy (1980) this text probably represents an abridgment of both parts. Such of *Lady Jane* as survives in *Sir T. Wyat* is an uninspired history play, heavily influenced by Shakespeare, in which motivation is glossed over, action is fast and confusing, and the odd mixture of comedy and sentimentality suggests that the authors had not quite got their act together. But the condition of the text makes any attempt at critical assessment, or even guesses toward the dramatists' shares in the play, virtually impossible.

In October 1602 Webster and Heywood were advanced money by Henslowe for a play called *Christmas Comes But Once a Year*; in November more payments were made, to Chettle and Dekker, and again to Chettle alone, for the same play, which was in production in November and December. The omission of Webster's name from these later entries does not imply that he had dropped out, since Henslowe's bookkeeping was always erratic. At this time his connection with Henslowe seems to have ceased. Webster's only other literary activity in 1602 was to produce a set of stilted verses prefixed to the third part of Anthony Munday's translation of *Palmerin of England*, printed in 1602.

Toward the end of 1604, Dekker and Webster collaborated in *Westward Ho*, which was produced by the Children of Paul's. This satirical and scandalous city comedy engendered a riposte: the even more scandalous *Eastward Ho*, produced by the Children of Her Majesty's Revels at the Blackfriars and written by Marston, George Chapman, and Ben Jonson; Dekker and Webster returned to the fray in *Northward Ho*, presumably in 1605. Both *Westward Ho* and *Northward Ho* were printed in 1607. Critical opinion is unanimous in thinking *Northward Ho* to be the better of the two Dekker/Webster plays, but there is good satirical comedy in both of them, and unmistakable signs of Webster's style as early as the first scene of *Westward Ho*. In a 1980 article Charles R. Forker makes a good case that these plays have been undervalued and stresses their self-conscious theatricality and the ambiguity of their support for middle-class morality. Despite their predictable, and rather confusing, plots, they might well bear revival.

VVEST-VVARD HOE

SCANE LONDON.

Actus Primus, Scæna Prima.

Enter Mistris Birdlime and Taylour.

Birdlime. Stay Taylour, This is the House, pray thee looke the gowne be not rufled: as for the Iewels and Pretious Stones, I know where to finde them ready presently. Shee that must weare this gowne if she wil receiue it, Is Maister *Iustinianos* wife (the *Italian* Marchant) my good old Lord and Maister, that hath beene a Tylter this twenty yeere, hath sent it. Mum Taylor, you are a kinde of Bawd. Taylor, if this Gentlewomans Husband should chaunce to bee in the way now, you shall tell him that I keepe a Hot-house in Gunpowder Ally (neere crouched Fryers) and that I haue brought home his wiues foule Linnen, and to colour my knauery the better, I haue heere three or foure kindes of complexion, which I will make shewe of to sell vnto her: the young Gentlewoman hath a good Citty wit, I can tell you, shee hath red in the Italian Courtyer, that it is a speciall ornament to gentlewomen to haue skill in painting.

Taylour. Is my Lord acquainted with her?

Bird. O, I.

Taylor. Faith Mistris *Birdlime* I doe not commend my Lordes choyce so well: now me thinkes he were better to set vp a Dairy, and to keepe halfe a score of lusty wholesome honest Countrey Wenches.

A 2 *Bird.*

once with a Pottle-pottand now with old iron.

Par. Gentlemen hasten to his rescue some, whilst others call for Oares.

Omn. Away then to London.

Par. Farewell Brainford.

Gold that buyes health, can neuer be ill spent,
Nor howres laid out in harmelesse meryment. *Exeunt.*

Finis Act. Quint.

SONG.

Oares, Oares, Oares, Oares:
To London hay, to London hay:
Hoist vp sayles and lets away,
for the safest bay
For vs to land is London shores.
Oares, Oares, Oares, Oares:
Quickly shall wee get to Land,
If you, if you, if you,
Lend vs but halfe a hand.
O lend vs halfe a hand. *Exeunt.*

FINIS.

First and last pages of text from the 1607 quarto edition of Westward Ho *(British Library)*

However, though Webster remained a lifelong collaborator with Dekker, Heywood, and others, he did not follow them into an entirely professional career. His next work was done for a different company, the King's Men, and consisted of an induction to Marston's revised version of his play *The Malcontent*, which the King's acted probably in 1604; it was printed in 1604. The early editions of *The Malcontent* are a considerable bibliographical and textual puzzle, the chief question being whether Webster contributed more than the induction to this "augmented" version of *The Malcontent*. The studies of the most recent scholar to examine the problem, Adrian Weiss, conclude very plausibly that only the induction is Webster's. The induction shows Webster's undoubted talent for satirical comedy directed at the citizen class (a vein much exploited in the plays in which he collaborated with Dekker) and his interest in matters theatrical.

Shortly after this, Webster married Sara Peniall and started a family. His eldest born, also called John, was baptized in 1606; the record survives because the baby evidently was born in the house of Webster's in-laws, whose parish, St. Dunstan's in the West, escaped the Great Fire. Sara, the eldest girl in the Peniall family, had been born in 1589; she was thus about ten years younger than Webster, and a mere seventeen years old when the baby was born. Other baptismal records are lacking, but from a neighbor's will it is clear that the Websters had a large family and were citizens in good standing with the community. But records are very sparse, and Webster's poetic and dramatic work seemed to have come to a halt; instead of pursuing his connection with the King's Men, he evidently had sufficient means to live an independent life. His next published work is *The White Devil*, which was printed in 1612.

In 1985, however, scholars Edward Saunders and Felix Pryor made a fascinating discovery in the muniments room of Melbourne Hall: a folded leaf which had originally been used as a wrapper for a bundle of Sir John Coke's correspondence and was now in a box containing plans for the garden. Upon examination, this leaf was found to consist of four manuscript pages of a hitherto unknown Jacobean play. The manuscript is "foul papers" (that is, an author's final working draft), much corrected in the course of composition. Its unique significance is that it is the only fragment of foul papers yet discovered. The handwriting is unlike that of any known Jacobean dramatist (though of course there are no surviving autographs of many dramatists, such as Francis Beaumont, Ford, and William Rowley, as well as Webster). The subject of the scene is a conversation between Alexander de Medici, the duke of Florence, and his favorite, his kinsman Lorenzo, in which Lorenzo manages to deflect Alexander's suspicions of him. The style very much resembles the sort of scenes Webster wrote in *The White Devil* between Bracciano and Flamineo.

Pryor claimed that the manuscript was a fragment of a hitherto unknown play by Webster, and tentatively titled it *The Duke of Florence*. This manuscript was put up for auction on 20 June 1986, but failed to reach its reserve price. The evidence for attributing this play fragment to Webster is equivocal, but his authorship is by no means impossible, and the similarities with Webster's style make the identification attractive. Against such an attribution must be set the entire lack of external evidence, and the fact that of Webster's habitual linguistic preferences, his fondness for contractions such as "i'th'," "o'th'," and " 's" as an abbreviation for "his" do not occur in the fragment. It is true that aspects of the Moor, Zanche, in *The White Devil* might derive from the fact that Alexander's mother was Moorish: the association might well have lodged in Webster's mind. And the image of the "Jacobs staffe" which occurs in the manuscript is an uncommon one, yet one that recurs in Webster. At present the matter must be regarded as undecided, but if it should turn out that the balance of evidence confirms Webster's authorship, then it will add a new work to his canon, and a further evidence that after 1605 (an allusion in the fragment to Jonson's *Sejanus* shows that it cannot have been written earlier) Webster determined to mine the increasingly popular area of Italianate intrigue tragedy.

This, at any rate, is the subject of *The White Devil*, which was printed (very badly) by Nicholas Okes in 1612, having been acted by the Queen's Men in the Red Bull theater sometime in the period from January through March of that year. Webster complains in his preface that "it was acted, in so dull a time of winter, presented in so open and black a theater, that it wanted (that which is the only grace and setting out of a tragedy) a full and understanding auditory." Clearly it had not been a success, despite its sensational subject matter, and Webster in publishing the play was hoping to restore his good name. In a postscript he praised the acting and especially

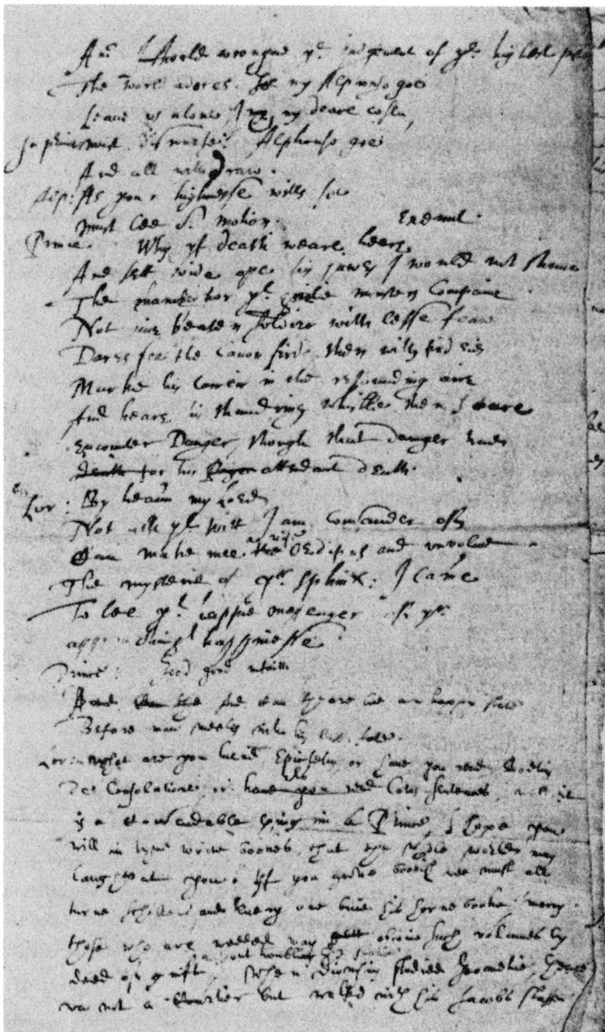

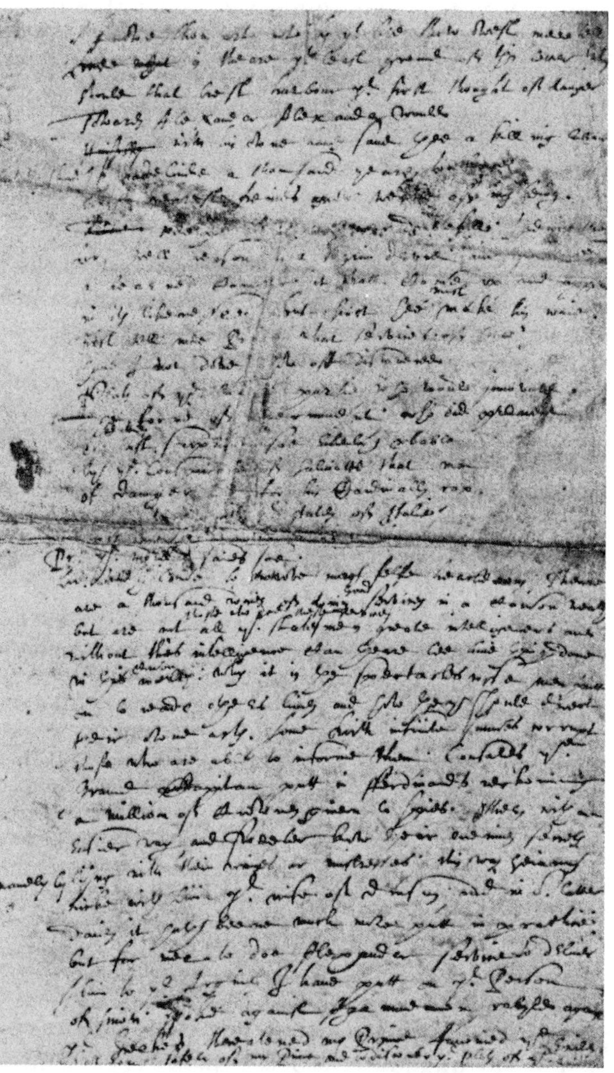

The Melbourne Manuscript (pages 1 and 4, left; 2 and 3, right), a fragment of a final working draft, discovered in 1985, of a previously unknown Jacobean play that has been assigned the title The Duke of Florence. *There are no surviving examples of Webster's handwriting with which to compare this fragment, but stylistic evidence suggests Webster's authorship (Bloomsbury Book Auctions catalogue, 20 June 1986).*

the work of Richard Perkins (who almost certainly played Flamineo): the first such tribute in the history of English drama.

The play deals with the adulterous passion of the Duke of Bracciano for Vittoria, which leads to his murder of his Duchess and of Vittoria's husband. His careless arrogance earns him the enmity of his Duchess's powerful brother, Francisco, Duke of Florence, and of the Cardinal Monticelso, who in the course of the play becomes Pope. Bracciano is ensnared in a plot and poisoned; subsequently Francisco's hired killers end Vittoria's life. It is an immensely powerful play, in which the conventional structures of social restraint (religious, political, and personal moralities) no longer have the capacity to control the characters' vigorous passions. Francisco succeeds in his plan of revenge not because he is in any sense a better man than Bracciano, but because he is more astute, a better Machiavel, a smarter operator. At the center of the play is the ambivalent figure of Flamineo, Bracciano's secretary and Vittoria's brother. Whatever moral scruples he may have had have been overgrown by a lifetime of dependency; the corrupting atmosphere of the court has warped all his ethical reactions. He has no objections whatever to soliciting his sister for his master; his only complaint throughout the play is that his dedicated service to Bracciano's willful sensuality has never brought material rewards. He dies, as he has lived, in a state of lack of knowledge. Flamineo is a classic malcontent (Marston's play, with which Webster's had a close association, is an undoubted influence). He is a kind of litmus paper, through whose reactions we can sense the level of tension of the rest of the court, and through whose corruption we can gauge the decay of the entire society.

Vittoria marks a new departure in Jacobean drama, a heroine whose morality is thoroughly corrupt, but with whom it is impossible not to sympathize. She has elected to live by the truth of her own sensations, and this decision leads her to welcome the passionate relationship with Bracciano, so different from the milksop Camillo to whom she is married. When Bracciano's injudicious actions land her in court, she seizes the opportunity to defend her life-style in the vigorous and characterful scene called "The Arraignment of Vittoria," in which she eloquently challenges the mean and narrow-minded morality expressed by her accuser, Monticelso. It is a great scene for a self-confident actress and is succeeded by two more: the great quarrel scene in the House of Convertites to which she is condemned, where her fury at Bracciano's allowing her to take the blame melts gradually under his masterful influence; and the final scene, in which she confronts death first at the hands of her malcontent brother, and then in the persons of Francisco's assassins. No one who saw Glenda Jackson's superb performance at the Old Vic in 1976 will ever forget the way she reconciled the conflicting aspects of Vittoria's character into a performance of great power and consistency. No other heroine in Jacobean drama is quite such a challenge to the actress or the audience: not even Cleopatra, who for all her moral evasions is never party to a pair of nasty murders of convenience. Yet because she is a woman, Vittoria's freedom of action is very much circumscribed by a wholly male-oriented society, a society which she must manipulate as best she can in defense of that independence of mind which characterizes her. The only quality which remains to Flamineo and to Vittoria in the drawn-out scene of their deaths is a sort of personal integrity, a courage in the face of unavoidable suffering.

Neither Vittoria nor Flamineo is in any sense an admirable character, but Webster creates for them, and the other denizens of his corrupt world, a language so full of vitality and poetic strength and energy—Webster is by far the most "conceited" of the Jacobean dramatists—that they cannot fail to attract attention and even sympathy from the audience. Their evil actions are largely inexplicable to themselves, which leaves them intriguing enigmas to the audience. The work of scholars such as Fredson T. Bowers, Harold Jenkins, and Richard W. Hillman has shown that both *The White Devil* and *The Duchess of Malfi* employ many of the techniques of the revenge play, but not at all for the usual purposes of such plays. In *The White Devil* Francisco carries out the role of revenger, but is never subject to the moral dilemmas that most revengers suffer from, which makes their plays interesting. Nor is the corrosive evil of the revenge ethic the subject of the play. In many ways, Flamineo is evil, but his evil is not the explanation (in dramatic terms) of either his character or the structure of events in *The White Devil.* Nor are the plays structured according to the revenge-tragedy paradigm; as A. J. Smith has suggested—in an essay in *John Webster* (1970), edited by Brian Morris—Webster's way of re-creating reality, by a series of seemingly random juxtapositions of scenes of very different tone and style, reflects powerfully the instability of the imaginary yet persuasively real-seeming world he has created.

Many critics have held *The White Devil* to be inferior to *The Duchess of Malfi* on the grounds that there is little or no sense of hope in the earlier play and that it is impossible to identify wholly with any of the characters. These objections have led more sophisticated critics to search for structures of meaning at a deeper level in *The White Devil*, with some success; there is also the undeniable fact that it is an overwhelmingly powerful play in performance. It can be played as a very bleak representation of the selfishness and carelessness of worldly people, revealing as grim a view of society as some of Samuel Beckett's plays. It is also possible to play it more in sorrow than in anger, so that the excesses of the characters seem to arise from a society that has lost its roots in traditional morality and religion, people who have no star of guidance by which to steer their lives. This, surely, is the more intelligible understanding of the play and aligns it with such other works as Shakespeare's *Macbeth* and *Antony and Cleopatra*, plays that show individuals trying to derive from their own personal resources the moral judgments to control their lives. Macbeth turns away from the values he knows perfectly well; Antony seeks in his own will a value higher than his society's. The similarities are striking, except that both Antony and Macbeth are heroic in status, which is not true of any of the characters of *The White Devil* (saving, in her special way, Vittoria). But the dramaturgy is the same: the sense of people lost in their selves, struggling and, necessarily, failing to make sense out of their lives in a world from which sense had been banished.

Shortly after *The White Devil* was performed, an event occurred which cast down all of England: the sudden death in November 1612, at the age of eighteen, of Prince Henry, King James's eldest son. Webster expressed his grief in an elegy entitled *A Monumental Columne*, which was published in two formats: on its own, and with companion elegies by Cyril Tourneur and Heywood as *Three Elegies on the Most Lamented Death of Prince Henrie*. Nicholas Okes was the printer, and the elegies were published in 1613. Webster dedicated his poem to Sir Robert Carr, who was one of James's favorites and shortly to be created earl of Somerset; almost immediately Carr became involved in the Overbury scandal, which also produced a connection with Webster.

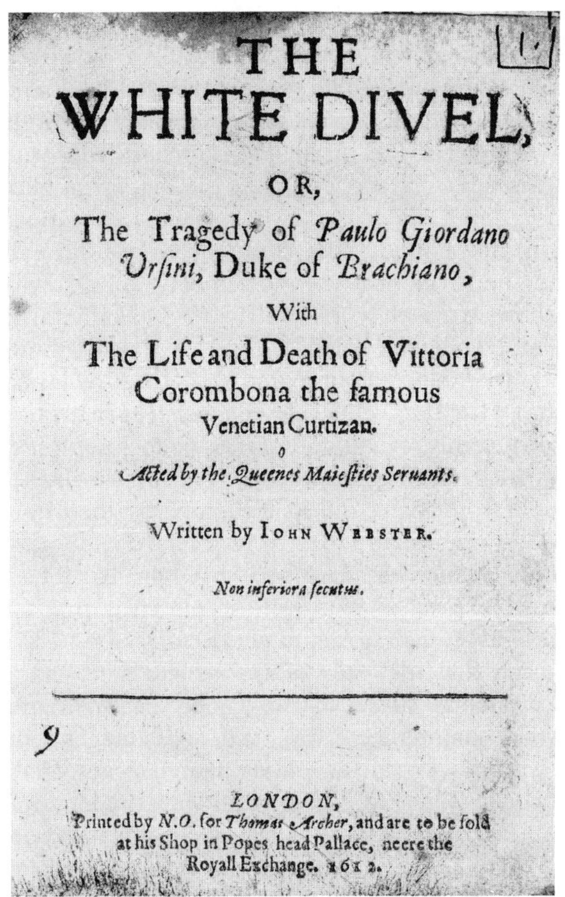
THE WHITE DIVEL, OR, The Tragedy of *Paulo Giordano Ursini*, Duke of *Brachiano*, With The Life and Death of Vittoria Corombona the famous Venetian Curtizan.

Acted by the Queenes Maiesties Seruants.

Written by IOHN WEBSTER.

Non inferiora secutus.

LONDON, Printed by *N.O.* for *Thomas Archer*, and are to be sold at his Shop in Popes head Pallace, neere the Royall Exchange. 1612.

Title page for the 1612 quarto edition of one of Webster's best-known plays. Webster complained in his preface that its first production "wanted . . . a full and understanding auditory" (Henry E. Huntington Library and Art Gallery).

(Robert B. Bennett's suggestion that the dedication was ironical and cynical is preposterous.) Clearly Webster felt powerfully the untimely death of this hopeful prince; he compares him in the elegy to the Black Prince and uses all the usual elegiac machinery. But the poem remains obstinately earthbound: the brilliance and originality of Webster's imagery seemingly deserts him in the formal couplets of this poem. Nonetheless, as has often been remarked, some of the ideas stillborn here come to vivid life in *The Duchess of Malfi*, which Webster was probably already at work upon: the play becomes, as it were, the objective correlative for the grief occasioned by Henry's death upon which the elegy choked.

The Duchess of Malfi, by common consent Webster's greatest play, was probably written in 1613 or 1614; it was performed by the prestigious King's Men and must have been staged before 16 December 1614, because William Ostler, who played Antonio in the original production, died that day. Unique among dramatic quartos of its period, that of the *Duchess* (printed by Nicholas Okes in 1623) gives two partial casts for the play, one for the original production, the other presumably for a revival near the date of publication (John Thompson, who played Julia, apparently did not join the company until 1621). In both performances the bluff, portly John Lowin, rather surprisingly, played Bosola (his other roles included Shakespeare's Henry VIII and Falstaff, and Jonson's Volpone and Sir Epicure Mammon). Richard Burbage played Ferdinand in 1614; in the revival, the part went to Joseph Taylor. Richard Sharpe, who is listed as playing the Duchess, probably did so at the revival; the principal boy actor in 1614 was Richard Robinson, whose name was favorably brought by Jonson into *The Devil is an Ass*. It seems clear that the play was initially given at the Blackfriars theater, though the title page of the quarto adds that it was publicly acted at the Globe. Many writers have commented on the advantages the Blackfriars would have had for the scenes of the Duchess's torment and murder; but the idea that the stage could have been artificially darkened for these scenes has been exploded, and the fact that they worked on the Globe's daylit stage shows that the special effects were emblematically rather than realistically achieved.

It seems evident that in Webster's own time, as subsequently, *The Duchess of Malfi* was his greatest success. In the Duchess herself, we are given one of the greatest of tragic heroines, who tries to establish a good, Christian life in the context of the deranged hostility of her brother Ferdinand and the less unstable but equally cruel machinations of the Cardinal. Despite her brothers' urging against her remarriage, she secretly weds Antonio, her master of the household, and lives with him some years before Ferdinand's spy, Bosola, uncovers the truth. (The notion, expressed by several critics, that the Duchess herself becomes somehow guilty by marrying her social inferior is, in terms of the play's overall structure and mood, grotesque.) Harried from her home, separated from husband and children, the Duchess is imprisoned and tormented in the famous masque of the madmen; she is finally murdered, in one of the most powerful scenes in all Jacobean drama. Initially she acts with stoic resignation (her celebrated line, in response to Bosola's attacks, "I am Duchess of Malfi still," is only one of many stoical responses). But at the last she attains a mood of Christian resignation, well described by David Gunby (in an essay in *John Webster*, edited by Brian Morris). After her death, the evil that men have done lives after them and is worked out in the final act, which brings all the other principals to their deaths.

Most writers find the structure of *The Duchess of Malfi* easier to apprehend than that of *The White Devil*. The powerful conflict between the Duchess and Ferdinand—and the role of Bosola as the intermittently reluctant agent between them—provides a clear and direct dramatic organization that Webster had not attempted in *The White Devil*, and indeed, only achieved elsewhere in *Appius and Virginia*. Ferdinand's obsession with his sister is darkly motivated—there are enough hints that it arises in suppressed incestuous feelings about her to have convinced most critics—but so is the rest of his unstable, haughty personality. It is not enough for him to separate the Duchess from her family: he organizes her torment and murder, actions which finally drive him into that particular form of insanity known as lycanthropy. He has, in theatrical terms, made himself into a beast. A development of Flamineo, Bosola adds to the earlier character's readiness to do evil for personal advancement an uncertainty very characteristic of Webster. At one moment Bosola plays the spy with evident relish and skill; the next he laments his degrading employment and begs Ferdinand to abandon his campaign against the Duchess. But only after the deed has been done, and Ferdinand has refused to reward Bosola for it, does his latent hostility become overt. Like Flamineo, Bosola never becomes entirely sympathetic, or wholly unsympathetic; and he does worse things than Flamineo ever did. He too is a malcontent, but despite his personal confusions, his actions are crucial to the destruction of the evil brothers, and thereby to the eradication of evil from the world of the play. And in his confusion and uncertainty, he finds himself acting in ways which are deplorable but by no means inexplicable. Like *The White Devil*, *The Duchess of Malfi* achieves its dramatic power through the vivid, brilliant, and flexible verse in which Webster has caught his characters' dilemmas. The play continues to excite the admiration of critics and the enthusiasm of theatrical companies. Without wishing to belittle Webster's other achievements, there is no doubt that common consent is that *The Duchess of Malfi* is Webster's supreme achievement.

At the height of his success, he was obliged to suffer the grief of his father's death: Webster senior must have died by 1615, because in that year Webster was admitted free of the Merchant Taylors by patrimony; his brother had been already admitted through apprenticeship in 1612, and it was Edward who carried on the family business after the elder Webster's death. The image of John Webster and his family that one arrives at is of successful and prosperous members of the urban middle class. Unfortunately the biographical record for the dramatist fades out in his middle years. However, in 1615 Webster contributed thirty-two new "Characters" to the sixth edition of Sir Thomas Overbury's popular Theophrastian collection, *New and Choise Characters, of Several Authors*. Whether Webster knew him before the *Characters* were published is unknown, but as Overbury had been a member of the Middle Temple, it is not inherently unlikely. Overbury's death rather cast into shade his life and literary achievements: he was poisoned by agents of Frances Howard, Countess of Somerset, who brought suit of nullity against her first husband, the earl of Essex, in order to marry Robert Carr, the earl of Somerset, King James's favorite. Overbury was Carr's friend, and allegedly he wrote the poem "The Wife," printed in *New and Choise Characters*, to dissuade Carr from marrying Frances. The king had Overbury imprisoned in the Tower for refusing to accept a diplomatic appointment, and there he died, in September 1613, probably with Somerset's connivance. The tale became a public scandal of monumental proportions, and led to the fall from favor of the entire Howard family.

Overbury may be credited with the fashion in England for "characters"—generalized thumbnail sketches of classes of people, often satirically pointed. They survived as an essential aspect of biographical treatments and fictional handling of biography for more than two hundred years: one can still find the descendants of the "character" in Charles Dickens's novels. Webster liked them, and had already written some into *The White Devil*: Flamineo gives a "character" of the cuckold in his description of Camillo in I.ii.; Monticelso has his famous "character of a whore" in "The Arraignment of Vittoria" (III.ii.): "This character 'scapes me," ripostes Vittoria, dryly. There are also Antonio's "characters" of Ferdinand and the Cardinal to Delio in *The Duchess of Malfi*, and many more. The thirty-two "New Characters" in the sixth edition generally believed to be by Webster (on the basis of close parallels with *The White Devil* and *The Duchess of Malfi*) include the celebrated "An excellent Actor," apparently written as a rejoinder to the abusive character of "A Common Player," in J. Stephens's *Satirical Essays, Characters, and Others*, also published in 1615. This precipitated a reply from Stephens, who criticizes Webster's "hackney similitudes" (without actually naming him); and another satirist, Henry Fitzgeffrey, attacks Webster in his book *Satyres and Satyricall Epigrams* (1617), which contains a poem (in execrable verse) called "Notes from Blackfryers":

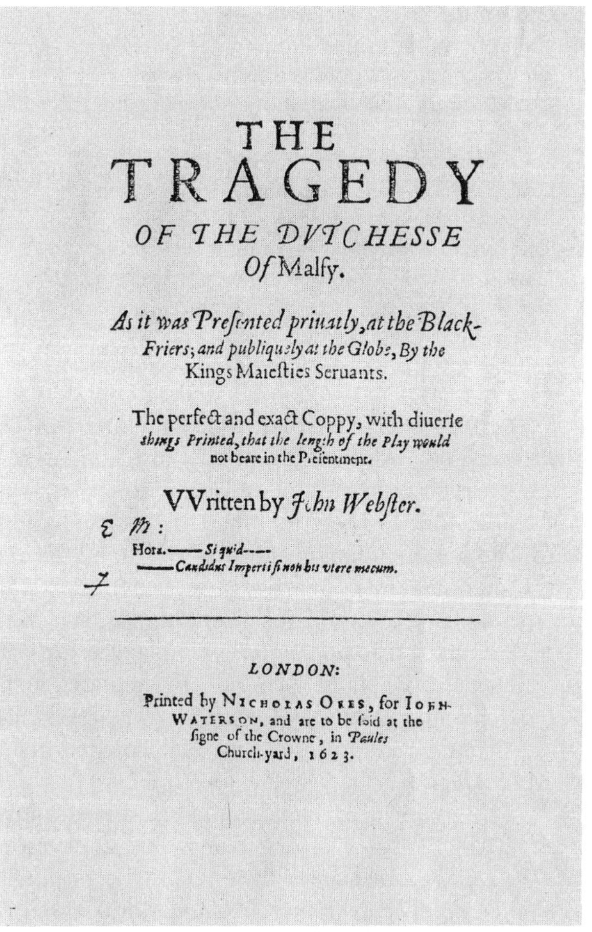
THE
TRAGEDY
OF THE DVTCHESSE
Of Malfy.

As it was Presented priuatly, at the Black-Friers; and publiquely at the Globe, By the Kings Maiesties Seruants.

The perfect and exact Coppy, with diuerse *things Printed, that the length of the Play would* not beare in the Presentment.

VVritten by *John Webster.*

Hora.—— *Si quid*——
——*Candidus Imperti si non his vtere mecum.*

LONDON:

Printed by Nicholas Okes, for Iohn Waterson, and are to be sold at the signe of the Crowne, in *Paules* Church-yard, 1623.

Title page for the 1623 quarto edition of Webster's most successful play (Anderson Galleries auction catalogue, sale number 2217, 10 January 1928)

But h'st! with him Crabbed (*Websterio*)
The *Play-wright, Cart-wright*: whether? either! (*ho*—
No further. Looke as yee'd bee look't into:
Sit as ye woo'd be *Read*: *Lord!* who woo'd know him?
Was ever man so mangl'd with a *Poem*?
See how he drawes his mouth awry of late,
How he scrubs: wrings his wrests: scratches his Pate.

A *Midwife*! helpe! By his *Braines coitus*
Some *Centaure* strange: some huge *Bucephalus*,
Or *Pallas* (sure) ingendred in his *Braine*—
Strike *Vulcan* with thy hammer once againe.

This is the *Crittick* that (of all the rest)
I'de not have view mee, yet I feare him least,
Heer's not one word *cursively* I have *Writ*,
But hee'l *Industriously* examine it.
And it some 12. monthes hence (or there *about*)
Set in a shamefull sheete, my errors *out*.
But what care I it *will* be so obscure,
That none shall understand him (I am sure).

Behind the petty malice of this libel can be distinguished that both Stephens and Fitzgeffrey knew enough to associate Webster with the coaching trade, that Fitzgeffrey knew of his association with Dekker in the *Ho* plays, knew of his liking for Italianate plots (hence "Websterio"), and was aware of his reputation for slow composition. Before one takes this poem too seriously (no author in those heady days escaped detraction), it is worth recalling the respectful and generous poems that Middleton, Rowley, and Ford contributed to *The Duchess of Malfi*.

The major enigma of this period is the lost play, *Guise*. Webster refers to it in his dedication of *The Devil's Law-Case*, where he lists it with *The White Devil, The Duchess of Malfi*, "and others" which his dedicatee, Sir Thomas Finch, has seen. Whether this means "seen in print" or "seen on the stage," no one can tell; and what the "others" are—did he mean the collaborative plays, or was he hinting at other lost plays (perhaps *The Duke of Florence*?)—can only be guessed at. It seems fair to assume that a play about the notorious duke of Guise would be a tragedy of intrigue; that the *Guise* was written before *The Devil's Law-Case* is only a plausible inference.

The Devil's Law-Case was written for the Cockpit (later known as the Phoenix), built by John Best in 1609, and converted by Inigo Jones to its final form in 1616, when Christopher Beeston leased it for Queen Anne's Men, the same company as had formerly produced *The White Devil*. It is a reasonable inference that Richard Perkins, the actor Webster had praised in *The White Devil*, was entrusted with the leading role of Romelio in *The Devil's Law-Case*, though no cast list survives. The play was printed in 1623, the same year as *The Duchess of Malfi*, but by a different printer (Augustine Mathewes). The date of composition is uncertain: the title page described it as "A new Tragecomoedy," but such assertions are not to be trusted. There are some lines which seem to be derived from Jonson's *The Devil is an Ass*, which was acted in 1616, but the topical allusions discovered in the play are difficult to depend on: such as they are, they suggest 1619, which in itself is a plausible enough date; it must have been played before 1622, when Queen Anne's Men disbanded.

Most critics agree in finding it the most difficult of Webster's works to assess. It uses many of the materials and styles of *The White Devil* and *The Duchess of Malfi*, but for an entirely different dramatic end. The key event in the play is the law case itself, where Leonora attempts to disinherit her son Romelio by alleging his bastardy. Unfortunately for her scheme, the judge trying the case turns out to be the man she is claiming to be Romelio's father. But this is only one of a huge number of plots in the play, many of them originated by Romelio himself, whose scheming is untinged by moral considerations, and who goes so far in his designs as to disguise himself as a Jewish doctor and attempt to stab to death the wounded Contarino. By an ironic reversal, the blood-letting actually saves Contarino's life, and none of the other immoral plots in the play actually comes to fruition. Both David Gunby (in a 1968 article) and Elizabeth M. Brennan (in her 1975 edition of the play) have argued that there is a providential moral in this plotting, without carrying conviction to all critics. The chief obstacle to finding *The Devil's Law-Case* intelligible is the incoherence of the plot (though Ralph T. Berry amazingly calls it the "most skillful" of the plays). Wildly different from the Fletcherian model of tragicomedy, *The Devil's Law-Case* is full of actions which are both absurd and shocking. Romelio seems to owe something to Marlowe's Barabas, and certainly to Jonson's Volpone, and the general tone of corruption and folly is hard to reconcile with the overly hasty, careless ending. No account of the play has made a wholly plausible case for its unity, least of all Lee Bliss's extraordinary view that the conclusion was *deliberately* made unsatisfactory. The one test that remains is that of performance, which might show possibilities that have eluded the critics. But, alas, apart from a production in York, England, in 1980, *The Devil's Law-Case* has not been revived since its initial production.

The years 1623 and 1624 mark the high point of Webster's public celebrity. Both *The Duchess of Malfi* and *The Devil's Law-Case* were printed in that period, as were his verses prefixed to

The Deuils Law-case.

OR,

When Women goe to Law, the Deuill is full of Businesse.

A new Tragecomædy.

The true and perfect Copie from the Originall.

As it was approouedly well Acted by her Maiesties Seruants.

Written by IOHN WEBSTER.

Non quam diu, sed quam bene.

LONDON,
Printed by *A. M.* for *Iohn Grismand*, and are to be sold at his Shop in Pauls Alley at the Signe of the Gunne. 1623.

Title page for the 1623 quarto edition of one of the plays that lends credence to the theory that the dramatist was the John Webster who entered the Middle Temple to study law in 1598 (Anderson Galleries auction catalogue, sale number 1405, 4-5 March 1919)

Henry Cockeram's *The English Dictionarie.* In 1624 he was responsible for the most public activity of his life, the Lord Mayor's Pageant of 1624, which represents the uniting of his poetical career with his position as a Merchant Taylor and important citizen of London. (The reason Webster was given the job is that John Gore, the incoming mayor, was also a Merchant Taylor: the guild therefore produced the pageant.) There were two water tableaux; then in Paul's churchyard a Temple of Honor was erected with Troynovant (that is, London) surrounded by presentations of other famous cities and celebrated poets, doing her honor. Following this was a triumphal chariot containing eight famous English kings who had been free of the Company, preceded by the representation of Sir John de Hawkwood, an eminent Merchant Taylor soldier in the time of Edward III. A troupe of famous notables who also had been free of the Company followed, all costumed; there were also representations of famous maritime events. These were succeeded by two more pageants, the first, the Monument of Charity, fashioned like a garden, which represented the foundation of St. John's College, Oxford, by Sir Thomas White, a former mayor and Merchant Taylor; a speech by Learning was included as part of this pageant. The last pageant was the Monument of Gratitude, focused on the figure of the late Prince Henry, presented on a rock of jewels. This last pageant is the original note to what was otherwise a grand but entirely conventional set of pageants. The praise of Henry represented a kind of indirect criticism of the government of James I. According to Bradbrook in *John Webster, Citizen and Dramatist,* "Henry represented a decency in the monarchy which Webster's commentary spells out, and which had vanished in the final squalid stages of James's ignoble reign." (In "The Politics of Pageantry," 1981, Bradbrook discusses the City pageants and their political and theatrical connections in general.)

In September of the same year (1624) was licensed a play called *The Late Murder of the Son upon the Mother* (also known as *Keep the Widow Waking*), by Webster and Ford, in which Dekker and Rowley probably also had a share. The text is lost, but seems to have been a topical piece about a foolish widow intimidated into marriage, a scandal that was a nine-days' wonder at the time. The dating of the other plays with which Webster is more or less securely associated is virtually impossible. *Appius and Virginia,* which was acted by Christopher Beeston's company at the Phoenix in 1634, was printed, with Webster's name on the title page, in 1654. However, most scholars believe the play to have been written in collaboration with Heywood (for the most recent bibliographical and linguistic discussion of it, see MacDonald P. Jackson's article in *Studies in Bibliography,* 1985). Most writers also think on the basis of prosodic tests that the play dates from the end of Webster's career. Such tests, however, are only marginally reliable in view of the entirely different character of *Appius and Virginia* from Webster's other plays. Michael P. Steppat suggests it should be dated 1615, as Robert Anton of Cambridge included a reference to "Virgineaes rape" in a diatribe (published in 1616) against the "lustfull Theatres" of the time. The context hardly suits Webster's chaste tragedy; it is conceivable that Anton had another (lost) play in mind.

Appius and Virginia is a Roman tragedy about a corrupt judge, Appius, who seeks to possess the heroic general Virginius's daughter, by claiming her to be the child of a dead slave of one of his corrupt associates. The centerpiece of the play is another trial scene (IV.i.), in which Virginius fails to defeat Appius's schemes, and kills Virginia rather than allow her to fall into Appius's hands. The army rises in support of its general, and Appius and his associates fall. The play was much liked by nineteenth-century critics, who felt relief at the absence from it of the sort of irregularity and horror that characterize *The White Devil* and *The Duchess of Malfi*; in the twentieth century its status has slipped. Bradbrook accounts for its formal style and classical simplicity by supposing it to have been written for a children's company.

The other plays, *A Cure for a Cuckold*, *Anything for a Quiet Life*, and *The Thracian Wonder*, form a bibliographical group: they were part of a series of plays printed by Thomas Johnson for the bookseller Francis Kirkman in 1661-1662. Kirkman obviously had obtained these theatrical manuscripts and was anxious to get them into print as quickly and as inexpensively as possible. The quartos are monuments to meanness in printing, with almost all the verse printed as prose and the layout as squeezed as possible, in order to contain the plays within as few sheets as could be managed. In the circumstances, much of the evidence that would have helped to date the plays and to assign shares in them to the various authors has disappeared. Most scholars agree in refusing Webster any share in *The Thracian Wonder*, a very foolish play indeed cobbled up out of Robert Greene's *Menaphon* and Shakespeare's *The Winter's Tale*. But Webster is by general consent allowed a share in *A Cure for a Cuckold* (Webster's name appears with Rowley's on the title page) and (less universally) *Anything for a Quiet Life* (which Kirkman published as by Middleton).

A Cure for a Cuckold is a peculiar play: it has a preposterous main plot, involving a totally unnecessary duel between two friends at the instigation of Lessingham's beloved, Clare, "whose acts are so obscure as to be indecipherable," according to Bradbrook. Although a most tedious traversal of some of the love-and-honor territory that the Fletcherian tragicomedy had made popular, this main plot is in some respects not unlike the plotting of *The Devil's Law-Case*. But the virtue of *A Cure for a Cuckold* lies entirely in the subplot, which almost certainly featured its fat coauthor, William Rowley, as the mariner Compass, who returns home after having been given up as drowned to find that his wife has had a child by a gentleman, Franckford. Both Franckford and Compass wish to keep the child, and the issue is decided in a comic trial in a tavern, where Compass's arguments in favor of maternal rights persuade everyone: a surprising conclusion in an age so dominated by patrilineal thinking. Compass divorces his wife and instantly remarries her, thus obviating the cuckoldry he has sustained. If the whole play lived up to the subplot, *A Cure for a Cuckold* would be well worth revival, but the obscurity and tediousness of the main plot are insurmountable obstacles. There is no plausible indication of date, nor any that the play was ever revived. Rowley, as a leader of Prince Charles's Men, presumably presented it with his company, either at the Phoenix or at the Curtain.

Even less can be said about *Anything for a Quiet Life*. As Middleton died in 1627 it must be earlier than that; F. L. Lucas draws attention to a reference to the Standard in Cheapside as new; this monument was restored in 1621, and as none of the other allusions in the play are of much help in dating it, it seems plausible to locate it sometime in the early 1620s. H. Dugdale Sykes was the chief champion for Webster's presence in the play, and though his methodology has come under attack subsequently, his attribution was accepted by Lucas, and by Richard H. Barker and David J. Lake in their books on Middleton. Many recent authors have tended to bypass it, and the most that can be said is that at present the majority opinion concurs in assigning Webster some share in it. Cyrus Hoy has given good reasons for thinking that Webster had a share in *The Fair Maid of the Inn*, which he assigns to a team of Philip Massinger, Webster, Ford, and John Fletcher. It was printed in the Beaumont and Fletcher folio of 1647. He thinks it was the last play on which Fletcher worked; it was licensed in 1626. Another play claimed in part for Webster from the Beaumont and Fletcher folio is *The Honest Man's Fortune*, which also survives in a scribal manuscript written by the prompter of the King's Men, Edward Knight. It appears that the play was originally written in 1613 and subsequently revived in 1625. Although some of the play recalls Flamineo's satirical vein, Hoy dismisses Webster's participation, showing that on linguistic grounds Nathan Field probably wrote most of the play, with Massinger working in act 3 and Fletcher in act 5.

It seems as well at this point to reject two other ascriptions to Webster. There is a very bad pseudohistory play called *The Valiant Scot*, printed in 1637 and described on the title page as being "By J. W. Gent."; the publisher was John Waterson, and the identity of his initials with the author's is suggestive. In a 1965 article R. G. Howarth made a vague, impressionistic case for Webster as author, which was refuted by George F. Byers in his 1980 edition of the play. There is also a letter-writing manual called *A Speedie Post*, by I. W., printed in 1625, which was also claimed for Webster by Howarth in another 1965 article on the grounds that the phrase "worms in libraries" occurs in it and in *The Duchess of Malfi*. This does not by any means exhaust the number of works which have been attributed to Webster (see, for instance, Carol A. Chillington's 1981 article in *ELH*). So far, computer-aided studies of authorship have not produced any evidence of an unequivocal or self-evidently reliable nature which would enable them to be applied to the Webster canon. There can be no question that computer applications will continue in the future, and little doubt that at some stage a program will be devised which can add data to the kind of linguistic tests perfected by Hoy, which so far are the most reliable indicators in authorship determination. But even these are subject to uncertainty. One of Webster's most characteristic uses in *The White Devil* and *The Duchess of Malfi* is a very strong preference for "hath" rather than "has." Yet in *The Devil's Law-Case* we find "has" almost universally. Is this a change in linguistic habit? Or is the fact that *The Devil's Law-Case* was printed by Augustine Mathewes, while the two other plays come from Nicholas Okes's shop, relevant?

The date of Webster's death is unknown: Heywood mentions him in the past tense in *The Hierarchie of the Blessed Angels* (licensed 7 November 1634) along with other dramatists then dead, but how long before that he died cannot be determined. (Howarth, in 1954, tried to discount the Heywood reference because a John Webster was buried in Clerkenwell in March 1638, but as this John Webster was not described as a householder, it was almost certainly not the poet.)

Webster's critical reputation, like those of most of his Jacobean contemporaries, has fluctuated enormously (Don D. Moore has made a good survey of this subject). His work never vanished entirely from critical or theatrical awareness: he was one of the relatively few Jacobean dramatists whose plays continued to be given in the Restoration. John Downes, the prompter, described *The Duchess of Malfi* in his *Roscius Anglicanus* (1708) as "one of the Best of Stock Tragedies," noting that it had "fill'd the House 8 days Successively"—a very good run indeed; he also lists *The White Devil* as an old play that was acted now and then. In the period during which adaptations were popular, three of Webster's plays were so treated. Joseph Harris adapted *A Cure for a Cuckold* as *The City Bride* in 1696; more surprisingly, Nahum Tate altered *The White Devil* as *Injur'd Love* in 1707, and Lewis Theobald in 1735 produced a version of *The Duchess of Malfi* which he called *The Fatal Secret*.

Revival of critical interest in Webster really begins with Charles Lamb's *Specimens of the English Dramatic Poets* (1808), which printed excerpts from the plays, with a commentary which stressed Webster as a master of the emotions of fear and horror and of intenseness of feeling generally. This view was reiterated through the nineteenth century, culminating in an enthusiastic article by Algernon Charles Swinburne (1886; republished in his *The Age of Shakespeare*, 1908), which ranked Webster next to Shakespeare, chiefly on the grounds of his poetic genius. There was an opposition party, which grumbled about the violence and extravagance of the plays, and complained that Webster could not construct: this school of thought reached its apex in the writings of William Archer, between 1893 and 1924. Archer complained that the Webster enthusiasts only concentrated upon selected passages of poetic splendor, ignoring the structural weaknesses and unrealistic tone of the plays. Archer's complaints were responded to by T. S. Eliot, among others, who pointed out that Archer's criteria were those of the late-nineteenth-century well-made play, and thus totally inappropriate to Renaissance poetic drama.

In the meantime scholars had been working on Webster, beginning with the first collected edition (by the Reverend Alexander Dyce, in 1830). Much nineteenth-century scholarship was devoted to the attempt to establish the canon, and if possible to assign shares in the collaborative plays. The major figures in this work are H. Dugdale Sykes and E. C. H. Oliphant (who is still worth reading, though superseded by the more analytical studies of Cyrus Hoy). Both Sykes and Oliphant attempted to use various kinds of internal evidence to establish authorship; and although the detail of their work and many aspects of its methodology have been questioned, on the whole their opinions are still widely accepted. Their conclusions were at any rate enshrined in what is still the standard edition of Webster, Lucas's *Complete Works* of 1927, which includes many of the doubtful texts.

Since the 1920s an extraordinary amount has been published on Webster: the first 70 pages of Samuel Schuman's bibliography take us up to the watershed year of 1927; another 184 pages are needed to bring the record up to 1981, and more than 100 of these pages record the preceding mere twenty years. By far the great majority of studies stay with *The White Devil* and *The Duchess of Malfi,* since—as Hoy remarked in 1976—many critics feel uneasy in attempting structural analysis or close reading of the other texts, whose authorship rests upon a thin thread of inference. Many writers find the central issue of Webster's work to be whether or not he was expressing any kind of coherent moral or spiritual concepts in the plays. Eliot, though more sympathetic to Webster's dramaturgy than Archer, believed that his was "a very great literary and dramatic genius directed towards chaos," and his lines from "Whispers of Immortality" (1920) have been used as catchphrases by critics and directors alike:

Webster was much possessed by death
And saw the skull beneath the skin;
And breastless creatures under ground
Leaned backward with a lipless grin.

Daffodil bulbs instead of balls
Stared from the sockets of the eyes!
He knew that thought clings round dead limbs
Tightening its lusts and luxuries.

The critics who feel that Webster's outlook was fundamentally negative outnumber those who believe his plays to express positive values (Ian Jack's attack on him is one of the most vigorous); and those who find him truly positive (such as Gunby) are in turn outnumbered by those, such as Travis Bogard, who will allow only that in the existentially chaotic universe Webster's plays reveal, an individual can still assert personal integrity. This view makes Webster into a kind of stoic-Senecal dramatist, a view appropriate enough to the ideology of the later twentieth century, but not, one hopes, the last word. Influential studies, such as Hereward T. Price's, have sought to find structural patterns in Webster in his imagery, while others have focused on particular texts or upon staging questions. Among the more influential studies have been Clifford Leech's book (1951) and Inga-Stina Ekeblad's celebrated essay on Webster's "Impure Art" (1958), which shows how the images of dance in the Duchess's death scene are emblems; instead of stressing the unity of creation they reveal the disordered state of the Duchess's collapsing world.

One of the most important developments has been the systematic study of Webster's sources and methods of composition. Robert W. Dent and Gunnar Boklund both deal with this subject and reveal that Webster was more of a borrower than perhaps any of his contemporaries, that he wrote, as it were, with commonplace book open before him. Some critics, unreasonably, have felt that this diminishes his imaginative originality; they might have pondered on Eliot's *The Waste Land* (1922), and Eliot's (or James Joyce's) compositional methods: "These fragments I have shored against my ruins." That Webster was a great borrower is interesting information, but marginal to the indisputable fact that he was a great tragedian.

Interest in Webster continues to increase. The publication in 1979 of the concordance to Webster by Richard Cornballis and J. M. Harding provided an essential tool (though they did not include *Anything for a Quiet Life* and *The Fair Maid of the Inn*). A new full-length critical study by Charles R. Forker was published in 1986, and the Cambridge University Press will publish a new, complete, critical edition in old spelling in the near future. Performances of at least *The White Devil* and *The Duchess of Malfi* continue to be fairly common (the former at the Bristol Old Vic in 1983; the latter in a disappointing production by the National Theatre of Britain in 1985); David Carnegie's list of productions is surprisingly long. It is reasonable to conclude that Webster's remoteness, the very difficulty of seizing the "author's intention" that has led so many critics to disagree so violently, will ensure continuing controversy, while the undeniable power and passion of his best work will continue to attract readers and audiences. It is to be hoped that the subsidized theaters will take the risk of producing one or more of the other works, to give them the only true test of drama, a professional staging.

Bibliographies:

William E. Mahaney, *John Webster: A Classified Bibliography* (Salzburg: Institut für Anglistik und Amerikanistik, 1973);

Inga-Stina Ewbank, "Webster, Tourneur, and Ford," in *English Drama (Excluding Shakespeare): Select Bibliographical Guides*, edited by Stanley Wells (London: Oxford University Press, 1975);

David Carnegie, "A Preliminary Checklist of Professional Productions of the Plays of John Webster," *Research Opportunities in Renaissance Drama*, 26 (1983): 55-63;

Samuel Schuman, *John Webster: A Reference Guide* (Boston: G. K. Hall, 1985).

References:

William Archer, *The Old Drama and the New* (London: Heinemann, 1923);

Richard H. Barker, *Thomas Middleton* (New York: Columbia University Press, 1958);

Robert B. Bennett, "John Webster's Strange Dedication: An Inquiry into Literary Patronage and Jacobean Court Intrigue," *English Literary Renaissance*, 7 (Autumn 1977): 352-367;

Ralph T. Berry, *The Art of John Webster* (Oxford: Clarendon Press, 1972);

Lee Bliss, "Destructive Will and Social Chaos in *The Devil's Law-Case*," *Modern Language Review*, 72 (July 1977): 513-525;

Bliss, *The World's Perspective: John Webster and the Jacobean Drama* (New Brunswick, N.J.: Rutgers University Press, 1983);

Travis Bogard, *The Tragic Satire of John Webster* (Berkeley: University of California Press, 1955);

Gunnar Boklund, *"The Duchess of Malfi" Sources, Themes, Characters* (Cambridge, Mass.: Harvard University Press, 1962);

Boklund, *The Sources of "The White Devil"* (Uppsala, Sweden: Lundequistska Bokhandeln / Cambridge, Mass.: Harvard University Press, 1957);

Fredson T. Bowers, *Elizabethan Revenge Tragedy 1587-1642* (Princeton: Princeton University Press, 1940);

Muriel C. Bradbrook, *John Webster, Citizen and Dramatist* (London: Weidenfeld & Nicolson, 1980);

Bradbrook, "The Politics of Pageantry: Social Implications in Jacobean London," in *Poetry and Drama 1570-1700: Essays in Honour of Harold F. Brooks*, edited by Antony Coleman and Antony Hammond (London: Methuen, 1981), pp. 60-75;

Nicholas Brooke, *Horrid Laughter in Jacobean Tragedy* (London: Open Books, 1979);

Rupert Brooke, *John Webster and the Elizabethan Drama* (New York: John Lane, 1916);

John Russell Brown, "The Printing of John Webster's Plays," *Studies in Bibliography*, 6 (1954): 117-140; 8 (1956): 113-127; 15 (1962): 57-69;

George F. Byers, ed., *"The Valiant Scot" by J. W.: A Critical Edition* (New York: Garland, 1980);

Carol A. Chillington, "Playwrights at Work: Henslowe's, not Shakespeare's, *Book of Sir Thomas More*," *ELH*, 11 (1981): 439-479;

Richard Cornballis and J. M. Harding, *A Concordance to the Works of John Webster*, 4 volumes (Salzburg: Institut für Anglistik und Amerikanistik, 1979);

Robert W. Dent, *John Webster's Borrowing* (Berkeley: University of California Press, 1960);

Jonathan Dollimore, *Radical Tragedy: Religion, Ideology and Power in the Drama of Shakespeare and his Contemporaries* (London: Harvester Press, 1984);

Mary Edmond, "In Search of John Webster," *Times Literary Supplement*, 24 December 1976, pp. 1621-1622;

Inga-Stina Ekeblad, "The 'Impure Art' of John Webster," *Review of English Studies*, new series 9, no. 35 (1958): 253-267;

Ekeblad, "Storm Imagery in *Appius and Virginia*," *Notes and Queries*, new series 3 (January 1956): 5-7;

Ekeblad, "Webster's Constructional Rhythm," *ELH*, 24 (September 1957): 165-176;

T. S. Eliot, "Four Elizabethan Dramatists: A Preface to an Unwritten Book," in his *Selected Essays* (London: Faber & Faber, 1932);

Una Ellis-Fermor, *The Jacobean Drama: An Interpretation* (London: Methuen, 1936);

Charles R. Forker, *Skull Beneath the Skin: The Achievement of John Webster* (Carbondale & Edwardsville: Southern Illinois University Press, 1986);

Forker, "*Westward Ho* and *Northward Ho*: A Revaluation," *Publications of the Arkansas Philological Association*, 6 (1980): 1-42;

H. Bruce Franklin, "The Trial Scene of Webster's *The White Devil* Examined in Terms of Renaissance Rhetoric," *Studies in English Literature*, 1 (Spring 1961): 35-51;

J. Gerritsen, ed., *The Honest Man's Fortune: A Critical Edition of MS Dyce 9 (1625)* (Groningen, Djakarta: J. B. Wolters, 1952);

David Gunby, "*The Devil's Law-Case*: An Interpretation," *Modern Language Review*, 63 (July 1968): 545-558;

Antony Hammond, "*The White Devil* in Nicholas Okes's Shop," *Studies in Bibliography,* 39 (1986): 135-176;

Hammond and Doreen DelVecchio, "The Melbourne Manuscript and John Webster," *Studies in Bibliography,* 40 (1987);

Richard W. Hillman, "Meaning and Morality in Some Renaissance Revenge Plays," *University of Toronto Quarterly,* 49 (Fall 1979): 1-17;

R. G. Howarth, "John Webster's Burial," *Notes and Queries,* new series 1 (March 1954): 114-115;

Howarth, "*The Valiant Scot* as a Play by John Webster," *Bulletin of the English Association, South African Branch,* 9/10 (1965): 3-8;

Howarth, "Worms in Libraries," *Notes and Queries,* new series 12 (June 1965): 236-237;

Cyrus Hoy, "Critical and Aesthetic Problems of Collaboration in Renaissance Drama," *Research Opportunities in Renaissance Drama,* 19 (1976): 3-6;

Hoy, *Introductions, Notes, and Commentaries to Texts in "The Dramatic Works of Thomas Dekker" Edited by Fredson Bowers,* 4 volumes (Cambridge: Cambridge University Press, 1980);

Hoy, "The Shares of Fletcher and his Collaborators in the Beaumont and Fletcher Canon," parts 4 and 5, *Studies in Bibliography,* 12 (1959): 91-116; 13 (1960): 77-108;

Ian Jack, "The Case of John Webster," *Scrutiny,* 16 (March 1949): 38-43;

MacDonald P. Jackson, "John Webster and Thomas Heywood in *Appius and Virginia*: A Bibliographical Approach to the Problem of Authorship," *Studies in Bibliography,* 38 (1985): 217-235;

Harold Jenkins, "The Tragedy of Revenge in Shakespeare and Webster," *Shakespeare Survey,* 14 (1961): 45-55;

David J. Lake, *The Canon of Middleton's Plays* (Cambridge: Cambridge University Press, 1975);

Clifford Leech, *John Webster: A Critical Study* (London: Hogarth Press, 1951);

Leech, *Webster: "The Duchess of Malfi"* (London: Arnold, 1963);

Don D. Moore, *John Webster and his Critics 1617-1964* (Baton Rouge: Louisiana State University Press, 1966);

Brian Morris, ed., *John Webster,* Mermaid Critical Commentaries (London: Benn, 1970);

Peter B. Murray, *A Study of John Webster* (The Hague: Mouton, 1969);

E. C. H. Oliphant, *The Plays of Beaumont and Fletcher: An Attempt to Determine their Respective Shares and the Shares of Others* (New Haven: Yale University Press, 1927);

Robert Ornstein, *The Moral Vision of Jacobean Tragedy* (Madison: University of Wisconsin Press, 1965);

Jacqueline Pearson, *Tragedy and Tragicomedy in the Plays of John Webster* (Manchester, U.K.: Manchester University Press, 1980);

Hereward T. Price, "The Function of Imagery in Webster," *PMLA,* 70 (September 1955): 717-739;

Samuel Schuman, *"The Theatre of Fine Devices": The Visual Drama of John Webster* (Salzburg: Institut für Anglistik und Amerikanistik, 1982);

Michael P. Steppat, "John Webster's *Appius and Virginia,*" *American Notes and Queries,* 20 (March/April 1982): 101;

E. E. Stoll, *John Webster: The Periods of his Work* (Boston: Mudge, 1905);

H. Dugdale Sykes, "A Webster-Middleton Play: *Anything for a Quiet Life,*" *Notes and Queries,* 141 (5 March 1921): 181-182, 202-204; (19 March 1921): 225-226; (9 April 1921): 300.

Index to Volume 1

Index

This index includes proper names: people, places, and works mentioned in the texts of entries for Volume 1. The primary checklists, which appear at the beginning of each entry, are not included in this index. Also omitted are the names London and Dublin, because they appear so frequently. Volume 8 of the *Concise Dictionary of British Literary Biography* includes a cumulative proper-name index to the entire series.

Cumulative Index of Author Entries for Concise Dictionary of British Literary Biography

Cumulative Index of Author Entries

ISBN 0-8103-7981-3